6/02

WILD MAN

THE LIFE AND TIMES OF DANIEL ELLSBERG

TOM WELLS

FOR ST. MARTIN'S PRESS

WILD MAN
Copyright © Tom Wells, 2001.

All rights reserved. No part of this book may be used or reproduced in any manner whatsoever without written permission except in the case of brief quotations embodied in critical articles or reviews.

First published 2001 by
PALGRAVE™
175 Fifth Avenue, New York, N.Y. 10010.
Companies and representatives throughout the world.

PALGRAVE™ is the new global publishing imprint of St. Martin's Press LLC Scholarly and Reference Division and Palgrave Publishers Ltd. (formerly Macmillan Press Ltd.).

ISBN 0–312–17719–4

Library of Congress Cataloging-in-Publication Data
Wells, Tom, 1955-
Wild man : the life and times of Daniel Ellsberg / Tom Wells.—1st ed.
    p.   cm.
Includes bibliographical references (p.) and index.
ISBN 0–312–17719–4
1. Ellsberg, Daniel.   2. Pentagon Papers.   3. United States—Politics and government—1969–1974.   I. Title: Life and times of Daniel Ellsberg. II. Title.

CT275.E38518 W45   2001
973.923'092—dc21
[B]   2001019452

Design by Letra Libre, Inc.

First edition: June 2001
10 9 8 7 6 5 4 3 2 1

Printed in the United States of America.

To my son, Willie

CONTENTS

ACKNOWLEDGMENTS

I WISH TO THANK ALL THOSE PEOPLE WHO AGREED TO BE INTERVIEWED for this book. Their help was enormous. I particularly wish to thank J. Norvill Jones, Carol Cummings, Vincent Davis, Jan Butler, and Robert Sachs for providing collections of documents. The documents were of immense value. Thanks to David Paynter of the National Archives for expeditiously processing my Freedom of Information Act request for Watergate Special Prosecution Force records, which were voluminous and revealing. Pat Anderson of the Nixon Project at the National Archives was also helpful, as was Carol Leadenham of the Hoover Institution Archives and Mark Coir of the Cranbrook Archives. Judy Salm helped out with Cecil Currey's papers. Robert Beyers, Richard Townsend, and Vale Rabe sent me old Cranbrook newspapers and other material. Other people who provided me with written materials include Daniel Ellsberg, Paul Warnke, Richard Elms, Stanley Sheinbaum, Anne Blair, Simon Bourgin, and Margaret Brenman-Gibson. Thanks to Kirby Hall, Carol Cummings, Jan Butler, Richard Townsend, Stanley Sheinbaum, and Anthony Russo for providing photographs. Doric Wilson compiled the index. I also wish to acknowledge the advice or help of Lisa Bryant, Jess Cook, Richard Leo, Eric Schroeder, Bob Blauner, Gus Shubert, Anthony Russo, John Shultz, Tom Varbedian, Mike Walbridge, Cecil Currey, Ralph Cole, and Brady Sullivan.

My editor, Michael Flamini, offered wise advice. The National Endowment for the Humanities, the John F. Kennedy Library Foundation, and the Lyndon Baines Johnson Foundation provided financial support. And a special thanks to Lisa Bryant for her love, support, and tolerance.

PREFACE

THIS IS AN UNAUTHORIZED BIOGRAPHY, WRITTEN BY SOMEONE SYMPA-
thetic to Daniel Ellsberg politically but critical of the man. Ellsberg did not want
this book written. He talked to me at length, granting many hours of interviews.
But he did so warily, and more so as we went along. He felt he had been burned
badly by some people who had written about him in the past. Also, he wanted to
write a memoir. He had wanted to write a memoir for over twenty years, but hadn't
felt psychologically ready to do it, and he had torturous problems writing. He
didn't want to be forced into writing the memoir because of my book. He asked me
whether I would be interested in working with him on a memoir. His wife, Patricia,
had been enthusiastic about a collaborative book, he told me. I said I was not interested in collaborating on a memoir. He initially entertained some hope (faint as it
may have been) that this book would present him in the ways that he sees himself,
or at least in the ways that he wants other people to see him. He spoke highly of a
previous book I had written. He told me early in our discussions that he couldn't
think of a better person to write a biography of him—if one was going to be written. But he eventually stopped talking to me. "I've heard enough," he told me with
a chuckle in our last discussion, at Washington's Mayflower Hotel in November
1995. "I get the picture."

Ellsberg had found many of the comments I relayed to him from my
sources painful. Tormenting. They had made his stomach bubble. "This has
been from the beginning, as you know, a difficult, uncomfortable, unpleasant
process for me," he told me in our final discussion—which ended acrimoniously,
with Ellsberg turning off my tape recorder, although he treated me to dinner afterward and when we parted outside the restaurant he bowed. "And I want to
free myself from it. I don't enjoy it. . . . I'm not in such wonderful spirits. This
doesn't do much."

Ellsberg thought I wasn't being critical enough of information I was getting
from people I interviewed. "He feels that people are going to try and do him in,"
his friend Noam Chomsky told me. "And he has good reason to feel that." Many of

Ellsberg's former colleagues had been angry at him for releasing the Pentagon Papers to the press in 1971, and thus they might have reason to get back at him. That should be kept in mind when reading this book. But it was my perception that, with perhaps a few exceptions, their unhappiness with Ellsberg's release of the Pentagon Papers did not distort the characterizations of him that they offered for this book (though some of his traits were brought into sharper relief because of his action). Those characterizations were shared by many people who knew Ellsberg, including people who applauded his release of the Papers.

There had been other problems. Ellsberg didn't like the fact that, at the beginning, I had informed him in a letter that I was going to write this biography, apparently whether he wanted me to or not. "We got off on not a good foot," he told me later. He felt "closed in on." He said it was as if I was telling him, "I'm moving into your house. I'm taking over your life somehow." He had a strong emotional reaction, he told me, and felt harried and depressed. Seriously depressed. He didn't like to even think about this book. It was "driving me nuts," he said. But it was not clear, he told me, why he was reacting so strongly.

Ellsberg also came to believe that we, biographer and subject, had an adversarial relationship. It was not unlike the relationship between a prosecutor and a defendant, he argued. Moreover, he didn't think I understood him or empathized with him, nor was I sufficiently like him to be able to do so. "The truth is, we don't seem to resonate well," he told me in our final discussion. He didn't think my book would be true to him. "I think he doesn't feel you get him," Patricia told me. Ellsberg worried, in particular, about how I would describe his motivations for releasing the Pentagon Papers. That topic is, of course, central to this book. He feared that I would psychologize too much about his act, point to some sort of personal problems. He clearly worried that I would attribute his act to a desire for fame.

He felt that some of my questions were insensitive. He was right. I apologized for that. He thought I was asking too much about his sexual life, for example (a topic he brought up first—making it, I thought, fair game—and talked about at length with me). But the fact is Ellsberg absolutely loves to talk about sex, at great length, and does so unsolicited. It is one of his most marked personal features. Sex is a big theme in his life. But he worried about the image readers would have of him from this book. "I don't want to talk about sex," he once told me, after talking about his sexual past in a prior session. "I don't want to be perceived as talking about sex." And he distrusted his own judgment, his discretion, about discussing it and other matters. He consequently wondered if he should expose himself to being interviewed for this book. "I haven't served myself well in the past," he pointed out. But three days after making these comments, Ellsberg talked about his sex life extensively with me. He apparently could not restrain himself, even with a biographer.

I had also pushed and provoked Ellsberg, striking some raw nerves, more than was in my interest as a biographer. On occasion, I had become almost antagonistic, virtually pouring salt on his wounds. I had provoked him in part because he had provoked me (which I'm not proud to admit). He had not always followed through on what he had told me he was going to do (as I came to learn, that was not atypical behavior for him) and generally played a bit hard to get. "I've given you reason to be angry at me," he granted. Some of his answers to my questions led me to bore in on him more than I would have otherwise. I thought I was getting a fair number of self-serving responses from him. I had begun to question his honesty. He talked often about lying by U.S. government officials. He said it was a mission of his life to reveal to the public the costs of this lying. He also stressed that he would never lie to me, or even mislead me. If I wanted to get something *right*, I should ask him about it. "I don't lie to the public," he told me, and when talking to me, he was talking to the public. "I lie only when necessary to my immediate family." Ever since the Pentagon Papers came out, "I have never told a conscious lie" to the public, he claimed. It was my perception, however, that Ellsberg did sometimes lie to the public, and to me. Or that he had convinced himself that what he was saying was true when it was not. (I usually could not tell the difference, though at points he struck me as clearly self-delusional.) And it was not uncommon for Ellsberg to speak with great self-assuredness and self-righteousness about doubtful matters.

Apart from questions of honesty, I lost some confidence in the powers of Ellsberg's memory. He acknowledged that his memory—which "used to be totally amazing"—was not what it once was, that he now gets things wrong at times—names, dates, time sequences. But the problem seemed to me to go a little beyond that. Some of his memories struck me as having little to do with reality. "He can't tell a story straight," one person who knows him quite well told me. Sanford Ungar, formerly the dean of the School of Communication at American University and the author of a book on the Pentagon Papers, related,

> He remembers things in a very peculiar way. He acts on them in a very peculiar way. One of the most bizarre experiences I ever had with him is that I interviewed him at considerable length at their apartment in New York when I was working on my book. I have tapes of those interviews. But he claimed many times—*many* times—to other people that I had never interviewed him for my book. And, you know, either there was somebody posing as him, which clearly there wasn't, because I knew him at the time, or he just has this capacity to rewrite his own experience in history.

This posed a problem for this book. What to do with a subject whose memory is erratic and who tends to exaggerate? My solution, in a nutshell, was to compare his recollections with what I learned from my many other sources and to evaluate them within the array of evidence. Many of his recollections I let stand in context for readers to judge for themselves, some for entertainment value, for Ellsberg is a fine raconteur.

At one point, Dan and Patricia Ellsberg had me over to their home to hear "the Tom Wells story," as Dan put it, in a condescending tone (one he employed often with me). They wanted to learn more about me, to hear where I was "coming from," to learn what my "motives" were. They had their own tape recorder rolling on their dining room table next to mine (Dan taped most of our interviews). Dan had woken up at four that morning, they told me, his mind churning about this book, specifically over a recollection someone had given me. This person had said that, according to Ellsberg, his first wife, Carol, had told him when their marriage went south that she had never hated anybody so much in her life. "It's horrible stuff to have to deal with," Ellsberg told me.

He asked some people not to talk to me. To at least one he said that I couldn't be trusted. But he gave the green light to others. A couple of years after he had stopped talking to me, his son Robert told my editor at a conference, "My father would practically pay people not to talk to this guy now."

It crossed my mind that Ellsberg might go after me in some way, perhaps try to discredit me. His former friend Martin Garbus, the civil liberties lawyer, advised me, "If Dan turns on you, he will turn on you brutally and hard. And he will turn on you with righteousness and justification." That is consistent with what I know.

———◆———

My research for this book was extensive. I interviewed 236 people and have quoted them often to help bring Ellsberg's story to life. Some people I interviewed also gave me documents of various sorts—notes, letters, memos, papers, essays, trial transcripts and exhibits, old newspaper articles, photos, and the like. This material and the interviews were extraordinarily valuable. I utilized a number of archival collections available to the public, including the Cranbrook Archives in Michigan; the John F. Kennedy Library in Massachusetts; the Neil Sheehan Papers in the Library of Congress; the Lyndon Baines Johnson Library in Texas; the Nixon Presidential Materials at the National Archives in Maryland; Watergate Special Prosecution Force records at the National Archives; the Edward G. Lansdale Papers in the Hoover Institution Archives at

Stanford University; the Meiklejohn Civil Liberties Library in Berkeley; the Indochina Archive in Berkeley (later moved to Texas); and material from the Cecil Currey Papers at Fort Hays State University in Kansas, the J. William Fulbright Papers at the University of Arkansas, and East High School in Denver, Colorado. Through a Freedom of Information Act request, I was able to obtain and get released to the public thousands of Watergate Special Prosecution Force records bearing on the break-in at Dr. Lewis Fielding's office, Ellsberg, the Pentagon Papers, the Plumbers, and related matters. I also obtained some Nixon Presidential Materials records through mandatory review and re-review requests. Ellsberg himself provided me a few documents, including papers, essays, notes, briefing and speech transcripts, letters, and articles, as well as "corrections" to books bearing on him. The RAND Corporation provided some papers and access to interview transcripts. I listened to many newly released Nixon White House tapes at the National Archives, watched video footage of Ellsberg at the CBS News Archive and the UCLA TV and Film Archive, and viewed other videos people gave me. In addition, several people provided me copies of interviews of Ellsberg or speeches by him. And I perused numerous newspapers and read widely in other secondary sources.

My work on this book was funded mainly by a National Endowment for the Humanities Fellowship.

BREAK-IN

BERNARD BARKER WAS A 54-YEAR-OLD REAL ESTATE BROKER IN MIAMI when E. Howard Hunt approached him in August of 1971. Born in Cuba, Barker had worked for the CIA for almost seven years in the 1960s and had been Hunt's principal assistant during the Bay of Pigs fiasco in 1961. Hunt, who had used the code name Eduardo during the Bay of Pigs mission, commanded Barker's unswerving loyalty. "Eduardo represents the liberation of Cuba," Barker would say. So when Hunt asked him if he would participate in a surreptitious entry to obtain information on a traitor who had apparently passed classified documents to a foreign embassy, Barker was eager to help. He hoped to obtain Hunt's help in overthrowing Fidel Castro. Hunt, who believed that killing Castro was the route to liberating Cuba, informed Barker "that he was considered the expert in the White House on Cuban affairs." Barker was eager for clandestine action again. "In the process of doing these things in the past, you get to like the adventure," he said later. Hunt, too, desired action. After being recruited the previous month to participate in a secret White House Special Investigations Unit that was investigating the traitor, he had been "dying to get with it" but had then begun complaining about his job, saying that the unit wasn't doing enough.[1]

Hunt informed Barker that he would need the assistance of two of his experienced associates for the covert entry. He wanted dependable men who, like Barker, had been through the Bay of Pigs and who had received CIA training. Barker recruited Felipe DeDiego and Eugenio Martinez, two salesmen in his real estate company. Martinez had worked for the CIA since 1961 and had been on retainer to the agency since 1969, though Barker was apparently unaware of this last fact. All three Cubans "were really highly motivated," G. Gordon Liddy, another member of the Special Investigations Unit, remembers.[2]

After getting a look at Martinez and DeDiego, Hunt prepared a memo to David Young, the cochairman of the Special Investigations Unit with Egil Krogh, that included enough "vital statistics" to allow for a "five-way index check" on the three Cubans. Hunt and Liddy also viewed their CIA training files, which showed that they could perform covert entries. According to Liddy, their CIA training "final exam" was breaking into a building in New York City—"getting in and getting out." The men were cleared in Washington. Hunt stressed to Krogh that they would accept only expense money for their work, as the bag job was a contribution to national security and no profit should be obtained.[3]

At CIA safe houses, Hunt and Liddy obtained pocket litter (i.e., false identification), a small experimental camera concealed in a tobacco pouch, wigs, thick glasses, two sets of false teeth, and a limp-producing shoe insert. For a related covert operation, Hunt obtained a tape recorder from the CIA. His CIA contact person considered that transaction "an unmitigated pain in the neck" and perceived Hunt to be "an over-graded semicompetent case officer" whose clandestine request for the recorder was "ridiculous since he could have purchased it himself in an untraceable manner by paying cash over the counter." Following other unreasonable requests by Hunt, including one that the CIA immediately recall a 24-year-old secretary with an "average IQ" from Paris for his use "and explain to all concerned that she was urgently needed for an unspecified special assignment," the CIA cut off relations with Hunt. CIA Director Richard Helms told John Ehrlichman, a top White House official who was supervising the Special Investigations Unit, that Hunt was "bad news" and that the CIA "had perhaps kept Mr. Hunt on a little longer than we should have but that we had several years ago separated him from more operational tasks because he was overly romantic, and at the same time we had continued him because he had some serious financial problems relating to a sick child and we did not want to have a disgruntled ex-employee."[4]

In the late afternoon of August 25, Liddy and Hunt flew from Washington to Los Angeles for a reconnaissance of their target. They took a taxi to the comfortable Beverly Hilton, where they registered under aliases. On the travel request he filed with the White House before leaving that day, Liddy stated that the purpose of his trip was a "meeting with Bureau of Customs official re drugs." David Young informed John Ehrlichman at the White House, "Hunt and Liddy have left for California." In his hotel room, Liddy did around a hundred push-ups before retiring.[5]

The next morning, after putting on their disguises, Hunt and Liddy cased the building that housed their target. The target was the small Beverly Hills office of a private, shy, scholarly man of 62 years who had a slender build, leathery dark skin, and egg-shaped bald head. He looked a bit like Yul Brynner. "He walked with a certain confidence, which in a sense belied his quietness," recalls Dr. Alfred Goldberg, who was probably his closest friend in Los Angeles, at least until 1967 when Goldberg moved from an office adjacent to his. "There was a kind of, at times, a swagger, but not in an obnoxious way." He was "quietly self-confident. He was not a cocky person." The man was not easy to get to know and, in fact, very few people knew him. "He kept most things to himself," Goldberg remembers. He "was not a hail-fellow well-met. . . . He was like a Buddha. He'd sit there like that, you know, with a knowing smile on his face, as though he knew something, but he wasn't telling." He possessed superior intelligence, which was well recognized by those around him. "He was very wise," Dr. Roger Gould recalls. "He spoke sparingly, but when he spoke, people listened very carefully. He had a great deal of respect. . . . This was a man of great integrity and great depth." Although he had earlier owned a home in Beverly Hills and he was not hurting financially, he now lived modestly in an apartment in West Los Angeles, and his office was also decorated simply. He was a highly principled man of liberal political beliefs with, some suspected, "a lot of very pent-up passion—for human dignity and for honesty—and a lot of sympathy for the underdogs," Gould remembers. Yet few actually knew his political views. Even Goldberg, who used to ride to and from work with him every day for years after they opened their adjacent offices on the same day in 1950, didn't hear a lot about them. "He kept his political views to himself," Goldberg reminisces. "He was very discreet."[6]

The man whose office Hunt and Liddy were targeting was a psychoanalyst, Dr. Lewis Fielding. He had been Dr. Gould's personal analyst for his psychoanalytic training; Dr. Goldberg was also a psychoanalyst. Born and raised in New York City, Dr. Fielding had received his medical training in Switzerland and Vienna. He had served as a psychiatrist in Patton's Third Army during World War II. He had left the army as a lieutenant colonel in 1946 and joined the Veterans Administration in Los Angeles as a staff psychiatrist and instructor in clinical psychiatry. In 1971, the year Hunt and Liddy were casing his office, Fielding was probably the most highly regarded psychoanalyst in Los Angeles. The internationally known psychoanalyst Dr. Ralph "Romy" Greenson, who was a friend of his and of Goldberg, and who directed some patients to them, was probably the most prominent analyst in Los Angeles. But Fielding commanded the highest respect from his fellow analysts, including Greenson, even though few knew him personally. "Fielding was not a Hollywood doctor," Goldberg recalls. "He would avoid the limelight. That's one of the things I think people respected. . . . You knew Fielding was there, but he was quietly on the side."[7]

The traitor who had allegedly passed classified documents to a foreign embassy was a former patient of Dr. Fielding. Gould had trained under Fielding at the same time the traitor had seen him, so Gould and the traitor had lain "on the same couch probably within the same two-hour period several days a week," Gould surmises.[8]

———◆———

The traitor was an odd man with an intriguing past. He was a genius who had been raised to think of himself as special and marked for major achievement. But his considerable academic accomplishments aside, he had experienced difficulty realizing his gifts. Following impressive successes as a student at Harvard, and despite an enduring reputation for brilliance, enormous ambition, and a substantial capacity for personal charm, his once promising career had fallen short of expectations. First as a defense intellectual at the RAND Corporation, then as a lowly Pentagon staffer, and later back at RAND, he had problems completing work. Though unusually creative, energetic, and brimming with ideas, he was chronically disorganized and lacked self-discipline. He had a hard time sitting still. He was self-indulgent, and he habitually ran late. His judgment was questionable. After his work habits had damaged his reputation in the Pentagon, and following a devastating marital breakup and other disappointments in his love life, he had behaved recklessly and exhibited a death wish during a stint as a gun-toting warrior in Vietnam. "He had sought to discharge internal tension by taking action; his analytic treatment was unsuccessful in altering this propensity," Dr. Bernard Malloy, chief of the CIA's psychiatric staff, later analyzed. He had even fantasized about being the first American killed by regular North Vietnamese Army units. That would be one hell of a way to go, he thought. He felt he had already lived long enough.[9]

The man had developed a harmful reputation among colleagues for indiscretion. He enjoyed letting others know about the high-level state secrets he learned. He reveled in working with highly classified material and loved knowing secrets. He also enjoyed telling colleagues about his personal life. "It was very important for him that we, us men, knew that he was a stud," one former RAND man recounts. "And that these beautiful women really went for him. And that he was not really bound by the normal rules and conventions of tedious society. That he needed it, he kept saying." His indiscretion about sexual matters and seemingly rich sex life became widely known. The Special Investigations Unit showed interest in them. "I have been advised by a neutral source who directly observed the premises that the bedroom of the subject's California oceanfront former home contained an extraordinary amount of mirrors," G. Gordon Liddy transmitted to Dr. Malloy in October 1971 for the CIA's work on a psychological profile of him. "The source, a moving man, said that in all his experience he had never seen so many mirrors in a bedroom."[10]

The man also had a marked need to be prominent. There was something almost childlike about his zeal to be close to power and part of important events.

In the early spring of 1971, after undergoing a 180-degree about-face on the war in Vietnam, this man, Daniel Ellsberg, then aged 40, had provided a top-secret history of U.S. decision making in Vietnam to a reporter from the *New York Times*. The June publication in the *Times* of reports on the history had alarmed the Nixon White House. It was a cataclysmic event in the history of leaks of government secrets to the press—"the most extensive release of classified documents and information ever to occur in this country," U.S. National Security Adviser Henry Kissinger wrote President Richard Nixon. The White House feared that Ellsberg might also release other state secrets. And it worried he might be part of a communist spy ring. According to a Soviet double agent who reported to the FBI, an unidentified man using an alias had provided a complete copy of the history to the Soviet embassy in Washington. Ellsberg was the prime suspect, though intelligence was murky. "We did not know whether Ellsberg was what he was purporting to be—a romantic loner of the left acting out of conscience—or whether he was in with the show with the KGB," G. Gordon Liddy told me. "We also didn't know what else he had. We didn't know where he had it. Nor did we know what his intentions were." There were even doubts inside the government that Ellsberg himself had provided the documents to the *Times*. Maybe a co-conspirator had done so and he was just trying to take credit for it to become a hero. Nixon told an aide, "If you could get him tied in with some communist groups, that would be good. . . . That's my guess, that he's in with some subversives."[11]

Now, after publication of the top-secret documents in the *Times*, Ellsberg's emotions were in great conflict. He was reveling in the limelight—which he had long considered his due—generated by his release of the documents. "He loved it," one of his lawyers, Charles Nesson, remembers. "He just plain loved it." He had always sought praise, and he was now getting it in spades. And he felt the satisfaction of having accomplished something big. He struck some as quite self-important about it all. But Ellsberg's anxiety and frustration were immense. Although he had striven to secure legal cover for his act and thereby to avoid jail, he had been indicted and faced a possible long prison sentence. Virtually all of his ex-colleagues and friends had disowned him over his disclosure. "I lost every friend I had in the world, at least every male friend," Ellsberg would recall.[12] His pain was gargantuan. One of these friends had been perhaps his best friend, Harry Rowen, who lost his job as president of the RAND Corporation largely because of Ellsberg's release of the documents. Many former colleagues doubted Ellsberg's character.

Ellsberg's ex-wife was furious with him. He had involved their two children, ages 10 and 13, in copying the documents. She thought that psychotic. "You do not take children along to commit felonies," Carol Cummings says evenly. Though antiwar, she also opposed the release of top-secret material. A Ph.D. student in psychology, Carol Ellsberg (she later reassumed her maiden name, Cummings, because of unwelcome attention from the whole affair) had been concerned that Dan had started "flipping out" years earlier. She had testified about his copying before a grand jury and in a federal affidavit. That was a "bonehead" move, Dan had told their children during a visit in early July of 1971. He informed Carol then that she had made a bad mistake, although he was friendly and he wrote around six checks to her for expenses, she told the FBI. He also "appeared to be seeking her approval for the disclosures he had made," she reported to the bureau. "He just can't stand the idea that I won't praise him," Carol told Charles Nesson a year later. Ellsberg informed Carol around this time that it was her fault he was on trial. He couldn't understand why she was angry at him—nor did he seem to understand just how angry at him she was. "Can you relax and enjoy it now?" he would say to her.[13]

Infuriatingly, Carol was refusing to cooperate with Dan or his lawyers, who considered her possibly the most damaging witness of all. She was also spilling to the FBI (at least insofar as she had information to spill). During her initial meeting with FBI agents four days after the documents had first been published, Carol had "expressed a desire to cooperate with the FBI" and said that she was "willing to furnish information regarding Daniel Ellsberg," an FBI document reveals. "She stated that she is completely patriotic and if Daniel Ellsberg is responsible for disclosing classified information, he should be in jail." On several occasions in the days that followed, Carol had even phoned the FBI's office in Los Angeles (where she lived) and "volunteered information" about her former husband. She provided information on a range of matters, including his finances, lifestyle, former girlfriends, and, most extensively, his copying of the documents. Many girlfriends and associates she named were contacted by the bureau. The material Carol provided on Ellsberg's copying of the documents was incriminating. Some of the information she furnished probably fed into two psychological profiles the CIA did on him. She also related that Ellsberg had previously seen a psychoanalyst, and that he had assured her that he had told this analyst all about what he had done.[14]

That caught the FBI's attention. Following a request by the bureau originating at the highest level, Carol had telephoned the FBI to give them Dr. Lewis Fielding's name. To obtain Fielding's name, she had contacted a psychiatrist who had treated both Dan and herself in the early 1960s. She had earlier considered calling Fielding to get him to talk sense to her former husband about his copying of the documents.[15]

After learning Fielding's identity, Dr. Bernard Malloy of the CIA did "a background check" on him and found him "a solid, capable, talented and responsible psychoanalyst." Malloy even believed that Ellsberg "would be better off if he continued analysis."[16]

Daniel Ellsberg's life was a maelstrom at most times, but particularly so now. On top of the problems already discussed, his two children were caught in the middle of his crossfire with Carol and disquieted by their mother's anger. It was "just a terrible experience," his son Robert remembers.[17] Though Ellsberg's current wife, Patricia, the likable heiress to a toy company fortune, was tremendously supportive, she had her own family problems to deal with: her famous father, the "toy king" Louis Marx, was irate over his son-in-law's action.

Anthony Russo, Ellsberg's partner in copying the top-secret documents, was becoming an albatross around his neck. That July, after refusing to testify before a grand jury investigating the release of the documents, Russo had traveled from Los Angeles to Cambridge, Massachusetts, to speak with Ellsberg. He knew that he would probably face criminal charges too. But Ellsberg did not want to share either the limelight or the courtroom with Russo, who had been a close friend at RAND. Ellsberg worried about being sullied and damaged by Russo, a countercultural radical. He began to distance himself from Russo. "I went there to Cambridge wanting to sit down and talk about the damn thing," Russo recounts. But Ellsberg "didn't want to talk to me. . . . He was trying to ignore me." Ellsberg wished Russo would go away.[18]

A highly sensitive and emotional man, Ellsberg was also enraged by unflattering media portrayals of him. Like most celebrities, he had far less control over his press than he desired. "He didn't like things written about him that implied that he was anything less than this historic, heroic figure," Sanford Ungar, who was then a reporter for the *Washington Post*, recalls. Maddeningly, Neil Sheehan, the reporter at the *New York Times* to whom he had provided the

Pentagon Papers (as the top-secret documents became known), had secretly copied them behind his back and then neglected to forewarn him of their publication. Adding insult to injury, *Times* articles were describing Ellsberg as the man who *said* he gave the Papers to newspapers, failing to give him certain credit for his act. "It drove him nuts," remembers the *Times*'s Marty Arnold. Ellsberg came to believe the *Times* hated him. He was also frustrated that newspapers weren't publishing more of the documents and that his disclosure wasn't having greater political effect. "That was always a discouraging point with him," Russo's lead attorney, Leonard Weinglass, reminisces. "That it didn't move people as much as he thought it should have."[19] In addition to all of this, Ellsberg was by nature a restless man never really at peace with himself.

Wearing their disguises, Hunt and Liddy took photographs of Lewis Fielding's office building from all sides. Liddy posed as a pipe-smoking tourist to allay suspicion. In one photo, Liddy stood next to Fielding's parking space looking "proud as punch," White House Counsel John Dean would later inform President Nixon. Hunt and Liddy also timed the drive between Fielding's home and his office; that might prove useful if the psychoanalyst unexpectedly got "out of pocket" during the actual entry. Upon returning to their hotel, Liddy angrily jettisoned the shoe insert he had received from the CIA, which had turned out to be painful. Still wearing his wig, he decided to go for a walk in the park, only to be "cruised" by another man. Liddy decided not to wear the wig again.[20] The risk that the operation could be traced to the White House thereby increased.

Liddy and Hunt had assured David Young and Egil Krogh that they could carry out the mission without it being traced to the White House. After all, they had both had experience with bag jobs in the past. Hunt, a secretive man who "had a habit of locking himself in his office," had participated in break-ins overseas during his many years as a CIA operative. Liddy, an intelligent and articulate gun freak who played Nazi songs in the Special Investigations Unit's offices, had some experience with break-ins from his earlier work as an FBI agent.[21]

Liddy had hoped that his former employer, in fact, might be able to obtain Fielding's files on Ellsberg. He had approached the FBI about it.[22] But the approach the bureau took (on its own initiative) had been unsuccessful.

After Carol Ellsberg had named Fielding, FBI Director J. Edgar Hoover had sent an "Urgent" teletype to the Los Angeles FBI office directing, "You should immediately interview Dr. Fielding to obtain any information he may be willing to furnish regarding his knowledge of background and activities of Daniel Ellsberg." Perhaps Fielding could shed light on Ellsberg's suspected communist connections, the bureau believed. Hoover and other FBI officials surmised that if Fielding had "only a Ph.D." he might talk, but that if he had a medical degree he might refuse on the grounds of doctor-patient confidentiality. When FBI agents attempted to interview Fielding, the psychoanalyst turned them down; he refused to even acknowledge that Ellsberg had been his patient. "Fielding would never tell anybody who his patients were," Dr. Alfred Goldberg recalls. Fielding's attorney told the FBI that Fielding did not wish to discuss any matter with the bureau. (When Fielding again refused to talk to the FBI two years later, after the penetration of his office had been revealed publicly, the FBI felt that "indicated strongly that Fielding is in complete sympathy with Ellsberg.")[23]

This was not the sort of thing Liddy and Hunt had had in mind. "We were hoping the FBI would do what, when I was back in the FBI, back in the earlier days, they did on a regular basis, which were called black bag jobs—would go in and out," Liddy remembers. "But they were no longer doing that." The "specially trained cadres" who used to conduct entries for the FBI had "been allowed to wither on the vine" and had "lost their skills," Hunt perceived. The White House may also have been concerned that if the FBI undertook the job, Hoover might later use it as "leverage" against Nixon, perhaps even as insurance against being fired. The Plumbers, as the Special Investigations Unit later became known, would have to become operational. "It occurred to me, 'Well, if they won't, I've done it in the past, we can do it again,'" Liddy recalls. "'We will do it.'"[24]

To assure that the operation would not be traceable to the White House, Hunt and Liddy had agreed, they would use some of Hunt's former Cuban associates in the CIA to actually enter the "target area." They would use "the Cuban asset." If captured, these men could be relied on not to talk. On a memo he later attempted to remove from the Plumbers' files, John Ehrlichman signed off on their plan "if done under your assurance that it is not traceable."[25] By that stroke of his pen, the White House had authorized a burglary.

After casing Fielding's office building in broad daylight, Hunt and Liddy returned to the building that night under the conditions in which the actual break-in would be made. They entered as if they owned the building, then walked down a hallway and up the stairs to the second floor, where Fielding's office was located. Maria Martinez, a cleaning woman, noticed them there. "I am the doctor," Hunt announced in Spanish before she could say anything. Hunt told her that he and Liddy (also purportedly a doctor) had to leave something for Fielding that he was expecting. After eyeing them "suspiciously," Martinez let them into Fielding's office. Liddy snapped pictures of the inside and the lock on the front door while either Hunt engaged her in conversation (his version) or she "went on to another office to do my cleaning" (her version). According to Hunt, Martinez asked after a time, "What's he doing in there?" Martinez later said she noticed Liddy "taking pictures of the walls of [Fielding's] office." If so, so much for the tobacco pouch. Liddy observed that Fielding had "files equipped with locks I saw I could defeat easily with a torsion bar and pick." After Hunt slipped Martinez some money (effectively a bribe and thus possibly a crime in itself), the two covert operatives retreated to their car. From there they noticed that both the front and rear doors of the building were "kept open as late as 1:00 o'clock in the morning." Hunt would say later, "We did a rather thorough, I think, professional study of the objective."[26]

Hunt and Liddy then immediately flew back to Washington, arriving at 6:20 A.M. At Hunt's request, they were met by an employee of the CIA's Technical Services Division, whom Hunt directed to promptly develop their film. Hunt picked up the photos at a CIA safe house later that day. The CIA made copies of the photos and later gave them to the Watergate prosecutors. "These fellows had to be some idiots," John Dean would say to President Nixon of Liddy and Hunt.[27]

Upon returning to Washington, Hunt and Liddy met with Krogh and Young to discuss the break-in. They passed their photos of Fielding's office around a table in a small room in the Plumbers' offices and presented a detailed entry plan and a diagram of the target area. The plan included a proposed budget and "a simple plan for escape by using 30 feet of nylon rope." Young was bothered that Liddy and Hunt had encountered the cleaning woman and had actually been in Fielding's office; that increased the risk that the operation could be traced. Liddy and Hunt emphasized that they could carry out the entry in a way that no one could tell anyone had been in the office. It would be a clean in and out. Hunt said to Young words to the effect, "I think we have a perfect situation here for a clandestine surreptitious entry." "Good," Young replied. Given Liddy and Hunt's assurances, Krogh thought the chance of their getting caught was "very remote." Ehrlichman would later tell Krogh that, if they were caught, "we can always say that Hunt and Liddy were out in California on an investigation and went beyond anything we contemplated."[28]

Liddy and Hunt decided that Labor Day weekend would be an optimal time for the break-in. For three days, doctors and cleaning people would be away. "D Day," Hunt called the weekend. In military fashion, he and Liddy began subtracting the days to go.[29]

———◆———

In the minds of the Plumbers, there was a mix of reasons for the break-in. They thought Fielding's office might contain a "rich lode of material" on Ellsberg, "the best instant source of a full read-out" on the man. The material might help determine his motives, capabilities, and intentions, as well as his co-conspirators. "The FBI told us—they didn't identify this as having come from a wiretap, but I'm morally sure that it *was* from a wiretap—that although Ellsberg had terminated the services of a psychiatrist named Fielding in Beverly Hills, he still would call the doctor at all hours of the day and night, almost on a daily basis, to discuss with him the most intimate details of his daily life," Liddy remembers. "That being the case, it seemed to us logical that he might have discussed with the doctor what else he had, what he intended to do with what else he had, and whether he was involved with the KGB." Hunt later testified: "Dr. Ellsberg, by virtue of his contact with foreign nations, particularly foreign women . . . his experimentation into hallucinogenic drugs, all of this created to me a pattern of bizarre conduct that I thought the Soviets, at the very least, would be quick to take note of." That Ellsberg "consorted with females of foreign birth and extraction . . . was a danger signal to anybody in the counter-espionage field," Hunt said. Krogh thought it imperative to determine whether Ellsberg was acting in concert with a foreign power.[30]

The Plumbers had hoped the CIA might be able to illuminate Ellsberg's character and motivations by constructing a psychological profile of him. The profile could also be used to smear Ellsberg through leaks to the press, they envisioned. "Hunt was heavily into that," Liddy recalls. Hunt hoped to be able to use the study "to refer in a knowledgeable way to Dr. Ellsberg's oedipal conflicts or castration fears." The CIA's psychiatrists had produced the first profile two weeks before Hunt and Liddy's reconnaissance mission to Fielding's office. They had done so with great reluctance. The information they had on Ellsberg was quite sparse (it came largely from the media and FBI reports), and studying a U.S. citizen violated the CIA's charter, which "might come to light during any legal proceeding," the CIA's psychiatrists feared. Also, their efforts "could be misunderstood, misinterpreted, and mistakenly considered to have derived from the doctor-patient therapeutic relationship which was in fact far from the case," Dr. Bernard Malloy, who directed work on the study, later said. "All concerned were very uncomfortable and uneasy about this task and strongly desired and preferred to have the Agency relieved of responsibility for meeting it," another CIA staffer stated.[31]

The CIA's assessment of Ellsberg had been handed to David Young by a special security courier on August 11. It observed:

> There is nothing to suggest in the material reviewed that Subject suffers from a serious mental disorder in the sense of being psychotic and out of contact with reality. There are suggestions, however, that some of his longstanding personality needs were intensified by psychological pressures of the mid-life period and that this may have contributed significantly to his recent actions.
>
> An extremely intelligent and talented individual, Subject apparently early made his brilliance evident. It seems likely that there were substantial pressures to succeed and that Subject early had instilled in him expectations of success, that he absorbed the impression that he was special and destined for greatness. And indeed, he did attain considerable academic success and seemed slated for a brilliant career.
>
> There has been a notable zealous intensity about the Subject throughout his career. Apparently finding it difficult to tolerate ambiguity and ambivalence, he was either strongly for something or strongly against it. There were suggestions of problems in achieving full success, for although his ideas glittered, he had trouble committing himself in writing. He had a knack for drawing attention to himself and at early ages attained positions of considerable distinction, usually attaching himself as a "bright young man" to an older and experienced man of considerable stature who was attracted by his brilliance and flair.
>
> But one can only sustain the role of "bright young man" so long. Most men between the ages of 35 and 45 go through a period of re-evaluation. . . . For the individual who is particularly driven towards the height of success and prominence, this mid-life period may be a particularly difficult time. The evidence reviewed suggests that this was so for Ellsberg, a man whose career had taken off like a rocket, but who found himself at mid-life not nearly having achieved the prominence and success he expected and desired. Thus it may well have been an intensified need to achieve significance that impelled him to release the Pentagon Papers.
>
> There is no suggestion that Subject saw anything treasonous in his act. Rather, he seemed to be responding to what he deemed a higher order of patriotism. . . .
>
> Ellsberg's reactions since emerging from seclusion have been instructive. Initially there was jubilation, an apparent enjoyment of the limelight. This was succeeded by a transient period wherein there was a sense of quiet satisfaction, of acceptance of his new-found stature, as if his personally significant action had accomplished what he sought to achieve. But then, embittered that Con-

gress and the press had not wholeheartedly supported him, he turned against them. This is not surprising, for there would seem to be an insatiable quality to Ellsberg's strong needs for success and recognition.[32]

The profile was pretty much on the mark. But the Plumbers found it unhelpful. It "was a very poor psychological profile," Liddy remembers. Only hours after receiving it, Krogh and Young reported to John Ehrlichman, "We have received the CIA preliminary psychological study . . . which I must say I am disappointed in and consider very superficial. We will meet tomorrow with the head psychiatrist, Dr. Bernard Malloy, to impress upon him the detail and depth that we expect. We will also make available to him here some of the other information we have received from the FBI on Ellsberg." Young told Malloy the next day that the profile was "too general to be useful" (prompting Malloy and his colleagues to respond, effectively, "Garbage in, garbage out. Give us better material," as Liddy remembers it. "Don't complain to us about the quality of the psychological profile when you don't give us much").[33]

Hunt and Liddy believed Fielding's files on Ellsberg might provide grist for an improved profile. "That was the second reason that pushed us towards going in and getting the doctor's office files," Liddy told me. "One, we could get that information [on Ellsberg's capabilities, intentions, and collaborators]. Second, anything else that was in there we were going to give to the CIA. . . . They had said, 'Give us better information, we'll give you a better profile.' Which made sense to us. . . . 'We're going to be in there anyway for our own purposes, and the CIA wants this, and they can give us . . . a real profile on this guy.'" It was, in fact, upon receipt of the CIA's first profile of Ellsberg and "in this connection" that Krogh and Young recommended to Ehrlichman that they undertake a covert operation to examine Fielding's files on Ellsberg.[34]

But another motivation for obtaining Fielding's files was to collect dirt on Ellsberg. Hunt, who approached the Plumbers' investigation of Ellsberg from "the psychological warfare point of view," proposed the mission to White House Counsel Charles Colson as part of a "skeletal operations plan" for determining "how to destroy his public image and credibility." Fielding's files might contain evidence of Ellsberg's psychological problems, drug use, and deviant sexual practices, Hunt believed. "They expected to find evidence to corroborate what Hunt had been saying about Ellsberg's mental unbalance: that he was a drug user; he shot at peasants in Vietnam from a helicopter; he had a *ménage à trois* with two women," Ehrlichman would say years later. "The catalog went on and on." The evidence would be leaked. The Watergate Special Prosecutor Leon Jaworski later concluded that the primary purpose of the

break-in was "to obtain derogatory information about Ellsberg in order to release that information publicly and thereby destroy Ellsberg's public image."
Jaworski erroneously rejected the conspiracy investigation motive.[35]

———— ·◉· ————

As planning for Special Project #1 (as the break-in became known inside the
White House) proceeded, funding arrangements had to be made. At Ehrlichman's behest, Krogh asked Charles Colson to obtain $5,000. Krogh, who "didn't
speak very highly of Colson," specified cash. Krogh recognized that Colson was
the man to go to for money for operations no one wanted traced to the White
House. It was perhaps best that Krogh rather than his partner David Young approached Colson for the money. Colson didn't think highly of Young's abilities
and would later recall being annoyed on one occasion when Young stopped him
in the hall and he didn't want to talk to Young.[36]

Colson called Joseph Barody, a Washington lobbyist and consultant who
had worked with him on White House propaganda projects in the past. Colson
told Barody he needed $5,000 in cash "right away." Barody gathered the money
that afternoon and evening, largely from his office safe. To avoid the possibility
of tracing it, Colson arranged to have Barody repaid with laundered funds from
the Associated Milk Producers. When Colson's secretary, Joan Hall, subsequently made out a personal check from Colson to reimburse Hunt for additional expenses, Colson "refused to sign it" and directed Hall to reimburse
Hunt through the White House. Hunt would bill the White House for eight
hours of work per day as a "consultant" for his involvement in the break-in, and
would arrange for Bernard Barker, Eugenio Martinez, and Felipe DeDiego to
receive a "modest" sum beyond operational expenses, since they "might have
been able to sell substantial real estate in Florida" had they not been away.[37] So
much for pledging they would eschew any financial gain.

On the same day that Hunt and Liddy took pictures of Fielding's office
building, David Young asked John Ehrlichman, "How quickly do we want to
try to bring about a change in Ellsberg's public image? . . . If the present
Hunt/Liddy Project #1 is successful, it will be absolutely essential to have an
overall game plan developed." The next day Ehrlichman wrote Colson, who
was spearheading the White House's effort to smear Ellsberg, "On the assumption that the proposed undertaking by Hunt and Liddy would be carried out
and would be successful, I would appreciate receiving from you by next
Wednesday a game plan as to how and when you believe the materials should
be used." As a member of the Watergate Special Prosecution Force would later

note, "Obviously Ehrlichman knew something important was going to happen in the next few days."[38]

Upon receiving Ehrlichman's memo, Colson, who claimed to detest the term "game plan," acted surprised. As usually happened when he was surprised, Joan Hall remembered, he raised his eyebrows and his ears went back. Hall herself recognized the significance of the memo and had immediately "marched it" into Colson's office. Colson remarked to Hall that it was "stupid to put it in writing." "Unbelievable to be in writing," Hall later told the Watergate Special Prosecution Force. Shortly after the break-in, Ehrlichman would tell Colson to "forget the memo" and not to discuss Hunt and Liddy's operations "with anybody *at all*," Colson told the prosecutors. "Ehrlichman was emphatic on this point."[39]

On August 30, while vacationing in a Forest Service cottage used by government officials on Cape Cod, Ehrlichman gave his final approval for the bag job. Krogh and Young, who had just spoken to Hunt and Liddy about the results of their reconnaissance mission and their plans for the entry, were on two phone extensions in Krogh's office on the first floor of the Executive Office Building. They told Ehrlichman that Hunt and Liddy had reported that the operation was feasible and could be carried out without being traced to the White House. They didn't discuss specifics or possibly even mention Hunt and Liddy by name, as they were speaking on a regular phone line and worried it might not be safe. Ehrlichman asked Krogh and Young what they thought. They should "continue on," both said. They attempted to assure Ehrlichman that the break-in could not be traced. "Fine," Ehrlichman said. They should proceed and let him know at once if anything important was discovered.[40]

That same day—D minus four—Hunt instructed Bernard Barker to fly with his men to Los Angeles and to meet him there in three days. "Barker didn't tell me where we were going and I did not ask," recalled Eugenio Martinez. "I was an operative."[41]

On September 1, when Joseph Barody arrived at Colson's office with the $5,000, Colson directed him to Krogh, who accepted a plain white envelope from him and looked inside to see if the money was there. "I might have counted it," Krogh said afterward. He hurriedly took the envelope to the Plumbers' offices, where Liddy and Hunt were waiting for their expense money before departing for the break-in. Krogh was late and they were worried about missing their plane, but he insisted that they go out and exchange the cash for other bills so that it couldn't be traced. Liddy "cleaned" the money at two banks near the White House. "For God's sake, don't get caught!" Krogh told Liddy before he departed. "He seemed nervous," Liddy remembers. "He said, 'Call me—I want to know as soon as you're out of there and it's safe. Whether you get anything, whether you don't get anything,' he said, 'call me immediately. Because I need to know that we're out of jeopardy here.'"[42]

Hunt and Liddy then hopped on a flight to Chicago and registered at the Sheraton Hotel under their aliases. Liddy was packing a folding Browning knife—"deadly and quiet," he wrote afterward in his memoir. Should he need to dispose of someone during the bag job, "a gun would be too noisy without a silencer, and none of mine, including a sterile (that is, nontraceable) CIA 9-mm assassination piece I now owned, was threaded to receive one." A mere pencil might have served Liddy well, however. "I could kill a man with a pencil in a matter of seconds" by jamming it into the victim's neck, he claimed. (Two years after the break-in, Liddy would find himself in the Watergate prosecutors' office with John Dean, whom he despised. "The thought did occur to me that there were pencils on the desk," Liddy writes. "I thought to myself, 'My God, maybe they put me in here to 'off' Dean." Liddy restrained himself.)[43]

In Chicago, Liddy and Hunt purchased $559 worth of electronic and photography equipment from Allied Radio and Altman Camera under their aliases. They would soon become unhappy with the quality of the equipment and deem their expense account inadequate. "It was a source of constantly needling of me by Hunt," Liddy recalls, "that our radios were stuff we went down and bought from Radio Shack." Years later, when I interviewed him, Liddy would still have much of the equipment from "the Fielding job." Why did they fly to Chicago rather than purchase the equipment in Washington? "Too close to the origin of the operation," Hunt explained.[44]

By this stage of their investigation of Ellsberg, after digesting many intelligence reports, Liddy and Hunt's portrait of him had taken greater shape. It was not flattering. "Unstable, self-righteous, egotistical, and the kind of guy who would go over to the other side and rationalize the hell out of it," Liddy responded when I asked him about his perception of Ellsberg at the time. Ellsberg was "sufficiently disturbed emotionally" to have seen a psychiatrist for two years, Liddy observed in a memo to Krogh and Young on August 18, and he had also been involved in "several breaches of security," first in the U.S. Marine Corps and later at both the Department of Defense and RAND. And although Ellsberg was obviously highly intelligent, his research habits were questionable. His work on the Pentagon Papers study had apparently not been up to snuff; he had been more into reading than writing, it was reported. On the same day that Hunt and Liddy began their reconnaissance of Fielding's office, the *New York Times* disclosed that Dell Publishing Company had canceled a contract with Ellsberg because he had failed to complete an introduction to a book of his Vietnam writings. And there were those "strange sexual practices." Liddy wasn't sure what to make of them. He knew about the mirrors and orgies, Ellsberg's general "promiscuous sexual life" and "sexual exhibitionism," as he reported to Krogh and Young. But was there even more? "Maybe he was into whips and leather," Liddy thought. "I didn't know. But it was just strange sexual practices were alleged to be associated with Ellsberg. And I heard that years later, that he apparently still had strange sexual practices." "The picture that emerged," Hunt recalled, "was that of a brilliant, unstable man" with a "rather peculiar background" who "had evidently a great many sexual problems" and led a "rather bizarre life." ("I did not go to an analyst because of any sexual problems, I can assure you," Ellsberg told a reporter when informed of Hunt's comment.)[45]

Hunt and Liddy were not on firm ground in criticizing another man's interest in sex or his behavior, however. Though married, on the very day of the Fielding break-in Hunt would meet one woman with whom he would have an affair. According to an FBI interview report, he later attempted to involve this woman in a *ménage à trois* with him and a new paramour after she had married another man.[46]

One evening, Hunt, a woman named Mary Denburg, Liddy, and his date, Sherry Stephens, were having dinner. To impress Stephens with "the power of his mind," Liddy had her hold a lighted match or cigarette lighter under the palm of his hand. "He held his hand over the match until his hand was badly burned," Denburg recounted to the FBI. "He showed his burned palm to [Denburg] and to Sherry, then wrapped it in a cloth napkin. During this exercise, Liddy did not show any sign of pain. Based on his conduct generally, [Denburg] considered him 'quite intense and a little weird.'" Liddy, who recalled that Stephens seemed badly frightened as he stared into her eyes while "the flesh turned black" and "the scent of burning meat" wafted into the air, burned his left hand rather than damage his gun hand. He was unable to do his customary hundred push-ups the next morning.[47]

When Liddy and Hunt arrived in Los Angeles on September 2, they met up with Bernard Barker, Eugenio Martinez, and Felipe DeDiego, who had flown in earlier from Miami. The men checked into the Beverly Hilton under fake names. Barker, Martinez, and DeDiego did not yet know the target of their mission or even whether it was in the United States or overseas. Hunt informed them it was to be an entry operation right there in Beverly Hills, and that night they all went out to evaluate the target—"what you guys call casing the joint," Barker told me. Hunt briefed the three Cubans on the operation. They would be entering the office and searching for certain material. If they found it, they should photograph it and leave it in place. Ellsberg's name was not mentioned. The briefing did not sit well with Martinez. It "was not like anything I was used to in the Company"—the CIA, he wrote afterward. "There wasn't a written plan, not even any mention of what to do if something went wrong." "At that time Martinez had objected to me that we're not going by the book, according to the old CIA tradition," Barker recalls. "And that he thought the security was very lax. . . . This very same thing was what happened the day of the Watergate disaster." (When Martinez got upset over the quality of the first Watergate break-in some eight months later, Hunt told Barker "that Martinez was not there to think, but to follow orders.") Martinez also apparently had doubts about Hunt himself, despite his legendary status among anti-Castro Cubans. "There was something strange about this man," Martinez wrote. "His tan, you know, is not the tan of a man who is in the sun. His motions are very meticulous—the way he smokes his pipe, the way he looks at you and smiles." But to DeDiego, Hunt's involvement suggested it was a legitimate government mission.[48]

The next day, as John Ehrlichman was relaxing on Cape Cod, the burglars purchased camera equipment, deliverymen's uniforms, a large footlocker-type suitcase, nylon rope, surgical and work gloves, masking tape, and black plastic. They also bought a glass cutter and crowbar in case they had to make a forced entry. They obtained the items at stores in the Los Angeles area—far from the operation's origin, per Hunt's concern, but in the backyard of the operation itself. The men then regrouped in their hotel, "went over the operation plan again, checked out each item of equipment from the checkoff list, and decided that all signs were go for that night," Hunt later testified. Hunt made some telephone calls to determine Fielding's whereabouts. Meanwhile, Richard Nixon was in Chicago addressing a convention of the Associated Milk Producers—bankrollers of the break-in.[49]

Barker and DeDiego donned the deliverymen's uniforms, as well as the thick glasses and wigs obtained earlier from the CIA. "They looked kind of queerish," Martinez recalled. "But that was not my responsibility." Carrying the suitcase filled with burglary tools and covered with Rush and Air Express stickers, Barker and DeDiego went over to Fielding's office building with the others, who took up positions behind the building. Efrain Martinez, a janitor who was standing outside the building, saw Barker and DeDiego there at around 10 or 11 P.M. They were dressed in black pants, black shirts, and black hats, Efrain Martinez would later recount. He thought they might be UPS or postal employees. They greeted him in Spanish. Martinez told Dr. Fielding the next evening that "they talked in an accent which he recognized to be Cuban and that he would know such an accent." Barker and DeDiego then walked into the unlocked building. Maria Martinez, the cleaning woman Hunt and Liddy had encountered during their earlier reconnaissance mission, was cleaning on the first floor. She was Efrain Martinez's mother and worked with him. Barker and DeDiego told her they had to make a delivery to Dr. Fielding. Though both mother and son thought this late-night drop off was a bit unusual, neither gave Barker and DeDiego any trouble. "We just told them we were making a delivery," Barker recounts. "She said something about it was after hours. We said, 'Well, we'd like to get the thing done. It's not real important.' You know, we went very low key on that." Fielding subsequently stated, "I, of course, had made no arrangements for that or any other delivery. I had expected no suitcase and found no suitcase on my arrival at my office" the following evening.[50]

Maria Martinez unlocked Fielding's office for Barker and DeDiego. "They entered the office and put the valise on the floor near a table," she testified afterward, despite being frightened to talk about the break-in. "They asked me what time I was leaving that night and I said that as soon as I finished my work I would leave." Barker or DeDiego pushed in the button on the doorknob so that the door would be unlocked when they returned that night for the bag job. They also pushed in the button on another door on their way out. But "apparently the cleaning woman was very sharp," Barker told me. "We did it twice, and she turned them off twice."[51]

Meanwhile, Hunt had driven over to Fielding's apartment building and assumed a position there. His job was to keep tabs on Fielding and to warn the others if, at this late hour, he got out of pocket. Reassuringly, Hunt saw that the lights were on in Fielding's apartment. He also determined that Fielding's Volvo was in the garage. "I set upon fixed surveillance on that," he later testified.[52]

Sometime after midnight, Barker and his men met with Liddy for their final briefing. Liddy, who had been surveying the office building from a slumped position in a car parked behind it, gave Barker a slip of paper with Daniel Ellsberg's name on it. They were to look for Ellsberg's file and photograph the documents in it, Liddy instructed. It was now only about a half an hour before the actual break-in. "They didn't know what the target was until we sent them in," Liddy remembers. Barker said afterward that the name Daniel Ellsberg "meant nothing to him" at the time. Did he know anything about the Pentagon Papers? "No," Barker told me. "I don't know anything about that."[53]

When I interviewed him over the phone, Barker, who worried I was "some leftist" and suggested three times that we end the interview, showed greater awareness of Ellsberg. "Ellsberg is a *fucking traitor*," he said angrily. "Anybody that turns over information to a foreign country is a traitor to this country. You can be very sophisticated—and it's a lot of *bullshit*—and you're still talking about a fucking traitor."[54]

After they observed Maria Martinez leaving for the night, Barker and his men proceeded to the rear door of the building. To their surprise, it was locked. Barker checked the front door and it, too, was locked. He had been instructed to avoid forcing the entry if possible, but with the building sealed, it was now impossible to conduct a clean in and out. After further reconnaissance and deliberations in the car, the burglars decided to enter through a locked ground-floor window concealed by shrubbery off a small back parking lot. As they made their entry, Liddy decided that he would watch their backs, despite instructions from Krogh that he stay away from the building. "I drew the Browning knife from the case attached to my belt and unfolded the blade," Liddy recounted. He assumed a position in a narrow space between two buildings shrouded by more plants. "If somebody could not be distracted, you'd have to take him out, or at least hold him or something," Liddy explains. "A weapon is a weapon, and a weapon is to be used." But if the police came, he would flee to distract attention. "I can run for miles, and there were numerous deeply shadowed hiding places in the area from which I could pause to warn the men inside with the transceiver," he wrote.[55]

Eugenio Martinez approached the window and tried to use their new glass cutter. "It was bad, bad," he later recounted. "It would not cut anything!" One can imagine his frustration. On a smaller scale, this was like the Bay of Pigs, where he had also been saddled with substandard equipment. Martinez and DeDiego placed masking tape on the window and either hit the glass with their hands (DeDiego's version), the crowbar (Martinez's version), or both. "Unknown perpetrator(s)" with "unknown" motives used an "unknown object," young Beverly Hills police officer Michael Haigwood, then five years on the force, would write in a report the next day. Before putting tape on the window, Martinez had removed his gloves. They would remain off during the rest of the mission. So much for preventing fingerprints. (Afterward Hunt would "certify" to Young and Krogh that "none had been left.") Martinez and DeDiego then reached up, unlocked the window, and climbed through, with Barker somewhere behind. They tore a curtain on their way in and left what remained of the window in an open position, duly noted by Dr. Bernard Sosner, a psychiatrist who discovered the break-in the next day. (Sosner recalls that the burglars had first attempted to enter the building by "smashing" a plywood-covered window of an adjoining x-ray room, though that is not in the police report nor recollected by others.)[56]

Unbeknown to the burglars, they were now in the consultation room of Dr. Ashley Lipshutz, a 37-year-old cardiologist, then away on vacation. In the darkness, they knocked over "some books or something," DeDiego recalled. They then moved out into the hall and up the stairs to Fielding's office. They still did not know exactly what they would be doing once they got inside. They turned the knob on Fielding's door and were surprised to find that it, too, was locked. This was the third locked door encountered by these operatives that they had expected to be unlocked. They got out their small crowbar and pried it open. "The wood part of the door near the lock had been hacked away," Fielding would observe the next evening. Once inside the office, Martinez and DeDiego opened the suitcase Barker and DeDiego had delivered earlier and took out their equipment. "Really, it was a joke," Martinez wrote afterward. The nylon rope for escaping down the side of the building "was so small, it couldn't have supported any of us." The men covered the windows of the office with black plastic. As Martinez finished setting up their equipment for photographing the documents, they heard Barker's "familiar knock" at the door and let him in. Barker gave them last-minute instructions. "We are here because we are doing a great job for the country," Barker stated. "We have to find some paper of a great traitor to the United States, [who] is an s.o.b." "We asked who was the guy," DeDiego remembered, "and he said, 'Daniel Ellsberg.'" Barker likely then showed them the piece of paper with Ellsberg's name on it. Martinez wrote afterward that Barker had earlier whispered Ellsberg's name to him because Barker worried he'd forget it and that "the name meant nothing to me."[57]

Meanwhile, Howard Hunt was panicking. Fielding's parking space at his apartment building, he noticed to his astonishment, was now empty. Hunt frantically tried to reach Liddy over his walkie-talkie, but to no avail. He got in his car and sped over to Fielding's office building. Hunt "passed me, circled, then parked and entered my car," Liddy recounts. "He was quite agitated." Hunt urged Liddy to order Barker and his men out. Liddy agreed to check up on them over their walkie-talkies, but again there was no response. The equipment purchased at Radio Shack did not seem to be up to the task. Liddy cursed it. Hunt, who suffered from a duodenal ulcer, would not calm down and urged that either he or Liddy go in and bring the men out. Hunt and Liddy argued in the car. Hunt's panic showed weakness, Liddy thought. He detested weakness in men. He thought disclosure of the Pentagon Papers showed "the problem of human weakness," he had written exactly one month earlier. "Hunt was too old for this game," Liddy told me. "Whatever he once was and everything, he no longer was. And he just didn't have the stomach for it, really, anymore. Hunt

was no longer strong. . . . He stayed in the game too long. He should have stayed out of it."[58]

Liddy likens Hunt's panic to his response when the second Watergate break-in started going down the tubes the following year. He and Liddy were in a hotel command post when they learned that the Watergate burglars had been captured by police. Hunt, Liddy recounts, squealed and jumped slightly, jerking one knee upward. Liddy got up from his chair to demonstrate Hunt's reaction to me. "I mean, he made this violent gesture . . . like he was really shaken by it. See, now, if you're in the business like that, you get very, very quiet and very, very calm, and you get very, very analytical. And you know exactly what to do, and you do this and the other thing. You don't go like that. He'd lost his nerve. That was the problem." Liddy, who was a national radio talk show host when I interviewed him, added, "Hell, if I fail at radio, I can go back to burglary tomorrow. You know, I've still got the nerves. But he doesn't." After Hunt "collapsed" and declared he was cooperating with the Watergate prosecutors, Liddy, who has not spoken to him since, even plotted to have him killed. "It occurred to me that Hunt had in his head a huge amount of stuff," Liddy explains. "Never mind just Watergate. I mean, God knows what he had and what he was going to reveal. And that they [the White House] might find out Hunt was being disloyal, they might know that I was loyal, and want Hunt killed. So I made arrangements with a black organized crime guy, who's now deceased, to poison Hunt on my order." The poison would be put in the "diet tray" Hunt received in prison because of his ulcer. "This fellow had the connections," Liddy says. "I could have had Hunt killed like that [snaps fingers]. But I would only do it if I was ordered to. And the order never came. . . . He may have found out about that. So Hunt has no love for me, and I have no love for Hunt."[59]

Back in Fielding's office, Barker and his men went to work on a locked wooden cabinet. Using their crowbar, they pried it open, bending the lock "completely out of shape." Behind the wooden cabinet they encountered Fielding's metal file cabinet. It was also locked, so they pried it open as well, again mutilating the lock. Their entry was getting messier. This was not what Ehrlichman, Krogh, and Young had envisioned. With Barker taking the lead, the burglars then began going through Fielding's files. "I was looking for any paper with the name of Daniel Ellsberg on it," DeDiego recalled. They also rummaged through Fielding's desk. "We looked anywhere," DeDiego said. Martinez and DeDiego snapped photographs of file and desk drawers so that, they later explained, they could put them back in place. With the cabinets already mutilated, however, that seems a questionable objective. But they also wanted proof of their search. Barker subsequently testified that they photographed the cabinets "to prove that we had forced them open." Joan Hall, Charles Colson's secretary, would see a photo afterward of someone wearing rubber gloves displaying files. The burglars piled Fielding's files on the floor. Judging by all the financial records present, Barker thought Fielding's office looked more like that of an investor than a psychiatrist. "It looked like the guy was a big bond or a stock man," he remembers. "He looked like a very rich man who had investments all over the world." "That's surprising," Dr. Alfred Goldberg comments. "He didn't live that way," though Fielding wasn't the type to talk about his investments. Barker says he was not interested in Fielding's financial records. "Once I would glance at stuff like that, I'd put it away. I mean, that was a man's personal life. We were not interested in anything like that."[60]

For somewhere between 30 minutes and a little over an hour, Barker and his men combed Fielding's small office. But they could find no Ellsberg file. "We found nothing there that I believe they were looking for," Barker remembers. "I don't know whether the raw files were not there or whatever." The operatives found only a card in Fielding's address book showing "that Ellsberg was a client," Barker says. "When I followed up that card into the files and so forth, I couldn't find anything." They found "absolutely no material . . . with the name of Ellsberg on it of any sort," Hunt would testify. Fielding's office had been "a dry hole," John Ehrlichman told Charles Colson several days later. Martinez took a photograph of the listing of Ellsberg in Fielding's address book "just to have something."[61]

"Okay, now we have to leave," Barker then directed his men. Rather than straightening up the office and putting the files back in place, however, they were to leave the premises in disarray. That way, it was hoped, the break-in would look to be the work of a drug addict, allaying suspicion. Martinez took a small plastic container of vitamin C tablets and spilled the contents on the floor. The burglars also stole some prescription pads and Fielding's Saturday mail from his desk. They may have also overturned a chair and taken a pair of glasses. "Office had been ransacked," veteran Beverly Hills police officer Clinton Brickley reported at 10:50 the next evening. "Possible burglary," he perceived. "Looked like a junkie rip-off."[62]

So far so good, in that respect.

Lugging their suitcase full of equipment, Barker and his men then proceeded back down the stairs. They reentered Dr. Ashley Lipshutz's office, where they "messed up things," Dr. Bernard Sosner recalls. "Perpetrator(s) open[ed] desk and drawers," police officer Michael Haigwood reported. "Only light ransacking noted. . . . Doors left ajar and papers in disarray."

Some books and other items were strewn in the middle of the room. "We had *thought* there was a burglary," Lipshutz told me. "Nothing was missing. . . . I had no idea what was going on. . . . It was a very strange thing. . . . I was totally in the dark."[63]

Like officer Brickley, Sosner thought it was a drug raid. "I made absolutely no connection to the fact that the break-in that I found had anything to do with the Fielding-Ellsberg matter," he remembers. It was not until he was called by the Los Angeles District Attorney's office two years later that Sosner realized he had been the one who had discovered the famous Fielding job. "For two years, I thought somebody broke into [Lipshutz's] office looking for drugs," he says. The break-in had not been a big topic of conversation around the office building. "Analysts are a funny breed," Sosner comments. "They stick to themselves. . . . They're usually not a very talkative lot. . . . For the people I talked to, it just wasn't a big deal." "Fielding obviously didn't tell anybody," Dr. Alfred Goldberg recalls. "Because a story like that would have spread like wildfire. So he kept it to himself. . . . I would say nobody knew anything about it." Goldberg didn't even discuss the break-in with Fielding after it had been publicly revealed. "Because right at that point, immediately, I know we're treading on something that has to do with his patient," Goldberg points out. "And that's off limits. . . . He'd clam up."[64]

The month after the break-in, Beverly Hills police charged Elmer "Spots" Davis with it. A toothless 43-year-old convicted burglar and drug addict, Davis copped to the break-in and a series of other burglaries after police offered him a deal for his confession so they could "clean up the books." "Subject stated that he did make this entry, looking for narcotics," the police report said. Davis soon recanted, however, and he was never prosecuted. It turned out that Davis was in jail at the time of the break-in. Beverly Hills police never informed Fielding of his arrest.[65]

It was not a stellar performance.

Upon discovering the break-in at about 4 o'clock the afternoon of September 4, Sosner called Dr. Jerry Port, Lipshutz's 39-year-old partner who had an adjoining office. Port came out to inspect the damage and then called the police. At 4:45 officer Haigwood arrived and filed his report, without, apparently, venturing to the second floor of the building. "Investigation revealed unknown perpetrator(s) entered only victim's [Lipshutz's] office and no signs of perpetrator(s) were found in the other connecting offices," he wrote at 6 P.M. Two hours later, however, while doing his cleaning, Efrain Martinez, the janitor, noticed Fielding's office door was open. He went inside. The janitor told his mother that "something strange had occurred in the doctor's office where the men had left the valise. To wit, that he had discovered that the office had been burglarized." Maria Martinez recalled that days earlier she had encountered two men at the same office. "I think they were Americans," she later testified. "They were not the same men who came to bring the valise. . . . The strange thing is that these men were taking pictures of the walls of the same office where the two men left the valise and where my son, Efrain Martinez, on the following day discovered the burglary." Efrain Martinez called the police. When officer Brickley arrived, Martinez told him about the delivery of the suitcase. But now, Martinez said, the suitcase was missing. Brickley dusted for prints on the door and cabinets and took the vitamin C container to police headquarters for a fingerprint examination, which yielded a print, but not that of Elmer Davis.[66]

A police officer notified Dr. Lewis Fielding of the break-in at about 9 P.M. that night. Fielding had first started treating Daniel Ellsberg in March of 1968 and had done so for nearly two-and-a-half years. Ellsberg says he depleted his savings to pay for the treatment. He had returned from Vietnam in 1967 extremely debilitated and depressed. His realization that he had a desire to be killed in Vietnam had shaken him; he questioned his sanity. And he continued to have problems writing and completing work. Maybe psychoanalysis would free up his pen. More than one person at RAND had encouraged him to get help. His failures at romance and other problems also likely shaped his decision to seek treatment.[67]

Dr. Fielding was not eager to drive over to his office. After all, it was Saturday evening on Labor Day weekend. Fielding called the building manager, who suggested he come over, however. When he arrived at his office, his wife at his side, Fielding "found my papers and records strewn about," he testified to Ellsberg's lead attorney the day after the break-in was publicly revealed in April 1973. He noticed that his cabinets, which "contained information and records concerning my patients including Dr. Ellsberg," had been forced open, and that "the files in my cabinet were in considerable disarray. My personal papers, including those pertaining to Dr. Ellsberg, appeared to have been thoroughly rummaged through." Fielding told his own lawyer within the next two days that "Dr. Ellsberg's papers had been removed from his folder," according to the FBI's account of a telephone conversation it had with his lawyer. But Fielding "made no connection of the incident with the Ellsberg case" at the time of the break-in, a spokesperson for Ellsberg's attorneys told the press. He, too, thought it was probably a drug raid. "As I looked over the office," Fielding also recounted to Ellsberg's lead attorney, "I attempted to do some rearranging. I could not tell what was missing, although the incoming Saturday mail which was usually neatly stacked on my desk by the cleaning people was not there and never turned up." (Hunt had thrown it in the trash.) Fielding advised officer Brickley that he "didn't know of anything missing," however, and further investigation confirmed his belief that "nothing had been taken."[68]

In June and July of 1973, Fielding would testify slightly differently. He stated that he had noticed upon arriving at his office that his file on Ellsberg, which he kept under Ellsberg's name in the fourth drawer of his metal filing cabinet, "had been rifled and had distinct marks and impressions to indicate that [it] received special attention from the burglars." A thick envelope containing two "documents" bearing on Ellsberg (he didn't say what type of documents), one of about 25 pages, the other of 35 or 40 pages, had been examined. "These papers, as I found them, were outside the envelope. I know that I had left them inside the envelope. Beyond that, there was evidence that these papers—you know, again, if you have been with a file long enough and lived with it, you know what your papers look like. And this looked as if it had been fingered, had been fingered over, you know, people had done something with it." Fielding's testimony also showed that he noticed that "his personal file had received special attention from the burglars. Because both the Ellsberg and his personal files were in more disarray than the others and also because of the story of deliverymen leaving a suitcase in his office the night previous to the burglary, Dr. Fielding was somewhat suspicious of the theory that the burglary was nothing more than a drug addict looking for a fix," members of the Watergate Special Prosecution Force who interviewed Fielding recorded. Fielding, they wrote, "said he was 'tormented' by the suspicion that the break-in was associated with Ellsberg. He must have wondered about the connection between the FBI attempt to interview him and then the break-in." Yet Fielding told grand jurors in June 1973, "I could not believe the inconceivable." It was hard to fathom that the U.S. government had actually done this. While "it seems a little simpler now," he said, "at that time it was not so [simple]."[69]

Fielding left his office late that Saturday night "in considerable distress," he recounted. "He wasn't a person who would be very voluble in that regard, but he would have split a gut," Goldberg says. "He was angry and outraged . . . that his office would be broken into, and that his work with his patients would have been so violated. . . . If your home is your castle, the analyst's office is your castle squared." And the burglars had even gone through his files. That's quite a violation.[70]

Fielding did not report any suspicions he had to either Ellsberg or the police. That suggests that he either didn't tie the break-in to Ellsberg immediately afterward or at least was uncertain about it. Had he been convinced that

Ellsberg was the target, professional ethics and his own moral code probably would have led him to inform Ellsberg. Fielding's statement that he was "somewhat suspicious" of the drug raid theory came after fuller public disclosure of the facts of the break-in and may have been shaped by it. "I would question whether or not Fielding ever even thought about the connection, knowing what I know about this man," Dr. Roger Gould comments. "I think that if he seriously thought that they were after Ellsberg, if he had that foresight rather than hindsight, that this is one of those dirty tricks, I think he would have contacted Ellsberg," Goldberg argues. "I do not think he would have kept that from Ellsberg. . . . That's the way he operated, and that's the way I would have operated." But Fielding would never have told the police, even with good evidence. That would have meant revealing that Ellsberg had been his patient.[71]

Two months after the break-in, Ellsberg may have given Fielding more reason to be suspicious. But if so, it wasn't reason enough for him to say anything to Ellsberg. The son of a South Vietnamese political leader told Ellsberg that he had learned that the U.S. government had tapes of Ellsberg's psychiatric sessions. Ellsberg called Fielding and another psychiatrist he had seen and asked if they had ever taped their sessions. Fielding said no.[72]

Fielding would have been loath to say anything that might generate media attention. He was horrified by the publicity he received following the later disclosure of the break-in. "He tried to avoid it at all costs," Gould reminisces. "He hated the attention. He was actually angry about the people chasing him and everything. . . . This thing seemed to be a great trauma to him. . . . All of a sudden he was hoisted in the middle of this circus, and he felt totally violated." Fielding may have also considered how Ellsberg would react. Though he had not treated Ellsberg since the summer of 1970 and Ellsberg had since seen another psychiatrist, Ellsberg, as we have seen, had been calling Fielding frequently and at odd hours. The FBI reports Liddy saw indicated "he's just as liable to pick up a phone at three o'clock in the morning and call him." If so, that's a man in trouble. Ellsberg phoned Fielding after he left the RAND Corporation in 1970 to tell him "how free he felt," Ellsberg later remembered. According to his phone records, he made "a series of calls" to Fielding shortly before the Pentagon Papers were published. "Now I'm free," Ellsberg told Fielding again after leaking the Papers, Liddy reported to the CIA.[73] Fielding may have worried that telling Ellsberg about the break-in would prompt even more calls, more demands on his time, and that his former patient would be overwrought. It would just be a headache, and, again, there was no proof.

Ellsberg was later irritated and probably angry with Fielding for not informing him of the break-in. "It is still amazing to me that he didn't," he said in

1973. Ellsberg would subsequently claim that Fielding had "no doubt that it had been a White House operation against me," but that Fielding didn't tell him on the advice of his lawyer and that consequently he developed an ulcer. In fact, Fielding had suffered gastrointestinal problems for some time. "I think Ellsberg ought to do a little soul searching," Goldberg chuckles. "And instead of talking about Fielding feeling guilty, he probably should deal with Ellsberg feeling enraged that he didn't call him." Ellsberg also maintained that when he called Fielding on the day the break-in was revealed, Fielding said he was unaware that a burglary had taken place, though Fielding testified that he "confirmed" to Ellsberg that a break-in had occurred.[74]

What really happened inside Fielding's office that night? Most likely, Fielding did not keep any notes on Ellsberg and his office really was a "dry hole." The White House apparently made a gargantuan miscalculation. "I know they found nothing, because that's not the way Fielding operated," says Goldberg, even before I inform him that the burglars reported coming up empty. "I would have been surprised if he'd kept notes. Anybody who was that careful to preserve the privacy and confidentiality of his patients as Fielding was. . . . It's very unlikely that he would have had any notes about Ellsberg or anybody else." Goldberg adds, "Nor do I have anything in my files. So that if anybody breaks in, they find nothing." Ellsberg would later state that Fielding told him he didn't keep any notes on his sessions with him, but that he had given Fielding copies of papers he had written, and that one of them was found outside the envelope on top of the file drawer.[75]

All parties to the break-in reported afterward that they had found no Ellsberg file, so a conspiracy to conceal otherwise is unlikely. When I told Bernard Barker that Fielding testified that his Ellsberg file had been rummaged through, Barker responded, vehemently, "Untrue, untrue. . . . If I would have found it, I would have rummaged through [it]. I would have photographed the damn thing, and that would have been the end of it. I don't think he's telling the truth there. Or he may be and we didn't find anything." The two "documents" Fielding said had been "fingered over" were probably papers written by Ellsberg, and one of the burglars may have had his hands on them without noticing their relevance. The burglars were operating under pressure, and they had only been given Ellsberg's name right before they went to work. When asked before the grand jury whether he had seen "two large documents" or "any envelopes" with Ellsberg's name on them, Felipe DeDiego said no. Liddy doubts the burglars could have missed any Ellsberg file. "These were not a bunch of amateurs," he asserts. "We didn't take any of them on until we had viewed their CIA training files." And Barker is "a cool customer. He's not somebody who gets hurried under pressure or anything else."[76]

But Ellsberg told Watergate prosecutors he couldn't "conceive" that the burglars would miss his name on his paper found outside the envelope. And they "probably did" photograph Fielding's "records" on him, Ellsberg told the press. "The records were there. . . . They were prominently in disarray," although "the records we know about would not have been very helpful to them." Hunt, Ellsberg believed, may have later seen his paper. "I think they did photograph more than they admitted," he said. "I'm virtually sure they lied when they said they photographed nothing that had my name on it."[77]

As Barker and his men emerged from Fielding's office building, looking "sweaty and disheveled," they were met by a nervous Hunt, who directed them back to the Beverly Hilton. A police car trailed briefly behind them. "I thought to myself that the police car was protecting us," Eugenio Martinez wrote. "That is the feeling you have when you are doing operations for the government." At the hotel, Barker held up the piece of paper bearing Ellsberg's name. "There's no file with this name on it," Barker informed Hunt. "I don't think we found anything that was worthwhile." "Are you *sure?*" Hunt, who was disbelieving, responded. They were. They'd gone through "every goddamn file in that office," Barker reported, "and there was nothing there." Barker and his men felt "very bad," Martinez recalled. "We had failed." "Well, we know that, but they don't," Hunt said, curiously. Barker and his men didn't know what to make of this remark. Perhaps, Liddy and Ellsberg would both later theorize, Hunt meant that Ellsberg might *think* they found some material on him. Hunt had a bottle of champagne on ice and was in a mood to celebrate. That perplexed Barker and Liddy. "I didn't know why he was so [upbeat]," Liddy remembers. "I guess because they'd gotten out. And maybe he was apprehensive and he felt a great sense of relief that we'd gotten away clean. To me, it was just an unproductive bag job." Martinez told DeDiego and Barker that "this had to have been a training mission for a very important mission to come or else it was a cover operation. I thought to myself that maybe these people already had the papers of Ellsberg. Maybe Dr. Fielding had given them out and for ethical reasons he needed to be covered. It seemed that these people already had what we were looking for because no one invites you to have champagne and is happy when you fail. The whole thing was strange." But Barker didn't give it any more thought. "They were supposed to know what they were doing," he points out. "And according to the way we were trained [by] the agency, we didn't have need for any additional information." Barker and his men departed the Beverly Hilton in darkness at 4:46 A.M. and flew back to Miami.[78]

When Liddy called Egil Krogh from a pay phone at around 4 A.M. to report the results of the break-in, Krogh, like Hunt, didn't seem disappointed that it had failed. "He was just so elated that nobody had been caught, he didn't seem to care," Liddy remembers.[79]

Liddy and Hunt were not ready to abandon their pursuit of Ellsberg's psychiatric records, however. Fielding probably had "a basement full of closed files," Liddy thought. "And that's why I almost immediately said, 'Okay, we'll see if we can get permission to go into his home.'" Liddy and Hunt drove over to Fielding's apartment building, Liddy taking photographs and scrutinizing Fielding's front door lock. Afterward the two flew to New York. They bragged to two stewardesses that they had just done a "big national security job" (Hunt later sent one of the stewardesses a book with an accompanying letter on White House stationery). Liddy and Hunt registered under their real names and displayed their White House passes at the Pierre Hotel that night.[80]

Apparently sobered, Ehrlichman, Krogh, and Young elected not to penetrate Fielding's apartment, however. "They were, I think, too scared to do it," Liddy chuckles. "They had lost all their stomach for black bag jobs out of the White House." Ehrlichman later denied even hearing about the plan. The Plumbers also discussed breaking into Ellsberg's own apartment in Cambridge, but the talk "never came to anything," Liddy says.[81]

Krogh was certainly scared, and he had a right to be. On Tuesday, September 7, the first working day after Labor Day weekend, Liddy and Hunt visited him. They showed him their suitcase full of burglary tools—which Hunt had brought into the Executive Office Building—and photos of "a very damaged office," Krogh later testified. He found this "very distressing" and immediately felt that "a mistake had been made." Liddy and Hunt tried to assure Krogh that damaging the office made the break-in less traceable since police would suspect a drug raid, but "it was hard for me to understand that and it is still hard to understand it," Krogh testified. Hunt's assurance that no fingerprints had been left was "met with some expression of relief," however. When Liddy asked Krogh if he should get rid of their suitcase full of equipment, Krogh responded, "No, hang on to that. You may need it."[82]

Krogh walked over to Ehrlichman's office on the second floor of the west wing of the White House to discuss these troubling developments. Ehrlichman "conveyed a sense of being quite disturbed by what had happened," Krogh would recall, "but more than that, I think he was disturbed about the way it had happened." Evidence had been left at the scene of a crime they had authorized. That was reason to be disturbed. Ehrlichman felt the operatives "didn't evidence good judgment."[83]

Also on September 7, Hunt visited Charles Colson to brief him on the break-in. Hunt caught Colson as he was entering his office. "He came in with a long stride, and I said, 'I have something that might be of interest to you,'" Hunt recalled. "'It has to do with my activities this past weekend.'" Hunt started to take out some photos of Fielding's rifled cabinet from a brown envelope. "I don't want to hear anything about it," Colson replied. He declined to look at the photos and went straight into his office and closed the door. Hunt decided to show the photos to Joan Hall, Colson's secretary, explaining that they were of Daniel Ellsberg's psychiatrist's office and that "we" had been "out there" over the weekend. Hall remarked to Colson afterward that Hunt "talked too much." Hunt also showed David Young's secretary a pair of rubber gloves and pictures of Liddy standing in front of Fielding's building. Young's secretary "knew something funny was going on." She also observed Hunt and Liddy thumbing through a copy of the *Los Angeles Times* "as if they were looking for something."[84]

John Ehrlichman met with Richard Nixon in the Oval Office the next afternoon. "We had one little operation . . . out in Los Angeles," Ehrlichman related. After a pause, he added, "which I think it's better that you don't know about."[85]

The men in the White House were trying to distance themselves from the break-in. They had committed the seminal criminal act in a series of criminal acts that became known as Watergate. The episode would mark a turning point in the Nixon administration, send several of the participants to prison, and play a key role in undoing Nixon's presidency.

But what of the man whose release of the top-secret documents had prompted the break-in? His story starts 40 years earlier and is one of the stranger tales of those men whose actions shaped the Vietnam and Watergate eras.

ONE

LONER

"DANNY WAS JUST NEVER ONE OF THE GUYS. . . . HE WASN'T LIKE THE rest of the boys," agree two of Daniel Ellsberg's neighbors and grade school class-mates in Highland Park, Michigan, where he grew up in the late 1930s and early 1940s. Ellsberg had an unusual childhood. He spent little time with other children outside of school. "I didn't know kids in a social way," he remembers. "I had a good feeling about my classmates. . . . But I had no social life with them at all. I never saw them after school." "He was a little different," says Tom Varbedian, who lived on the same street as Ellsberg. "I don't think we walked to school with him ever. . . . He never fraternized with any of the young people in the neighbor-hood." Ellsberg was shy and quiet and kept to himself. He was not the sort one befriended easily. Some found him very solemn. Although he had a sense of humor, people didn't see it much outside of class. "He *never* played with us," re-calls Eugene Paul, who also lived on Ellsberg's street. "What I remember more than anything was the fact that he never wore clothes the way we wore play clothes. I don't remember him in play clothes. They always seemed to be school clothes. I don't even know if he *had* play clothes."[1]

Ellsberg was, to use a cliché, a mama's boy. His mother was the focal point of his existence. "She was my best friend, my mentor," he recalls. "I was really in love with her. . . . All meaning in my life, all value, came from my mother. . . . I wanted to make her happy, consciously, and to make her laugh. . . . Do things that would make her proud of me." Other kids in the neighborhood thought his parents didn't really want Danny to be one of the boys. "I really had a feeling that [Mr.] Ellsberg did not *want* his children to associate with the local gentry,"

Paul remembers. "I think the parents really kept us apart from him." Ellsberg later told his daughter, Mary, that his mother didn't allow him to have any friends.[2]

The whole Ellsberg family tended to be quiet and to stick to themselves. Though the Pauls and the Ellsbergs were among the few families of Jewish origin in the neighborhood, and the Pauls lived only two doors away for a number of years, "that didn't necessarily mean that we associated with the Ellsbergs," Paul recalls. "That's how aloof they were."[3]

Danny Ellsberg was a short, fairly slight boy, with wide hips, pudgy legs, and dark curly hair. He was not the athletic type. "There was a nice red blotch on either cheek," Alfred Gannon, who lived almost across the street from him, remembers. "A skin that wasn't exposed to the hardiness that young kids have who play all summer in the sun." And while Gannon's friends were into hair styles, "Danny's hair looked wiry and it lacked styling."[4]

Ellsberg had one friend in grade school, Myron Poe, who was also short, with thick glasses, unattractive, and perhaps shyer than Ellsberg. He, too, was often by himself. Today he'd be called a nerd. "He was my only friend," Ellsberg recalls. One of Ellsberg's happiest memories from his childhood is of the time he and Poe spent many hours building an elaborate World War I–style trench system, with barbed wire, bunkers and everything else. "Danny didn't play baseball, and he didn't play kick the can, and he didn't do some of the other things that I perhaps did," Poe remembers.[5]

Yet Ellsberg claims he was "known as a fighter" in grade school: "I used to take on four or five or six people at a time. They would try to drag me down." But Poe has no memory of that. "Danny was never the roughhouse type," Norma Lawrie, another classmate, remembers. Some classmates were surprised when I informed them that Poe was Ellsberg's friend. They didn't know he had any friends.[6]

Both Ellsberg and Poe were bright boys, Ellsberg especially, who was a cut above his peers. "We all knew that he was very gifted in almost every respect," Lawrie recalls. "I don't think that there was anything he attempted that he didn't do well." Ellsberg seemed particularly gifted in math and music (common strengths of gifted children). "I thought he was going to be a world famous pianist," Poe remembers. "Danny certainly had an unusual and unique talent." When Ellsberg played the piano at grade school one time "it was awesome," Alfred Gannon reminisces. "Awesome." Although Gannon had been around music all his life, he couldn't help but be impressed. Back then there wasn't air conditioning and people left their doors and windows open on warm days. The neighborhood boys would be out playing baseball "and you could hear Danny playing concertos," Tom Varbedian recounts. "And he was accomplished, there was no question about it."[7]

Like many gifted children, Ellsberg was an avid reader. He and Poe were both heavy users of their grade school library. "He had a great depth of understanding," Poe remembers. "He and I would talk about the various books that we had read, and he was very sensitive to the characters, to the plot, to the situations in which people found themselves." Ellsberg also had an exceptional memory. He liked to memorize things. His mother once took him to a radio station in Detroit to recite Lincoln's Gettysburg Address, apparently in a competition. He memorized the poem "Horatius at the Bridge" too. Ellsberg was also unusually curious, another common characteristic of gifted kids. Lawrie recalls running into him in a neighborhood park at age 14 after she had just returned from a stint modeling in New York: "He was as interested in my going to New York as if it had been some great academic achievement. . . . He wanted to know every minute detail of the trip to New York and what it was like. . . . Which was typical."[8]

Ellsberg's giftedness contributed to his distance from other children, particularly outside of school where their interests would have diverged most. But his mother's influence was pivotal. She had a brilliant young son, her first child, of whom she was enormously proud, and she was going to make the most of his gifts. Playing with other kids would have to take a back seat to developing his genius. "His mother was very possessive, and she tried to promote him as much as she could," Varbedian recalls. "She was a rather guiding type of a mother, to put it in a gentle way." Alice Tipton, who also lived in the neighborhood, puts it this way: "She was very ambitious and very focused, and not the usual kind of mother. She wasn't easy going. . . . She wasn't like other mothers. She was different. She was focused very much on her kids and very much on accomplishment." Two of Ellsberg's teachers at Cranbrook prep school remember her as being "pushy." One also found her overbearing and thought she viewed Daniel "as an establishment of hers. And she felt a proprietary interest in his success. His father took him a little bit more for granted. He was much more human about him and about their relationship." Other mothers in the neighborhood also pushed their kids, but not, it seemed, as much as Adele Ellsberg. "Some of us were academically oriented as well," Varbedian points out. "But we weren't that focused. . . . We weren't *forced* to be that focused."[9]

Adele Ellsberg was a Russian Jew raised in Denver, Colorado, the youngest of six children. Her father, a very intelligent man, had been in charge of planting and marketing for a large estate in Russia. His second wife, Adele's mother, was much younger than him. "I'm sure it was an arranged marriage, and it was certainly not congenial," his granddaughter Charlotte Miller, whose mother,

Clara Charsky, was one of Adele's two sisters, recalls. It would break up when Adele was a girl. Adele's parents and their first child, Harry, traveled to the United States probably during the early years of the period of mass immigration of Eastern European Jews from 1880 to 1920. They initially settled in a Jewish community on the east coast, but Adele's father was unsuccessful as a farmer there and lost his farm, so he and his family followed his oldest daughter from his first marriage to Denver, where he worked as a cutter in a pants factory and they lived in a Jewish enclave. Most everyone there was poor, but they were among the neediest.[10]

Adele's three brothers, Louis, Nathan, and Harry, were bright but not exemplary boys. They often skipped school and *heder*. "All they did was play marbles all the time," Miller chuckles. "The *heder* was of no interest to them." They would arrive home in the afternoon with sacks of marbles, which their father disgustedly threw in the toilet. "He was a real tyrant," Miller says. "My mother was very, very incensed about it. He would always beat the boys." Lou and Nate would become successful as young adults, though. Lou developed a flourishing wholesale drug business and set up Nate with a drugstore. Lou was a millionaire by the time he was 25 and both brothers retired at early ages.[11]

Lou would later give Daniel Ellsberg money and other gifts, though Ellsberg did not maintain close ties with his uncles and aunts. "Daniel Ellsberg was never appreciative or attentive with regard to his relatives," one remembers. "They never came to his attention. . . . He never made an effort to stay in touch. . . . The only thing he was concerned about was what was good for Dan Ellsberg. Not what was good for others." Shortly after Lou died in 1987, Ellsberg telephoned the assistant of Lou's attorney "to see if he was coming into some money," according to one relative, though Lou, bedridden before he died, had not heard from Ellsberg.[12]

Adele Charsky, who did not complete high school, worked for Lou in Denver, designing brochures and ads and doing secretarial work. She subsequently worked in Philadelphia for the National Jewish Hospital as a fund raiser, traveling a lot.[13]

Adele Charsky was a fairly tall woman, with dark hair, high cheekbones, a prominent nose, slender angular frame, and slim hands. She was refined, dressed beautifully, in good taste, and carried herself well. A "lovely woman," one of Ellsberg's teachers at Cranbrook recalls. "Very attractive." Adele was generally on the reserved side and not, it seems, an especially warm person, but she could be quite charming and gracious. She was intelligent and literate. Like many Russian Jews, Adele educated herself, Charlotte Miller remembers. She and her sister Bertha "read literature constantly. Whatever was really fine, they read . . . the very, very best. . . . Anything that was intellectual," although they stuck pretty much to novels, from authors like Galsworthy and Tolstoy. Others in Highland Park, Michigan, where Adele would eventually become active in local organizations and be elected president of the junior high school PTA, would see her as well educated. She was also artistic, interested in all kinds of music, and talented with energy to spare. She was an accomplished pianist. She had wanted to be a concert pianist but had not been able to do so. She danced well and had even given small performances in Denver. She made beautiful batik curtains. "In the basement we had laundry tubs," Miller recounts. "And Adele bought this beautiful silk, raw silk, and did these *gorgeous* drapes. You can't imagine how beautiful they were." Often, she made the curtains after working all day for her brother Lou. Making the curtains was arduous work. She heated the wax on a little gas stove in her sister Clara's basement, applied it to parts of the cloth, dipped the cloth in the tubs, then applied wax and dipped over and over again until there were maybe ten or twelve colors on the drapes and the weight of the cloth had grown significantly. Some in Highland Park would speak highly of Adele as an especially talented person.[14]

She was enormously ambitious. "She had this driving ambition," Miller stresses. "The fact that she would work all day and then come to our house at six o'clock to work on those drapes. Look at how she pushed herself." She focused some of her ambition on Charlotte, her niece. "She was just determined that I develop into something more than I was," Miller recalls. "She was persistent. I would take dancing lessons. She found the instructor. . . . She pushed me into the dancing." Miller later thought that Adele shifted her ambitions from her to Daniel after he was born.[15] And if she pushed her niece, think how hard she might have pushed her own son.

Adele was not raised in a religious home, but she had spiritual longings. She became a devout Christian Scientist and pursued it with her typical zeal.[16]

After declining at least one marriage offer, Adele struck up a relationship with Harry Ellsberg while working for the National Jewish Hospital. She quit her job, they married, and they settled in Chicago in the late 1920s or 1930. Adele was then in her late twenties.[17]

A short, stocky man some twelve years older than Adele, Harry Ellsberg was also a Russian Jew and had grown up largely in the same Jewish enclave in Denver. Their contact then had apparently been only casual, though Lou and Nate Charsky had known Harry when they were boys. Joseph Ellsberg, Harry's father, owned a loan office and was a "dealer in diamonds, jewelry, watches, and guns." Joseph was an intellectual man, well read, and an atheist. The Ellsbergs "had nothing to do with Judaism," Miller recalls. They were "evidently the only family there in that area where they lived who had no connection with Judaism at all." Like many Eastern European Jews, Joseph Ellsberg and his wife, Edna, whom Daniel Ellsberg says had a small shop, held radical political views. "He was a philosophical anarchist," Ellsberg says. "Socialist—that was the word I *always* heard about them," Miller remembers. According to Harry Ellsberg, who had a tendency to embellish stories, he and his father twice went to a saloon in Denver to bring a drunken Big Bill Haywood home to dry out. He would also say that his mother was always convinced that his father, who "had a lot of lovers," as did his mother (Daniel says), had an affair with Emma Goldman. "Probably true," Daniel surmises. Harry Ellsberg recalled accompanying his father to hear Goldman speak when he was a boy. Harry would later become a Republican and vote for Richard Nixon in 1972, though Nixon had condemned his son's release of the Pentagon Papers.[18]

Harry "Shorty" Ellsberg earned a B.S. in civil engineering from the University of Colorado in 1913. Daniel told me his father graduated first in his class, but I managed to obtain his academic transcript, and although he performed well, that is unlikely (a conclusion shared by a university employee who also perused his transcript). Harry Ellsberg married a gentile and had two children, Margaret and Harry, Jr., with her before she died and before his marriage to Adele.[19]

Despite a successful career as an engineer, Harry Ellsberg had the misfortune of living in the shadow of his well-known younger brother, Edward "Ned" Ellsberg. Ned graduated from Annapolis (according to Daniel, he too graduated first in his class) and earned a doctorate in engineering from the University of Colorado. He eventually advanced to rear admiral in the U.S. Navy and became fairly famous as a submarine salvage expert and author of both nonfiction and fiction, most notably salvage and adventure stories. His 1958–59 *Who's Who in America* listing says that he invented the torch for cutting steel underwater and designed the navy's system for salvaging submarines. Daniel, who resembled him somewhat in appearance, told me that his uncle wrote "seven or eight best sellers, seven or eight Book-of-the-Month Club sellers," and was "one of the big sellers in America." (According to his *Who's Who* listing, only one of Ned Ellsberg's books was a Book-of-the-Month Club selection, and the club itself has no record of carrying any of his books.) Daniel and Myron Poe read them. "Danny was proud of him," Poe reminisces. But Adele's family felt differently. "My mother and her sisters had absolutely no use for Admiral Ellsberg," Charlotte Miller remembers. "Because he was so indifferent to Harry and to Dan and so forth. . . . He had no contact with the group, with anybody who knew him" after he left Denver. Ned Ellsberg's exploits undoubtedly shaped Daniel's own taste for adventure, and perhaps his drive for accomplishment and recognition as well. Given the Charskys' feelings about the admiral, it's ironic that her niece believes Adele and Harry Ellsberg first made meaningful contact at a ceremony honoring him in Denver.[20]

Daniel Ellsberg was born in Chicago in 1931 in the midst of the depression. A sister, Gloria, came a year or two later.[21] Adele's sister Clara visited the Ellsbergs in Chicago around the time Gloria was born. "She felt that it was a very cold household," Miller remembers. "There wasn't any warmth. . . . She came back with a very cold feeling about the family." Not only was Harry lacking in warmth, but his two children from his previous marriage, particularly Margaret, didn't seem to get along especially well with Adele. There were also some marital problems, which Miller heard got sharp at times and which may have contributed to Adele's focus on her son. Harry Ellsberg was out of work for two or three years around this time (some one-fourth or one-third of U.S. workers were unemployed in 1933), and his mood was surely not enhanced by his plight. Indeed, many households were probably cold during these difficult years. And he now had four children. His unemployment did not help his standing with his in-laws either. Lou Charsky supported the Ellsbergs financially then.[22]

Daniel never developed a relationship with his half sister, Margaret, but he would become close to his half brother, Harry, Jr., who was ten or twelve years older than him. He looked up to Harry. "I worshipped my brother," Ellsberg recalls. "He was my ideal, and I loved him." He was a mentor, role model, and hero to Daniel. Harry's left-wing politics would have a major impact on him.[23]

The Ellsbergs moved to Highland Park, Michigan, in 1937 after Harry, Sr., obtained a job as a structural engineer with the renowned architectural firm of Albert Kahn in Detroit. Adele's sister Bertha was instrumental in his getting the job. Harry Ellsberg helped design some of the biggest factories yet built. According to Daniel, after working on "all the tallest buildings" in Chicago, his father was the "chief engineer" on the colossal Willow Run bomber plant, which was the largest industrial structure in the world at the time of its opening in 1942. But though Harry Ellsberg worked on Willow Run, Kahn's records indicate that he almost certainly was not the chief engineer. Daniel also told me his father "designed" the huge Dodge Chicago and *Philadelphia Inquirer* plants and Cobo Hall. But while he probably was the head designer for the Dodge Chicago project, he was not for the other two structures. Ellsberg has also claimed that his father was the "chief structural engineer" on the Hanford nuclear reservation plant that produced plutonium for the atomic bomb. That, too, is almost certainly untrue.[24]

Harry Ellsberg apparently had two main foci in his life: his work and Christian Science, to which Adele had converted him. "My parents amounted to religious fanatics," Daniel remembers. "It dominated their lives," and probably contributed to their remove in their neighborhood. Metaphysical healing is primary to Christian Science, and Harry Ellsberg claimed that it cured Harry, Jr., of polio (though he retained a limp). His letters to Daniel later were "always full of Christian Science piety," Carol Cummings, Daniel's first wife, recalls. Harry Ellsberg was given to lecturing others and dominating conversations, and his topic of choice was Christian Science. "He would give a lecture on Christian Science and . . . he was unstoppable," Daniel recounts. "There was simply no way to stop him. You would just leave the room. You could hit him over the head with a mallet and it wouldn't stop him." Also a raconteur, "he could tell, very dramatically, stories of everything that happened in the office during the day." Harry Ellsberg enjoyed telling jokes and could be genial, but Daniel would describe him as cold, as would other members of Adele's family, who did not think much of him and felt he treated Adele badly. "My family just really didn't care about him at all," Charlotte Miller remembers. "They didn't like Harry," who seemed "unable to relate to people." He "had a very bad disposition." What's more, they felt he did not adequately appreciate Adele and her talents; indeed, they had been opposed to her marrying him. Miller recalls having a phone conversation with Harry in which he was "very, very antagonistic" because "he felt that the family was anti-Harry." His tone stunned her: "I didn't really know just how to cope with it."[25]

Judaism was not part of Daniel Ellsberg's life as a boy. Indeed, it never would be, at least to any significant degree. Although his mother and father "thought of themselves as Jewish," he recalls, "it wasn't clear what that meant exactly. Except it had something to do with background." The poet Donald Hall, who became friends with Ellsberg at Harvard, remembers, "He didn't know he was a Jew. . . . He thought of Judaism as a religion. In his naïveté." Ellsberg would anger relatives during one discussion when he didn't exhibit particular concern for Israel and, according to Hall, "talked about being a Jew as if somebody else was a Jew, not him. Because he was a Christian Scientist. And he didn't know. He just didn't know." Hall adds, "It *is* strange of Dan, with all his intelligence, by that time, and maybe he was eighteen . . . not to realize, after Hitler, that the word Jewish did not just mean a flavor, like . . . a Methodist."[26]

The Ellsbergs lived in a largely upper-middle-class neighborhood of professionals and small businessmen in Highland Park. The town was virtually the creation of Henry Ford. The original Ford factory (designed by Albert Kahn), site of the first moving assembly line, was only six blocks from two homes the Ellsbergs occupied successively on Winona Avenue. Whole sections of Highland Park were laid out according to social class: there were the workers' homes, those for the foremen, the managers' and professionals' homes, and those of the wealthy. Winona was one of the nicest streets (though not the tops), lined with tall, gracious elm trees that canopied it. When the trees bloomed, "it could be raining hard somewhere but your street really didn't get wet in the drizzle," Leo Keshishian, who lived across the street from the Ellsbergs, recalls. People came from outside the area to drive under Highland Park's beautiful elms. The lawns in the neighborhood were well kept. Crime was scant, as was traffic; most families on the Ellsbergs' block did not own a car, though the Ellsbergs did. A milkman, iceman, vegetableman, and junkman—all with horse-drawn carts or wagons—regularly made their rounds, as did a small bread truck. Neighborhood boys raided the ice wagon. Ford and the other automobile companies (Chrysler's headquarters was right down the street) had attracted immigrants from around the world, and the neighborhood was a melting pot: there were Syrians and Lebanese, Armenians, Italians, Poles, Germans, and French.[27]

Beneficiaries of Ford tax money, the Highland Park schools were outstanding and earning a national reputation. Robert E. Barber elementary school, which Ellsberg attended, was a gem. It had an impressive music department, an orchestra and band, an indoor swimming pool, a gymnasium with locker rooms, a shop, and well-equipped home economics and art rooms. There was a medical clinic with a doctor and nurse always on duty, and a beautiful library. In a class called "Auditorium," taught by a specialist and held in a large room with an elevated stage, plush seats, and striking red velvet curtains, students performed. Barber's principal was highly regarded.[28]

Adele Ellsberg surely appreciated Barber's excellence. Perhaps that's one reason the Ellsbergs moved into the neighborhood. She also set high standards for Daniel and Gloria at home. In fact, that would be an understatement. "Bertha would go and visit them," Charlotte Miller recounts. "And constantly she said, 'It was just a culture factory.' . . . She'd come back and say, 'A culture factory, a culture factory. Everybody's pushed, pushed, pushed.' . . . Gloria was being pushed, Dan was being pushed. . . . Intellectually. Scholastically." And musically. The children of Adele Ellsberg would have the chance to be artists. That was the greatest thing in the world. Daniel would recall that his mother had pianos in two rooms so that both he and Gloria could practice at the same time. "There was an awful lot of piano playing from that house," Leo Keshishian reminisces. Adele arranged for her son to take tennis lessons, too. "It was her idea," Ellsberg remembers. She wanted him to be "more well rounded."[29]

Bertha and Clara thought Adele's relentless pushing of Daniel was too much, even unfair to him. "And then they'd laugh," Miller remembers. "Not that they felt they should interfere . . . or that there's anything you could ever tell Adele."[30]

His mother's driving approach undoubtedly fostered Ellsberg's intellectual and musical development and fueled his great drive to excel throughout his life. "Not only was he bright, he was an achiever," Norma Lawrie emphasizes. "I think he had a great deal of pride of accomplishment." Many who knew Ellsberg later would detect considerable ambition and an immense desire to prove himself, whatever the task. But, it seemed, it was never really enough. He was always running, striving, almost with a sort of desperation, perpetually restless. He "seems almost incapable of satisfaction," one journalist observed.[31]

Daniel was the favorite of the Ellsberg family. He was clearly brilliant, and he showed greater aptitude at the piano than did his sister Gloria, who also seemed unsure of herself. Of course, many families at the time focused their ambitions mainly on their sons, who had greater opportunities. "Adele wasn't as ambitious for Gloria as she was for Dan," Miller remembers. "She put all of her energy into Dan. . . . I don't think she cared that much about Gloria's intellect. I think that it had all gone into Dan." Miller recalls that Adele's letters to her mother and sisters back home "all came, 'Well, Dan does this so . . . Dan did thus and thus and so.' And the letters were all about Dan. She didn't include anything that . . . she personally had done." In the letters, Gloria's doings were eclipsed by Dan's achievements, including his winning awards for piano playing. "Of course, it was a great source of pride for her, too. He'd won the silver medal, or something. And that was a big thing."[32]

When I told Fred Dockstader, who was one of Ellsberg's teachers at Cranbrook prep school and who met regularly with his parents, that it was my understanding that they considered him the jewel of the family, Dockstader immediately responded, "Oh, yes! . . . He was the apple of their eye. . . . As a matter of fact, one reason that they used to come out to the school, I think, was to hear about how good he was doing. Because they always wanted me to tell them over and over again about his accomplishments." During Mr. and Mrs. Ellsberg's visits to Cranbrook, "her interests were centered solely on Dan," Dockstader recalls. Carol Cummings remembers that when she walked into Harry Ellsberg's study at home when Daniel was a graduate student at Harvard (and after his mother and sister had died), "all the pictures were of Dan. You wouldn't have known he had any other children." It was "as though he had been an only child." Cummings was startled. And "he'd save Dan's letters and take them to church and read them aloud to people." Dan "was definitely considered the jewel of the family," Cummings says. "Everybody was telling him how bright and gifted he was. . . . He was the star."[33]

In all likelihood, Ellsberg's sense of specialness took root when he was a boy. He learned that he was different from other kids and destined for big things. Many parents of gifted children convey to their child that he or she is special, and Ellsberg's mother was talking about his future in grandiose terms. He had the ability to be a world-renowned concert pianist, she told him. "I was indoctrinated from before I was five, or from the time I was five . . . in the notion that I had a great talent," Ellsberg remembers. "I was given the notion that I had an outstanding talent. And that it was . . . my opportunity and my destiny to be a great pianist, not an ordinary pianist. Like a Horowitz." Vladimir Horowitz, the great Russian pianist, considered by some to be the greatest pianist of all time, was "my idol and my model," Ellsberg says. "We only talked about being a top-rate" concert pianist. "His mother thought he was a young Mozart," Merrell Condit, another of Ellsberg's teachers at Cranbrook, remembers.[34]

According to Ellsberg, his mother valued his talent at the piano more than his intellectual abilities. But she did arrange for him to transfer to Cranbrook in the seventh grade. Cranbrook was even more exceptional than Highland Park's schools and had a special reputation and allure. Adele Ellsberg's son would not be a regular boy. "She thought he was overqualified for the Highland Park school system, which was a stupendous school system," Tom Varbedian remarks. Very few kids from Ellsberg's neighborhood went to Cranbrook. His mother arranged for him to compete for a scholarship, and to no one's surprise, he won it. "He didn't come to Cranbrook for music," Robert Bates, his music teacher there, says. Music was quite secondary to academic studies at Cranbrook. Yet, the piano may have taken precedence in his mother's eyes. "I was definitely made to feel guilty if I was ever reading instead of practicing," Ellsberg recalls. He says his mother even took books away from him at times:

They'd disappear, let's just say. I can't accuse her. I didn't catch her with a smoking book. But the books did disappear if I got too engrossed in them. On one occasion I remember I'd been looking for months for a book that I was just entranced by, *Little Women*. It had disappeared. Because any time I was reading a book when I should be practicing, the book would disappear. I never actually saw her. She never copped to it. So I remember looking through the laundry hamper for some reason, or putting something in, and there at the bottom of the dirty clothes was *Little Women*. And I can still remember going around in this great triumph, saying, "Look! *Little Women!* It's back. How in the world did it ever get in the laundry hamper? I found *Little Women*." Because everybody knew I'd been looking for it—I'd been asking everybody about it. And within an hour it had disappeared again. I never got it. . . . There's now no question what happened. But I think there was some question in my mind at the time as to how these books would disappear.[35]

Such episodes may say as much about Ellsberg's practice habits as his mother's priorities. He told me he practiced "about six or seven hours a day" on weekdays during grade school, since his mother got him released from school "half days throughout grade school," and "twelve hours on Saturday." "I did nothing but practice the piano," he says. His mother "insisted that I practice." Ellsberg is an undisciplined person with a long history of jumping from project to project and failing to complete work, however, and it is thus hard to imagine him practicing at the length and with the regularity and self-discipline he remembers. More likely, his mother had her problems keeping him on a practice schedule. The promise of specialness was probably, in part, a lure to keep him practicing. Ellsberg acknowledges that he didn't always show the expected level of dedication, and that "where I fell short of that . . . I ran into immediate obstacles and disapproval." Myron Poe remembers him breaking away from the piano to listen to the radio or develop film. At Cranbrook, Ellsberg was not much of a practicer, as Dockstader, who was the housemaster in his dorm part of the time, recounts: "He tended to play pretty much in the lobby after class. . . . He never practiced in the sense that a, b, c, d, e and so on. . . . It was mostly just playing, and enjoying the playing of it. . . . Practicing was not Dan's style. He was good enough that he didn't. . . . He didn't do the scales and that sort of thing, to my hearing. He just simply played pieces. And they were complicated, and he played them well. . . . I never had the feeling he was practicing." Robert Bates agrees that Ellsberg was not the practicing type.[36]

That his mother got him released from school afternoons to practice is one sign of her priorities (though Ellsberg exaggerates the extent of this regimen). He recalls that his mother arranged for him to be given an IQ test so that he could be excused afternoons. His release from school would have been quite unusual. Barber's principal would have needed strong cause to grant it, and an exceptional IQ score might have provided that cause.[37] It may have also taken determination and persuasiveness on Mrs. Ellsberg's part.

Adele Ellsberg surely imparted to her son that he had no small intellect, too. In school, where he was also getting plenty of plaudits, Danny Ellsberg seemed sure of his abilities. He knew he was gifted. "Danny was confident. There was no question," Myron Poe recalls. "Danny had a good deal of self-presence and knowledge. I don't think that Danny was unsure of himself at all. . . . Danny, I believe, felt he was a superior person. Danny was, in fact, a superior person." Ellsberg's half brother, Harry, Jr., would say more bluntly, "Dan knew he was going to be a very important person. He was never too humble." Others who came to know Ellsberg believed he thought the rules others lived by didn't necessarily apply to him, given his genius. "He thinks that he's above that," one friend told me. "I think Dan, in a sense, felt that his genius allows him a free ticket. Because, you know, his gift to humanity is so great that he's allowed to do what he wants." Ellsberg's celebrity that followed his release of the Pentagon Papers fed that self-perception.[38]

Socially, Ellsberg may have been unsure of himself as a boy. Hence, in part, his distance from his peers. "I don't see how he had any way to develop any social skills," Eugene Paul reflects. "He was a very sensitive kid," Poe remembers. "Dan was sensitive to other kids, to people, to situations." But he took to the stage in grade school with noticeable self-assurance; his piano recitals nurtured his stage presence. "I remember we were in Miss Walker's English class," Norma Lawrie recounts. "And we all had to read books and give a book report. And Danny was the only person I have ever known in my life who could make a child's book report more interesting and lively than the book itself. I remember the class was almost on the edge of their seats. And then peals of laughter at the funny parts. His reports were not just a synthesis of something. It was in great depth. He practically retold the book. It was fascinating. . . . They were classics. They were *wonderful.* He probably made us want to read more than Miss Walker ever did." Poe recalls Ellsberg giving a report on Mark Twain's *A Connecticut Yankee in King Arthur's Court.* Ellsberg recited the episode of the eclipse of the sun, which saved the Yankee's life. "The kids wet their pants," Poe says. "This was really very racy in the classroom. And the class was in an uproar, because Danny did such a great job." Lawrie adds, "He could have become an actor. . . . There's an old southern expression that says, 'He could charm the skin off a snake.' . . . He was a raconteur even then. . . . You were spellbound." Further, "I think he enjoyed *performing.* I think he enjoyed being the center of attention."[39]

That continued as an adult. "He likes to be in the spotlight," his friend Doug Dowd comments. "Or to put it differently, he seems to *need* to be in the spotlight."[40]

Ellsberg was the vessel for his mother's ambition. She had not been able to become a concert pianist. But her son could become one. She was determined

that he would. "We'd laugh: 'This is her goal in life,'" Charlotte Miller recounts. "We didn't have the sense to see it. . . . We didn't look at it as this terrible thing, destroying his life. Or maybe we saw it and felt there was nothing we
could do about it." When a parent lives vicariously through a gifted child, it is
"a dangerous emotional state," as one scholar put it. Ellsberg has said that his
mother decided even before he was born that she would raise him to be a great
concert pianist. He did not know this as a boy and was not happy upon learning
it later. "I'd always been told I had to do all this with the piano because I had
showed such talent. When I found out it had been determined before I was
born, it was . . . shattering. It's very difficult to realize that your mother, in
whom you've always placed such trust—that what she'd always told you was a
myth." She was talking about his piano career when he was only two years old,
he would recall, and had him banging away on a paper keyboard not long afterward. If true, it is unlikely that she had spotted any talent yet; while musical talent tends to appear early, it does not usually appear that early. When Ellsberg
was around six, he began taking lessons from Margaret Mannebach, a well-
known instructor of young piano students at the private Detroit Institute of
Music. She was something of a guru there.[41]

Ellsberg's mother was not, it seems, a nurturing sort. "My mother rarely
praised me—that's one characteristic—for a performance," Ellsberg told me.
"She would mainly tell me what I had done wrong. . . . 'Well, on that part you
need more practice' or 'You could have done this differently.' . . . I was not to
be satisfied myself. She was not to be satisfied. . . . 'Well, you did it *that* time.'"
When he stumbled in a recital, she let him know about it. He threw up before
recitals. "I found that it made me feel calmer," he says. Ellsberg undoubtedly
felt his mother's criticism more than a less sensitive child would have; combined with his own high standards of achievement, that surely produced stress.
He may have felt alone when he could not please his mother. And his mother
"wasn't very physical" with him, he remembers. Ellsberg may not have gotten a
lot of unconditional love. To get emotional support from his mother—the center of his existence—he apparently had to meet her expectations. But it was
hard to meet those expectations. His subsequent desire for center stage can be
seen partly in this context. "Mummy said when you were a very little boy, 'I will
only love you if you are a successful performer.' So he's a performer. Why are
you surprised?" his friend Joan Cleveland remarks.[42]

Ellsberg believes his mother misled him when she told him that he had
great talent as a pianist. "I had a moderate talent. I wasn't without talent. . . .
But I had no outstanding talent. . . . I wasn't any budding concert pianist." His
mother herself was a much better pianist than he was, he concluded. And she

had to have been aware that he had no outstanding talent. That realization angered him later in life.[43]

Ellsberg's father did not take a particularly active role in child rearing. Ellsberg would later tell others that he was a nonentity in the family and that he and his mother excluded his father from their relationship. When it came to his son's piano playing, "he had no interest in it," Ellsberg told me. "He never commented one way or the other." Asked whether his father praised his playing, Ellsberg responded, "No, not at all." But his father helped monitor his practicing.[44]

Ellsberg missed out on much of his childhood because of his mother's designs for him. "Practicing deprived me of a social life," he says. He never had a chance to be a regular boy. In his retelling, his mother forbade him from playing sports that might risk injury to his hands, though he was not inclined toward sports anyway. "Nothing existed outside the piano," he recalls. Other boys in the neighborhood sensed his mother's desire to turn him into a great concert pianist. "We all had that feeling," Tom Varbedian remembers.[45]

As a boy, Ellsberg realized he was missing out on things. Above all, he would have liked to read a lot more. And after enrolling at Cranbrook, "I would have loved to do activities, like theater, like drama," he recalls. "And I would have liked to have more time off. Go into town. I couldn't go into town the way people did on weekends. I had to practice all day, from eight to eight." Ellsberg had a sense of being "confined" by the piano, but "it wasn't exactly a feeling of resentment. Just the feeling, 'There are other things I'd like to be doing.'" His frustration did not reach the point of thinking about giving up the piano, he says. His feelings toward his mother "were only loving. I had no feelings of being oppressed by her or anything. Because I accepted the indoctrination. It was many years later that I looked back on it somewhat differently." Before that, "I accepted the notion that she was simply supporting me, like a good coach, in a talent and a vocation. . . . Although everybody else's perception, I learned later as an adult, was that I was doing it for her. . . . My awareness of it was never that I was being forced to do this by my mother. . . . She was just keeping me at it, because it was what I wanted." He didn't feel any conscious anger toward his mother, he says. And he did enjoy playing the piano, which was also a way of making her happy. "I would have said I had a happy childhood," Ellsberg told me. "I would never have said I had an unhappy childhood. . . . Given, a lot of strain."[46]

But Ellsberg would conclude after being psychoanalyzed that he had felt considerable unconscious resentment toward his mother. And "looking back on it, I think I lived unconsciously with the awareness—fatalistic awareness—that some day a crisis was going to come when my mother recognized that this wasn't working and that . . . I would fail," he says. "And that that would be a terrible confrontation. That would lead to a breach. . . . And I would lose the interest of my mother." He thus felt tremendous pressure to succeed. "Unconsciously, I think I lived with the thought that my world was going to collapse at some point. My relation with my mother would collapse. . . . And that would be like death. Because my mother was everything to me."[47]

One wonders if Ellsberg felt more conscious resentment than he now describes, however. When children are held to unrealistic standards by their parents, it can be punishing to them. Ellsberg later told one friend that he hated the demands of the piano. He told another that he would purposely neglect to practice one piece before recitals and thus would stumble. Some gifted children perform poorly by design to escape the pressure of their parents and others. The pressure Ellsberg felt from his mother may even have been traumatic for him. It is quite likely that he felt anger at her at times, perhaps even hate. "He just did not enjoy the pressure that was put on him," Fred Dockstader perceived. "I think that his mother always felt that he could be a little better. . . . I think it frustrated him and annoyed him. . . . She wanted him to be the world's greatest pianist, and he wasn't doing it." Perhaps Ellsberg resented and tried to distance himself from his mother's pressure while simultaneously attempting to please her.[48]

Dockstader and other teachers at Cranbrook did notice a distance between Ellsberg and his parents. "There seemed to be kind of an invisible curtain between them," Dockstader recalls. "I remember many times talking to his parents about him. And they really couldn't get through to him. . . . On occasion his mother would comment that she didn't completely get through to him." Ellsberg, as we'll see, was withdrawn at Cranbrook, and Dockstader suspected that he was withdrawn at home, too. Indeed, Dockstader thought, that was partly why he was withdrawn at school. "I blamed it partly on his parents," he remembers, particularly on his mother.[49]

Harry and Adele Ellsberg's devotion to Christian Science may have also contributed to the distance. The family apparently studied the day's "lesson sermon" and prayed every morning. They attended Wednesday night meetings at which people would rise to testify to the religion's healing powers and other benefits. They attended church every Sunday morning. According to Christian Science, the cause of sickness is mental, illness is an illusion, and medical examinations tend to promote sickness. Thus, Daniel Ellsberg could not see a doctor. As Christian Scientists of Jewish background, his parents also wouldn't allow him near toy guns. "That sent me into the marines, eventually," he chuckles. Although Ellsberg likely weighed Christian Science's tenets in depth, he didn't buy the religion. From an early age, "he discounted it," Carol Cummings says. "He didn't go for those ideas." Ellsberg challenged his Sunday school teacher; his questions were not lightweight. When he was in his late teens, he found a book at the Detroit public library called *Mrs. Eddy Purloins from Hegel*, which provided evidence that Mary Baker Eddy, the founder of Christian Science, had plagiarized "with lavish abandon" and that this "grew habitual" over the years (not uncommon observations). Ellsberg showed the book to his father and would later tell others how crazy the religion was.[50]

When they were both adults, Ellsberg's half brother, Harry, Jr., would often remind him that Daniel had tried to quit playing the piano a couple of times, and that his mother had "just ignored me as though I didn't exist," Ellsberg remembers. "And wouldn't pass the bread at the table. I asked for the salt and there was no response. . . . After a day or so of this, I'd go back to the piano." Ellsberg believes he retained from these episodes that if he tried to quit, it would end his relationship with his mother. But he has no memory of the actual events: "I totally repressed it." People sometimes repress memories of traumatic events. When Ellsberg and Myron Poe subsequently discussed their childhoods, there were things Ellsberg could not remember that Poe would have sworn he would have remembered. "I ascribed that to, undoubtedly, selective repression," Poe recalls. "Because, obviously, there *is* that problem over his piano and his mom and what may or may not have been expected." Yet Poe never observed Ellsberg's mother acting in a way he thought overbearing, and he later wondered if Ellsberg was exaggerating some of her behavior.[51]

Recollections of some who knew Ellsberg at Cranbrook do not create a picture of an enthusiastic pianist. "He played really quite well mechanically, but with no oomph," his teacher and lower school housemaster Merrell Condit recounts. "It was very mechanical. And quite accomplished, but no zip to it." His piano teacher Robert Bates agreed with that description. "He was a sphinx when he played," his classmate Ken Wright remembers. "He wasn't one of these guys who does it with style and panache and all that stuff. He just played."[52]

As an adult, Ellsberg has sometimes seemed angry or bitter over the pressure his mother placed on him. "I've done my time in hell," he told a journalist in 1971. His daughter, Mary, recalls that when she talked to Charlotte Miller about Adele Ellsberg in the 1990s, it "was the first time I'd heard anything remotely positive about her." During interviews with me, Ellsberg occasionally seemed resentful of his mother while appearing to try to avoid that impression. In his *Who's Who in America* listing, he left out his mother. That is rare and was quite possibly done on purpose. Ellsberg likens his mother to the father of one of his former psychoanalysts, who was quite cruel to his son.[53]

———◆———

Narcissism is a term that comes readily to mind when examining Ellsberg and his childhood.[54] It is probably an overused and certainly a nebulous concept, and there are degrees of narcissism (psychoanalysts talk of a continuum of narcissistic disorders). But among the more commonly attributed features of narcissism are self-involvement, a grandiose sense of self, insecurity, and an inordinate need for approbation and admiration from others.

The narcissistic personality develops in early childhood, most experts agree, and the mother's personality is generally considered key in its genesis. The mother is typically controlling, unnurturing, even cold (though her responses may fluctuate), overprotective, and ambitious for her child, and quite possibly even narcissistic herself. She considers her child, who is in many cases the vehicle for her own aspirations, to be special, and the child comes to see himself or herself that way. The mother often uses the promise of specialness as a lure for shaping the child in the image she desires. The mother and child typically have a close, "special" relationship. One psychoanalyst wrote of narcissists, "These patients often occupy a pivotal point in their family structure, such as being the only child, or the only 'brilliant' child. . . . A good number of them have a history of having played the role of 'genius' in their family during childhood."[55] All of this sounds much like Adele and Daniel Ellsberg.

The package of narcissistic personality traits also describes Ellsberg fairly well. He is a self-centered person in many ways. He tends to think that his current focus of interest is extraordinarily important, and that others should accord it the same importance. As his half brother, Harry, would recall, "He was obsessed with everything he did. Whatever it was, it was the most important thing in the world. He was one of those guys who tells you what he's doing when you don't want to hear it. He couldn't figure out why you weren't as interested as he was." ("That's a good quote," Ellsberg comments. "That's very true. . . . This is what my wife finds very difficult to live with.") More than one person over the years has watched Ellsberg steer conversations to his areas of interest, including himself. "If Dan's not the center of attention, he sits there and kind of sulks and pouts, and he's not a lot of fun," one friend would observe. Ellsberg's self-centeredness is "one of the things that makes him not an easy friend," another person who knows him says. "He's *extremely* self-absorbed. And the great question then is, How much are you getting back? And on something like Vietnam—so important—you're getting back a lot. But when you go onto a normal footing, then I think it's very hard for him."[56] Ellsberg tends to do things at his convenience, often at the last minute, inconveniencing others; he can be very inconsiderate of others.

Ellsberg also has a famously enormous ego. He habitually exaggerates his significance to historical events and his impact on them (one reason for his unpopularity among former colleagues, who know better). He has often claimed to be the only person or the first person to have done something or to have known something. His boasting seems almost out of control; he appears to have difficulty reining in his ego. His ego feeds his indiscretion. After beginning to think of himself as special as a child, he would continue to see himself in large terms as an adult. "He saw himself as a swashbuckling kind of figure, powerful through his intellect, and he was going to influence history," Roman Kolkowicz, a former RAND Corporation colleague, remembers. "He wasn't playing just for little bureaucratic scraps. . . . One could see he saw himself as a great historical figure who would save the world on the one hand, or destroy the enemy on the other."[57]

At the same time, Ellsberg was, and is, an insecure man. Indeed, that may largely explain his boasting, his chronic exaggeration, and even his fabrications. His insecurity also probably feeds his grandiose view of himself and his self-absorption. One person who worked for him for many years thought that he was one of the most insecure persons who didn't need to be whom she had ever known. "Don't underestimate his vulnerability or his sensitivity to criticism," a friend of his told me. "If you think his self-esteem is anywhere near what you might call secure, forget it." Like many narcissists, Ellsberg sometimes becomes enraged when he feels he's been slighted. But he told me, "Criticism in general doesn't bother me. I try to learn from it, and see if it seems possibly accurate. Even if it's in malice."[58]

Ellsberg also has a marked need for approval and admiration from others. One person who knew him found him "so narcissistic, it's almost touching," as "he's like a little boy, so in need of praise." In some of the many conversations Doug Dowd has had with Ellsberg, "I've often felt that in some sense he wants me to say, 'You've been a good boy,'" Dowd relates. "I think that Dan needs to have the back-patting done for him."[59]

Narcissism tends to cut people off from others, to impede their ability to fully relate and feel connected to others, and to empathize with their feelings. The narcissist's feelings are, to some extent, out of whack. People have commonly observed that Ellsberg often seems oblivious to what those around him are feeling and has difficulty tuning in to their feelings. Donald Hall speaks of "the oddness of affect" shown by Ellsberg ever since he got to know him at Harvard, where "I felt sometimes that Dan was expressing feelings because that's what the script said, and this is what people said and did, and not that he was feeling that. It was not that he was without feeling. It was that they were strange. They were not like other people's." Hall adds, "He was, of course, and is a strange man. He's always been. . . . I think Dan's personality or character structure is very strange and unlike anything else I know. There's no category of personality type that it really fits." Ellsberg is a highly emotional man, almost uncontrollably so, and his emotions are sometimes expressed at odd or inappropriate times; friends have been surprised at the circumstances in which he has cried. He can seem almost childlike emotionally.[60]

Narcissism is a strong element of what some Jungian psychologists call the *puer aeternus*, or eternal youth. The *puer aeternus*, who is in large part the product of an ambitious, dynamic, controlling, overprotective mother, feels special and superior to others, yet suffers from "an inferiority complex"; tends to be hungry, restless, and impatient; finds it hard to be satisfied and to complete work; is often a risk taker; has a heroic sense of self (which sometimes progresses to megalomania); can be quite charming and stimulating company; and tends to be a womanizer.[61] That description, too, fits Ellsberg well.

Ellsberg has read extensively on narcissism, but, at least publicly, he rejects it as a characterization of himself. He also rejects the descriptions "self-absorbed" and "egotistical." "It's not clear to me what that means," he says in both cases. "It has a ring to it that doesn't quite ring true."[62] My own experience with Ellsberg is that he can appear both acutely aware of his personal shortcomings (and impressively candid about them) *and* strikingly self-delusional. Like many of the rest of us, Ellsberg may not want to probe too deeply into himself for fear of what he will find.

TWO

OUTSIDER

WHEN 12-YEAR-OLD DAN ELLSBERG ENTERED CRANBROOK SCHOOL IN the fall of 1943, he was entering one of the country's elite prep schools. Cranbrook's founder, George Gough Booth, a Detroit newspaper publisher, saw the school as training the leaders of the next generation. Most students came from well-to-do families; many of their fathers were automobile industry men. In Ellsberg's junior year, students voted the Cadillac their favorite car. "Being well off was considered very important," remembers Gunther Balz, a former student. At Kingswood, Cranbrook's sister school, dancing classes were held for "would-be socialites." Cranbrook is located in Bloomfield Hills, a wealthy suburb and home to captains of industry in rolling countryside some ten miles north of Detroit. Designed by the Finnish architect Eliel Saarinen and located on 90 pastoral acres, Cranbrook was nationally recognized for its beauty.[1]

Students were largely apolitical. There was no television, only seniors could have radios in their rooms, and most students did not keep up with newspapers. But conservative views far outnumbered liberal ones. Students voted overwhelmingly for Republican candidates in a mock election in November 1946, and in a straw poll of both students and teachers in 1948, Thomas Dewey swamped Harry Truman. All of Cranbrook's teachers but one were men (the lone woman taught typing).[2]

Ellsberg entered Cranbrook after the United States had joined the fighting in World War II. "We were intensely patriotic, and really wanted the war to be over," remembers W. Laird Stabler, a member of Ellsberg's class who would later become Delaware's state attorney general and the state's Republican national committeeman. "All of us had relatives who were fighting; some had been killed." When one teacher, or "master" (as they were called), Bradley Patterson, who later became a powerful man in the Republican Party, invited a Nisei student at Cranbrook Art Academy to talk to his seventh grade social studies class, it did not sit well with school officials. "Gee, a real Jap," one student remarked. Students were urged to purchase war bonds and stamps "regularly!"[3]

Cranbrook unofficially limited Jewish admissions. Ellsberg was picked on and called anti-Semitic names by one classmate, an anti-Semite who also disliked bookish types, in part because he was very unbookish himself (and apparently lacking in good judgment: he crashed into two trees one night when attempting to drive home blindfolded). Ellsberg remembers this person as "a very big guy" and "a football player," but, in fact, he was fairly average in size and played other sports. "I decided to become a boxer to learn to deal with him," Ellsberg recalls. As a result, "I became a reasonably good boxer in high school. And waited then to get into a fight with him. . . . I had a more aggressive attitude as a result of that, and he then backed off of me, and he never gave me any trouble. He gave other people trouble after that." But when told this account, another of Ellsberg's classmates, Ken Wright, called it "bullshit." Ellsberg adds, "Not that I could beat him, of course, but that I could take a few swings and hurt him. Even though he would end by creaming me. I assumed that he would destroy me."[4]

Students at Cranbrook led a highly regulated existence. Coats and ties were mandatory in class and in the big barrel-vaulted dining hall. Before dinner, students would open the doors to the hall and line up as the masters entered. At long tables, dinner would open with a loud prayer. Rumor had it that saltpeter was mixed in their food to depress their sexual appetites. (According to a poll, the favorite topic of conversation of the class of 1947 was "sex," their favorite type of girl was "rich and innocent," and Cranbrook's greatest need was "co-education.") Students could not leave the school grounds without permission. Girls from Kingswood came over for Saturday night movies and dances "under lock and key." A Cranbrook boy who was caught with a girl in the bathroom was kicked out of school. Mandatory chapel services were held twice a week. Yet few students challenged the school's rules or criticized their masters "because *there is no cause for complaint*," according to an editorial in the student newspaper, the *Crane*, in December 1945. "You are a student in the best school in the world and lucky to be one."[5]

Shortly after Ellsberg arrived at Cranbrook, he and his seventh grade classmates gathered in their coats and ties to introduce themselves and to state their ambitions. "Dan was easily the most poised," his classmate Richard

Townsend recounts. Ellsberg declared, in effect, "My ambition is to be a dictator." That was rather audacious; the United States was then fighting dictators. "But he said it with a smile," Townsend recalls. "Everybody took it in good humor." Ellsberg "had, even then, the wit. And he spoke, I think, in paragraphs. The rest of us mostly just kind of stuttered, stammered something. He had a twinkle. I sort of recall taking to his spunk too. . . . There was sort of a shyness there, but he seemed to be winning us over by his mind and so on." Jack Sheldon, later a well-known musician and comic who was also in Ellsberg's entering class, was confident when introducing himself too, Townsend remembers. "But he didn't have as much eloquence, I think, as Dan," who "seemed to be kind of a stylist." And Ellsberg "was a bit impudent, always. From the dictator introduction [on]."[6]

Ellsberg remained a physically unimposing presence. Perhaps shorter than average, he also had "a bit of a potbelly," Townsend recollects. "He was your typical scrawny adolescent with acne, not knowing where to put his feet and not knowing what to wear," Dora Crouch, a Kingswood student, remembers. "He also had sort of shambling body posture. . . . He had all the drawbacks of being an adolescent." Walt Denison recalls Ellsberg walking around at Cranbrook hunched over, head down. Crouch would be surprised by Ellsberg's physical appearance at their fortieth class reunion in 1988. "He's wearing this fantastic tan suit and I think it was a blue tie, and he's looking very handsome, and he's got a terrific haircut, and just really put together very well. . . . He is very upright and has really learned how to control his body and make a good impression with the body." Crouch found him charming and physically attractive, which had not been the case earlier.[7]

To Gunther Balz, Ellsberg's physical appearance at Cranbrook stuck out. There he was in his "perpetually worn, funny double-breasted suit and his black briefcase," Balz recounts. "I think he only had one suit, and he wore it, I think, for four years. And he had this black businessman's briefcase. He looked like a Politburo lawyer or something going to work everyday." It was well out of the ordinary. His peers did not carry briefcases. "He dressed very simply, very plainly," Charles Maxwell, who entered Cranbrook with Ellsberg, reminisces. "I think Gunther may be right that he wore the same suit. And he may not have worried about it. . . . He had absolutely no affectations of wealth." Crouch, who saw the double-breasted suit one Sunday when Ellsberg came over for tea at Kingswood, also remembers "a sort of stringy tie" and "a loose vest" that "was really way out of the mainstream."[8]

Ellsberg was on the fringe of student life at Cranbrook. An outsider. He was quite reserved. "He really didn't have any friends there," faculty member

Fred Dockstader recounts. "He was a very, very withdrawn chap, wrapped up in his own life. . . . It was his outstanding feature. He did not have friends. He was a loner." He seemed remote and very private to many around him. Robert Beyers, who lived in the same dorm Ellsberg's senior year, recalls, "He was the kind of guy that . . . if you wanted to talk to him, you went to his room. He never came to yours." Ellsberg didn't enter easily into conversation. Balz, an extroverted type, remembers making one or two attempts to get him to open up, but to no avail. "If he had a social life, it sure as hell wasn't part of the school," Balz says.[9]

Ellsberg tended to be a solitary presence at meals. "In the dining hall, he was almost a nonentity," Dockstader recounts. "And the dining hall, in a way, was part of the way kids let off steam. . . . But with him, as I remember, most of the time he just sat down and ate and that was it." Physically, students couldn't eat by themselves at those long tables, "but he would just be by himself at the table."[10]

But Ellsberg was not simply an island unto himself at Cranbrook. He opened up with some of his classmates, probably those he found most interesting, and increasingly over time. "When you tried to bring him out, then he entered into the spirit of the thing," Maxwell found. "He never sort of said, 'Oh, your mother's mustache,' and pushed off to the library. That was not characteristic of him at all. . . . His personality was amenable to all kinds of things if you made the initiative." One time Maxwell approached Ellsberg with a question and asked to discuss it, "and he very quickly joined in. . . . I think he liked relationships, but I think he liked relationships that had some content to them, rather than sitting there and thinking brotherly thoughts." Maxwell remembers "just how friendly he was when you said to him, in effect, 'I'd like your friendliness. I'd like to see the friendly side of your personality. I need some help. . . . ' He was just very quick to help." There was a day at Cranbrook when students could wear anything they wanted. "Some people didn't dress up at all, but he did something kind of slapdash," Townsend recalls. "So he got in the spirit of things, it seems to me." One photo in his senior yearbook shows Ellsberg mugging for the camera with a group of his peers. Ellsberg ultimately formed at least a couple of good friendships and had a small peer group he was comfortable with.[11]

And he was not unpopular with other students. "Everyone respected his intelligence, respected his artistic talents," Ken Wright remembers. "He was not one of these guys who people disliked. I mean, you had no basis to even measure him." Other students "left him alone." Some were a little jealous of his intelligence. Ellsberg skipped eighth grade and consequently was less mature physically than most of his classmates. But "I don't think he enjoyed very much browbeating from the others," Maxwell recalls. "I think there was a respect that suggested that people were not interested in picking on him. Once he advanced a year or so, there were an awful lot of bigger boys that could have made fun of him. I don't think I ever saw anybody make fun of him. I think he was so brilliant that people at some stage just accepted him as the school genius. And I think that he accepted that role, because it was the one assigned to him by everybody else." One rumor at Cranbrook had it that Ellsberg had earlier missed qualifying to compete with other young wizards on the "Quiz Kids" radio program by only a hair.[12]

But Ellsberg did exhibit a certain sense of superiority that didn't sit well with everyone around him. He had "an air of cockiness," Dockstader told me. "He knew he was good and made no bones about it. . . . He tended a little bit to parade that around with the other kids." Ellsberg knew he was a good piano player and would show off his skills. "And also in the intellectual line," Dockstader remembers. "He made no bones about the fact that he knew the answers. I would not say he was pompous. But I would say he was very aware of his abilities and made the other kids know it." Dockstader adds, "He did not unbend graciously. . . . I have a sense of rectitude with him. Remote and, I guess, stiff a little bit. He was not a likable person." When I asked Floyd Bunt, another of Ellsberg's teachers, whether he exhibited a slight cockiness or sense of superiority, Bunt replied, "Maybe a little more than slight." Ellsberg had a supercilious smile. "I think he maybe thought the rest of us might have been a bunch of jerks. Not up to his mental capacity," Stabler recalls. "I think maybe he would have desperately liked to have been one of the boys, and wasn't, and so you react by just putting up a little wall there and going around acting like you don't give a damn about anything."[13] That may well be true. Many people compensate for feelings of insecurity with outward self-assuredness, or seek to protect themselves by not risking too much in social interaction.

But where some saw cockiness, others simply saw great confidence in his abilities. Ellsberg was "not someone who would strut around and pour it down your face," Wright remembers. "He didn't do that at all. He was very sort of modest about his accomplishments. He wouldn't step forward and take charge, or come into a room and start playing the piano. None of that." But Ellsberg wasn't about to play dumb to fit in. The inscription aside his picture in his senior yearbook observes, "Almost everything he attempts has an accomplished air about it, for Dan knows what he wants and he is sure to get it."[14]

The wall Fred Dockstader noticed between Ellsberg and his parents, the distance he saw between Ellsberg and other students, also separated Ellsberg from his teachers. "It was with us too," Dockstader remembers. "There was a curtain between us. I never felt any closeness to Dan. He was a good student and I gloried in his good work, and I enjoying looking over his papers and all that sort of thing, and enjoyed having him in class. But I never felt any companionship with him. . . . He was a distant chap. . . . It was hard to get close to [him]. . . . He didn't welcome confidences. He was always friendly enough in a way, but there was a barrier between us and him. All of us." Dockstader doubts Ellsberg was close to any of his teachers, another of whom remembers him as "a nonentity. . . . He just sort of faded into the wallpaper." His music teacher, Robert Bates, did not know much about him, and another teacher also found him introverted and withdrawn. His remoteness concerned some of his teachers. "I think that a few of us were aware that there were some shortcomings that needed some attention," Dockstader says.[15]

Ellsberg's parents were certainly aware of them. They visited Cranbrook regularly. Adele Ellsberg "was the flowering blossom, and [Harry] was a bit more in the background," Dockstader reminisces. Aside from being interested in their son's academic progress and accomplishments, "I think that in part they were trying to see if we could loosen him up some," Dockstader says. "That was my reading." They were concerned about his difficulty mixing with his peers. "I think that troubled them some," Dockstader recounts. "Particularly his father. I would say his father was a bit more bothered about that than she was." (His father would also later describe Ellsberg as a loner at Cranbrook.)[16]

That Ellsberg had enjoyed little social life in grade school could not have helped his situation at Cranbrook. He seemed "awkward socially" to one classmate and "kind of a nerd" to another. "He was the classical egghead: the real smart guy, but didn't have much else on the ball," Stabler thought. "He didn't have many social graces." And he was still very sensitive and astute about how others saw him.[17]

Ellsberg's giftedness continued to distance him from his peers. He struck Thomas Fennell, another classmate, as by far the smartest student in their class, a head above everyone else. His classmates voted him the smartest their senior year. "His personality was defined, in a way, by his intelligence," his classmate Jo Isaacson remembers. One of Ellsberg's teachers referred to him to other students as "the professor in the fourth-year class." He was the best student Dockstader had. "It was hands down," Dockstader says. "He had a brilliant mind. . . . He didn't have to work to do well at Cranbrook. It came very easy to him. He could read something and take it in very quickly. As a matter of fact, I think it was *too* easy for him." Charles Maxwell found Ellsberg remarkably knowledgeable about the world, even if "one had to literally pull things out of him. And when you did, it was quite a panoply of good things. Delivered in a fairly monotone [voice], so as not to somehow throw himself emotionally into the fact that he was so much more knowledgeable than the rest of us. . . . And I think he deliberately underplayed himself so that people would understand that he understood himself that this [reputation for] brilliance was not going to be imposed on him."[18]

Ellsberg also had different tastes than many of his peers—more refined ones, music and books preeminently. "I listened to records all the time," he remembers. "Incessantly. Piano records." He had a collection of classical and semiclassical records in his room. That would have been unusual. "I have a memory of him having a typewriter in his room [too], whereas I don't think most of us did," Townsend says. "He had it on a special table to the side there." Ellsberg wasn't into athletics, which were a big part of Cranbrook student culture. Culturally and intellectually, his background may have been more sophisticated than that of most of his classmates.[19] Perhaps he didn't find many of them particularly interesting.

In seventh grade, Jack Sheldon received the dreaded Black Spot for being "a bad citizen" and consequently had to push a small cart down the hall of his dorm toward the showers. His peers hit him on his rear end with Ping-Pong paddles or snapped towels at him. Sheldon then had to take a cold shower. Ellsberg seemed somewhat repulsed by the exercise.[20]

Perhaps more significantly, Ellsberg was focused on achievement. His tremendous drive to excel and great intellectual curiosity seemed to take precedence over social activities. Even as a teenager, he was animated more by ideas than by people, even then he was an intellectual. "He was very intense," Isaacson recounts. "He was very studious and very interested in a lot of things. I think it wasn't a conscious choice. He just enjoyed that." Ellsberg set high goals for himself. "He would set out to read ten books a month," Isaacson says; "he mastered many subjects. . . . It wasn't light reading. . . . They were books of great weight, let's say . . . scholarly books on subjects." "Tough things," Townsend recalled. "Like a book on economics. He read a lot on economics." By his senior year Ellsberg had read "several substantial books on the subject," Townsend wrote in the *Crane*. Ellsberg seemed a voracious consumer of information. "He was a great reader, and it was very important to him to digest a great deal of material," Maxwell remembers. "He would absorb maybe a book every two days. . . . And he was *really* going through the library. And a vast mass of things." Ellsberg recalls reading "the entire modern library book of the basic writings of Sigmund Freud" his senior year. "And I read that very closely."[21]

All this seemed to be less to compensate for being introverted than to ed-ucate himself and excel beyond the norm. "He just had his goals and he was very focused on them," Isaacson reminisces. "He had an agenda. Which a lot of people at that age don't have. . . . He had a much more deliberately planned agenda." Ellsberg appeared to want to maximize his life—to do as much as possible, to learn as much as he could, to attend a superior college (he was talking Harvard early on), to distinguish himself. He remained a serious boy who didn't smile a lot. The inscription aside his picture in the 1948 student yearbook says, "To the casual observer Dan appears to be nothing more than a sober genius." Absorbing knowledge was also entertainment for him. As a re-sult, he didn't seem to need to be one of the boys, Maxwell thought. "I think that he probably gave that up a long time before. . . . He had built a kind of life for himself in which he didn't need the approbation of his peers to find self-esteem in his work and his life." But "I think when it came his way he en-joyed it. I think he really did."[22]

In an advanced English course his senior year, Ellsberg wrote a thesis on semantics, and one of his first readings was *The Meaning of Meaning: A Study of the Influence of Language Upon Thought and of the Science of Symbolism*, a highly complex, esoteric, and dense book that many, if not most, college professors would find challenging; some would find it inaccessible. But it fascinated Ells-berg—at age 16. He also read other semantics texts, including the popularly written *Language in Action* by S. I. Hayakawa, whom he met at Cranbrook. Hayakawa "was very impressed with my knowledge of semantics," Ellsberg re-calls. Ellsberg's thesis and performance in the English course greatly im-pressed his teacher, Carl Wonnberger, who awarded him an A+ and wrote in his grade report: "In every department of the work Dan is definitely superior. His rating on the American Council English Test exceeds anything by which we can measure; his thesis deserves to be published, and he has a wider read-ing knowledge in the field of semantics than many alleged experts in the field. I wish Dan every success in what should be a brilliant future."[23]

Ellsberg also wrote poetry; most students did not. When fellow student David Osnos told him he liked a poem Ellsberg had written entitled "Christ-mas," which was published in the *Crane*, Ellsberg responded, "Oh, you're a sucker for sentimentality." Three other poems that Ellsberg wrote won a re-gional writing award in 1947. "I think he did poetry to show that he could do that, too," Osnos aptly comments.[24]

Ellsberg would much later act as if he wanted to be one of the boys. He phoned Jo Isaacson from an airport to talk one evening in the 1960s, although they had not been close at Cranbrook. Ellsberg also called or visited Isaacson several other times. "I've always been sort of struck that he would be approaching me," Isaacson says. "So he must enjoy or at least value certain contacts that bring him back to his earlier days." Perhaps Ellsberg wanted, in part, to talk about what he had done since (the conquering hero), or simply had become more comfortable. When he attended his fortieth class reunion, to the surprise of other alumni, "he sort of latched himself onto me" while walking around, Ken Wright, with whom he had exchanged few words at Cranbrook, remembers, "and finally I just wanted to go along by myself. It got to the point where it was cloying to me, and I just wanted to get away." During introductions at the Bloomfield Hills Country Club, Cranbrook and Kingswood alumni took turns saying something about their lives. But when Ellsberg stood up, he also "revealed his sexual fantasies," Wright, who was the emcee, recounts. "He said that he had fantasies at night about certain girls at Kingswood. . . . I was sort of, 'Wait a minute, Dan. We didn't want to have you stand up and deliver your sexual fantasies. . . . ' All of a sudden this came out from left field. . . . It was sort of an admission that took everyone by surprise. Because no one really knew much about Dan. But there he is, you know."[25]

Ellsberg had not had much experience with girls at Cranbrook. The *Crane* published the names of students and their dates who attended the big dances, and his name is listed only once. He accompanied a girl named Sonja Dahlgren to the commencement formal in June of 1947. Ellsberg describes her as "a girlfriend that I was very serious about." That summer, he recalls, "we saw each other everyday" and "I was on the phone to her constantly." But they split up shortly thereafter. "She said something that made me feel she didn't want to go steady the way we were. . . . So I broke up with her."[26]

In the middle of his senior year, Ellsberg dated Dora Crouch. Crouch was also brilliant. She had earlier convinced Kingswood to arrange for selected students to compete for four-year Pepsi-Cola scholarships to the college of their choice; Cranbrook also offered the competition as a result. Crouch scored in the top one percent in the country on the tests. Ellsberg got a perfect 800 score on the verbal section and 783 in math. (He would recall scoring 800 on the verbal section twice, which is not as unlikely as it might sound, as the competition required him to take the tests twice.) Ellsberg scored highest in the state of Michigan. He, of course, won a scholarship. "He took it in stride," Richard Townsend remembers. "He was very cool about it." Ellsberg elected to go to Harvard. He posed for a picture in the *Crane* drinking Pepsi. "As a matter of fact I never touch the stuff," he remarked. "Wouldn't want that to get around, of course."[27]

Crouch remembers their dating: "It started, I think, as a blind date, when somebody fixed us up. And it was awkward. I was young and gauche, and he was young and gauche. . . . And we'd be dancing and neither of us could think of anything to say. Or you'd go to a movie together and, 'Should we or should we not hold hands?' We were completely green. And on top of it, we were both brains—this type of person doesn't cope very well with the teenage pressures to be a regular person and do a lot of dating." But Ellsberg appreciated Crouch's intelligence, and they could satisfy the social pressure to date by dating each other. "I think that one of the things that kept us talking with each other over a couple of months was that we both had what's come to be called the liberal point of view about society, and about what was right about it and what was wrong about it, and what ought to be fixed," Crouch says. She recalls "a couple of conversations about how things were really bad with the world and that there was a big need for improvement." But more than anything, she remembers the emotional tone of their relationship, which was, "I can't imagine that this is going to go anywhere."[28]

Hence Crouch's surprise and discomfort during introductions at their fortieth reunion when Ellsberg, who was sitting next to her at a table, stood up and "proceeded to tell them a story about the two of us dancing together when we were teenagers," Crouch recounts. "I've blocked some of it, because I didn't like it. But what I can remember is that we were dancing together—and the kind of dancing people did in those days was very close dancing—and that he talked about us dipping way back, and placing passionate kisses on my forehead or my neck or something." Crouch has no memory of either kissing or dipping. "Now, neither of us was adept enough at dancing to do that kind of dramatic dancing either," she points out. She found Ellsberg's memory curious. He hadn't made those types of sexual allusions back in high school either: "I remember thinking that this was different about him."[29]

<hr />

Ellsberg participated in some student activities at Cranbrook. In seventh grade, he played a droll detective in a play. He had one line about a woman being thrown out of her home that went something like, "Thrown out into the cold and in the snow." He repeated it several times. Ellsberg served on a bowling committee and bowled regularly. Perhaps partly in rebellion against his parents, he was a member of the rifle club for two years. Students shot in a basement rifle range; the NRA provided guns and ammunition and presented awards. Ellsberg was a middling marksman; he ranked at the third lowest of eleven skill levels in May 1945. "He was a fairly good shot. He wasn't an outstanding shooter," Floyd Bunt, who helped coach the club, remembers.[30]

Ellsberg was a nonvarsity member of the tennis team for two years. He claims that he was the eleventh man on the ten-man team his sophomore year. "I was the first substitute. Which was very good. The others were nearly all seniors." He was the only sophomore that close to making the varsity, he says. (Ellsberg was actually on the team his freshman and junior years.) When he later applied to enter the U.S. Marine Corps, he claimed that he played four years of varsity tennis in high school. (He also told the Marine Corps he had no talent at musical entertainment.) Ellsberg was a member of the soccer team his senior year. "I was terrible at soccer," he acknowledges. His physical coordination was not the best.[31]

Ellsberg was required to participate in intramural sports, and in seventh grade he was selected by chance to be captain of his intramural basketball team. When the Pentagon Papers came out later, his father told *Time* magazine and possibly the *New York Times* that he had been captain of *the* basketball team at Cranbrook. The fable was picked up by the CIA and included in its second psychological profile of Ellsberg. Ken Wright was actually the captain of Cranbrook's basketball team. Peeved, Wright fired off a series of letters to *Time* demanding an apology and charging the magazine with trying to portray "essentially a nerd"—Ellsberg—as "this well-rounded individual, which he wasn't."[32]

Ellsberg was a member of the debating club for two years. He was probably something of a natural at that. In a competition in November 1945, he argued for compulsory one-year military training:

> If the United States is to take an active part in the fight against aggression, a force which can be quickly mobilized and thrown into action is essential. Moreover, the possession of armaments by other major powers provides a constant threat to our sovereignty. . . . At best the present United Nations Organization provides no assurance of safety from attack by a major power.
>
> We don't think that war can be averted simply by ignoring the possibility of future aggression. If in the future a situation arises where the military can save America, we must be prepared to meet it.

Ellsberg argued against reducing the legal voting age to 18 in another debate, but he may not have been taking personal positions in the competitions.[33]

Politically, Ellsberg was of liberal Democratic bent. "Definitely a New Deal supporter, definitely the sort of person who idolized Roosevelt, and who liked Truman, and who was very civil rights conscious," Maxwell remembers. But "I wouldn't have characterized him as having an attachment to any particular causes. I mean, he would speak animatedly about things like raising submarines from the deep, or something like that that he knew something about because of his uncle. . . . We know that in later life he became a person of causes. But I would not be able to find any such cause that he was adopting when he was in seventh or eighth grade."[34] That's not surprising, of course: few 12- or 13-year-olds have political causes. But by his junior and senior years, Ellsberg would be interested in socialism.

His half brother was the reason for that. Harry was a graduate student in economics at Wayne State University and active in the Young People's Socialist League. He "was extremely sympathetic to the Soviet Union," Ellsberg recalls, and refused to register for the draft during World War II until the Soviet Union was invaded by Nazi Germany. "My father claimed that through influence with the draft board person he kept them from either imprisoning him or inducting him. This could have been true, or it could not. My father was given to stories of that sort." Ellsberg's half brother also talked to him about racial discrimination in the United States. During Ellsberg's junior year, Harry gave him an economics textbook for Christmas, another heavy read, and one for college students; it was critical of capitalism and sympathetic to democratic socialism. The book "made me very interested in economic issues," Ellsberg recounts. "And I got fascinated by that. And then—again, partly reacting to some things my brother said—I got into a study of the labor movement in the thirties at Cranbrook. And decided to be a labor leader or organizer—an organizer, not a leader—or a union economist. I was going to work at a different kind of work every year for experience." Walter Reuther, the head of the United Auto Workers, became "the ego-ideal of Dan's youth," Harry would recall. Labor strikes were then widespread in the United States. Ellsberg would work a punch press in the night shift at a Dodge plant in the summer of 1948 between Cranbrook and college.[35]

"Dan says he has not as yet decided whether after graduation from Harvard to revive the IWW [Industrial Workers of the World] or to be personal adviser to future-President Henry A. Wallace," Richard Townsend wrote in the *Crane* in April of that year. Wallace was then running against Truman as the Progressive party candidate for president. Probably with a smile on his face, Ellsberg listed himself as the *Crane's* "Labor Adviser" the following month; in the same issue, he likely wrote the following short piece:

> Charges of "repressing civil liberties" are being brought against certain Cranbrook masters this week, it was disclosed today. The case centered around a request by several politically-conscious boarders to attend an educational program in Detroit (featuring, as it happened, presidential candidate Henry A.

Wallace). The petition, it was reported, was promptly scotched by one of their housemasters. The students vigorously protested the edict ("Reactionary! Bourgeois! Fascism!"); they intend to make a test case of the incident.

It is feared that this unfortunate occurrence may signal the opening of a new "clamp-down" policy by the administration. As this paper goes to press, it is rumored that fifth-form nominees for prefectship are being asked to sign a loyalty pledge and plans for repainting the seats in the assembly hall have already gone into effect. *Crane* editors can only view with alarm such distressing evidence of war hysteria at Cranbrook.

The following month, Ellsberg anonymously composed a humorous list of predictions of what graduating seniors might be doing 20 years later. Either he or the newspaper's editor wrote that Ellsberg himself would be *"The Worker's Wit* in American edition of *Pravda."*[36]

All this was fairly daring and brash behavior, even if done anonymously and at the end of his tenure at elite Cranbrook, at a time when domestic redbaiting was beginning to take hold. Perhaps it's one reason Cranbrook's headmaster wrote in Ellsberg's final grade report, "He is an independent thinker (which is fine) but I hope that he will keep a sense of balance and will avoid radical extremes in either direction. He must be on his guard lest he become the 'victim' of his unusual wit and brilliant mind."[37]

But Ellsberg was not generally vocal about his politics or inclined toward activism at Cranbrook. He did not participate in student government and apparently was not high on it. "If the student government has accomplished anything so far this year, the student body hasn't heard about it," he said in his junior year. "I remember him particularly for his *not* being very interested in political involvement," Robert Beyers recalls. During Ellsberg's senior year, Beyers was attempting to organize at Cranbrook a chapter of the United World Federalists (UWF), a primarily student organization that advocated strengthening the United Nations "into a world government of limited powers adequate to prevent war." He remembers talking to Ellsberg about the UWF, NATO, or some other political topic, and "really trying to get him interested in political stuff. You know, 'Why don't you come out?' . . . He wasn't interested." Though Ellsberg would maintain that he already believed in 1944 that the development of an atomic bomb would have horrible consequences for mankind, and that he was quite upset and disturbed by the subsequent U.S. atomic bombings of Hiroshima and Nagasaki, others at Cranbrook at the time seriously doubt both claims. One of his teachers, Bradley Patterson, thought Ellsberg's first memory was a product of his sentimentally interweaving his Cranbrook period with his later political ideology, and Charles Maxwell says of the atomic bombings, "I don't think that anyone that I knew of ever expressed dismay."[38]

Ellsberg anonymously wrote the "Cranium" humor column in the *Crane* his last year or two at Cranbrook. It was a way to express his sardonic, droll wit and participate in student life from a distance. "He was a little bit above it all," Stabler recalls. "Like he was in an ivory tower and kind of looking down and benignly casting barbs here and there." But Townsend noticed a significant improvement in the Cranium after Ellsberg began writing it. "It wasn't canned humor," he remembers. "It was something that he developed from the situation, and kind of put it through his prism. It had a sort of delectable zapper to it. . . . It seemed to get the character of people, I think, or the events." One of Ellsberg's items: "We have been asked to request the person who made off with Dan Bellinger's entire stock of underwear (size 28) last week to please return some of it, as the owner is getting desperate." Others:

> At least one junior can feel that he has already made a permanent contribution to the school. When Dick Townsend's copy of *Silas Marner* disappeared mysteriously two years ago, he bought another, but continued his search for the lost classic (after all, one can't have too many copies of *Silas Marner*). At last he ran it down—on the library shelves. He identified it by the inscription printed inside: "This Book Generously Donated to the Library by Dick Townsend."

> Mr. Rickets: "Larry Williams, what is the name of the present emperor of Japan?"
> Williams (without much conviction): "Hiroshima?"

> Of course, they won't take just *anyone*. Before even taking their physical, boys applying for NROTC had to pass a rigid psychological exam, consisting of the following questions: (a) Which member of your family is in an insane asylum? (b) Do you like to take orders? (c) Has your father been released from jail? (d) Do you think you could handle a mop and bucket?[39]

Ellsberg used the byline "The Country Wit" in some columns, after Cranbrook's headmaster, whom some thought pompous, used the term "country wits" to characterize misbehaving students.[40]

Ellsberg also showed interest in sexual matters, characteristic of teenagers, but which would soon become a quite pronounced personal characteristic:

The library lost its main current attraction last week when someone saw fit to tear out page 98 from this month's issue of *Holiday* (a full-page picture of a custom-built bathing suit on a custom-built model). Meanwhile, the library may as well close up shop. The only clue we can offer is that Mr. Wonnberger was talking about the picture first period.

With all these dances coming around, many boys have become more conscious of their ballroom technique. In particular, several boys felt that their timetested, "Ya wanna dance?" was sometimes inadequate, so they finally came to us for help. This request sent us (as what doesn't?) to that monumental work, *Etiquette* by Emily Post. According to Miss Post (p. 326, "Asking For a Dance") the approved formula is, "May I have some of this?"

If anyone is still doubtful, the procedure continues as follows:

"The girl either replies, 'Certainly,' or 'Yes, I'd like to very much,' or usually she says nothing but gets up. (And what if she doesn't, Miss Post? What then?) At the end of the dance the man says, 'Thank you!' Sometimes he adds, 'That was wonderful!' . . ."

Highlight of the Religious Conference: "?? But it won't go in!"

In a farewell statement he wrote in Townsend's copy of the 1948 school yearbook, Ellsberg said he had "been cleansed of all coarse-minded humor," however, and added, waggishly, "May you prosper in your life-work, whatever it may be—insurance salesman, usher, proofreader. . . ."[41]

As for the piano, Ellsberg played largely classical music at Cranbrook—his mother wouldn't let him play much else—mainly in a room adjoining two dorms. "He was not reluctant to play in front of the kids," Fred Dockstader remembers. "Although I don't think he played for them, and yet I think he played for them [laughs]. . . . He played for himself, but also to show other kids how good he was." Ellsberg was called Cranbrook's most promising pianist. "He was by far the best of us at the school," Dockstader says.[42]

Ellsberg played in school events, and in his senior year he accompanied a singer billed as having been one of the premier falsettos in the country, Ken Wright recounts. But the singer's "balls descended and he lost it. And it was one of the most pathetic things." His voice "was all over the lot. And there's Dan playing the piano behind him. . . . It was sort of sad." Ellsberg teamed with a classmate on drums to win Cranbrook's Amateur Night competition that year.[43]

For two years, Ellsberg played in the school orchestra, whose main activity was accompanying annual Gilbert and Sullivan operettas. But Ellsberg had difficulty with them. "I don't think Dan could ever do it," Robert Bates, who directed the operettas, recalls. "He just couldn't read [music]. . . . He wasn't able to handle that kind of piano playing." Like many piano students at the time, Ellsberg played rather difficult pieces readily, but he "didn't know what it was all about on the keyboard," Bates remembers. In those days, students were typically given a piece to play at a recital and performed it largely by rote. "That was the kind of playing that he did," Bates says. "I mean, he did Beethoven, Brahms, and so forth. But he didn't read music well. . . . He did not sit down and read music and play it. He learned intricate pieces sort of mechanically." So Bates began working with Ellsberg on really understanding the keyboard and reading music.[44]

Adele Ellsberg visited Bates after he'd worked with her son for a while. "His mother came to me and she said, 'I'm so glad you're working with him on his keyboard reading,'" Bates recounts. "She was happy that we were working on getting him used to the keyboard and reading music." Bates adds, hesitantly, "You're not supposed to talk about ethnic things, but she was a typical Jewish mother. I'm used to that kind of thing. You know how great they are in music. If they have a son or a daughter who shows any talent, they really will push it. And it's great, because we get some great musicians out of that. But it didn't work with Dan, I guess."[45]

Margaret Mannebach, Ellsberg's teacher in Detroit, prepared her students to shine in recitals. Thus, Ellsberg would practice the same pieces over and over again until he had them down pat and knew every note perfectly; sight-reading was not emphasized. And while some music students have a gift for sight-reading, others don't; Ellsberg apparently didn't.[46]

Around the time of his fifteenth birthday, Ellsberg gave "my biggest performance yet," he remembers. He played Beethoven's third concerto with "most of the Detroit Symphony." There were "300" people in the audience, he says, including "a lot of people from church, a lot of people from my father's office," and the recital went "very well. . . . But right after that, my mother thought the time had come to move to a more professional teacher." Someone who trained concert pianists. So Adele Ellsberg took her son to a man named Mischa Kottler.[47]

Kottler was the leading teacher of piano concertizing in Detroit. He was the official pianist of the Detroit Symphony, a professional solo pianist, and the musical director of a big radio station. He was very exacting about whom he took on as a student. He didn't take on many and had a reputation for refusing people. A person had to show exceptional promise; he sought those who demonstrated the potential to become concert pianists. That Adele Ellsberg went to Kottler shows the largeness of her ambition for her son. "He would be the top one to go to," Bates says.[48]

"I was to play for him and he would decide whether he would take me as a student," Ellsberg recounts.

> And I played a number of pieces as well as I could. Very well. And he asked me all the pieces I knew and what my repertoire was. . . . Finally, he says, "I won't take you. . . . I won't train you to be a concert pianist. Because your repertoire is very inadequate. And you're not a sight-reader." And he says, "You couldn't acquire the repertoire adequate to [concertizing]. . . . Your tone is very good. Your technique is very good. It's fine. Your feeling is good. . . . But you know about six sonatas. You should have read all of Beethoven's sonatas. . . . You should have just at least read through dozens and dozens of concertos. . . . You should have at least read this stuff."
>
> Of course, I didn't *just read* anything. I'd learned note by note. That's the way I'd been taught. And he said, "That's not preparation for a concert career. You have to learn sight-reading, so you can just sit down and play a piece adequately just by reading it." I couldn't do that at all.

Kottler was telling him, in effect, Ellsberg says, that not only did he lack the repertoire of a concert pianist, but "'you can't acquire it. Too late.' I was now 15 [chuckles]."[49]

Though Ellsberg apparently was not advanced enough for Kottler, he may also not have shown the ability to absorb music and the quickness that Kottler sought (which may have shown in his sight-reading; those who are quick about picking up music are often good sight-readers). When Kottler told Ellsberg he didn't have the necessary repertoire, it may have been his way of saying that Ellsberg was not apt enough or didn't have a great instinctive grasp of music (though Kottler's evaluations could also be arbitrary).[50]

"Now, that meant that on that day, suddenly at 15, my piano career had been jettisoned," Ellsberg remembers. "It was clear that I wasn't going to be a pianist." But "we didn't question it. He was the most professional guy we'd ever met. And he was very positive about it." Ellsberg's mother seemed saddened, Ellsberg recalls, though accepting of Kottler's decision. For Ellsberg himself, it was "kind of a relief," partly because even before then he had worried that he wasn't going to make it as a top concert pianist. "For a couple of years I'd increasingly come to think . . . 'I'm not going to be Horowitz, or Rubinstein,'" he remembers. "So I was feeling rather despairing." He later told one relative that he and his mother had agreed that if Kottler didn't judge him concert material, they would drop the whole idea.[51]

If Ellsberg had feared that failing at the piano would cost him his mother's interest, the possible repercussions of this setback may have unsettled him. He says his mother had also begun to question the whole enterprise, however, and that this might have muted her own reaction to Kottler's decision. She had been talking about his doing conducting or composing instead. These "odd" little comments of hers "did not pass unnoticed in my ears," he recalls. "Because that was an amazing contrast with everything I'd ever heard. *Nothing* but being a concert pianist mattered at all to her." Ellsberg himself had no interest in conducting.[52]

They both agreed he would continue playing the piano, however. His mother somehow convinced Kottler to teach him for his "own pleasure," Ellsberg remembers. That would not have been Kottler's usual practice and may have required some convincing on his mother's part. But it was now understood that Ellsberg would no longer be going to a music college. Before Kottler had turned him down as concert material, that had been taken for granted by his mother. Ellsberg would later tell others that his mother seemed to lose interest in him after Kottler's decision, and that she focused all her energy on the PTA.[53]

But several months after he auditioned for Kottler, an event occurred that made all that moot.

———◈———

On a warm Fourth of July, a Thursday in 1946, when Daniel Ellsberg was 15, his family was driving through Iowa in their sedan on their way to Denver. They were passing cornfields; the high temperature that day in Davenport was 86 degrees. They were going to attend a big party for Adele and her family thrown by her brother Lou Charsky. Lou was a sociable man with plenty of money, and it was going to be a grand affair. "He had somebody taking care of the whole thing," Charlotte Miller remembers. "And when they did them, they always did them beautifully, generously. . . . It would be a very generous affair. Very, very warm." And "everybody had been invited," including "all of Lou's friends, all of Adele's friends. . . . Everybody she had known was invited." Denver was, of course, Adele's hometown. Other relatives would also be there; it would be a reunion. "It was a family affair," Miller recalls. A newspaper article called it a birthday celebration.[54]

The Ellsbergs had left their home in Highland Park, Michigan, the day before. They had been late getting started, Daniel Ellsberg would remember. His mother had not gotten everything together and been ready to leave as scheduled. So when they arrived at their slated destination that night, they found that their reservations had been canceled. "We'd slept out on the dunes at Lake Michigan," Ellsberg recounts. His mother and his sister, Gloria, slept in the car, while he and his father slept outside. "It was too cold and he hadn't been able to sleep a wink," Ellsberg recalls. "And I'd slept a little bit. We slept together; we shared a blanket." The family departed early the next morning.[55]

It is unlikely that Harry Ellsberg was in a good mood. He was completely exhausted, and it was a hot day. Moreover, it was not his fault that his family had lost their reservations. He may not have been looking forward to the party either. Adele's family did not think highly of him, it will be recalled, and he apparently knew it. But Adele had insisted that they go to Denver. Daniel Ellsberg would later speculate that his rejection by Mischa Kottler had fed his mother's interest in going to the party; like the PTA, it was a new focus, a way of moving on. Harry Ellsberg would tell an interviewer that he had been concerned his wife wanted to go to Denver partly out of interest in another man who would be there.[56] If true, that would not have helped his mood.

The Ellsbergs stopped for a picnic lunch in a little park, perhaps in Davenport. Gloria Ellsberg had been sitting in the right front seat—the "death seat" (this was before seat belts)—during the morning's drive. "It was my turn to sit next to the driver, so I could see out," Daniel Ellsberg remembers. "Because she'd had it all morning. But after we had lunch . . . Gloria ran to the front seat again and said, 'I'm going to sit'—my father always told this story—'I'm going to sit here if it kills me.'"[57]

Daniel sat facing the right side of the car on some suitcases stacked on the floor behind the driver's seat. There were blankets on top of the suitcases. His father was driving. His mother sat in the back seat behind Gloria, with her legs across the back seat.[58]

The family drove west on Highway 6. Harry Ellsberg wanted to get some rest before driving much further. He told his wife "that he couldn't go on. That he was too sleepy," he would later tell Daniel, who recounts: "And she said, 'We've got to go on.' He said, 'I've got to stop and sleep by the road, or preferably we've got to find a motel, and let me sleep a while.' And she said, 'No, no. Then we won't make this party' that her brother was giving in her honor, to meet his friends. He said, 'Well, then you've got to drive.' And she said, 'I can't drive. I've got to be fresh for this party. I'm going to meet all his friends.' So he drove on."[59]

His mood may have soured further. Harry Ellsberg would later tell a reporter that the family planned to stop at Durant early that afternoon and then proceed to Des Moines the next morning.[60]

At around 1:10 in the afternoon, with the Ellsbergs only about three miles from Durant, Harry Ellsberg apparently fell asleep at the wheel. The sedan drifted off the road. A concrete bridge loomed 75 yards ahead. Harry Ellsberg evidently awoke when the car went off the road. He tried desperately to get it back onto the road, but the car's right rear tire blew out, making it difficult to control. The Ellsbergs crashed into an abutment of the concrete bridge. The right side of the car was "practically demolished," according to a newspaper article on the crash. Another article says "the entire right side of the vehicle was torn away." Given his seat position, Daniel didn't see anything.[61]

Adele Ellsberg was killed instantly; she was 45 years old. "Death of Mrs. Ellsberg was attributed to a fractured neck and crushed chest," a newspaper article recounts. Daniel says his half brother told him later "that my mother had been decapitated in the accident. And that it took the side of the car off, and it had cut her head off, and that the head was separated from her body."[62]

Daniel's own head was badly gashed by a metal fixture behind the driver seat. "So there was a big flap of skin just up to my skull," he recalls. He went into a coma. Daniel also suffered a broken leg and, according to a newspaper article, several broken ribs.[63] He would bear a scar on his forehead the rest of his life.

Harry Ellsberg suffered a broken nose, facial lacerations, and possibly a broken jaw. He survived the crash. Gloria Ellsberg, who was then 13 years old (according to newspaper articles), was not so fortunate. After state highway patrolmen arrived on the scene, she was rushed with her father and brother in an ambulance to Mercy Hospital in Davenport, but was unconscious when she arrived and never regained consciousness. She died at 4:25 P.M. "of a basal skull fracture," according to a newspaper article. Harry Ellsberg would later repeatedly tell others of Gloria running to get into the right front seat after lunch, "and then he would start crying and saying, 'And it *did* kill her,'" Daniel remembers. "Of course, when he would tell me this story, I realized later, it kind of had mixed feelings for me. Because he was crying about the fact that she was killed instead of me."[64] That could not have improved their relationship.

Daniel says that after spending 36 hours in a coma, or perhaps during the middle of the coma, he regained consciousness in the hospital in Davenport. "I can still remember it. It was a white room. Everybody's wearing white. Sort of white tile. Everything is white. . . . I'm lying on this hospital table, and everybody is all around." In a short story he wrote under a pseudonym three years later (which he told me was "totally autobiographical," in fact, "word for word"), he recalled "open[ing] his eyes to the crowd of relations and nurses filling [the] white-walled room. A doctor was bending over him, adjusting his blankets: 'You were in an automobile accident. You are very lucky to be alive.'" "How is my mother?" Ellsberg asked. "She died instantly," someone said, according to Ellsberg's story, which continued: "And that was all; he [Ellsberg] made no sign, then or later. The blankets were too warm and he moved inside them, and the gray-haired nurse at the bedside caught at his hand and said, 'You're a brave boy.' 'Yes,' the relatives were to echo many times, 'he is a very brave boy.'" But "after it had ended so suddenly, what he had really felt was nothing. Just nothing at all."[65]

Ellsberg was probably in shock. Numb. That would be common for someone in his shoes. "I didn't feel sorrow," he remembers. "I didn't grieve." Then *or* later. His ambivalent feelings toward his mother—not to mention any anger he felt toward her or emotional deprivation he suffered as a boy—undoubtedly contributed to that. After coming to in the hospital room, "I went back into unconsciousness, in about a minute," or maybe "a couple minutes," he says.[66]

Ellsberg would recall that his only thought after learning of his mother's death was, "Now I don't have to play the piano anymore." That is a stark response and quite telling. It, of course, suggests how great his frustration was over the piano. Ellsberg, who felt guilty about it afterward, comments, "Of course, it seems to imply a terrible hatred or unconcern about my mother. You know, resentment . . . indifference to her death or something. Or release, that the main feeling is liberation. Which implies either that I didn't care at all, or my feeling was very negative and very angry. Oppressed." At least unconsciously. His reaction suggested to him later "that I had wanted not to be a pianist. I wanted a release from that."[67]

In all likelihood, the death of his mother lifted a burden from Ellsberg. "It seems that her death was mostly a relief for him," his daughter, Mary, told me. After getting out of the hospital in Denver, Ellsberg stayed with Charlotte Miller's family in Estes Park, Colorado, before returning to Cranbrook. "There was a release" after the car accident, Miller perceived. "He seemed to be so free." During Ellsberg's stay and later summers in Estes, "he did just as he pleased. And there was no supervision at all. . . . He just lived his own life so completely."[68]

During the following summer in Colorado, Ellsberg recounted in his short story, an aunt tried to get him to talk about the car accident. "'How did your mother's death really affect you?'" she asked. "He wanted to be able to tell her, and she said, 'You know, we all want you to feel that you can talk to us.' But he had discovered then there was really nothing he could say to her, or any of them." But riding home from his mother's grave after his uncle had coaxed him to visit it, "he closed his eyes, and suddenly he knew the feeling and the memory raced very close behind him, and in a little while would catch up to him. And all he could do was hold them off a little longer."[69]

Ellsberg's disclosure that his only thought after learning of his mother's death was that he wouldn't have to play the piano anymore would cause him great distress. It was printed in *Time* magazine and elsewhere following publi-cation of the Pentagon Papers. "I knew that I was going to have to explain that to my relatives," he recalls. He heard from them about it, he says. "My *father* had said, 'Did you tell that to *Time?*' My uncle asked that, my aunt asked that. . . . And they said they had never heard that before. . . . I had never told it to any of them. Naturally. . . . They said, 'Did you really feel that?' I said, 'Well, I did have that thought. I have to admit it.'" His father was upset. Ac-cording to Ellsberg, "I had told a former lover this story, and she naively men-tioned it to a reporter."[70] But he told the story to a number of other people as well, including at least several I interviewed for this book.

Ellsberg's distress would turn to rage when J. Anthony Lukas wrote a piece on him for the *New York Times Magazine* after the Papers came out. Lukas quoted Ellsberg as telling him, "I can remember standing in the wreckage, looking down at my mother and thinking, 'Now I don't have to be a pianist any more.'" Ellsberg claims Lukas lifted the last part of the quote from *Time*, then "hyped it up . . . made it a little more dramatic" by placing him over his mother's dead body. But Lukas told me that Ellsberg made the remark while they were drinking champagne on an airplane, although he conceded he could have erred on the context of Ellsberg's thought. When Ellsberg read Lukas's piece, "I nearly threw up when I got to this part," he recounts.

> I imagined myself standing over my mother and looking down at her headless body, or actually at her severed head. . . . I couldn't get the image out of my head for days and days. . . . It drove me crazy. The image of my mother, my *beloved* mother's beloved face as a head was now for the first time in my head. And I couldn't get it out. . . . I think it was a large part of a year that thing haunted me. . . . The thought that I would have had that thought looking down at my mother's corpse was just sickening. Now, the impression it made on other people was of course exactly the same.

The quote gave readers "an impression of me that I was a kind of monster," Ellsberg says. He talked to everybody about the article; he couldn't stop talking about it. Though Ellsberg denies it, one of those he apparently talked to was his half brother, who wrote a letter to the *New York Times Magazine* question-ing the accuracy of many of Ellsberg's quotes.[71]

Nate or Lou Charsky, perhaps both, took a plane from Denver to Daven-port the day after the car accident. They arranged for the bodies of Adele and Gloria Ellsberg to be sent to Denver for funeral services and burial. They also arranged to have Daniel and his father brought to Denver by train three days later. His relatives could tend to Daniel better in Denver, where he spent two to three months in a hospital. "I couldn't get out of bed for three months," Ellsberg recalls. "I couldn't go to the bathroom. I had to use a bedpan. So I was confined to the bed straight for three months." Nate's wife, Eleanor, "was just marvelous to him," Charlotte Miller remembers. "She came every day to visit him." Lou Charsky also spent time with his nephew. The Charskys worried that Harry Ellsberg could not, or would not, provide the emotional support his son needed. Clara Charsky remarked to her brother Lou at one point, "Lou, this boy has a father. You can't be his father."[72]

The Charskys also wanted to make sure Daniel received good medical care. They, of course, knew that his father was a Christian Scientist who opposed seeing doctors. Nate "just picked up Dan and took him to Denver to be treated by a doctor in a hospital," Miller recalls. "It was certain that Nate was taking Dan to Denver to a hospital and to a doctor that he knew, that they knew. That was very definite." Nate was determined about it. When Harry Ellsberg saw a doctor himself—after years of lecturing against seeing doctors and not taking his children to doctors—"the family was very angry," Miller remembers. "Harry wanted a doctor for himself, and maybe he didn't want one for Dan. . . . The family was so angry. . . . Because there were no doctors in their lives at all. . . . He was so reluctant for the whole family to see a doctor. . . . All these years, no doctors. . . . Now *he* sees a doctor." The Charskys were bitter about it. Daniel Ellsberg's later comments suggest that his father didn't, in fact, want him to see a doctor after the accident. He remarked to Lukas, "I don't think I ever saw a doctor until I broke my leg in a car crash. The reason I still have this scar on my forehead is that my father wouldn't let them stitch it up until my uncles arrived and insisted."[73] One wonders how long his resentment over that lasted.

As one might expect, Harry Ellsberg's standing in the Charsky family plummeted after the car accident. "The family always blamed Harry for it," Miller remembers. "Everybody was concerned about Dan and nobody cared about Harry. We just didn't care what happened to Harry. . . . They held him responsible for the accident. They were very unhappy about it. They were very unhappy about Adele's death, about Gloria's death. Very bitter. But, well, what happened to Harry, nobody even cared."[74]

Ellsberg didn't see his father while hospitalized in Davenport. "He was in a separate room," Ellsberg recounts. And "he was very groggy, because they'd sedated him." Ellsberg didn't see his father on the train to Denver either: "He had a different compartment." Ellsberg says that he only learned all this later from his half brother, who came out from Detroit after the accident and accompanied them on the train:

The only memory I have from that period after the accident is this one moment of waking up in the hospital. [Also] one other moment at night, when I
felt confined by my traction and I tore the traction off my leg. Which the doctors mentioned at the time took a kind of superhuman strength. Demonic
strength. I tore off all the bandages and the weights and everything else. And I
can remember doing that, pulling at these things and tearing. And then the
third memory is being lowered into the railroad compartment from outside on
a stretcher through the window. . . . I was on a hospital bed. They put me in
through the window. And then I remember Harry [Jr.] reading to me a book
called *The Feather Merchants*, by Max Shulman. Which made me laugh so hard
I was crying and the tears were rolling down my cheeks. And I kept telling
him, "Harry, stop it. It hurts me. My cast is hurting me. It hurts. Don't read
that." Because I was just hysterical with laughter at the thing. And I remember
that very well. And that's the only memory I have from the first 30 days.[75]

Harry Ellsberg, Sr., returned to Highland Park, Michigan, following the funeral for his wife and daughter in Denver six days after the accident. He never returned to Denver to visit Daniel in the hospital. Harry, Jr., later explained to
Daniel that their father was busy with work, the trip would have been expensive,
and he wasn't in good shape. But Harry Ellsberg probably didn't know how to respond to his son after the accident. He would acknowledge later that "he felt
very, very guilty about [it]," Ellsberg remembers. "I asked him once how he had
felt about the accident. And he said, 'My main feeling was that I was afraid you
would never forgive me.'" Racked by guilt that kept him from seeing his son, he
was not, in all likelihood, eager to spend time with the Charskys in Denver under
these circumstances. Also, "he was hemorrhaging blood from an ulcer at that
point," Ellsberg recalls. "He was vomiting up blood." The ulcer was caused by
stress from his guilt, Ellsberg believes. "Harry tried to get him to a doctor, but he
wouldn't think of a doctor, wouldn't hear of it, as a Christian Scientist." By then
he may have decided he'd had enough of doctors again, and his religion was
probably particularly important to him at this time. Ellsberg adds, "He was
dying. I said [to Harry, Jr.], 'Didn't you try to get him to a doctor?' He said, 'God,
yes. I kept telling him, "You've got to go to a doctor, or you're going to die."' But
he would never. He would have died before going to a doctor, I'm sure. And finally, and like other Christian Scientists, he had a healing. He got over it."[76]
     He may have been overwhelmed by the accident. Harry, Jr., later told
Daniel their father was "obsessed" with it:

> Harry said he just had nightmares, he couldn't sleep. And that he talked about it
> all the time, and tried to figure out how it had happened. He wanted to believe,

Harry says, that it was carbon monoxide. His brother, Ned, the admiral, visited him and said that he thought it was probably carbon monoxide. My father said, "Well, the windows were open. It was a very hot day." . . . And the uncle said, "Well, you could still get carbon monoxide poisoning even if the windows were open." But I said, "Well, for Christ's sake, you don't have to have any very deep explanation. He hadn't had any sleep the night before at all."

Ellsberg wasn't aware of his father's agony over the accident, since he was in Denver and then, after returning to Cranbrook, only saw his father on weekends. "We never discussed the accident," he says.[77]

The failure of Ellsberg's father to visit him in Denver is difficult to defend. Ellsberg had just lost his mother—the one person in the world to whom he was deeply connected—as well as his sister. He was probably at least somewhat frightened. Now his father was keeping his distance from him. Most likely, Ellsberg felt abandoned. His mother's death and his father's distance surely fed his insecurity, with powerful lifelong effects. A secure place in the world would be hard to find. He may also have blamed his father for the accident. If so, he must have been angry at him, or at least deeply resentful. And there is the question of how Ellsberg felt about his father's resistance to his getting medical treatment. A friend of Ellsberg who has read some of his autobiographical writing told me that his relationship with his father, which had always been unsatisfactory, went downhill following the accident. The CIA's psychiatrists would speculate that Ellsberg held his father responsible for his mother's and sister's deaths as well as his own injuries, and that he felt rage toward him. But Ellsberg says, "I became very close to my father after my mother died. [We had been] much less so before."[78]

Myron Poe remembers that Ellsberg came home from Cranbrook less frequently after the accident. He didn't see him at all the next year, Poe says, and when they did talk, Ellsberg didn't say anything about the accident. "We *never* talked about it," Poe recalls. Poe noticed a change in Ellsberg: "There's no question that after the car accident, the few times that I saw Danny, he was more subdued than he had been." A classmate at Cranbrook perceived that it was without a doubt quite difficult for him.[79]

Who *could* Ellsberg have talked to about the accident? Aside from his half brother, other relatives, and perhaps a couple of friends at Cranbrook, Ellsberg was fairly alone in the world. He did not talk much about the accident, if at all, to Cranbrook classmates. Many of those I interviewed had never even heard about it. "He couldn't bring himself to talk about it with his friends," a journalist who studied Ellsberg's Cranbrook years wrote. "He notified his classmate Michael Mooney by mail—not with a letter, but by sending him a newspaper clipping about the tragedy." Ellsberg returned to Cranbrook on crutches, with a cast on his leg, in the fall of 1946, and was in that condition for some time. His classmate Lauren Otis, who would be voted second smartest in their class, had broken his ankle severely the previous spring and also was on crutches for much of a year. But although they had common ground, they never discussed their plights. "Because he didn't talk about it"—the accident—"we didn't talk about it," Fred Dockstader recounts.[80]

It is difficult for adolescents to grieve fully when they lose their parents at such a young age. Indeed, it would probably not be healthy to do so; "it would incapacitate them," Bob Blauner writes. It is even harder if the remaining parent is not fully responsive. But when I interviewed Ellsberg nearly a half century after his mother's death, he still had not grieved for her. "I've never cried," he says, and "I cry a lot." (However, Ellsberg says his half brother told him that, just after his mother's funeral, when he visited him in the hospital, "You were very morose. . . . You *were* grieving.") Ellsberg's inability to grieve has perplexed him. "When I tell [people] about the accident, it's always in a very affectless, flat way," he relates. "Which may seem rather creepy to people. I understand." In our interviews, Ellsberg showed emotion during his discussions of the accident once, then said, "Maybe we should finish with [this]."[81]

Ellsberg would conclude that his failure to mourn reflects survivor syndrome. Many survivors of the U.S. atomic bombings of Hiroshima and Nagasaki did not grieve fully for the dead around them either. And like these survivors, Ellsberg speculated, he had feelings of guilt (in his case unconscious ones) that he had survived rather than the others. "In the typical survivor fashion, I could say, 'I was supposed to be sitting in that seat,'" he argues. "'Gloria was killed because she was in that seat instead of me. It could have been me. It *should* have been me.'"[82]

Unresolved grief often leads to psychological difficulties, including depression, flatness of affect, and problems empathizing with other people's feelings.[83] Perhaps self-absorption too. It may help explain some of Ellsberg's problems in these areas, even that "oddness of affect" and those "strange" feelings that his poet-friend Donald Hall spoke about.

———◉———

Ellsberg was late returning to Cranbrook for his junior year. He continued to play the piano there, but now he played some jazz and romantic pieces—ones his mother wouldn't have allowed—along with the old classical stuff. He continued to excel in his studies. Ellsberg was awarded the Harvard Book prize for "high achievement while a junior" by Cranbrook's headmaster and faculty—he obtained the highest grades in his class his junior year—and won that Pepsi-Cola scholarship to Harvard with those exceptionally high scores. Ellsberg also graduated first in his class his senior year, edging out Lauren Otis. "An excellent mind!" his physics teacher commented on Ellsberg's final grade report. Cranbrook's headmaster wrote: "Dan ends with a fine record! . . . May Harvard and Cranbrook become increasingly proud of you." "Obviously he's brilliant," the assistant to the headmaster remarked after reviewing Ellsberg's academic records years later.[84]

But Ellsberg didn't always maintain the highest grades in his class or even in his dorm at Cranbrook, nor did he dominate the academic awards. That is hardly a major failing. Yet occasionally he didn't even make the monthly honor roll, which only required grades of B- or better in all subjects. Where he fell short, at least in light of his enormous intellectual potency, it may have reflected his work habits on top of the strong competition. "There was quite a restlessness, quite a lack of seeing it through to the end," Fred Dockstader recalls. "Either to drop a project . . . just drop what he was working at, or to move on to something else. A disinclination to keep on at the other. . . . He dillydallied from one thing to another. . . . It was a butterfly [approach], in a way. He flitted from place to place." Ellsberg also showed a tendency to be late and rather disorganized.[85]

These traits were apparent when Ellsberg stayed with Charlotte Miller's family in Colorado during summers after his mother died. Miller's children "were always laughing at him, because he was always late, he was always doing something," Miller recalls. Ellsberg took Charlotte's son, Bob, on rock climbs and hikes with him. "I recall that they weren't well planned out," Bob Miller recounts. "We'd load a bunch of fruit and stuff into a knapsack, load some water in, and take off . . . I mean, we'd just go." But "Dan was *sure* that everything was going to work out perfectly." Ellsberg was always "forgetting things, losing things, looking for things. . . . I remember us always saying, 'Oh, Dan. . . . ' And we'd start laughing." One morning, Ellsberg and a friend were going to climb Long's Peak. That required getting started at three or four in the morning. When Ellsberg was found still at home at seven, he remarked, "Well, I'll find a smaller mountain."[86]

But Ellsberg could perform spectacularly at Cranbrook even without the greatest self-discipline or personal organization. "Real stuff," wrote a member of Harvard's admissions committee. "May warm up, too; notice that he writes a humor column for school paper. I'd like to see what he calls funny." His classmate Stuart McCombs recalls, "You just knew that whatever gift he had mentally was not going to be wasted."[87]

THREE

LIBERATED

DAN ELLSBERG THRIVED AT HARVARD. RELEASED FROM THE PIANO, HE could now pursue his interests without inhibition. "I just had a wonderful time at Harvard," he reminisces. "I had four to six hours more in the day than I'd ever had before, because I didn't need to practice. I was on my own; nobody was telling me what to do. . . . I seemed to have time and energy to do everything." He also recalls, "I was popular in a new way. I was outgoing. . . . Harvard was just a wildly happy four years for me. . . . The second half of my sophomore year, I'm spending *hours* every afternoon making love to Carol [Cummings] in my room." One evening not long after he arrived at Harvard, Ellsberg grabbed a Hemingway novel and a beer and began reading on a bench in Harvard yard: "I felt so strange. I couldn't figure out what it was. Then I realized: I felt *free*, for the first time in my life."[1]

Some who knew Ellsberg at Harvard doubt that he was "wildly happy," however. He still seemed a very serious young man. "He was not given to moments of levity," Philip Cronin remembers. "Our discussions were always quite serious." Ellsberg had a particularly strong way of expressing what he thought; his intensity continued to stand out. Carl Kaysen, who was a young economics professor at Harvard then, felt "he was always wound up. And he talked fast. And he was lively; he had high spirits." Kaysen remembers "a person with strong feelings that are under tight control." Ellsberg appeared to harbor a lot of emotion beneath the surface.[2]

He was given to powerful enthusiasms. He pursued his interests fervently. "He was bright and energetic and sort of pouncing on things," Donald Hall remembers.

"He wants to be everything and do everything. . . . Eat the whole world. . . . He was zapping here and zapping there. . . . Very interested also in extending his competence over all fields." Ellsberg's hunger for achievement remained quite pronounced. "Dan was ambitious; he wanted to make himself known," one class-mate would remember. "But he was then a quiet person; he wouldn't talk about himself. He wasn't easy to know." And there was still a restless quality to his striv-ing; his desires were diverse, seemingly insatiable, and fluctuating. Hall recalls: "He wasn't intense in that he was focused on a particular thing. He wasn't, I don't believe. You know, he became focused later on game theory. . . . And he was cer-tainly focused on sex. But there was no set of ideas or values. . . . There's a curi-ous way in which Dan was someone who had tremendous energy and tremendous curiosity without having values . . . [or] any sort of intellectual or moral center. The center was in *generalized* curiosity and a *generalized* wish for su-periority." But while many other driven people Hall knew "seemed to have a kind of a murderous hostility in their attitudes, I never felt that with Dan at all. . . . This was a curious thing about him. That he was *enormously* driven, or driving, and eager to conquer everything, but he didn't seem eager to rub anybody's face in it. He didn't seem particularly eager to be better than other people. . . . He was just being terrific."[3]

Ellsberg's great drive to prove himself was also evident during his sum-mers. In Colorado, he got into rock climbing long before it became popular, and made it up the east face of Long's Peak when few were climbing it. Ells-berg's father later told a reporter that Daniel learned "from an Alpine guide" and that "anything that's tough he wants to do." "He was very ambitious," Charlotte Miller remembers. "I mean, if Long's Peak were a difficult peak, he was climbing Long's Peak. He always had to be up on top, at the very top of everything." Ellsberg's masculinity had been repressed as a boy; now he was expressing it. One summer he worked on a ranch in Wyoming, stacking hay and performing other manual labor. "It was the first time I'd ever really used my hands in hard physical labor," he recalled later. "That was very im-portant to me."[4]

Ellsberg's dynamism and razor-sharp mind were attractive to many who met him at Harvard. He held people's attention. He would question people re-lentlessly. "You felt as if you were the most interesting person in the world when you were with him," Kirby Hall, who married Don Hall in 1952, remem-bers. "Because he wanted to know everything about you, as though he was col-lecting you." And "it was fun to watch the gymnastic of his mind. . . . It was like quicksilver." In social situations, however, people typically only watched it one on one. When Dan and Carol got together with the Halls, "he focused on

Don," Kirby recounts. "Dan *never* was able to participate in a group." He "ze-roed in on whomever he was talking [to]."[5]

Ellsberg also began to evince a tendency to lecture people, which got more pronounced over time and became a very prominent personal characteristic when he was an undergraduate. "In those days I found it quite charming," Carol Cummings laughs. "I thought he was so smart. I was impressed." But "he isn't an expert on everything, I finally noticed. It's just that you find yourself discussing the things he's an expert on."[6]

Ellsberg continued to show great confidence in his abilities. He struck Cummings as quite self-assured. Six of Ellsberg's classmates from Cranbrook also went to Harvard. "It was rather intimidating," Jo Isaacson recalls. "So for the first few months, those of us that knew each other more or less clung together, in a way. We branched out, but we maintained our friendships. But he just took off" and "did his own thing." It is unlikely Ellsberg felt intimidated for one minute at Harvard. He would distinguish himself. Put differently, he would show off. Richard Townsend received a letter from him relating, in ef-fect, "This place is interesting, and perverse, but we're going to get through it grandly. We're not just going to soldier on and muddle through."[7]

But behind Ellsberg's confidence in his intellect was probably a lingering anxiety about his social skills and a considerable neediness. He yearned for the approbation and admiration of others. He "was a very needy person," Joan Cleveland, who became friends with him, remembers. "He was hungry, he was lonely. I mean, there was this intelligence, but intelligence doesn't keep you warm at night, as it were." Ellsberg wanted "constant adulation, constant ap-plause. . . . He needed *endlessly* to be told how wonderful he was, how smart he was. And he was all these things; that's true. But it was 180 degrees from the people who *enjoy* being smart, or enjoy playing the piano, or enjoy whatever it is they've got. It made him anxious. It didn't give him pleasure." Cleveland adds, "Like the rest of us, he was very gifted and very screwed up." Although Ellsberg spoke as if he were sure of himself, and even arrogantly at times, "looking back I would say that there was a sense of instability, that he was on a kind of narrow edge, and that he might well have had a dark side in the sense of being depressed or uncertain of himself or whatever," his classmate Donald Blackmer recalls.[8]

Ellsberg's confidence in his musical abilities was put to the test soon after ar-riving at Harvard. He enrolled in the notoriously difficult Elementary Harmony course. Music had been such a huge part of his life that it was "unthinkable" to him to go without taking at least one music course. Richard French, who taught the course, remembers Ellsberg as "a person who sort of wanted his own way."

Ellsberg found the course the toughest of his college career. He earned a B in it, and that took some rallying. "But that did it," he reminisces. "That was the end of my musical career."[9] Following his half brother, he majored in economics.

Donald Hall was probably Ellsberg's closest male friend at Harvard. Hall was extroverted, charming, and witty, and, like Ellsberg, brilliant and highly driven with a large sense of self. "Don was very ebullient and outgoing," Cleveland remembers. "He was a show-off. He was very full of himself." Cleveland recalls a verse that went, "Donald Hall is fat and tall, but the ego within the matter is even taller and fatter."[10]

Ellsberg met Hall while trying out for the *Harvard Advocate*, the undergraduate literary magazine, toward the end of his freshman year of 1948–49. Hall was an *Advocate* editor. The magazine had been disbanded in the early 1940s after some trustees determined that its editorial board was full of homosexuals. It had started publishing again in 1947, with low circulation. Hall recalls that the night Ellsberg was interviewed by *Advocate* editors, Ellsberg was wearing a loud necktie. John Ashbery, who like Hall would become a prominent poet, remarked, in a nasal, effeminate voice, after Ellsberg had left the room, "Well, he *was* intelligent, but I wish he'd throw that tie away."[11]

Ellsberg and Hall quickly took to each other. "We were pals," Hall remembers. "He was my second best friend at Harvard" after another poet and writer, Robert Bly, also an *Advocate* editor. Hall was drawn by Ellsberg's intelligence. "I decided he was smart," Hall says. "This was in this sort of aggressive Harvard world. I mean, the word was, 'He's rather bright.' And that was the highest compliment. Or, 'He's not very bright.' And that was the other thing to say. And there was nothing else. . . . And Dan was rather bright, to put it mildly." Hall was also attracted to Ellsberg's energy and his humor. "He was laughing all the time," Hall recounts. "He always found sexual meaning in everything. . . . And that's still true. . . . He still talks about [sex] a lot." For Ellsberg, talking about sex would be one way to establish an intimacy with people and to capture their attention. At Harvard he often found a sexual implication in something that wasn't so obvious but that was amusing to discover. When I asked Hall how his and Ellsberg's interests overlapped, he responded, "Well, literature and sex. I don't remember that we talked about anything else." After Hall wrote a poem that contained a metaphor of putting coins into vaults, Ellsberg sent him a postcard at his family home in New Hampshire over the summer that asked, "Have you been coining any vaults?" Hall was embarrassed; other people could read postcards. (Ellsberg would again show poor judgment years later when he called Hall in 1994 after learning that Hall's wife at the time, the poet Jane Kenyon, had leukemia. "We talked about that for awhile," Hall recalls. "And then he started talking about sex. I got really pissed off. . . . 'I don't want to hear about this anymore! I've heard about it for forty years.' . . . And he was full of it.")[12]

Early in their relationship, Ellsberg told Hall about his "weird childhood" (Hall's words) and about the death of his mother in the car accident. "He was very moved when he told me," Hall recounts. "And he was very young when he told me." Ellsberg seemed to Hall to harbor only mild animosity toward his mother. "She was determined that he would be a piano virtuoso, and he didn't understand that," Hall remembers. "But he didn't sound actively hostile toward her. This is part of what I call the oddness. The oddness of affect." Ellsberg told Hall about his first thought after learning his mother was dead. Hall found the whole situation curious. Ellsberg didn't *talk* about rebelling against his mother as a boy, yet his first thought upon learning of her death was relief. "The attitude was very strange," Hall says. And "he knew how strange he was." When Ellsberg first met Jane Kenyon later, "Jane didn't like him, and that was why. The feelings seemed sort of out of kilter." Hall asked later in our interview, "I've known him all these years, and do I know him at all?"[13]

———◦◦◦———

Ellsberg wrote two short stories for the *Advocate*. Both involved car crashes, which had begun to haunt his sleep. The first, "The Long Wait," harks back to a crash he was in when riding as a passenger in a DeSoto convertible several months earlier (that time he was not hurt). Ellsberg "takes his central character through a dreaming flashback and unconquerable optimism before the car hurtles off the road and overturns," wrote an unenthusiastic reviewer in the *Harvard Crimson*, the student newspaper. The reviewer called the piece "a new wrinkle in an old face." The story begins:

> When he looked up the car was in front of them, big and blue and shiny in the headlights, straight ahead in the middle of the road. He heard Sam say, "Here it is," and he took one look ahead and thought, *this is the time, all right,* because the big Buick stretched from one side of the road to the other and there didn't seem to be any way to miss it. . . . He thought, *why doesn't Sam turn to the left?* and then he thought, *it doesn't matter because we aren't going to miss it . . . this time we can't get out of it.* So he relaxed, and when they hit he was lying back and his hand was resting lightly on the side of the car.[14]

In the story, Ellsberg's character is a tough guy and a loner. Shortly after entering Club Rhumba, an attempted marijuana deal goes bad. "I was already beginning to wonder if I'd done the right thing bringing Sam along," Ellsberg wrote. His character liked to work by himself—there were fewer mistakes that way—and he had Sam go sit in the car outside. "So long as I didn't have to depend on anybody else I always had a feeling that I could get through anything that happened." This is the type of masculine, daring figure Ellsberg had long wanted to be, one suspects. He has brought together two of his most personal themes in the story: his desire to be tough and his memory of the event that violently killed his mother and sister. His character tells the stocky club manager he needs some "tea . . . about a pound of it." But the suspicious manager, standing aside "a huge Negro" named Tommy, says he runs "a clean place." "I'm talking straight, but I don't know if you are," Ellsberg's character replies. "I came here to do business." Then "I ducked to one side and something swung past my ear and glanced off my shoulder. The colored boy [who worked the bar] was off balance behind me and I put a quick jab in his stomach with my elbow. Tommy made a dive for me. . . . I brought my knee up hard in his face. I turned for the stairs but he had his hand around my ankle. I tried to jerk loose and then I was falling" down the stairs. He expected to hear a gunshot next. But "partly it was from experience that I didn't think anything would happen to me, because plenty of times I'd been in scrapes where everyone around me was killed or caught and I walked away, but partly it was just a feeling I had. It's a feeling you have to have in my job to last, and I had it. So I slid down the stairs as fast as I could . . . and the knife hit the wood a few steps above my head."[15]

At the end of the story, Ellsberg returned to the car crash:

> After the crash the car kept moving and there was still nothing to do but wait. There was always the long wait. . . . He had waited the time Billy was shot at the wheel, when they slid off the road just ahead of the oncoming car and rolled over against a fence-post and he got out of the car before it started to burn. Now he was waiting for the car to turn over or the dashboard to rise up and explode around their heads, but mostly just waiting to stop.
>
> The car was rocking dizzily from side to side and he ducked his head. He coughed and choked a little as though he had swallowed too much water. . . .
>
> . . . Now the car was rolling heavily, balancing uneasily first on one side, then the other. Abruptly the sharp tips of the trees sank past the steep side of the convertible, the moon swung across the sky and was eclipsed by the rising darkness, and the long wait began to end. He thought, *not this time, either,* and then the side of the car hovered darkly and fell across him.[16]

In Ellsberg's other short story, "Social Call," written under a pseudonym, he recalled waking up in the white hospital room after the crash that killed his mother. The story recounted a reluctant visit to his mother's grave with an uncle (probably Lou Charsky) one year later. Following convention at the *Advocate*, Ellsberg used the pseudonym "Andrew Hunt." He says he wrote the piece anonymously for fear his uncle would see it and dislike it.[17]

"'I thought perhaps you'd like to go to the cemetery this afternoon,' said Uncle Henry over the phone," Ellsberg wrote. But Ellsberg, or "Dick," wants no part of this. "'No, I don't think so, Uncle Henry,' he said. It was not the right answer. 'You shouldn't go back home without ever having seen your mother's grave. . . . You know you'll have to go before you leave.'" They drive to the expensive cemetery in his uncle's Cadillac. "'I'm a little bit surprised at you,' Uncle Henry said. 'You should want to come out here. . . .' 'Does it really mean so much?' Dick asked. ' . . . You're old enough to know that there are a few things in life you have to do . . . ' Uncle Henry said. 'You know, just because a person is gone doesn't mean you have to forget them right away.'" After visiting his mother's grave, Dick recalls feeling "nothing" when she had died, then questions whether that was true. "'Now, aren't you glad you went after all?'" his uncle asked him. "Not very, Dick began, and then he shrugged and said, 'I don't know Uncle Henry.' He looked ahead into the darkly falling rain and tried to think of other words to say, and couldn't."[18] Ellsberg's lack of grief, his failure to feel, pervades the essay.

According to Ellsberg, he considered pursuing a writing career early on at Harvard. He took an advanced English composition course his freshman year taught by Harvard's president, James Conant. "I did flirt with the idea of becoming a writer instead of an economist," he remembers. "More than flirt. I thought strongly about it." But people who knew Ellsberg at the time question that. "He never mentioned it," Carol Cummings recalls. "I never heard anything about it. He wanted to be an economist." And Don Hall says, "He wasn't a serious writer. He was trying it out. He tried out everything. And then he got more interested in economics. And spare time at the *Crime* [*Crimson*]. So the *Advocate* was a hill he climbed. Then he probably lost interest in it. . . . He's not a writer at all." Hall adds, "I don't recall that I was ever excited about him as a writer. As I was about many people."[19]

Ellsberg ultimately became president of the *Advocate*. That was unusual for an economics major. "He used to brag about the fact he was the only person who ever got a summa [cum laude] in economics and edited the literary magazine," his later friend Sam Popkin remembers.[20]

Ellsberg went out for the *Crimson* his sophomore year. The *Crimson* was a quality newspaper on which many well-known journalists got their start; it may have been one of the better journalism schools in the country. Ellsberg's move was a rare one for an *Advocate* man. "They were the enemy," Hall says of the *Crimson*. So was the *Lampoon*, the humor magazine. "It was unthinkable that anybody would belong to two," Hall remembers. "And there were people on the *Advocate* who . . . certainly were annoyed by it." That may have been part of Ellsberg's point. But "he was unconventional, and he wasn't trying to be unconventional," Hall says. Ellsberg claims to have been the first *Advocate* person since John Reed to join the *Crimson*. "There must be something to that," he told an interviewer. "When he went on to the *Crime*, he was wanting to be more," Hall observes. "He wanted to risk, to be more." Ellsberg was elected to the *Crimson* editorial board.[21]

Ellsberg says the *Crimson* was the core of his social life, but his colleagues there don't remember him hanging out with them much. "The *Crimson* was not *at all* central to Dan's life," Philip Cronin reminisces. "We were both on the editorial board of the *Crimson*, but Dan was not in the group," Ned Sack recounts. "Some of us used the *Crimson* as sort of a social headquarters. Our social life swirled around it. . . . He came in and wrote his editorials and went somewhere else. . . . He didn't come to the parties or anything like that."[22]

But Ellsberg was one of the newspaper's best writers, if not a prolific or quick one. "He tended to take his time," Cronin recalls.[23]

After writing about an advising program at Harvard for married students and about cloud seeding, Ellsberg wrote a three-part series critical of the American Medical Association. "The AMA has been waging last-ditch battles against socialism for 30 years," he argued. He assailed the AMA's opposition to various health and social programs, and lamented disparities in health care in the United States, but questioned government medical insurance. In the *Crimson* "comment book," one editor criticized his writing as "a socialistic blurb in *Daily Worker* style." "Typical AMA smear," Ellsberg responded. Though of diverse viewpoints, the *Crimson* leaned toward liberalism. Editorials were consistently critical of the red scare and witch-hunting then taking place in the country; Harry Truman's loyalty program had begun in 1947, communists were being prosecuted and fired from their jobs, HUAC was holding hearings, and Senator Joseph McCarthy was running at the mouth. "To shut him up, the nation must first put an end to the hysteria that has produced him," one editorial stated. Ellsberg wrote a piece disdainful of two witch-hunters in Massachusetts, using their own words to hang them.[24]

Ellsberg remembers being "quite political" at the time and distributing leaflets on election day in 1948 for a Progressive party senatorial candidate. "I was unusually political for a Harvard freshman at the time" and "a left-wing Democrat," he says. But Don Hall does not recall Ellsberg talking about politics at all. "I *really* don't believe that politics were a part of him," Hall says. William Simmons, who became the *Crimson*'s president Ellsberg's junior year, also has no memory of any political discussions with him. When Cronin saw Ellsberg on television following publication of the Pentagon Papers years later, he noticed that "he was much more involved in a cause at that time—much more forceful, rhetorical, espousing a point of view—than he had at any time previously." This was not the Dan Ellsberg he had known at Harvard, Cronin thought. He seemed "very different. Very different."[25]

Ellsberg also wrote a piece in the *Crimson* ridiculing the book *Dianetics* and another one mocking an ROTC recruitment comic book. Both exhibited his dry, droll sense of humor. There was typically a point behind Ellsberg's humor. "It was not raucous," Cronin remembers. "It was mild." "Playful low-key," John Sack, another *Crimson* writer, calls it. "He found life funny, and found situations funny." Ellsberg liked to deadpan. He once gave a mock economics lecture at the Signet Society, the campus literary club. "In the parody of the talk, he said, 'Now, let us take case A,'" Hall recounts. "And then he lifted up this placard with a capital A on it. And then he lifted up another one with capital B on it. And that was his illustrated lecture. . . . It *was* funny." After Ellsberg and Carol Cummings married, they debated whether to call one of their two cats Wendell Furry (after a Harvard physics professor and ex-Communist of that name), or Nathan Pussy (after Nathan Pusey, the new president of Harvard). Pussy won out.[26]

Ellsberg joined with other young *Crimson* men in stealing an ornamental ibis from the roof of the *Lampoon*. They then ran a series of pictures in the *Crimson* showing the ibis in different settings—a lunch counter, the *Boston Globe*, a barbershop, a burlesque theater. Ellsberg wrote a mock editorial entitled "Deplorable" assailing the thieves. "It has become obvious that the Ibis's repeated public appearances have been engineered by some calculating, conspiratorial group," he wrote, according to a later retelling. "It is absurd to maintain that a copper bird could have arranged a series of audiences with notables, or eluded pursuers unaided." During an interview 20 years later, Ellsberg repeated the last line twice, paused, then said, "I *loved* writing that."[27]

Ellsberg specialized in reviews of movies, plays, and literature for the *Crimson*. He showed considerable talent as a critic and seemed well versed in the relevant fields. He did not hold back. In a review of the play *Right You Are*, he wrote:

> The weakness of Idler's production must be blamed largely on the director,
> who gambled on surmounting the thinness of the material by turning the play

into a farce. He seems to have convinced the actors that the tongue is swifter than the ear, so that by misdirecting the audience with frenzied gestures, meanwhile speeding through lines, they might hide the fact that the dialogue makes no pretense at being funny. . . .

An alternative would have been to play the roles straight, delivering the speeches slower, at a lower pitch, and with more subtlety. Dramatically, "Right You Are" would then have had to stand on its intellectual content, which could have been bolstered by more conviction on the part of the actors.

Reviewing the novel *The Poor in Spirit* by Otto Friedrich, Ellsberg criticized the incessant and "incongruous" intrusion of Friedrich's own voice into the story and asserted, "Before the end the reader may care very little what Otto Friedrich thinks of this and that."[28]

Ellsberg took on some big names. Of Jean Paul Sartre's *Troubled Sleep*, he wrote, "Sartre is a great novelist; but if his work is to be more than a record of failure, the final section" of his series of novels then titled *The Paths to Freedom* "will have to answer some difficult problems." It "will test Sartre's philosophy severely. In particular, so far Brunet seems to approach most nearly his model of the man acting on the basis of commitment, yet it is hard to believe that Communism can be the goal of 'The Paths to Freedom.'" Ellsberg said that a play written by John Ashbery "showed typical defects" and knocked Thornton Wilder for chiding the audience for its behavior during a Frank O'Hara play.[29]

Ellsberg wrote a brazenly critical review of John Kenneth Galbraith's book *American Capitalism*. Galbraith's observation that Americans are, paradoxically, insecure economically despite the U.S. economy's impressive performance, he argued, "seems to be made largely of straw. What he calls the 'depression psychosis' is reasonably explained by the fact that we recently emerged from a catastrophic depression, during which the economy performed anything but brilliantly. It is not obvious at all that a fear of unemployment and deflation is psychotic." And Galbraith's claim that the market is regulated by "countervailing power" to society's benefit, Ellsberg contended,

is very incomplete. Not once does Galbraith offer a precise definition of the key word, "power." Nowhere does he suggest clear-cut operations for measuring power or even for comparing different degrees of power. . . . These distinctions and comparisons are absolutely crucial in a practical application of the theory, yet they are so vaguely defined that even the author seems to fall into inconsistency. . . . The argument that remains standing is that it can be better for the consumer to have two powerful firms facing each other than to have one monopoly unopposed. This hardly seems the basis for a general theory, but it does set up significant questions: when is it better, how much better, when is it worse? Instead of sharpening his concepts to attack these questions, Galbraith ignores the last possibility and bases broad policy programs on the implicit assumption that the appearance of countervailing power is always to the consumer's benefit. This he has not proved; he cannot, for it is not true.

Ellsberg recalled later that Galbraith, who taught economics at Harvard, phoned the *Crimson* after the review appeared and asked, Who is this Daniel Ellsberg? But Galbraith told me, "I'm sure I didn't. I would remember that, and I didn't."[30]

Ellsberg loved James Jones's *From Here to Eternity*. "There has not been a better book written about soldiers. In recent years, I believe, there have been few better books written." Rather provocatively, he titled his review "Soldiers and Whores."[31]

Ellsberg tended to write into the wee hours of the morning at Harvard. "One night I think I was famous [because] I stayed up for a night and wrote everything on the Ed page," he recalls. (For the record, other *Crimson* editors also performed that feat.) On that occasion, Ellsberg criticized the Catholic Legion of Decency's role in censoring the movie *A Streetcar Named Desire*. His accompanying review of the movie began, a bit overheatedly: "Like a cannon rolling loose on the deck of a frigate, Marlon Brando crashes through 'Streetcar,' malicious and violent. Screeching like a cat, walloping tables and women, peeling shirts off his sweaty muscles and tossing away his lines in a punchy, thick-lipped Polish accent, Brando fixes the attention of camera and audience until the sound of his voice seems a separate presence on the screen." Ellsberg was critical of Elia Kazan's direction of the movie. As the night wore on, he remarked on his siege in the comment book: "4 A.M. Boy, I want you to know, this is the last time D.E. signs up for two pieces in one night. . . . 9 A.M. D.E. is sick."[32]

Crimson writers subjected each other to strong, even savage criticism, particularly in the comment book. Ellsberg relished the competitive atmosphere and the male bonding it nourished: "I loved the *Crimson*."[33]

In May 1952, as he was set to graduate, Ellsberg wrote a piece recounting an episode of a radio series he had followed the previous summer. "He Walks Alone" told of the adventures of one Bob Barkeley, a womanizing American undercover agent. Barkeley walked alone "through a dense jungle of intrigue." "In two action-packed minutes," Ellsberg recounted, "with the announcer keeping score, Bob's brisk punches K.O. five more comrades. . . . He rescues Rita, who breathes, 'You're wonderful.' 'Save that for tea,' says Bob, clubbing a reviving Red to the deck. . . . 'Listen, Rita,' says quick-witted Bob, 'what color petticoat are you wearing?' 'White.' 'Then strip it off.'" The series appealed to Ellsberg's taste for adventure, not to mention his growing cold war views. In the vernacular of the day, Ellsberg himself referred to communists as "Reds."[34]

He had become a cold warrior. The Soviet blockade of Berlin in 1948 was one reason. He felt it necessary "to keep Berlin free." He accepted the U.S. government's position on the issue. Ellsberg began to think that his half brother sounded like an apologist for the Soviet Union on it. The establishment of Communist Party rule in Czechoslovakia the same year also disturbed him. Although Ellsberg liked Henry Wallace on domestic issues, Wallace started to sound naive to him about the Soviets. The Hiss case was also formative. In 1948 Whittaker Chambers accused Alger Hiss of having been a fellow Communist Party member while in the government. Chambers went on to accuse Hiss of espionage. (Hiss was ultimately found guilty of perjury.) "All of my friends assumed that Hiss was innocent," Ellsberg recounts. "And it was the general assumption around Harvard." He began reading extensively on the case. He consulted both the English and American editions of Earl Jowitt's *The Strange Case of Alger Hiss* and found discrepancies that were disquieting. Jowitt, Ellsberg deduced, had modified unwarranted statements in the English edition for the American edition (though Jowitt still claimed that Hiss was innocent). "I was shocked by the comparison," Ellsberg says. The changes seemed significant and made him suspicious. Ellsberg also read Chambers' massive 1952 memoir, *Witness*, which impressed him. "And so I really made a study of it," he remembers. "I read everything I could read on the thing.... And I became convinced that Hiss was guilty." The evidence seemed conclusive to him.[35]

Ellsberg's newfound freedom at Harvard also included the liberty to pursue his interest in young women. He attended Sunday brunches at Hillel House, a Jewish student center, to try to meet them. "He found that if you went to a Radcliffe [event] and met a Radcliffe girl for the first time—and he was always chasing them—he would take her hand and look at it, and look at her, and say, with one of these patented looks, 'Do you play the piano?'" Don Hall recalls. And "all these middle-class girls played the piano growing up. Every one of them! So they were flattered.... It worked every time." When Ellsberg told Hall about this, he would be laughing uproariously. In his scheming about girls, "he was like everybody else, only more so and more clever," Hall says. "More assiduous and more clever. But clearly ... the sexual drive or the need for sexual expression is extraordinary." It's "another way to eat the world, if you pardon the expression."[36]

Ellsberg had not had much sexual experience. He had lost his virginity in "surreal circumstances" in Laramie, Wyoming. The summer after his freshman year at Harvard, he met a Chicano woman in Denver. He had earlier read a book entitled *Ideal Marriage: Its Physiology and Technique*, which included three chapters on "The Sexual Physiology of the Adult Woman" and five on "Sexual Intercourse: Its Physiology and Technique." The book emphasized the importance of variation in technique and giving pleasure to one's wife. It was a serious medical and scientific work written by a Swiss gynecologist and directed to the medical profession and married men. The book was right up Ellsberg's alley: it combined intellectual rigor with sex. He likely found it absorbing. He certainly found it instructive: "the Dr. Spock for fucking," he would later call it. He remembers having "marvelous" sex with the Chicano woman. During a drive in his uncle's roomy pink Cadillac convertible afterward, she "just slid off the leather seat and curled up on the floor," he told me. "She was like a puddle of butter."[37]

Before classes had resumed at Harvard that fall, Ellsberg attended a get-acquainted dance for freshmen at Radcliffe. He was, of course, a sophomore. He approached a number of young women that night—"one girl after another"—departing "with lots of names in my Harvard Coop book," he reminisces. But one young woman, Carol Cummings, apparently made a particularly strong impression on him. Cummings, who had just arrived at Radcliffe days earlier, would later describe Ellsberg as "circling like a shark around her" at the dance and then "diving in" (in his words). Ellsberg liked her right away and walked her home from the dance. But Cummings would later be disconcerted to discover that hers was not the *last* young woman's name that he had taken down in his Harvard Coop book that night.[38]

Carol Cummings was from a military family. Her father, a recently retired marine officer, had participated in the invasion of North Africa in World War II and then spent the rest of the war largely in the Pacific. He had retired from the Marine Corps in June 1949 as a brigadier general and was then an attorney in Colorado. Carol had lived a peripatetic life. It had been a difficult and painful one. One brother had died as a small child; her other brother had died at Guadalcanal. In December 1943, when Carol was 12, her mother had died of cancer. She had been put in a boarding school as her mother's condition had deteriorated. Meanwhile, her father's life had been at risk in the Pacific. She had had her own checking account when she was 12 and paid her own bills. Her father had remarried, but his second wife had also died of cancer. Her father was a quiet, withdrawn, perhaps depressed man, yet sweet and gentle, and far from your stereotypical marine general.[39]

"One of the first words that comes to my mind when I think about Carol is pain," Joan Cleveland recalls. "There was pain behind her eyes." And "there was something lamblike about Carol. She just sort of took it, whatever *it* was. It started with the death of her mother; there must have been fear about her father. And then this husband"—Ellsberg—"who glittered but he didn't have the resources to be considerate. . . . She was stoic and she was long suffering." But Carol rarely complained and had a fine sense of humor; she laughed a lot and was often bubbly and cheerful. Also, "propriety was always very important to her," Kirby Hall reminisces. "She wanted to have her table look nice and stuff like that. Just a kind of opposite of Dan. And taste was important to her." Carol was considerate, compassionate, and generous; she was widely liked. "Everybody loved her," Hall remembers. She was also sensible and down-to-earth. "I thought she was very good for him [Ellsberg], because I think she gave him a sort of balance of somebody who was very practical and more social in her own way," Philip Cronin recalls, adding with a chuckle that she "could engage in more general social conversation than Dan was inclined to." She was also less calculating.[40]

Carol Cummings was a very intelligent person. She had been her class valedictorian and president of the student government at St. Agnes boarding school in northern Virginia. But she lacked confidence in her intellectual abilities. "I got to Radcliffe and I felt that everybody was smarter than I was," she remembers. "I was sort of pluckily doing my bit, but it was clear that I was with the heavy hitters now." Carol wasn't particularly intellectual. One didn't usually discuss books and such with her. Like most young women at Radcliffe at the time, she was not career-focused. "None of us had any career plans," she says, though she later earned a Ph.D. in psychology and became a psychologist. "The only career plan we had was to be wonderful wives and mothers. I'd always been very interested in medicine, but I didn't think I was smart enough to go into that. So I went into something that I thought I could do, which was literature. But I've never had much admiration for a field that I could do well in," she laughs. Yet Cummings would graduate magna cum laude from Radcliffe. Ellsberg later told their two children that Carol was smart—then he would add, Of course, he was a summa and she was only a magna. "A person's intelligence is very important to Dan," Cummings points out. "It's a quality he values a great deal."[41]

Carol Cummings was an attractive young woman, with a roundish, pretty face. At Radcliffe, her hair was already beginning to gray, and she had an ample chest. "She was very sexy," Andrew Norman recalls. "Very charged. A lot of energy that was very attractive." Though John Sack thought Carol had a slightly mischievous smile that suggested "she might be very exciting with sex," she was an innocent girl. "She was very virginal," Don Hall remembers. "She had had no experience at all, in my recollection. . . . She was very straight. . . . A very good girl. Naive." According to Ellsberg, she had only kissed a boy once in high school.[42]

Cummings was not strongly attracted to Ellsberg initially. "I didn't go out with him the first few times he asked me," she recounts. "I made some excuse." But Ellsberg was very persistent. One evening, he sat patiently with Carol while she answered the phone and signed people in and out of her dorm. Next time, she thought, she was going to go out with him. They started dating. "I was attracted by his sense of humor," Cummings recalls. "And I suppose I was attracted by the fact that he was interested in me." She found his persistence flattering. Carol was, of course, an 18-year-old girl in an intimidating new environment. "So she found this nice boy that glommed onto her," Kirby Hall analyzes. "She chose him because he chose her." But Ellsberg was also entirely different from any boy Carol had ever met in Virginia. There was his prodigious intellect for one thing. She admired it. "I'd never known anybody that smart," she reminisces. "Well, I'd never known anybody who displayed it as much. I had grown up in an atmosphere where people were much lower key. . . . He didn't hang back, any more than he does now. This was very different from what I was used to." So was his intensity, as were some of his topics of conversation. "He was reading a lot of Freud at the time, and he'd give me lectures, sort of, on infantile sexuality," Cummings recounts. "It was racy stuff for me. . . . A subject I knew nothing about. . . . He would sit and lecture me for a long time." Perhaps this was partly a way to broach the whole topic of sex. To score, in other words. Ellsberg also talked about sex in other ways with Cummings. Given her lack of experience, she didn't know whether it was out of the ordinary or not.[43]

Ellsberg's effort to get Cummings into bed was waged with his typical zeal. "One of the major things I remember from my friendship with him as an undergraduate was the strategy and tactics of the seduction of Carol Cummings," Don Hall told me. "He would talk endlessly about his plans. He was a wonderful schemer. And I find this very amusing and not everyone would. . . . He certainly wanted to seduce her. And he managed." Ellsberg was attracted to Cummings' personality, her sense of humor, and her intelligence; he simply enjoyed being with her. But his initial focus was sexual, Hall believes. "He wanted to go to bed with her. . . . He appealed to her sympathy, because he had lover's nuts and how terribly it hurt. . . . He appealed to her sympathy because he was in such pain."[44]

Hall later wondered if the fact that Carol's father was a marine general also attracted Ellsberg. "That made her more formidable in a way," he reasons. "It made it more of a challenge."[45]

It often didn't take much more than a young man's sexual desire to initiate a relationship resulting in marriage in those days, and that seems to have been the case here. "I don't think they hardly had anything in common," Hall recalls. "I didn't have anything in common with my first wife [Kirby]. And it didn't work out well in either case." Their painful childhoods may have also drawn them together. They'd both lost their mothers; they were both needy. And Ellsberg recognized that Carol would be there for him. Asked if he thought their parental losses helped bring them together, he responded, "I'm sure it did. . . . We wanted a home. . . . I think the idea of clinging to each other and taking care of each other probably appealed to both of us. I'm sure it did to me." Ellsberg told Carol about waking up in the hospital after his mother had died and thinking that he wouldn't have to practice the piano anymore, but he didn't talk about the car accident much, she remembers.[46]

Cummings responded to Ellsberg's talk of lover's nuts. "She was a plum ripe for picking," Kirby Hall comments. "And Dan picked her." He "just swallowed her up," a subsequent friend of Carol deduced. Their courtship was somewhat precocious for the times; they were seriously involved in pretty short order. According to Ellsberg, "We had insane sex, every day." One of their neighbors, a music teacher, would lie on his bed next to the wall and listen to them, Ellsberg recalls. Ellsberg's neediness would eventually spell trouble for their relationship, however. He was "overeager," Kirby Hall observed:

> This man for some reason has to demonstrate at all moments that he is totally virile. . . . He has to constantly prove it. And I imagine he was after her three times a day. And that's not making love—that's proving that you can do it. . . . And Carol was very romantic. I mean, we were raised on Lauren Bacall and Humphrey Bogart . . . Cary Grant and Katharine Hepburn. And to have someone . . . coming at you two or three times a day—which I'm *sure* he did—would be the biggest turnoff in the world. . . . I think a normal woman does not respond to that kind of neediness. I mean, it's the neediness of it—prove to me that I'm lovable—more than that, I'm virile.

Ellsberg, Hall argues, was like any oversexed man who

> can't accept that he's a needy little boy and he's got to have his mama tell him he's lovable three times a day. . . . That's what Carol responded to when he said he had lover's nuts. He was saying, "I can't stand it if you don't love

me. . . . The pain is too intense." But he expressed it in terms of his physiology rather than in terms of his heart. . . . He would come after her saying, "Oh, I'm such a stud and I'm so sexy and you should be turned on," and she didn't know that this was this infant sucking on her. You can see how irritating it would be to a woman. And the restlessness—"Can't I ever satisfy you? Why do you have to come back in two hours for more?" . . . And Dan, of course, wouldn't have any comprehension of that. Because his need had to be met. Because he felt so terrible if it wasn't. He was so vulnerable.[47]

Ellsberg fell in love with Carol fairly quickly. "There was a curve," Don Hall recounts. "At the beginning there was all this sort of wonderful, funny, young-man humor of manipulating her and seducing her, and what he said now and what she responded to, and so on. . . . I mean, at the beginning he liked her. He clearly liked this girl. And he told stories about her naïveté that were very affectionate stories when he told them. . . . After he got what he wanted, he became very fond of her." Cummings says, "I had kind of fallen for him by Christmas time."[48]

But first Ellsberg had to surmount an obstacle in the form of Robert Bly. Or at least he thought he did. Bly was older than Ellsberg and one of the many military veterans attending Harvard after World War II. "He was the first person I dated in college," Cummings reminisces. They went out together a couple of times. "He hit on her," Don Hall remembers. "And Dan felt a rivalry." Bly "is a very rivalrous fellow," Hall adds. "Bly has this high energy and a great interest in sex. And did as a child. So we talked about nothing but poetry and sex." Ellsberg recounts:

After I'd met Carol and been out with her several times, [Bly] mentioned one night at the *Advocate* that he had been out with a girl that knew me: Carol Cummings. And he said, "She's a very intelligent girl. A very attractive girl." He said, "I was very impressed. We were lying in front of the fire"—they'd been on either a ski weekend or I think it was up on the Cape or something . . . "and she was talking. She was really very interesting." And I thought, "Oh, my God [laughs]. I can't compete with this guy. So either I nail her down very quickly, or she's lost." So I called her up and made dates for every night the next week. And at the end of the week we were in love, or I was in love. I later learned that this great weekend had been with about five other people, and that "lying in front of the fire," yes, they had their fire, but with about five other people in the room. But I had this image of them being in a hunting lodge together somewhere—this wild older man, you know.[49]

That same year, Carol attracted the interest of another literary man. Dylan Thomas gave a poetry reading at Harvard and attended a party thrown for him afterward at the *Advocate*. Cummings and Ellsberg attended the reading, and afterward she changed into a taffeta dress in Ellsberg's room. Don Hall remembers:

> She wore a low-cut dress at this party. And Dylan, who was drunk as a skunk and could be cruel, put his hands on Carol's waist and rocked back and forth. And Carol said, "I liked your reading very much, Mr. Thomas." He said, "Did you wear that dress to my reading?" . . . He was short, but Carol was very short . . . so he could peer down her dress. And he was doing this. And, "Did you wear that dress to my reading?" Well, this was the question she was terrified somebody would ask, because she had just changed it in Dan's room. And that was a compromising thing to do. . . . She turned purple, and mumbled. . . . [Ellsberg] was standing there feeling awkward.

In Ellsberg's version, Thomas "got fascinated by her cleavage. He was sort of staring at it. And finally his head bent lower and lower . . . until his forehead was sort of resting on her chin and he was simply staring down at her cleavage." "Looking down her blouse at her bosom," recalls Kirby Hall, "he said, 'I would rather suckle those paps than go back to my old wife in Wales.' So Carol said, 'Oh, that's very nice of you, Mr. Thomas.' . . . That's the sort of thing she would have said. She would have been very respectful." Despite Carol's acute embarrassment, Ellsberg was flattered that Thomas was so attracted to his date. Thomas subsequently "passed out," Ellsberg remembers. "Somebody walked him around the block. He went on later to a faculty dinner . . . during the course of which he picked up a chair and reduced it to kindling. He just smashed it . . . against the floor."[50]

The next summer, Ellsberg worked on the ranch in Wyoming. He gave Carol a reading list for the summer "to bring me up to snuff," Carol recounts. "I dutifully read it all. I was quite caught up in it." In retrospect, "it's hilarious," she laughs. "I was majoring in literature!" When they returned to Cambridge for the school year, Ellsberg reminisces, Carol "was very disconcerted at how muscular I was. I'd left . . . an intellectual, thin, willowy type, and I came back . . . with large shoulders and arms. From stacking hay." He'd also returned with a propensity for swearing, which had been seeded while working in the Dodge plant two years earlier. He would interpolate "fucking" into the middle of words or phrases, as in the peanut-fucking-butter. "I could swear better than anybody I knew and I was likely to run into at Harvard," he remembers. "But Carol hated that. And so she got me totally out of swearing."[51]

Carol also set about to change Ellsberg's dress, which was unusual for a Harvard student. "He was only 18, but he was wearing double-breasted pin-stripe suits and wing-tip shoes," she recalls. His uncle Lou Charsky "had given him a lot of stuff," including "white-on-white shirts, and he'd be wearing hand-painted Sulka ties. It was quite an outfit." Carol accused him of dressing like a gangster. "He was a mess," Kirby Hall recounts. "There was a disorganized quality to him . . . that showed in his appearance." Ellsberg later told an interviewer that he had been deriding convention through his odd dress. "Dan is a world-class brat," Joan Cleveland comments. "And he did outrageous things sometimes just for the sheer joy of being outrageous."[52]

Carol was troubled about being intimate with Ellsberg. "I think she felt really bad about fucking and not being married," Don Hall remembers. "This is an ancient world we're talking about. . . . She wasn't brought up to fuck without being married. And it didn't get easier as it went on. . . . I think that she wanted desperately to get married, because it was wrong." Ellsberg says that Carol put "very heavy pressure" on him to get engaged. He told her they were "too young to get married," however, and that he wanted to get at least two or three years of graduate school under his belt first. "But I just want to be engaged," Carol said, according to Ellsberg, who "took it as, 'Let's get engaged to be married.'" He was wary of getting engaged, believing she would then pressure him to get married. "I certainly wasn't putting pressure on him to get married," Cummings remembers. "I wanted to get engaged. . . . It certainly meant a lot to me." Ellsberg finally assented. But he assumed it would be a long engagement, like three or four years. Ideally, they'd get married after he got his Ph.D.[53]

"So I called my rich uncle," Ellsberg recounts. "I asked whether he could find a diamond at a wholesale price." Ellsberg used $1,200 of $20,000 he had inherited after his mother had died to purchase a nicely cut diamond ring. And that was at half price. He proposed to Cummings the weekend of the annual big football game with Yale in late November 1950. "She was amazed and very, very happy," he remembers. "The diamond really astounded her."[54]

Cummings visited her father in Colorado over that Christmas break. Around the day after Christmas, Ellsberg called her up "and said, 'Let's get married,'" Cummings recalls. "And I was startled." They'd just gotten engaged. "I had had no idea that we would get married soon," Cummings says. "I was very surprised at that. And I still don't exactly understand it. . . . He wanted to do it right away. In fact, he'd already been around to the church to see which weekend was free, and that sort of thing." In Ellsberg's memory, when he spoke to Carol over the phone about getting married, "she was sort of breathless" and said at one point, "Do you really want to get married?" Cummings thought they should put it off a while. "It didn't seem like very good timing," she remembers. "It seemed a little rushed. But then when I came back, he was enthusiastic, and I got enthusiastic too." Cummings returned to Cambridge early, but not before Ellsberg had already lined up the minister and reserved the church. This was a young man in a hurry. The fall semester reading period and midyear exams at Harvard were upon them; their wedding would take place February 10, two days before the new semester began. "So all during the time I should have been studying for my exams I was sending out wedding invitations and finding a place to live and so forth," Cummings recalls.[55]

Ellsberg explains the timing this way: He believed he would be drafted for the Korean War by June. That fall, Chinese army troops had entered the war after the American troops had moved up to the Yalu River on North Korea's border with China. "Waves of Chinese Communist infantry smashed today at the turned right flank of the United Nations in northwest Korea," an AP article that ran in the *Crimson* reported the Tuesday after the Yale weekend. "The Reds attacked all along the 75-mile front, forcing new withdrawals and imperiling the entire UN line." It was clear that the war would not be over by Christmas as General Douglas MacArthur had predicted. Further, in mid-December the U.S. Army had called for a doubling of draft calls, and the draft law itself might have to be changed; universal military service, an option being considered, would exclude deferments. "I'll be in Korea for a year or two," Ellsberg remembers thinking. "Who knows what I'll feel when I get out. We may not even stay together." Ellsberg discussed his predicament with his half brother over Christmas. Harry, who was keen on Carol, suggested that Dan marry her now. This was a new thought to Ellsberg. And Harry was influential with him. Ellsberg also reasoned, he says, "Well, if I don't get married, I'll go to Korea and she'll feel abandoned. She'll feel terrible. . . . If we get married, we'll have six months together, and she'll know I'm coming back to her, and she'll feel much more secure." Given her family history, Carol feared abandonment, he says. She would even tell him that "she had been afraid she was going to be an old maid" before meeting him and that "I had saved her from this," he claims ("which is such nonsense," Kirby Hall says). To his mind, then, he did it for her, but his decision may have reflected his own insecurities as much as hers.[56]

Carol's father was not pleased. He "was extremely unhappy" and "looked very sad," Cummings recounts. Her father didn't like Ellsberg very much, she believes, "and I was young. . . . I think he was sad to see his 19-year-old daughter marrying a young man who didn't strike him as just what he would have wanted. . . . Actually, he never really said a word against him. But I knew my father and the kind of person he was, and what his friends were like, and the things he admired in people, and Dan did not have those qualities. So I knew that this wasn't going to be the kind of person he would be happy with my marrying." Before she and Ellsberg got married, Cummings remembers, they went on a skiing trip with her father and his future third wife for a day: "We were supposed to pick up Dan early one morning at his house, and he wasn't ready when we got there. . . . We were supposed to pick him up at six o'clock. . . . We were all ready, all in our ski clothes, all three of us waiting in the car ready to go. He was still in his pajamas. My father was very prompt. This wasn't the sort of thing to establish a good relationship. . . . It would annoy him if we'd made some arrangement and Dan was late." Her father also found Ellsberg boastful.[57]

It was unusual for Harvard students to marry at age 19. "I was sort of shocked that somebody our age would get married," Jerry Goodman, a classmate who later became known as Adam Smith on television, recalls. Many people assumed it was because Carol was pregnant. But "pregnancy had nothing to do with it," Ellsberg says.[58]

Carol would later seem bitter about the circumstances in which she got married. She suggested to her friend Mary Marshall that Ellsberg virtually "tricked her" into marrying him "because he was so lecherously pursuing her" and then "just insisted on it," Marshall remembers. This was not something she'd wanted to do, Carol told Marshall. According to Ellsberg, the following exchange took place with Carol years later during a heated argument in the dining room of their Los Angeles home:

Carol: "Well, you were the one who wanted to get married. . . . I did not want to get married."

Ellsberg: "You pressed me and pressed me to get engaged."

Carol: "I wanted to be engaged. . . . I didn't want to get married."

Ellsberg: "Could you please explain the difference."

Carol: "We had been making love for nine months, and all my friends knew. I was afraid we'd be found out, my father would find out, we'd get kicked out of college. . . . I'd be humiliated."

Ellsberg: "Why did you not want to get married?"

Carol: "I was young. . . . I wanted to be free, to be on my own. . . . I developed self-confidence. . . . I felt attractive now. . . . I was thinking about meeting other people."

Ellsberg: "Why did you accept my proposal then?"

Carol: "I didn't want to refuse over the phone. I thought I would tell you as soon as I got back to Cambridge that I didn't want to."

Ellsberg: "Why didn't you?"

Carol: "When I got back, you'd already hired the minister, gotten the church, the invitations. . . . I pressed you to get engaged. Now that you wanted to get married, I felt I had to. . . ."

Ellsberg: "Why didn't you tell me this before?"[59]

All that rings true in its broad outlines. Most likely, there had been a colossal miscommunication. Or shall we say, a failure to communicate.

The scene of their wedding was the oldest church in Cambridge. Christ Church had opened in 1761; it was an Episcopal church (Carol was an Episcopalian). Their fathers and other relatives attended along with friends and people from the *Crimson* and the *Advocate*. Males who participated in the ceremony were to wear blue suits, but Don Hall, who was an usher, didn't have a blue suit so he rented one. "But it was absolutely bright blue," he recounts. "Everybody else had the proper dark blue. . . . I didn't know how bad it was, because I was a social clod. But I think Kirby and Carol were both kind of appalled." After the ceremony, a reception was held at the Signet Society, where the guests munched on little sandwiches and cake and drank champagne punch.[60]

In Ellsberg's retelling, Carol seemed sad and depressed that day. "What the hell is wrong with her?" he says he thought. "Why isn't she more happy?" And for a time afterward Carol continued to seem unhappy, he remembers. "She was sleeping all the time" and her grades slipped. "I suspect this is part of a scenario that has developed over the years," Carol responds. "If we were still married, I doubt if he'd be remembering that I was sad on our wedding day. And I don't remember being sad on my wedding day." Also, "It's not surprising I didn't do very well in school that [semester]. He maintained his focus. He kept on studying. But I was learning how to be a wife, and cooking, and doing laundry, and so forth." Their sexual division of labor was fairly standard stuff. Ellsberg did "nothing" in the way of domestic chores, Carol recalls. "He never did. Even when we were both students." That frustrated her then. Early in their marriage, she had hopes of sharing the burden, but later she didn't expect it. Kirby Hall observes: "She was grumbling about Dan, because there's a lot to grumble about. . . . It was kind of grumble, grumble . . . right back from the beginning. . . . She noticed—I mean, you notice—that he was really absorbed with himself. . . . She found him to be very trying. He was just inconsiderate. . . . He'd be the sort that she wouldn't have a clue when he would be there for supper. And just no team spirit. No 'I'm going to be two hours late for supper.' A woman can deal with that. But she had no way of getting him to be cooperative."[61]

The Ellsbergs moved into a basement apartment after marrying. They saw a lot of Don Hall and his girlfriend Kirby that spring, and also became friends with Joan and Leonard Friedman (later Joan Cleveland). But Dan Ellsberg's circle of personal friends was not a large one. "I wouldn't have thought it would be easy for him to have friends, given his intellectual and personal style," Donald Blackmer reflects. "He certainly wasn't going to relax and hang out with people." The Ellsbergs, Halls, and Friedmans would see a lot of each other later in the 1950s in Cambridge. They were a bright group interested in ideas and became quite close. Ellsberg and Cleveland would develop their own close relationship. "Joan and Dan were very much attracted to each other," Don Hall recalls. (After his divorce, Ellsberg would also show interest in Kirby Hall. "He flirted with me," she recounts. "And he brought me . . . some earrings from Morocco, a great big medal from Vietnam on a chain, a little pin . . . with a mirror on the back." Ellsberg brought Cleveland a piece of some sort of metal from Vietnam. "I had no idea what I was supposed to do with this," she remembers. "All of his Vietnam stuff, I found it repugnant.")[62]

———◦◉◦———

Ellsberg was meanwhile making quite a mark academically at Harvard. His professors judged him to possess truly exceptional intellectual promise. Carl Kaysen told me that Ellsberg was one of the four brightest students he had in the twelve years he taught at Harvard. The other three became professors. "I would say that they were all extraordinarily gifted," Kaysen remembers. "He was one of the four that I think of as being unusually bright." In a rare decision, all three economics professors who read Ellsberg's senior honors thesis on game theory graded it a summa. "We all thought he was an extraordinarily able guy," Kaysen says. "He was very imaginative. And he mastered quite a difficult literature." He also had superior analytical power and wide interests, including music. Wassily Leontief, a distinguished economist who would later win a Nobel Prize, was among those who read Ellsberg's senior thesis. He too found Ellsberg's an unusually impressive intellect. "He had intellectual passion," Leontief recalls. "He really thought about problems. He really discussed the problems. . . . He really analyzed problems." Asked if Ellsberg was one of the brightest students he ever had at Harvard, Leontief responded, "Oh, yes. No doubt." One would have thought that he would go on to have a good Harvard career, Leontief said. After I mentioned to him that Thomas Schelling, another brilliant scholar who became Ellsberg's mentor at Harvard when Ellsberg was a graduate student, referred to Ellsberg as a "genius," Leontief remarked, "I think that Ellsberg intellectually is better than Kaysen and better than Schelling."[63] That's quite a statement.

"Dan was one of the exceptional students who knew all his professors," Carol Cummings recounts. "And they knew who he was. He was a shining light. . . . And he was like a colleague in a way, you could say, of a lot of the professors."[64]

Ellsberg's closest mentor was Richard Goodwin, an introverted, some would say quirky, young professor, also of truly exceptional intelligence, a mathematical economist with a powerful mathematical gift and strong aesthetic interests, including painting. He had left-leaning politics. (Ellsberg later had to name him as a former associate when receiving clearance for highly classified material.) Goodwin's politics shaped the economics department's decision during Ellsberg's junior year not to grant him tenure. Goodwin influenced Ellsberg to pursue mathematical economics and game theory rather than labor economics. Ellsberg talked humorously about using game theory to make money. "There was a little private joke about how he was going to go to a casino someplace and take ten dollars of my money and turn it into ten million," Joan Cleveland recalls. "Well, he didn't turn it into ten million." Ellsberg applied game theory, which considers rational decision making under uncertainty, to events later in his life; uncertainty fascinated him. "I think that he still has this curious combination of being himself a very passionate person and still being heavily influenced by the intellectual framework of game theory and rational calculation and so on," Kaysen observes. "There's a certain contradiction there."[65]

Ellsberg's senior thesis, "Theories of Rational Choice Under Uncertainty," critiqued and analyzed game theory and utility theory, in particular a pathbreaking tome by John von Neumann and Oskar Morgenstern entitled *Theory of Games and Economic Behavior*. (Another writer would call von Neumann "possibly the most brilliant man . . . of the twentieth century.") That Ellsberg's thesis earned him a summa was a major honor: Harvard's economics department had not awarded any summas in 1950, and only two in 1951. Ellsberg's was the only one in 1952. Unusual too was the publication of two articles from his undergraduate thesis, including one in the prestigious *American Economic Review* entitled "Theory of the Reluctant Duelist." "He loved the title," Don Hall remembers. "And that was Dan so much." The piece is a coiled, systematic, highly complex critique of von Neumann and Morgenstern's theory; Ellsberg contended that one of his insights was "crippling" to their argument. Other people also found it persuasive. Ellsberg distributed copies to old friends and others. His other article, a less tightly constructed and also highly complex piece, contrasted two concepts of utility. In both articles, Ellsberg showed no hesitation about taking on the big boys in their fields. Each article also benefited from discussions he initiated with Morgenstern at Princeton. Ellsberg noted in one that he was indebted to Morgenstern, the noted economist Paul Samuelson, and others "for the opportunity to discuss problems and to read unpublished writings on the subject." He mentioned receiving such unpublished papers twice. He was a young man with access, talking to the best. But one of Ellsberg's Harvard professors wrote in a report to the economics department: "If there is one principal shortcoming in his work, it is an unfortunate tendency to be somewhat erratic in the pursuit of a single line of investigation, which leads to a lack of depth and completeness."[66]

There was another problem. Late senior theses were penalized at Harvard, "and his was extremely late," Cleveland remembers. "And I said, 'Why are you bothering to write it? You've already got an F.' He said, 'This is going to be a summa thesis, and I'm going to get a summa.' And it was, and he did. This was part of, 'The rules don't apply to me, because I'm so smart.'" "Because he was such a distinguished student, needless to say, there were no consequences," Cummings recalls. Ellsberg often turned in papers late at Harvard. "He had trouble getting things done on time, and getting things done," Cummings says. "More so than the usual person." And he was "late to everything." Classes at Harvard started at ten minutes after the hour, but he usually arrived twenty minutes after the hour.[67]

But Ellsberg graduated third in his class of 1,147. His academic future looked bright. That June, he would recall, Leontief and Kaysen took him to lunch at Harvard's faculty club and told him they were going to nominate him for junior membership in the prestigious Society of Fellows at Harvard. Selection as a junior fellow was one of the top academic student honors in the country, superior, one could argue, to receiving a Rhodes scholarship. It was a three-year fellowship to do whatever one pleased. No classes were required, no exams, no teaching, only attendance at a nice, leisurely, intellectual Monday night dinner preceded by drinks in a wonderful wood-paneled dining room (at least for a time, the senior fellows and junior fellows took turns choosing the menu and wine list). "It's the nearest thing to a high table at Oxford or Cambridge that I saw," Thomas Schelling, who was himself elected to be a junior fellow, remarks. "It was the best thing in the world!" Don Hall, another junior fellow, exclaims. "To be a junior fellow was three years of free time." The Society of Fellows had originally been created by A. Lawrence Lowell, then president of Harvard, who judged the Ph.D. program too narrow, too confining for the most powerful and creative intellects. These people, the superbrains, needed more freedom to develop ideas. Only seven or eight junior fellows were elected a year, few straight out of college before doing any graduate work (as Leontief and Kaysen were apparently proposing for Ellsberg).[68]

The recommendations of Leontief and Kaysen would have carried considerable weight with the senior fellows (who chose the junior fellows), but Ellsberg had already decided to study at Cambridge University in England for a year. He had a Woodrow Wilson fellowship for that. He said later that he thought he was the only Woodrow Wilson fellowship holder who chose to go overseas. Going to Cambridge or Oxford was, of course, a badge of distinction. Ellsberg's mentor Richard Goodwin would also be at Cambridge. "I went to Cambridge to be with him," Ellsberg recalls.[69]

Fine, Leontief and Kaysen responded when Ellsberg told them his plan. They would nominate him for the Society of Fellows after he returned.

But his junior fellowship would be delayed when Ellsberg chose an unusual career path. Here again we see an unconventional young man.

FOUR

SOLDIER AND THEORIST

THE ELLSBERGS TRAVELED IN EUROPE THE SUMMER BEFORE CLASSES began at Cambridge. Carol had to delay her senior year at Radcliffe to accompany Dan to England. They drove to Denmark with Jerry Goodman, who was off to Oxford on a Rhodes scholarship. In Cambridge, the Ellsbergs lived in a big house with a well-to-do, conservative English couple. At one political meeting at their home, Carol noticed, the working-class conservatives were making the tea and the more affluent conservatives were drinking the tea, giving her a lesson in class divisions in England.[1]

Ellsberg studied advanced economics at Cambridge. He tried to get a job at a steel mill in England but was unsuccessful because of red tape, he said later. If so, it was an uncommon step for someone studying at one of the premier institutions of higher learning in the world. In England Ellsberg read about Stalinist repression in the Soviet Union, which strengthened his cold war views. He was an increasingly anticommunist young man with a lingering (and shall we say romantic?) attachment to the working class. "I was a liberal on domestic matters and, on foreign policy, a tough guy," he would recall.[2]

The Ellsbergs visited Don and Kirby Hall in Oxford, where Don was then studying. There, Ellsberg spoke with Hall about a source of frustration in his marriage. As they were walking around Christ Church Meadows one day, Ellsberg expressed dissatisfaction with his sex life with Carol. "He was frustrated," Hall recounts. "He was criticizing her or him or the combination of them." Hall adds, "And I'm sure that Dan, you know, would give a lecture and talk about it, and make it the be-all and the end-all. . . . And this would be, of course, off-putting. . . . That would put you apart." Kirby Hall remembers that while in England, Carol, in turn, spoke of her own marital frustrations.[3]

After returning to the United States in 1953, Carol completed her A.B. in history and literature at Radcliffe and Dan started graduate school at Harvard. His performance on his general exams in economics was so impressive that he received the technically nonexistent grade of "excellent plus." The plus "simply means that he's exceptional," Wassily Leontief explains. Another of Ellsberg's professors remarked afterward that his performance was the best he'd ever heard. "The guy was absolutely bowled over," Carol Cummings remembers.[4]

But Ellsberg's thoughts were on the military. He had enlisted in the marines after returning from England, but the Officer Candidate School class he wished to enter was then full and he was placed on inactive status. Had the class been open, he said later, he would have gone right into the marines. Ellsberg wanted to explore life in the military. He loved to experience new things, and he wished to grasp and prove his masculinity. "I joined the marines for the same reason the posters recruit most people: 'Are you man enough to be in the marines?'" he would tell one writer. "To test myself." His *Crimson* colleague William Simmons points out, "He was the sort of person who would go in the marines. I mean, Dan was all man." Carl Kaysen and Leontief were both surprised that Ellsberg would volunteer for military service, but "I thought it was in some way characteristic of him to do that, and . . . to volunteer for the Marine Corps," Kaysen remembers:

> You know, the most gung ho of the military services. Dan had a kind of macho way about him, and this was an expression of that. . . . He took it as a challenge, to show that he wasn't going to go into, let's say, the air force, which was the most intellectual of the military services, where he could almost certainly have gone in and used his academic training and his academic interests [to get] an operations research job or an intelligence job or whatnot. . . . I do think it was Dan's competitive instinct that led to him [joining the marines]. I mean, if I think of some of the other people [at Harvard then] . . . I simply can't imagine them doing this.

Kaysen had left graduate school to work for the OSS (Office of Strategic Services) during World War II, but the last thing he would have done was volunteer for the marines.[5]

Ellsberg's thirst for adventure and drama also entered his decision to enlist. Don Hall observes:

Dan's always an adventurer. Sexually, intellectually—in every way. I said [ear-
lier] he didn't have a subject or a center, been moving around from one thing
to another. The adventurer was the constant. And I think it still is. And I think
that the Pentagon Papers was an adventure. And getting arrested, as he has
been so many times, is an adventure. . . . I think a great deal of the fuel that
drives the engine is his excitement. And the excitement of adventure and risk
taking and so on. So, the first time I saw this in a mortal and military way was
his desire to go into the marines. I mean, my great desire was to stay out of the
damn service. . . . I was doing everything I could to stay out. As were the other
people most of us knew. And he joined up.

Joining the marines "was just unthinkable in that world that we lived in," Kirby
Hall recalls. "It was odd. It was completely out of keeping with his experiences
at Harvard or his experiences at Cambridge." Donald Blackmer found Ellsberg's decision astonishing: "Here was a guy who was an intellectual, and the
thought that somebody with those credentials could leap . . . feet first into the
military, enlisting in the marines, it just didn't compute. . . . The guy was a pa-
triot. Or at least that's the impression you had." Ellsberg seemed to Blackmer
to approach questions from a different angle than others, and his marine enlist-
ment was one sign.[6]

Ellsberg says he also felt obligated to join the military. "I thought it was my
duty. I had been deferred for a couple of years, and the time had come now to
do my duty." "I think he had a strong feeling about his country," remembers
Ann Elms, who got to know Ellsberg when he was in the marines. "You were
patriotic and you served." Kaysen recalls Ellsberg telling him that "he just felt
strongly that it was unfair for some people to be subject to the draft and for
people like him not to be subject to the draft. . . . He *said* that he felt it was
wrong to take advantage of his status as a student to avoid military service."
Ellsberg says he could have obtained a physical deferment since he still had a
bad right knee from the car accident.[7]

But in all likelihood, expediency also informed his decision. When he was
in England, he told Carol that it was pretty clear that he would get drafted
when they came back. "He had had all these years of the draft board letting
him get educational deferments. So he couldn't keep it up," Carol recalls.
While military service could be delayed, it was hard to avoid it forever. "In England he was exploring other possibilities," Cummings says. "I remember
specifically he was not interested in the Marine Corps at that time." But if a
young man obtained a commission in the marines in those days, he only had to
serve two years, and two years as an officer beat two years as an army private.

"And a lot of guys liked the kind of intensity of it—*a marine*," Jerry Goodman remembers.[8]

Ellsberg told me he joined the marines largely for another reason. For Carol, who "loved the Marine Corps," in which she'd grown up. That "had everything to do with it. Because I was doing it for her, in the main. To make her happy. I was going to go into one service or the other, and I knew she would be very happy going back to the marines." His friends assumed the fact that Carol's father was a retired marine officer shaped his decision. "That was the only way that I made sense of it," Blackmer recalls. Carol was surprised by it.[9]

After becoming an antiwar activist many years later, Ellsberg's time in the marines would remain very important to him. "I think he still thinks of himself, in part, as a marine," one friend says. "Because of his sense of being a real manly man."[10]

⸻ ◈ ⸻

Ellsberg had a rough time in Officer Candidate School (OCS), which he entered in April of 1954. Perhaps it's not hard to understand why. His self-discipline and personal organization fell short of military standards; he was neither athletic nor physically tough; and he carried a touch of snobbery into the marines. He was "overweeningly conceited," Joan Cleveland recalls. "And the notion that, 'If I'm going to your camp, I've got to pay attention to your rules and maybe play by them,' that was not part of the equipment. It was sort of, 'My rules are better than your rules. . . . Refined people drink sherry.' Well, you don't drink sherry in the marines. . . . It was a real unwillingness, at the beginning at least, to value the rules of the group which you have just joined." Ellsberg was not a follower. "He had a hard time accepting the change," Cummings recounts, "getting used to the routine." Ellsberg told me: "They were *all* varsity football players [in OCS]. I'd never *met* a football player until I went into the marines. The captain of my own team was there; I'd never come near to meeting him at Harvard. So they lived a different life. They were used to barracks, in effect. They were used to locker rooms. I wasn't. I didn't know anything about rifles. I had trouble with the inspections on rifles. It was all a very new life to me."[11]

Adhering to a military schedule was difficult for Ellsberg. And, as we've seen, he was not the most careful dresser. Carol Ellsberg, who was then still at Radcliffe, took a train from Cambridge down to OCS in Quantico, Virginia, to visit him one weekend. "They had had an inspection and his trousers had been sewed up a tiny bit too short, so that they came out of his boots," she remembers. "And so he'd got dinged for that and was confined to barracks for the weekend. . . . [I] traveled for ten hours down, got there, and he was confined to the barracks. So whoever was in charge that weekend . . . took pity on him and let him sit on the lawn. . . . I hung out on the lawn with him."[12]

Although he earned "the top grades" on written tests in his class, Ellsberg recalls, he received low peer ratings and consequently ranked "near the bottom" in his class overall:

> The reason I was so low was that out of the ten-week course, my first month was spent essentially crying all the time. Because I had intense hay fever. . . . My eyes were constantly itching, constantly filling with tears. I couldn't see anything. I was wheezing at night. I had asthma. And I was afraid to turn myself in to get an antihistamine because I'd heard that if you had asthma, they'd run you out right away. And we couldn't leave the base to get an antihistamine. So I had to live through this for the first month. . . . It was so bad that I used to go into the latrine at night to keep from waking up the guy above me with my wheezing. I would just go into the latrine and wheeze. . . . And I just lay around all the time. When we weren't working, I would lie on my bunk, weakly.

Ellsberg also recounts:

> I got on all right with my platoon, but the peer ratings were based on both platoons. And the other platoon you didn't work with directly. . . . They would see me around and all they saw was this weak-looking, passive [person]—I couldn't volunteer for anything. I just felt terrible all the time. Even so, my own platoon felt pretty well about me and gave me sort of middling ratings. But the other platoon just didn't know—"Totally unfit. . . ." So they just all gave me totally bad ratings. . . .
>
> Then after the first month, I got antihistamines. My breathing cleared up. I now had some energy. . . . And now I got fairly high ratings from my own platoon. But continued to get horrible ratings from this other platoon. Because they continued to think of me . . . as being very unfit to be an officer. You know, very weak looking, very nothing. A nerd.[13]

As a result, "I was doomed for the cutting board," Ellsberg says. That meant he would be weeded out of OCS and enter ordinary enlisted men's training. That wouldn't look good, including to Carol, her father, and his friends and relatives. And enlisted men's training was tough. Then, one day, Ellsberg recounts, another guy in his platoon, a football player, "took me aside and told me what my problem was. . . . He said, 'We know you're a good guy. But these other guys in the other platoon don't realize that you're good. . . . They think you're a pussy.'" Some of them also didn't like the fact that he didn't swear at all. Ellsberg found that ironic: "I figured, 'Shit, I know all that. I've done all that. But I don't need to pick something up just because they're imitating some sergeant or enlisted man.' . . . I somehow thought it was beneath my dignity to learn this now." What's more, "They said, 'You don't go out with women. You don't go looking for women at all.' And, again, I thought, 'Well, shit, you know, I'm married.' I was the only married man. . . . And it didn't seem dignified. Frankly, if I went out looking for women, I did it on my own. I didn't go with these guys, because I thought it didn't look good. . . . I did go out looking a couple nights, but I didn't get anywhere. . . . Didn't have enough time. But I certainly wasn't going to go with them. I thought that wasn't right to do it that way."[14]

Ellsberg told me he didn't have any affairs in the marines, but saw "many whores." Once, a fellow marine informed him that he didn't like getting a blow-job. "That piqued my curiosity: 'What was your experience?'" Ellsberg remembers. It turned out it had been during the winter in Korea, and a whore had sucked him through a barbed-wire fence. "You mean you took your cock out at 40 below zero and stuck it through a barbed-wire fence?" Ellsberg replied. "I don't think you've given it a fair shake."[15]

Ellsberg mulled over his poor image among other marines and thought, "Well, hell, now. I can give a better impression than that." Not only did he know how to swear, but he could show some toughness. He'd done some boxing. "I thought, 'Well, they want me to be aggressive. I know how to be aggressive.'" One afternoon, he recalls, he went to the gym "to find somebody to box with. To get back in the spirit, just the psychology of boxing. Of hitting somebody. But mainly of being willing to get hit. It gets you in a more aggressive mood." When boxing, "you get used to being hit in the face. . . . And it hurts, but you understand that you're not made of sugar anymore. . . . So you don't flinch. . . . And you then look at people in a different way, much more aggressive. . . . You're going to hit them back and hurt them badly." At the gym, "there was somebody who did want to box. And I beat the shit out of him. I remember this guy as some loser of some kind. And I really remember beating on him quite hard."[16]

That same afternoon, Ellsberg recounts, the football player in his platoon who had told him about his problem invited him out for beers that night with some friends, including some from the other platoon. "They were all football players that night," Ellsberg remembers. "I drank about a dozen beers. We all did. A tremendous amount of beer." When they returned to the base, a marine on guard duty, one who thought poorly of Ellsberg, remarked, "What are you doing with him?" The guard was "the top football player," Ellsberg says. In fact, "he was an All-American football player, and he was going to be on the marine team." But Ellsberg was in an aggressive mood after his boxing match that afternoon, having beaten that poor loser to a pulp, and he took offense at the guard's remark. "I said, 'What the fuck are you talking about?' He said, 'What's that?'" Ellsberg recounts. In bayonet drill, Ellsberg had learned how to take the rifle away from an attacker, "so I took his rifle away from him." Marines on guard duty are not supposed to let anybody even touch their rifle. The All-American football player "swung at me," Ellsberg recalls. Then "these guys sort of pulled him back. And I swung at him. Then they pulled me away. And we went into town and drank more beer."[17]

After this encounter, Ellsberg's reputation among the other men improved. When they heard that he had traded punches with the guard, "everybody was looking at me with new eyes," he remembers. But "I had to call my wife and say, 'Darling, it looks as though I'm going to be court-martialed. . . . ' So that was a catastrophe. Because of her father."[18]

But Ellsberg was sent before the cutting board instead. He claims that the reason he was not court-martialed is they couldn't court-martial him without also court-martialing the guard, and "they were counting on him for the marine football team." Moreover, "No one who went to that cutting board survived. . . . I was the only exception." Both of these claims strain belief. Ellsberg also says that the members of the cutting board "realized I was telling the truth and this guy was lying," and that "my tone from the beginning was, 'Sir, I have no excuse. I did what I'm accused of.'" In the end,

> I made a very strong impression on the major who was in charge of it. . . . I made such a marvelous impression on this major that at the end of it, he said . . . "The votes for you to be cut are two to one. But since I am the senior officer on this board, you have passed. . . . I think you could be an outstanding officer. . . . You're not a natural officer. You're not a natural leader. . . . But you should be able to make up for that with intelligence . . . and you will learn how to do what you have to do." Which, again, was very shrewd. . . . I read a lot and I listened to people a lot, and I became a very good officer. An outstanding officer.

And the major, Major Faser, "got to be a fan of mine."[19] Faser may have been disinclined to let such an unusually bright young man get away. The marines probably did not get many of quite this intellectual caliber very often.

Faser, incidentally, "was famous for having introduced the Marine Corps to two things: knife fighting and night fighting," Ellsberg says. "Both."[20]

———◦◦◦———

Newly commissioned second lieutenant Dan Ellsberg entered the Marine Corps' Basic School outside Quantico in July 1954. He now "had the hang of it," he remembers, and his performance improved greatly. "I did extremely well in Basic School" and "got very high peer ratings." He apparently told two interviewers that he graduated number one in his class of more than 1,100 in Basic. "I don't think that's true," responds Richard Elms, who shared a bunk bed and locker with Ellsberg in Basic. Ellsberg told me that the only people who finished ahead of him were Naval Academy graduates, sergeants, and some ex-enlisted men. "But I was ahead of everybody in my Officer Candidate class. . . . I was in the top ten" of those who didn't have regular commissions. This Elms would not dispute, but he wonders how Ellsberg learned about it, "because I don't recall being told how we ranked." However, "he was always tops in terms of the academic work and the tests. . . . Dan's scores were always very, very high compared with the rest of us. . . . I think people admired the fact that he did very well on the exams."[21]

Not surprisingly, Ellsberg's intensity stood out in Basic. "He took the training very seriously," Elms remembers. Fueled by his travails in OCS, Ellsberg's drive to succeed was quite marked. "I think Dan felt it very important to excel," Elms says. "Being a Marine Corps second lieutenant didn't come as easy to him as it did to others, and he worked hard to be successful at it." He "wanted very badly" to "prove himself able," as reflected in his interest in the infantry. "Dan really wanted to be an infantry platoon leader," Elms recalls. "That's what he wanted to be. And that was very clear from the beginning." Being an infantry platoon leader was the most challenging of the options available to officer trainees in Basic. "He wasn't as athletic as some of the rest of us were and . . . it was important to Dan to prove his macho-ness, if you will," Elms recounts. And Ellsberg took the written examinations a good deal more seriously than most of his cohorts.[22]

In Basic, marines had to run obstacle courses and undertake a ten-mile hike carrying a heavy pack. Ellsberg, who was somewhat short and wiry and still far from physically prepossessing, hung in there, Elms recounts: "He didn't fall out of the hike; he didn't fall to the wayside. Some people did. When we had to go over the ten-foot wall, he got over it. Some people didn't. But I just had the distinct impression at the time that it was more difficult for him than for some of the rest of us that had played ball and that sort of thing. But he didn't fail. And my impression is that he was more concerned about it, about not failing. And I think he put a lot of energy and intensiveness into making sure he didn't fail." Also, while some people would get lost during map exercises and consequently others made fun of them, "I was not conscious of anybody making snide remarks or laughing or anything behind his back," Elms says. (But Don Hall remembers that when Ellsberg visited him years later at his old farmhouse in New Hampshire, "he would sleep upstairs, and come down through that door there, and have no idea where he was. He would have no idea where the bathroom was. He was here several days, and he could never figure [it] out. . . . I said, 'How the hell did you find your way around Vietnam?' And Dan said, 'With a map. With a map.' So I said, 'Should I make you a map of this room?' He would always come down and just stand there absolutely puzzled.")[23]

Ellsberg's mechanical aptitude is not high, and he continued to have problems with rifles in Basic. The trainees had to show proficiency in taking a rifle apart, cleaning it, and then reassembling it as fast as possible. "As far as knowing the names of all the components, he was perfect," Elms remembers. "But as far as actually physically doing it, he was not the best at that." Because of his bad knee, Ellsberg was unable to fire a rifle from a kneeling position. But he had better luck with pistols in the marines, he has often stated. He told an interviewer for *Look* magazine:

> I fired expert with the pistol with both hands. . . . The first time, I failed to qualify with the .45, like most people. That irritated me so much that the next two years I fired successively with the left and right hand and fired expert with both. I shouldn't tell this, but that was really suggested to me by a line in *The Secret Life of Walter Mitty*, where he's having a fantasy he's on trial for murder, and his defense lawyer points out to the judge that Mr. Mitty had his right hand in a sling and the victim was obviously shot by a right-handed person. And Mitty's voice is heard in the courtroom: "With any known make of gun I could have killed Gregory Fitzhurst at three hundred feet *with my left hand.*"

Ellsberg told another interviewer that he strengthened his forearms and hands by holding the pistol with his arm outstretched while reading at night, and improved his aim by shooting a pencil at a target on the wall. He claimed he was the only person who learned to shoot Expert with both hands. "He did qualify as an Expert with the pistol and was very proud of it, because not very many people did," Elms recollects. But "whether right and left hand[ed], that sounds a little extravagant to me."[24]

Ellsberg also had trouble staying on schedule in Basic. He and Elms lived with their wives off base, and Ellsberg had a hard time getting up and getting off in the mornings. "I don't think he liked to get up early," Ann Elms, Richard's wife at the time, remembers. "Sometimes Carol would be shining his boots as he was running out the door and grabbing them. . . . There are stories about [others] having to wait for him outside early in the morning when he runs out carrying his boots." Ellsberg "was one of the last ones to arrive in the morning and get squared away," Richard Elms recounts. "I was always worried about the fact that he wouldn't make the formation on time. But he always did." Elms and Ellsberg had to arrive before the formation at seven o'clock to make sure their bunk beds were in order, and sometimes to change clothes. "Dan tended sometimes to cut it a little close. . . . I do recall several mornings when he'd cut it just about as close as you can cut it."[25]

Ellsberg enjoyed the camaraderie of military service. But his circle of friends was again small. "He wasn't, I don't think, one of the popular guys," Ann Elms remembers. "If you'd go to something social, it was always obvious . . . that Carol was a lot more comfortable than Dan was." Ellsberg joked that perhaps the way to get everyone to like you was to buy them all "nutty buddies," a type of ice cream cone. After a hard day, you set up everyone with a round of nutty buddies.[26]

Ellsberg had a reserve commission in the marines, and in his retelling he was offered a regular commission coming out of Basic. A regular commission carried some prestige and the obligation to serve three years on active duty (a reserve commission required two). "They offered ten people out of my class, out of more than a thousand who didn't have regular commissions, regular commissions at the end of the Basic School," Ellsberg claims. "And I was not only in the ten, but I was told that I was the top of the ten. So in that sense, I was the top of the class." But he didn't take it, he says, because he was unsure how he'd perform in the Fleet Marine Force with a real platoon ("it turned out I did extremely well"). Both Carol Cummings and Richard Elms doubt Ellsberg's account, however. "I never heard of anybody switching from reserve to regular at this stage," Elms says, and as for Ellsberg specifically, "I never heard that, [and] I think I would have heard about it." "I don't know who told you that," responded Peyton Robertson, Ellsberg's first company commander, when I asked him about it.[27] Most likely, Ellsberg was offered a regular commission later in his marine tour.

By now, Ellsberg had come to enjoy military life. "I loved the Marine Corps," he recalls. It was satisfying to succeed in this new world. He was quite proud to be a marine officer. After he obtained either his reserve or regular commission, he called on Carl Kaysen at Kaysen's home in Cambridge. "I just have this image of Dan in his uniform, his swagger stick, the whole bit," Kaysen recounts. "Just was amusing. And again I thought, you know, 'That's Dan.' . . . Dan was and is an actor. And he loves to be on stage. And he's good at it. . . . He was there with his bars. And he may have had a specific impulse to show off to me. I'd been in the army during the war." Joan Cleveland remembers, "He used to come back periodically dressed in these funny clothes, and tell us about his exploits. And it was something that I—all of us, really, I suppose—neither understood nor valued. It was sort of, 'Who cares? What are you doing all this for?' . . . I just thought this whole marine thing was sort of incomprehensible." Ellsberg came to a New Year's Eve party at Cleveland's (then Joan Friedman's) home in Boston in his dress blues. She had a long-haired white cat, and Ellsberg "wound up spending a very long evening sitting on a bridge chair, because it was the only chair in the house that didn't have cat hair on it," she recounts. "And I thought, 'Why did you do this?' I mean, this was not a formal party. . . . But it was sort of, 'I'm getting dressed up in my costume, and I'm coming to your party.' A woman would have done that." Wassily Leontief recalls Ellsberg coming to the Society of Fellows at Harvard one day with his marine uniform on— "the most remarkable thing." He was "a peculiar man."[28]

<hr>

Ellsberg chose to use his 30 days leave after finishing Basic School to fly to Europe and North Africa on a free, space-available basis. He brought home some artifacts. About three years later, shortly after Kaysen and his wife arrived to have dinner at his home, "Dan disappeared," Kaysen recounts. "And five minutes later or three minutes later . . . an Arab in complete Bedouin costume stepped into the room. And it was Dan. It took a minute to realize it was Dan. He was made up. He was so convincing. It was kind of an odd thing to do. He picked this costume up in North Africa when he was there. . . . Again, I thought it was a kind of performance. But knowing Dan, it was not a performance that surprised me excessively." Ellsberg also gave the performance later at his home in Los Angeles. "He came sweeping down the stairway with a burnoose on and a cape," Mary Marshall laughs.[29]

After his trip overseas, Ellsberg was sent to join the Second Marine Division in the Fleet Marine Force at Camp Lejeune in North Carolina. He was probably in the best physical condition of his life by this point: this was Dan Ellsberg in his physical prime. He and Carol lived for three months in a small trailer, then moved into a small apartment. Carol wanted to teach in a local school, but she didn't have the required North Carolina teachers certificate.

"Carol had terrible trouble getting a job," Joan Cleveland remembers. But she didn't resent being a military wife. "This was a life I understood very, very well," Carol recalls. "And I thoroughly enjoyed it." But the Ellsbergs' marriage continued to have its problems. One can only speculate on the variety of those problems, but Ellsberg's self-centeredness and inconsiderateness were among them. His lecturing was also beginning to bother Carol. "When I began to notice it was when I found that I didn't like it even when he was talking about something I was interested in," she says with a laugh. "By the time we were in North Carolina, I was aware of having that feeling."[30]

Ellsberg was assigned to a marine company at Camp Lejeune and reported to his company commander, Captain Peyton Robertson. Robertson's wife had earlier known Carol Ellsberg and the two couples formed a bond. (Robertson would remain friendly with Ellsberg in later life and decline to do a full interview for this book after hearing from Ellsberg that it was "not going to be very favorable.") Ellsberg was assigned a rifle platoon. "I don't mind telling you—anybody can repeat this—Dan Ellsberg was the finest officer I had in my company," Robertson told me over the phone. "Out of five lieutenants, he was the top one. . . . I can go down all the leadership traits and name every one of them. . . . I think they are unique traits that he had. . . . Whether you're talking about loyalty, enthusiasm, endurance, whatever, he was the top one." Ellsberg wanted his platoon to be the best one in Robertson's company. That company was named the honor company of their battalion, and Ellsberg had a lot to do with that, Robertson told me. He or another commander at Camp Lejeune would tell *Life* magazine that Ellsberg was "bright, innovative, and dedicated." Robertson emphasized using incentives rather than punishments to get the best out of marines and to induce them to work together, and Ellsberg followed Robertson's approach with his own men. "Dan Ellsberg did that better than anybody else in my company," Robertson told me.[31]

After he had commanded several rifle platoons, Ellsberg recalls, William Barber, a Korean War hero and Medal of Honor winner, picked him to be his assistant operations officer. Barber "was a father figure to me, and was very keen on me," he says. Ellsberg's promotion would have been an honor and fitting for a bright young officer who had performed well as a platoon leader. (It may have been around this time that he was offered a regular commission.) According to Ellsberg, "as the assistant operations officer, I was in charge of training for the battalion for a number of months." But most likely, he was issuing training orders under the guidance and approval of superiors. After this, Ellsberg recounts (his military records are unclear on the sequence), he was the executive officer of a rifle company, hence the number two man in the company:

My company commander was a major. When he left, he recommended me to replace him. And I did replace him. And I was the only first lieutenant in the Second Marine Division who had a rifle company. Out of more than 40 companies. They were all captains or majors. And several majors, who wanted to have that on their record of having a rifle company, wanted to replace me. But they didn't. The battalion commander would not replace me, despite frequent requests to do so. Because I had the best company in the battalion and, in fact, in the division. By a lot of different criteria. . . . By every criteria, actually, we were the top. We always were the top in the division. And partly by using principles I'd learned from my first company commander, Peyton Robertson. A very good philosophy.

His company garnered more awards than any other company in his battalion and possibly even in the regiment, Ellsberg recalled. He has bragged often that he was the only first lieutenant in his division to have a company. However, Ellsberg was probably given the company temporarily, in an acting capacity, and was able to hang onto it for several months, quite possibly because of its performance.[32]

"I would say the happiest time in my life probably was the three and a half months as a company commander," he reminisces. He felt quite close to his men. Ellsberg and his platoon leaders encouraged those who lacked high school degrees to take correspondence courses to earn them. Many did. Ellsberg also urged his men to retake the General Classification Test if they had done poorly on it. "As far as I know, this has never been done in the history of the services," he says. And "*no one* reduced their score. The average increase was like 30 to 40 points. It was incredible." But out in the field, things were different: he gave his men very tough preparation for combat. If there was a hard job, they were going to volunteer for it:

I set them very hard tasks, and I set them a very strong example. . . . I often wouldn't sleep at all. I would go without sleep for two nights in a row. . . . I did everything the hard way. . . . I made it no easier on myself. When we were on a march, we would take the longest marches. But I would carry a fifty-caliber machine gun. It's the heaviest piece of equipment. . . . At times when people were getting droopy, I'd borrow a fifty-caliber machine gun, and I would walk up the line from the back of the line to the front. . . . And I was one of the smaller people. . . . Walking like Groucho Marx, you know, the loping stride. . . . I would just pass everybody carrying this fifty caliber.

One fellow marine would remember Ellsberg as a "tough, hard-nosed hatchet man."[33]

Ellsberg never experienced combat, but he wanted to. He was set to finish his marine tour in June 1956, so that May he had to relinquish his company. Then he read in the newspapers that there was a good chance of war breaking out in the Middle East that summer over the Suez Canal. His battalion was due to go to the Mediterranean, so he applied to extend his tour, "because it looked as if there might be the possibility of some action," Don Hall remembers. "He hoped to see action. . . . 'Action' was the word." Hall was completely bewildered. "I mean, this is *absolutely* alien to me," he fervently recounts. "And it was alien to everybody else at Harvard. . . . I hadn't ever known that he was a war lover." "We were all outraged," Kirby Hall recalls. "To have this friend who was a hawk was really quite startling. And he was a hawk." "It was the talk of all of us," William Simmons laughs. "Everyone said, 'Did you hear what *Dan* did?! Boy, is that gung ho.'" But "I think everybody thought it was just typical Ellsberg to do something like that."[34]

Ellsberg had by then been elected to be a junior member of the Society of Fellows at Harvard. His three-year term was scheduled to start after he got out of the marines that June. But when he extended his tour, "I gave the whole thing up," he claims. "I had to reapply, from scratch. . . . They told me—emphasized— 'You're up against a different group of people, and there's no guarantee you'll get in,'" although he thought his chances were good. As it turned out, he gave up six months of his junior fellowship. His decision was, again, an unusual one, but he probably did not have to reapply "from scratch"; rather, he likely requested to delay his tenure and was successful.[35] Of course, to look down one's nose at the Society of Fellows is a fairly impertinent thing to do.

Ellsberg denies that his primary motivation for extending his tour was to see combat: "It was totally a question of my battalion. . . . I had trained these men for combat without having been in it myself. . . . So the idea that these men . . . might be in a combat operation using my training, but I wouldn't be there with them, I just couldn't bear the thought of that. . . . It wasn't just that I wanted to be with them, but I wanted to do what I could, you know, to help save their lives. . . . I wouldn't have dreamed of extending . . . if it had been some other battalion. But it was my battalion." Ellsberg felt a sense of loyalty and responsibility to his men, and most marines want to do what they've been trained to do. When I asked him whether the state of his marriage had anything to do with his decision, however, he responded, "Well, that's the trouble. Well, of course it had something to do [with it]."[36]

His first child, Robert, had been born six months earlier. Carol was not happy that her husband, who had already been away a lot in the marines, was now going off to the Mediterranean, though according to Ellsberg she didn't complain about it at the time. At Camp Lejeune, however, Carol had complained about it. "He had been away most of the time before [Robert's birth] on maneuvers and stuff," she recalls. "So he had been around very little." Then the day after Carol got home from the hospital after giving birth to Robert, "he went up to have an interview for the junior fellows in Boston; he was gone about five days. Then he came back. Then, I think when the baby was a month old, he went on maneuvers" for around two months. Then he left again for six months.[37]

Some people from Harvard also questioned Ellsberg's decision. "Some of us were startled," one remembers. "I was a bachelor, but that struck me as a little odd. . . . It just didn't seem to me to be very fair to the family and to the wife."[38]

Ellsberg was an assistant operations officer aboard a ship in the Mediterranean. It turned out to be a demoralizing six months for him. He served "under a very poor battalion commander who . . . knew nothing about the infantry," he recounts. "He was a very passive, very poor officer. . . . And I didn't like the staff officer." Ellsberg was "miserable, basically." He was disappointed there wasn't a war. "He was frustrated with standing on the deck of some warship and the whole thing was over so fast," Jerry Goodman remembers.[39]

While in the Mediterranean and elsewhere in the marines, Ellsberg wrote long letters to Carol and others describing his experiences. Carol suspected, with some cause and annoyance, that they were really designed for publication. "They often had a quality that seemed aimed at the ages rather than at me particularly," she remembers. "Writing for a larger audience, perhaps. To be in the future."[40]

It was in the Mediterranean that Ellsberg was first privy to top-secret information, he would say later. He saw war plans in preparation for making landing plans. "We didn't know which side we would be fighting at that point," he recalls. "I felt that any war was better than none. . . . I was more than prepared to fight any enemy designated by my commander in chief."[41]

Military intelligence investigated Ellsberg for a security violation when a carbon copy of a long letter he had written to Crane Brinton, the head of the Society of Fellows at Harvard, that described some U.S. plans in the Mediterranean was found in his desk. Ellsberg hoped to impress Brinton with his knowledge of the plans—he was "fluffing it up for Brinton," Carol Cummings remembers.[42] Ellsberg got off the hook, but his indiscretion with classified material would cause him problems later.

———◦———

Ellsberg joined the Society of Fellows in February 1957, and it is hard to imagine a more desirable situation for him. He now had complete freedom to satisfy his immense intellectual curiosity and drive. The Monday night dinners were surely enjoyable affairs. Highly articulate, Ellsberg loved intellectual exchange. His manner, however, was typically quite serious. And there was all that disposable time. Joan Cleveland recalls, "I had a piano, and for weeks in the early days of his tenure at the fellows he used to come over every day and spend a day practicing. And he said, 'Wouldn't it be funny if I spent my whole . . . two and a half years . . . as a fellow learning all the Beethoven sonatas?' . . . It was sort of, you know, that would be bratty to the economics department, who thought that they had a little star here. . . . He didn't do it. But it was that sort of attitude."[43]

Ellsberg enjoyed the distinction of having been in the marines. William Simmons, who attended some Monday night dinners with him, recalls "Dan and I chuckling over the fact that somehow the fellows would find out that Dan and I were both veterans. And this was unusual in the Society of Fellows." Ellsberg could also be humorous on the subject of his brilliance. During the quiz programs on television around this time, Carol Cummings recounts, "he said, 'Now, there ought to be a program where all the questions are about Daniel Ellsberg. . . . For example, who first compared Ellsberg to Leonardo?'"[44]

Ellsberg continued to do research in decision theory and game theory. He explored decision making that took place under conditions in which the probable occurrence of events relevant to the decisions was uncertain, and information about other people's intentions was incomplete. He used complex mathematical models. Ellsberg asked the question, Are there situations in which people do not assign probabilities to the occurrence of uncertain events or even act as if they do? He believed there were. It was widely (though not universally) assumed among those who studied decision making that there were not. Rational people don't behave that way, others argued. Ellsberg questioned what were known as the "Savage axioms," roughly described as postulates of rational behavior in the face of uncertainty. Leonard "Jimmy" Savage was perhaps the most influential person in the field of decision theory. Ellsberg, then, had his sights set high.

"He loved analyzing risks," a friend would remember. "He talked about it all the time. It fascinated him." Philip Cronin was a trial lawyer in Boston at the time and Ellsberg picked his brain extensively on the subject. In their many conversations, "the primary thrust . . . was risk analysis," Cronin recounts. "We were taking various events—the Suez Crisis is a good one . . . and applying risk analysis. And he was interested in my involvement, because obviously a trial lawyer engages in risk analysis day in and day out."[45]

Ellsberg also studied bargaining and threats, which fell within game theory. Thomas Schelling, a professor of economics at Yale (soon to go to Harvard), had recently published an important article on bargaining that was influential with Ellsberg and stimulated his work. Ellsberg visited Schelling at Yale sometime before the summer of 1957. "It was clear to me that he was sort of breathless to meet me," Schelling remembers. "He had read at least some of my stuff. And I think he thought that in all the world I was the person most likely to appreciate what he was doing. Because I was doing that kind of thing myself." Schelling, an original thinker with a powerful mind, came to have enormous regard for Ellsberg's own intellect. In an interview with me, he twice referred to Ellsberg as a genius. After I pointed that out to him and asked him to explain, Schelling replied, "First, Dan, I think, considered himself—but not with complete confidence—to be a genius. I think he was somewhat insecure; he wasn't simply quietly confident of himself. But I think Dan felt that for the kind of thing he did, for things having to do with subtlety rather than rigor, maybe, that he had insights that hardly anybody else in the world could get. I tend not to use the word 'genius' except in quotation marks, but I would say Dan was one of the brightest people I ever knew."[46]

Schelling thought one aspect of Ellsberg's genius was seeing something in a situation that others don't see. In his work on bargaining and threats, Ellsberg was very good at "finding dramatic illustrations of an idea," Schelling remembers:

> Dan read a lot, and he read with his eyes open for examples and illustrations of whatever he was working on. . . . Dan could read a story, a novel or something, and take certain twists of plot and convert them into little bits of theory. . . . He can look at that and say, "Gee, you know, there's something great there." And it's that kind of perception, coupled with a theoretical bent, a desire to see something that is paradoxical, and then to find "how can you formulate that theoretically so that people can understand exactly what's going on?" And I tend to think that's what I have been good at. But I would say that, among the people whom I've known who try to do the kinds of things I do, I think Dan did them best.

In a Harvard seminar and paper in 1958, Ellsberg illuminated the psychology of military deterrence by quoting from Joseph Conrad's novel *The Secret Agent*. In the novel, a small bespectacled man who always kept some nitroglycerin and a detonation system on him claimed that the police would never try to nab him because they believed he had the will to blow up both himself and them.[47]

Ellsberg felt competitive with Schelling. He was, of course, a graduate student, Schelling a noted professor. "I think Dan was in a position that I think a lot of geniuses get in," Schelling comments. "Namely, there's somebody whom they admire almost to the point of worship that they want to surpass, and they don't want to seem like an upstart. And there's sort of a combination of boast-fulness and apology. Without putting down their mentor or whatever you call the person, they want to get a little off at arm's length in order to say, 'I didn't learn all this from him.' . . . So I think Dan always had the problem of saying either 'This is different from Schelling,' or 'even if this is very much like Schelling, I did it on my own.'"[48]

In 1958, while in London, Schelling wrote a long essay extending the scope of game theory. The essay was published in the *Journal of Conflict Resolution* that September. Probably in early September, Schelling flew from London to Califor-nia to spend a year at the RAND Corporation in Santa Monica, where Ellsberg was then finishing a summer working as a consultant. Schelling remembers:

> I had mailed my manuscript from London to the *Journal of Conflict Resolu-tion*. When I got to RAND, Dan gave a seminar, a brilliant seminar, a main point of which, or maybe the climax of which, was exactly the point that I had made in this article. And I was shocked and embarrassed, because I didn't know what to tell Dan. I hated to go up to him and say, "I scooped you on your favorite idea." And I didn't know how he'd react if I said, "We both independently came upon the same formulation." And I was wondering what to do, and I never said anything, and he left. And I remember meeting him the following December at the annual meeting of the American Economic Association. And he had been stunned, and he asked me, "When had I last revised my article?" And I said, "I didn't. I mailed it from London at the end of August." And he said, "You didn't change it?" And I said, "No." And then I think Dan's wife told me that Dan had been in a terrible stew, because he thought that I had been guilty of an unethical practice by plagiarizing him without acknowledgment.

In a preface to a RAND reprint of a lecture Ellsberg gave on threats, he point-edly noted that "at the time this was written Schelling had not presented any *formalization* of his path-breaking notions on bargaining and threats, and it was a major aim of my lectures to accomplish this." (Schelling responds, "I had done all that before I left London.") In two footnotes, Ellsberg seemingly went out of his way to emphasize his unique contributions to the study of threats. Ellsberg accused another scholar of plagiarizing his work, too. This scholar "published something that Dan was sure was cribbed from him," Schelling re-calls. But "I think it very improbable." (The accused party told me, "I would rather not reopen this very painful episode. I did not plagiarize Ellsberg.") Schelling observes, "Dan is a very sensitive, egotistical person, and I think it's easy for him to think that somebody stole his stuff."[49]

In the summer of 1957, Schelling was at the RAND Corporation when Ellsberg passed through Santa Monica. Ellsberg was then taking a seminar at Stanford in advanced mathematics for social scientists. He dropped in to see Schelling, who arranged a lunch with the head of RAND's economics division, Charlie Hitch, and the economics section head, Joe Kershaw. "I remember Dan showed off so egregiously that I was embarrassed and sorry I had arranged the lunch," Schelling recounts. "I just remember thinking, 'Oh, shit, he's showing off in a very juvenile fashion.'" But "I just totally misjudged the effect he was having," as Hitch "was so charmed that he immediately went to work to hire Dan. . . . Apparently he made a great hit with those two people." One of Ellsberg's personal skills is charm. "He's a little too charming," Schelling comments. "He's a little too inclined to be the life of the party."[50]

During Ellsberg's consultancy at RAND the summer of 1958, he and Schelling became close in the two or three weeks they overlapped. Schelling helped him get acquainted with people after he had himself arrived, though Ellsberg didn't need much help, as he had been energetically introducing himself to people. "I think by then he was no longer in awe of me," Schelling recalls. "I think he was quite comfortable. I was still ten years older, but I think he became pretty confident that we were good friends." Schelling often took talented and energetic, yet troubled, young admirers under his wing, and his son Andrew believes his father would have put Ellsberg in that category—"absolutely brilliant, full of insight, but not that capable to really get his life together." Schelling became quite fond of Ellsberg; they exchanged intimacies (Schelling would tell Ellsberg in the 1960s that he was contemplating suicide, and they then discussed it rationally).[51]

Ellsberg was the young rapporteur of "a big strategy group" at RAND that summer. He saw a lot of RAND heavyweights like Albert Wohlstetter, Herman Kahn, Harry Rowen, and Andrew Marshall. "I met them all, the key people at that time," he remembers. "And certainly made an impression on all of them. . . . I don't think there was any way I wasn't going to get offered a job at that point. I did very well that summer." "Dan gave some very brilliant talks," Wohlstetter would recall. "He was very brilliant, no question about it." For several years, Wohlstetter had been studying the vulnerability of U.S. Strategic Air Command (SAC) bases to a surprise Soviet attack, and Ellsberg saw classified information on the situation. He also saw reports of a missile gap between the United States and the Soviets. Preventing a surprise Soviet nuclear attack seemed to him "the most important problem in the world." And U.S. retaliatory capacity was key.[52]

Ellsberg worried about the prospect of a nuclear war. Richard Townsend was studying city planning in graduate school at MIT at this time and remembers visiting him at his home in 1957 or 1958. "He said I should be working on plans for underground bomb shelters, as a city planner," Townsend recounts. "I should do a master's thesis on that. Because he was very worried about the state of the world . . . the possibility of catastrophe and accidents. And that there was a real need for this." Scientists and government bodies were then advocating massive shelter programs. Ellsberg seemed to Townsend to have inside information on the situation. Townsend was thinking as he surveyed Ellsberg's home, "Here is a much more rich place than his Cranbrook room. There's some art on the walls and an appreciation for those kinds of things." Ellsberg went on to tell Townsend that he was so concerned about a nuclear war that he had developed a contingency plan of sorts. He knew someone who had a boat, Townsend remembers,

> and if he had a sense from his inside information that the bomb was going to go off and the end of the world was coming, he was going to get himself and his family on that boat and go down to Chile. . . . Well, I laughed at that. . . . But years later, when I was working in Washington in the State Department, the Cuban missile crisis happened. . . . And my boss at the State Department said he was going to West Virginia to get away from the possibility of catastrophe, and we didn't have to come in anymore. The whole city at least was on edge, it seemed. So I tried to call Dan to see if this was it, to see whether it was going to blow up. . . . And no answer. . . . I thought, "My God, he's gone to Chile. And that's all."[53]

Ellsberg was offered a full-time position at RAND. He would start in 1959 after his Harvard fellowship ended. Charlie Hitch hired him but Albert Wohlstetter probably influenced Hitch's decision. "I was the one who hired him," Wohlstetter told me. "He came to work with me."[54]

Ellsberg was considered a great find at RAND, perhaps even a future Nobel Prize winner.

———◦◦◦———

Ellsberg first met Henry Kissinger while a junior fellow at Harvard. He participated in Harvard's Defense Studies program, of which Kissinger became director in 1958. Ellsberg and Kissinger would see each other sporadically over the years, never becoming friends, though Ellsberg would make a big production out of their association at one RAND seminar both attended (it was a "sort of lovefeast," one witness remembers). Ellsberg presented his ideas on bargaining and threats at the Defense Studies seminar. "He was one of the most interested students," Deirdre Henderson, who was the administrative assistant to the program, recalls. "He was really intrigued with all this." And "very intense, always. . . . Very zapped in." Ellsberg spoke of deficiencies in the United States's military posture and its preparation for nuclear war. "He was saying, 'Look, we need to build up our forces,'" Henderson reminisces. "That we were in serious trouble."[55]

Ellsberg would first meet Richard Falk, to whom he would later give a large chunk of the Pentagon Papers, at this time. In 1958 a mutual friend invited both Ellsberg and Falk to dinner, thinking they would enjoy each other, but they did not. "It was during his very conservative period," Falk, later a well-known legal scholar, remembers. And "the chemistry wasn't particularly good."[56]

Ellsberg's cold war views were evident in lectures he gave under the prestigious auspices of the Lowell Institute at the Boston Public Library in March of 1959. Entitled "The Art of Coercion: A Study of Threats in Economic Conflict and War," they examined patterns in "the art of influencing the behavior of others by threats." That Ellsberg, a graduate student, was invited to give them was an honor. "He was very excited by the whole thing," William Simmons recalls. Those in attendance included Gloria Steinem, who "wanted to get me on a TV show," Ellsberg would subsequently tell a journalist. (Ellsberg also boasted to the journalist, Frank Rich, about some sort of alleged personal involvement he had with Steinem later.) In his opening lecture, entitled "The Theory and Practice of Blackmail," Ellsberg used tools of game theory to examine, abstractly, conditions shaping the influence of threats. He argued that threats can increase the chance of an undesired war, but that they can also be used to deter aggression. Ellsberg considered the problem of how to convince the Soviets that the United States would retaliate strongly if the Soviets attacked. "It is a peculiarity of thermonuclear threats that they make cowards of practically everyone. Very few are the objectives that would seem worth— to anyone—a *high* probability of nuclear retaliation," he wrote. He approvingly quoted John Foster Dulles, "The ability to get to the verge without getting into the war is the necessary art." Ellsberg also contended that if a blackmailer appeared "irrational" it might make him more effective. Ellsberg seemed, to some, a fan of blackmail. He later denied it. But in a variant of this lecture given the next year for a seminar on arms control, he coolly discussed the use of nuclear threats by the United States to restrain the Soviet Union and to end a war without surrendering. He noted that the atomic bombing of Hiroshima had increased the credibility of U.S. nuclear threats.[57]

Ellsberg concluded his first Lowell lecture by dramatically telling listeners, "In the next lecture, we shall hear the *sound* of blackmail; the words that Adolf Hitler spoke, and their echoes, that won him half [of] Europe before the firing of a shot. There is the artist to study, to learn what *can* be hoped for, what can be done with the threat of violence." Ellsberg's second lecture, on Hitler's diplomacy, was provocatively entitled "The Political Uses of Madness." He observed that Hitler had been a bold and successful blackmailer. When practicing blackmail, "it pays to be mad" in certain situations, Ellsberg asserted, or at least "convincingly mad," and Hitler was "erratic, unpredictable." Hitler promoted his reputation for unpredictability to make conquests, he noted. ("I think you'll find in some ways maybe this is Dan," his later friend Sam Popkin comments. "Trying to decide how to act on the basis of what he wants to get, not of who he is.") Ellsberg also pointed out the risks of Hitler's approach. But to some listeners, he, again, seemed a fan of blackmail, even of Hitler's use of it. Richard Barnet, later with the Institute for Policy Studies, remembers being "rather put off" by Ellsberg's analysis of Hitler's tactics when he read it. "The way it was written, the way it came off the page, he really got excited about [them]," Barnet recalls. "And that left me troubled." Ellsberg later denied that he was recommending the use of blackmail or admired Hitler's diplomacy. But in his presentation before the arms control seminar in 1960, he argued that some controlled madness might be helpful in U.S. dealings with the Soviets, and noted that Hitler had done well with it.[58]

President Richard Nixon would later practice what he called his "madman theory" of war in Vietnam, threatening the North Vietnamese with major escalation. Ellsberg believes Nixon probably got the madman idea from Kissinger, "who, in turn, almost surely got it from me, as a phrase to describe a concept." Nixon applied the idea "almost so precisely to the concept that I had in mind. In those days it was very unfamiliar." But, in fact, Kissinger did not need Ellsberg to entertain the idea, nor did Nixon. "By the time Nixon became president, the idea that a madman might be more credible than a fully rational person, in terms of willingness to do something enormously self-destructive— that was no longer a novel idea," Thomas Schelling points out. Schelling himself had made that point in his writings, as had others.[59]

⸺ ◉ ⸺

Though junior fellows were not required to write a Ph.D. dissertation, most did and had since the postwar years. Ellsberg planned to earn a Ph.D. "I think originally he probably thought that his Lowell lectures would be a dissertation," Schelling says. More, they could have been a book. "If he had managed to get them all nicely on paper at the time, I think the Harvard University Press might have been happy to publish them," Schelling recalls. "But he just couldn't do it." Ellsberg would ultimately write his dissertation on decision making under uncertainty. But it was a tough go. "I knew he was disappointed that he wasn't able to finish his thesis and get his degree" while at Harvard, William Simmons remembers. "He was upset because he wasn't finishing his thesis." Ellsberg eventually completed it in 1962 at RAND. "I wrote it from start to finish in six months," he says. "I worked night and day on it." "It astonished me he completed it," Schelling recalls. "I don't think he would ever have got the dissertation done if I hadn't just nagged at him for a couple of years." Gus Shubert, who was also in the economics department at RAND, recounts, "A number of us in the department kept pressing and pressing and pressing him: 'Get it done, get it done, get it done.' We gave him the time, we gave him everything he needed, the secretarial help to get it done. I think only that pressure from outside got him to do it here. . . . We were all beating him over the head to get him to finish it."[60]

Ellsberg denies he was pressured to finish his Ph.D., however. "Nobody even *encouraged* me to do it," he says. He became quite agitated discussing this issue with me. "Most things that I have written have had to be pulled out of me, by some way or other," he grants. "The Ph.D. happens not to be one of those things." Ellsberg acknowledges that Schelling pushed him to publish a seminal article he wrote based on his research (more on it later). "He dragged it out of me. It would not have happened without his pulling at me. That did not happen to be the case in the Ph.D." Moreover, "I was not getting a Ph.D." and RAND "didn't give a flying shit whether I had a Ph.D." The reason he got his Ph.D.: "In one sentence, I was tired of having to explain that I was not a Ph.D. when everybody called me Dr. Ellsberg." Harvard awarded him his Ph.D. in 1963.[61]

———— ◆ ————

Meanwhile, the state of Ellsberg's marriage remained unchanged. A pulse of gnawing dissatisfaction beat under the surface. One day Ellsberg came across a section in *Ladies' Home Journal* entitled "Can This Marriage Be Saved?" that described various problems married couples faced and listed an institution called the Institute of Family Relations. At his initiative, he and Carol then saw a marriage counselor at the institute in the late summer of 1958. "It was one of those quickie things," Carol remembers. "Four visits or something like that." They saw another counselor at the institute the following summer. At least one of these summers, their counselor was a Baptist minister. Carol and Dan saw the counselors separately. Dan was frustrated with their sex life, which he considered "a very strong limitation in the marriage." He concluded years later that, rather than loving him, Carol felt anger at him, and that that was one reason for their sexual problems. But it remained unclear in his mind exactly why she was angry with him. Ellsberg told me his problems in the marriage were confined to sex: "Otherwise I was happy in the marriage." He recalls telling the counselors, "My marriage is great in every other respect." He loved Carol, and he loved their children, Robert and Mary (who was born in November 1958). But Ellsberg was probably emotionally frustrated too. He noticed a larger reserve on Carol's part. "Of course, in retrospect, the reserve may have reflected the real distaste," he says. "Which I certainly wasn't aware of. I thought she loved me."[62]

Ellsberg would conclude that the Baptist minister had used a dubious approach. He had basically advised them to stay together, to accept their marriage, to adapt. The minister was into saving marriages, Ellsberg thought. Any problems Carol was having were never brought to his attention during these sessions, he remembers, although he believes she did voice complaints about him to the minister: "I thought *I* was the one that had problems. *I* insisted we go to a marriage counselor. I insisted twice, two different times. And I poured out my heart to these guys on the terrible problems I was having and I was not aware *she* was having. She was not communicative on that score. So in retrospect she was obviously very resentful of lots of things. But I was not aware of it at all." In sum, "We communicated zero," Ellsberg says. "If we had talked about things, we could have worked it out."[63]

Kirby Hall saw a lot of Carol Ellsberg in the first half of 1957 in Cambridge. They were both young mothers with young sons, married to ambitious junior fellows at Harvard. Carol and Dan then lived in an apartment on Massachusetts Avenue. "I was over there, and she showed me this god awful furniture that Dan had bought," Kirby remembers:

> I mean, just bought. Usually you consult. When you're young and poor, you consult about what you're going to buy if it's a large item. . . . He got it in France or something, and he brought it all the way to the United States. It was just shoddy stuff. It was the sort of thing that he would kind of pop on her. He had no sense of teamwork with her. I mean, *none*. . . . He simply didn't think about other people.

> One day . . . he and Don decided that they would take care of the little boys, and Carol and I could have a whole day together to poke around Boston. . . . So she came back at the end of the day and Robert [Ellsberg] was still in his night clothes . . . with his diaper on. He was one and a half. I mean, Dan. I don't know why my then-husband didn't notice. You got a little fragrant by that time. . . . That would be something that Dan would do. . . . He wasn't trying to be mean. He's simply unaware of other people. . . . I don't remember *any* relationship between him and Robert. I'm sure he liked Robert, but . . .

Ellsberg "was such an obnoxious husband," Kirby recalls. "I mean, he was *terrible*." Terrible "in terms of other women, in terms of being intensely interested in everybody but her." Joan Cleveland speaks of Ellsberg's "sins of inconsiderateness: 'I don't really care what you need or want, I am writing the great American thesis.' Or 'I am doing whatever it is I am doing, and I am brilliant, and you're supposed to admire this.'" Ellsberg would complain toward the end of his marriage that Carol did not admire him. One person who knew them both quite well offers: "He is not what you would call a considerate man. And after a while you get tired of it. . . . He thought what he was doing was so important. Everybody thinks what he's doing is so important, but other people learn to conceal it somewhat and act interested in what their spouse says."[64]

Carol was not considering divorce at the time, her complaints about Dan aside. In fact, she was very opposed to divorce. Marriage was a lifetime commitment, she felt, and her religious beliefs disposed her against divorce. Moreover, their two small children needed a father, even one with shortcomings. And what would she do for money? Besides, Dan could be a lot of fun.[65]

Outwardly, the Ellsbergs' marriage did not seem to be in trouble. "Everything seemed fine to me," recalls Ann Elms, who stayed in touch with Carol after their husbands finished the Marine Corps' Basic School. "I never got any hints in the letters that things weren't going well." Polly Cronin, the wife of Philip Cronin, remembers:

> There wasn't anything in the air that seemed a problem. The only time I saw Dan lose his temper was once, and it was at me. . . . For some reason we were out at their house [in Belmont, Massachusetts]. Carol wasn't there. . . . So we had gone out to have dinner with Dan. He'd been alone for two or three days. . . . I got out there, and the kitchen was a mess. . . . And there was a bowl caked with the rest of the frosting for a cake after you've scraped everything out. It'd been on the counter for so long it was all hard. And I washed it. I thought Dan would be so pleased with something like that. He was *furious* at

me. He was saving the frosting to eat afterwards. And that was a side of him I'd never seen before.[66]

When the RAND position was offered to Dan, though she recognized it was a big opportunity for him, Carol was not enthusiastic about moving. "I hated it," she remembers. "I didn't want to move to Los Angeles. I thought it was like moving to Las Vegas, Miami Beach, or someplace."[67]

Although she opposed the move, Carol went along with it. The situation provided fertile ground for increasing resentments.

FIVE

SUPERGENIUS

EACH WORKDAY, IN THE LOBBY OF THE RAND BUILDING NEAR THE Santa Monica pier, armed guards checked employees in for work and issued them passes that would allow them to go through locked doors. Visitors were to be escorted at all times. This closely patrolled "brain factory" had been established in 1946 to advise the air force on air warfare. Warfare would be a science. The air force was still overwhelmingly RAND's chief sponsor when Ellsberg reported in June of 1959 at a monthly salary of $1,000.[1]

Much research at RAND was highly classified. Simon Bourgin began working as its public affairs officer in the early 1960s "with the job mostly of keeping people out of the place," he recalls. "RAND had a certain mystique and [we] didn't think it ought to be dispelled by making it ordinary."[2] Most RAND analysts believed they were doing important work for their country. But those outside the temple didn't know just how important their work was, since the analysts couldn't discuss classified matters with those lacking security clearances or publish reports on them. Some consequently felt they didn't get the credit that was their due. Their reactions veered from feelings of insecurity to displays of self-importance.

The intellectual environment at RAND was loose. Analysts had considerable autonomy in choosing research projects. The building was never closed. Some analysts worked odd hours; insomnia was common. The approximately 500 professionals at RAND included mathematicians, engineers, economists, political scientists, and physicists. But interdisciplinary work was hazardous, as the place was cliquish.[3]

Cutting up other people's ideas was a popular sport at RAND. "It was a very competitive, vicious environment," Roman Kolkowicz, a RAND sovietologist at

the time, remembers. "RAND was a ball-busting place." When analysts presented papers, many of their colleagues came as if wielding knives. When one
abrasive RAND mathematician attacked another man's presentation, the pre-
senter "grew so nervous that he finally fainted."[4]

One of the sharpest knives at RAND was wielded by Albert Wohlstetter, a
powerful and controversial figure who would have a big impact on Ellsberg's
life. "He did it with style," Kolkowicz recounts. "Walking in very late, looking at
the victim—then *destroy*. . . . He was *nasty*. Ruthless and nasty." Many analysts
were intimidated by him. "He managed to have an enormous store of facts at his
fingertips," Norman Dalkey, another RAND analyst at the time, recalls. "If you
raised an objection to something he was saying or proposing, he could bring out
that stack of facts with amazing facility." The nuclear strategist Bernard Brodie,
who became an enemy of Wohlstetter, almost had a nervous breakdown because
of him. "He became so broken down in the presence of Albert," Thomas
Schelling remembers. "Just tongue-tied. And I'm sure Dan [Ellsberg] never did.
Dan would just never be intimidated by somebody like Albert."[5]

A mathematical logician eighteen years older than Ellsberg, Wohlstetter
was brilliant, suave, sophisticated, a Renaissance man. A perfectionist, he had
problems completing work and was difficult to work with. He learned that the
way to write was to pick an adversary. "He was very good at talking about the
things he was writing, but very poor at getting them done until he found an adversary," Schelling recalls. "And then he just threw himself into it very successfully." Wohlstetter had headed two original and highly influential studies on
the vulnerability of U.S. SAC air bases to a surprise Soviet attack. He had also
written an influential article on the "precarious" thermonuclear balance entitled "The Delicate Balance of Terror."[6]

Wohlstetter and his wife, Roberta, also a talented RAND analyst, and
their unconventional daughter lived in a glamorous, distinctive home in the
Hollywood hills. It had a spiral stairway, pool, bamboo, view, the whole bit.
Albert and Roberta entertained frequently, in high style. Albert liked to hold
court and be the center of attention. He would "talk at length, at nauseating
length, about a fine little wine or some cuisine," Kolkowicz recounts. "He was
a great Francophile. . . . And monomaniacal monologuer." Wohlstetter was a
big name-dropper. But he could be charming. "If you're willing to listen, he is
indeed entertaining," Schelling says. "And if you're willing to listen, he gets to
like you." Wohlstetter's ego was gargantuan. "His attitude was sort of, 'I'm the
only smart person there is,'" a former RAND engineer remembers. "And
when you listened to him carefully, what he would really be saying is, 'Those
other guys are pretty dumb, aren't they?' And always criticizing everybody

else." Wohlstetter sought admiration and minions. "He sits on his throne," another ex-RAND researcher recounts. "And he expects people to kowtow, to kneel, and so on. He will bestow favors. If you're one of the favored, he would be very generous. If you're not one of the favored, forget it. . . . He can't take anybody who doesn't adore him, and kneel in front of him, and kowtow, and praise his bamboo."[7]

Wohlstetter turned off many people at RAND. But many others admired him and wished to be like him. If they could only be as smart, glamorous, sophisticated, and powerful. Some competed to impress him. "Wohlstetter was a mentor to quite a few of us," Frank Trinkl, a RAND mathematician at the time, recalls. "We looked up to him."[8] Wohlstetter tried to woo bright new arrivals at RAND to his circle. He was successful more often than not. His boys included Harry Rowen and Dan Ellsberg.

Ellsberg was an understudy of sorts to Wohlstetter and his favorite boy. "I think Albert was very fond of Dan, and really had a great deal of respect for him," David McGarvey, another RAND mathematician at the time, remembers. Ellsberg's brilliance attracted Wohlstetter, who hoped he could use it to his benefit. Wohlstetter may have also hoped to be able to point to Ellsberg with pride later, as Ellsberg's star rose. And Ellsberg was attracted to Wohlstetter. He admired him and his sophistication. Certainly Wohlstetter's brilliance and flair, not to mention his stature and influence, caught Ellsberg's attention. Ellsberg would have liked to carry Wohlstetter's status. Wohlstetter was hyped on SAC's vulnerability to a surprise Soviet attack, and Ellsberg was concerned about it, too—"because Albert was," Jim Digby, a former colleague of both men, recalls. In a December 1960 paper, Ellsberg called Wohlstetter's "Delicate Balance of Terror" article "brilliant and authoritative." He was "sort of a junior Wohlstetter," Trinkl chuckles. "He was trying to really imitate, in a sense, Wohlstetter. In his abrasiveness, in his bragginess. In a lot of [ways]."[9]

So close was their relationship that Ellsberg became almost a member of Wohlstetter's family. He was the son that Wohlstetter never had. Ellsberg told me that Harry Rowen "was my older brother, and Albert was my father." Both "were like family to me. . . . I told them anything, everything . . . about my personal life, about everything I was doing." Ellsberg didn't suffer Wohlstetter's knife. Wohlstetter was careful with Ellsberg. "He treated me as an intellectual equal," Ellsberg says. Ellsberg's voice seemingly started to break when he told me, "In fact, he used to say that I was very appreciative of him."[10]

Ellsberg would also become close to Bernard Brodie, another older man. Brodie, too, was drawn to Ellsberg and viewed him almost like a son. Ellsberg would have a history of attraction to powerful older men. They helped him and advanced his career.[11]

In several cases, however, Ellsberg would ultimately bring these men grief.

———— ◦◉◦ ————

Touted by Wohlstetter, Dan Ellsberg, then 28 years old, was considered to be a golden boy when he started at RAND—"a supergenius," the nuclear physicist Arnold Kramish says. "Everybody was raving about him," Kolkowicz found when he arrived at RAND in 1961. "He was considered the whiz." As at Harvard, those around him believed Ellsberg possessed extraordinary intellectual potential. "He was considered the brightest person in RAND," Guy Pauker, who was a RAND political scientist, remembers. "He was considered sort of our pride and joy. 'How wonderful to have Dan Ellsberg.'"[12]

Ellsberg struck some as unusually imaginative and inquisitive. "He was fast on his feet," Norman Dalkey recounts. "Impressive in that respect. . . . He latched onto ideas, and gnawed away at them." He was an exceptionally fast reader. Gus Shubert recalls, "I think in general the economists thought that Dan was potentially a world beater. He had all the assets. He had this very quick mind. He was very, very sharp with understanding substance and being able to put it together and fit the pieces together. That he had all the potential for being either a great theorist or maybe an empiricist or whatever. . . . Everyone sort of regarded him as a man of *great* potential—as I certainly did. . . . He certainly gave you the impression that he was *it*." Ellsberg would go places, Frank Eldridge, a RAND physicist, thought: "He had a presence that people paid attention to."[13]

Ellsberg's intellectual reputation at RAND came mainly from his work in decision theory and game theory. He gave talks on it at RAND. At Schelling's invitation—and repeated prodding, as Ellsberg acknowledged—Ellsberg published an article on decision making under uncertainty entitled "Risk, Ambiguity, and the Savage Axioms" in November 1961. It was a seminal, ground-breaking article. More than any other writing, it made Ellsberg's reputation in intellectual circles. One need only read it to see the enormous power of his intellect. The article remains important in decision theory and in the foundations of probability. "It's one of the few articles that still gets cited," Richard Zeckhauser, a Harvard professor who studies decision theory, points out. "It's very unusual. I don't think it alone had such a great impact, but it was very important as a very clear and very early contribution to this field."[14]

In the article, Ellsberg described a class of situations in which many reasonable people make choices that do not conform to the "Savage axioms," those postulates of rational behavior in the face of uncertainty, specifically choices not conforming to the "sure-thing principle" (perhaps the most controversial of Leonard J. Savage's postulates). These reasonable people included Savage himself, "when last tested by me (I have been reluctant to try him again)," Ellsberg wrote wryly. Ellsberg found that highly ambiguous situations commonly elicit behavior that violates the axioms. People undervalue ambiguous information. Ellsberg's contribution to the field became known as the "Ellsberg paradox." "The results were just of a lot of interest to a lot of people," Dalkey, also a decision theorist, remembers. "He clearly was getting at a very basic issue in the foundations of probability."[15]

But some felt Ellsberg tended to exaggerate the significance of his findings. He was not shy about advertising his insights. "What Ellsberg didn't do is give some rules of how you should behave under those circumstances" in which you don't know the probabilities of relevant events, Dalkey recalls. "He didn't really have much to say about that." Ellsberg "just said, 'Hey, here's a real problem that needs addressing.' But he didn't really address the problem. He just raised it," dramatized it, and gave illustrations, though they were ingenious ones. Some scholars pointed out that the issue had been raised before (as Ellsberg explicitly recognized).[16]

Ellsberg shot onto the scene in decision theory at a young age. He then left it to pursue other interests. "It fits with other things that he was involved with," Dalkey observes. "He was much more interested in making an impact, creating an effect, than in pursuing something to a solid contribution, if you please. And I don't think I'm disparaging the guy when I say that. He wanted to rouse people."[17]

One wonders what Ellsberg might have accomplished had he stuck with it. Though he was not in their class, several decision and game theorists went on to win Nobel Prizes. "I don't think he was ever able to figure out what he wanted to do," Zeckhauser argues. "I saw him figure out that he wanted to do each of a variety of things. And my guess is that if he had pursued one of those things assiduously, he would have figured out in the middle that that's not what he wanted to do."[18]

But Ellsberg would talk about getting back into decision theory later in his life. "Whenever I see him, he asks me, 'What books should I be reading? What are the great books that have come out in our field in the last five years?'" Zeckhauser told me. "And he's always wanting to get back to this field. Which is very hard to do." After Zeckhauser recommended some recent work to Ells-berg, "I saw him again three years later and he hadn't read it. . . . He's told me that he wants to write an article."[19]

Ellsberg's brilliance was his most compelling attribute at RAND, but he had other appealing qualities as well. He had a warm side. "He could be a cold bastard when the occasion demanded," Kolkowicz remembers. "Steely-eyed; cut you right to the ankles. But at the same time, there was a warmth there, which the others" at RAND didn't always have. Ellsberg charmed people. "He was one of the few people whom I could bring to dinner almost anytime with-out my wife objecting," Guy Pauker recalls. His wife, Ewa, a RAND research associate, found Ellsberg dashing and fun-loving, and a good-looking young man. Ellsberg had piercing blue eyes. He drove an Alfa Romeo sports car. "He was always very gallant," Mary Marshall, whose husband, Andrew, was a RAND economist, reminisces. "And he was a kind of breath of fresh air, in a way. Because a lot of people at RAND—men as well as their wives—are pretty stodgy, and tend to be dull." But he and Carol were fun to be with: "We used to laugh a lot. . . . And they were in the real world. They weren't off someplace." Ellsberg picked up Mort Sahl's style of humor, though again there was usually a point behind his wit, which was often at another person's expense. "There's a very deep edge to his humor," Sam Popkin would find. "There's a lot of scoring of points and pinning things down."[20]

Ellsberg's energy continued to attract people. It was electric. "He would jump from one subject to another without having exhausted the first," Simon Bourgin remembers. Ellsberg was gung ho about whatever he set out to do. If he was committed, he was committed 110 percent. "He was very enthusiastic about all this cold war analysis that we used to do—first strike, second strike calculus, all that," David McGarvey recounts. "He approached anything like that with a terrific amount of enthusiasm. And he was good at it." Ellsberg was not the type to suggest a leisurely stroll or a leisurely talk. He was a man of ac-tion, always doing something.[21]

Ellsberg was also a romantic and an aesthetic, made in part of artistic ma-terial, with what seemed to be a volatile emotional make-up. "He was a strange mixture, perhaps, of great intelligence and great emotions," Paul Langer re-calls. "And they don't mix too well." But he also seemed to be "a real human being, not a cold analyst," Langer points out. "So people felt with Ellsberg, and no doubt with Wohlstetter also, 'Here was an unusual combination.' A man who excels, on one hand; on the other hand, he is not averse to showing emo-tions and idealism and romanticism. . . . You cannot help but be intrigued by a person who combines that."[22]

To some, Ellsberg's tendency to show his emotions (perhaps more marked during his second stint at RAND in the late 1960s) was among his alluring qualities. Guy Pauker remembers: "On one occasion I'd brought Dan along to dinner, straight from the office. . . . And during the dinner, Dan says, 'Oh, I'm so glad I'm not alone. It's my birthday today.' And for some reason, Ewa, who doesn't always do that, had made a chocolate cake, which was in the kitchen. And she sneaked into the kitchen and stuck a candle on it and lit it and brought it in. And Dan started crying. He said, 'That's my favorite cake, and nobody has made one for me in so many years.' He'd been divorced by that time. . . . He was emotionally deprived."[23]

And while some at RAND held on tightly to information, Ellsberg liked to share his knowledge and experiences with others, including quite personal experiences. His openness oiled relationships and encouraged the exchange of intimacies. Ellsberg's broad interests appealed to colleagues, too. He remained interested in poetry, literature, and music. One could talk about many things with him, and at a high level.[24]

Some women around RAND found him particularly charming. Rosemary Enthoven, whose husband, Alain, was a RAND economist, "was just mad about Dan," Mary Marshall recalls. "She thought he was wonderful." On the beach one day during his second period at RAND, Ellsberg remarked to Thomas Schelling's wife, "Corinne, you can really fill out a bathing suit." "I remember my mother sort of blushing with enthusiasm," Andrew Schelling recounts. She seemed "very, very pleased. . . . For a few days, she kept bringing it up." Ellsberg appeared to be comfortable with women. "He's more relaxed," Kolkowicz comments. "With men, he's tense. He has to dominate. He has to be in control."[25]

Though appealing in some circles, there were those among Ellsberg's RAND colleagues who felt reserved about him. A few even found him repellent and couldn't understand why others sang his praises. Some were jealous of his brilliance and his reputation as a *Wunderkind*, but a more common reason for their disfavor was his large ego. He seemed to Gus Shubert to have a "general air of superiority." "He struck me as arrogant," Kolkowicz recalls. "A pretty boy. Very self-assured. It was an intellectual arrogance." Ellsberg was enormously prideful of his intellect and seemed to take himself quite seriously. "I remember once I borrowed some money to pay a bill that he and I [had] in the restaurant," Kolkowicz recounts. "And then the following day I went to his office, and I was going to write him a check. . . . And I wrote it, 'Dan Ellsberg,' whatever the amount is. He takes the check, he says, 'Why Dan? *Daniel.*' Who gives a shit? I mean, it's a check. He says, 'No, I will not accept this check.' I didn't have a checkbook with me . . . so I actually have to kind of fit in

'Daniel.' . . . He was *deadly* serious. It was the most amazing thing." Ellsberg, Kolkowicz continues, "was extremely self-aware and self-conscious about himself and his role. . . . He sometimes would refer to himself almost like in the third person. . . . There was an extreme sense of self, an extreme ego. . . . He thought he cast a very large shadow. . . . The way he looked at others it was like . . . he wasn't interested. *He* was the only [one], always at the center stage. His thing was always central. . . . By and large, he walked alone. And we, the rest of us, were sort of the dim periphery." Ellsberg seemed to have a desperate desire to stand out. As a government consultant, he was "a kind of Zelig," Kolkowicz remembers. "He was everywhere. And at important event[s], he always made sure he was up front. . . . There was almost something childish [about it]. He wasn't aware, particularly, that what he was doing was kind of crass and obvious."[26]

"Ambitious, I think, is the word," Dalkey comments. "You could see it. He was going places. He wasn't going to be mundane." Some thought him an opportunist. Ellsberg seemed to see himself in heroic terms. "He pictured himself as destined for some heroic role," another RAND analyst, who enjoyed his company, recalls. "Being an individual at the leading edge who could make a big difference was an important motivator for Dan. . . . There was a lot of acting out." Of course, that's a perception easier to offer in retrospect, but it's not an uncommon one of Ellsberg, including among people on the left. "Always, there was the romance of Ellsberg," Kolkowicz says. "He had a romantic sense of himself, a vision of himself, and his role in the larger scheme of things. . . . And there was sometimes a euphoria. He would talk . . . and he would get *carried away*."[27]

Ellsberg's competitiveness also rubbed some of his RAND colleagues the wrong way. William Kaufmann, a modest man, had difficulty working with him. "I have to confess to you, I never did like Dan from the outset," Kaufmann told me. "I found him just not my style. . . . I thought he was very abrasive." Ellsberg "was sort of immediately attacking you, whether he had any basis for it or not. I just frankly always felt very uncomfortable around him. . . . He was very critical of other people's work. And I don't know whether that was related to his concern about what other people would say about his work." Often, when Ellsberg fired off a series of questions at one of his colleagues, he was not only trying to learn from the colleague, but probing for weaknesses in the colleague's arguments. ("In asking questions, he would be as intense as in making a statement," his later friend Howard Zinn would find. "He would *bombard* you with questions . . . one after the other, without a second in between. Almost as if he's said, 'Okay, I'm going to interrogate.'" "Dan knows how to zero in and *get* you in that spot," Sam Popkin discovered. "He knows how to get to *the* spot where you're pinned, and you have no choice but to give the answer he wants. . . . He knows how to skewer you.")[28]

Norman Dalkey, another modest man, had his own problems working with Ellsberg. Not long after Ellsberg started at RAND, they collaborated on a project on the command and control of nuclear weapons. "I didn't find him comfortable to work with," Dalkey remembers. "He didn't like to listen to other people's ideas that weren't quite in his [perspective]." Ellsberg was a man who was "pursuing his own course. He was not a team player." Dalkey found him pushy and always charged up (not a good combination). Ellsberg insisted on publishing separately his part of a paper they'd worked on together (though his paper was likely never published).[29]

Other colleagues also found Ellsberg too sure of his own ideas. He struck some as a true believer and a zealot. He sometimes sounded like "some Baptist minister," Trinkl thought—"the founder of a revealed truth." Many would conclude later that he was the kind of man who could move from one extreme to another, another judgment easier to offer in retrospect, but one that fits nonetheless.[30]

Many questioned Ellsberg's judgment. Some thought him on the immature side. He often spoke ahead of himself. Konrad Kellen, who knew Ellsberg in the late 1960s at RAND and liked him, thought Ellsberg's mind tended to "run away with him a little bit once in a while." And Ellsberg showed a "poor sense of proportion," Kellen remembers:

> For example, we were talking about the treatment of blacks in this country, which he didn't like. He says to me, "*Well.* . . . The way we treat the blacks here, it's exactly like the Nazis treated the Jews." I said, "*Dan.* I mean, Auschwitz? Women, children, and old men being shot with machine guns and thrown into ditches that they had first to dig. I mean, how can you—a Jew, an intelligent person, and a man who has traveled—how can you say that? I mean, the blacks are obviously treated very poorly in this country, and it's a shame. But how can you make such a statement?" . . . It shows this sort of exaggerated mind. At that moment, he believed it! Now, who would come to such a conclusion? Either an extremely unknowledgeable person who doesn't know what Auschwitz is, has no idea what went on with the Jews in Germany, or somebody whose mind runs away with him in a strange way. . . . Also, it's sort of a powerful statement to make—like a powerful statement if you put out these [Pentagon] Papers.

Ellsberg was excitable, even mercurial, which clouded his judgment; his emotions seemed to carry him away like waves at times. Some thought him a little unstable (though he was hardly the only RAND analyst in that boat). Some of his colleagues simply found him too intense. One didn't really have casual conversations with Ellsberg. ("The words have all rung in my ears of a British girl that I'd fallen briefly intensely in love with," he told me. "I can hear her words saying, 'You're too *intense* for me.'")[31]

——◦◦◦——

Though Ellsberg enjoyed the RAND social scene, his wife was less pleased with it. Carol was generally well liked in RAND circles, but RAND gatherings were not her cup of tea. The RAND men would always be clustered among themselves in another part of the room, or even in another room altogether, or out on a porch or deck. They liked to talk shop, and their wives were not supposed to hear classified information. It was a man's world. Ellsberg and other analysts weren't even supposed to tell their *own* spouses about their classified work (though Ellsberg would sometimes try to pass on confidential information to Carol, which she would tell him he shouldn't be talking about). Carol consequently didn't know much about Dan's work.[32] They were on separate tracks.

Carol did become friends with a few RAND wives, though. "She and I used to exchange cracks about people," Mary Marshall remembers. "There was a kind of rapport," and "because she didn't find so many people there that were a lot of fun, she glommed onto me."[33]

"I loved RAND," Daniel Ellsberg told me a number of times, once with some emotion. "He thrived in the place," Thomas Schelling remembers:

> That was exactly where he wanted to be. I think it's partly that RAND let him do what he wanted to do. He could do theoretical things, he could get involved in very practical things. He had sort of carte blanche. It was almost like being a junior fellow in a classified environment. . . . And I think there were people there whom he could genuinely admire. . . . Dan was surrounded by very interesting people doing very interesting work, and people who knew a lot about weapons and command and control and things of that sort, which intrigued him. . . . I don't think Dan could have imagined a better place to work.

Ellsberg would later look back on his time at RAND as an idyllic sort of existence: "I'd pick my own problems; no one would ever ask me what I was doing from one month to the next, and they would supply me with any books I wanted and copies of journal articles almost instantly." As at Harvard, Ellsberg reveled in the intellectual sparring and the blunt criticism, particularly when he was doling it out.[34] Not least attractive, through his writing, through consulting in Washington, he could influence people in positions of power. Ellsberg was attracted to power. In his position, he could get close to the center of real power, and maybe even exert some power.

One source of power was information, and one type of information was secret information. Ellsberg loved having access to highly classified information at RAND and in Washington. It fascinated him and made him feel important. "He *loved* to have the inside dope," Gus Shubert remembers. "Then he'd also feel free to criticize: 'And that's why I'm asking this.' . . . He *loved* to be in the know. You know, peeking through the window and seeing what's going on inside where nobody else could see in." Reveling in classified information was a pervasive illness at RAND, but Ellsberg sometimes carried it to extreme lengths.[35]

He occasionally visited Joan Friedman in New York in the early 1960s. "Everything was supersecret, and he couldn't talk about anything, because it was all classified," she remembers. "This was part of, 'I'm a genius, and they trust me. I'm better than you. I'm smarter than you. I'm more trustworthy than you.'" And I know things you don't know and I can't tell you about them.[36]

Ellsberg would later acknowledge to a journalist that reading classified documents in the Pentagon initially gave him a tremendous feeling of power. "It's a power to manipulate, and it's an extremely heady feeling to be on the inside, having secret knowledge. . . . Those first tastes of secrecy are extremely heady and addicting." Ellsberg told me: "I understood the value of knowing secrets that other people didn't have, and what one could do with that, in the way of changing policy, in the way of getting access to other secrets. . . . You couldn't know too many high secrets. Because they would be useful one way or another in getting done what I wanted done." Those secrets would also allow him to promote himself, both in Washington and at RAND. For one way to make yourself valuable to others is to convey that you possess something they need. There was also the appeal of "the secret as ornament: 'I know something you don't know,'" Ellsberg acknowledges. And he simply had a boyish enthusiasm for knowing secrets. "I took to it very much. . . . Definitely more than many."[37]

Ellsberg would ultimately have very high security clearances and access to quite sensitive material (apparently mainly for his work on nuclear command and control, and then later for a study of crises). At one point, he had "about a dozen" security clearances above top secret, he would say. He also claimed that he had one more clearance than did the chairman of the Joint Chiefs of Staff, General Earle Wheeler.[38]

Discretion was not Ellsberg's strong suit; indeed, it never would be. He liked to tell others about his high clearances. He boasted about it. "I remember that we all knew that Dan would brag about being privy to highly classified stuff," Jim Digby remembers. "He was always telling us if we knew what he knew," Roman Kolkowicz says. "This was the truth that we didn't have. . . . It was part of his myth. That he is seeing things we will never see." Ellsberg was forever "grabbing people in the hall and saying, 'Step in here. I have to tell you what's going on,'" Shubert recounts. He obviously derived great pleasure from it. Adam Yarmolinsky, who was Secretary of Defense Robert McNamara's special assistant, remembered that Ellsberg developed a reputation for loose lips among some people while consulting in the Pentagon (though Yarmolinsky did not know of any instances in which he violated security). Some colleagues grew to dislike Ellsberg in part because of his indiscretion, which could come back to harm them. But his ego and insecurities apparently compelled him to talk; he hoped to impress people and sought recognition.[39]

Ellsberg's loose talk also reflected another facet of his personality. "It's an aspect of Dan that may be the most important aspect of his entire temperament," Thomas Schelling argues:

> I think Dan had a youthful enthusiasm. And the thing that distinguishes Dan from anybody else I knew is that whenever Dan discovered something that he thought was original and important, he couldn't wait to tell you. . . . And that was the way Dan was whenever he got a game theory idea or a strategic idea. He just *had* to let you know it. . . . And that, I think, is exactly what I was reminded of when the Pentagon Papers hit the streets. I said to myself, "That's got to be Dan Ellsberg. . . . When Dan knows something, he just can't hold it back." . . . And part of it's getting credit. I think Dan is . . . like any scientific genius who just is enraptured by his own discoveries, but they're no good unless somebody else can appreciate them.[40]

But while some RAND colleagues wondered at times if Ellsberg's indiscretion risked security and thought his boasting was a bit unusual, they didn't worry about him a great deal, Digby recalls, as they felt his talk would be kept within proper channels. And he could be cautious and calculating. "Dan Ellsberg is a person who is both the most guarded and the most blurty person you'll know," Sam Popkin aptly comments. "One minute he's talking about his intimate sex practices. The next minute he's playing a multilevel game so deep that nobody, even a Kissinger or a Schelling, could see what he was doing or where he was going."[41]

Ellsberg maintains he was careful with classified information:

> If I was a person with a need to tell a secret, I would never have gotten the secrets that I got. I don't need to tell a secret. . . . I was trusted, I was given jobs that required discretion, that simply no one had ever been given at RAND. . . .

I had an acute sense of what, in my profession, it was alright to tell this person, and what was not. . . . The idea of saying he had to boast about what he knew that other people didn't know—I'm just telling you, had I had that strongly and had I not been able to rise above that early in my career, I would never have gotten to where I got. And where I got was to have twelve clearances higher than top secret.

"I used extremely good judgment as to who I would tell what," Ellsberg claims.[42]

Todd Gitlin, who spent a lot of time with Ellsberg between the mid-1970s and the early 1980s, came to conclude that divulging secrets was "central to him," however:

I was quite fascinated by him as a human force. And I developed something of a psychoanalytic theory of him and what makes him tick. I saw him as a man for whom the center of his existence was leaking. . . . This is what he did, in meetings or through the course of conversation . . . : "Here I'm going to tell you something I've never told anyone. I'm going to leak it to you." I think he has a passionate need to reveal secrets. But it's not what it appears to be on the surface. His obsession with revelation is, I think, a kind of hiding in plain sight. In other words, a keeper of deep secrets goes around making many smaller revelations in order to convince himself that he is an open book. Many people like talking about themselves. But I've never heard anybody else couch so many factual revelations in this form: "Here's something I've never told anyone before." So it's not just the need to talk. It's also the need to be the center, to be riveting another person one to one. . . . He compulsively needs to leak to a person.

The attorney Marty Garbus, who got to know Ellsberg in the late 1960s, says with a laugh, "If you want to keep a secret—badly—you tell it to Dan." Ellsberg admitted to me in 1995 that his judgment was "not what it used to be"— prompting his wife, Patricia, who was sitting with us, to remark with a laugh, "I'm not sure it ever was that good."[43]

"Don't tell me a secret that cannot be told to somebody else," Ellsberg cautioned me. "If there's something that I should absolutely, must not tell anybody, don't tell me."[44]

———※———

The RAND of Ellsberg's time was a place where men were thinking about nuclear war, how to deter it but also how to wage and survive it. Many felt a nuclear war with the Soviet Union was not unlikely. SAC bases were vulnerable to a surprise Soviet attack, many believed (following Wohlstetter), and the Soviets might well take advantage of that. Some analysts felt a sense of urgency. It was still the age of the missile gap, when most believed the Soviets had growing missile superiority. Ellsberg and others worried that the Soviets might use that superiority to destroy the United States's retaliatory capacity. Many Americans built bomb shelters at their homes. Robert McNamara apprised President Kennedy in 1961 that "without fallout protection, even a missile attack on SAC that avoided cities would probably result in the deaths of 50 to 100 million Americans." "It was scary," Frank Trinkl recalls; many felt that the United States was on a collision course with the Soviet Union. Ellsberg and a lot of others were "really afraid that nuclear war was imminent," Schelling remembers. Ellsberg referred several times in a 1960 paper to the *first* thermonuclear war, as if he expected it.[45]

The hawkish RAND nuclear physicist Herman Kahn, a gregarious and obese man whom the Wohlstetters once weighed "by displacement" in their swimming pool, was a leader of work at RAND on developing a nuclear war-fighting capability. Kahn, who viewed himself as someone not afraid to ask the hard questions, came out in 1960 with a remarkably insensitive tome entitled *On Thermonuclear War*. Kahn argued that nuclear war with the Soviet Union would not necessarily bring about mutual annihilation, and that U.S. preparations and war strategy would significantly affect the amount of destruction. If "we can cut the number of dead from 40 to 20 million, we have done something vastly worth doing!" Kahn exclaimed. As for the question, "Will the survivors envy the dead?," he contended that all the destruction and suffering "would not preclude normal and happy lives for the majority of survivors and their descendants." With the right preparations, "the restoration of our prewar GNP should take place in a relatively short time—*if we can hold the damage to the equivalent of something like 53 metropolitan areas destroyed.*" While "it would not be surprising if almost everybody vomits," Kahn said, the distribution of radiation meters would help boost morale. Say a person gets sick simply from anxiety or such: "You look at his meter and say, 'You have received only ten roentgens [of radiation], why are you vomiting? Pull yourself together and get to work.'" Kahn also argued for a credible U.S. first strike capability. Ellsberg read and commented on Kahn's manuscript. In one paper, he favorably cited Kahn's (bloodless) discussion of war strategy and how and why a nuclear war might get initiated—which included such statements as, "A nation such as the United States might be willing to fight to the last man, but there are *almost no circumstances that are likely to occur* in which it should be willing to fight to the last woman and child." Ellsberg looked up to Kahn "intellectually," Carol

Cummings remembers. "I think Dan enjoyed Herman Kahn," Schelling says. Kahn may have had similar feelings about Ellsberg since he quoted extensively from Ellsberg's Lowell Institute lecture on Hitler's diplomacy.[46]

Some remember the Dan Ellsberg of this time as a nuclear hawk. In discussions at RAND on nuclear matters, "there was a kind of callousness about him that stunned the hell out of me," Kolkowicz recalls. Both Kolkowicz and his friend Arnold Horelick, also a RAND Soviet expert, were struck by his callousness and "the facile way" he spoke about nuclear weapons, Kolkowicz recounts:

> We all know how Herman Kahn spoke: "Six months later, after a big nuclear war, we'll come back and da da da da da." You know, this kind of [stuff]—that's Herman. And we all made fun of Herman at the time. But in a different way, Dan was . . . romantic about nuclear weapons. Not the use of them for killing people, but the way you can manipulate other people. The various means— clever means—you can use them in a way either to maintain the peace or destroy the enemy. He had . . . a primitive view of the Soviet adversary, the Communist adversary. . . . It was the evil Bolshevik, you know, and we are the good guys.[47]

Richard Barnet had some contact with Ellsberg when Barnet was in the government in the early 1960s. He, too, remembers Ellsberg as "a real nuclear hawk" at the time. Ellsberg and others talked of "options," making nuclear weapons "relevant," and "tailoring deterrence" to "all levels of conflict," Barnet recalls. "It's always the paradox of whether you have the weapons in a state of untouchable horror, or whether . . . you try to make them usable in different actual war plan scenarios. And I think that was very much his line." Richard Elms remembers that Ellsberg was eager to see Edward Teller, the father of the hydrogen bomb, during one of Teller's visits to RAND. "He was excited about seeing him," Elms chuckles. "He knew he was in the building and made it a point to go down the hall and see if he could catch a glimpse of him."[48]

But Ellsberg may have had a more sensitive moral compass about war than most RAND analysts. "The thing that I remember most strongly was the feeling on his part that everybody, but in particular national leaders and national military leaders, should have a strong moral sense and a strong moral sense of responsibility," Norman Dalkey reminisces. But as far as Ellsberg expressing concern for potential war victims, "I never heard that," Kolkowicz recalls. RAND men were expected to act like detached surgeons with a knife, and Ellsberg would be "the coolest surgeon."[49]

Ellsberg became immersed in nuclear command and control, a process within the U.S. military that involved gathering and communicating information, and planning and directing military actions. Ellsberg explored questions such as: How might the process of going to war get started? How clear are the lines of authority? How well understood are the procedures? How reliable and efficient are the communication channels? In a 1960 paper on nuclear command and control, which he provided to me, Ellsberg argued that the United States must be prepared to fight a thermonuclear war with the Soviet Union and to achieve the best possible outcome, one serving U.S. interests. A nuclear war was not impossible or unthinkable, he maintained, nor should deterrence be the United States's only strategic objective. He opposed an all-out attack on enemy cities but considered a retaliatory strike on population possible; he argued that a surviving control capacity might greatly increase the strike's efficiency. He also left open the possibility of exploiting Soviet vulnerability through a preemptive first strike (though he now says, "I was totally against a first strike"). Ellsberg contended that strategic threats were a powerful means of improving the war's outcome. He stressed that the United States must have a reliable and efficient command and control system, one capable of surviving a Soviet attack, with a capacity for flexibility and discrimination, rather than one programmed simply for an all-out response. But it should have the capacity to wipe out a substantial portion of remaining Soviet forces. Kahn's manuscript for *On Thermonuclear War* was one of the five references Ellsberg cited.[50]

In a February 1961 paper, one circulated in the Kennedy administration, Ellsberg argued the advantages of hardened and fixed primary command centers. Without them, he wrote, the United States might be relinquishing any chance of exploiting weaknesses in a Soviet attack and might even allow the Soviets to paralyze U.S. retaliatory capacity.[51] Ellsberg was clearly a man who judged the U.S. nuclear war–fighting capability important.

His research on command and control impressed some colleagues. Frank Eldridge, an expert in the field, thought "he was very good at setting up the measures of effectiveness of operations or systems and determining what should go into different decision-making processes." Ellsberg did a complex analysis of time lags and uncertainties in the communication process. "He kept telling me things that I didn't know that were useful to know," Adam Yarmolinsky recounted. "The most striking I remember," Yarmolinsky told me, resulted from a trip Ellsberg took to the Pacific to study nuclear command and control for the Office of Naval Research in late 1959. In Okinawa or Japan, "he looked at the airplanes that were kept on alert there that were supposed to be dual purpose: nuclear and nonnuclear," Yarmolinsky recalled. "But he came and told me that the bomb racks for the nuclear bombs were rusted on . . . frozen on to the airplanes. That was the kind of thing that he came up with. And he had a knack for ferreting out that kind of thing."[52]

In the Pacific, Ellsberg viewed classified war plans affecting the Pacific Command. "I became probably as familiar with the content of those war plans . . . as any civilian in the country," he bragged later. The plans troubled Ellsberg. They seemed to be inflexible, and he was told that President Eisenhower had delegated the authority to use nuclear weapons to a number of unified and specified military commanders if Washington was out of contact. Thus, generals and admirals might be using their own judgment about whether to launch nuclear weapons. Their judgment might not be good or even based on accurate information. Ellsberg later told Carl Kaysen and others about the situation. "He was saying, in effect, he doubted that the commanders really thought they had to wait for a presidential order," Kaysen, who was a member of the Kennedy administration, recalls. "And he doubted that the chain was as strong as it was supposed to be." And "I'm sure he was correct." Kaysen also worried about the military's judgment on using nuclear weapons. He had personally heard General Curtis LeMay say, "The Russians will attack us early some morning. Somebody will wake the president up at 4 A.M. and tell him we're under attack. What does the poor son of a bitch know about it? What will he know about what to do? *I* know what to do." Also, the Joint Chiefs of Staff killed a proposal to build a deep underground shelter and command post for U.S. officials beneath the Potomac River, "and we used to believe the chiefs were opposed to it because they thought, if there was a war, they would be better off without the president and secretary of defense," Kaysen says.[53]

But Kaysen felt that Ellsberg's assessment of the situation reflected the element of extremism in his personality, his tendency to push things a little too far. "It isn't that I thought Dan was exaggerating the basic situation," Kaysen says. "I don't think he was. But somehow it was always sort of slightly larger than life." Kaysen knew there was "a very complicated set of authorizations" on using nuclear weapons to which Ellsberg was probably not privy. Further, Eisenhower had made delegations to use nuclear weapons in emergency situations to just three of the unified and specified military commanders, "not to anyone else," Kaysen remembers. (But Ellsberg may have thought three were plenty.) Also, "the issue came up in the Kennedy White House about these delegations," Kaysen recounts. "The question was whether they were valid or not, since Kennedy had made no such delegations. And the best view of the president's legal advisers . . . was that the delegations . . . couldn't be from the past president. . . . And the question was, Should he revoke them?" The answer was no, Kennedy and Robert McNamara decided, "that this might raise a political storm, and that the commanders would themselves be sort of dubious enough about whether they existed that they would hardly want to rely on them." Kaysen remembers having "the renewed sense that Dan is one hundred and ten percent. Intense, hyped."[54]

In 1961, Robert McNamara constituted a task force for planning a unified national command and control system. Ellsberg claimed later that he was a member of the task force; in fact, he said, he jointly represented both the National Security Council and the Defense Department on it. McGeorge Bundy, the national security adviser, had requested that he serve on it, Ellsberg said. But Kaysen, who was one of the two White House representatives on the task force with Tazewell Shepard, says that isn't true. "Dan was certainly not on the task force," Kaysen recalls. "I was a deputy special assistant to the president. Shepard was the president's naval aide. It was at that level. And Dan was not at that level. Now, he may have gone to several meetings," and "I do remember talking to him a lot. So he was involved." So was Frank Eldridge, who says, "I don't remember him contributing too much to the task force."[55]

<hr>

While in the Pacific studying command and control in January 1960, Ellsberg met Gary Snyder, the Beat poet. One day in Kyoto, Japan, after visiting the Ryoanji rock garden and checking out a number of hostess bars with "gorgeous hostesses" sitting on the stools, in a district westerners usually did not visit, Ellsberg came across what looked like a beer hall where the waitresses were "wearing nothing at all but transparent shortie nightgowns," he would recount. "I decided to go in." There he encountered Snyder, whom he already knew as the character Japhy Ryder from Jack Kerouac's *The Dharma Bums*. Ellsberg looked quite out of place and was having a hard time communicating with the waitress, so Snyder helped him order and they ended up talking for hours. The next day, wearing his green marine raincoat and short hair, Ellsberg visited Snyder at the poet's home outside Kyoto. Snyder was a pacifist, and "we argued about pacifism," Ellsberg wrote later. Snyder found Ellsberg a worthy opponent, and there was nothing like one of those. Ellsberg "sized up my host that day as—something I was not used to feeling—a better man than I was. His life was more together. I was as smart as he was, but he was wise. That was an unsettling thing to find in someone who was almost exactly the same age. . . . He seemed to me very much my senior." Snyder exhibited "a composure, a capacity for sudden calm . . . that I lacked," Ellsberg recalled. He told Snyder his story—"rarely shared," he would claim—of how he lost his virginity in Wyoming. "I had, then as now, a passionate obsession with preventing nuclear weapons from being used by anyone ever again that he probably would have respected if he had known it," Ellsberg also recounted.[56] In reality, it is unlikely Snyder would have cared much for Ellsberg's views on nuclear strategy.

---·◆·---

In 1960, after viewing the war plans affecting the Pacific Command, Ellsberg spent time in Washington further studying command and control. He met several colonels on the air force staff, who, he said later, divulged to him some of the war plans of the Joint Chiefs of Staff (JCS) and air force. These plans were also inflexible and undiscriminating, he learned. It was also unlikely that they would be executed as designed; the timing and coordination of U.S. bombings were problematic. The air force colonels talked to him for several days—six to eight hours at a stretch—about the plans, Ellsberg recalled. But retired Major General Robert Lukeman, who was one of the colonels, told me "these conversations were extremely brief" and probably occurred only "three or four times." Ellsberg's recollection of six-to-eight-hour talks over several days is "pure fantasy," Lukeman said. "He used to drop by the office and lean on the edge of the desk and ruminate and disturb our work," Lukeman remembered. But Ellsberg says, "I dealt a lot very closely with Lukeman." Lukeman acknowledged discussing with Ellsberg the need—also felt strongly by the colonels—for greater flexibility in nuclear war planning but seemed reticent to admit to any relationship with Ellsberg. Another of the colonels, retired Lieutenant General Glenn Kent, did, too, when I phoned him. When told that Ellsberg remembered discussing JCS and air force war plans with him and the other colonels, Kent responded, "I don't recall any such conversation," though "that didn't mean he didn't have them with somebody else."[57]

Ellsberg also recalled that the colonels showed him the Joint Strategic Capabilities Plan (JSCP), one of the JCS's strategic planning documents. One annex of the JSCP contained prescriptions for the use of nuclear weapons. The JSCP called for launching a nuclear attack on all cities and military targets in the Soviet Union, Eastern Europe, and China as quickly as possible in the event the United States and Soviet Union were engaged in armed conflict, Ellsberg remembered. And it could be executed by military leaders, he believed, if the president was out of contact. Ellsberg would claim to be the only civilian—including the president and secretary of defense—to have seen the JSCP. Both Lukeman and Kent denied showing it to him.[58]

Ellsberg spoke to RAND colleagues and Kennedy administration officials about the JSCP. He would remember talking to incoming officials Paul Nitze and Walt Rostow about it in the fall of 1960 (though Rostow has no memory of that). Ellsberg briefed McGeorge Bundy on the JSCP in early 1961. Bundy was extremely impressed by his briefing, Ellsberg said later, and allowed him to talk much longer than was usual for briefers. Bundy also thanked him effusively, according to Ellsberg. "I made a lot of effort to try to get the president to read the JSCP," Ellsberg recalls. Kennedy never did, though Bundy and Kaysen "read all my quite detailed memos on what was wrong with the plan."[59]

Gus Shubert recounts that after Ellsberg read the JSCP and returned to RAND, he "was scurrying around the halls—as only Dan could do—'You won't believe what I've seen! . . . It's incredible! Do you know what they're going to do!? . . . RAND has to get in there and fight against that.' Which I think was basically right. But it's just his style. . . . He was very, very much taken aback by it. And at that point he did translate it into the number of lives that would be lost, and that sort of thing. He thought it was a great crime to rely on a plan like this."[60]

But Ellsberg exaggerated the significance of the JSCP. It was guidance to the unified and specified military commanders, who each prepared their own nuclear war plans, rather than an operational war plan per se. "It's a kind of big-think document," Kaysen says. It did not fully control the commanders' plans, which, in turn, would not fully control the course of a nuclear war. And it was assuredly not *the* U.S. war plan, as Ellsberg has often stated (though, in theory, it guided the war plan of SAC, which controlled most of the country's nuclear weapons). U.S. nuclear war planning was not yet centralized. "Oh, good God, no," Lukeman replied when I asked him if the JSCP was the central U.S. war plan. And it "was not a war plan in any sense of the word. It was a general capabilities plan. . . . You could have handed a copy of it to the Kremlin and they wouldn't have known a hell of a lot about anything. . . . Nobody at the time paid any attention to the JSCP." William Kaufmann says, "It's mostly a collection of contingency plans. . . . The chiefs had been very fussy about making the JSCP available, but I'm not sure that it's because of the sensitivity they assigned to the JSCP or because they just don't want the civilians poking around in their planning." Ellsberg would claim that the JCS called the JSCP a capabilities plan as cover to hide the fact it was an operations plan. "There was no real war plan," Lukeman scoffs. Ellsberg "blew that up way out of proportion."[61]

That he did reflected not only his genuine horror at the specter of an all-out nuclear war but a desire to promote himself. He was a man with unusual access, Ellsberg was telling others, one who knew something so powerful that even President Kennedy should be informed of it. This was secrets as power.

Though Ellsberg was a skillful manipulator of the Washington scene, it seems unlikely he was the only civilian to see the JSCP. "Something like that is probably absurd," Kaysen comments.[62] Robert McNamara, for one, surely could have obtained the JSCP if he wished. But whether he did is another question.

More interesting is what Ellsberg's claim says about him. As noted earlier, he has frequently professed to be the only person or the first person to have done something or to have discovered something. "This is standard with Dan," Kolkowicz observes. "He was always the first, the best, the youngest, or whatever." Such talk reflects, in all likelihood, Ellsberg's extreme need to stand out, doubts about his actual achievements, and insecurity. "He did many, many important and exciting things," Kolkowicz points out. So "why does he need to brag beyond it, so it actually cheapens [the accomplishment]? . . . But there was a compulsion."[63]

Ellsberg also tends to overstate his involvement in events of this period (and other periods), probably for the same reasons. Frank Trinkl will sometimes be reading about defense issues in the early 1960s and think, "Oh, was I really in the Pentagon at that time, or was it all Dan Ellsberg?" When working on nuclear command and control in 1959 and 1960, Ellsberg likes to say, he was working for President Eisenhower, or when consulting later for Harry Rowen that he was working for President Kennedy. He will speak of "my former boss Lyndon Johnson." He was "a kind of assistant" to Robert McNamara, McGeorge Bundy, Paul Nitze, and other senior officials, Ellsberg would claim. He has often stated that he served "15 years in the executive branch"—a period that would include time he spent in the marines and at Harvard. He also claimed to be the first person at RAND to learn there was no missile gap. Others there didn't know the gap was a myth until he gave a top-secret briefing at RAND on the gap in the fall of 1961, he said.[64]

"That's baloney," Andrew Marshall responds to Ellsberg's last claim. Marshall had felt the gap was a myth during Kennedy's 1960 presidential campaign (which had exploited the notion of a gap) and had doubted the actual number of Russian missiles even before then. A few others at RAND had also questioned the gap, though most did not. Marshall remembers that Ellsberg himself had arranged for Marshall to speak to Deirdre Henderson of the Kennedy campaign specifically to tell her what he thought about the gap. Robert McNamara had unguardedly said there was no gap at a background press briefing in February 1961, and the following month McGeorge Bundy had written in a secret memo, "The phrase 'missile gap' is now a genuinely misleading one." No one from RAND that I talked to could remember Ellsberg's RAND briefing, but assuming it occurred, some may have doubted his message for another reason. "Dan was obviously so wrapped up in not only conveying the truth, but conveying the idea that he is the man who found the truth," Shubert remembers. "And people don't know whether he's exaggerating what he's saying in order to make himself more important or what."[65]

Ellsberg has also often claimed that he wrote the guidance to the JCS for developing a new U.S. nuclear war plan in 1961. McNamara assigned him the job, he told an interviewer. McNamara "gave my draft, under his name, to the joint chiefs without any change," he said. Taking it a step further, Ellsberg has also often claimed that he wrote the war plan itself. "I drafted the nuclear war plan for the Kennedy administration," he told another interviewer. "I wrote the fucking war plan," he told me. He said he did it for Harry Rowen. "I wrote every word of it." Then Ellsberg quickly stopped himself and acknowledged, "I didn't write every word of the war plan. I wrote every word of the Sec Def guidance to the Joint Chiefs of Staff on war plans. . . . Which is quite detailed guidance." The actual plan was developed by the Joint Strategic Target Planning Staff.[66]

New guidance was indeed drawn up, as was a new war plan. In late 1960, the Joint Strategic Target Planning Staff had put together a Single Integrated Operational Plan (SIOP-62) for fighting a nuclear war. It was an attempt to strengthen coordination of the military's nuclear war plans. SIOP-62, which came into effect in April 1961, planned for launching the entire U.S. strategic force, including 3,500 nuclear weapons, against the Soviet Union, China, and satellite countries in the event of hostilities. It could be executed either in retaliation of a Soviet nuclear attack or as a preemptive strike. The idea was to destroy all targets in one gigantic spasm. Casualties would have been unimaginable. The plan was "dangerously rigid," McGeorge Bundy wrote Kennedy in July 1961. "In essence, the current plan calls for shooting off everything we have in one shot, and is so constructed as to make any more flexible course very difficult." Both McNamara and Kennedy were disturbed when briefed on SIOP-62.[67]

In March 1961, McNamara assigned 96 projects to the Defense Department, the first being to "prepare a draft memorandum revising the basic national security policies and assumptions, including the assumptions relating to 'counterforce' strikes and the initiation of the use of tactical nuclear weapons." The second was to "prepare and examine a 'doctrine' which, if accepted, would permit controlled response and negotiating pauses in the event of thermonuclear attack." Ellsberg recalls that Harry Rowen (then in the Pentagon) assigned him the first project, and that the memorandum he drafted revising the United States's basic national security policy (BNSP) was sent by McNamara to the JCS as McNamara's guidance for developing a new nuclear war plan, SIOP-63. His memorandum was around "five times longer than any previous

BNSP," he says. "I was totally revising the BNSP." His memo argued against "indiscriminate initial attacks on all major urban-industrial centers," but said U.S. forces should be retained to "threaten those targets." Ellsberg felt there had to be choices. Options.[68]

But two authors who examined U.S. war planning suggest that while Ellsberg's draft was part of the guidance McNamara sent the JCS, it was not the guidance as a whole. McNamara issued "a series of guidelines," one writes. Ellsberg's draft was the "central war section" of the guidance, the other says. It also seems unlikely (though not impossible) that McNamara sent Ellsberg's draft to the JCS "without any change," as Ellsberg has claimed. Ellsberg was a quite junior figure, and whatever he wrote would probably have been vetted by others. One author says Alain Enthoven and Frank Trinkl (both in the Pentagon) took Ellsberg's guidance and developed it further, providing more detail and specifying options. But Trinkl himself doesn't remember working with Ellsberg on this piece of guidance, or even working with any draft memorandum by Ellsberg—"not at all." He and Enthoven wrote the guidance for constructing SIOP-63, Trinkl recalls. "We did our own draft. . . . If a draft [by Ellsberg] had existed, it wasn't shared. And I don't know why it would not have been shared."[69]

Ellsberg recognizes this subsequent work on the guidance, but argues, "Mine is sort of the basic document." The later work that involved defining the options occurred "after my thing had been accepted by McNamara as his guidance." And he contributed extensively to the later work too, he says, and shaped the result significantly.[70]

One has to be skeptical of Ellsberg's boast, or the boast of anyone that they alone wrote a major government policy. That's not the way it usually works, and it certainly doesn't appear to have worked that way in this case. The bottom line seems to be that Enthoven, Trinkl, Ellsberg, and Rowen all contributed to the guidance. Robert Lukeman, who was assigned the second of McNamara's 96 projects, and whose advocacy of flexibility and graduated options may have also fed into the guidance, was incredulous when I told him that Ellsberg claimed he wrote it himself and that McNamara signed his draft unchanged: "That's nonsense." Rowen later seemed to equate Enthoven's work on the options with the guidance. Carl Kaysen, who was also involved in efforts to get SIOP-62 changed, and who helped write a memo for Kennedy and McNamara on what was wrong with it, does not believe Ellsberg's claim. William Kaufmann also worked on McNamara's project number one; in a sign of Rowen's liking and respect for Ellsberg, Rowen had assigned Kaufmann the section on conventional forces, Ellsberg the section on nuclear forces, although

Kaufmann, by experience and expertise, would have been the natural choice for the nuclear part. Kaufmann doesn't recall that Ellsberg ever wrote anything for his section.[71]

The guidance for constructing SIOP-63 called for greater flexibility and discrimination. The "balls out" strategy of the previous plan would only be pursued if less severe, prior options failed to yield satisfactory results. But the options "all involved large attacks, and civilian damage, at least from radioactive fallout, would have been very heavy," Rowen wrote.[72]

Ellsberg also has been known to suggest that it was the alarms he sounded about the murderous character of U.S. war plans that led to the revision of SIOP-62. "One of my missions was to get the secretary of defense to take command of that issue and to tell the joint chiefs what the plan should be," he told me. "And that was accomplished. I was very proud of that, and felt that it was an improvement." But while Ellsberg's efforts may well have heightened concern over the military's plans, the fact of the matter is that McNamara, Enthoven, and Kennedy, among others, didn't need him to tell them that SIOP-62 was a bad plan.[73]

Walt Rostow of the State Department ultimately took over revising the BNSP. "I spent all night writing comments on his draft," Ellsberg remembers. "He asked me to read it over. . . . And I said, 'Wow, I have a lot of things I think that are wrong with this.' So . . . I stayed up all night and wrote, very densely, about twenty or thirty pages of changes. . . . All of which went in. . . . They accepted all of my points." Asked to comment on this account, however, Rostow called it "nonsense." He denied soliciting Ellsberg's opinion on the BNSP.[74]

In 1960, as the Democratic presidential convention had approached and John F. Kennedy looked to be its likely nominee, many RAND analysts had their sights on a job in Washington. Attending the convention in Los Angeles, Dan and Carol Ellsberg listened to Kennedy's acceptance speech with Richard and Ann Elms. Ellsberg "was very much in favor of Kennedy's election," Richard Elms recalls. "He was so admiring of JFK," Mary Marshall says. "He thought he was wonderful." Kennedy was, of course, a cold warrior. After he became president, Ellsberg heard that Kennedy shared McNamara's concern about an all-out nuclear war, though. Also, "he had learned all about JFK's peccadilloes and his sexual drive," according to Mary Marshall. "And he was so admiring of it. I mean, insofar as anybody knew at the time. With all the rumors, guys were talking about it."[75]

Jan Butler, Ellsberg's later lover at RAND, first met him at a party during the convention. She thought he seemed quite excited, even a bit awed, about attending the convention. He talked excitedly but without real authority, she noticed. He seemed quite young to Butler, who was young herself. Carol Ellsberg, Butler thought, showed greater maturity. Dan and Carol appeared to have something of a mother-son relationship; when Dan got overly excited, Carol would bring him back down.[76]

Ellsberg had done some work for the Kennedy campaign. Deirdre Henderson, whom he had befriended at Harvard, worked with Kennedy's academic advisory group in Cambridge. She had stayed at the Ellsbergs' home during the convention. It was through Ellsberg, Henderson believes, that she involved other RAND analysts in advising the campaign. Albert Wohlstetter, Rowen, Enthoven, and Ellsberg, among others, gave advice on strategic and defense issues. "They were concerned that the Eisenhower administration had let things slide a bit," Henderson recalls.[77]

Ellsberg was again a junior figure. "He certainly was a player. But he wasn't in the forefront," Henderson reminisces. Ellsberg "offered assistance and help. . . . He wrote papers. . . . Some of which I sent to Washington. Some of which weren't incorporated." Ellsberg eagerly offered his assistance to Henderson. "I can remember that Dan Ellsberg was always there on the periphery saying, 'Now, Deirdre, can I help you with anything?' And handing me papers, and doing this and doing that. . . . I didn't call him up and ask him. It was usually he coming to me and saying, 'I've got this, I've got that. And I want you to pass this on.'" It was a harried time for Henderson, and "of course if you needed something, Dan was always ready and willing to do it." Sometimes she had to keep him at arm's length.[78]

David Halberstam later wrote that Henderson called Ellsberg to seek his advice on bolstering Kennedy's defense credentials, saying that Kennedy needed to be identified with a weapon, and that Ellsberg responded, "What about the infantryman?" Henderson questions this account. "That is definitely overplayed," she says. Ellsberg "called on me. . . . I would say he was one of the junior players in a scene and that he has since rewritten his part."[79]

Ellsberg had his eyes on a position in the Kennedy administration. But, having now gotten settled in Los Angeles, Carol opposed moving to Washington. "He wanted to go to Washington, and I wasn't too keen on it," Carol Cummings remembers. "My position at the time was, 'I never see you here, and if we go there I'll *never* see you. And there I'll be in Washington, D.C., and I won't know anybody.'" Carol had started nursing school at UCLA in 1959. "The children would be uprooted, I'd be uprooted," she felt. "From my standpoint, there was nothing in it for us to go to Washington." But to Dan, "that's where the action was" and he seemed quite caught up in the new Kennedy administration. He and Carol attended many inaugural events in Washington. Ellsberg says he could have "easily" obtained a job in the Kennedy administration. "I didn't have a definite offer, but I didn't seek one. I was there all the time anyway. I was doing exactly what I wanted to do in Washington," as a consultant.[80]

Ellsberg had doubts about where his career was headed, though. Thomas Schelling spent the summer of 1961 at RAND and saw a lot of him then. "Dan was suffering his thirtieth birthday," Schelling recounts. "And I remember talking to him about kind of a pre-midlife crisis he was going through. . . . He was saying he was 30 years old and he didn't know whether he was on a trajectory to go someplace, and he was having to think about his future."[81]

Consulting in Washington must have been an exhilarating experience for Ellsberg at times, moving in the corridors of the Pentagon, talking to officials, frequenting war rooms. "I was in nearly every war room that we have," he later boasted. He loved being near the decision makers. "He was a real political operator, a bureaucratic operator," Kolkowicz recalls. "It gave him his identity, really."[82] Washington was another new world to him, one rife with intrigue, and where there was plenty of action.

As at RAND, some in Washington considered Ellsberg a young hotshot. But there, too, his ego and hunger to stand out rubbed some colleagues the wrong way. "He was always showing off," Adam Yarmolinsky remembered. Ellsberg "would sort of drop in and want you to stop what you were doing and talk with him," Robert Komer, who was then on the National Security Council staff and who came to respect him, recounts. "He was very pushy in advancing his own views. Very pushy in insisting on talking about all the big people he knew in Washington. Which I never [found] to be the fact." Some in Washington also questioned Ellsberg's judgment and maturity. He appeared at times to Yarmolinsky to be an eternal adolescent.[83]

It was important to Ellsberg that others knew he was close to power. William Kaufmann remembers him talking about how he allegedly persuaded President Kennedy to get involved in a war game. ("I never met Kennedy," Ellsberg told a journalist.) Joan Friedman received a phone call from Ellsberg one Saturday, probably in 1962 or 1963, in which he said he had a meeting with McNamara:

He had flown east from wherever he was. And he called me up and said, "I'm going to have an interview in Washington with McNamara. And then I'm going to come to New York. Let's have dinner." So I said, "Okay." And he said the interview was at 11:30 in the morning or something, "so I should be there by two or three." So I said, "That's okay, it doesn't really matter." And I started getting phone calls: "McNamara is so interested in me this interview is going to go on for hours." . . . There were several phone calls. . . . I suppose every time he left to go to the men's room he called up.

Friedman soon "realized that the purpose of these phone calls had nothing to do with me" or "my convenience." Rather, "they had to do with, 'I need to tell somebody how smart I am. And McNamara thinks I'm wonderful.'" Ellsberg's calls "*appeared* to be considerate," Joan (Friedman) Cleveland recalls: "'Oh, I'm going to be late, and I'm calling to tell you so that you aren't inconvenienced.' And I thought, 'No, no, no, that's not what's *really* going on here.'"[84]

Ellsberg eventually showed up quite late, Cleveland recounts, "and we went out to dinner. And my position basically was, 'Yeah, big deal. You're smart; we all know you're smart. . . . ' Which was really not what he was looking for. . . . And I can now remember that as being a very argumentative evening. And I felt badly, because I understood what he was looking for. If I had been nicer, I would have given it to him. But I really couldn't bring myself to lie about it and say, 'Wasn't that wonderful that he thinks you're a genius?'" Cleveland chiefly remembers from the evening "this tremendous need to be thought a genius."[85]

In Washington, Ellsberg consulted mainly for the office of the assistant secretary of defense for International Security Affairs (ISA), which played a key role in formulating the Kennedy administration's foreign and defense policies. RAND had a contract with ISA. Harry Rowen was deputy assistant secretary of defense for ISA. He gave Ellsberg consulting assignments and promoted his career considerably. The two became good friends. "We became buddies," Ellsberg remembers. "In fact, I lived with him when I first went to Washington. We got very close." When Ellsberg worked as a Pentagon aide a few years later, their bond grew. Rowen "knew all my personal life," Ellsberg says. "He knew everything I was doing. And agreed with everything I was doing. Our minds ran totally together." Rowen was then Ellsberg's closest friend, five-and-a-half years older (though Ellsberg remembers him as "eleven years older"), and treated him as a sort of younger brother. "I could imagine that Harry thought of me as his best friend," Ellsberg reminisces. In fact, "I would say we loved each other."[86]

Rowen was a former chemical engineer who had studied economics at Oxford. At RAND, he too had gravitated to Albert Wohlstetter and seemed to often take his cue from him. Rowen was a very intelligent man, if not in Ellsberg's league or with the same breadth of interests. He loved to debate issues. He knew how to get things done in the Pentagon. In the world of great power politics, he was not a stickler for principles or torn by moral considerations. Advancing U.S. interests was key, and whatever worked was okay. Rowen possessed limited social skills. "He impressed me as a guy that had no social graces, who didn't talk to people easily," Richard Best, who was RAND's security officer, recalls. "He was not a guy you'd warm to." "A peculiar bird," Jan Butler calls him. "He's stiff, and I suppose shy, or contemptuous, or all of those things. He had a marvelous opinion of himself and of nobody else, except Albert and the in-boys. . . . Harry was just a cold fish." Rowen was one of the most arrogant of the "whiz kids" in the Kennedy administration. He was clipped, brusque, and rude, and could be quite difficult if you crossed him.[87]

By the time Rowen would become president of RAND in January 1967, and probably before then, he would be trumpeting Ellsberg's virtues to others. "Harry Rowen was not reluctant at all to convey to others—on more than one occasion—that he felt that Dan Ellsberg was a superior person, and the kind of person RAND should give power to," Alexander George, a RAND colleague, remembers. "Harry Rowen's extolling of Dan was quite extreme. And it was controversial, I think, within RAND." Rowen, who had great respect for Ellsberg's intelligence, "held him up as a model—'People should listen to Dan,'" George recalls Rowen saying.[88] When the Pentagon Papers hit the newspapers several years later, however, Rowen would wish he had never met Ellsberg.

As a consultant in Washington, Ellsberg wrote papers, briefed officials, helped draft speeches. "I had certain qualities that made me very valuable," he remembers. When giving briefings, he could speak straight to the point, giving his listener precisely what he wanted, he says. "Other people at RAND were not capable of doing that." Ellsberg says he excelled in fast moving operational situations. "I could write very fast, and cogently and persuasively, under pressure in Washington." He claims he ultimately got paid more than others at RAND because of that. "I could deliver more reliably than other people. And fast, and better." That's "what got me my promotions, and why I did zip up the hierarchy." But Fred Hoffman, a former RAND colleague, remembers, "He's not a succinct conversationalist, briefer, or writer."[89]

Ellsberg had to move quickly during the tense period of the Cuban missile crisis in October 1962. He was called to Washington as a consultant nearly a week into the crisis on the day of Kennedy's speech announcing the existence of the Soviet Union's missiles in Cuba, he would recall. It was Rowen, most likely, who requested his services. He served as an intermediary between a crisis work group at RAND and the Pentagon, Roman Kolkowicz remembers. "He would fly in, spend time with us . . . and then he would fly back and brief" people in the Pentagon. "We were to serve him so he could then assist." Ellsberg took pride in his role. "Again, he was this mysterious powerful man who would fly [in]—a military plane would fly him in—and he would . . . spend a couple of hours with us, and then fly out," Kolkowicz says, whisking his hand up in the air.[90]

Ellsberg says he was a member of two of three working groups aiding the Executive Committee of the National Security Council (ExComm) during the crisis. One was at the State Department under Walt Rostow, the other was at the Defense Department under Rowen. But Rostow "definitely" recalls that Ellsberg "wasn't on my group at State," adding, "He tells all sorts of stories." William Kaufmann was involved in the work group under Rowen. "I don't remember Dan really being involved in that," Kaufmann says. But he was "running in and out."[91]

Kaufmann does recall one memorable episode involving Ellsberg during the missile crisis. It took place on Saturday, October 27, the day Nikita Khrushchev demanded removal of the U.S. Jupiter missiles from Turkey in exchange for removal of the Soviet missiles from Cuba. Kennedy, who felt the Jupiters were obsolete, decided to remove them, but without putting that in writing, for political reasons. Assistant Secretary of Defense for ISA Paul Nitze, who was his usual hawkish self during the crisis and favored an air strike on Cuba, came back to the Pentagon from the White House that day "in a very dark mood," Kaufmann remembers. Nitze opposed removal of the Jupiters. Rowen, Ellsberg, and Kaufmann were there with Nitze, who was Rowen's boss. Nitze asked the others for their ideas on how to "frustrate" (to use Kaufmann's word) Kennedy's decision. Ellsberg "got very emotional, and thought this was an outrage, what Kennedy was doing," Kaufmann recounts. "And Harry and I were trying to get to work, to see whether we had any ideas about what to give to Paul. And Dan was just, if I remember it correctly, was just ranting and raving. And Harry and I just took him and pushed him out of the Pentagon, and went back to work."[92]

After the missile crisis, Ellsberg returned to RAND and briefed people on events. "There was a big turnout in the basement auditorium," Alexander George recounts:

> Two things stand out, which struck me and some of my colleagues at the time as really quite striking indications of Dan's limitations. One of them was, he

said, "We were working night and day. We slept there," etc. "We were so busy," etc. "We were sending these memos upwards to Rowen, who in turn was sending things up to Nitze, who in turn was sending things upwards to somebody else. . . . Then one day in the middle of the crisis, I happened to get hold of a couple of newspapers. And I was shocked to learn what had been going on that I wasn't aware of."

George, who liked Ellsberg, wondered how he could be providing well-considered advice when he wasn't staying abreast of newspapers, which are often used by government officials to send signals. Also, "he said, 'It was only after the crisis was over that I learned that Kennedy and Khrushchev had been exchanging secret letters during the crisis. I didn't know that statesmen in a crisis talked to each other.' That really was a shock to me."[93]

Ellsberg contributed to several important speeches in Washington. He was probably the main author of a major and provocative speech by the Pentagon's Roswell Gilpatric to the Business Council in October 1961 during the Berlin crisis. That speech, which was vetted at the highest level, including by President Kennedy himself, was on U.S. strategic posture and directed in large part to the Soviets. Designed to bury the missile gap and warn the Soviets on Berlin, it was a major flexing of U.S. military muscle, perhaps an unprecedented one. "Our confidence in our ability to deter Communist action, or resist Communist blackmail, is based upon a sober appreciation of the relative military power of the two sides," Gilpatric declared. And "the fact is that this nation has a nuclear retaliatory force of such lethal power that an enemy move which brought it into play would be an act of self-destruction on his part. . . . The United States does not intend to be defeated." The speech explicitly did not rule out the use of tactical nuclear weapons. Ellsberg told me it "ended the Berlin crisis and started the Cuban missile crisis," or at least was "critical" on the first count and had "a major effect" on the second. That is, it gave the Soviets pause on Berlin, made them back off, and provoked to a significant degree the shipment of missiles to Cuba. But although the speech probably did influence the Soviets to ease off on Berlin and fed into Khrushchev's decision to ship missiles to Cuba, Ellsberg's first claim is typically exaggerated and self-aggrandizing.[94]

Ellsberg also worked on a major speech on U.S. nuclear strategy by Robert McNamara at the University of Michigan in June 1962, but, as with other claims he has made, it's difficult to say how large his contribution to the speech actually was. McNamara's address announced the U.S. "counterforce," or "no cities," strategy, which entailed hitting only Soviet military targets initially in response to Soviet military action but threatening the destruction of Soviet cities if the Soviets did not desist. McNamara had given a classified version of the speech to NATO ministers in Athens, Greece, the previous month. William Kaufmann, a key counterforce advocate, had written that speech, with help from Rowen. Ellsberg told me that he wrote McNamara's Ann Arbor speech. When I responded, "You among others," he replied, "Well, I wrote the last draft," then acknowledged that it was "mainly Bill Kaufmann's Athens speech." Adam Yarmolinsky had earlier revised that speech for delivery in Ann Arbor, then showed it to him and asked for his comments, Ellsberg recounts:

> I said, "Jeez, this is terrible." And I think I spent a lot of time going over it in detail. . . . As I was talking to him, he gets a call from McNamara. He said, "Yes, Bob, yes." And he said, "Well, actually I have Dan Ellsberg in my office right at this moment. . . . And he has just given some very searching criticisms of this speech. . . ." So he listens for a minute, and hangs up. He says, "Well, McNamara says that if you don't like the speech, why don't you write your version of it. . . ." So I worked on it all afternoon and all night, and had it for him at eight o'clock the next morning. . . . I used Kaufmann's speech a lot.

But Yarmolinsky told me with some assurance that he wrote the speech. He was McNamara's speechwriter then, he pointed out, and he and McNamara worked on the final draft together—the one "that I brought to him and that he marked up, and that was it."[95]

In 1963, Ellsberg worked on NATO policy for Rowen and was probably the main author of two speeches that fall by McNamara on NATO and U.S. strategic posture. McNamara "personally" asked him to write the second of the two speeches, Ellsberg recounted, "and he said also at the request of Mr. [Dean] Rusk," the U.S. secretary of state. "I wrote this speech on my own, totally," Ellsberg told me. McNamara "didn't change a word." Through Yarmolinsky, McNamara also requested that he write the other speech, Ellsberg remembered, and again "McNamara didn't write a word of it." But Kaufmann would later describe that speech (which took place four days before President Kennedy was assassinated) as "one of the last results" of the "most fruitful collaboration" between McNamara and Kennedy, who "typically" contributed to McNamara's major defense speeches.[96]

Ellsberg revered Robert McNamara. "I loved McNamara," he recalls. "I was a total fan." Vincent Davis, who got to know Ellsberg in the Pentagon in the summer of 1965, remembers, "He was a hero worshipper, and McNamara was his hero. He was totally devoted to McNamara. He thought McNamara was a genius. He wanted to emulate McNamara. There was nothing McNamara did that could conceivably be wrong." Davis thought Ellsberg seemed apologetic of McNamara. But Ellsberg never attained the personal relationship with McNamara that he desired. In 1966, he would wonder if McNamara even remembered his name.[97]

———◦———

Meanwhile, back at RAND, some of Ellsberg's colleagues were beginning to wonder about his work habits. He seemed to have difficulty completing projects on time, if at all, and tended to jump from one thing to the next. Ellsberg, they noticed, was lacking in personal organization and self-discipline. "A number of us . . . began worrying about Dan's output," Jim Digby recalls. "We began to worry that this promising young man was not turning out very useful written reports." Though those concerns would be more widespread during Ellsberg's second stint at RAND, his problems finishing work had been apparent from day one. "It was always deplored that a man with his brilliance" didn't produce more, Guy Pauker remembers. "I think he was an underachiever if there ever was one."[98]

Ellsberg was not known for his papers at RAND. His challenge to the Savage axioms aside, his reputation was based in large degree on his verbal brilliance. "If he weren't in the process of trying to beat up on somebody, he had a lot of fascinating things to say," Kaufmann thought. Ellsberg could be a force in seminars. Kolkowicz, who participated with him in some seminars on nuclear issues, recalls that "he was invariably the intellectual leader in these meetings. He was very articulate, very enthusiastic," and unintimidated by others. He offered insightful observations about colleagues' projects. "Dan's involvement in something typically meant that he sort of came up to you, read over your shoulder, said, 'Oh, is that so?'" Shubert remembers. "He's a combination voyeur and corrector."[99]

Ellsberg could write a trenchant short paper. But longer projects proved harder for him. "He had terrible trouble—witness his dissertation—in ever bringing a piece of work of his own to conclusion," Shubert recounts. "He was high energy on everything except when it came to producing something. In the [economics] department, we had a *terrible* time with him to get him ever to finish anything." Ellsberg's seemed a hard intellect to get into a productive mode. Brilliant but erratic was a common perception of him. "Great on ideas, but hard to follow through on them," David McGarvey recalls. "I remember a number of briefings, and the briefings would be engaging and so forth, and there would follow some length of draft—and then nothing," Fred Hoffman reminisces. After the draft, "then pretty much it would dwindle."[100]

Ellsberg would get excited about one thing and then excited about another, and seemed unable to focus on any single issue for very long. And he was
still always running late. He also sometimes left work for others to finish up.
That happened to Kaufmann on the BNSP, and then later (probably after Ellsberg began working in the Pentagon in 1964), "I remember some very grand
briefing that he was supposed to be preparing," Kaufmann recalls. The briefing
was for McNamara. "And I finally had to do it. Not give the briefing, but prepare the talking points. . . . It was supposed to be some big presentation."[101]

RAND's records of Ellsberg's writings during his first period there, 1959 to
1964, include only two short "Ps" (or cleared papers) and one brief "D" (or
draft)—a total of 27 pages. One of Ellsberg's "Ps" was "based entirely" on one of
his 1959 Lowell lectures. The other was a response to a critique of his seminal
paper challenging the Savage axioms (which is also listed in RAND's records
and which he may have further developed there). Ellsberg planned to publish "a
much longer" version of his first "P" with RAND, but apparently never did,
based on RAND's records.[102] "Ds" were the least polished and least valued form
of written output at RAND; they were internal first drafts. It was the more finished "Rs" and "RMs" (reports and RAND memoranda) that really counted.

Ellsberg also wrote his long 1960 working paper (another "D") on nuclear
command and control (probably the paper that he had insisted to Norman
Dalkey that he publish separately). Ellsberg had hoped to publish it as an
"RM," but, again, there is no sign in RAND's records that he did. Kaufmann
recalls Ellsberg talking about undertaking a command and control study in the
context of counterforce strategy, but it, too, is nowhere to be found. Dalkey remembers that "our command and control study was delayed *long* beyond the
target date" because Ellsberg was late on his end. "I didn't feel he was a serious
researcher, in the sense in which RAND defines a serious researcher," Dalkey
says. Besides hopping too readily from one topic to the next, "he didn't seem to
have a research framework. When you're tackling your research subject . . .
you try to get to the basic factors that are involved in that research area. And
you didn't have the feeling that that was the first thing he focused on."[103]

Ellsberg spent the first six months of 1962 writing his Ph.D. dissertation at
RAND. But, as we've seen, it took repeated prodding from others for him to
get it done. He planned to publish it as an "RM," which was "forthcoming," he
indicated, but, again, never did. "The tragedy was that Dan was absolutely incapable to [sic] turn it into a book," Guy Pauker remembers. "He was just unable. Everybody was begging him. . . . And all the people who really wanted to
see him become a Nobel Prize person were begging him to . . . publish his thesis. He never did." While his seminal article may have contained the gist of a

book and was itself a great triumph, Ellsberg himself says, "It was a publishable Ph.D. thesis. . . . It's publishable now. I'd be happy to publish it now. . . . But that is not what my life has been about."[104]

Ellsberg says that people who criticize his written output at RAND "just don't know what I wrote." He is acutely sensitive to such criticism. His "important writing," Ellsberg argues, was in Washington as a consultant—the nuclear guidance he drafted, the speeches he prepared, his other papers, which were "often very lengthy." "RAND didn't see any of that," he says. "They didn't have access to it," and thus "most people did not know" about it. To argue he wasn't fulfilling his promise, Ellsberg maintains, is to judge him by "a standard which I did not share. Namely, academic achievement." He "wasn't big on publishing anyway. The final stuff. And you didn't need to at RAND." During his time overall there, "I chose to write only Ds, essentially. . . . There was no advantage to me of writing [an] R or RM."[105]

But Ellsberg clearly did have trouble finishing papers and other work at RAND. The reasons are probably multiple. He was raised by his driving, demanding mother to have very high standards of achievement. His subsequent experience in school fed the belief that he was a superior person marked for major achievement. But like his mother's, Ellsberg's standards may have been too high, even impossible to meet. He may have feared failure. That could have inhibited his writing. One could even go so far as to speculate that, if only subconsciously, Ellsberg wrote with a vision of his exacting, critical mother in mind. And RAND was in a sense another authority figure with high expectations of him. "I think he was a perfectionist," Dalkey recalls. "And he didn't want to put out something that wasn't really great." Yet the need to be great is different than perfectionism. Ellsberg's writing had to be explosive, powerful, eye-grabbing. The stakes in his writing were probably higher than they are for most people. He and others would sometimes refer to his problem as writer's block, and in some cases writer's block is rooted in an unrealistic sense of self and what you need to accomplish.[106]

Also, as we know, Ellsberg was an insecure and sensitive man with an inordinate need for approbation and admiration from others. That, too, could have inhibited his writing, certainly for publication. It is difficult to write and always be looking over your own shoulder.

And there was Ellsberg's exceptional curiosity about all manner of things. His mind zipped all over the place. Perhaps ideas kept coming too fast to him. "I think maybe it's that ideas just came in an undisciplined fashion, so that every time Dan got something on paper—damn it, something else would stick into his mind, and it was never finished," Thomas Schelling says. Moreover,

Ellsberg would rather be doing things than writing about them. "He's got to be moving all the time, and talking, and meeting with people," Howard Zinn notes. His liveliness probably reflects, among other things, impatience, which of course does not lend itself to sustained effort.[107] And people who are tied in knots (as Ellsberg often appears to have been) often have difficulty writing. Or, perhaps, writing simply becomes tiresome to him.

Ellsberg's undisciplined and disorganized qualities obviously hampered his work greatly. But whether he had always been undisciplined or was still rebelling against his mother's demands, or both, is hard to know (though the first possibility seems most likely and most consequential). Perhaps an orderly life bores Ellsberg. He's not wired to work on a strict schedule. "I can't write nine to five," he says. "I've never done it. . . . It's just not my rhythm."[108]

But Ellsberg's erratic work style was by no means rare at RAND, and he was still considered a valuable asset, partly because he tended to ask the right questions and to offer incisive criticisms. It wasn't easy to get papers out of some others either. And many of his colleagues believed Ellsberg could still blossom in a major way. Then he would *really* be a credit to RAND. Thus, "they were always excusing him, indulging him," Mary Marshall believes.[109]

Ellsberg's problems completing work would continue to plague him in later years, however. His genius would, to a disturbing degree, lie fallow. By November 1965 he would see his difficulty publishing his writings as a career tragedy.[110]

"He never quite made it," Gus Shubert reflected in 1995. "Because he could never quite get over that last hump, producing the great work, whatever it was. . . . He just never got there. And he certainly isn't ready to get there now."[111]

SIX

REJECTION

IN THE EARLY 1960S, AS ELLSBERG WAS PROVIDING ADVICE TO THE U.S. government on the use of nuclear weapons, he was also experimenting with LSD. Twice, he would remember.[1] Taking LSD was not illegal then. The drug had been used for years by therapists with their patients. Some therapists thought it aided self-insight and even helped unearth repressed childhood memories. Many researchers had also dispensed it to their experimental subjects, and hundreds of papers had been published on it.

Ellsberg's curiosity about LSD had been piqued by a 40-year-old former Hollywood actress and writer of slick fiction named Thelma Schnee Moss. Ellsberg had met Moss at a party, probably at his friend Jerry Goodman's house. Moss was then studying psychology at UCLA. Sallie Goodman, Jerry Goodman's wife and a friend of Moss, had introduced Dan and Carol Ellsberg to Moss. Sallie Goodman was an actress herself, under the professional name Sallie Brophy, and had appeared on live television shows and in westerns.[2]

Moss was a bright, intense woman who had undergone LSD therapy in the late 1950s. To her happiness and relief, it had cured her of sexual frigidity, and after only nine sessions. Under LSD, she experienced "a genuine *physical* orgasm, unique in my life," she would write later.[3]

Moss had encouraged Sallie Goodman to undergo LSD therapy, too. The person running the LSD program that Goodman participated in was Dr. M. A. Hartman, a psychiatrist whose claim, Goodman recalls, "was ten sessions and you were a changed person for life. So we all did that because we didn't want to do seven years of analysis." "It was very fast therapy," Jerry Goodman reminisces.

"Because you didn't have to go through all the bullshit that you yourself throw up. But it took a lot of skill to handle it." Sallie Goodman saw people's lives change after taking LSD. "Possibilities open up," she says. "My life changed. Thelma's changed. Some people's lives changed dramatically." She became an enthusiast.[4]

Sallie Goodman also convinced her good friend Betsy Drake Grant to participate in Hartman's program. Grant then got her husband, Cary Grant, involved. "He was very enthusiastic about the whole thing," Goodman remembers. "It was absolute release," Grant would recall. He thought after taking LSD, "Oh, those wasted years; why didn't I do this sooner?" On one LSD trip, "I imagined myself as a giant penis launching off from Earth like a spaceship." But learning about himself was painful. "That moment when your conscious meets your subconscious is a helluva wrench," Grant recounted. "You feel the whole top of your head is lifting off."[5]

Encouraged by his wife, who kept talking about "this wonder drug," Jerry Goodman joined in LSD experiments at UCLA run by Dr. Oscar Janiger. Goodman was then a financial portfolio manager. Janiger was studying LSD's effects on creativity in artists, musicians, and writers. Under the influence of the drug, the subjects in the experiments were observed by a "baby-sitter," usually a graduate student. Jerry Goodman's baby-sitter was Thelma Moss. The LSD was dispensed in the form of little blue pills. "You were really like a guinea pig," Goodman recalls. "Thelma Moss says, 'Oh, what are you thinking? What are you seeing?' And you're saying, 'Get lost.'" LSD enhanced creativity among some artists and musicians, it turned out, but Goodman found he couldn't write a thing. So did most other writers.[6]

Moss spoke enthusiastically about LSD to Ellsberg. The drug intrigued him. He and Carol "both thought that sounded great, and were very interested," Ellsberg remembers. But he was not without concern. "My feeling was, 'Gee, if you're that much out of control and so forth, I have too many secrets in my head,'" he recounts. "So Carol did it first. . . . And the effect it had on her seemed so good, beneficial—it looked wonderful. . . . It loosened her up . . . in a way that I'd never seen her—ever—in my life. . . . So I thought, 'Well, that looks terrific. . . . Fine. Sign me up.'" Ellsberg, who would enjoy LSD later in his life, adds, "I know that I've never told secrets on LSD."[7]

But Carol recalls that she was, in fact, a reluctant participant. "I only did it because Dan wanted me to do it so much." She didn't approve of the experiment. "I did not think it was good science. I mean, I was her 'housewife control.' I didn't think I was a housewife control anymore by that time. I was in school." Further, Moss had told Carol that the experiment was being conducted in an M.D.'s office, but when she arrived, Carol found it was in the office of an osteopath who (she later learned) was interested in LSD. Carol remembers her experience:

> First she gave me a card and gave me a bunch of crayons, and I was to color or expand on the drawing [on the card] in any way I wished. And so I did something very pedestrian. . . . Then she gave me the acid. And I was so uncomfortable in her presence that it took forever to have any effect on me. She said, "*Go* with it." She was a very "*Go*-with-it" sort of person. . . . "Shut your eyes. You're ascending a staircase. At the top of the staircase there's a door. You open the door and what do you see?" "Nothing." So she gave it to me again. And I drew a little Freud guy or something. Not much better than the first one.
>
> But then finally it began to get to me, and she gave it to me again, and this time I started doing sort of a cross between Gauguin and Rousseau—you know, bright colors and mysterious animals peeking out among the bright flowers.
>
> . . . During this time I could hear screams from rooms in this [office complex]. I don't know what the guy did, what kind of therapy he was doing. . . .
>
> But she said, "Well, got to go. I'll call Dan to come pick you up." And she plunked me down in the waiting room full of these people. . . . It was terrible. . . . And I said, "Well, can't I have some crayons?" So she gave me some crayons. So I was sitting there happily coloring, making these drawings and stuff, while these people were looking at me. . . . Finally Dan came and picked me up. And I said, "I don't think I should go home like this. . . . I have little children."

So Dan called up Jerry Goodman, who found a place for them to stay for a while. Carol still wanted to do some coloring. She was getting into this now. "So we went to FAO Schwartz in Beverly Hills," she recounts:

> They didn't have any plain white paper. . . . I was standing there very still, not wanting to give away the fact that I was under the influence of drugs. . . . So [Dan] said, "Well, we'll just take one of these big coloring books." . . . And there was an Alice in Wonderland [book]. . . . So [the saleswoman] said, "Will that be all?" and "Is everything alright?" And I said, "No." They looked over at me kind of nervously, both of them. . . . "I want Peter Rabbit." "Certainly."[8]

Thelma Moss, who took LSD every week (according to her daughter), was also exploring the reactions of people on the drug to paintings and music. Moss showed Ellsberg classical paintings before and during his trip, and observed his reactions. Not surprisingly, on LSD, he viewed the paintings differently. She also had him do some drawings. "That was the one time in my life when I did draw," Ellsberg remembers. "I did very good drawings while I was [on] the LSD. [While] tailing off."[9]

Ellsberg participated in another LSD experiment headed by Dr. William H. McGlothlin, a member of RAND's logistics department. A psychologist, Mc-Glothlin was interested in determining some of the long-term effects of LSD and other hallucinogens on "normals." McGlothlin thought LSD had beneficial and enjoyable effects. "Almost everyone who takes LSD finds it a fascinating experience for which it is difficult to find adequate superlatives," he wrote. But, as might be expected, McGlothlin was unable to attract RAND's support for his research, and some RAND analysts would later say he went off the deep end. Some sampled LSD, however, including Herman Kahn (not while writing *On Thermonuclear War*, one would hope) and an administrative employee who took it on his own and "was urging everybody to try it," Arnold Kramish remembers. "My impression is that he eventually went stark raving mad."[10]

Carol Ellsberg would tell the FBI after the Pentagon Papers were published that Daniel Ellsberg had talked about LSD and marijuana with McGlothlin, who "had told him of a place in New Mexico or Mexico where experiments with drugs took place," an FBI teletype records. (McGlothlin was interested in the use of peyote in Indian rituals.) The FBI would also report that Ellsberg "volunteered to assist a doctor at UCLA specializing in matters of the brain, who was seeking volunteers to study the effect of LSD on brain waves."[11]

Ellsberg loved LSD. Sallie Goodman believes it changed him. "This experiment was the beginning, I think, for him of the big change, where he . . . was truly becoming liberated and becoming a sixties child," she contends. "It all started back there." Yet Ellsberg likely intellectualized his experience to a large degree. "It's like his whole liberation," Goodman chuckles. "He did it so mechanically: 'Well, now, we take off all our clothes, because there is a cost-benefit thing to this.'"[12]

Among the insights Ellsberg obtained on LSD was an unsettling one (how many users have had that experience?) that led him to urge Carol to participate in marriage counseling again. Not long after he and Carol had seen counselors in the summers of 1958 and 1959, he had started seeing a psychiatrist by himself, probably in 1960. This was, of course, well before he went to Dr. Lewis Fielding (and was treatment that the Plumbers apparently never learned about). Dr. Ronald Koegler, whose name Carol Ellsberg would later provide the FBI, was the psychiatrist who gave her Fielding's name, which, as we've seen, she then phoned in to the FBI. Roberta Wohlstetter referred Ellsberg to

Koegler, Carol believes. Just why Ellsberg started seeing Koegler is unknown, though he told me that he "started seeing a psychiatrist to get [Carol] to go," and "in hopes that something would turn up that [would indicate] what the problem was" in their marriage. Ellsberg describes Koegler as a "mutual psychiatrist we were going to for marriage therapy."[13]

The psychic epiphany Ellsberg experienced on LSD coincided with a sexual epiphany that he experienced as he began having affairs with women, unleashing another troubling undercurrent in his already shaky marriage. Starting in about early 1960, Ellsberg told me, he had had "a number of affairs." These affairs took place "in different parts of the world." He had an affair in Japan with a Japanese woman, probably while studying nuclear command and control there in early 1960. He fell in love with her, he told me. He had these affairs for about a year and a half, he said, "up to June 1961." After one lover wanted to have a child with him, "I quit."[14]

For about a year, anyway. He then commenced a "long affair" in Washington.[15]

When he was on LSD, Ellsberg recounts,

> I sort of saw myself with all these various women that I had known. . . . The thing that struck me was I realized that I was embracing them all the time. I had my arms around them or I was holding hands with them. . . . Which is my way. . . . I sort of like to be close. And I realized that what was a particular lack with Carol was that she was very reserved, very reticent. . . . She hated to hold hands in public. Her father, her marine colonel father, had given her the idea that it was very disgusting to see people necking in public, or even showing any affection in public. . . . And she was very self-conscious about any show of affection in public, in particular. And I suddenly realized that it was very important to me to be very close to someone, to anybody. And that what I was lacking was a kind of intimacy, physical intimacy. And that that had to change . . . or I couldn't stay married, now that I'd had this other experience.

Ellsberg realized his frustration with his marriage wasn't simply sexual. He craved an intimacy that just didn't exist between him and Carol.[16]

"He wanted me to see Koegler," Carol recounts. "And I was kind of reluctant. Because I figured Koegler would have formed his opinions about the context, what a terrible person I was." Koegler "was *his* psychiatrist," Carol points out. "And, then, he obviously must have been talking about the problems he was having with his wife." But Carol finally consented. "I thought that what was going to happen was Koegler was going to size me up and then refer me elsewhere," she recalls. "Because I think Dan thought I was pretty screwed up and needed therapy." But "we ended up with Koegler seeing both of us." Separately. Never together. Ellsberg would later judge this approach to marriage counseling ridiculous.[17]

In one of their conversations in the early 1960s, Ellsberg told Joan Friedman that during his marital therapy, "the problem was that, although things were getting better, which is to say certain unacceptable behavior on his part had been identified and he was really fixing it . . . the uncovering of all these old wounds was happening at such a clip that there was no way to make it better fast enough to make up for all of the wounds that were being uncovered." As for the nature of those wounds, Ellsberg was never specific, Joan (Friedman) Cleveland recalls. But her impression was that there were two categories: "Episodes of neglect: 'You should have been there and you weren't'" (Carol "had to deal with all these crises and he was always not there") and "episodes of infidelity." "It was as if the dynamic of the therapy was—to put it in numbered terms—when she went into therapy she thought the marriage was a 6 and he was going to fix some behavior so it would become an 8," Cleveland remembers. "As she went into therapy, the marriage went from a 6 to a 5 to a 2 to a minus. And then nothing he could fix could possibly make up for how bad it was. . . . And that's what really killed it."[18]

According to Ellsberg, Koegler told him after his marriage collapsed that Carol had declared during her "first visit" that she intended to get a divorce after finishing nursing school. "I'm telling you this so that you don't have any delusions about getting back together again," Koegler said, in Ellsberg's retelling. "She didn't start [nursing school] until she was determined to get divorced," Ellsberg contends. Thus "she had been thinking [about divorce] for four years without telling me." Carol finished nursing school in January 1963. She asked for a divorce nearly a year later. Yet Ellsberg insisted to me that Carol requested a divorce a week after she finished school. Ellsberg's erratic memory—often understandably aggravating to Carol when it involves her life—particularly irks her on this point. "Dan's got it wrong in his mind," she told me. What's more, "he apparently has been telling it to the children since they were little children. So it certainly has fossilized into truth as far as he is concerned." But it's simply not true, she says. "Also, I never discussed divorce with Koegler at all, until the day I came in in October of 1963 and said, 'I want a divorce.' And I remember Koegler kind of jumped, because he was startled." Ellsberg tried to argue the issue with Carol some 30 years after their divorce, during a dinner that nearly broke down in acrimony. "I just said, 'I don't want to talk about it anymore,'" Carol recounts. "'Well, don't you think it's interesting?' I said, 'No, I don't think it's interesting. I think it's morbid, and I'm not interested in discussing it, and I'm not going to discuss it.' And I would have walked home if we hadn't been so far away." Later, "I mentioned it to the children, and they said they'd been hearing it for years." When Carol pointed out to Ellsberg that she graduated from nursing school a year before they parted, "Dan said, 'Oh, that can't be.' And I said, 'Dan, I know when I graduated from college.' 'So what did you do when you graduated?' 'I worked in the operating room at UCLA.' And he said, 'Yes, I remember you weren't very good.'"[19]

Carol adds, "It's so annoying to be accused in such a public way. . . . He tells people all this stuff. And I'm the only one that knows it's not true. And I don't have any way of defending myself. And it makes me mad when he does that. . . . You know, I've never intended to talk about this sort of thing . . . but . . . if he's telling you a story that isn't true, I think I have a right to defend myself. . . . I'm so sick of it. You tell him it's not true, and he thinks a little bit, but then, 'No, it can't be. She's wrong.'"[20]

Ellsberg claims he did not realize his marriage with Carol was in trouble until the moment she asked for a divorce in late December 1963. "I was not aware she had strong problems with the marriage," he says. She wasn't voicing her resentments, and "I wasn't picking up [on] things." Further, "I would have said that she loved me throughout, til that moment," that "she loved me as much as I loved her. And that just shows how wrong somebody can be. . . . It may show my character as to how insensitive I am. . . . And, of course, it's an extremely unsettling thing to realize in one's life, from then on. Because you know that both because of people not communicating and because of my own problems in hearing certain things, it leads you to question any relation[ship] you have." For Ellsberg, this included the relationships he had with his own children.[21]

Ellsberg knew that Carol held things against him—lots of things—but he would have thought they were small irritations. It had been the "premise" of their discussions that he was the one who had a problem. Ellsberg says it never even *occurred* to him that Carol would want a divorce, partly because of her opposition to divorce. "It was easier for me to imagine dying than divorce." It had never even come up before, he believes.[22]

But in retrospect, it's clear Carol was feeling tremendous resentment, he acknowledges, even hatred. He later told a friend that Carol once said to him, "I've never hated anybody so much in my entire life." Ellsberg now strongly denies that Carol ever said this to him, though he finds it easy to believe that she felt it. He found it "unhappily plausible," he told me, that she made the remark to someone else.[23]

One wonders if Ellsberg was more aware of Carol's resentments at the time than he admits. He was not only in marital counseling but keenly attuned to what other people thought of him. He had to have been aware that Carol was unhappy. Most likely, the divorce came as a surprise to him mainly because he didn't think she would ever ask for one.

Carol's irritations with him were sometimes evident to others. "She called his bullshit," Roman Kolkowicz remembers. "Directly. Sometimes at parties. And he didn't like that." At one party at his house, Ellsberg told Kolkowicz he wanted to show him an issue of the *Harvard Advocate*. "He says, 'Come. Come to the bedroom,'" Kolkowicz recounts. "That's where he keeps it. And Carol says, 'Is he going to show you the goddamn [thing]? He didn't write anything there.' I mean, she just put the whole thing down. . . . It was so startling. She was kind of unkind to him. She didn't know me very well. New person, you know. And she essentially said, 'Is he going to show you these again?' . . . It was almost like, 'Don't pay attention to him.'" Kolkowicz also recalls,

> What's always struck me [is] that she did not kowtow to him. Far from it. She just looked at him as a kind of spoiled brat who was putting on airs. And she called him on this. I've seen it. . . . There are all kinds of incidents, but they simply will support that . . . she did not . . . tend to this flame of the genius. Far from it. . . . And it was sad, because I don't think he took it seriously. He was surprised that she asked for a divorce. Because he couldn't believe . . . that she would do it.[24]

Carol was not inclined to complain about her husband to others. She was used to disappointments in life and tended to be stoic about her marital problems. "I don't think she would have ever told anybody," Mary Marshall says. Carol had never even said anything to her father about what bothered her about Dan. At home around their children, she tried to keep her anger to herself. Robert Ellsberg was eight years old when his parents separated. "I was not aware that there was serious tension or unhappiness in the house," he remembers. But Carol would sometimes make snide remarks about Dan to Marshall, or compare him to some other husband: If he was only like so and so, she would say.[25]

Ellsberg expressed his frustrations with Carol openly to others. "She's a nurse," he once told Kolkowicz, in a deprecating tone of voice, "I can't talk to her about things." In so many words, "he was telling me she was a good mother, and she was an okay wife, but she's not sharp," Kolkowicz recalls. "He used to complain," Marshall remembers. "One of the things he complained about was what she read . . . *Ladies' Home Journal, Good Housekeeping*. . . . I think he wanted her to be a little more intellectual." Ellsberg had little, if any, interest in nursing. But "I always told her, and believed, she was very, very bright," he recalls. However, "people have different kinds of intelligence. And she didn't have the kind of analytical intelligence which . . . I have."[26]

According to Ellsberg, he never felt any animus toward Carol. "I loved her from beginning to end," he says. During a discussion I had with both him and his second wife, Patricia, Ellsberg remarked, "I could love her still." And he would have never asked for a divorce, he remembered. His marital frustrations weren't *that* great, and he couldn't imagine leaving their children.[27]

Toward the end of their marriage, Ellsberg did worry about Carol's fidelity. He spent most of the fall of 1963 in Washington. "He called a couple of times, and both times he thought there was a man there with me," Carol recounts. "One time it was the TV, it was the news—Walter Cronkite or something like that [laughs]. And the other time I said, 'Excuse me'—I had the washing machine on and I went to turn off the washing machine—and he said, 'Who's there?'" Ellsberg had "a general feeling that I was up to no good," Carol remembers. "But it wasn't true. . . . I never went out with anybody or had any romantic interests in anybody while I was married." To others, Ellsberg accused Carol of having an affair. A RAND man she dated for a few months after their separation told her that Ellsberg was casting aspersions on her. "So, I thought, all those people at RAND think I'm an unfaithful wife who was terrible to the great man," Carol recalls. Ellsberg would subsequently explain Carol's decision to divorce him by referring to her alleged affair with a man at UCLA. Andrew Marshall later thought that was the only way he could imagine her wanting a divorce: it had to be another man rather than hatred or it would have been too big of a blow to his ego.[28]

Ellsberg tried to keep his own affairs hidden from Carol. "I took great pains, on the whole, that she should not know," he told me. And "she never said anything about it to me. . . . At the time she asked for a divorce, I expected to hear some comment on it, possibly." But she still didn't say anything. Ellsberg is "certain" that Carol was not aware of his affairs. But she made irritable remarks to him later that she had learned of them, he recounts. "Then she said, 'Well, I felt like a fool,'" or words to that effect. But she also "thanked me for not knowing," Ellsberg claims. Carol told me: "He was philandering, but I didn't suspect it. . . . I was sort of innocent that way. I mean, looking back on it, there were many signs. Diner's Club bills and stuff, flowers and stuff. You know, it was always that he was collecting it [the flowers] for other guys in the office. . . . I mean, I would see the Diner's Club bill and I would say, 'Why were there these flowers?'" Or, "Why did you rent a Jaguar?"[29]

But others doubt Carol was so innocent. "She suspected his philandering," Mary Marshall recalls. "That was one of the sore points: the women," Kolkowicz says. Robert Ellsberg would later tell a friend of his father, according to the friend, that his mother's "big complaint" was that "'every time I needed him he was off in some foreign country cohabiting with somebody.' That's my memory of the word—'cohabiting,'" the friend says. "It might have been 'fornicating' . . . but it was a fancy word," but spoken after the fact. Carol told me that Dan's affairs had nothing to do with their divorce. But as Donald Hall says, "They didn't help. They helped to draw him away and they helped to push her away."[30]

Ellsberg's affairs were known to others. He was less than discreet about them. It didn't take much, if any, prompting for him to talk about sex. He obviously enjoyed talking about it tremendously. Some of Ellsberg's colleagues probably joined in such discussions happily (more than they might acknowledge now, perhaps), while others were taken aback, ill at ease, or embarrassed. "He engaged in what I thought was childish, almost infantile sexual braggadocio," one RAND analyst told me. "I was sort of stunned that he would volunteer that stuff. . . . It was not barroom macho talk. It was Dan exploring the lower depths and higher limits, and a felt need to convey this to other people for the purpose of letting them know that he was there. . . . To convey to others that he was living at the upper edge." And to forge an intimacy. Ellsberg would talk about sex with the same intensity that he talked about strategic issues. His boyish enthusiasm for sharing secrets and discoveries was evident. "He was, I think, exactly that way whenever he discovered what it felt like to be in bed with a woman," Thomas Schelling remembers. "He just couldn't wait to tell you. And it wasn't bragging. It was just, 'Gee, mom, look what I found out.'" Ellsberg's sexual discoveries were "like those classified nuclear secrets," Schelling observes. "He knows something that he finds so startlingly interesting that he can't help talking about it."[31]

Ellsberg's sex talk would become more common after his divorce, but it was nonetheless quite marked when he was married. "There were all these women," Don Hall knew. "He was unbelievable," Kirby Hall remembers; "he made the rest of them look tame." Ellsberg exhibited "this sort of juvenile lasciviousness," Hans Heymann, another RAND analyst at the time, chuckles. "It was very apparent that he had this thing." Simon Bourgin recalls:

> He's a great womanizer. He's so bloody attractive. And then I think he's one of those men who doesn't have to have a natural line with women. I think he just sidles up to them and everything is done. He's the kind of guy who women like to sort of adopt, because he's boyish and he looks as if he needs mothering. . . . We talked about women a lot. . . . As a matter of fact, my secretary. . . . She was a tall, good looking Radcliffe girl . . . well built and very smart, and knew her measure of men. And she and Dan liked each other.[32]

Kolkowicz recounts:

> He bragged about his macho and what a stud he is. . . . For example, he
> bragged to me once that he just took off one evening—he walked out. You
> know, he was bored at home, he walked out to get . . . a pack of gum, I guess
> he said. And he went straight to the airport, went to Tahiti. Stayed two weeks.
> Picked up a very young, beautiful native. And he didn't tell Carol a thing. His
> great kick was to sit by the pier where the tourist boats would come in several
> times a week with this beautiful young girl, and hold his arm around her and
> watch these fat ugly old tourists sort of schlep down the gangway. . . . I asked
> him why does he go to this Tahiti bullshit. "You didn't tell your wife for two
> weeks?" He says, "I needed it. I needed to get away." . . . There was a sense
> like the rules are not made for him.

Ellsberg told me he did take off to Tahiti once while married but declined to
talk about the episode, beyond saying "I love the story."[33]

Ellsberg, who was an amateur photographer and at some point an accomplished one, showed Kolkowicz nude photos of a young Tahitian woman. "He
had them in his briefcase," Kolkowicz recalls. "And he would pull them out."
Kolkowicz remembers Ellsberg displaying photos of Swedish stewardesses too.
"Amazingly enough, I don't recall ever sleeping with a stewardess," Ellsberg
told me. "It's been a nightmare of mine that I will meet some woman some day
that I have slept with that I won't remember. But it never happened to me
yet. . . . And I would say that I have never slept knowingly with a stewardess."
But others also recall Ellsberg talking of his involvement with one or more
Swedish stewardesses. Over time, there were "various pictures," Kolkowicz
adds. "Whenever he had a new set of pictures, I would see them."[34]

Other RAND colleagues also recall hearing of Ellsberg's adventures in
Tahiti. After all, he returned to RAND bragging about his exploits. Hans Heymann recounts: "He'd had a lovely encounter with a beauteous young lady,
whose picture he paraded around in dishabille. . . . It was a bit juvenile. But,
anyway, he was all full of enthusiasm. . . . That was his big secret. . . . He never
called it a secret, but he obviously had this great mystique about it. You know,
that he was unveiling to the beauties of romance and passion and what have
you. It was never a case of his saying to me, 'You're sworn to secrecy. Don't tell
anybody.' Because he was going around showing these [pictures] to everybody."
He even had the photos up on his bulletin board in his office at RAND. "In any
case," Heymann continues,

> we were invited to a party. It was either at his house or somebody else's house
> in Santa Monica. And somehow the conversation turned to the Pacific and the

South Sea islands and so forth. And somebody said, "Gee, what are the nicest islands to go to?" And I said, "Well, you ought to ask Dan. Because he's been to Tahiti. He obviously can tell you about that." I said it innocently. Well, his wife happened to be there. And he looked at me in absolute horror. And he said, "Who? *Me?* I've never been to Tahiti. What are you talking about? . . ." So I said, "Gee, I must have got you mixed up with somebody else."

Carol seemed stunned, Heymann recalls. "She didn't say anything, but it was clear that she was extremely embarrassed. And very uptight. I had caused a little problem for him." But "from that day on, that guy Ellsberg went around telling everybody, 'Heymann's a nice guy, but you can't trust him with secrets.'"[35]

During a visit I made to RAND in 1994, as a secretary was escorting me to an office, she asked what had brought me to RAND. When I told her I was interviewing people for a biography of Daniel Ellsberg, she responded, out of the blue, "He's the guy who showed the photos of the nude women in Tahiti to everyone." She had been a young secretary at RAND at the time, and Ellsberg had shown her some pictures, too. Most men who roll out sexy photos of women (and most probably keep them to themselves) do so before other men. "But I think he would rather show it to girls," Konrad Kellen chuckles. "To get around to the sexual area. And then go on from there." Others also remember Dan Ellsberg and his photos. "There was one time when he had a thick wad of photographs of Asian women," Don Hall recounts. "Some nude. . . . And he was showing them very inappropriately. That is, people didn't know how to react. And he was showing them around anyway." It was "at some inappropriate place, some academic place. . . . I didn't even want to sit down just the two of us and look at them. . . . But that he was doing it. And people were obviously feeling distaste, and he didn't even *notice* it." Hall believes Ellsberg was married at the time. Later, after he was divorced, Jim Digby amusedly recounts, "we invited him to dinner here, and he said, 'Oh, I've got to show you my slides from the Ile du Levant.'" (The Ile du Levant is a famous French nudist island.) "Dan had taken these slides of whatever girl he was with at the time on the Isle de Levant," Digby says. "He showed them to me, and probably Mary Jane," Digby's wife. "There was specifically some of a woman that he had been dating at the Isle de Levant."[36]

According to Kolkowicz, Ellsberg had a romantic little spot in Malibu for some of his affairs. "It was a sort of a cheesy little motel, but it was right on the water. . . . You could be hidden down there below. . . . Well, that was his *pied-a-terre* . . . his top-secret hideaway." Although "it would have been nice," Ellsberg told me, he denies maintaining such a place while married. "When I lived out of the house, I went to a motel right next to RAND. . . . What he may be confusing here is that there were a few occasions when I slept with somebody at the Surf Rider Motel. . . . I certainly had affairs. But I didn't have a place down there. I went to their place."[37]

While in Paris for a NATO meeting in December 1963, before Carol asked for a divorce, Ellsberg had dinner with Andrew Marshall (who had recently been stationed with NATO in Paris), Mary Marshall, Harry Rowen, and others. "He was talking about buying scarves for this girl and that girl," Mary Marshall recounts. "He was coming home with presents for every woman he knew, practically. . . . It was like he was buying for three or four. . . . I have this feeling that we were standing out on a street, either before or after dinner. And he was full of vim, vigor, and vitality, and laughing. And he was telling me, basically, that he had done this shopping. And he may have even shown me something." Marshall was puzzled: she was a friend of Carol. "It was said with a smile, a little laugh, and so forth," Marshall remembers. "He wasn't really boasting. It was hardly more than a couple of sentences, but you understood." Andrew Marshall (who would also later remember the scene) and the other men present "were rolling their eyes at some of this stuff," Mary Marshall recalls. "Everybody always seemed to be extremely indulgent of Dan. . . . Like the 'bad boy,' or 'Isn't he adorable?' . . . All the men were smiling, like, 'Well, this is our little Dan.' He amused them." Some probably envied him.[38]

One of the women Ellsberg was buying presents for was Yvonne Svenle. He had met Svenle in 1963, she would later testify in his Pentagon Papers trial, probably in Washington. Ellsberg was having an affair with her. It may have been the "long affair" he mentioned earlier. He was "rapturous" about her, Jerry Goodman reminisces, "everything about her." Svenle was a young Swedish citizen who worked at the Swedish embassy. She was a very nice person, by all accounts, bright—though not as bright as Ellsberg wished, it would turn out—blonde, and fairly attractive. "That fine figure of a woman," one male juror would call her. Svenle lived with Ellsberg in Malibu after his divorce.[39]

Kolkowicz would notice over the years that Ellsberg had "a powerful influence on women. And he always goes for the good-looking women. . . . It was important to him." Deirdre Henderson thought Ellsberg considered himself "quite the ladies man." Henderson saw him socially in Washington in the early 1960s. Ellsberg would call her up and ask to get together; one might say they dated, though Henderson stresses that she was not interested in Ellsberg romantically. Ellsberg made overtures to Henderson, but "he didn't get beyond the verbal nuances," she says. "I just couldn't take that much of him. Even for lunch. I mean, he would start on this business of nuclear weapons and . . . deterrent and everything.

It was just so boring. . . . Then he'd say something about, 'You're so beautiful.' . . . He always tried to say [softly] . . . 'You're the most beautiful person I've ever met.' . . . That was the line. . . . So at every stage, if he'd start on that baloney line, I would just turn him right off." Ellsberg was "always very self-conscious about his projection of his words and his voice and his manner," Henderson remembers. And, he was "very good at theatrics. The voice, the words, the slight slippage in his [tone]."[40]

Ellsberg told me his sexual frustration in his marriage fueled his affairs. But sexual satisfaction was surely not his only motivation for seeing other women, nor is it, of course, for most men who have affairs. Richard Zeckhauser recalls that when he listened to Ellsberg describe his sexual adventures, probably after his separation from Carol,

> I didn't have the impression that he was getting incredible sexual pleasure from all of this. I mean, I don't think it was promiscuity because he was basically a promiscuous person. And I don't think that he was a satyr or anything like that. I think it was sort of the game and the pursuit and "look at my power." . . . Once again it was proving himself, but in another field. Because, "Here I am, I'm real good and I'm well respected at RAND. But when I'm in a bar or when I'm picking up stewardesses, I'm just a guy with charm." . . . In other words, it's more to see, "Can I get this attractive woman to like me?" Or, "Can I get them to do things that they haven't done before?" . . . Having women like you is sort of a very unambiguous measure of your magnetism. . . . "I'm not going to give them money, so it's not that I'm rich. And particularly if they're just stewardesses, it's not even that I'm a great scholar. It's just I personally am so dynamic."

The reasons for Ellsberg's affairs could have been numerous. He has spoken of his need for intimacy and affection that wasn't being met through Carol. It's a need that might have had roots in his childhood since he was raised by an unnurturing mother. He may have been looking in part for someone to tell him that he was lovable, to express warmth towards him. Ellsberg may have also been attempting to confirm his masculinity and physical attractiveness through his affairs. ("He has always been so sensitive about, 'Am I an attractive sexual male?'" one friend of his observes.) Ellsberg could obtain "narcissistic supplies" from his lovers too. He might have been looking, to some extent, for admiration. Joan Cleveland believes Ellsberg's womanizing and that of some of his contemporaries "was filling a really neurotic need on the part of these young men to find people who would constantly tell them how wonderful they were. And they particularly liked people who didn't know them very well, because they didn't know yet anything bad about them. I mean, the first meeting you're just plain wonderful. After six meetings, I know that you have all these nasty habits. And so I think there was sort of constant requirements for fresh supplies of people who would be in the first stages of, 'Gee, aren't you wonderful.'"[41] Ellsberg's affairs may have also been outlets for internal pressures or ways to add excitement to his life. The possibilities are, of course, endless.

—◦◦◦—

Meanwhile, Carol Ellsberg was doing a slow burn. Or a not so slow burn. "She didn't like him," she would tell Kirby Hall later. "She did not like him," Hall stresses, and "he would be hard to like." "She really disapproved of him," Mary Marshall noticed. "She had contempt for him and his silliness, a lot of these things that he did that finally got on her nerves. Like drumming on the drums . . . in the living room . . . or he'd [have] his flights of fancy . . . I think she was no longer beguiled by his brightness." That is undoubtedly true. Carol grew increasingly impatient with her husband. "I think she thought he was a kind of a fool," Marshall recalls. "This guy that she was married to was wild and woolly . . . and in her rather self-disciplined and ideal world, this was driving her nuts. . . . I just had the feeling that as she looked around, she was wondering why in the hell she had to be married to this wild man, who wasn't particularly sympathetic. Not because he can't feel these things; they just never occurred to him. He's insensitive to these things, to all this sort of thing."[42]

"There were so *many* reasons" for wanting a divorce, Carol told me with a laugh. "I mean, it wasn't any big secret." For starters, Ellsberg was not only inconsiderate and self-absorbed, but apparently incorrigibly so. He was also a poor listener. "She was being treated as an appurtenance, more or less," Gus Shubert perceived. Don Hall, who talked to Ellsberg about his divorce afterward but didn't get any great explanations from him, recalls Ellsberg saying "that she wasn't interested in what he was doing, and he wasn't interested in what she was doing. They had grown apart." Ellsberg thought his own work was extremely important, more important than Carol's. "Yes, I thought what I was doing was very important, of course," he told me. "It's interesting she would compare the two." And there was that problem of him always being away when Carol needed his help. It was as if she was on her own most of the time anyway. She may have wondered what good he was. She would later complain to Mary Marshall, "And there he was, not here." Ellsberg traveled on *his* schedule. He spent increasing time in Washington—doing exactly what, Carol didn't know—while she had to take care of their children and go to school. But although "he was always away," she told me, "I didn't mind it." It was "sort of a relief. . . . I felt happier. I didn't seem to cry as much when he was away. Life was rather peaceful." Who knows, if he'd been home every night, she might have asked for a divorce earlier.[43]

Ellsberg's travels were a source of irritation to Carol in December 1963, when he was in Paris for the NATO meeting. "Robert got sick and was in the hospital," she recounts. "I was kind of scared. It turned out not to be serious. But I guess the doctor was a little scared, too. He had a lot of symptoms." Carol worried that Robert might even have juvenile arthritis, leukemia, or some other serious disease. But once again, Dan was nowhere to be found. "I called and I couldn't reach him," Carol remembers. "Then, the next I knew, Beverly Rowen called and said he'd gotten this wonderful chance to go to France." Ellsberg says he flew off to Paris "on very short notice. I was in Washington. . . . I was supposed to be out with somebody that night. I had to cancel that appointment from the plane, it was on such short notice. . . . I had a date for dinner that night." Ellsberg had been walking out of the Pentagon with Harry Rowen, who was going to Andrews Air Force base to fly to Paris for the NATO meeting, he recounts, and expressing concern that somebody else would rewrite the speech he had drafted for McNamara to deliver at the meeting. Ellsberg thought he was the man to do that. "So Harry says, 'Well, hell, why don't you come to Paris? . . . You can come on the plane with me,'" he remembers. Although Ellsberg did not have any extra clothes with him,

> we just left from the Pentagon. . . . It was about 4:30 in the afternoon. I thought that was a rather dashing thing to do. . . . The whole thing had this wild, sort of fun aspect to it. Here I'm going to Paris on one hour's notice. . . . We dashed to Andrews to get on the plane. We dash onto the plane, the plane takes off. I ask, "Is there some way I can phone back to this hotel and tell the person I'm supposed to meet?" They said, "Yeah, we have a radio phone here." So I left a message at the hotel for my dinner date to say, "I'm sorry, I'm off to Paris." . . . So there I was that night in Paris, without even a toothbrush or anything. A game thing to do.

Ellsberg says he didn't know Robert was ill. He also saw no reason to contact Carol: "I don't even know if I would have bothered to call home. Because what does it matter? I'm only going for a couple of days." But Carol was upset. Although she had already decided to get a divorce, "it sure didn't make me want to change my mind, I'm telling you," she recalls.[44]

There was also a continuing difference of opinion over the desirability of moving to Washington. Dan's wish to take a job there had grown after he had completed his Ph.D. dissertation. "I said, 'Now it's time for me to go to Washington,'" he recounts. "That's when she said, 'I won't go to Washington.'" Ellsberg got hot on going again after the Cuban missile crisis. Then, in 1963, Carol told him that he could go to Washington as much as he wanted, so he spent a lot of time there that year, perhaps six months or so. Carol later told him when she demanded a divorce that December, he recalls, "I wanted you to be away. I didn't want to be with you. I couldn't stand to be around you."[45]

That fall, in Ellsberg's retelling, Adam Yarmolinsky, Robert McNamara's special assistant, asked him to be his deputy, in fact urged him quite strongly to be his deputy. Ellsberg says they were friends at the time. Yarmolinsky denied it when I interviewed him. (One episode may summarize the nature of their relationship. Ellsberg interviewed Yarmolinsky in 1964 for Yarmolinsky's oral history for the Kennedy Library. In the interview, Ellsberg spoke much more frequently than did other Kennedy oral history interviewers and was notably well informed about the issues. He seemed to be showing off his knowledge at times. Yarmolinsky, in turn, often offered short answers, which perhaps suggests that he was either feeling insecure about his own knowledge compared to Ellsberg's or was simply getting annoyed by Ellsberg's showing off.)[46]

Ellsberg remembers that Yarmolinsky told him when offering him the job that he'd be "a top candidate" to replace him as McNamara's special assistant later (though the decision would be McNamara's). The job offer was extremely attractive to Ellsberg. "I thought, 'Wow, I'll work right next to McNamara. . . . I'll see an awful lot of what comes into the secretary . . . and be in on things.'" But Carol told him, "No way."[47] For her, the marriage was over by that point.

Yarmolinsky told me he did not have a deputy, however, and thus couldn't have offered Ellsberg such a position, though he might have considered hiring him as an assistant of another sort. Ellsberg may have come to him and said he'd *like* to be his deputy, Yarmolinsky recalled, "and my reaction was probably some flattery, because he was a hotshot kid."[48]

In any event, on November 22 Ellsberg was having lunch in Washington with a former boss at RAND, Burt Klein, another father figure to him. Toward the end of the lunch, Ellsberg recounts, as he was about to drive Klein back to work,

> I said, "You know, Burt, I have decided that I will come to Washington. That I've just got to do it. And I will hope that Carol will be joining me. And I will try to get her to join me. . . . But in any case, I have got to come to Washington."
> . . . It was raining. . . . Just before he got out of the car, he said, "Dan, if you give up your marriage for your job, I will never forgive you." I said, "Jesus

Christ, Burt. How can you say such a thing?" Because I loved him, and I had a feeling that he loved me, as far as that goes. He said, "Well, that's what wrecked my first marriage. . . . Your wife is basically right. You shouldn't come to Washington. And it will break up your marriage. . . ."

. . . Far from saying or ever hinting that she wanted a divorce, the warning she was saying was, "I will not go to Washington, because if we go to Washington, this marriage will not survive. . . ." I hardly knew what she meant, exactly. It didn't quite make sense to me. . . .

He got out of the car and closed the door. I started crying. And I just was sobbing. And I was thinking, "God, I've got enough problems. With Carol, and my kids, and my family. And now I'm hearing that my friends will not forgive me. . . ."

So I was crying all the way back to the Pentagon, to the river entrance. I think the rain stopped about that time. I parked in the parking lot in front of the river entrance, which is a very choice parking space. . . . So I walk up the stairs, and everybody else is crying. I said, "What are they crying for?" . . . Kennedy had been shot. . . . I had no emotional energy. None at all: "I've got my own problems here [laughs]. I can't think about that now."[49]

There were other sources of strain in the Ellsbergs' marriage. Like, perhaps, Dan's failure to devote more attention to their children. He would later conclude that it influenced Carol's decision to divorce him. But "for all my sins of being away when Robert was six months old," he says, referring to his extension of his marine tour, "by the time she went to nursing school . . . I had more of the children for those four years than she did. Considerably more. . . . Except when I was away out of town, which was a lot in the last year." One wonders what Carol would think of that recollection. She would not discuss Ellsberg's parenting with me, saying, "That's getting into an area that I don't want to get into, because I don't want to be too bitchy about this." But once, when showing me a photo of him and Robert (who was then a baby) sitting at the piano together, she made a sarcastic remark about the seemingly doting father. "Certainly he was not very domestic," she says.[50]

But Ellsberg obviously loved his children, and Carol knew that. Mary Marshall, who never heard her complain about his parenting, thought he always treated them like "little adults." He would try to engage Robert in particular (who was three years older than his daughter, Mary) in intellectual discussions. Robert told me his father always treated him

as a dialogue partner whom he took very seriously. Sometimes that was maybe a burden. And sometimes it made me feel intellectually inadequate, or not able to hold up my own. . . . He always talked with me pretty seriously about the things he was reading and the things that he was intellectually concerned with. At a time when I was too young to have developed maybe my own thoughts on these subjects . . . and not always feeling capable of returning much of value. . . . He clearly got something out of it. . . . That's the kind of relationship we had.[51]

As for the sexual strain in the Ellsbergs' marriage, Ellsberg would later tell a journalist, "I'd always been very uninhibited about sex, but hadn't had a chance to express that during my marriage." He also probably wanted to discuss their sex life more than Carol did. He would subsequently discuss it with Thomas Schelling, who remembers, "I think he didn't so much blame her as say, 'We should never have gotten married.'"[52]

Not least important, the Ellsbergs' marriage had not been planted in solid ground. They had married at age 19, based on an apparent misunderstanding; they were short on common interests. It's not surprising their union didn't last. Ellsberg would remark after their separation that "the marriage was a misunderstanding from the beginning," Schelling says.[53]

———⊙———

It was in October of 1963 that Carol finally decided she'd had enough. Her husband was then in Washington. "One day I just thought, 'I could get divorced,'" she recounts. "'Why didn't I ever think of this thirteen years ago?' . . . He'd been away and things were going well [laughs]. I was enjoying my work, and the children were doing well. I thought, 'Maybe it's [time].'"[54] She was now a nurse; she had a marketable skill. That could not have been irrelevant.

But Carol didn't tell Dan of her decision right away. "For one thing, he was in Washington and it would have had to be over the phone," she explains. "And secondly, Christmas was coming up. My parents were coming to visit for Christmas—terrible timing. So I told him the day after, or a couple of days after, Christmas." Ellsberg, who would claim later that she told him on Christmas day, had just returned home the week of Christmas. Carol's parents were still there when she made her move. "I didn't do it on purpose," she recalls. "It came out in the course of our talking," as demands for divorce often do. Her father noticed some tension in the air afterward, and as he was leaving he asked Carol if something was wrong. She told him. "He looked very upset," she remembers.[55]

Ellsberg recalls that his fateful conversation with Carol took place in their upstairs bedroom. "It was just a short conversation," lasting only "maybe 40 minutes," he says. When Carol told him what she wanted, he was startled. "It was just *astonishing* to me," he recounts. "It just came out of the blue." He had thought things were getting a little better between them. He seemed "awful sad," Carol remembers. ("How often have you wanted to take Dan Ellsberg by the shoulders and say, 'What did you think was going to happen when you did that?'" Joan Cleveland remarks, pointing to his behavior that led to his divorce as a prime example. "And he was genuinely surprised by the consequences.") According to Ellsberg, Carol wouldn't tell him why she wanted a divorce. "I asked her, 'What's the problem?' She said, 'I don't want to talk about it.' . . . She said she wanted a divorce, that was it." "I didn't really want to get into it," Carol reminisces. "And Dan always likes to talk about things. And I had already decided. . . . I'd had a couple of months to think about it. So I just was determined." Whatever she told him, it wasn't enough, as he kept pushing for an explanation.[56]

In Ellsberg's retelling, Carol told him she didn't love him. "I said, 'Well, how long have you felt that way?'" he recounts. Carol replied, he says, "'I never loved you.' And then I said, 'That's ridiculous. How could you say that?' . . . She said, 'Well, of course, at the beginning I was in love with you.' . . . But she implied that *before long*" that had changed. After Ellsberg told the journalist Joe McGinniss that his wife had informed him that she'd never loved him, he added, "I wish she had remembered to tell me that a little sooner. Like before we got married." Carol was not pleased when she read Ellsberg's quotes. "That always has annoyed me very much," she told me. She strongly denies telling Ellsberg she never loved him. And "he knows I never said that." Ellsberg told their children he was sorry he said it to McGinniss, yet said it again to me. He also told me he didn't recall discussing Carol's purported remark with any journalist, and added, "If you find that in print, I'll be very surprised."[57]

Ellsberg was not ready to simply give up his marriage. "As is typical, he went out and bought some books about divorce," Carol recalls. "Wanted to read those and discuss them." "That's what he'd do," Don Hall comments. "Set her up. Set her up." Hall adds, "I think the man who handed Carol the books on divorce is absolutely the same man who set out to figure out how to seduce [her at Harvard]. He probably read books about seduction." Carol was not interested in the books, however. "I'd made up my mind. I mean, this was no time for marriage counseling or anything like that," and with Dan Ellsberg "you don't really want to start in it, because then you have to argue over every single [point]. . . . He'd say, 'Well, you've got it wrong,' or 'You've misunderstood.' Da da da. . . . But I'm sure it would have been extremely frustrating to him, because he wasn't getting a chance to talk about it."[58]

In some marriages, spouses reach a point where there is nothing more to be said, and Carol had apparently reached that point. "Dan would chew a bone forever, thinking he could get some meat off it, when there was none," Kirby Hall comments.[59]

Feeling devastated, depressed, and probably angry, Ellsberg moved out of the house a few days later. He attended a New Year's party at Jerry and Sallie Goodman's house first. Carol had originally planned to attend as well, but not now. "I remember my strange disoriented feelings," Ellsberg recounts. "Here I was without Carol." For a time, he focused his attention on a woman at the party: "She looked stunning."[60]

Ellsberg went skydiving shortly thereafter. He'd always wanted to and now he had an opportunity to go with a RAND guard: "I leaped at it." There were times in Ellsberg's life when depression led him to take risks, and this was evidently one of them. "He was with a girlfriend," Carol remembers.[61]

Ellsberg also wanted to take his children along. "I didn't think that sounded like a very nice day for the children," Carol recalls. "To go stand with daddy's new girlfriend and watching him jump out of planes. I thought that was too tense and nerve-wracking." And what if something happened? "So I said, 'No, they couldn't do that.' . . . He said, 'You don't have the right to refuse me the company of my children.' And da da da da da. And I said, 'Well, I do. It's not going to happen.' . . . That's the only time I can think of when I said, 'Absolutely, they can't go on this excursion.'"[62] Until the Pentagon Papers, that is.

One has to question Ellsberg's judgment here. Yet he also missed Robert and Mary acutely after his separation from Carol. He cried when he spoke to his children about the divorce, he said later.[63]

Ellsberg may have felt abandoned again after his marriage collapsed. There had been the death of his mother earlier, and his father's subsequent remove. This was another powerful blow to his sense of security. His internal turmoil, his emotional frenzy, must have been truly immense. "He was very upset," Andrew Marshall recalls. Asked how long it took him to recover, Ellsberg responded, without wanting to get specific, "In a certain sense, I never recovered." Perhaps he meant the doubts he said he consequently feels in relationships.[64] Certainly, Carol's rejection of him fed his insecurities enormously.

Gus Shubert, among many others, got a taste of Ellsberg's distress and his anger. Shubert was then the acting head of the economics department at RAND. He recounts:

> When I sat down with him during his divorce—which I was doing almost on a two or three times a week basis—he would come in and tell me about what was going on. It was clear there was a real hostility building up there, and his

dominance was being challenged. . . . For some reason, I really don't know why, Dan singled me out as a person [through] whom he wished to seek release from all this. So he would come in and say things like, "Oh, you'll never guess what she's done to me now!" And I said, "Well, I'm not going to try." And then he would list some particularly—in his mind—heinous crime that she had committed. [This] really did go on and on through the whole divorce. Which I think he found sort of an insult. The divorce. I know he was very unhappy. But that's really all we talked about in those sessions, was about the divorce and what *she* was doing. Never what *he* was doing. Always what *she* was doing to him.

To Ellsberg's way of thinking, Shubert remembers, "the divorce was an attack. He interpreted some of her actions as *deliberately* designed to thwart him and frustrate him. And he may have been right." For example: "I remember one day he came in and he said, 'You won't believe this. . . . Last night we were dividing up the property, and we were dividing up the phonograph records. And we laid them all out on the floor, every record that we owned. And we arranged them by records that she liked and records that I liked. And our tastes in music were very different. And she took every one of those that I liked. Leaving me with all that stuff of hers that I didn't like at all.'" Relations between Dan and Carol were only going further downhill.[65]

Kirby Hall also got a dose of Ellsberg's anger. He took her out for a chocolate soufflé in Washington, perhaps in part to vent. "He was *furious* at [Carol]," Hall recounts. "Because there was some vacation that they had scheduled. And so they all went on this vacation. And *then* she told him" she wanted a divorce. "He was determined to feel exploited. And if there was any exploiting, it wasn't on [her side]."[66]

Ellsberg was reaching out to whomever he could for support. Discussions turned into angry monologues. "It was very, very [consuming], in terms of time and in sort of emotional drain on him and me," Shubert recalls. "But we never discussed the cause. In fact, I don't even think we discussed who . . . had filed for divorce." The nuclear strategist Bernard Brodie took Ellsberg under his wing, in a sense. Alexander George got the impression (probably from Brodie) "that Bernard was really holding hands in a very serious and constructive way with Dan." Brodie's biographer would later see letters from Ellsberg to Brodie in which Ellsberg was "reaching out to him." "With me at least, he claimed he was hurt," Roman Kolkowicz remembers. Also, "he felt guilty. But he says he doesn't know why. And he says she doesn't understand." Ellsberg seemed to another colleague at a loss to figure out the divorce.[67]

Carol Ellsberg sometimes vented her own anger to others. "She made a big fuss over something that I balled her out for, and I never convinced her," Mary Marshall recounts. "She brought up the fact that he had squandered her inheritance. . . . He had invested it, and the stocks went down. I said, 'Come on! . . . You're married! If he'd made a million, you'd have thought it was wonderful.' Well, anyway, she wanted it back, is what she really wanted." After the Pentagon Papers were published, Carol told the FBI that she had earlier inherited "approximately $13,000 that had been in trust for her," according to an FBI memo:

> Shortly after their marriage, Daniel became avidly and financially involved in the stock market and often spoke of the success he had made in this field. However, at the time of their divorce she learned that he had not been successful to the extent claimed and had lost her entire $13,000. This was one of the circumstances that led to her being given title to the home they had purchased in 1959 and which home she currently occupies with her children.
>
> Carol stated that Daniel handled their checking account and it was continually out of balance. She explained that Daniel would write checks and at times have no idea of the status of his account, having to call the bank to determine the amount of money currently on balance.[68]

In RAND circles, Carol was somewhat of an outcast after their marital breakup. "Everybody took Dan's [side]," Mary Marshall recalls. "And nobody even inquired about hers." Virtually everyone assumed Dan had asked for the divorce. But some would have leaped to Carol's defense, including James Schlesinger, the future defense secretary and CIA director. Schlesinger expressed concern for her well-being. He was "quite offended" by some of Ellsberg's behavior, Carol remembers. "I know he did let me know that some bad things were being said to people" about her by Dan.[69]

When I interviewed him in 1995, Ellsberg was still wondering why Carol divorced him. "She didn't tell you?" he asked me. "I've never really known what it was. . . . I can only speculate. . . . She's never told me."[70] But Ellsberg surely has a better sense of it than he lets on.

At Christmas in 1993, he visited Carol's home (his former home) because his children Robert and Mary were there. "He was in one of these introspective moods, where he wanted to know why I wanted the divorce," Carol recounts. "I guess it's irritated him that I've never wished to discuss it with him. So he began discussing it with the children." Ellsberg stayed up into the wee hours with them, talking about it. "He wasn't really that interested in hearing what they had to say and what I had to say," Carol recalls. "He'd had these [ideas] that he was trying out."[71]

As would be expected, the dissolution of their parents' marriage was not easy on Robert and Mary. They missed their father, who provided, among other things, excitement and surprises in their lives. Robert reminisces:

> I think that I felt a kind of sadness and loss. And it made me a little more introspective. I tended to turn inward somewhat. . . . I don't think I was an unhappy child growing up, or prone to sadness or depression, but . . . maybe it contributed to my kind of thinking more about serious aspects of life. . . . I didn't see my father for long periods, especially when he moved to Washington and when he went to Vietnam. . . . When I think of my relationship with my own children now, how much that's a part of my life, I feel sad to have not had that kind of a family life.

Asked how her parents' breakup affected her, Mary Ellsberg responded, "I would say that Robert and I were pretty stoical about everything that happened to us. . . . Dad wasn't around much before the divorce either, so I don't think it was that big a change."[72]

Ellsberg would claim later that Carol badmouthed him to their children after their separation, turning them against him. But Robert recalls, "My mother didn't tell me anything." Mary, who would come to have very resentful feelings toward her father, for a complicated mix of reasons, told me:

> I was probably more demanding than Robert, and more aware of feeling let down by him [her father]. Dad was a difficult person to be around. He was unreliable, chronically forgetful or late to pick us up, would wander into bookstores or record stores on the way to a restaurant for dinner and would become so absorbed that he would spend what seemed like hours reading and forget all about dinner, or whatever plans we had. He would bring newspapers to the table and start reading out loud or lecturing on whatever subject he was researching at the time (in the early years it was the [Vietnam] war, then nuclear holocaust, then the nature of evil, etc.). He almost invariably got our birthdays confused and often our names (he often confuses me with my mother, or his sister [Gloria] who died when he was young, and he often confused Robert and Michael's [his son by Patricia] names, even though there are 21 years between them). He seemed to love us passionately in [the] abstract, but had a hard time focusing on us as children. Most of the time we were simply resigned, but probably I resented it more, and showed it more than Robert.[73]

Carol Ellsberg filed for divorce in July of 1964. Owing to financial arrangements over their house, she soon withdrew her petition; but when those financial matters had been cleared up so that she could gain title to the house, she filed for divorce again in March 1965 (there was no reconciliation of any sort in the meantime). Ellsberg was a bit perplexed when Carol proceeded with the final judgment of divorce in 1966 when he was in Vietnam. "I [had] urged Carol not to make it final so that she would get my [government] benefit from Vietnam, in addition to my alimony that I was paying," he remembers. "She would get, as my wife, quite a hefty allowance for my being away in Vietnam. Which cost me nothing and was good for her." But she gave it up when their divorce was finalized, "for reasons that I've never known. . . . I wasn't hardly bothering her; I was in Vietnam. What difference did it make? . . . I know I called back to her and I said, 'This is foolish. You're just giving up free money here. . . . Why are you even thinking of giving this up? It doesn't make any sense.'"[74]

But "she wanted to be divorced, period," Ellsberg observes, adding, "That's wanting to be divorced quite a bit."[75]

SEVEN

DAMAGED GOODS

REELING FROM HIS MARITAL BREAKUP, ELLSBERG MOVED TO WASHINGTON in 1964. He did not have a job offer. Rather, he had been invited to conduct a study. Thomas Schelling, who ran some military crisis games in the Pentagon, his close friend John McNaughton, who was the incoming assistant secretary of defense for International Security Affairs (ISA), and a couple of other officials "worked out a kind of study that we wanted an imaginative person to do," Schelling recounts.

> And I remember thinking, "Dan Ellsberg is the man for the job. And now that he's left his wife, maybe he'd like an excuse to move 3,000 miles away." . . . We thought, much as he liked RAND, we could probably spring him loose now that his family was breaking up. . . . I thought he was perfect for this job. . . . I thought (a) he's got the kind of intellect and curiosity that we need, and (b) he has been immersed in command and control. And that combination of experience and quality of mind, I thought, meant that there was nobody else in the world that could do what he could do.

But "he never did the study," Schelling remembers. "I never knew why. . . . Very likely, Dan got there and decided there were other things he'd rather do."[1]

Ellsberg did embark on a study that winter under the sponsorship of Walt Rostow, who was then in the State Department. "I'd heard of him vaguely as an economist," Rostow, also an economist, recalls. "He was a talented young fellow." Rostow had received a telephone call from Harry Rowen:

He said, "We have this young fellow rattling around in the Pentagon, and we don't know what to do with him." . . . Harry called me up and told me that he was a nuisance around the Pentagon and he wasn't doing anything, and he was poking his nose every[where]. . . . Ellsberg was a very difficult character in the Pentagon to nail down to doing a routine job. . . . Harry was very honest with me about what the problem was with him. He was like a cat on a hot tin roof. . . . That was what he conveyed. He was all over the place. . . . He obviously was a fairly able fellow, but he couldn't focus.[2]

Rostow knew of Ellsberg's research on decision making under uncertainty and thought he might be able to put it to good use in a study of crises the U.S. government had faced in recent years, including the Suez, Berlin, and Cuban missile crises. "I thought that he was going to produce a really important paper, which would take the framework for his thesis and apply it to a new field," Rostow reminisces. And "I was hoping that, in the Pentagon, it would solve the problem of his rattling around." Rostow outlined the project to Ellsberg. "He seemed to like the idea," Rostow remembers. "It caught his imagination." Then "the next thing I knew he wanted a [special] clearance to get at the papers" he would need to conduct it. Ellsberg would later recall receiving "unprecedented access to data and studies in all [government] agencies" on the crises and "several special clearances." He boasted of having "very high-level access to all our secrets in the State and Defense Departments and the CIA." He also pointed out that he was "the sole researcher" on the project—which indeed he was. "No one worked with him," Rostow chuckles. "I assigned him that."[3]

Rostow, of course, assumed that Ellsberg would then produce the paper. But "then he didn't have enough clearances, and then his mind wandered," Rostow recounts. Ellsberg spent over six months on the study, but he failed to complete it.[4]

He later testified that he delivered "a formal briefing" on his research, however, "presenting my main conclusions to an international panel that had been set up to help me and watch over this project." And he completed "a good deal of manuscript" of "preliminary writing." "I never saw anything," Alexander George, who also studied crises, remembers. "I never heard of anything in writing. And I think that he had probably a well-deserved reputation for having this problem of not finishing things." Ellsberg told his friend Seymour Hersh that one reason he failed to turn in a paper to Rostow was that "it would have been so highly classified nobody would read it." That's a dubious remark, at best. "It's nonsense," Rostow says.[5]

Ellsberg did share some of his findings with colleagues, though, including the State Department's Helmut Sonnenfeldt, who found them quite illuminating and was impressed. Fred Iklé, who had been a RAND colleague, remembers Ellsberg giving a talk at Harvard on crises that was "a flop. It was just unprepared, I must say."[6]

John McNaughton asked Ellsberg to be his special assistant the summer of 1964. Schelling had testified to Ellsberg's talents to McNaughton. So had Harry Rowen. McNaughton valued intelligence greatly and was looking for brains. "Mr. McNaughton was very high on young men who had high IQs," a McNaughton aide told me. "And a guy by the name of Harry Rowen talked Mr. McNaughton into hiring Dan. . . . That's how he got hired." Rowen told McNaughton, according to this aide, who worked quite closely with McNaughton, that Ellsberg was the smartest person ever hired at RAND. Fred Haynes, who also worked in ISA, heard this account from several people. But Ellsberg recalls, "John McNaughton knew me at that point. I don't even think a recommendation from Harry added a tremendous amount." Ellsberg told one interviewer that McNaughton hired him because of his expertise in nuclear issues, and that McNaughton admired him a lot.[7]

Other people from RAND were also touting Ellsberg's brilliance in Washington at this time. Vincent Davis, who would work with Ellsberg the following summer in ISA, remembers that "people like Guy Pauker just sung the praises. They said, 'Gosh, this guy is extraordinary.'"[8]

Ellsberg was excited by the opportunity to be McNaughton's special assistant. He would be on the inside, near the highest levels of power in the Pentagon, with access to a great deal of important and sensitive material. And if he performed well, he would be in line for a promotion to deputy assistant secretary. The job was a stepping stone.

John McNaughton himself cut an impressive figure. He had been a Harvard law professor when he joined the government in 1961. His father owned a chain of newspapers and a radio station, and McNaughton had been a columnist and editor at the main family newspaper in Pekin, Illinois. He wrote well and concisely. He had run for Congress and been an assistant district attorney. Like Robert McNamara, of whom he was enamored and eager to please, McNaughton was a hard and conscientious worker, wrapped up in his work. He was high energy and intense. "He was the most intensely action-oriented man I think I've ever come across," Fred Hoffman, who began working in the Pentagon in January 1965, reminisces. "John viewed himself as the principal agent in seeing that what McNamara wanted done got done, in the way McNamara wanted it." McNaughton put in long hours. Before arriving at his office at eight o'clock each morning, he played tennis. He played it hard and he played it well, despite a bad knee. A gangly six feet four, he would arrive at his office wearing his tennis clothes, shower and change, then hightail it down to Bob McNamara's office. "McNaughton made a point, and clearly it was a model to me also, of running down the hall to McNamara's office," Ellsberg recounts. "It was a strange sight to see him loping down the hall. The only person who ran in the Pentagon."[9]

McNaughton was a highly intelligent man, and a clear-headed thinker. His mind was quick, orderly, analytical, precise. He taught an evidence course at Harvard and had a lawyerly tendency to cross-examine people. He was extraordinarily well organized. "He was the most organized person I ever met," one aide recalls. He expected the same level of organization on the part of his staff. And he was decisive. Aides always knew exactly what John McNaughton wanted; he would even spell it out on paper for them. McNaughton knew how he wanted things done: he wanted them done right. He sometimes had his main secretary check up on his aides' work. Efficiency was important to him as he admired and tried to emulate McNamara's own efficiency. He could be short with people. "He was rather hard bitten," Townsend Hoopes, who was a McNaughton deputy, remembers. "He spoke and wrote very tersely. . . . You'd go in to see him, state your case, make your recommendations, and leave." Some people hated him. Once, when one of his two secretaries laughed as he was dictating something, McNaughton snapped at her, "When I'm dictating, I'm like an automaton. And I don't expect any laughter about anything I say." McNaughton demanded punctuality. He was keenly conscious of deadlines and precise about them. If he wanted a memo the next day, he wanted it the next day. He expected aides to work quickly, as he did, and to stay on schedule. His trips to airports were planned down to the minute. He also required the sense from aides that everything was under control, but he tended to be distant from them. "He never got close to any of his employees," one remembers. "He was all business."[10]

Ellsberg revered John McNaughton in the way he revered Robert McNamara. "Dan's posture toward McNaughton and toward McNamara was one of great respect and deference," Vincent Davis recounts. "I never heard him say anything negative about either one. And the little comments that occurred from time to time indicated to me . . . that he admired them enormously and had no reservations about it." Nine-and-a-half years older than Ellsberg, McNaughton was one of those senior men whose power and stature attracted him and whom he sought to please. He and McNaughton were "close friends," Ellsberg told an interviewer. "I think he really liked me and respected me and liked talking to me." Ellsberg felt "a sense of love" for McNaughton, he recalled, and there was a "very, very strong" bond between them. Indeed, it was "one of the closest in my life."[11]

More likely, McNaughton kept an appropriate distance from Ellsberg. One McNaughton staffer remembers that Ellsberg

> wanted me to tell him every social engagement that Mr. McNaughton and Mrs. McNaughton had. And if he didn't get an invitation to the same one, he wanted me to call up and see if I couldn't get him invited. And *this*, I said, "This is the last time I'm doing it." McGeorge Bundy and his wife had invited the McNaughtons over for dinner at their house. And Dan didn't get an invitation. He wanted me to call McGeorge Bundy's office and see if I could get him invited. I called, because I was good friends with McGeorge Bundy's secretary. . . . She said, "Well, no, it's just the four of them." Well, the next week, I thought, "If he asks me to do this one more time, I'm going to tell Mr. McNaughton." . . . I think he thought that as a special assistant he should go every place John McNaughton went. And this isn't necessarily true. . . . I thought this was very wrong, to seek another invitation for yourself. It made me angry. . . . [McNaughton] wouldn't have liked it at all. . . . [Ellsberg] wanted to be a big shot. . . . And he wanted to go to all these good places.

That kind of behavior was characteristic of Ellsberg, Fred Haynes recalls. "He tried very much, I think, to do that, and never was really pulled in."[12]

***

Ellsberg says he began working for John McNaughton on the evening of August 4, 1964, the time of the phantom second attacks by North Vietnamese torpedo boats on U.S. destroyers in the Gulf of Tonkin. "I was reading the cables" on the alleged attacks "as they came in," he told me. That is probably true, but RAND records indicate that Ellsberg was not officially off RAND's rolls until mid-October, so he must have been on consultant status in the Pentagon during the Tonkin affair.[13]

Ellsberg's job as McNaughton's special assistant was "a very lowly one," he would testify frankly in his Pentagon Papers trial. He did whatever McNaughton wanted him to do. RAND's Richard Best wondered if the job wasn't beneath Ellsberg's talents. "It seemed to me a step backward for a technical guy, and a guy of promise, such as Dan was considered to be," Best remembers. Ellsberg would later describe his position in more elevated terms. "I worked at a high level in the Defense Department," he said. He helped McNaughton "on particularly sensitive issues of various kinds which were not handled in the normal staff work."[14]

Ellsberg's civil service rank was certainly high. As he has frequently pointed out, he carried the "supergrade" rank of a GS-18, which was then the highest in the civil service. It was "equivalent to the military rank of major general," he wrote later. More truthfully, he wrote on another occasion it was "equivalent to lieutenant general." "Dan always bragged that when he traveled abroad, he always traveled the military equivalent of a three-star or four-star general," Roman Kolkowicz remembers. A special assistant would normally have had a much lower rank, Ellsberg noted, but he requested the GS-18, and since McNaughton wanted "a lot of substantive input" from him, he got it.[15] Certainly somebody had to have gone to bat for him.

A person wouldn't have guessed Ellsberg had a high rank from the looks of his small office, which was much smaller than that of McNaughton's two secretaries. Paper was stacked and strewn about everywhere. "You should have seen his office," Harry Harris, who also worked for McNaughton, recalls. "What a mess. . . . Dan I would not classify as an organized manager." His nearby River House apartment was not in much better condition. "His apartment was a shambles," Vincent Davis remembers.[16]

Ellsberg's job was demanding. He had to be at work when McNaughton was at work, though he would usually arrive a little late. He couldn't leave until McNaughton left and worked 12-hour days, he recounted later. One McNaughton staffer remembers Ellsberg working a Saturday (nothing unusual about that) despite a badly infected thumb. "He'd been to Fort Myer" to see a doctor, the staffer recalls. "And he told me that they had wanted to amputate his thumb, because it was so infected. But he was sitting there with his thumb in a cup of hot water. And I went and told Mr. McNaughton. I said, 'You better send him home.'" He did.[17]

According to Ellsberg, McNaughton directed him to work full time on Vietnam. But Alvin Friedman, Ellsberg's predecessor as McNaughton's special assistant who was then a deputy assistant secretary of defense, was probably McNaughton's top aide on Vietnam at the time. "Dan Ellsberg didn't start out getting into Vietnam," Friedman told me. That occurred

> over an extended period of time. . . . I was the person that was primarily working with John McNaughton on Vietnam. . . . That was my region. . . . I don't remember all during that time a major involvement of Daniel Ellsberg in Vietnam matters in the Pentagon. . . . I don't remember Daniel Ellsberg going down to the joint staff and discussing bombing targets. I don't remember Daniel Ellsberg going down to the joint staff and discussing what divisions should be introduced into Vietnam first, and how they would do it, and so on. And that was all what I was doing. . . . I can't conceive of why he would have so much to do with Vietnam when I was doing it. . . . McNaughton and I would sit for hours in his office. But I don't remember Dan Ellsberg being there. On Vietnam.[18]

But Ellsberg claimed later he was extensively involved in Vietnam planning. From the first day he began working for McNaughton, he said, "I participated in all the planning between State and the Defense Department representing Mr. McNaughton or assisting Mr. McNaughton in the planning related to the bombing program against North Vietnam . . . in particular in a planning group on which I was a member under the chairmanship of William Bundy . . . to consider alternative bombing plans against North Vietnam." Ellsberg said he represented McNaughton on the group. But Bundy, who was then an assistant secretary of state and who doesn't recall any specific contacts with Ellsberg in the group, remembers, "He certainly wasn't the principal representative [from ISA]. It was an admiral from the navy." And McNaughton "was so much the man in charge, I dealt with him constantly." Ellsberg also testified that he helped McNaughton "in the planning and execution of the sending of . . . ground units for combat in Vietnam in the spring of '65, and finally in . . . the planning that went into the open-ended commitment of American troops. . . . In the course of that I also did a number of special assignments for Mr. McNamara and . . . in some cases McGeorge Bundy."[19]

Ellsberg's work for McNaughton on Vietnam included reading a steady stream of cables. They poured in from U.S. embassies, military commands, the JCS, CIA, State. Ellsberg was to decide which cables merited McNaughton's attention. He asked to see all of them. "Dan Ellsberg was into everything," Harry Harris, who was screening cables in the office each morning before Ellsberg arrived, remembers. "Dan wanted all the cables. . . . He saw everything." One military officer in the Pentagon would testify later that Ellsberg was a "paper collector" who appeared to keep "everything that came through distribution." (When subsequently leaving the Pentagon for Vietnam, the officer said, Ellsberg attempted to take "boxes and boxes" of such documents with him without having them inventoried or cleared.)[20]

Screening cables swiftly was important in McNaughton's office. But Ellsberg found the flood unmanageable. Most people probably would have, but one suspects that Ellsberg got overly absorbed in some cables. The traffic on Vietnam consisted of "about two stacks of paper daily, seven feet high," he would testify in his Pentagon Papers trial. But when I told Friedman that, he responded, "That statement is ridiculous. . . . I was in the same office, and you'd read cables, but there were no stacks of cables several feet high." Ellsberg tried to pare down the traffic to a manageable flow by ordering that he receive only messages with higher security classifications. Some he directed to McNaughton, others he filed away so that they would be quickly available later, it was hoped, if necessary.[21]

Ellsberg would later apologize in dramatic fashion to "the American public" for not releasing some of the classified information he was seeing at this
time. In 1997 he declared that he had had documents in his possession showing
that President Lyndon Johnson planned to escalate the Vietnam War after the
November 1964 election. He was speaking at a symposium marking the career
of George McGovern. McGovern, who was not fond of Ellsberg ("he's an abrasive guy, as you probably know by now," McGovern had told me during an interview the year before. "He's kind of an egomaniac"), acted surprised by
Ellsberg's comments. "I didn't realize he had so much information so early,"
McGovern remarked at the symposium. "I learned a lot today."[22]

Ellsberg represented McNaughton at some meetings, and he traveled to
the Philippines around this time as a Pentagon representative to a conference
of U.S. ambassadors. James Thomson, who was then in the State Department,
hit it off with Ellsberg at the conference and on the plane home. "He got out in
California . . . to give to his children . . . spears and other tribal paraphernalia
from the Philippine mountain people," Thomson laughs. "Spears and ma-
chetes for his little children."[23]

Ellsberg also did a lot of writing for McNaughton, and early on Mc-
Naughton asked him to put together some papers on ways that the United
States might "lose" Vietnam, how to leave, if necessary, and how to justify that
departure. "As a Cold Warrior I found this assignment not at all congenial,"
Ellsberg recalled. But he did not turn out to be a big idea man for Mc-
Naughton, who would frequently invite three or four aides in to consider pos-
sible scenarios for getting out of Vietnam. Ellsberg was not present at these
sessions, Peter Solbert, who was McNaughton's principal deputy, remembers.
The participants were deputy assistant secretaries, "and Dan was just among
the assistants to McNaughton."[24]

Solbert himself tried to get Ellsberg's ideas on an issue once, but Ellsberg
made it clear that he was exclusively McNaughton's assistant "and wasn't terribly helpful," Solbert recounts. If the request didn't come from McNaughton
himself, Ellsberg wasn't inclined to respond. It was an attitude. "It took him an
awful long time to get anything together," Solbert recalls. And then when he
did, "it didn't look as if he'd thought very hard or worked very hard on it."[25]

One key McNaughton staff person, who attended many meetings on Vietnam, remembers that "every now and then Ellsberg would put his hand up and
come out with something rambling. . . . And it was glossed over. . . . He had
some ideas. . . . But they . . . never got any place." But Harry Harris thought
Ellsberg was "rather incisive on certain things," even if he sometimes put forward ideas that were "a little far-fetched . . . a little bit too way out." But "I

think he was just kind of searching maybe for a scenario or something. . . . He wants to take it to the next step. To carry it out. And he was always hypothesizing." Asked how much McNaughton listened to Ellsberg's advice on Vietnam, the other McNaughton aide quoted above responded, "Not much. I think he was disenchanted soon after he [Ellsberg] was hired." Sometimes at meetings, McNaughton "would just shut him up," this aide recounts. "You know, cut him off. . . . And Mr. McNaughton was the type who would listen to everybody for their views." Thomas Schelling recalls, "John McNaughton confided in me that he had a hell of a time getting Dan to shut up and go get to work. That Dan would love to sit in John's office and talk and talk and talk. And when John had work to do, and John thought Dan had work to do. But it was, again, this ebullient sense of sharing his discovery. Every day Dan had an idea and he just had to go talk to somebody." As for going on too long, "he has to make you understand," Schelling observes. "And if you don't look sufficiently shocked, he figures you don't understand yet. He'd better repeat it. . . . He knows that the idea he's got is a good one and an important one. And if you haven't understood it, you're missing something terribly important." McNaughton "found Dan sort of a pleasant nuisance," Schelling recalls.[26]

Ellsberg was also thought to be argumentative. McNaughton accepted some of that, but then he would want to bring matters to a close. He didn't want to use every memo as an occasion for redebating an issue. "I think Ellsberg was more inclined to keep arguing what he thought should be done," Alvin Friedman remembers. "Which is really not the role of a [special assistant]."[27]

Dan Ellsberg was, without question, a hawk on Vietnam. "When he came in, he was gung ho," Harry Harris vividly recalls. "And he said, 'We're going to blast these [North Vietnamese].' He had the Curtis LeMay outlook. . . . He was going to get 'em." The day the United States launched its "reprisal" strikes against North Vietnam after the Gulf of Tonkin incidents, Harris remembers, he and others were waiting for a cable on the strikes. "Ellsberg was there. And he said, 'We're going to'"—Harris smacks his fist into his palm. "'We're going to really strike these guys. . . . You can't attack an American ship on the high seas, and anybody that does has to pay for it.' . . . Ellsberg was right in there. . . . I didn't know Dan Ellsberg until he showed up on the scene. . . . He says, 'We're going to really sock it to these guys.' . . . And we had the air power, and we're going to go after 'em. And this was kind of a chance to teach the North Vietnamese a lesson, to leave our ships alone." Asked if Ellsberg was more gung ho than he was then, Harris responded, "*Oh, yes.* You know, I wasn't in the Marine Corps. He was. . . . In retrospect, I found him to be extremely militant. . . . I found his views on Vietnam to change 180 degrees." Ellsberg recommended that U.S. ground forces be committed to Vietnam. He believed that an irrevocable U.S. commitment would ensure victory, he acknowledged later. He felt the war was a test of the American will to thwart communist aggression. He "flatly rejected" the idea of negotiations with North Vietnam.[28]

Guy Pauker consulted for ISA during this period and had many talks with Ellsberg in Washington. "He was an ultrahawk," Pauker remembers. Once, Pauker dropped by his office and said,

> "Let's go to dinner." . . . And he said, "Oh, dammit. I can't get away. I have to finish this speech for McNamara." And the speech was about the Viet Cong. . . . And I looked at what he had done—and . . . he was not an easy writer—and he was making McNamara say . . . that the Viet Cong can best be understood if one compares them with the Capone gang in Chicago, Illinois. . . . That they're like an organized crime group. And I said, "Dan, you cannot make McNamara say something that's stupid like that. . . . These are dedicated political soldiers. These guys are not gangsters." [But] that's how he saw the Viet Cong when he was working in the Pentagon. . . . Like Capone gangsters. That's hawkish.[29]

In the spring of 1965, Ellsberg collected data on assassinations and kidnappings by the National Liberation Front, or Viet Cong, for release to the American public to justify the U.S. bombing of North Vietnam. He became steeped in such data. In speeches at colleges defending U.S. war policies, Ellsberg likened Viet Cong assassinations to murders by members of organized crime. In a speech at Antioch, he said that while the Viet Cong were not *actually* gangsters, but hard-core political cadre, they were using the methods of gangsters. Ellsberg stated that he had been critical of the U.S. government internally for not releasing data on their assassinations and kidnappings earlier and had been urging that it be done. In another speech he drafted that spring (probably for someone else), Ellsberg underscored the brutality and scale of Viet Cong terrorism and argued that its similarity to that of organized gangsters in large U.S. cities in the 1920s was quite strong. In Chicago in the late 1920s, Ellsberg said in his talk at Antioch, the rate of bombings was very comparable to Viet Cong terrorism. In the other speech he drafted, he painted North Vietnam as expansionist outside Vietnam and emphasized the role of its infiltration into the South in fueling the insurgency there. Antiwar protesters were emotional, he said.[30]

William Simmons, his former colleague on the *Harvard Crimson*, who dined with him in Washington around this time, recalls that Ellsberg felt that U.S. intervention in Vietnam was necessary "to keep the commies, wars of liberation, and that sort of thing from taking over huge chunks of the world." Ellsberg seemed "excited" to be "on the side of the policies coming out of that office [ISA], including the policies involved with the buildup in the Vietnam War." Ellsberg argued with Don Hall about the war when he came to Ann Arbor to speak at a teach-in and stayed at Hall's home. He was "very calm and rational," Hall, then a professor at the University of Michigan, recounts.

> It infuriated me. . . . You would say something angry. . . . He won't get mad back! And that makes you *madder*. . . . So we had real arguments. But I was the one who lost my temper, and not him. And we didn't enjoy our friendship. Of course, it's partly this refusal to respond, to get angry, that makes Dan sort of strange. There was a woman across the street, a very attractive woman, who was passionate and very irrational with her politics. Left-wing politics. And he found her attractive, as everybody did. And he tried to argue with her, and she just got so mad. Started screaming. . . . He would argue with anybody.[31]

Jerry and Sallie Goodman also clashed with Ellsberg over the war. "We would have these violent arguments," Sallie Goodman recalls. "And Jerry was always saying, 'This is a stupid war for us to be in, and we've got to get out.' . . . We were all *screaming* at one another at the dining room table. And Dan finally said, 'Well, we can *try not to lose*.'" During one evening, a revved up Ellsberg kept saying, "We can't win, but we cannot lose." Wassily Leontief also had a long and intense discussion with Ellsberg about the war. "He defended it," Leontief remembers. "I was very opposed, and he was very in favor."[32]

Many would come to see in Ellsberg's hawkishness on Vietnam and his later sharp turnaround prime evidence of the extremist in him. "At any given period, he seems to be utterly a true believer," the journalist J. Anthony Lukas concluded. "Because he's going due north today doesn't mean he's going to be going due north tomorrow. But wherever he's going, he's going at the same pace and with the same conviction," Gus Shubert observes. First Ellsberg was an ardent hawk, then anybody who had anything to do with the war was "a fool or worse. It was really unbelievable."[33]

Ellsberg remembers being pessimistic about Vietnam in 1964 and 1965. He had spent a week there several years earlier as a member of a Pentagon task force. The situation didn't look good to him then, he said; U.S. involvement might even be doomed. By the fall of 1964, Ellsberg recalled, "that war looked like a hellhole." But if the United States quit Vietnam, he worried, it would hurt U.S. status and influence in the world and benefit the Soviets and Chinese. Ellsberg would also remember being "totally against" the U.S. bombing of North Vietnam. He thought it would fail. And killing people without military or political benefit, he said he believed, was murder. He considered the U.S. air campaign against the North and the use of B-52 bombers in the South "criminal," he claimed. But when told that Ellsberg said he had opposed the U.S. bombing in November 1964 as his Vietnam working group was meeting, William Bundy replied, "I doubt very much that's true. Because it would have stuck out like a sore thumb. That was not the case." And "insofar as I had any idea of his views, I think there was a definite gung ho feeling." Ellsberg strongly defended the bombing in a speech he drafted that spring.[34]

But he was not a crude hawk by any means. "He was the only hawk I'd heard who made any sense at all," Stanley Hoffmann, a Harvard professor who debated Ellsberg at Radcliffe in the spring of 1965, remembered. "There was something extremely genuine and human in him that I didn't see in other hawks. . . . He was not a government mouthpiece or an intellectual adding machine, but a human being you could argue with. Not a Bundy." Hoffmann liked Ellsberg and was impressed by him. "He seemed to me more open, more sensitive, than many of my colleagues. . . . I found the man very attractive. . . . I had a sense that this was an honest disagreement, but each one could try to argue."[35]

On campuses, Ellsberg artfully defended the war. He criticized aspects of U.S. policy. "I was on the whole quite candid on the thing," he recalls. "I was presenting my view; it wasn't necessarily the official government view." He told listeners that he found certain criticisms of U.S. policy *plausible*. (Saying an opposing view was plausible would become virtually a staple of Ellsberg's in debate. Some would wonder, however, just how plausible he really believed that opposing view was.) The South Vietnamese government might not be filled with wonderful men, Ellsberg would tell students, but what about the Viet Cong? "Are we sure to win?" he would ask. "No. But should we quit without trying?"[36]

In their debate, Hoffmann threw Ellsberg for a loop by conceding a number of government arguments for purposes of the debate, then doubting U.S. prospects in Vietnam. Ellsberg admitted feeling somewhat disarmed. "He presented the sort of standard administration defense, which was [to consider] the balance of power," Hoffmann recounts. Ellsberg subsequently told Hoffmann that he had been taken "completely off guard" by him, Hoffmann remembers:

> Because he expected me to make a moral argument. And I essentially chose the
> same ground he had chosen and made the sort of "realistic" attack on the war.

Saying that I didn't believe in dominoes, that I thought it would have very bad consequences for American power in the world. And I didn't say much about morality. Because I thought that with somebody like him—and I knew that he was essentially an economist by training, and training in game theory—moral arguments wouldn't have been a dialogue. So I preferred to meet with him on his own ground.[37]

After Ellsberg went to Vietnam several months later, he sent Hoffmann letters. Hoffmann was surprised, as he had first met Ellsberg at the debate. That debate had obviously meant something to Ellsberg. Curiously, he denied writing Hoffmann later. "It was very interesting," Hoffmann recalls. "I could almost trace the evolution. The first letters were, 'You may have had a point. Things are not going the way I thought they would be going. And I wanted just to tell you that I'm thinking about your kinds of arguments.' And then . . . there was this gradual evolution" to passionate antiwarrior. Hoffmann came to believe Ellsberg's approach to politics was "insufficiently distant. It's a strange parallel, because he's a much more appealing person, but it's a bit like McNamara. His capacity to go from one extreme to the other without stopping in the middle. . . . He started seeing things in black and white. . . . So while I liked him, I found some things excessive or impulsive in his psychological make-up. . . . Frankly, the impression he gave me is that of an extremely intelligent and very, very decent man, but not somebody whose political judgment I would necessarily trust. Because of this capacity to go a bit too far."[38]

Ellsberg would tell Hoffmann, on more than one occasion, that Hoffmann had been right about Vietnam in 1965, and that he had been wrong. "Each time I saw him: 'You know, that debate was very, very important. I kept thinking about it,'" Hoffmann remembers him saying.[39]

―――――◦―――――

The year Ellsberg spent working for John McNaughton was a difficult one for him. He seemed troubled, erratic to co-workers. "He was sad," one remembers. "And I thought maybe it's because of the breakup of his marriage. . . . He was like a scruffy, lost puppy." It seemed clear to Fred Haynes that "he was suffering a kind of psychological blow from this"—his marital collapse. "It was talked about by a number of people." Ellsberg seemed "unable to come to grips with his divorce. . . . And you could understand it." Some in McNaughton's office felt sorry for him. For Ellsberg was a nice person, they thought, and friendly. "I liked Dan," Haynes stresses. "I felt either empathy for him or sympathy for him or whatever. . . . Again, the puppy syndrome. He *was* likable. You felt like taking him by the hand and leading him to the trough to drink," Haynes laughs.[40]

Vincent Davis thought Ellsberg was "a bit mixed up emotionally" and "a bit unstable just now," he wrote two friends in 1965. That was partly because "the breakup of his marriage left a few scars, and he has a few immature streaks in his personality," Davis told one of the friends, John Paul Vann. Davis believed there might be "certain unstable elements in his personality which have deeper roots" than his current troubles, he wrote his other friend. "He certainly lacks the kind of solid maturity which you . . . have—indeed, there are certain streaks of childlike behavior in his make-up. . . . I like Dan personally very much, but I hope his traces of instability do not result in any problems either for him or for OSD" (Office of the Secretary of Defense). Davis felt Ellsberg's work problems and creeping doubts about Vietnam were contributing to his shakiness. He would later conclude that Ellsberg was "right on the edge that summer. . . . Dan was really unraveling."[41]

Some people suspected that Ellsberg might be manic-depressive. "Dan certainly fit the pattern," Davis thought. "When he was manic, he was super-enthusiastic, very talkative, garrulous, gregarious. And when he was depressive, he was very blue, moody, angry, upset. And these appeared to be moods [that] occurred in fairly clear-cut cycles." But Ellsberg's ex-wife, Carol Cummings, is skeptical. "I wouldn't have described him as manic-depressive when I knew him," she told me. Neither would some other people.[42]

Some who worked around Ellsberg in ISA thought him overly needy because of his marital breakup. He seemed lonely, looking for companionship. "Dan always wanted to be loved by people," Harry Harris remembers. "Wanted to be part of the group." Both in ISA and in later encounters with Ellsberg, Fred Haynes recalls, "he always seemed to me to be someone who was on the outer fringe but wanting to be a part of the in-group. . . . It's like a puppy or a little kitten sort of wandering around the edge" trying to get in.[43]

Yet Ellsberg seemed distant to some. Haynes, a friendly, easygoing man, worked with him for several weeks in ISA on a study analyzing the efficacy of graduated military pressures in Vietnam in particular, but also elsewhere. Haynes recounts:

> We would sit together in the Pentagon and be working on a particular problem, trying to talk it through. And he would sit for long periods without saying anything. . . . And then he'd come forth with a very interesting thought. . . . One could sense a kind of strangeness, which may have been an early manifestation of the capacity to switch gears completely. . . . In the time that I worked with him there was this odd capacity to fade away from you. You'd be talking

to him about an issue and . . . he would focus way out of where you were. I mean, he'd be looking at nothing, and obviously in his own mind be thinking about something. And then, as I indicated, he would come forth with some fairly good points. But there was this strangeness to him. I don't want to be too judgmental over it, but I think there was a strange form of coldness about him. No matter how much we worked together, and how many times I've seen him since . . . I could never get close to Dan. I just couldn't. And I am basically a fairly warm individual. I mean, I like people and I get along well with them. And I never could really get close.

When Ellsberg seemed off in a zone, "his eyes would glaze," Haynes recalls, "and you almost felt like he was on another planet. And I think it was his way of thinking. And I was never sure whether he was thinking about what we were working on, or whether he was thinking about something else. . . . And sometimes I would just say to him, 'Dan, we need to get some work done.' And he'd come back to battery. And he would talk. But he would just fade out." Harry Harris sometimes wondered if Ellsberg was hearing everything he was saying, or whether Ellsberg was already one step ahead. It wasn't clear to Harris either just where Ellsberg's mind was at times. Yet his strength lay in his capacity to sit back and think, Haynes noticed: "He was *very* good at that. And he could take relatively complex issues . . . and he could run it through a whole series of machinations in his own brain. I found it very fascinating to work with him. He also could express himself quite well. . . . A very bright, bright man. . . . I found him remarkable to work with on that particular project. Because he could see right away, and he would raise the issue."[44]

Another co-worker remembers observing Ellsberg walking oddly along the hall with his back to the wall at times. "It was weird. . . . I thought, 'Boy, is he goofy.' . . . He's like in another world." Ellsberg later worked under General Edward Lansdale in Vietnam, and Lansdale's secretary remembers him often pacing or walking in an odd manner in Vietnam, too. "He seemed to be oblivious," she recalls. To the co-worker in ISA, Ellsberg's mind seemed "fogged up." He often acted absent-minded as well, which led another co-worker to envision a funny scenario:

Somebody who had worked with him over in our place and who now worked in a different organization came over to a farewell for somebody in ISA who was leaving. And at this time Dan was over in Vietnam. And a lot of people would come back, our people in ISA, and they'd tell this and that about Ellsberg, and wild stories. So, anyway, I said to this person, "Well, I'm afraid that Dan is never going to come back alive from Vietnam." And he said, "Well, that's probably true." He said, "He'll either get caught in bed with somebody else's wife and get shot, or he'll jump out of an airplane and forget he doesn't have a parachute."

This co-worker also remembers driving Ellsberg to his apartment and observing him trying to get out of the car while forgetting he had a seat belt on. "I thought he might have had a high IQ, but he didn't have sense enough to come in out of the rain," this person says. "It was like he wasn't all there." Some McNaughton aides laughed about him behind his back.[45]

Ellsberg's work habits left something to be desired. In terms of staying organized, when compared with McNaughton "Ellsberg was flip side," Harris recalls. One wonders if those cables that were to be quickly available later were always quickly available. Also, "Dan had rather irregular office habits, in terms of when he came to work, how late he worked," Harris recounts. He was in and out a lot, and sometimes it seemed as if he was more out than in. Harris amusedly remembers one morning when Ellsberg arrived at the office looking disheveled and unshaven. "He was up in New York. . . . I said, 'McNaughton's going to kill you.'"[46]

It became known in McNaughton's office that Ellsberg had an active love life, which contributed to his irregular schedule. "He was traveling away for weekends . . . or having some activities in Washington," Harris recounts. "He came in unkempt—he had a long night. Came in late or took the shuttle in the morning. . . . He would always have kind of a travel bag coming in. He'd kind of have a ten-o'clock shadow." Another McNaughton aide noticed that at one point Ellsberg had his eye on one of McNaughton's two secretaries, Janie Harris. "But she was *not* interested," the aide remembers. This aide, too, recalls Ellsberg arriving at the office Monday mornings disheveled and carrying a travel bag. "Sometimes he stayed overnight in the office. . . . I didn't know what he was *doing*. But he would sometimes arrive and shave and all. And one time I guess he used Mr. McNaughton's bathroom in Mr. McNaughton's office. And Mr. McNaughton told him not to use it again. . . . He even left his shaving stuff in there one morning." This aide doesn't think Ellsberg's comings and goings created any significant problem, but one time this aide, McNaughton, and others were leaving Andrews Air Force base to fly to Europe for a meeting, and although Ellsberg was on the manifest to go, "he didn't show up and he didn't show up," the aide recounts. "And so Mr. McNaughton said, 'Close the airplane doors.' Well, after they closed it, just as they closed it, he showed up and then got on the plane."[47]

Ellsberg would develop a habit of swearing angrily at himself when he found himself running behind schedule. He told me he feels "tremendous self-loathing and despair" when running at least twenty or thirty minutes late, rather than his customary ten minutes late. But he also claimed, "When I've got a boss—which I *notably* have not had for 25 years, and have chosen not to have, and I don't want to have—but when I have a boss, who not only demands promptness, but needs it . . . I'm on time. But that's the only time I am."[48]

A more serious problem for Ellsberg in McNaughton's office was completing work on time. "Dan, when he had to get a speech out, would do an overnighter," Harris remembers:

> If he had to get something out for McNaughton, he was really working right down to the wire. He'd put it awfully close. . . . Dan was always [into] the research, and he wanted as much information as possible, and then putting it together. . . . On one occasion I thought McNaughton was going to kill him, because he didn't get something finished on time. . . . I said to myself, "Mc-Naughton, he's going to kill you." . . . He *never* got the thing [finished]. And I remember he would sometimes lean against the wall. . . . He wanted to have some sort of intellectual discussion. . . . I said, "Listen, I've got to get this thing out. I mean, *I'm* going to get killed if I don't get it out."

"He didn't ever finish anything that he started," another McNaughton aide recalls. "A lot of things he never did get done." Another of Ellsberg's co-workers in ISA recounts:

> He could not hack it. He simply was congenitally unable to do the kinds of things you had to do for that group [ISA]. They demanded that you produce immediately. No matter what it was. Whether it was a mobilization plan for Vietnam or whether it was five speeches that had to be done by Monday morning at eight o'clock for delivery to Congress to particularly sympathetic people on the Hill, or whatever. You *really* had to go hard at it. And Dan could not do that. . . .
>
> It was difficult to work with him in [that] sense. . . . I was used to moving fast. Dan was not. And it was a little frustrating for me.

No two ways about it, Ellsberg couldn't keep up with his workload, Fred Haynes remembers. "He had to think. . . . He couldn't hack the speed required to do these various tasks. . . . People like McNaughton, people like Harry Rowen, and McNamara himself, could move at extraordinarily high speed to do whatever they had to have done. There was no foolishness about it. And you had to adapt to it. And that's the one thing that Dan couldn't do. . . . He couldn't grab hold and produce in a hurry. . . . Ellsberg wasn't geared for that." While Vincent Davis and Ellsberg were theoretically working together on a project, "basically Dan used me as a sounding board for his own ideas," Davis recalls. And "to tell you the truth, there was no work. Dan was a walking gadfly going around talking to people. But he had a hard time sitting down and putting stuff on paper."[49]

Ellsberg continued to be indiscreet. Early on the job, he discussed some highly classified cables he was seeing with the State Department's Michael Forrestal, who did not have access to them. Those cables were quickly taken off the list of cables to go to McNaughton. The blame "came down on my head, since there was a flurry of investigations as to who had fucked up on this, and I had to admit what I had done," Ellsberg recalled to a journalist. "I never got chewed out more," he told me. "I nearly got fired for it." The husband of one McNaughton staffer remembers that whenever he would go to the airport to meet his wife when she was arriving on McNaughton's plane, "Ellsberg would be there. And I'd sit down and say hello. . . . And he'd hand me papers. And he'd have a briefcase full of papers . . . He'd say, 'Look at this. What do you think of that?' . . . And I'd say to [his wife], 'That character handed me stuff that, to me, it looks like I shouldn't have been reading it.' . . . You know, I didn't know him at all. . . . I thought it was a little out of line, considering the number of people I met before and after that that were in very responsible positions. . . . He was different." Ellsberg, who met McNaughton's plane so that McNaughton could peruse the papers while riding in the car, seemed impressed with his responsibilities.[50]

In September 1965, Vincent Davis wrote John Paul Vann in Vietnam (shortly after Ellsberg arrived there) that Ellsberg's job in ISA "was going a bit sour. Confidentially, a few key people had decided that he was something of a security risk in his old job, because he had a tendency to talk out of school too much. He told me a lot of stuff that he had no business revealing. . . . One word of warning: Don't tell him anything which you would not want repeated in his circles. At the same time, this aspect of his personality might be of use to you if you wanted to get an indirect message relayed via him, without him even being aware that he was the messenger." In Vann's response to Davis, who had also mentioned Ellsberg's emotional problems and immaturity, Vann said he had already come to similar impressions of him, though they had just met a little over a week earlier. Vann came to believe that Ellsberg could use some more discretion.[51]

It had also become known in the Pentagon that Ellsberg had a habit of running out of his office leaving file drawers open and classified papers scattered on his desk. Consequently, "some kind of action had been taken, which did two things," according to Davis: "it notified Dan that his sort of careless habits in this regard were not appreciated, and urging him to clean up his act."[52]

Patrick Sullivan, who was then a psychologist at RAND, remembers visiting Ellsberg in the Pentagon in 1964 with a colleague to discuss some research Sullivan and the colleague were doing. "His office was pretty well stacked with material," Sullivan recounts. "And with lots of red-bordered stuff—TS [top-secret] stuff—around. And I think he was called away, but for whatever reason he left, and he left the two of us sitting there with all of this stuff. We looked at each other: 'My God,' kind of. He should have parked us out in the hall and locked his door." Ellsberg also seemed nervous, fast reacting, and distracted to Sullivan.[53]

But Ellsberg's behavior was probably not uncommon in the Pentagon. Classified stuff was frequently left lying around. And there were undoubtedly those who appreciated his loose lips.

<hr>

Ellsberg continued to talk openly about personal matters. His propensity for talking about sex fairly mushroomed after his marital breakup. "It's really quite strange," Thomas Schelling, who saw quite a bit of Ellsberg then, recounts:

> Dan was very unprivate about his sexual discoveries. Every now and then, I would be talking to somebody who I didn't think was so terribly close to Dan, and one of us would make some remark about, "Dan is beginning to learn about women." And somebody'd say, "What did Dan tell *you?*" And he'd say, "Well, Dan told me this." And I'd say, "Jesus Christ, he told me the same!" And it turned out that Dan had told a number of people what a joy it was to discover sex after he'd come to Washington and left Carol behind. And the implication was that he never had any of that with Carol. He probably as much as told me that. But at least that was a strong impression. Not only the impression he gave me, but the impression he seemed to *want* to give me. . . . He began this period in which he was, I thought, remarkably indiscreet in talking about what he'd discovered. . . . [He was] talking about how he was essentially being introduced into the wonders of sex.
>
> At that time, I never got the impression that he was anything but exhilarated. I never found him to be depressed. I never got any hint that he regretted divorcing Carol. . . . I think if he was ever depressed, he may have been depressed about abandoning his children. But he sure didn't act like somebody who was suffering the depressing aftermath of a painful divorce. He seemed like a released person. . . . He was still quite talkative, in an almost exhilarated mood.

Schelling later anonymously told a journalist that Ellsberg had talked as if he "had never known what the inside of a woman's thighs felt like" before. Ellsberg read the quote and knew it was Schelling. "I thought, 'Well, maybe that's the one thing that he only told to one person, so he's got me coded in his memory,'" Schelling humorously recalls.[54]

Another friend of Ellsberg remembers him talking about "doing a tremendous amount of fucking" right after his marital breakup. "He suddenly discovered that there was a whole world out there of an awful lot of girls who were fucking. . . . I had the feeling that for several months it was one or more girls a day. He may even have said that." Ellsberg told this friend, "out of a sense of wonder," about "some girl who had muscle control in her vagina, so that she was actually fluttering and fluttering or masturbating with her vagina. And he was just full of *amazement*. . . . He was just *amazed* at this: 'What is she *doing?* What is happening? Ooohhh. I can't believe it.' . . . After Carol Cummings, it was definitely that he discovered a brave new world. . . . He was just amazed at what was out there. . . . He described it as like, 'Holy crow. I never knew this was going on out there. Why didn't somebody tell me?'"[55]

"He was totally obsessed with sexual stuff," recalls Kirby Hall, who heard about it from her husband at the time. "He's a gross man. And yet he was so appealing." Fred Hoffman similarly remembers Ellsberg's "intense desire to recount his sexual exploits at great length . . . at a level of detail that I hadn't experienced since adolescence . . . with no encouragement at all." Though Hoffman suspected that Ellsberg noticed his discomfort with it, "it never fazed him."[56]

Later, in California, Richard Zeckhauser also got a heavy dose of Ellsberg's sex talk, which contrasted with his previous experience with Ellsberg. "My first image of Dan was as Dan Ellsberg, successful American, 1950s married man" living a very conventional life, Zeckhauser, who spent three summers at RAND, reminisces. "And then the next time I see Dan . . . he's talking to me about the stewardesses." Ellsberg "would come in and say, 'Did you see the cute little blonde in Logistics? God, I had her over the other night. . . . ' I mean, it was sort of some vague sexual story. And then he'd sort of say, 'You've got to go to this bar up on Zuma Beach, where I picked up three women in three nights, and then I had two stewardesses staying with me last night.' . . . And he would sort of offer to be a procurer. . . . But I presume that after he left my office and talked to me about the two stewardesses, he probably went three offices down the hall and talked to somebody else." Zeckhauser had also been a junior fellow at Harvard (starting in 1965) and had a lot of common interests with Ellsberg. They would talk about Tom Schelling, their mutual Harvard adviser. They would talk about decision theory, perhaps a little about Vietnam. "And then," Zeckhauser remembers, "with never any prodding from me, we would move into some sexual stuff."[57]

There would also be talk of Ellsberg carrying on with two young Swedish women, which he was very proud of. Helmut Sonnenfeldt, who like others found Ellsberg stunned and perhaps guilt-ridden by his marital collapse, thought women were one of his responses to it. "Dan was an attractive man, and he attracted certain kinds of women who felt sympathetic," Fred Haynes comments. "The lost puppy is a good one to hang your hat on. And women who liked to talk to him were of the type who would be sympathetic to the lost puppy." Haynes adds, "I didn't have time to do that, and he really didn't either."[58]

Patricia Marx, whom Ellsberg met in 1964, would have been sympathetic to lost puppies. She was vulnerable yet warm, caring, and giving, a supportive person and a good listener. "Pat was always adored by people," her cousin Marlene Twaddell remembers. "The idea of competing against anybody else she wouldn't dream of doing. She thought it should be shared. . . . There is no meanness in her." Almost everybody liked Pat Marx.[59]

Born in 1938 and thus seven years younger than Ellsberg, Marx was a product of wealth and privilege. She had been raised largely in a white-pillared mansion on a 20-acre estate in Scarsdale, New York. Her father was the famous toy-maker Louis Marx, variously referred to as a "toycoon," "the Henry Ford of the toy industry," "the hawk of the toy industry" (for his war toys), "the Toy King of America," or simply "the toy man," in Richard Nixon's words. Louis and his younger brother, David, had started their toy business during World War I. "Zippo the Climbing Monkey" and the "Alabama Coon Jigger" (a tap-dancing minstrel) were sources of their first fortune. The Yo-Yo, however, would be Louis' "greatest success," according to one piece on him. He was reportedly a millionaire by age 26. By 1951, Louis and David Marx had over a dozen factories around the world. "He makes and sells more low-priced, mass-produced toys than anybody, anywhere, any time," an article on Louis in *Reader's Digest* in 1955 stated. That year his face graced the cover of *Time* magazine.[60]

Louis Marx was short, stocky, and bald, a Jew whose Jewishness was not important to him, hard driving, always working, with energy to spare. He found it hard to sit still. "He talks, walks, and gestures tirelessly, like one of his own wound-up toys," a journalist observed. He had "enormous gusto," his daughter Patricia Ellsberg reminisces. One of his favorite phrases was "Live It Up." He had it embroidered on silk neckties that he gave away. Marx had a strong personality; he liked to lecture and could be dogmatic. Once at a formal banquet in Japan, after some Japanese had apparently dealt underhandedly with him, Patricia Ellsberg remembers, "they said, 'Mr. Marx, there have been mis-understandings.' And so Dad got up and said, 'There have been no misunder-standings. The problem is,' he said, 'I know just what you've been doing.'"[61]

Perhaps insecure about his intellect or lack of a college education, Marx was intent on expanding his vocabulary. He was known to bask in the sun at the bottom of his drained swimming pool on winter days, smoking long cigars while dictating letters to his Audiograph or reading the dictionary, marking the words he wished to learn. A secretary then typed the words onto pages in small black books, which Marx studied at free moments. With a black book in hand, he would jog up and down his driveway or on the roof of his office building in Manhattan, memorizing words. He purportedly read the dictionary from front to back. He gave vocabulary tests to his daughters' boyfriends.[62]

Louis Marx had famous and powerful friends. That was important to him. He was "in love with power," John Simon, the theater, film, and literary critic, and a former boyfriend of Patricia, recalls. "And power for him was gener-als. . . . He collected four-star, three-star, five-star, however-many-star gener-als. And he knew them all. They would be godfathers to his numerous children. And they would be regulars at his house. There was a big friendship between him and these various generals," who included Curtis LeMay, Rosie O'Don-nell, Omar Bradley, George Marshall, and Dwight Eisenhower. Marx named his sons from his second marriage after his generals.[63]

Despite her family's wealth, Patricia Marx's childhood had not been easy. Her mother, Renee Marx, had died of breast cancer at age 33, when Patricia was only six. "Our childhood when she was alive was very happy," Patricia re-members. But her mother's year-long illness and then death were "just awful. . . . My father got just terribly depressed. He was just completely bereft. . . . Everybody was bereft. And so there was a lot of sadness." Louis Marx had purchased the Scarsdale mansion before his wife's death, but she died before they moved in. "I'd get to feeling morose," he said later, "and hit the bottle." "My father became like my mother," Patricia recounts. "He really adored me. So all those early years, I was very, very close to him. I think he needed me, too." And "he really poured himself into being a father. He'd al-ways tell us what was right and what was wrong."[64]

Lou Marx may have seemed easygoing to the casual eye, and he was per-missive in some ways, but his round, smiling face was backed up by an iron fist. "If you did something he thought was wrong, you'd never hear the end of it," Patricia recalls. And "he had a big capacity to get angry over little things. So he was not easy to live with." One never quite knew when he would go off. Spilling your milk or even rattling your ice at the table might do it.[65]

But Louis Marx loved children, and he had plenty of help raising his own. The Marxes had governesses of various types, including a cook and a maid, and lots of tutors. "It was like a camp for my brother," Patricia says with a laugh. "We'd learn judo, and then we'd have piano teachers and singing teachers and tennis teachers. And we lived . . . isolated on a fairly big estate. And it had a tennis court and a swimming pool." The Marx children were also given French lessons, and classical music was piped into their rooms at bedtime.[66]

Louis Marx was a striver, and so, in large part, were his children. Louis, Jr., Patricia's brother, became a very successful businessman. He was a proud man who knew his own worth and could show the arrogance of the rich. Patricia's sister Barbara became a well-known futurist or New Age philosopher. "She was very grand and dictatorial," John Simon thought, with "that same kind of power-play attitude toward the arts that the father had toward business and the military establishment and so on. And she was very dogmatic." Her uncle, David Marx, who had his own group of famous friends, also instilled the value of achievement in his children. Patricia, her two sisters, and David's daughters also had their sights set high when it came to men. "There had to be something very special about the guy," Greg Wierzynski, who knew the family, recalls. "That by and large was drummed into the Marx girls."[67]

Patricia would gain five half brothers after her father remarried when she was around eleven. Idella, Louis' new wife, was a secretary in his office, as Patricia's mother had been. She was taller and 28 years younger than him, flighty, slender, blonde, and quite beautiful. "What on earth did you marry him for?" one of Lou's friends asked her. Idella had previously been a starlet and had toured overseas with a U.S.O. troupe. According to Simon, she had been involved with the striptease business. "She came from a very dubious background," Simon says. Many people thought she was a gold digger. She, too, could be quite sure of herself. "Finally, I guess, she was caught out in all kinds of adulteries, and that's when papa dumped her," Simon remembers.[68]

After finishing boarding school, Patricia Marx spent two years at Stanford, then transferred to Radcliffe, graduating in 1959. "I was just a fish in water in Radcliffe," she recounts. "Because it's just so vibrant intellectually, and so rich. I was just swooning with delight." Like Carol Cummings before her, Patricia participated in Radcliffe's honors program in history and literature. "I loved the arts and literature and intellectual history," she remembers. "I really loved to learn. . . . I loved ideas." She'd hit her dates with existential and philosophical questions when they might have had their minds on something else.[69]

After graduating and moving to New York, Patricia did a weekly public radio program called "Patricia Marx Interviews" for which she interviewed recognized people in the arts and sciences, as well as political types like Howard Zinn. "That's how I got my education, was by talking to these people," she recalls. "I read and I think, but I'm really moved by the personal." She became much more political. "She asked soft questions," Marlene Twaddell remembers. Louis and David Marx "helped her get the interviews. They had to be softer questions, because she got the interviews through her family. So it's very hard for her to be a journalist under those conditions." Patricia didn't have an easy way with words on the air. One friend who listened to her program recounts, "It's a little girl asking a big person about their achievements. And what you hear if you hear the radio programs carefully is her quavering voice."[70]

Some people thought Patricia liked to hang out with recognized men. Celebrities. She struck Richard Falk, whom she interviewed and got to know a little bit, as being strongly attached to elite perspectives and backgrounds and having an almost instinctive attraction to the establishment. John Simon recalls:

> Pat was always interested in the people whom she considered interesting, deserving, talented, influential, in the good sense of the word. And she pursued them. But she pursued them in a nice way. There was nothing pushy or ugly about it. She just was interested in them and tried as much as possible to get to know them. But out of very sincere admiration and a sense that getting to know them would improve her in some way, would further her own thinking in some of those areas, and so on. In other words, it was all rather high-minded and noble. If anything, too noble. But there was nothing low or self-promoting about it.[71]

Patricia, who had earlier been an Eisenhower-style Republican, also got her political education through going out with men, such as the author Walter Karp. Her main man was Simon, a recognized and influential force in New York cultural and intellectual circles. Quite brilliant, Simon had a Ph.D. from Harvard and was someone whose views people paid attention to. But he was also controversial; some found him meanspirited, arrogant, an intellectual bully. But Patricia apparently saw his vulnerable and sweet side, and she was particularly attracted to noted intellectuals. Simon recounts:

> Her stepmother, Idella, had watched me on television from time to time and heard me on the radio from time to time, and was much taken [chuckles] with my performances. And I guess she got Pat to watch . . . and listen, too. And I guess Pat was moderately impressed or something. And so what they did is— that was Idella's strategy—they had a box at the Metropolitan Opera, and they would call up people and say, "Would you join us for dinner and a night at the

opera?" And that way they could usually get most people. And they certainly got me. That's how we met. . . . It was sort of intellectual admiration, fan-club stuff. And if anything else came from it—which in this case it did—that was just gravy. But it wasn't the intention.[72]

Simon, who often helped Patricia prepare for her radio interviews, found her enormously sincere and full of good will. She was "in love with humanity and doing good things, and helping mankind in whatever way possible," he remembers. "At this point she was thinking that one could change mankind through ideas. . . . She was very big on round-table discussions." Patricia was on the board of the 92nd Street Y, which sponsored cultural events, and Simon was often either the moderator or a participant in discussions. Also, "she was so *serious*," Simon recounts. "I mean, in a nice way. . . . There was something very earnest about her. . . . And there were intensities of other kinds about her that people who knew her superficially obviously didn't suspect . . . emotional, sexual . . . very loyal, very involved friendships." And, she could have a temper: "For example, in one of these round tables she thought that I was rude to Susan Sontag—as if one could possibly be rude to Susan Sontag. And she was very angry at me, and she wouldn't talk to me until I apologized. And yet it was all perfectly within the bounds of civilized round-table opposition. There were one or two times when she really got very, very mad. But otherwise she was very even-tempered." Though very attractive physically, in a quiet, understated way, Patricia tended to look older than her age. "She complained that people were always saying, 'You're looking so much better,' and that they were never saying, 'You're looking so good,'" Simon recalls.[73]

Patricia's relationship with Simon got off to a lightning quick start and became quite serious. "We both thought of marriage," Simon recounts. "But she, in those days, was very much . . . under the thumb of her father . . . very much in awe of him, and desperately wanted to impress him." And "she knew that her father didn't really approve of me, or wouldn't approve of me. And her elder brother, Louis, Jr., would not approve of me as a member of the family. . . . Pat felt that she could never really take me home to the family in any kind of easy, unafraid, sort of carefree, spontaneous way. She was always afraid I would say something to offend them or pick a fight or something." Patricia's father found Simon overly critical, too cranky—why didn't he write a play himself instead of tearing them apart all the time?[74]

Aside from this, Simon's cynical view of humanity did not jive with Patricia's, and she was disappointed that he didn't talk about ideas more. "This was something she couldn't get over," Simon remembers:

She thought that people like us [he and others in the arts] sat around discussing noble, lofty, mighty, humanitarian things, rather than chitchat, gossip,
humdrum, mundane, everyday things. This to her was terribly disappointing.
And she kept saying, "Let's talk about *ideas*. I mean, let's talk about *ideas*." And
I said, "Pat, you don't understand. Writers and others in similar fields do not
sit around talking ideas. Yes, occasionally, sometimes it happens. But they do
that in their writing, and they're very happy to get away from it when they're
just socializing." This was very disconcerting to her. It was kind of sweet. I
mean, I was charmed and amused by it. Nevertheless, I was not going to spout
ideas just to oblige her or anybody else.

Patricia would also become disappointed in the arts and their capacity to
change the world for the better.[75]

By the time she met Dan Ellsberg in the spring of 1964 in Washington,
her relationship with Simon had cooled. "I went to Washington in part because
it was pretty well over with John," Patricia told me. She had broken up with
him. But despite the cooling, Simon recounts,

We were still nominally close, although I had strayed into some other relationship and she had strayed into other things. . . . There were one or two other
men who were of slight importance in her life, and there was one woman who
seemed very important to me, and even perhaps two. But still somehow we
were still more or less together, as I recall, despite all that, because I remember
that I was sneaking away and trying to keep it all hidden from her. And she had
one or two involvements that she was more or less trying to keep hidden from
me. Although we both found out about [them]. . . . So I think it would have
probably ended even without Dan. But perhaps not so soon.

By the time Patricia started seeing Ellsberg, Simon was no longer living in her
apartment. "She told me that it was over, as far as that sort of thing goes," he
recalls. But Simon and Patricia would continue to see each other after she
started seeing Ellsberg.[76]

Patricia met Ellsberg at a party that a mutual friend had offered to help
throw at her home in Washington. The friend had told Patricia that if she ever
met Ellsberg, "be careful, because he's brilliant, but dangerous." That piqued
Patricia's interest. But at the party, "I thought Dan was interesting . . . but it
wasn't like love at first sight or anything," she remembers. Afterward, they and
others went out to dinner. Then they had no contact for a while. "But just as I
was about to leave and go back to New York, I got a call from Dan asking me
out," Patricia recalls. She declined since she was returning to New York.[77]

The following spring, in 1965, Patricia was back in Washington. She decided to invite Ellsberg to a gathering at her sister Jacqueline's home in Washington that her sister Barbara was throwing for Jonas Salk. Barbara was a friend of Salk. Patricia remembers: "When Dan walked in the door of my sister's house . . . I was a goner. Because they had these . . . sunken lights in the ceiling . . . and one of them would shine on the door. And I opened the door—and I hadn't seen him for a year, and I hadn't really connected—and somehow the light hit his blue eyes. . . . I hadn't seen those blue eyes in that way. And he walked in . . . and I just instantly went, 'Ah!' [laughs] And I was a goner. That was it."[78]

Ellsberg asked Patricia out soon afterward, their first date apparently taking place the Friday night before the first national anti–Vietnam War demonstration, which was sponsored by Students for a Democratic Society on April 17 in Washington. During the course of what turned out to be "a very romantic evening," Ellsberg asked Patricia what she was planning to do the next day. She replied that she was going to go to the demonstration, but that he could accompany her if he wanted to. Patricia was planning to do some interviews for her radio program there. She opposed the Vietnam War. Ellsberg was reluctant, but he was curious about the protest, and he wasn't going to pass up this opportunity. The next day, they went to see the cherry blossoms. "We went for this romantic picnic," Patricia recalls. "And I just fell totally head over heels."[79]

Patricia ran into some friends at the antiwar demonstration, including Martin Garbus, a left-leaning lawyer, and his girlfriend or wife, Ruth. Marty had been influential in Patricia's political education, and Ruth was her best friend. Patricia introduced them to Ellsberg—"and then later heard, 'How could you be going out with somebody from the Pentagon?'" she remembers. Actually, Marty Garbus was not wondering why Patricia was going out with someone from the Pentagon so much as "why she was going out with this particular person from the Pentagon, who had a political sense and a political vision that was certainly abhorrent to me," he recalls. For Ellsberg was not only a hawk, but "very critical of us. And I remember Dan's, I guess, disparaging of us and our politics at the demonstration. And he really thought at that point in time that the demonstrators were irresponsible and didn't understand what the realities were." Garbus saw in Ellsberg "a kind of closed, militaristic figure" not unlike Patricia's father. "Dan had a certainty about himself," Garbus recalls. "The same certitude that he had when he was a hawk, he had as a dove. Dan *appeared* to listen to other people's views, and appeared to listen to other people's opinions. I'm not so sure that he did." Ellsberg was critical of speakers at the demonstration.[80]

But Patricia was quite taken by him. One person who observed them in their early stages remembers, "If you saw them in the room, they were sort of

hanging on each other. So there was an obsessiveness there at that moment."
Patricia thought Ellsberg absolutely brilliant, "and he just seemed like such a
mover—he was going places," Marlene Twaddell recalls. That Ellsberg was a
man of stature surely attracted Patricia. He would have fit the bill of somebody
special. There was also a physical attraction between them, and mutual intense
intellectual curiosity; one imagines Ellsberg appreciated Patricia's own mind.
Patricia may have found Ellsberg's sensitivity and vulnerability appealing too.[81]
And Ellsberg needed a care giver and source of support, if not an admirer.

Perhaps with some cynicism, some people would come to feel that they were
a great catch for each other: Ellsberg because of his later celebrity, Patricia because of her money and thus Ellsberg's ability to pursue a life he wanted without
having to make a large living. "I think Dan got married because of the meal ticket
aspect of Pat," Anthony Russo, Ellsberg's co-conspirator in the Pentagon Papers
case, says. "I just always had the feeling that that was a meal ticket for him." Ellsberg had managed to obtain a Marx foundation fellowship, some thought.[82]

They were in some ways an odd couple: she a dove, he a fervent hawk; she
a warm, giving, and empathetic person, he centered largely on himself and his
career, with that strange, faraway, cold side.

Meanwhile, Ellsberg's career in Washington was in trouble. In fact, it lay in
shambles. His shortcomings, of course, had not gone unnoticed by John Mc-
Naughton, who had become disillusioned with him, probably fairly early on.
McNaughton "became disenchanted because he wasn't all that he thought he
would be," one close McNaughton aide remembers. "He expected a lot, and he
didn't get it."[83]

The main thing he didn't get was work on time. Ellsberg couldn't be
counted on to get things done when McNaughton wanted them done, if ever.
His disorganization was also troublesome. "It was like oil and water," Harry
Harris recalls. "They just didn't mix." Ellsberg "was gathering all this stuff and
he wasn't really producing." Thomas Schelling concurs: "Dan was a disappointment [to McNaughton]. John couldn't count on him to take a job and finish it. And John was a kind of person who liked to decide what to do, do it, do it
on time, do it right. And John had little patience for things that were pure conversation. If the conversation wasn't going to lead to a memorandum that
would go to the secretary of defense or something, that was play, not work. And
there was limited time for play. And Dan always wanted to play." McNaughton
would say afterward that the job didn't really suit Ellsberg.[84]

Ellsberg's loose tongue also troubled McNaughton. "A need to boast about what he knew made Ellsberg somewhat indiscreet under normal circumstances," Neil Sheehan later wrote. "His emotional distress was making his indiscretion worse." Ellsberg denies that McNaughton worried about his discretion, however. Sheehan's account "has to be wrong," he told me. "McNaughton couldn't have been concerned about that. Because I'm telling you, that is a characteristic that precludes your getting the kind of access that I had. . . . That would be a cover story for something else." Ellsberg, who did not want to talk to me about how things worked out between him and McNaughton, admitted, "We did have a breach in our relationship. Not fatal. I mean, I continued to work for him, and continued to be very friendly. . . . He was willing to see me go. But not for that reason."[85]

In August 1965, Ellsberg joined a U.S. team headed for Vietnam led by General Edward Lansdale. McNaughton's disillusionment with him was a major impetus to that, and perhaps the most important one of all. McNaughton was "happy to see him go to Vietnam with the Lansdale group," Harris recalls. "Had he not left, I think John McNaughton would have fired him." Another McNaughton aide I spoke to also believes Ellsberg would have been canned otherwise. When Lansdale's team was being formed that summer, "it was suggested to him that he be part of it," Harris remembers, possibly even by McNaughton himself, "which would have taken care of McNaughton's problem. Because he wanted him out. At that stage. Because it got to be rather serious toward the end. . . . I know that he was unhappy." McNaughton appeared to have written Ellsberg off. "Everybody knew that he joined the Lansdale group because he was pushed out," Harris adds. "That was common knowledge." Ellsberg was transferred to the State Department for a short period before going to Vietnam. McNaughton almost certainly aided that move. "I don't think that Ellsberg would have done it on his own, because it was a better job over where he was with us," the other McNaughton aide argues. This aide, too, recognized why Ellsberg was heading to Vietnam: "I figured it was because we had organized his going over there. . . . [McNaughton] must have organized something to get rid of him, but without actually firing him."[86]

McNaughton usually "fired" people by taking them out of the loop and not giving them important work rather than actually terminating them. That, in fact, was Ellsberg's fate before he went to State. McNaughton gave him other tasks in ISA. "McNaughton just finally said, 'Well, we've got to do something with him,'" one McNaughton aide recalls. Fred Haynes, who worked with Ellsberg in the policy planning staff of ISA, believes this change took place fairly quickly. "He can be best described, I think, as a floater during that period," Haynes says. "He was one of those people who floated, because . . . he couldn't hack the speed required to do these various tasks."[87]

Ellsberg was apparently floating when Vincent Davis worked with him in June and July of 1965. Rather than working in his small office next to Mc-Naughton's office, Ellsberg was then in an office somewhere in the outer perimeter of McNaughton's empire. It was one of those Pentagon offices where two desks are pushed up against each other, and two people face each other across the desktops. Ellsberg was already there when Davis arrived. "I was told that would be my desk, and I would be working with Ellsberg on some items on his agenda," Davis remembers. Ellsberg was evidently put on another project later in July. "I am especially pleased that you have been selected to do some long-range thinking on behalf of OSD," Davis wrote him on July 23 (shortly after Davis returned to Denver). "I will be interested to hear how your new assignment is coming along. . . . I had the feeling that your former work in Mr. McNaughton's outer office had put you under great pressure." Davis believes Ellsberg's new assignment involved Vietnam. He wrote a friend in ISA that among the possible reasons for Ellsberg's instability was that "he feels his new assignment is something of a demotion." Davis some years later wrote that McNaughton "terminated" him.[88]

Ellsberg would acknowledge in one interview that he was moved to another office toward the end of his tenure with McNaughton, partly to do some long-range planning on Vietnam. He stopped being McNaughton's special assistant then, he said, but continued to see him, and claimed that he had proposed the long-range planning.[89]

Unable to cut it with McNaughton, Ellsberg's hopes for a higher position in Washington had been dashed. "There was no way," Harris says. "Sure, he wanted a deputy assistant secretary [post]. Like Mort Halperin, [who] came in after him. Mort came in, and what did Mort get? He *got* a deputy assistant secretary. . . . But with Ellsberg, there was no way he was going to get anything. He was damaged goods." Another McNaughton aide, who supports that appraisal, comments, "He didn't have it to get any further. He shouldn't have been where he was in the first place."[90]

This was a pivotal career setback and a crucial period in Ellsberg's life. His star had dimmed considerably. Ellsberg, who has never acknowledged this career failure—indeed, has bragged often about how impressively he performed in Washington—may have wondered where his career was headed now.

In all likelihood, Ellsberg went to Vietnam in late August 1965 with feelings of disquiet and despair, possibly even desperation (mixed with a fair amount of excitement). "He had really kind of played out his string in the United States,"

Davis observes. "He was sort of Lawrence of Arabia in a sense. No jobs for him in London, so he might as well go over and do big things with the Arabs. Again, the marriage had broken up. He had alienated McNaughton, or at least wasn't [wanted] by McNaughton. He never got on any kind of relationship with Mc-Namara," and "without it ever being said officially, he had a mental health problem." Perhaps Ellsberg hoped to lose himself in Vietnam. Davis wrote John Vann in September 1965, "I am not surprised that Dan Ellsberg is a member of the new Lansdale team. Dan has a kind of gung ho Peace Corps mentality—wants to be out on the firing line," and he was suffering those career and personal problems. "I think he wanted to go to Vietnam in about the same way that Frenchmen in the 19th century went to Africa and joined the Foreign Legion when things got fouled up in their private lives in France."[91]

Ellsberg also sought to fight the communists in Vietnam, and he loved adventure. Vietnam would be another proving ground. And as far as wars went, Vietnam was the only thing going, he later remarked.[92]

Ellsberg first hoped to go to Vietnam as a marine commander. That way, he could lead men into battle and see action, which he had not been able to do earlier in the marines. The war was escalating sharply then, and he didn't want to watch it from a distance. The way to go to war was as a marine, Ellsberg thought. "I called a guy I knew who was in charge of officer placement in the Marine Corps headquarters . . . and asked him what rank would I have to go back as," he would recount. "He looked it up and said, major, the same rank as if I had stayed in. I said I'll only go back if I can go as a captain . . . where I'll have at least a chance of getting a company to command." Ellsberg worried he'd get tabbed to be a speechwriter. Vincent Davis heard in the Pentagon that the marines didn't want him back, though, because he was "too old and grayed."[93]

Ellsberg was also eager to see the war for himself. By then he was skeptical of many government reports. He told Davis "that high U.S. officials have consistently and strongly 'lied to the public' in all the public statements concerning the war," Davis wrote John Vann. "He did not trust, by that point, the facts and figures that were being brought into the Office of the Secretary of Defense in the field reports," Davis remembers. What if the whole thing was actually a huge mistake?[94]

One day, Ellsberg invited Davis over to his apartment for lunch. "He said, 'I've got some records I want you to hear,'" Davis recounts. "He'd gotten some new music. . . . He said, 'We'll make sandwiches over there.' . . . By the time we got there, his mood had swung to one of his dark, foreboding, sort of angry postures. And he said, 'What the hell can you tell me about the war in Korea?'" Davis had been a naval officer and pilot during the Korea era:

And then he started throwing me these McNamara-type questions: "Exactly how many fatalities were there in Korea as of a given date? And three months later, how many fatalities had there been? And how many fatalities were there at the Chosin Reservoir?" . . . He wanted to be very precise. He wanted to have very hard numbers, on a very tight schedule. He wanted all this laid out in a way that an economist would lay out data for making some sort of projections. And it became clear to me that he was . . . trying to compare what had happened in Korea with what he thought might be happening in Vietnam.[95]

Ellsberg's doubts about Vietnam grew when he and Davis met with Bernard Fall, the French Indochina scholar and critic of U.S. policies, that July. Fall was living in Washington and was a friend of Davis. Ellsberg, who had read some of Fall's writings, had asked Davis to arrange the meeting. "He pushed the telephone that we sort of shared . . . across the desks," Davis recounts. "He said, 'Call him up.' And I said, 'You want me to call him, do you?' He said, 'Yes. Right now.' This was typical Ellsberg. So I said, 'Okay, I'll call him.'" As Davis was speaking to Fall on the phone, "Dan said, 'Get us scheduled right away, Vince.' So I said, 'Bernie, Dan is eager to talk to you.'" Fall agreed to see them at his home late the next afternoon. "Fall said he would give Ellsberg an hour, but he got all wound up in the conversation," Davis wrote John Vann two days afterward. Their talk ran about four hours. In Fall's office, amid his numerous file cabinets and papers, including original French maps and charts from Dien Bien Phu, Davis remembers,

Dan hit Bernard with a couple of questions, and that was enough to open the Pandora's box for Bernie. And Bernie began delivering this sort of magnificent monologue lecture that would have been beautiful for a large audience, but it was for an audience of one, Dan. . . . And Bernie got out maps. It was just an absolutely transfixing presentation. And I got a little nervous. I thought this was discourteous on our part, because I knew Bernard's wife, Dorothy, was upstairs fixing supper starting about six o'clock, because I could hear her rattling around up there, dishes, pots and pans. And I started trying to make little excuses: "Well, Bernie, Dan and I really ought to be leaving now." And then Dan would say, "Well, I do have one more question."

. . . When we walked into Bernard Fall's house that night, I think Dan was still a true believer. I think he was still a man who felt that, basically, official U.S. government policy as represented by McNamara was right. Maybe a few little problems with it that could be fixed, but it was basically right. But when he walked out of there [four] hours later, I think Dan was a changed man. I think that was the epiphany scene for Dan. I remember it was a beautiful clear [night]. . . . And Dan was kind of groggy, intellectually groggy. It was just the two of us, and we'd been exposed to this incredible performance by Bernard. And Dan didn't know quite how to react. And then there was a long period of silence. I hadn't seen him that way. He was rarely silent. He was either manically effusive or depressively angry. But he was never quiet. But he finally turned to me. We were in his car, and we were driving back down on Connecticut Avenue, and he finally turned to me and he said, "We've got to get that man in to talk to McNamara."

Which, according to one of Davis's letters to Vann, Ellsberg soon did.[96]

Ellsberg was then scrambling for ways to get to Vietnam. When he learned that the Lansdale group was being formed, he pleaded to get on it. "I do know that he begged to be on Lansdale's team," Frank Trinkl, who was in the Pentagon at the time, remembers. "He went to them," Guy Pauker recalls. "He wanted to go to Vietnam and he had to find a reason to be there." Ellsberg would remember approaching Lansdale about joining his team after a meeting. Gus Shubert heard from his contacts in the Pentagon "that he fought like a cat to get himself on that group. That Lansdale didn't really want him. He didn't fit in with the rest of the cast." According to Shubert's contacts, "he waged an extraordinary struggle to get on it. . . . It was sort of half over Lansdale's dead body. And probably John McNaughton had a lot to do with it." McNaughton did indeed help Ellsberg get on the team. One Vietnam scholar determined that Ellsberg was the last member originally selected by Lansdale, who hadn't wanted him, and that he had been assigned to the team by Robert McNamara. Similarly, a team member told me that a high-level Pentagon official got him on the team. Lou Conein, another member of the team, recounts, "Somebody in the Pentagon gave Lansdale Ellsberg's name. That was the way it happened." Lansdale then had Conein check up on Ellsberg. Conein called either the marine headquarters or the Pentagon. "I says, 'Is Daniel Ellsberg a good man, and everything like that?'" Conein recounts. "And they said, 'Oh, sure.' I don't know if that meant they wanted to get rid of him or what. . . . If you want to get rid of somebody, you flatter the hell out of him." In any event, "I said to our hero and our leader, 'Well, they approve him.' So in he come."[97]

Ellsberg, of course, later described his inclusion in Lansdale's group in a more favorable light. "I was the only volunteer that he ended up taking," he told *Look* magazine. He would also describe himself as a State Department "official," since State was his sponsoring agency, although in another interview he said he "represented the Defense Department." But he acknowledged that Lansdale accepted him essentially as an apprentice of his trade, which was counterinsurgency.[98] Other team members had experience in that trade; Ellsberg did not.

— ◦ —

As Ellsberg was preparing to go to Vietnam, his children, Robert and Mary, visited him in Washington. He had scant time to spend attentively with them during the day. "In between my shots, visas, and briefings, I took them to see historical monuments, mostly at night," he wrote later. It must have been an emotional visit for Ellsberg at times. He was going on an uncharted journey, one from which he might not even return. He expected to stay in Vietnam until the end of the war, he would say. "I'm here for the duration," he wrote Deirdre Henderson shortly after arriving in Vietnam. He knew the war wouldn't end anytime soon. In fact, he expected to die in Vietnam, he recalled. He didn't really have any thought of returning.[99]

Richard Elms was in touch with Ellsberg before he went to Vietnam. "He was excited about going over there," Elms remembers. His attitude was "let's go over there and win the war and do things that marines are supposed to do. . . . I think his mindset was he wanted to go over there and strap on a .45 and go out with the marines and really see what was going on and really get into the combat aspects of it. . . . I knew he hoped to get out with the marines in the field and see firsthand what was going on." Richard Zeckhauser remembers Ellsberg's frame of mind this way: "I'm going off to Vietnam, we can win this thing, we can particularly win it if we had a thousand people like me."[100]

EIGHT

DEATH WISH

THEY WERE COUNTERINSURGENCY MEN. OPERATIVES. THEIR TRADE was thwarting unwanted Asian rebellions. General Edward Lansdale, a steadfast anticommunist, was a legendary operative and intelligence agent: the Quiet American or the Ugly American of literature. His reputation had been established through his role in engineering the defeat of the Huk guerrillas in the Philippines in the 1950s. He was an expert in "psyops," or psychological operations. He had applied his trade in Vietnam against the Viet Minh, forerunner of the National Liberation Front (NLF). Propaganda, psychological warfare—"psywar"—and paramilitary operations had been his tools. He had then run Operation Mongoose, the clandestine campaign to overthrow and eliminate Fidel Castro. Lansdale was a rumpled-looking man with a pencil-thin mustache, unorthodox, secretive, devious, reserved, though he could be quite blunt. He was a master spook rather than the swashbuckling type. He loved undercover work. Some questioned the consistency of his judgment, however, and thought his reputation overblown.

Most of the men on Lansdale's small team in Vietnam had worked with him before, including Major Lucien (Lou) Conein, another legendary man. Conein had been a soldier in the French army. In 1945 he had parachuted into northern Vietnam as an operative of the OSS ("the office of sexual satisfaction," he joked to me). He had later directed sabotage operations in North Vietnam. Like Lansdale, Conein had a long association with the CIA ("the criminals, idiots, and asses," he called them, or, alternatively, "the cookie factory," because "there's nothing but fruits and nuts in the goddamn place"). Conein, who drank two Vietnamese beers the morning I spoke with him, had been one of the key players in the U.S.-backed coup that killed South Vietnamese President Ngo Dinh Diem and his brother Ngo Dinh Nhu in 1963. "They committed suicide," the coup leader told Conein. Conein had a safe house in Saigon. Like Ellsberg, he fashioned himself a swashbuckler. "He was always posing in front of mirrors," Lowell Hukill, who was Lansdale's secretary, recounts. "He never saw a mirror he didn't like." The Lansdale team was a motley group. "They looked like the Lavender Hill Mob, sent over from central casting," one official thought. A "houseful of oddballs," said an army officer.[1]

Their mission: to get South Vietnam on a strong political footing. They would defeat the North Vietnamese and NLF through building a democracy in the South and winning the hearts and minds of the people there. "The true struggle in Vietnam is being waged upon a political basis," Lansdale argued. His team would help "pacify" South Vietnam (to use that awful word of the day). That wouldn't be accomplished through massive application of U.S. firepower, Lansdale believed. "In a people's war, you never make war against your own people," he commented later. Adroitly, Lansdale and his men would get South Vietnamese leaders to do what they wanted them to do. With some hypocrisy, Lansdale criticized other U.S. officials for telling the South Vietnamese government (GVN) what was good for it.[2]

Lansdale's men saw themselves as an elite group on an important mission. Yet they were a team in name only. Lansdale "only loosely" controlled them. "Everybody that came out there was almost an independent operator," team member Joe Baker remembers. "He could do just about what he wanted to do." They also found themselves without a clear charter in South Vietnam, outsiders and distrusted among members of the U.S. establishment. U.S. Ambassador to South Vietnam Henry Cabot Lodge felt only *he* should deal with top South Vietnamese leaders, though Lansdale considered that one of his most important roles, and indeed insisted on playing it, thereby angering Lodge. Lansdale did not get along well with the U.S. embassy. He lamented the "artfully vicious back-knifings and self-serving crap that comes out of this place." The team became a side show. On top of that, its members often wondered what Lansdale wanted. "The only man I ever thought that halfway understood Ed was Dan Ellsberg," Baker says. "And Mike Deutch," another Lansdale man. "Both of them are all brains."[3]

Lansdale's men had been told before departing for Saigon that they might be the target of assassins there. Upon arriving in the late summer of 1965, they felt like marked men. Ellsberg's comrades thought him careless and naive. Conein poked fun at his innocence. A bounty was placed on Lansdale's head.

Lodge "got madder than a hatter, because the bounty on Lansdale's head was higher than it was on Lodge's," Hukill recounts. "Lodge got really bent out of shape on that."[4]

Danger was the main theme of a piece that Ellsberg wrote on the sights and smells of Saigon that September. He sent the piece as a letter to Harry Rowen, among many other people, and Rowen and Adam Yarmolinsky urged that it be published. Yarmolinsky got the piece into the *Reporter* magazine. Ellsberg was not high on the *Reporter* and had hoped for the more popular *New Yorker*. The essay was published anonymously, after being cleared by State Department censors, although Dan Jacobs, the man who had introduced Patricia Marx to Ellsberg, determined the author's identity from various clues, including the author's obvious liking for Vietnamese girls. Ellsberg's mood when he wrote the piece was colored by the recent death of a new acquaintance, Jerry Rose, an American adviser to the GVN who may have been on the CIA's payroll. Rose's death shook Ellsberg. He had visited Rose's apartment the night before learning of it, hoping to have dinner with him.[5]

In the essay, entitled "Vietnam Diary," the 34-year-old Ellsberg wrote:

> Hard to recapture, after three weeks, the trace of foreboding in moving through the streets and the crowds of Saigon, one's first night in Vietnam. . . . Which of the newsboys, the cyclo drivers, the soup peddlers is an enemy; why is the balloon seller crowding me? (Just recently, an American was asked to hold a long stick of balloons for a moment; they exploded.) Gradually, alertness is dulled. . . . Yet there are reminders. A policeman hails a passing Vespa, makes the two boys dismount and searches them ("They often stop Vespas with an extra passenger," says my companion. "The boy in back could be ready to throw a grenade").
>
> . . . "All weapons must be cleared before entering" say frequent door signs. At the cashier's desk at the entrance to the PX . . . is a jumble of Swedish "K" submachine guns, Thompsons, grease guns, and carbines, dropped by the owners while they shop inside. Sidearms are as varied: .45's, snub-nosed .38's, huge Magnum six-shooters, back-pocket Browning .25 caliber "pistolets."

When one reads the piece, it is easy to get the impression that Ellsberg was enjoying the danger. "I felt a bit uneasy," Paul Langer, one of many people at RAND who read it, recalls. "He was carried away. . . . He got a kick out of it. . . . He gloried in it."[6]

In the essay, Ellsberg acknowledged his carelessness about security. Walking through the jungle in the countryside, "the soldier walking with me grows very agitated, tapping my carbine," he wrote. "Finally I understand, I have not put a loaded magazine in the weapon." On the way to a restaurant with Lansdale and Joe Redick, another team member, when Ellsberg turned around to ask some questions he was met with a tap on the shoulder from the back seat: "Don't worry about talking now, you're sitting next to an open window . . . stay alert." Lansdale later wrote to his men, "Let's face it. Dan was a bright academic type who often behaved in rather naive fashion in the early days with us."[7]

And there were the young women in Vietnam, another big theme in Ellsberg's letter. The girls in the bars in their white nurses' outfits were "the prettiest whores in the world," he wrote:

> "I spend most of my off hours water-skiing," says the beautiful blonde secretary. . . . "Aren't the VC on the other side of the river?" "Oh, yes, they shoot at you sometimes . . . but they're terrible shots. . . ." The thought of the Vietcong having a blonde American in a bikini, on water skis, as moving target to practice on is irresistible; she promises to make a date with me soon, so I can watch. . . .
>
> The girls on the bicycles wear *ao-dais* ("ow-zai"), loose silk pajama trousers with long panels of silk fluttering down front and back, tight bodices. . . . There are men who stand around and say, "You know, I don't think you see so many of them [in the bars] that are really beautiful." I think you do.

Yet he did not think much about sex, Ellsberg wrote in the letter.[8]

Ellsberg was taken by Vietnamese children. They were friendly and cheerful, and reminded him of his own children. "They rush out with hysterical grins—and I remember my children running out to climb over me at the end of the day, and my heart turns over," he wrote. "They seem so *pleased* by your existence. . . . I love them, and I don't want to leave them." Other Vietnamese also seemed to welcome his presence. Cruising down a river, "my arm grows tired from waving, but the reaction is intoxicating—the people act as if we were liberating them," Ellsberg recounted. "Girls poling sampans grin at us . . . ; old ladies bathing by the shore, fishermen in their boats or drying nets, all smile and wave." But Ellsberg was romanticizing and, to some extent, misreading the reception that he and other Americans were receiving in Vietnam. He concluded the piece: "I'm hopeful, desperately glad to be here. I expect to work here a long time."[9]

At Ellsberg's request, his essay was widely circulated, and some who read it were a bit puzzled. "This was not the Dan we knew," Roman Kolkowicz remembers. "This was a new romantic self-image that he was creating. . . . In the past he would be the cool, rational RANDite. . . . So something happened. . . . This was the new romantic man of the people. It was a whole new Dan. . . . Some of us were scratching our head: 'What happened to Dan?'" Kolkowicz adds, "It's sort of like McNamara. The cold, calculating, rationalist originally, and then we used to see him at these close, small meetings weeping and whining."[10] But Ellsberg had not become a romantic in Vietnam: that was already in him.

Ellsberg was prickly about the idea of anyone editing his writing, and he was angered when Meg Greenfield, the Washington bureau chief of the *Reporter*, and the State Department made a number of changes in the piece, largely minor ones, without his approval. But he requested 50 copies of the published version, presumably for distribution.[11]

Ellsberg originally wrote the letter while laid up in bed with a case of amoebic dysentery. He drank some water without boiling and filtering it (despite being instructed to do so), "so, of course, he got very sick," Lowell Hukill remembers. "I almost had to carry him over to the dispensary. He was just dying. . . . His legs just turned to rubber. . . . I just saw him in the office, and he was so obviously sick. . . . But you almost had to talk to him like a little mommy or something," she laughs.[12]

As the young neophyte on the Lansdale team, Ellsberg realized he was being watched by his seasoned comrades. This was not an auspicious beginning. "He was a complete babe in the woods, not knowing about health habits in Asia and other kindergarten lessons that we all learned so long ago that we never think about them any more," Lansdale later wrote. Though Ellsberg had worked on Vietnam in the Pentagon, operating on the ground there was an entirely different matter. "I don't think it bore any relationship to any life experience that he'd ever had," Rufus Phillips, another team member, reminisces. "He was sort of a fish out of water." Moreover, while some people adapt readily to new situations because they relate to other people easily, Phillips points out, "I didn't feel that Dan had that facility. . . . There was a kind of nervous energy aspect to him. He didn't seem to me to connect very well with people easily. He seemed to be more of an academic in the ways that he approached things." Phillips thought Ellsberg was "lost, really, for quite a while in terms of what he might be doing that might be useful. . . . He was extremely bright; the problem was that you couldn't give him something to do, because he didn't understand the local context," and how that might affect what could be done, and in what ways. Lansdale appointed Conein to be Ellsberg's "big brother" and told another of his men to tutor him in counterinsurgency.[13]

Phillips, who had already spent considerable time in Vietnam, came to feel that Ellsberg never fully appreciated how Vietnamese realities affected what Americans could do there. For example, Ellsberg wanted to fire all the South Vietnamese province chiefs, many of whom were corrupt or incompetent. "I said, 'We're the U.S. government. How do we fire 45 Vietnamese province chiefs?'" Robert Komer, then an aide to President Johnson, recounts. "Well, he hadn't thought that through."[14]

Again, Ellsberg's indiscretion and ego bothered some of his colleagues. In the main, they were used to operating discreetly, secretively, and Ellsberg's carelessness and loose tongue could prove injurious to them. "He used to carry secret papers in his pocket," Lansdale would recall. "Jesus, I used to go crazy trying to keep him clean on that." One memo to team members instructed them to be "more careful regarding security. Several times the young ladies in the office have found classified material on the desks after everyone has left," and material for internal use only "has been given to outsiders." That fits Ellsberg's earlier behavior in the Pentagon. After Ellsberg returned from a breakfast meeting with U.S. officials in December 1965, Michael Deutch informed Lansdale,

> he only casually mentioned to me that the subject of the breakfast was to seek his views on the progress of pacification, the situation in the provinces . . . whether the job of running the pacification effort here should be given to one centralized authority . . . and on what the team has accomplished. With quite some glee he told [another team member] and me, separately, that if [the team] has no need for him, he has another job offer, but he is happy to stay on the team, although he feels that his knowledge of Binh Dinh [province] qualified him to take on Binh Dinh instead of Hop Tak. He told the visiting [officials] . . . that EGL [Lansdale] is not particularly well known in Washington for administrative experience. He described your talent of getting a rapport with the Vietnamese, and was asked if EGL has the same talent in getting along with Americans, and I gather that the kid answered "not to the same degree—he is too suspicious." . . . Since he is "the member of the team senior to all in civil service rank," it is my understanding that he took upon himself to give the assembled breakfast gathering his views on other matters, on which he did not debrief himself to me.

This report could not have pleased Lansdale. Either Joe Redick or Joe Baker (probably Redick) indicated that he "strictly agree[d]" with it and told Lansdale: "Frankly I always suspected Dan as being a dangerous person to have on the team. He knows most of the high ranking visitors or their aides and is always reporting to them. We both know that this can be dangerous because he is still wet behind the ears. To prevent any further occurrences such as above I am allowing Dan to take a three-week vacation in India to get him out of our way and to give Mike and me time to evaluate just what damage has been done to the team and to you." Deutch also suggested to Lansdale that he determine if RAND people in Vietnam had been "spying on us, and misinformed by the Kid."[15]

Ellsberg angrily reproached others for indiscretion, however, when he thought someone on the team had passed a "Secret-Sensitive" memo he had written critical of a South Vietnamese major to two strong devotees of the major. He had hoped to befriend the two men, he wrote in a frosty memo to the team, but now that might be impossible.[16]

Ellsberg did have the highest civil service rank on the team, equaling Lansdale's. He carried the foreign service grade of FSR-1/3, equivalent to his GS-18 in the Pentagon. He threw it around a bit. "Most of us were considerably lower in rank," Redick remembers. "I think there probably was a certain amount of envy." Ellsberg's rank ultimately got him a house by himself, a two-story villa on an alley with separate quarters for a *mamma san* who cooked, purchased groceries, and cleaned for him. Most other team members lived together. Ellsberg also threw around his Harvard Ph.D. some: he could be arrogant. He exhibited "a very firm belief in his own convictions," Barry Zorthian, the head of the Joint U.S. Public Affairs office in South Vietnam, recalls. Ellsberg was "contentious, stubborn . . . not an easy guy to have a debate, dialogue with. Because he was very convinced." He did not seem to lack self-assurance or poise. He used his superior intellect to tear holes in other people's arguments. His skills at argument impressed Lansdale. He could put people in their place calmly, icily.[17]

Ellsberg's womanizing in Vietnam worried at least one team member. Shortly after he arrived there, perhaps even within a day or two, "he picked up a girl at a bar and brought her home," Bernard Yoh remembers. Yoh thought that reckless. Who knew which side the girl was on? Ellsberg struck Yoh as undiscriminating in his choice of partners. Again he bragged about his adventures.[18]

Ellsberg spent many hours at the Cercle Sportif, the French colonial sports club in downtown Saigon, "because of the women," Lou Conein remembers. (When he left Vietnam, he was in arrears at the club.) He sometimes brought young women by the Lansdale team's houses. "I knew he was fooling around with some of those French women down on the strip," Joe Baker recalls.[19]

Ellsberg risked his own life when he became involved with a young Eurasian woman named Germaine who was the mistress of a Corsican mafia man in Saigon. The Corsican mafia ran rackets that included drugs, money, and prostitution. Germaine was attractive—"sexy" and "beautiful" by two accounts—perhaps in her early twenties, with "more flesh on her than the usual Vietnamese," remembers John Sack, who stayed for two months at Ellsberg's house in Saigon. "And more spirit." Germaine had attended a

French lycée. Ellsberg fell in love with her and wanted to marry her. Germaine's Corsican lover was the manager of a restaurant. He discovered the affair and threatened to shoot Ellsberg. Both Conein and Lansdale had to intercede. "The Corsican was going to slit Ellsberg's throat," Lansdale recounted. "I had to go to the Corsican, whom I wouldn't have otherwise touched with a ten-foot pole, and ask for Ellsberg's life." Conein told Ellsberg, according to one account, "Listen, my friend. You are in much more trouble with the Corsicans than with the Viet Cong. You know what they do when somebody fools with one of their women? They'll get you down on the pavement and whip your face with barbed wire." Conein told me he likely saved Ellsberg's life, then regretted it after Ellsberg released the Pentagon Papers. "If I hadn't interceded, he might have been bumped off," Conein said. "Because they don't play around with you screwing around with their girlfriends. . . . They would have taken care of him. . . . They would have gotten the Vietnamese to do it." Conein warned a top Corsican that if they shot Ellsberg, he would have some of *his* people plug some Corsicans: "I said, 'Look, lay off of the stupid bastard.'" After speaking with Conein, the top Corsican allegedly upbraided the restaurant manager and told him he should keep his woman in line. Ellsberg told Sack he was with Germaine in his car one night on a side street in Saigon when a Corsican stopped them and pulled a gun on him.[20]

Another evening, Sack was having dinner with a friend on the narrow side terrace of the Continental Hotel along Tu Do street, and "all of a sudden Dan came running up. Not looking scared, but looking very urgent and concerned. Saying something like, 'I need some help. I need some friends. Can you come with me?' He was going to a restaurant, and the Corsican people were supposed to be waiting for him at the restaurant. . . . He had that 1970s grave Ellsberg expression of concern on his face. That I need some help right now." The three hurried off to the restaurant, but found it pretty deserted. "We looked around and we looked around, and nobody was there," Sack recounts. "But we looked around feeling very dramatic."[21]

Ellsberg liked to live on the edge, and he undoubtedly got a thrill out of this whole episode. It was another adventure, more high drama.

Ellsberg had his sights on Lowell Hukill (then Lowell Kelso) shortly after arriving in Vietnam. "He used to ask me out all the time, and I never did go," Hukill chuckles. Hukill was a strikingly attractive young woman and may have been the blond secretary he mentioned in his *Reporter* piece. Although Ellsberg was a handsome man by some accounts, Hukill did not find him attractive. "He annoyed me," she remembers. "He seemed like he had a real lack of maturity."

Ellsberg "didn't seem all together. . . . He just didn't. . . . He didn't think at times. I mean, because otherwise you don't go out and drink the water when it even stinks." It was as if there were many types of intelligence, Hukill thought later, and Ellsberg had only one or two types. "I never even saw his brilliance," she recalls. "I didn't see him produce." Ellsberg didn't look all together either. "His dress was not really embassy dress," in terms of "the care that would go into that kind of thing. . . . This guy had been through the Marine Corps—you would think something would rub off." Further, "I got the impression many times he didn't understand the seriousness of things. Ah, he did have a good time, you know. That's the impression I got. . . . For the most part you'd think he was hanging loose." Hukill thought Ellsberg acted like "an undisciplined kid."[22]

Others in Vietnam also found Ellsberg erratic or a bit odd. Again, he didn't seem to focus on any one thing for very long and jumped from one thing to the next. His disorganization was evident. "There were some odd quirks to his nature" and a "strange side to him," Rufus Phillips remembers. Besides having a "compulsion" for going out on patrols and "trying to kill VC," Ellsberg had a collection of "sort of pornographic photographs," Phillips recalls. "Some sort of weird stuff. I mean, it seemed weird to us. . . . It was an odd quirk in his personality."[23]

After he returned from a trip to India, Thailand, and other spots, Ellsberg came into the Lansdale team's offices at the U.S. embassy one day carrying a book of photographs of erotic Indian sculptures. He had photos of such sculptures displayed in his house, too. The sculptures "obviously turned him on," says a person to whom he showed slides. Hukill felt the photos that Ellsberg brought into the embassy were "very pornographic. And the whole book was just full of them." Patricia Marx, who was then visiting him in Vietnam and who had accompanied him on the trip, was with him when he carried them in, Hukill recounts:

> He hands me the book! And I'm looking at this, and I said, "Pardon me?" Does this sweeten it up because it's in stone? . . . I mean, I'm a young female gal in my twenties, and he comes in and he hands me this book, and I'm supposed to appreciate the art. And his girlfriend is standing right there with him. . . . They're just enjoying the hell out of this. . . . And I wasn't really embarrassed, and I wasn't shocked. I was just kind of like, "What's the matter with you? I mean, this is just inappropriate." . . . They're just oblivious! It's kind of like, "Prudence? What's that?" . . . It's vacant. . . . I think when people do that they've got some kind of a deficiency.[24]

Bernard Yoh also found Ellsberg a bit immature. After the CIA had given Ellsberg a small .25 caliber automatic Saturday-night special to carry, "he was very sad," Yoh remembers. "He said, 'I only rate a twenty? Don't I rate something bigger?'" Ellsberg was "complaining to everybody" about it and "sort of almost crying: 'Is this all I rate?'"[25]

Members of the Lansdale group had expected more from Ellsberg: "I got the impression people were pretty disappointed with his performance there," Hukill remembers. "Everybody was saying, 'Why was he rated at the Pentagon as a whiz kid?'" Yoh recalls. "'Where is the whiz?' . . . In the entire team, no one could figure out" where it was. Deutch mentioned to Lansdale the possibility that he might have to "ditch" Ellsberg. To her astonishment, Hukill heard from others that Ellsberg was actually paid more than Ambassador Lodge, given his high rank. That is probably untrue, but Ellsberg's total compensation and benefits, totaling $37,678, exceeded Lansdale's.[26]

Ellsberg was an outsider on the Lansdale team. He didn't hang out with the others much. "I don't think I ever saw Dan socially out in Saigon," Joe Baker remembers. "I don't know where he disappeared at night. . . . I never ran into the man." "I don't think *he* thought he fit" on the team, Hukill says. "I don't think he really felt like he was a part of the group."[27]

Ellsberg got along well with the others if he made an attempt. He didn't always make an attempt. Nobody on the team actively disliked him, as again, he could be quite friendly and charming—"Dan had the polish," Baker notes—but he didn't get close to the others. "I think, by and large, that there was not an awful lot of love lost either way," Joe Redick remembers.[28]

Ellsberg dealt more with Lansdale than with the other men, in part a sign of his priorities. Lansdale was yet another father figure to him; he tried to please Lansdale and hoped to benefit from their association. (The more father figures we encounter, the more deficient Ellsberg's relationship with his real father appears.) "I would say I loved Lansdale," Ellsberg recalls. Lansdale was a hero to Ellsberg. Lansdale taught him a lot about the war and counterinsurgency; with his typical fervor, Ellsberg came to advance many of Lansdale's ideas. Ellsberg lauded Lansdale even after turning against the war. Lansdale, in turn, liked and felt affection for Ellsberg. "When the two of them were together, they got along very well, as far as I could tell," Redick remembers. Lansdale wrote in April 1966, "Dan's forte here has been to get below surface on conditions in the field, so that we could deal with the truth. . . . [He] demonstrated rather unique skill at obtaining, digesting, and analyzing field problems that somehow hadn't come to light before." Ellsberg was good at getting information from people. "I think that Ed thought that Dan generally did some useful things," Phillips says. But Ellsberg also frustrated and irritated Lansdale, with his carelessness, naïveté, self-promotion, and eagerness to participate in combat. Hukill thought Ellsberg was like "a gnat" to Lansdale at times. Ellsberg probably cornered him for conversations more than Lansdale wanted.[29]

RAND's Gus Shubert visited with Lansdale in Saigon in March of 1966. "It was like something right out of Graham Greene," Shubert recounts. "With the blinds all drawn, and no lamps on. The place was semidark. I'm wondering if we're going to get shot or something." Lansdale seemed "one very discouraged, tired old man." When Shubert asked Lansdale about Ellsberg, "he sort of rubbed it off as, 'Well, you know, everybody makes mistakes, and he was one of mine,'" recalls Shubert, who wondered why Lansdale was telling *him* that, as it was the first time they'd met.[30]

⸻⸻◆⸻⸻

The exact nature of Ellsberg's work on the Lansdale team was never clear to other team members. "My role was, as in the Pentagon, an extremely lowly and menial role," he later acknowledged. "I was to do what [Lansdale] told me to do, which was, to a large extent, often a clerk's job or the job of a patrol or someone finding out information."[31]

The team focused much of its initial work on cultivating relations with top South Vietnamese leaders, and Ellsberg helped draft a speech for Prime Minister Nguyen Cao Ky, a showy and corrupt man not highly regarded by many Americans (he was a "little bastard" and "goddamn little fool," John Vann wrote). Ky used most of the speech. Ellsberg also did a lot of other writing for Lansdale, including a paper on South Vietnamese "pacification doctrine" that impressed Lansdale. In addition, Lansdale had Ellsberg participate in meetings and committees so that he wouldn't have to; Ellsberg was "a real asset" on committees, one team member thought. Ellsberg also performed some liaison with the U.S. military, which he seemed to enjoy, and in February 1966 he acted as "sort of the spokesman for the military" on a tour he helped give for reporters covering a visit by Vice President Hubert Humphrey. Ellsberg was "militant" about the war and showed few doubts about it, one of those reporters, Tom Wicker, thought. Don Oberdorfer, another reporter who spoke with Ellsberg in Vietnam, remembers him as a "combative" and "swashbuckling character . . . wearing a gun around," without any qualms about the war.[32]

Ellsberg also met with other U.S. visitors to Vietnam, including high-level ones whom he probably sought out. During Humphrey's trip, he showed the National Security Council (NSC) staffer James Thomson around. Thomson remembers a "strange evening or afternoon" when Ellsberg took him to a large, second-floor room somewhere in Saigon where CIA people were gathered. It was "all a little spooky. . . . It was not all social, but there was plenty to consume. And they were sort of talking spook talk." Ellsberg became intrigued with spooks and their games in Vietnam. The place "would make sixteenth-century Medici Italy look like a Boy Scout camp," Douglas Pike, who was a U.S. foreign service officer in Vietnam, notes. "It's wheels within wheels, and nobody knows who was on what side." Pike felt Ellsberg had a spook mentality similar to Lou Conein's—"you know, these larger-than-life types." In the U.S. foreign service community in Vietnam, people would talk about Ellsberg. "He wasn't your ordinary bland civil servant, or your very precise foreign service officer," Pike remembers. And he "seemed to be all over the place."[33]

Ellsberg felt good intelligence was a key to defeating the enemy in Vietnam, and he went out with "Census Grievance" teams, which were advised by the CIA and acted as "intelligence specialists." They placed informers in villages to identify VC for elimination. Ellsberg advocated strengthening intelligence against the enemy. In a tough-talking, hard-line memo of October 1965 prompted by the possibility of negotiations and a cease-fire—which Ellsberg opposed, arguing that it would likely have a wide array of "disastrous" consequences—he urged that the United States and GVN "expand," "consolidate," and improve the "overall intelligence effort," particularly that of South Vietnam's CIA-run Police Special Branch, which targeted the VC infrastructure, and "expand interrogations and dossier files." The GVN's interrogation program should receive a "great expansion," Ellsberg advised, and the dossiers should be "detailed." The United States and GVN should also "move as rapidly as possible into effective Special Branch operations against the VC/NLF political apparatus." Ellsberg wanted "maximum intelligence exploitation" of any opportunities that peace talks provided:

> Nothing is more important—with or without negotiations—than to acquire and use as rapidly as possible the ability to operate effectively against the VC/NLF political/administrative apparatus. . . . As much of the VC/NLF political apparatus should be rolled up—by arrest, assassination, capture, defection—interrogated, and where possible used by the GVN in psywar and intelligence functions, *before* negotiations or ceasefire confer any legitimacy on the NLF agents who can now be treated as criminals. . . . The Police Special Branch should be losing no time in acquiring as accurate and complete a file of detailed political dossiers on members of the NLF as possible.

All of this presumably excluded torture, if we are to believe Ellsberg's later claim that he had decided before going to Vietnam that he would never "collaborate in" torture, and that if he learned Americans were "condoning or systematically engaging in torture," he would not only quit the government, but speak out publicly against it "very forcibly." But it did include, again, assassination.[34]

Ellsberg made his later claim in a joint interview with Anthony Russo, whom he met for the first time in Saigon shortly before writing his memo. A RAND analyst, Russo had heard of Ellsberg before meeting him, indeed, had taken note of the name, having worked for Professor Oskar Morgenstern during his last year of graduate school at Princeton and having learned about game theory. Russo had asked about Ellsberg after he began work at RAND in 1964. "I was told that he had left, and they said, 'Besides, he wouldn't talk to you anyway. He'll only talk to people of deputy secretary level or over,'" Russo recounts with a laugh. Russo was alone in RAND's French colonial villa in Saigon one afternoon when Ellsberg, who had arrived in Saigon only days earlier, knocked on the door. Ellsberg introduced himself and asked Russo to fill him in on things in Vietnam. As Russo talked, Ellsberg "took copious notes." Russo came to see this as one of Ellsberg's two main modes: "He's either in an intense monologue . . . or he's taking notes copiously. He always had his stenopads."[35]

Russo also got a taste of Ellsberg's gung ho spirit in Vietnam. "I clearly remember one time he said, 'Well, there's no question but that we'll win,'" Russo recalls.[36]

Ellsberg's main work on the Lansdale team involved assessing conditions in the field. He studied pacification efforts, pointed out problems, and recommended improvements. Lansdale wanted him to act as a "catalyst" for pacification. Ellsberg usually traveled by car or Scout, speaking with officials, military officers, and villagers. During one plane ride, he drew his pistol when the pilot spotted what he claimed were two VC on the ground. Ellsberg later testified to feeling a "very great sense of unease at the fact that humans, on the basis of wearing black pajamas, were being hunted like animals all over Vietnam at the discretion of pilots who decided who our enemy was and who it wasn't."[37]

Walt Rostow read many of Ellsberg's reports on his field trips, at least one of which Ellsberg sent him directly. "I read them religiously in the White House," Rostow remembers. "They came across my desk. . . . They were not very distinguished." Lowell Hukill, who did a lot of typing for the team, also read many of them. "He'd write things like [they were] going out into the provinces, and they were going by in their jeep, and there was this absolutely beautiful Vietnamese girl on the side of the road, and you'd just be admiring her beauty, but you had to remember that perhaps she had a grenade," Hukill recalls. She thought Ellsberg's reports were largely journalistic and therefore didn't merit much in the way of security classification. But "he wanted to have everything much more highly classified. Because then, of course, he'd feel more important." Ellsberg later testified that one "formal" report he wrote was "meant for the President."[38]

Ellsberg's field reports tended to be detailed, narrative, almost blow-by-blow accounts of his trips, travelogues of sorts, well written, with extensive dialogue (complete with pauses) and descriptions of the sights; some underscored the danger he faced. The following excerpts from one report, written in haste, impart some of their flavor.

> The ceremony was being held across the road, in a garden so filled with flowers and vines that the faces of the officials were hidden when they sat down on the porch. In a corner next to the porch stood the village notables, flanked by a double row of little girls, sitting up straight in white ao-dais. They were all pretty, all with long black hair combed smooth down their backs. . . .
>
> As we walked in file, the rice chest-high on either side, a distant shot rang out now and then. I had heard the first ones back in the outpost: some far, some fairly close. "Soldiers shooting birds," the captain said. "Or checking their weapons. Or having fun. . . ." Now artillery was firing sporadically, far off. The sound joined birdcalls, wind in the rice, bamboo clicking, low thrumming of a helicopter moving slowly a mile off: Delta sounds on a quiet, hot day. . . .
>
> "With that automatic weapon, it could be a squad," the captain said softly. "Three or four, anyway. . . . We can't very well go back the way we came, now; too open. I think we'd better try to get them before they get us. OK?" He asked me to cover him; he pulled back the bolt on his submachine gun and cocked it; I did the same. . . . The captain moved in a crouch along a paddy embankment toward a second grove, in the direction of the shots. It was now very quiet, except for the artillery. When he reached the grove he squatted next to a palm and gestured to me; I moved over to him, bending below the level of the tall rice, trying to remember what I had learned a long time ago about moving quietly. As I came up, he slid into the stream of water, moved across it, climbed up on the bank and disappeared into thick brush. After a moment I followed, feeling the cool water move up my boots, my pants, to my crotch as my boots hit mud at the bottom.

Lansdale would tell Ellsberg later that one of his field reports showed "an unusual talent for writing narrative based upon really sensitive observations of the scene around you—which some of your associates have felt that you are too self-centered to have."[39]

Out in the field, Ellsberg noticed considerable divergence between reality and other U.S. reports on the war. As he had suspected in the Pentagon, the cable traffic was often inaccurate. "Time after time in the history of U.S. involvement in South Vietnam," he wrote Lansdale, "major policy failures have occurred in part because our reporting system was not telling U.S. policy-makers what they needed to know, and too much of what it was telling them wasn't so." In letters and talks, Ellsberg tried to get officials in Washington to recognize this problem, while simultaneously keeping his name before their eyes.[40]

When Ellsberg had arrived in Vietnam, he had with him a must-see list of people. John Paul Vann was high on that list. Vincent Davis had earlier shown Ellsberg some letters Vann had sent him, hoping to use Ellsberg as a channel for bringing Vann's ideas to the attention of those at the top level of the Pentagon. Vann also wanted his ideas to reach the top. Davis had also helped put Ellsberg in touch with Vann, as had David Halberstam, who told Ellsberg that Vann was the most knowledgeable person in Vietnam about the situation there other than the reporters.[41]

John Vann was something of a legend in Vietnam. He was a former army officer with a promising future who had retired from the service in 1963 after an affair he had had with a 15-year-old baby-sitter—one of many sexual encounters he had had with girls—led the army to charge him with statutory rape. Though Vann got off, his army career was now limited. "His future had been washed out by a fatal flaw, a compulsive sexual need for teenage girls, often several a day," one writer recalled. Vann's was a strange and revolting form of womanizing; he had an "urge to use and abuse all women," another writer observed.[42]

Vann was an Agency for International Development (AID) province representative on pacification when Ellsberg met him. A moderate Republican, he was short, tough, and wiry, a tightly coiled redneck with, like Ellsberg, enormous energy and personal ambition; he would soon move further up the ladder of civilian command. Vietnam was, in part, a stage for drawing attention to himself. Vann was cocky and outspoken. He didn't mince words and "butted heads with everybody that there was to butt heads with," his widow, Mary Jane Vann, remembers. He had little patience for what he considered stupidity. In his criticisms of the U.S. Army, "he spoke in four-letter words, and he was very, very direct, and was looking at you," Harry Harris later found. "He said, 'These guys are assholes.'" Vann was very conscious of rank—his rank. "I outrank everybody else around here," he told Harris. "He was very expressive to me on that," Harris recalls. Vann was a leader and a manipulator. He sometimes took on other people's coloration as he talked to them. He was courageous and fearless, given to acts of daring and surviving them. "Nobody wanted to be in a car with him," Mary Jane Vann remembers. "In the family, lots of times, we'd be just white knuckles." But it was his life, Vann would say, and he was going to live it fast, short, and to the hilt. Vann's recklessness in Vietnam led some to wonder whether he had a death wish. But life off the high wire bored him, and "he was always one to look out for number one," Mary Jane says.[43]

That last trait would lead him to betray Ellsberg.

Vann was not a good family man. He had five children, four of them boys, and he gave them relatively little of his time. Mary Jane didn't fare much better. "I saw John three days a year," she remembers. And "when he would come back, he'd walk in the house and immediately be on the phone. . . . In fact, if he even said hello to one of us or one of the kids, that was boasted over. . . . I don't think he spent five minutes with the kids." Financially, Vann kept his family on a short leash. He wanted the money for himself. Like Ellsberg, Vann did what *he* wanted to do. His marriage to Mary Jane ended in divorce (later rescinded after his death because he had not signed the papers).[44]

John Vann was a forceful critic of U.S. policies in Vietnam. In far too many cases, he thought, the wrong people were in South Vietnamese command positions. He felt the United States should get the right people in. Vann was a relentless critic of the GVN and the South Vietnamese Army (ARVN). "Sometimes he said, 'Well, we're on the wrong side. We should have been with the Viet Cong,'" Mary Jane remembers. But Vann was a tiger about winning the war. He believed it essential to stop the spread of communism and felt it was winnable with different policies. But that would take major U.S. influence. The United States should "take over the command of this operation lock, stock, and barrel—but maintaining Vietnamese front men," Vann wrote a friend.[45]

Ellsberg met Vann only two days after arriving in Vietnam. "I am impressed with Ellsberg," Vann wrote Vince Davis after spending a day with him. "He is basically a very sharp cookie—and will work out well once he gets oriented with some practical experience."[46]

Vann and Ellsberg soon became buddies. Vann and Harry Rowen were his two closest friends in his life, Ellsberg told me. Vann was another hero to him, perhaps even a model. Ellsberg idolized Vann, who was seven years older. "He worshipped John Paul Vann," Gus Shubert recalls. Ellsberg admired Vann's idealism, his knowledge of the war, and his brashness, toughness, and courage. He may have seen something of himself in Vann when he witnessed Vann putting somebody down. Ellsberg could also learn about the war from Vann and get out in the field more by pairing up with him. And both men enjoyed danger and were intent on proving their manhood in Vietnam. Ellsberg also respected Vann's ability to lead other men, perhaps even his ability to manipulate them. "Ellsberg was a soloist. Vann was a conductor," Sam Popkin, who did counterinsurgency research in Vietnam, comments.[47] And Ellsberg probably thought it was beneficial to be close to a well-known man who was going places.

Vann, for his part, respected Ellsberg's brilliance and Harvard credentials. "Dr. Dan Ellsberg," he would refer to him to others. Vann gave Ellsberg's papers to others. He told David Halberstam that Ellsberg had the most powerful mind ever applied to Vietnam on the ground level.[48] Ellsberg's rank surely also made an impression on him.

On top of all this, both were highly charged men who could talk for hours without stopping, zealots in a cause, and egotists to boot. Each saw himself in heroic terms, playing big roles. Their mutual strong interest in sex also goes a long way to explain their friendship. "When Vann found a friend who regarded sex with some of the importance he did," Neil Sheehan wrote, "he interpreted the attitude as an invitation to confide the details of his exploits, which he liked to do." Ellsberg would recall Vann telling him, upon noticing him reading, that he should be out screwing.[49]

After meeting, Vann invited Ellsberg to join him for a tour of his province, Hau Nghia, and in mid-October 1965 Ellsberg spent two days there. He wrote a lengthy report on his trip for Lansdale and other team members. Typically, he struggled to get it into satisfactory form and then passed it to others; some recipients, including Harry Rowen, circulated it further. The paper was Ellsberg's best field report in Vietnam, and particularly illuminating on ARVN's failings.[50]

Riding with Vann through Hau Nghia "was an education for me," Ellsberg wrote. "With Vann's running commentary on this drive through roads and hamlets mainly abandoned by the GVN, I got a microscopic view of the guerrilla war and political campaign." Vann frequently drove fast, sometimes "very fast . . . with one hand on an AR-15 pointed out the window, extra ammo around his shoulder and grenades in his belt." Ellsberg carried a machine gun on his lap. Vann told him what to watch for and what to do if ambushed. A land mine blew up some South Vietnamese troops on a road they had traveled only four hours earlier, Ellsberg noted in the report. "You're safest in a single, unmarked vehicle, driving fast at irregular times, during the day," Vann instructed him. At one intersection, "Vann pointed right and said, 'if you want to meet VC with 100% certainty, day or night, just go into that treeline, 400 yards off,'" Ellsberg recounted. "'Some Polish journalists wanted to meet VC; the VC met them at the treeline, burned their jeep and kept them for three days. They got

a good story.'" At a marketplace, "I got out and took some pictures, till Vann
honked the horn," Ellsberg wrote. "'Let's move out,' he said, 'they're starting
to move away from the car.' There was now a noticeable empty space around
the Scout." Villagers were generally friendly, but "these people smiling at us
right now would smile just as warmly—and be perfectly honest about it—if
they knew that in another 10 yards we were going to be blown up by a mine the
VC laid last night; and they wouldn't say anything," Vann told Ellsberg.[51]

Ellsberg got an education on ARVN's habits. ARVN avoided contact with
the enemy, he learned, though the enemy's locations were not hard to determine. He found ARVN's behavior astonishing and appalling.[52]

Vann would have a great influence on Ellsberg's views on the war, and this
trip was enormously stimulating. Ellsberg devoted a section of his report to
Vann's views, which, he argued, "deserve the attention of the team." VC control of the countryside was often "thin," he observed, and could be reversed
with improved policies. But that would take much greater U.S. intervention
and control. So might the development of new South Vietnamese leadership, a
possible "requirement" for winning the war. Although Ellsberg raised questions about Vann's approach, he was becoming a devotee.[53]

The two men took many other trips out into the field together, deepening
their friendship. At times Vann directed Ellsberg to grab hold of his M-16 or
carbine and to make sure grenades were at the ready. (Ellsberg was also known
to take a "Swedish K" submachine gun, something of a status symbol—which
he liked to show off—into the field with him.) During one drive on a narrow
road through dense jungle foliage, Ellsberg "glanced down at his side to be
sure a grenade was handy and lifted the carbine he had been cradling in his lap
so that he could immediately open fire out the window," Neil Sheehan recounted, based on Ellsberg's retelling. "Vann started driving with one hand.
With the other he raised the M-16 automatic he now customarily carried."
The two kept their gun muzzles pointed out the windows and their hands on
the triggers. When they arrived at their destination, a small town near the
coast, the province military advisers were taken aback. According to Ellsberg,
no Americans had driven to the town for almost a year. "Is that road open?"
one of the advisers asked in amazement. "Well, it is now," Vann replied. Ellsberg and Vann took pride in their bravery, enjoyed the feelings of superiority it
gave them, and savored the advisers' reactions.[54]

They subsequently drove to the coastal resort town of Vung Tau, thereby
making a trip literally all Americans thought was suicidal and that hadn't been
made for over a year, Ellsberg claimed later. To lessen the chance of getting
ambushed, Vann had French license plates put on their car before embarking.

Down the road, they got stuck in a traffic jam. An ARVN officer explained that there were a "mil VC" up ahead. But Vann and Ellsberg drove on, the officer pleading wildly for them to stop—he didn't want to move out. Driving at great speed, weapons in their ready positions, Ellsberg and Vann continued without incident. The episode added to Ellsberg's education about ARVN.[55]

The writer Frances FitzGerald met Ellsberg for the first time not long after this trip. FitzGerald, whose father was Desmond FitzGerald, the CIA's deputy director for plans, and Jill Krementz, a photographer, were in My Tho in the Delta. It was FitzGerald's first trip out of Saigon. My Tho was some 40 miles from Saigon on a well-traveled road. Ellsberg offered to give the two young women a ride back to Saigon in his jeep. "I mean, we were about the only two going," FitzGerald laughs. "And Jill's very pretty." During the ride, "all of a sudden, Jill, who had been there [in Vietnam] longer than I had, picked up her feet and there were these grenades rolling around underneath the seat," FitzGerald recounts. "And it turned out there was some rifle, proba- bly an M-16, under there too. And he said, 'Oh, I didn't want to frighten you.' And Jill, who had certainly driven that road quite often, thought this was sort of strange. Because we were right on the outskirts of Saigon by [then]. He cer- tainly made an impression there." Krementz would later recall arguing fer- vidly with Ellsberg about the war when she was in Vietnam; Ellsberg was a fierce defender of it and seemingly a genuine war lover, she said. Krementz would come to see Ellsberg as a troubled and strange person, and one at- tracted to celebrity.[56]

Ellsberg and FitzGerald hung out together some in Vietnam. "He squired her around Saigon all the time when she was there," Joe Redick remembers. "He was going out with Frankie FitzGerald," John Sack says. Ellsberg helped her understand the war. "He was one of the few people in the government . . . who you could really have a serious talk with about the war," FitzGerald re- calls. "He was just sort of beginning to figure things out. . . . So we were put- ting ourselves through this rather intense course of trying to figure out what in the hell was going on." They had long discussions. Michael Deutch told Lans- dale that it was his understanding that FitzGerald was writing "dutiful and fa- vorable reports" on Ellsberg to her father.[57]

FitzGerald witnessed Ellsberg's coolness under danger. He drove her to a big Buddhist-initiated demonstration in Cholon, the Chinese suburb of Saigon. She recounts:

> You could feel sort of an anti-American mood at this demonstration. . . . So we
> decided at a certain point . . . that we ought to flee. So Dan started driving,

[amid] the fumes of exhaust, tear gas, everything, and lost his way. Which was really easy to do. . . . In, again, one of these Cherokee jeeps. And we kept going down narrower and narrower streets. We couldn't find the main drag at all. And finally the street was so narrow that the fences on either side were touching the car, and finally were too narrow to let the jeep go through. . . . We couldn't go forward and couldn't turn around. . . . People started throwing stones at the car. Really hard. . . . I really thought if we didn't get out of there, we were dead. And Dan, in a very cool manner, I must say, managed to turn the car around. Which I thought was impossible. . . . He was just very cool.[58]

Both Ellsberg and Vann took pride in their ability to stay cool under danger. Driving the roads made Ellsberg feel alert, like a hunted animal, he would recall. One could rationalize the need to drive the roads, and it did serve a purpose—helping one understand the war, primarily—but the excitement also offered relief from one's frustrations, he said. Neither he nor Vann felt fear when facing danger, Ellsberg said. He felt calm and efficient. "He didn't seem to show any fear," Lowell Hukill remembers. "He seemed to just think it was wonderful to get in some fatiguelike outfits or khaki outfits and go with someone else, and they'd have their rifles, and they'd go out into the provinces." The only time he *was* efficient was under danger, Ellsberg said.[59]

After Vann got him into the habit of driving the roads, Ellsberg came to spend much of his time that way. He drove thousands of miles alone, and on roads others wouldn't risk, he would recall. "I was probably the only civilian who had served at a high staff level who was then exposed to the realities of the war in Vietnam close up," he bragged. To a large degree, Lansdale team members lost track of him. "He'd go off on his own," Lou Conein remembers, or "he'd be with John Paul Vann, and hell, you didn't know where the hell they were." Ellsberg "was playing cowboy and Indian . . . most of the time," Conein says, and seemed "anxious to get into *something*."[60]

Sam Popkin heard about Ellsberg "all the time" when he was in Vietnam in 1966 and 1967:

He was always the guy going out there to find out what was really going on. But there was also a little bit of the strange loner. Picking up the gun and going out alone on patrol to see how things were. There was a little bit of a crazy edge. . . . He became the role model of what would happen to you . . . if you weren't careful around the heart of darkness. It was easy to turn into an Ellsberg. Ellsberg was the guy I always heard about going out there with his rifle when he should have just been analyzing things, and instead of writing memos would go out there with his gun.

Fred Haynes was a marine commander in Vietnam when he ran into Ellsberg a few times there. "He was very hawkish," Haynes recalls. "He carried a carbine and wore khakis. And he loved it. It was a great thing for him psychologically. . . . He liked to be seen as the guerrilla fighter, as the guy who was out with the boys and out in the brush. And he was a courageous guy. . . . I've always felt that he had a solid internal core of courage that he could call on." Haynes remembers that Ellsberg carried several types of guns with him in the field, though Haynes never saw him with more than two guns at a time.[61]

While others in Vietnam also succumbed to the romance of danger, members of the Lansdale team suspected that their young comrade was taking too many chances, behaving recklessly, even juvenilely. If Ellsberg was captured, they might also be in jeopardy. Had they known (and they probably did not) that he had experimented with some narcotic in Vietnam, and that he had been high on LSD or some other drug during one enemy assault, they might have *really* wondered about his judgment. "I had to keep telling him not to take a carbine on his civilian trips into the provinces, to stop playing soldier," Lansdale wrote later. In a memo in December 1965, Lansdale directed that Ellsberg "not take undue risks" during one field trip. "He should not display a weapon (it invites attack to seize such a prize from a civilian)," Lansdale instructed.[62]

Ellsberg joined a number of combat operations in Vietnam. "I did a lot of shooting," he would acknowledge. He was finally seeing the action he had missed as a marine. Proving his abilities and demonstrating his skills were probably important to him. He wished to show other men his marine qualities. "At one point he made quite a point of talking to Lansdale about his experience as a marine," Joe Redick remembers. "He seemed to be quite proud of his experience." Ellsberg would ask Lansdale for a week's leave and then "grab a rifle and go out against the Viet Cong," Lansdale recounted. "I told him that was wrong. I said, 'We're here to make friends with the people, to win them over to our side, and you don't do that by throwing a grenade at them.'" Team members reminded Ellsberg that he was not a marine anymore. "I used to think, 'You're going to get your butt blown off,'" Hukill recalls. Again, Ellsberg seemed naive. He told Joe Baker, "You know, Joe. That combat isn't that bad." Baker had been in the infantry during World War II. "I says, 'Well, Dan, it is fun, exhilarating, for a minute or two for a day,'" he recounts. "'But you go out there and sleep for three weeks and live in the jungle with those things.' And Dan never did. I said, 'If you're really interested in combat . . . sign up for a year. . . . Just sign up in Nam.' The marines were looking. . . . I was talking to General [Lewis] Walt [the commander of U.S. Marines in Vietnam] once. And he said, 'God, if Ellsberg wants to sign up, we'll fix him up. He's right here in the country, and we'll fix him up.'" But Baker couldn't convince Ellsberg to enlist. "Dan liked . . . to go out with these units," Baker remembers, "but he'd come back at night or he'd come back the next day and take a nice shower and sleep in his apartment."[63]

Ellsberg wanted to lead men in combat. Arnaud de Borchgrave was a *Newsweek* correspondent when he encountered Ellsberg "running around with an M-16" and exhorting U.S. soldiers on during Operation Masher in early 1966:

> I was introduced to him, and I was wondering why he was carrying an M-16, given the fact that he was not in the military. That had been made clear to me, that he was just there as an observer. I remember it was a very hot day, like most days, hot, sticky and wet. And we'd been walking, let's say for about two hours, with no action at all. And the platoon commander said, "Let's take five," or "Take ten." . . . And Ellsberg said, "Let's keep going. We've got to find Charlie [the NLF]." That was his big thing: Charlie, Charlie. Chase Charlie. I mean, we all felt very lucky to be able to rest for ten minutes. And he was indefatigable. He wanted to keep going. . . . [But] the platoon commander prevailed, and we did take five or ten.

One reporter in Vietnam would recall hearing loud shouts one day in 1966 from a U.S. infantry company. "There was Ellsberg, dressed in fatigues and jungle boots, telling the infantrymen to get off their goddamned asses, to get on the offensive and stay on the offensive. He carried a submachine gun and was practically taking over the company." The reporter Peter Arnett, who walked with Ellsberg for a time during an operation in Long An Province, remembered him "wading through a Mekong Delta paddyfield knee deep in mud, a Schmeisser submachine gun cradled in his arms, impatience mirrored on his face, not a soldier but a civilian eager to see the war won. 'These guys just don't know how to fight,' he gasps to a reporter in annoyance. He turns to the American infantrymen crouching down in the tall green rice behind him seeking cover from a persistent Viet Cong sniper. 'Damn it, this is no way to win a war!' he shouts. 'Move up.'" Ellsberg was chased away by the angry U.S. battalion commander at one point. He annoyed other American officers too. He later testified that he tried to educate the battalion commander, who was "brand-new to infantry operations," during his approximately ten days of combat in Long An. He "reported to him at the end of the day suggestions and recommendations as to how the battalion was doing."[64] Ellsberg was finally fulfilling his marine career.

Ellsberg's ten days of combat in the Delta took place during the Christmas holiday period of 1966–67 and was the heaviest fighting he experienced in Vietnam. This is apparently when he did most of his shooting. He had managed to get assigned to a U.S. Army battalion. He and the soldiers were often immersed in water and were "under a lot of fire, some days every half hour or so," he recounted. The firing emanated from "invisible snipers," guerrillas who moved from one clump of trees to the next, evading, it seemed, the firepower Ellsberg and the soldiers were able to lay down in their direction. While on the operation, Ellsberg thought about the old military argument about whether it was best to walk on the dikes in rice paddies or to walk in the paddies themselves; up on the dikes, it was thought, a person was more visible and thus more vulnerable, but in the paddies you're slowed up by water and mud. Ellsberg thought to himself, There was absolutely no question about it: you just can't get anywhere through that mud. It was best in most situations, then, to take your chances up on the skyline.[65]

In response to the guerrillas' sniping, "we did a lot of firing," Ellsberg recalled. Once, during this or another operation, when everybody else was firing, Ellsberg paused to take some photographs. That angered a U.S. sergeant, who reminded Ellsberg that they were engaged in combat.[66]

Ellsberg chose to walk increasingly with the lead elements of the infantry platoon in the Delta. He walked "point" with an advance party of several men. "The point travels fifty to a hundred yards in front to scout out enemy presence and draw fire if there's an ambush," he later explained to a journalist:

> I was walking through tall, thick rice, rice water up to my knees, and suddenly heard firing just to our rear, not coming at us but at the troops who were following us. We got down, turned around and saw what looked like boys wearing ragged black shorts and black jerseys. Backs to us, they were standing in the thick rice we had just moved through, firing AK47s at the troops behind us. They had let us move past them—we must have walked within a few feet without seeing them—so they could fire on the main body of troops following. . . .
>
> It was eerie to see Vietcong up that close. We couldn't shoot at them, because we would have been firing into our own troops, who, meanwhile, were busy firing in our direction. I kept my head down, but I watched them til they disappeared after a minute and a half or so into the tall rice and got away. Exactly the same thing happened a couple of hours later. I was very, very impressed by their tactics. . . . Both times the thought that came into my mind was very much like the line that kept recurring, later, in *Butch Cassidy:* "Who are these guys?"

Ellsberg forgot his helmet at points during the operation and had to borrow helmets from others (not always easy to do).[67]

In an interview later, Ellsberg would raise the question of the morality of his shooting at people in the Delta. "Well, I can testify when you're being fired at, you don't worry at all about the moral dilemmas involved in firing back," he said. But, of course, he wasn't out on combat patrols simply to return enemy fire. He and the soldiers were *scouting out* the enemy. Ellsberg was prepared to kill Vietnamese, perhaps even eager to do so. He felt it was okay to kill them, otherwise he wouldn't have been out on patrol. He claimed in one interview that he didn't know whether he actually shot anyone. The CIA's psychiatrists would later deem it quite possible that he killed the enemy.[68] And John Sack, who was staying at Ellsberg's house in Saigon at the time, remembers an account that Ellsberg gave him right after returning from the Delta that suggests he did.

Sack, who believes he was the first person Ellsberg spoke to about the incident save for those who were with him on the operation, says Ellsberg told it "not out of braggadocio," but "out of a sense of wonder." It was as if Ellsberg was trying to establish it in his own mind and give the incident reality by putting it into words. He told Sack that, during the operation, a Viet Cong machine-gun nest had pinned him and other men in his unit down. "They were wondering what to do about the VC," Sack remembers Ellsberg telling him. "And nobody knew what to do." Then Ellsberg began "moving out and around the back, just by himself, the back of the VC . . . nest, and sneaking up behind them from the rear, and taking a hand grenade and throwing it in and killing them. Which is the kind of stuff you win a Silver Star for if you're in the army." Sack has no doubt that Ellsberg's account is true. "I'm just very surprised that nobody else ever got that story," he told me. When I suggested to him that Ellsberg may not have wanted to reveal publicly that he had killed anyone in Vietnam, Sack quickly said, "He didn't say he killed them. He just said—what's the word he used?—he neutralized them, or they stopped firing, or whatever. He didn't go over to see if they were dead. He threw a hand grenade and the firing stopped."[69]

Ellsberg's willingness to risk himself in combat impressed some in Vietnam. He was obviously a brave man. But others questioned his judgment. When I asked one journalist who knew him in Vietnam if he had ever accompanied Ellsberg on a military patrol, he said no and added with a chuckle, "And I wouldn't have wanted to. . . . I was out on patrols, with units, moving through the countryside. But I don't think I particularly would have felt at ease. Dan was too much of a risk-taker. . . . If he were talking about what he was doing, telling sort of like locker-room stories, I wouldn't have gotten the impression of sort of quiet military competence."[70]

Ellsberg took pleasure in the danger of combat too, the sharpened sensitivity and alertness he experienced, the feeling of being hunted while he, now, was also hunting other men; he again took pride in his coolness. He gloried in combat. This was Ellsberg the romantic war lover at his most extreme. Combat also provided relief from his problems. Ellsberg doubted wars could be fought, he would say later, if they didn't offer people relief from the meaninglessness and boredom in their lives. Combat provided a break from his own depression and frustrations, he said. Again, he didn't feel fear. Combat was like being in a movie, he said. Ellsberg acknowledged to one journalist,

> The truth is, if you live through it, and if you don't get your legs or your genitals blown off, battle can be very interesting and exciting. For the most part I *enjoyed* the combat experience that I had. The kind of intense experiences that you see in the movie *Platoon*. . . . I hardly *breathed* through the last hour of *Platoon*. I came out and was hyperventilating for about half an hour. . . . I was reliving the experience. . . .
>
> Now, I can hardly imagine how I did things like go down into Viet Cong tunnels, like that guy in the movie did. I actually went into one tunnel and found lots of letters—which I had intelligence translate, they turned out to be love letters—and candles, warm candles, which meant someone had very recently been there. . . .
>
> It wasn't as good as lovemaking or body-surfing, let's say. But by the standards of most things, it was a very interesting way to spend your time. . . . It's as exciting as being in the Mafia. . . . Just recently—I don't know what brought this into my head—I was thinking of my experience in Vietnam as if I had participated in a gang rape, one that was not lethal to the victim. It can't be that everyone who participates in such a rape—after all, the perpetrators are legion—could honestly say they totally failed to enjoy it.[71]

Gus Shubert got an unforgettable glimpse of Ellsberg's ardor for fighting the Viet Cong. One evening in March of 1966, Shubert was walking to the RAND villa on Rue Pasteur street in Saigon when he glanced across the street and noticed what appeared to be an awfully familiar sight. "It can't be," Shubert thought to himself. But "sure enough," Shubert recounts, "here's this guy striding along the pavement, a gun over his shoulder, bandoleers across his chest, two .45s, a combat uniform, tin hat—the whole bit. I nearly dropped my drawers right in the street. So I walked across, and I said, 'Dan!' He said, 'Gus!' And I said, 'What the hell are you doing? Playing soldier?' That was not the right thing to say. It angered him deeply. And he said to me, 'I am here to kill communists.'" The incident spoke volumes about Ellsberg's zealotry, Shubert thought. "There is no doubt in my mind that when he first went out there, he really thought that his job was to go out and shoot communists. And when he came back, there's no doubt in my mind that he believed that killing communists was a totally unproductive, futile exercise, and a disgrace to the United States of America." The incident "was unbelievable!" Shubert exclaims. Ellsberg later denied that it took place. But when told Shubert's account, Richard Elms responded, "That does not surprise me at all. And that was my feeling about his attitude when he went over there."[72]

Bernard Yoh and George Tanham, a RAND counterinsurgency man, also remember Ellsberg's thirst for action in Vietnam. "He was a shoot-them-dead, superhawk," Yoh says. "When he first arrived, he just couldn't [wait]. . . . He was so violent that he was expressing all kinds of things." "He'd want to kill Viet Cong, the bad guys," Tanham remembers. "They were the bad guys and all that." Yoh heard from a U.S. military officer whom Ellsberg accompanied in a helicopter that Ellsberg wanted to shoot some VC from the helicopter. The officer told Yoh and others at Yoh's house about the incident shortly after it occurred. Ellsberg "pushed the gunner away," the officer related, Yoh recounts. "He just push the guy aside and grabbed the machine gun. I forgot whether he actually squeeze[d] the [trigger] or not. But, anyhow, he grabbed the machine gun, and he said, 'I want to shoot me some VCs.' He made that statement." The officer informed Ellsberg that, as a civilian, he couldn't fire unless they were under fire themselves, says Yoh, who swears by the story: "No doubt about it. . . . I mean, that's real." Either Conein or Lansdale later told one scholar that Ellsberg wanted to shoot some VC from helicopters. But when I asked Conein about it, he said that he personally didn't know whether Ellsberg actually did. "It's not beyond Ellsberg at all," Robert Komer comments. But Ellsberg has adamantly denied ever shooting at anyone from the air.[73]

Ellsberg made sure to let friends and colleagues back home know of his military exploits in Vietnam. Richard Zeckhauser saw him during a visit Ellsberg made to the States and heard accounts he gave others:

> There were stories of his great intended bravery. He would sort of like to go up to the top of a hill with a gun and . . . find the Viet Cong and shoot at them. . . . Supermacho types of things. . . . I remember his talking—it was just like a sexual exploit: "So I was with this captain, and he had a so-and-so gun. And the Viet Cong was just over the next hill, and we went up there to see what we could see. And I borrowed the gun and I fired some rounds." . . . I remember the incident as being very much consistent with his [sexual braggadocio]. You

know, it was really to me no different than, "So I went into the bar and I found these two girls, and I dragged them back to my place in Malibu."

Ellsberg boasted about "seeing action" to Donald Hall—"getting a rifle and telling me he wasn't supposed to," Hall recalls. "Went out on patrol." "Dan did have a little bit of gun-toting swagger," Thomas Schelling remembers. "I occasionally had letters from him when he was in Vietnam and it was clear that he enjoyed tramping around with a gun in one hand. . . . I had the impression that he loved what he was doing. . . . It seemed as if he was describing what he was doing so that I would know that he was facing danger. That he was right in the thick of things."[74]

Ellsberg also wanted his two children to know that he was in the thick of things. He sent Robert and Mary numerous letters, photographs, and audiotapes. With some disapproval, Carol Ellsberg showed Mary Marshall some soldier-of-fortune-style photos of him that he'd sent Robert and Mary. In at least one, Ellsberg was "standing on a hill waving a Kalashnikov rifle" or other gun, Marshall remembers. "Posing himself against the sky with the military weapon. . . . He just couldn't resist putting the most dramatic interpretation to whatever he was doing," even with his own children. "They were pictures of him in uniform and holding a gun," Carol Cummings recalls. "Going to dangerous places. . . . He sent albums of these." Carol was struck with some of his poses. "She was scornful of these poses," Marshall remembers—"'Typical Dan.'" Says Carol, "I always thought it was very different from my father, because I was a grown woman before he ever said much about his war experiences. And even then it was very little. And he'd actually been in a war. But I think he thought it wasn't proper. First of all, I thought it frightened Robert and Mary to hear the dangerous things. You know, he'd send a tape and there's a bomb going off: 'That's the sound of gunfire in the distance.'" Carol thought that outrageous. Ellsberg had John Paul Vann deliver to Robert a "deadly crossbow" during a trip Vann took to the United States. Vann also showed Robert, Mary, and others photos of Ellsberg.[75]

But Ellsberg sent more benign photos as well, including some of him playing with Vietnamese children, and presents, such as a plaster Vietnamese doll and a necklace to Mary, who gathered the impression from all of this that her father "was doing something glamorous and important far away." Ellsberg, accompanied by Yvonne Svenle, met his children for a vacation in Acapulco.[76]

Ellsberg also gave Lansdale photos of him running around with a carbine.[77] He apparently could not control himself—Lansdale had made his sentiments clear.

Ellsberg would later rationalize and soft-pedal his liking of weapons and combat in Vietnam. He claimed that essentially all civilians carried weapons outside Saigon, and that when participating in combat he was on the scene primarily as an *observer* of the pacification effort. And one had to take risks in Vietnam. Ellsberg claimed that he joined the fighting in the Delta to determine for Ambassador Henry Cabot Lodge whether it was desirable to commit American troops there, and to assess how it would affect civilians in the area. He was secretly assessing the performance of U.S. troops for Lodge, he said. Ellsberg wished to show that committing U.S. troops to the area would not be a good move, he recalled. "I was representing the ambassador, investigating pacification." And "I carried a weapon because the alternative was, if you didn't carry a weapon, other people would have to take care of you. I was anxious not to attract attention to myself." Further, he shot at people "only when I was being shot at." He had no desire to combat the VC, he said.[78]

Ellsberg would also later express unbridled anger at America's violence in Vietnam. One evening in 1990 at Ellsberg's home, the writer Tim Beneke was watching a television documentary with him in which a Vietnamese man who had been badly wounded as a child during the war met the American platoon leader who had been responsible. As the American was explaining to the Vietnamese why he got hit, "Ellsberg exploded with obscenities— 'Motherfucker! Goddamn shit! Sonofabitch!,'" Beneke recounts. "'So that makes it okay, you motherfucker!' I'd rarely heard so much profanity in so short a period of time. I remember thinking that this was another Daniel Ellsberg who was popping out."[79]

—————◦◦◦—————

Ellsberg was clearly a fervent believer in the American cause when he was in Vietnam, a genuine enthusiast of counterinsurgency. His questions about the war, his sources of discouragement—and they would be many and great—were always about means and results rather than the ultimate goal. He did not talk about the morality of the war then, Lansdale recalled. Ellsberg felt strongly that "Communist domination," "Communist agents," and the "Communist network" in South Vietnam (as he put it) had to be defeated. The enemy's "covert" agenda there was "forced-draft industrialization under totalitarian controls, capitalized by exploitation of the peasants and preceded by a bloodbath to destroy or terrorize potential opposition: a vision so stark and repelling it must be kept esoteric," he wrote a year into his tour. "He was extremely moralistic about it all," one friend recounted. "He really believed that the

Communists were bad people and that U.S. security was threatened." Ellsberg resembled a boy scout in his zeal for his work. "In 1966 . . . he was really hot for winning the Vietnam War," Robert Komer remembers. "He was *very* pro–Vietnam War, very pro-government, very anti-VC, anti-Hanoi. He later executed a 180-degree turn. Well, there were no signs of that when he was in Vietnam." Ellsberg was "just totally gung ho in everything that he said and did," Lowell Hukill recalls.[80]

Ellsberg's fervor is vividly captured in papers he wrote at the time. In his hard-line October 1965 memo, he also advised that the United States and GVN step up efforts to take control of contested areas of South Vietnam and "attrit by offensive action the strength of VC main force and regional force units, aiming at achieving military ascendancy in the near-term period and eliminating 'deep red' zones" of uncontested VC control. The prospect of negotiations "puts a premium on reducing the evident strength of the VC main force 'army' as quickly as possible," he wrote. "ARVN should be able to go *anywhere* in the country . . . with a battalion; but the road to that situation passes through a great deal of offensive action (initially, almost entirely U.S.) and a great many casualties." U.S. psywar operations should attempt to split the VC from North Vietnam and encourage VC troop defections, Ellsberg also argued, by claiming that Hanoi would sell the VC out in negotiations. Meanwhile Washington should ready a propaganda campaign "on the necessity and justification of continued operations" in Vietnam if domestic pressures for a "premature" cease-fire developed. If demonstrations against Americans arose in South Vietnam, Ellsberg advised, the United States should expand its support for "police and riot control activities" there. He theorized that if the United States escalated its operations in Vietnam, including its air strikes over the North, that might strengthen the U.S. position in any peace talks. And the United States should press for "key demands" from Hanoi as a condition for suspending the bombing of the North.[81] All this from the same man who later claimed that he considered the U.S. bombing campaign against the North criminal.

The month before writing this memo, Ellsberg visited the "Weapons Branch and Weapons Display" of the American high command in Vietnam. He wished to "learn the availability of captured Chicom [Chinese Communist] weapons for various purposes of exploitation"—that is, propaganda and dirty tricks. He found quite an assortment and stockpile of such weapons, including especially desirable ones with "good clear Chinese markings." In a memo Ellsberg wrote later that same day, and which Lansdale sent under his own name to Lodge, Ellsberg proposed that the weapons be distributed widely over the countryside of North Vietnam, dropped by parachute along with a starter-set of ammunition. They would be dramatic evidence to the North Vietnamese of the role their government—spurred on by the Chicoms—is playing in the South. And some peasants in the North might decide to put these toys away for a rainy day; they might even find a good use for them in the short run. . . . The DRV [North Vietnamese government] would have the fun of carrying on continuous nationwide searches for "returned" armament, never knowing how much had been dropped and how much might still be hiding in the hands of their loyal citizens. . . .

The first drops would be unannounced, but international newsmen could be briefed in a backgrounder fairly early, and photographers could be encouraged to inspect and photograph the material before delivery, or even to accompany some drops. . . . There would be obscurity (or even exaggeration) concerning the total numbers of weapons to be returned, and a variety of deception measures could keep NVN [North Vietnamese] internal security forces fully occupied. Meanwhile, the publicity on the program would be a dramatic way of reminding an international audience of the role of continuing infiltration from the Communist Bloc.

The weapons would be landed ready for use, accompanied by some such message as this: "This weapon was originally a gift from your Communist Chinese allies, for the purpose of killing Vietnamese. It was brought South by North Vietnamese soldiers, to be used on those, including women and children, who oppose Communism and do not want their country run secretly by the Chinese. We do not need these Chinese weapons in the South; so we are returning them to our brothers in the North, where perhaps they will be more appreciated."[82]

Lieutenant Colonel Tran Ngoc Chau was a South Vietnamese province chief when John Vann introduced him to Ellsberg in the fall of 1965. Vann had spoken quite highly of Ellsberg to Chau, a good friend of his, and wanted Chau to meet Ellsberg. "When I first met him, he was a *warrior*," Chau recounts. "Physically, psychologically, intellectually—in every way." Ellsberg was "very, very aggressive" about the war, Chau says. "'And this war, we will win it!' . . . That's my first impression, is a guy who says, 'We will win the war. There [is] no reason why we not win the war. And we're doing right.'" Ellsberg was confident about winning, Chau remembers. And "one thing that's sure is that he's working very, very hard." Chau soon came to admire and respect Ellsberg. They became good friends. "I loved Chau like an older brother," Ellsberg recalled.[83]

Chau was an intelligent, proud, and independent man, a devoted anticommunist who emphasized the importance of political mobilization over military action. He would become, for Ellsberg, a prime example of a "good Vietnamese," the type of political leader who could move South Vietnam in the right direction.

Ellsberg had both a scientific and romantic view of the war, and he offered specific ideas on the deployment and training of South Vietnamese soldiers and cadre. He strongly advocated more extensive "clear-and-hold" operations by ARVN. To pacify South Vietnamese hamlets, the Viet Cong needed to be "annihilated" or chased away, he wrote, then "destroy[ed]" if they returned. But Ellsberg felt damage to civilians from air and artillery strikes should be reduced.[84]

Under Vann's influence, he became a strong critic of the GVN and ARVN. Too many South Vietnamese leaders and officers were ineffective, incompetent, stupid, or corrupt, Ellsberg believed. Many kept their positions through payoffs, he knew. These bad apples had to be replaced. Ellsberg recognized that corruption was widespread in South Vietnam and being exploited by the enemy. On field trips, he found examples of corruption and brought them to the attention of the U.S. embassy.[85]

Ellsberg did not express moral opposition to corruption in his memos, however. Rather, he worried that the problem could "explode any day" in the media, resulting in "a major 'exposé.'" Corruption could become fodder for American opponents of the war, he worried, leading to "widespread revulsion by the US public with the GVN and its cause, and enormous pressure not merely for investigations and personnel changes but for withdrawal of US aid, troops and involvement. . . . This could happen, for example, next week, or tomorrow. It could happen with great suddenness, without warning." Ellsberg felt U.S. officials "would probably be implicated as accomplices. . . . At worst, *this issue could blast us out of SVN* and lose the war." And corruption had costs inside South Vietnam. Ellsberg recommended "quiet" efforts to combat corruption, as well as "closely-held *contingency planning . . . now* to prepare for a crisis in public confidence and support triggered by newspaper or Congressional charges or investigations."[86]

Ellsberg became increasingly dismayed by ARVN's passivity and lack of discipline. Its failure to fight like it needed to fight undermined pacification severely, he argued. Pacification was in trouble, he wrote in March 1966. "Drastic measures deserve consideration," including U.S. efforts to replace "incompetent or undisciplined unit commanders at all levels" and to abolish some units. Ellsberg sought to determine why ARVN wasn't fighting and to *get* it to fight and to behave properly: "ARVN discipline and combat performance *must* be improved."[87]

Ellsberg pushed more forcefully for greater U.S. control over the GVN and ARVN. He wanted the United States to run South Vietnam as a colony, in many ways, albeit from behind the curtain, and for the good, he thought, of the South Vietnamese. Such imperialism—benevolent, but imperialism nonetheless—was the only way to bring about the reforms necessary to win the war, he and Vann believed. In a memo in October 1966, Ellsberg recommended compiling a "central, confidential *biographic file*" on South Vietnamese officials and commanders in order to determine who should be replaced and by whom. The United States should also study "alternative modes and techniques of influencing the GVN and RVNAF [all armed forces of South Vietnam], with an eye to uncovering new or currently neglected channels and tools." Ellsberg argued against bypassing GVN authority completely, however, as he felt leadership must ultimately come from the Vietnamese: "A U.S. 'takeover,' whether blatant or tacit and pragmatic, does not provide an adequate answer. At the same time, the radical changes required *within* the GVN and RVNAF seem most unlikely to occur without the strong, focused, and coordinated exertion of U.S. influence at high levels." With such changes, Ellsberg contended, the war could be won.[88]

As would befit an emotional man, Ellsberg was up and down about the odds of success. Harry Harris remembers receiving a long letter from him sometime during Ellsberg's first year in Vietnam, the bottom line of which was, "It's not winnable." "You meet him on the street and you say, 'How are things going?'" Douglas Pike recounts. "And he said, 'Boy, they're really going great.' And he'd been out in the boondocks, and 'We're winning this war,' and so on. And then about three weeks later, you're at a cocktail party, and you say, 'Well, how are things going?' And he'd say, 'We're not going to ever win this goddamn [war].' . . . He'd get violently argumentative on one direction, and then the next time you hear him he was violently argumentative on the other. And this was more of a personal thing than something that stemmed from hard data."[89] Most likely, it reflected a growing and wrenching internal split.

Ellsberg advanced many of his ideas in a paper he wrote for a U.S. Roles and Missions team that was evaluating operations in Vietnam the summer of 1966. His paper would be commended highly by one of the Pentagon Papers' authors, he later pointed out. The Roles and Missions team was critical of the war effort and also advised greater U.S. influence over the GVN. But American turf battles, dissent, and inertia limited its impact. Ellsberg and others had hoped the report would spur more far-reaching changes. Ellsberg said later he was a member of the Roles and Missions team, but one memo calls him a "sub-team member," and Robert Komer believes that the team's head, George Jacobson (whose selection Ellsberg claimed "full credit" for) "would not have, independently, wanted to put him on the team. Because Jacobson was a very shrewd politician, and he knew that Ellsberg was actively disliked by many of the people in the [U.S.] mission in Saigon." Jacobson thought highly of Ellsberg's abilities, however, and would remember picking him first for the team. "Ellsberg was one of the most productive and maybe the brightest fellow on the whole task force," he said. Ellsberg clearly did a lot of work for the team.[90]

Jacobson and others found many of Ellsberg's ideas on the war insightful and refreshingly frank. Komer, an upbeat, gung ho, and abrupt man nicknamed "Blowtorch" because he figuratively put a flame to people's rear ends to get them moving, thought Ellsberg well worth listening to, despite the impracticality of some of his notions. "I found Ellsberg very interesting on Vietnam," Komer remembers. "A smart guy. He knew the Vietnamese business. . . . His advice was often given, and frequently sound. . . . Probably the only person who was willing to listen to Ellsberg and do something about what he liked was myself." That was partly because Komer found Ellsberg's ideas pretty similar to his own ideas. In an April 1966 memo to Deputy U.S. Ambassador William Porter seconding many of the ideas Ellsberg had expressed in one memo, Komer asked, "Any merit in making Ellsberg your unofficial *field inspector* of province operations? Judging from his memos he has a quick eye."[91]

But as in the past, Komer found Ellsberg overly self-promoting and a pest at times. "He would usually push himself to my notice," Komer recounts. "Say he wanted to come over and talk to me, or seek an appointment. And I always gave him one." Ellsberg was "quite elated" by one contact with Komer, Michael Deutch wrote. "Ellsberg was a constant bugger, I must say, about his own stuff," Komer remembers. "And not very good at doing what others wanted him to do. I regret to say that this was my experience." In 1966 Komer was trying to effect a reorganization of the U.S. pacification program in South Vietnam. "Well, Dan wasn't all that interested in talking about that," Komer recalls. "He wanted to talk about the things *he* thought needed to be done." And "he loved praise." More generally, Ellsberg was far more interested in talking than in doing, Komer noticed: "I couldn't corral Dan."[92] That, of course, was many people's experience with him.

When it came to distributing his writings on the war, Ellsberg "papered the Pentagon," Adam Yarmolinsky remembered. He wanted to reach those close to the seat of power. He also sent papers to those without influence. He was an inveterate promoter of himself and his views. He touted John Vann effusively.[93]

Ellsberg visited Washington in the fall of 1966 after orchestrating a mini-campaign to get Komer, Harry Rowen, or Alain Enthoven to invite him back for consultations. He wished to see his children in California, and he thought this might be "his last look at the States as well as old girl friends." Ellsberg brought some of his papers to distribute in Washington, but he cut short his visit when William Porter asked him to accompany the State Department's Nicholas Katzenbach to Vietnam. He was to brief Katzenbach, who was traveling with Robert McNamara.[94]

His flight to Vietnam would prove to be a high point of Ellsberg's career. He had brought with him on the plane a briefcase full of his writings on the war; he was seated across the aisle from John McNaughton, who was sitting across a table from McNamara. McNamara and McNaughton had brought "nothing else to read," Ellsberg later claimed. Based on Ellsberg's retelling, Neil Sheehan wrote that as soon as the huge, windowless, converted tanker lifted off, Ellsberg "opened the briefcase and passed a memo to McNaughton with the suggestion that he might find the reading interesting enough to while away flight time. McNaughton glanced through the memorandum and handed it to McNamara, who looked at it and then began to read. Ellsberg fetched another memorandum from the briefcase for McNaughton, who started to read carefully too. McNamara and McNaughton were both swift readers, and Ellsberg had emptied his briefcase before the plane had gone far toward Saigon." One witness to the scene was a bit amused "because of the almost obsessed manner of Ellsberg, a Dostoevskyan figure, and the fact that McNamara had no place to hide."[95]

According to Ellsberg, McNamara and McNaughton read his papers "page by page. . . . Both of them read all that stuff." Moreover, "I was a major influence on their thinking. . . . I have little doubt looking at their memos over that time that I had a big influence on their pessimism about the stalemate that was occurring" in Vietnam. McNamara sent a pessimistic report on the war to President Johnson upon returning to Washington; he observed that pacification was "thoroughly stalled" and "a bad disappointment." Ellsberg wrote later that McNamara "paraphrased" parts of his contribution to the Roles and Missions study. That is quite possible, as some of McNamara's remarks on pacification bear a marked similarity to Ellsberg's, although Ellsberg's observations would not have surprised McNamara or McNaughton. Ellsberg flew back to Washington with McNamara to resume consultations, again giving him papers and discussing them with him, he recounted.[96]

In Washington Ellsberg phoned a fellow member of Lansdale's team, Sam Karrick, who was also then stateside. During their conversation, Ellsberg informed Karrick that he had received several job offers in Washington, "all of which he turned down," Karrick wrote Lansdale. Ellsberg also conveyed that Harry Rowen, who had recently been named president of the RAND Corporation, wanted him "to report for work as soon as possible" after Rowen assumed office, Karrick wrote. Ellsberg intended to work at RAND again after leaving Vietnam, Karrick related, but "he has explained he may not feel free to come home so soon."[97]

Late that November, Ellsberg did accept a job offer. This one was in Vietnam. William Porter, who had been put in charge of all U.S. civil field operations in the South, offered him a position as his "personal assistant" (to use Lansdale's words) or "special assistant" (to use Ellsberg's). Ellsberg says he was *the* special assistant to Porter, but Porter also had other assistants, including "special" ones. (In his 1974–75 *Who's Who in America* listing, Ellsberg elevated his title to "assistant to U.S. Ambassador to South Vietnam.") Ellsberg had done tasks for Porter before—"for special investigation," he would say—including assessing pacification prospects, heading at least one task force, and studying psywar in the provinces. Ellsberg had lobbied to work full-time for Porter, who, it would now have been clear, would be a better man to link up with than Lansdale, whose team was going nowhere fast in Vietnam. Porter obviously noticed Ellsberg's strengths; he was impressed with Ellsberg's reports to Lansdale. Porter had also recently lost one or two people and was looking for experienced help. He wanted Ellsberg to make spot checks for him in the field and give him straightforward assessments—in effect, be his eyes and ears in the field. Ellsberg would later describe this new job as a "loosely defined post" in which he was to make "special evaluations" of pacification and military efforts for Porter "personally."[98]

But Porter, like John McNaughton before him, would apparently become disillusioned with Ellsberg. "He disliked Ellsberg," Komer recalls. "He was not very impressed with Ellsberg." Komer suspects Ellsberg pushed his own agenda with Porter too much and did not always do what Porter wanted him to do.[99] That is a reasonable conjecture.

Ellsberg was an extremely frustrated man by this time. The war was not going well, and his prescriptions for changing U.S. policy were not, in the main, being implemented. He may have taken that as a personal rejection. "I suppose I have never been so frustrated and depressed in my life," he said later.[100]

———◈———

In the fall of 1965, Ellsberg had sent Patricia Marx a postcard from Vietnam. It was a marriage proposal. Patricia was both surprised and delighted by it. "Not that I was ready to get married to Dan," she remembers. "But I was very ready to explore whether I was ready to get married to Dan."[101]

Marx flew to Vietnam late that December. She and Ellsberg "had the most magical trip," Patricia recounts. "We went to Thailand and Nepal and India. It was wonder. It was the most amazing trip of my life. I was so in love, and everything was magical." Yet despite being swept away, "it wasn't totally clear that this was a man that would be a reliable husband," she says, partly because Ellsberg "was so intense and taking so many risks."[102]

Ellsberg proposed to Patricia while they were bathing in the Ganges. She said yes. "It was unbelievable, off-the-charts romantic," she reminisces. "And Dan was so handsome. He was dashing, intense, and [had] this poetic beauty, as well as masculinity. You know, tenderness and sensitivity, as well as being so virile. He was an *extraordinarily* attractive man, not just in his looks, but in his presence. Just charismatic and energetic and sensual. Just utterly compelling."[103]

Yet marriage was a ways away. "I said yes in the sense of, 'Yes! But let's get to know each other,'" Patricia laughs. "I wasn't going to say no in the Ganges. That would have been a downer." They decided, in effect, to be engaged. Patricia felt they needed to get to know each other "in a more sane way" before getting married, "because we'd only had two months together" in the United States, "and then he was in Vietnam, and then this idyllic vacation. But that's not real life." Their differences on the war were also an issue. But "love is not rational," Patricia says with another laugh. "I was so attracted and so taken with his brilliance and his intensity and his integrity. I disagreed with him, but I always felt he was a man of absolute integrity. . . . And I didn't know enough to know if I was right or if he was right. . . . What I sensed was that this was a man who was totally idealistic." Also, "we were not discussing Vietnam on our travels. . . . It was one of those times in life where it's kind of out of time and out of context. . . . Everywhere we went was *so incredibly beautiful*."[104]

Patricia flew to Vietnam to see Ellsberg again in the summer of 1966. They had planned to take another trip out of the country, but Ellsberg was unable to travel, so Patricia did some interviews for her radio program. She filled most of her time working on a magazine article with Frances FitzGerald. "I had this idea for an article, which she loved," Patricia remembers. "And she said, 'Let's co-write it.' But I knew I wasn't a writer; she was the writer. But I said, 'Let's work on it together.'" According to FitzGerald, she had already planned to do the article on her own, and "I realized that there was going to be a lot of legwork for this piece, and if she wanted to do part of it, I thought that was fine." The article was a critical look at slums, squalor, and public administration in Saigon; it blamed the U.S. government for many of Saigon's problems. It was published in the *Atlantic* under FitzGerald's name only, despite Patricia's considerable research. And Patricia received no credit in it. She thought that she'd been treated unfairly and protested; FitzGerald felt compelled to write a letter to the editor in the *Atlantic* to "correct" the "serious omission" of Patricia's name from the title page. Rather than expressing anger, however, Patricia said she was hurt and that FitzGerald's behavior surprised her. She seemed wounded and disappointed rather than mad.[105]

Patricia's differences with Ellsberg on the war came to a head during this visit. Her exposure to Saigon's slums and the U.S. government's seeming indifference to them had fueled her opposition. "That's when I got furious about the war," she recounts. It "was in my face all the time. . . . I mean, these poor kids living in sewage and dislocated." She and Ellsberg argued a lot, "which wasn't very conducive to getting married. It really broke up our engagement." As idealistic as Ellsberg and John Vann might be, Patricia thought—and "they were the heroes that were there," she argues—they were also part of the war. "And that's what I laid on Dan," she remembers. "And he said, 'But I'm trying to stop these terrible things.' And I said, 'It doesn't matter. You're part of something that's so awful. And you seem to be engaged in it. You seem to be totally involved in it.'" Patricia appeared to Ellsberg to hold him accountable for every facet of the war. He thought that unfair. It "created a great deal of friction" and "split us apart," he recalled. He took Patricia's criticisms of the war as personal criticisms, leading him to withdraw from her.[106]

They had a particularly heated exchange the night of a farewell party for Neil and Susan Sheehan, whom Ellsberg had lunched with shortly after arriving in Vietnam. (Neil Sheehan had earlier been advised by David Halberstam to get to know Ellsberg because of his indiscretion.) Patricia had a drink or two at the party and became "very voluble."[107]

According to Ellsberg, he broke off their engagement that summer. When Patricia left Vietnam, "I wasn't really sure where we were," she remembers. "I didn't break off the engagement. I certainly wasn't about to get married. But I think I felt . . . 'to be continued.'" Then she didn't hear from Ellsberg. "I think he felt that it was at least ended for now," she says. "There was no formal breaking of the engagement. But we really drifted apart for a time," although "he wasn't out of my life," as "our connection was at a so much deeper level" than politics.[108]

Back in the United States, Patricia saw John Simon again on and off. Simon, who dedicated a book to Patricia in 1967, remembers that they were "very close" again for a while. "Because things had not gone as well as they were supposed to [in Vietnam]. But I do remember being very jealous at pictures of her and Dan, that she had lots of snapshots."[109]

Ellsberg was apparently seeing his Eurasian lover, Germaine, at this time. "He *really* liked her," one person who knew him in Vietnam remembers. "And he asked me once who he should marry": Germaine or Patricia. "It was a very serious question to a friend. . . . He was really considering which one to marry." Ellsberg seemed to be "trying to make up his mind between the two of them," says this person, who was surprised that Ellsberg's relationship with Germaine had reached this point. This person strongly advised Ellsberg to choose Patricia. Ellsberg "seemed surprised by my vehemence . . . by the force with which I said Pat," the person remembers. "And he said, 'Really?' Because he couldn't make up his mind."[110]

Somewhere around this time, however, Germaine left Ellsberg. He was crushed. He'd now suffered back-to-back failed romances on top of his divorce from Carol. In September 1967, after returning to the United States, he wanted to send Germaine photographs that he had taken of her as well as an audiotape, but was unsure whether she would be receptive; she had apparently rebuffed an earlier overture through a colleague in Vietnam. John Vann sent Germaine some pictures and Ellsberg's address through a girlfriend. Ellsberg would still be asking Vann about Germaine the following year. "Germaine left to go to New Zealand in July—to stay *forever*—took baby," Vann wrote him in August 1968. (Vann's letter doesn't say whose baby, though she had children with the Corsican.) Vann's girlfriend was then trying to get Germaine's address for Ellsberg, Vann reported. As late as August 1969, Ellsberg would still have been eager to see Germaine during a trip he hoped to take to Vietnam, he recalled later, but by then she was again living with the Corsican and there was no hope.[111]

After Germaine left him, "I decided, okay, that's really it," Ellsberg recounted. "I'm thirty-six, I've lived long enough." "It was a very strange thing," he said. "I tried to make myself care. I would make myself think about my future, my career, but nothing made any difference. Not even when I thought about my children."[112]

Ellsberg decided to die in a glorious way in Vietnam. "I went out on patrol week after week after that," he remembers. "I thought, well, I enjoy this, it's an interesting way to go. . . . There was one two-week period when I saw a lot of combat, went out with one patrol after another, almost around the clock, and got shot at a lot." Ellsberg's "plan" was "to go into the field with every single unit we had in Vietnam. Starting at the DMZ and working all the way down to the Delta."[113] That is an ambitious plan, and characteristic.

Don Hall remembers Ellsberg telling him later "how crazy he was. . . . He saw some Cong that turned out to be coming toward him. They were dressed in new uniforms. And he thought it was a North Vietnamese Army [unit] . . . because they had new uniforms, and the Cong didn't have uniforms. And his thought was, he told me, 'What a way to go.' He was going to be the first person killed by the North Vietnamese Army. . . . Like it would be very important to have been the first person killed." But Ellsberg recognized later "that he was nuts," Hall recalls. "Dan realized that this was crazy of him to be thinking of his death in these terms." And that was the reason for seeing Dr. Lewis Fielding, Ellsberg told Hall. He concluded that his lack of fear and failure to take reasonable precautions in Vietnam were signs of psychological trouble.[114]

One man who had contact with Ellsberg in Vietnam told me that he had a "hunch" at the time that Ellsberg had "a death wish." Ellsberg appeared to him to suffer from "a kind of MacArthurian syndrome." "I often think of Ellsberg and MacArthur together," this person says. "I think that Ellsberg, like Mr. MacArthur, would have been delighted to have a hero's death. And that was part of him."[115]

Patricia Marx noticed that Vietnam was full of desperate American men, adventurers who thought they had little to live for in the United States. They were rootless, unattached. The high number of divorced men, with their higher suicide rates (as Ellsberg would note), struck her.[116] Ellsberg would have fit in that group.

Some of his former colleagues at RAND were concerned about him. "They were worried that he was suicidal, doing these dangerous things," Carol Cummings remembers. "Everybody acted like I cared," she adds, with some incredulity. "I didn't care what he was doing."[117]

Like others in Vietnam, Ellsberg had thoughts of a fate worse than death. He would tell Jan Butler that, at one point, possibly when standing in a rice paddy, it occurred to him that he could be maimed and have to live with the consequences. "But death—he was prepared for death," Butler recalls. "That was easy." And "that's when he decided to give it up and go home," Butler believes.[118]

Ellsberg contracted hepatitis before enemy fire could get him, however. He thought he contracted it while spending a night in a rice paddy. As he was recuperating for several months, he pondered his future. The self-promoting, boastful tone of his fifteenth anniversary report to his graduating class at Harvard, written on April 7, his birthday, was probably shaped by recent disappointments in his life. He was "facing a considerable turning point," he wrote. "The alternatives before me are to stay on in the government in Vietnam, or to return home to research and consulting: a choice between the engine room and the belly of the whale. . . . But the prospect, now, of several months of light physical activity pretty much prejudices the decision. Before this, I would almost surely have stayed on, probably as special assistant to the incoming chief for civil operations, a long acquaintance, Robert Komer." Komer did want

Ellsberg. He had written him on March 31, "I hardly need say that I count on your being at my side for as long as you can stand it." Komer offered Ellsberg a job with the new pacification organization he was setting up in Vietnam, though nothing specific. "He said, no, he wanted to go home," Komer recounts. "He was not very optimistic then. . . . I think that prolonged bout with hepatitis really had a big influence on Ellsberg. Sitting there in a goddamn hospital."[119] For many hepatitis sufferers, the disease does carry with it a period of depression afterwards. William Porter's apparent dissatisfaction with Ellsberg may have also provided impetus for his return.

Ellsberg told his Harvard classmates that he was "proud to have served with Lansdale. . . . I'm more convinced than I could have been before that Lansdale's basic thoughts on political development, on nationalistic and democratic rivalry with Communists for leadership of revolutionary forces, and on counterguerrilla tactics are sound, relevant to Vietnam, and desperately needed here; but none of them are being applied in any degree."[120]

Ellsberg claimed later that when he left Vietnam late that May, "I had already reached the opinion that we should get out of the war." Indeed, he quit the government "in large part in order to oppose our policy." He "strongly believed," he said, that U.S. involvement in Vietnam "must be ended," and he was "determined" to see it ended. He thought "we could not achieve any legitimate purpose in Vietnam." And his hopes for success had died a year earlier, he said.[121]

This is all far from the truth and is contradicted by Ellsberg's own writings. In a paper he wrote on pacification prospects and strategy in Vietnam that spring, dated May 6, Ellsberg was still making a case for how to fight the war. That was not the way it was being fought now, he emphasized. "A much more serious effort to destroy, attrite, demoralize or neutralize the VC provincial forces" was needed, he argued. Only ARVN or other Free World battalions were strong enough to attempt "the destruction of VC provincial battalions and companies," a task "crucial to widespread or lasting expansion of government control," he wrote. Thus, "One of the most promising developments that could take place in Vietnam would be the effective employment of ARVN battalions in the task of destroying these VC provincial forces, under effective command arrangements and using, at last, appropriate antiguerrilla tactics." ARVN's effort should be sustained and proceed "aggressively," "offensively"—indeed "unequivocally" so—Ellsberg wrote, "in close coordination with police and all intelligence sources." It should include "small unit patrolling, quick reaction forces, night ambushes and night patrols." The ARVN battalions should be "under the operational control of the sector commander" or the "district chiefs" rather than "under divisional or regimental control" as had been the case in the past, Ellsberg advised. He argued that "if the battalions assigned to counterguerrilla operations under sector control executed their mission with appropriately effective tactics, it would be realistic to expect the area effectively accessible to GVN influence to expand significantly by the end of 1967."[122]

But political mobilization of the South Vietnamese populace was pivotal to pacification, Ellsberg stressed. "The *first* requirement for progress . . . is to change the character of the national government and its relations with its own instruments and the people, in such a way as to supply the missing, crucial factor of motivation at all levels without which no pacification concept or strategy will attain reality." Ellsberg wrote in another memo, dated May 4, "I do not think that a Vietnamese Government of the present character and relations with its public can win this war." Changes at the top, resulting in more representative and nationalistic government, were necessary, and that would take "conscious exertion of influence by the US." Ellsberg advocated "tactful, calculated and adroit acts of involvement in Vietnamese political affairs," including through the use of money.[123]

John Vann sent Vincent Davis copies of Ellsberg's memos, calling one of them (apparently the May 4 piece) "the best political analysis done here in Vietnam." Davis observed to Vann that Ellsberg's May 6 memo showed that Ellsberg had "bought" much of Vann's thinking.[124]

⸺❖⸺

While laid up with hepatitis, Ellsberg wrote long letters to Harry Rowen evaluating RAND and proposing improvements. Rowen was open to changes and to Ellsberg's ideas. He had Ellsberg's letters reproduced and circulated at RAND.[125]

Ellsberg also sent Rowen a cable stating in effect, or possibly precisely, "Harry—Take me. I'm yours." Rowen showed the cable to others. Now, with Rowen as RAND's president, they could really do some things together, Ellsberg probably thought. Rowen was eager for Ellsberg to return to RAND. "Harry brought him back," Richard Best remembers. "He was Harry's boy. . . . He thought he would be of tremendous value to RAND. . . . He was his candidate. He was the man he really wanted in the [economics] department there." Rowen had great confidence in Ellsberg.[126]

But others at RAND were a bit nervous. Given Rowen's extreme extolling of Ellsberg, "some people, I think, trembled, and figured, 'My God, when

Dan comes back, what's going to happen here?'" Alexander George recalls with a laugh.[127]

In his enfeebled state, Ellsberg took a slow return trip to the United States. His stops included the Ile du Levant. It was on this trip, most likely, that he took the slides he later showed Jim Digby. Meanwhile he had continued to be silent with Patricia Marx. Then he phoned her "out of the blue" from Europe and invited her to join him there. Patricia told him to "bug off." He hadn't called or written for many months, and now he wanted her to fly suddenly to Europe? "I was quite mad by then," Patricia recalls. But Ellsberg's behavior was again characteristic: he wants to do things on his time and expects others to be there for him.[128]

Ellsberg told John Vann he expected to stop in Denver and visit his uncle Lou Charsky on his way to California. Vince Davis lived in Denver and hoped to see Ellsberg during his visit. But when Davis phoned Charsky, "he made it quite clear that Dan is unreliable when it comes to making a schedule, keeping a schedule, writing letters, etc.," Davis wrote Vann. "In short, Mr. Charsky has heard nothing from Dan, and was not aware that Dan planned to visit here in Denver."[129]

When he finally arrived in California, Ellsberg was in poor shape.

NINE

WILD MAN

ELLSBERG RESUMED WORK AT THE RAND CORPORATION IN LATE JULY of 1967. Philip Cronin, his college friend on the *Harvard Crimson*, saw him at some length in California within weeks of his return. "He was quite ill," Cronin remembers. "He was really very weak. He was not in good shape at all. And exceedingly discouraged by the whole Vietnam scene. Just a very debilitated, worn out person." Ellsberg was depressed about Vietnam and more introspective than in the past. "It's one thing to say that he had hepatitis, but it's quite another thing to realize how *very* sick he was," Cronin stresses. "In the sense that he was just absolutely worn out. To the point that he had difficulty just moving around. . . . He had no vitality at all. He was flat out, absolutely flat out."[1] Ellsberg's disappointments in his love life in Vietnam surely contributed to the depression Cronin observed.

Rufus Phillips also saw Ellsberg at some point after he returned from Vietnam. Phillips, too, remembers him as being "down, depressed." Ellsberg seemed to be "struggling" about what should be done in Vietnam. "If my recollection is correct, it seemed to me that he was beginning to make arguments then about the fact that what we were doing out there was futile," Phillips says.[2]

But Ellsberg was still trying to get his and John Vann's ideas on the war heard and U.S. policy changed accordingly. Before arriving in California, he had given debriefings in Washington on the war. He claimed later that he reported to Robert McNamara, Nicholas Katzenbach, William Bundy, Averell Harriman, Walt Rostow, Paul Nitze, and Cyrus Vance—"virtually everyone connected with Vietnam except Rusk and Johnson." If so, that's impressive access. Ellsberg said he told McNamara and Katzenbach "in private" that they should get a government in South Vietnam that would negotiate with the NLF and "get us out of there." He argued for civilian rather than military leadership. He spoke with McNamara in his office "for about an hour, showing him some memos and going over what I thought he ought to do on Vietnam," he recalls. He told Rostow "there is no chance of victory over there," he said.[3]

Most likely, Ellsberg distributed his May papers on pacification strategy and South Vietnamese politics in Washington. But those papers did not advocate U.S. withdrawal. Rather, they urged different policies in Vietnam, including more aggressive military action by ARVN. His later recollections aside, Ellsberg was still trying to win the war.

In California, Ellsberg settled into a dilapidated, one-bedroom beach cottage in Malibu. It is unlikely that he spent as much time resting as hepatitis sufferers are advised to do, despite his debilitation. Richard Zeckhauser got the sense "that he was very good at coming back and instantly getting into the southern California lifestyle. . . . I just had this impression of the plane landing at LAX, Dan taking a cab over to RAND with his suitcases, having his place out in Malibu, sort of showing up, giving a seminar, dropping his stuff, shaving, going off and picking up some girls."[4]

Ellsberg could hear the waves from inside his cottage, and on a clear day he could see Santa Catalina Island from his bed without raising his head. His cottage, he remembered, was "a marvelous place. Every room in it was at a different angle, because it was settling differently on the beach. But they condemned it and the pipes broke and the electricity broke and the shower was electrified. In fact, at one point it would at random develop an electrical charge on the water. It was very exciting; it was like Vietnam, actually. I used to take a shower leaning slightly out of the shower, so that if the electricity came on at that moment you—the theory was—you could fall outside the shower."[5]

Jan Butler sometimes lived in the house when Ellsberg was out of town. One morning, she recounts,

I was using the faucets, and I kept getting these little shocks. Which I had been getting all week. And that morning I just decided not to take a shower for some reason. . . . And I got to work, and I called the real estate woman and told her that there must be something wrong with the plumbing because of the shocks. And she said, "Okay, I'll take care of it." And she called me back that afternoon, and she said, "You didn't take a shower this morning, did you?" And I thought, "My God, you can't get away with anything around here." . . . And she said, "Because if you had, you wouldn't be alive."[6]

Butler had helped Ellsberg find the cottage. Ellsberg had shown up one weekend morning in a bathing suit at Paul Langer's beach house where Butler was then living. Langer, a close friend of Butler, was in Laos at the time. Langer had earlier offered Ellsberg use of his house (an offer he subsequently rescinded), and Ellsberg had come to check it out. But when he arrived, Butler was living there. Ellsberg was disappointed, as he loved Langer's place. "Partly, probably the reason Dan started dating me was because he wanted to stay at that house," Butler says with a laugh. "In fact, it wouldn't surprise me at all." Butler knew Ellsberg, having met him at the party during the 1960 Democratic convention and then having spent time with him during a ski trip, when they had danced, apparently flirted, and talked for hours. Ellsberg had told Butler of his marital frustrations.[7]

Harry Rowen had also assisted Ellsberg's move. One weekend right after Ellsberg had moved in, Butler remembers, Rowen arrived at Ellsberg's cottage with several of his six children in tow and "boxes full of food and supplies . . . just every kind of cheese and wine and breads and vegetables. . . . He must have spent two hundred dollars on that stuff. . . . I was quite overwhelmed and thought it was a very nice gesture, and so did Dan," who didn't have any food in the house to speak of.[8]

On September 16, 1967, Butler's thirty-second birthday, Ellsberg went over to Butler's own place, where they had coffee on the terrace and discussed, among other things, the advantages of being unmarried. After Ellsberg took a nap, they lunched at the Sea Lion restaurant; they sat next to each other rather than across from each other, Butler later noted. Afterward they went house-hunting in Ellsberg's convertible sports car. Ellsberg then tired again, so they went back to Butler's house. After Ellsberg took another nap, they made love.[9] Perhaps that was one reason for Ellsberg's two naps; it was a way to get onto the bed.

One day shortly after Ellsberg had moved into his cottage, Butler was staying there alone when a moving van arrived with some of his possessions. There were boxes and crates and "big barrels full of things," Butler remembers. Ellsberg had earlier told her to feel free to open containers and put things away, so one Saturday Butler had some spare time and began opening. She found some documents stamped "Secret." She was RAND's Top Secret Control officer and took classified material seriously. "I was shocked," she recounts. "I just simply closed up the thing again and didn't open anything else. And I called the locksmith at RAND and asked him to come out and put really good locks on the doors. . . . I just felt like, 'If he's going to keep stuff here, at least let's take care of it.'" Butler decided she hadn't seen anything.[10]

After his beach cottage was condemned the winter of 1968, Ellsberg found another one nearby, a more substantial place though it was close to being a shack as well. Like its predecessor, it was a share, and Ellsberg had the upstairs share. "There was a hammock there," Richard Zeckhauser recollects. "That was a very big part of his sexual [activity]."[11]

At some point, after Ellsberg had resumed relations with Patricia Marx, he proposed a deal to Paul Langer, who was going to be away again: Could he use Langer's beach house, in return for which Langer could use Marx's tony apartment in New York? Langer turned down the offer, though on its face it was an attractive one. Langer did not expect to reside in New York for long, and he was apprehensive about Ellsberg. "I felt, in Dan's case, that here's a man who is . . . highly emotional, intellectually gifted, and highly troubled," Langer recalls. "I sensed something. . . . A troubled person has to find an outlet," and Langer thought sex was one of Ellsberg's outlets. He also remembered Ellsberg's earlier romanticizing of the Vietnam War and the way he'd gotten carried away by the danger. Ellsberg seemed "like a volcano, raging inside with likes and dislikes," and "full of himself," Langer remembers. He did not want to have too much to do with him. What would he be getting into?[12]

After his first beach house was condemned, Ellsberg threw a party there. He invited people at RAND to bring crowbars and wreck the place. There was a black light, music, and face-painting, and, according to a *Time* magazine article, "a number of tipsy RAND analysts dancing to rock music." Some got high on marijuana. "Dan was passing it around, and everybody was smoking pot," Ewa Pauker remembers. The party spilled outside. Police showed up, but Ellsberg, Harry Rowen, and another RAND man assuaged their concerns. "This was the most benign party you've ever been to in your life," Butler reminisces. "These people are all terribly square. Dan was the hippest of all of them, and he was not hip."[13]

Ellsberg's friend Vu Van Thai, a RAND consultant who would later be brought oddly into the Pentagon Papers case, attended the party. An urbane economist, Thai was a former South Vietnamese ambassador to the United States and United Nations consultant. He opposed U.S. withdrawal from Vietnam and had long discussions about Vietnam with Ellsberg that shaped Ellsberg's views. At the party, "because Vu Van Thai was there, Dan had a big bowl of Mai Tais, so he could say, 'Have a Mai Tai, Thai,'" Butler recounts. "I mean, the only reason he served Mai Tais was so he could say that."[14]

Butler was an attractive woman, big boned, and soft and warm in appearance. She was smart, and she was conscientious about her work; Ellsberg thought her overly officious. A nice person, she was short on self-confidence. "She chattered," Richard Best, RAND's security officer and her boss, remembers. "It was nervous talk, I think." Butler had her frustrations with men and "was always losing boyfriends," Best recalls. "She couldn't seem to keep a man. And she talked to me about it. You know, what was wrong?" Butler saw a number of men, including the zealous anticommunist Leon Gouré before dating Ellsberg (and possibly afterward, too). Butler had been hawkish then.[15]

Butler and Ellsberg saw and lived with each other on and off for about two years. "As far as she was concerned, she was dating Dan seriously," Best remembers. "From what Jan was telling me . . . it was very serious." Butler didn't date other people much during this period, but she certainly knew Ellsberg was seeing other women. "I never felt that we had an exclusive relationship," she recalls. "He wouldn't let me think that for five minutes. . . . Probably a month or two would go by without my seeing him at all. It wasn't a steady thing, because there were so many other people involved. It was such a team. . . . He was a team leader," she laughs. The team, of course, being his other women. Ellsberg was usually up front about them—more than Butler would have preferred. There were things she didn't want to know about, and there were many things she *didn't* know about. "But actually in the end I was glad," she says. "Because I had no illusions about our relationship at all. And it ended up we just had a lot of fun together. . . . It was one of the happier relationships I've had."[16]

Butler found Ellsberg exciting to be around. He was always surprising her. "He had a lot of stories," she recalls. He mesmerized her. And his enthusiasm could be contagious. "I think he can't control his enthusiasm," she says. "I've just never known anybody like that." His curiosities could be infectious, too. One Friday or Saturday night, Butler recounts,

> we were trying to figure out what we wanted to do. And he decided what *he* wanted to do was go down to the Whiskey-a-Go-Go . . . on the strip . . . in a rather unattractive part of Hollywood. . . . People used to just go and line up outside and just sort of stay there; they didn't go in. And he wanted to do that. So we were going to dress up in our hippie clothes and go there and mingle with the crowd. Well, neither of us had anything like hippie clothes, so we put our ski sweaters on, which was as casual as we could get. I mean, we were really square. And we went up there and we stood against that wall for a little while and met some peculiar people, and then left. . . . He just wanted to experience it. . . . He wants to know everything he can. And he doesn't just want to be told. He wants to *be* it.[17]

Ellsberg gave Butler a Valentine's Day card with a drawing of two birds kissing on the cover below the words, "I sure do like to kiss you!" Inside it read, "You're Indescribably Delicious!" (a play on an advertising slogan). Ellsberg's ability to express his emotions appealed to Butler. "He was going through a very emotional time," she recalls. In fact, he struck her as "almost uncontrollably" emotional.[18] Most likely, Vietnam and personal and career troubles were all stirring the mix.

One day, Butler remembers, they arrived at Ellsberg's beach cottage, and as he was getting out of his car "I got my finger caught in the gate. And the pain was so bad it took my breath away. And it was finally getting better, and he discovered what had happened and just fell apart. . . . He came in on the end of it and just emoted like crazy. But he just is very empathetic. But he overdoes it. . . . I think that his emotions certainly guided him through the Vietnam thing. It was a very emotional thing for him, partly because of his future wife [Patricia] and the trouble that they had in Vietnam."[19]

Butler sometimes stuck up for Ellsberg when others at RAND doubted him. Helen Kwake did some clerical work for Ellsberg and came to believe he was emotionally unstable and a security risk (though, again, that's a judgment easier to offer in retrospect). When Kwake mentioned her concern to Butler, "she was so mad at me," Kwake recalls. "Boy, she just about took my head off." But as Butler handled top-secret documents, Kwake thought, "It's your neck."[20]

Ellsberg broke off his relationship with Butler when he became engaged to Patricia Marx around the spring of 1970. Richard Best remembers Butler telling him that Ellsberg brought Patricia by to meet her after getting engaged or married. "She was miffed," Best recalls, and "certainly hurt." Best thought it "a horse's ass" thing for Ellsberg to do. "He didn't see outside of himself on things of that sort." But Butler recalls that, overall, Ellsberg

> handled the whole situation very sensitively. . . . We went for a long walk on the beach one night, and he told me about her [Patricia], and told me that they were engaged. It was a very nice way of finding out about it. And, "I'm in love with this woman." I was a little surprised, because I didn't know that they'd been seeing each other that recently. . . .
>
> I've always admired him for how he dealt with me in that situation. . . . Of all the men I've known, he and one other are the only ones who haven't hurt me. Because they didn't betray me. . . . He hurt me in little ways, but they were momentary and fleeting. And I still consider him a friend.[21]

At RAND, Ellsberg gave more briefings and talks on the war. He spoke to RAND's board of trustees that November. He was pessimistic, critical. Progress in the war was not being made, he told the trustees; it was effectively stalemated. The United States had underestimated the North Vietnamese and Viet Cong. But the military campaign should continue, Ellsberg argued. Indeed, military action against VC local companies was critical. But he was skeptical of ARVN's ability to do the job; he illustrated its ineffectiveness partly through the use of charts showing low numbers of VC killed in action. Ellsberg argued once again that radical changes in ARVN and the GVN were essential. "I think he saw himself . . . as the person who is the brain truster who picks the right people and we win," Paul Langer says. Ellsberg told the trustees that a peace settlement that fell far short of defeating the Vietnamese communists would be quite costly to the United States, but to accept such a settlement after two more years of war, or to accept a favorable settlement after five or ten more years, would be even worse.[22]

Ellsberg debated the conservative Harvard political scientist Samuel Huntington in Cambridge after returning from Vietnam. "The remarkable thing was that they virtually agreed on everything," Thomas Schelling remembers:

> The only thing they disagreed on was whether the White House had the guts to make the Vietnamese government do what it would have to do in order to win the war. They both agreed that without a transformation of the officer system, the war could not be won. They both agreed that without pressure from the White House, that transformation would not take place. Sam said the White House can do it, and Dan said the White House can't do it. Otherwise, they agreed—we should win the war. This was even when he came home depressed. He agreed this is a war that deserves to be won. But the fucking White House won't do what it has to do to win the war.[23]

Ellsberg was still making arguments for how to deploy U.S. and ARVN forces and fight the war most effectively. But he opposed open-ended U.S. troop deployments and favored reducing U.S. casualties, which he thought might make a protracted U.S. engagement more tolerable to the American people.[24]

———◆———

Ellsberg was meanwhile spending time with his two children again. "He did not neglect them at all," Mary Marshall remembers. "He really liked to be with the kids." But when asked if he saw them very often, Carol Cummings responded, "It was irregular." "Fairly sporadic," were Mary Ellsberg's words. When Philip Cronin visited Carol in the summer or fall of 1967, that was a concern to her. "Between a divorce and irregular visits, she did not think that was good for the children," Cronin recalls. Ellsberg would later fault himself for not seeing his children more. Robert Ellsberg remembers that his activities with his father had the flavor of a treat:

> I had a feeling that these were kind of like holidays more than everyday life. . . . To a certain extent I didn't feel he was part of my routine life. It was kind of a world apart. We'd stay with him for a weekend or something like that at various points, but it was always kind of a circus. . . .
>
> Maybe he had a feeling or need to squeeze into the time we had some way of sharing with me what he was going through and his thinking and his life. I felt I had a pretty good sense of what was happening with him, because he would speak pretty freely about [it]. . . . I felt to a lesser extent was he entirely engaged with what was going on in my life. And so there was a kind of different quality of relationship with my mother than with him. With him it was more sort of big ideas and books and that sort of thing. And with my mother it was what I was doing in school and who my friends were, and that kind of thing. . . . More typical parental interest in all the details of my life.[25]

Robert was closer to his father than Mary was, though there were periods when Ellsberg paid more attention to her. Mary was apparently less interesting to him intellectually because of her younger age. "He thought I was cute and bought me extravagant presents, beautiful dolls, Thai silks, French perfumes, Seiko watches, gold jewelry," Mary recalls. Helen Kwake remembers Ellsberg telling her that he had taken Mary to the musical *Hair*, which included nudity: "The kid was a very nervous child. . . . And I guess the kid didn't know what to do. It upset her. And I said, 'Why would you take a kid to see it? Take her to Disneyland.'"[26]

Mary Ellsberg was bright, highly demanding of herself, enthusiastic, emotional, and sensitive. (Who does that sound like?) "Mary was kind of jittery," Mary Marshall remembers. With some concern, Carol Ellsberg had mentioned to Marshall earlier how fascinated Mary was by fire. "She was a little worried about Mary for a while," Marshall says. "About how stable she was." Mary loved to read. Robert Ellsberg was also bright and bookish, less social and emotional than Mary, unathletic, artistic, musical, and "attracted to religious artists and reading the Bible." He attended Episcopal services and other church events regularly with his mother and sister; like Mary, he sang in the choir and was an acolyte. Robert was interested in moral, philosophical, and religious issues at a young age. His father "became focused on Robert as a confidant and intellectual partner, celebrating his accomplishments as a writer, which I think was a little embarrassing to Robert," Mary recounts. "He wanted to send one of Robert's poems called 'Courage' to the *New York Times*, which even we understood was overdoing it. At the age of nine or ten, I was not in a position to compete with this kind of adulation." Ellsberg continued to try to engage his children in deep intellectual discussion and to lecture them on assorted topics, including guerrilla warfare. Mary, whose relationship with her father has been difficult, and who found answering my questions "a painful process," says of such behavior by her father:

> To a certain extent I tuned it out. I don't think I ever went as far as Michael [Ellsberg's son with Patricia], who used to actually tell Dad that he was boring and would refuse to listen. We were at a disadvantage with Dad, since if we didn't behave minimally well, he could disappear, so I think we didn't dare to show our feelings as bluntly. However, it is true that as small children we spent a lot of time hearing about the war, and later, nuclear holocaust and disarmament. I remember his asking me once out of the blue, perhaps I was eleven or twelve, what I talked about with my friends, and it struck me as such a strange question coming from him that I couldn't think of an answer.
>
> I guess I felt that he was basically clueless about us. I may be wrong, but I don't believe that he ever met any of my teachers at school (I do remember him coming to my junior high school graduation, but I don't think he ever went to my grade school or high school). Maybe these are not uncommon experiences, especially among children of divorced parents. . . . We probably spent a fair amount [of time] with him, but it does seem to me that our time with him was mostly focused on his interests. I don't think of him as having been actively involved in parenting. . . . The only time I remember him having an opinion about anything around my upbringing was when I got my beginner's driving license at 15 and he was horrified.
>
> He sort of bounced back and forth between benign neglect, and then popping up with extravagant gestures, like a pool table, or crates of Marx toys after he started going out with Patricia. Once I had a birthday party at his house on the beach, and he bought a pint of all 31 flavors of ice cream to go with the cake. It was fun, but a little disorienting, since most of the time we [were] living under pretty tight circumstances. I think we didn't allow ourselves to enjoy it fully, out of loyalty to Mom and awareness that these moments of excess were fleeting. It was probably frustrating to him as well that we did not accept his efforts with more enthusiasm.
>
> In college the dynamic was different, but similar—if we shared our papers he would read up on whatever issue it was about, trying to have something to contribute, but the effect was discouraging to us, because it meant that he was invariably an expert on anything we were studying, and usually with much greater insight than anything we had come up with. I believe at this point his intentions were the best, trying to share something with us and show that he

cared about what we were doing. On the other hand, during this period I believe that I was also trying to write about issues that were interesting to him (nonviolence, dependency theory, etc.) and when I got more involved in health education, for example, I think he was less interested.[27]

One night, probably in 1969, Jan Butler and Ellsberg took Robert and Mary with them to an antiwar demonstration at UCLA. When one of the speakers called President Nixon a liar, Mary "became very disturbed," Butler recalls. "I could see that she was really unhappy about it." But "Dan was so wrapped up in what was going on that he couldn't separate himself from the event to take care of what was going on with Mary. And so I had to kind of comfort her. . . . But, really, Dan should have been addressing this problem with his daughter. I was just meeting her."[28]

———————

In the fall of 1967, Ellsberg had his first contact with the Pentagon Papers. He worked on this top-secret history of U.S. involvement in Vietnam in Washington. Robert McNamara had directed that the study be undertaken. McNamara explained later that he wanted scholars to understand what had gone wrong in Vietnam in order to prevent similar mistakes in the future. "I think his objective was to try and see to it that it didn't happen again," Paul Warnke, a senior Pentagon official at the time, recalls. McNamara had told a group of Harvard professors in November of the previous year that he wanted such a study undertaken for the use of scholars, although it's unclear when he envisioned they would actually have access to it. Deeply disturbed over Vietnam, McNamara may have also seen the study as a means to change U.S. policy; he had originally directed that it be completed in three months. A complex man, McNamara probably had other motivations as well. "I think he meant it to absolve himself of guilt," David Halberstam argues. "As his pathetic, dishonest little book"—his 1995 memoir *In Retrospect*—"is intended to show. That he had no choice" in Vietnam. "He is really just a lying son-of-a-bitch," Halberstam says.[29]

Ellsberg would later suggest that he himself had stimulated the study. That is almost certainly untrue. He also bragged that he had read more such studies done with classified material "than probably any other person." He had been "immediately assigned" to the Pentagon Papers project after returning from Vietnam, he said, having been "urged" to participate "from the outset." The last part, at least, *is* true, and it was Morton Halperin, a deputy assistant secretary of defense for Warnke, who requested his involvement. "The truth is, we were asking everybody who we thought was likely to be willing to participate and had sort of basic skills," Halperin recounts. "We were looking for people who had academic training, knew something about Vietnam, who had a security clearance, and might be free to spend several months working on the study. So anybody who fit that bill, we asked. It wasn't that we sort of searched the whole country and said, 'Dan Ellsberg is the one.'" But "he would have been sort of very high in all the categories."[30]

"They were very anxious to get me," Ellsberg claimed in an interview. "I was only willing to do it on condition that I would be able to profit from it intellectually by reading the whole study. That was the price I asked for participating as a researcher. So I was given the commitment that I would be able to read this thing ultimately. No other researcher got that commitment on the study. RAND was not given access. . . . I was the only researcher in the country with authorized access to the entire study. . . . I was authorized by the assistant secretary of defense to have personal access to the entire study."[31]

Warnke, that assistant secretary of defense, denies making any such promise. "I think he has a tendency to lay it on a bit thick at times," Warnke observes. Ellsberg testified in his Pentagon Papers trial that Leslie Gelb, who chaired the study's task force, was the one who made this promise. But Gelb strongly disputed Ellsberg's claim: "I did not in any way either say or imply that Dan would have access." "We were just not in a position to do that," Halperin points out. "Because we had no idea what would happen to the studies." One might charitably say this was all a misunderstanding: Gelb or Halperin may have said they'd *try* to get Ellsberg access, and then Ellsberg later blew up their exchange beyond that.[32]

Six researchers were assigned to the task force. They would be working with classified material, lots of it, mainly from Defense, CIA, and State.

Ellsberg's involvement elicited some concern. "The one person I'm worried about is Dan Ellsberg," Gelb reportedly told a colleague. Ellsberg's indiscretion and high-strung temperament were apparently reasons for Gelb's concern. The study was supposed to be hush-hush. One official warned Ellsberg against making any disclosures when it was finished. According to the CIA's psychiatrists, Ellsberg was eventually "nudged out of" the study "because his supervisors were uneasy with him." Hans Heymann remembers that he and several other researchers felt considerable ambivalence about Ellsberg's participation. "We had had a number of experiences with him that made a lot of us feel very uncomfortable with his probing and his searching and his record-keeping and his activities. . . . He struck people as different and worrisome." Ellsberg's emotional intensity was one reason, Heymann says. And there was his "curious behavior" of making "endless collections of information" for his own purposes. "Everywhere he was scribbling like crazy," Heymann recounts. He exhibited what struck Heymann as an "unhealthy and emotional probing into the failures of U.S. policy. A notion that there was a gigantic deception. . . . There were overtones of, 'I'm going to find what *really* happened underneath.'" People wondered about his motivations.[33]

Consequently, Ellsberg was assigned a relatively safe portion of the study, according to Heymann. "They were trying very hard to keep things compartmentalized. And some people had much greater freedom of looking at things outside of their assigned area. But Ellsberg did not. They really tried to isolate him." But he then edged further and further into other materials, "and there was more and more nervousness, and great effort to keep him cut off from that." G. Gordon Liddy later reported to Egil Krogh and David Young, "On at least one occasion, Gelb found it necessary to admonish Ellsberg as he was found to be reading widely in materials not connected with his assigned subject matter, and producing no drafts connected with a substantial amount of the classified material into which he was delving." But others on the task force probably also read widely in other materials (or at least read some of their colleagues' writings), and if Ellsberg did, it would not have been terribly unwarranted.[34] Moreover, it seems unlikely that anyone worried at this stage that he would actually *release* the study. That goes beyond indiscretion.

Ellsberg testified at his trial that Gelb told him "I could choose any area that I wanted particularly, and I chose the 1961 period of the early decisions by President Kennedy to do research on. . . . The first problem was to find what files were relevant to the period 1961. . . . I made some collection of documents for the 1950 period entirely, and in particular asked for the task force to receive the set of all NIEs, National Intelligence Estimates, relating to Indochina or Vietnam from the earliest period." Ellsberg read all the NIEs up to the most recent ones, he recalled. He became immersed in documents from the 1950s; he was intrigued with President Eisenhower's decision not to rescue the French in Vietnam.[35]

Ellsberg said he finished a first draft on the 1961 period in late December 1967. His draft was "almost 400 pages," he testified. "And I wrote that in one month," he told me. "That's a lot." But Ellsberg either did not get his draft done as quickly as Gelb wanted, or it wasn't what Gelb wanted, or both. "It wasn't ready on time," one of his colleagues recalled. "Very few of Ellsberg's words finally appeared," Gelb said. "Dan just didn't do his work." Howard Margolis, who also worked on the study, believes Ellsberg became engrossed in other work. But Ellsberg claimed later, "I drafted the volume of the study on the Kennedy decision making in 1961." Getting closer to the truth, he told me that the documents he selected from the task force's files were "used very much" in the final product, "and *some* of [his] theses. Not a whole lot." Margolis, whom Gelb asked to finish Ellsberg's section of the study, "rewrote" it, Ellsberg said. Gelb, Ellsberg pointed out, had all sections rewritten by another author. ("Reviewed" might be a better word, though almost all the sections did have more than one author.)[36]

Ellsberg further testified that he "helped" by "kibitzing" on other volumes of the study. "His role, as far as I could observe it, was one of kibitzer-in-chief," Gus Shubert, another member of the task force, recounts. "He would look over people's shoulders and look at their stuff: 'Oh, isn't that interesting.'" Shubert never saw any product from Ellsberg. "He certainly would want to talk to everybody in the group about their own studies," Halperin comments. "And have interesting ideas. But he would be much more interested in doing that than actually writing something."[37]

Margolis found what Ellsberg wrote of limited use and told Gelb he wanted to start from scratch. "My recollection is that Dan had essentially done a detailed account of the intelligence as of the time Kennedy took office . . . and he hadn't started at all on what actually happened in 1961, or perhaps had made some preliminary notes, but it was not what I wanted to use," Margolis recounts. "So I told Gelb that I had better make it my task to write that '61 period. . . . The volume on 1961 would have been wholly my volume and none of Dan's. . . . I'm quite sure I didn't use any material he wrote. . . . I certainly got a running start from what he did, but basically the volume on 1961 was what I did." This, of course, goes beyond "rewriting." When told that Ellsberg remembered writing almost 400 pages, Margolis responded, "If he says he did, he must have, but I don't know what it was."[38]

Harry Rowen saw advantages to Ellsberg's work style, however. When Shubert visited him after being asked to join the study and pointed out some potential pitfalls in it, Rowen responded, "Gus, why aren't you more like Dan? Just get in there and get everything you can."[39]

Ellsberg took time off from his work on the Pentagon Papers study to join the celebrated antiwar demonstration at the Pentagon in October of 1967. He says he participated because he was "totally sympathetic" to the goal of ending the war and wished "to be part of it," although he didn't feel he had a great deal to learn from antiwar protesters. One problem was they didn't have access to classified information and consequently didn't know the full story. After protesting, he observed the demonstration from inside the Pentagon. "To get a better view, I wandered into McNamara's office at one point, and there was McNamara, with his secretary," Ellsberg recounts. McNamara was standing at a window, surveying the crowd below, looking pretty grim. Ellsberg stood at a window near McNamara. "Ironically enough, we didn't say a word to each other," Ellsberg remembers. McNamara may have wondered what Ellsberg was doing in his office. "I hope this is making a strong impression on him," Ellsberg recalls thinking.[40]

Around two months later, Ellsberg phoned his friend John Sack from some command post or restricted room in Washington. Sack remembers it as the White House Situation Room, though that seems unlikely. Sack got the impression that Ellsberg was calling other old friends from the room as well. "He calls me laughing: 'I'm in the White House Situation Room right now. Do you have anything for me?'" Sack recounts. As it was, Sack *did* have something for him. Sack had had dinner a couple of nights earlier with Jerry Rubin, Lee Weiner, and Rubin's girlfriend, who were making plans for protests at the Democratic convention in Chicago in August 1968. And that very afternoon, Sack recalls, "Jerry had called me and said, 'I've got a great name for the group. . . . We're going to call ourselves the Conspiracy.' And an hour or so later there's a call from Dan in the Situation Room saying, 'So you got anything for me?' And I said, 'Yeah, I got some hot stuff. . . . Jerry Rubin has just formed a group called the Conspiracy.' . . . I'm sure he laughed. It would be very much like him to say, 'Okay, boys, put that up on the wall: the Conspiracy. . . . ' And then I called Jerry Rubin and I told him. . . . He was laughing." To impress Don Hall, Ellsberg showed him a pass he had to some restricted part of the Pentagon or other government agency. "He was wearing it, showing it," Hall remembers.[41]

In early December 1967, Ellsberg participated in a confidential conference on Vietnam in Bermuda sponsored by the Carnegie Endowment for International Peace. Discussion focused around the bombing of North Vietnam and the threat of a wider ground war. Fueled by his mounting pessimism about U.S. prospects in Vietnam and his frustrations over how the war was being conducted, as well as his increased exposure to antiwar views in the United States, Ellsberg made some of his strongest criticism of the war yet. A dove was beginning to emerge inside the same man who was still talking about how to fight the war most effectively. Moral concerns were evident. "Ellsberg was very ominous about the horror we were inflicting on the Vietnamese people," James Thomson, who was then a history professor at Harvard, remembers.

And the older folks, I think, began to think of him as some kind of outspoken kook. . . . He was for stopping the bombing and finding a way to get out. And he was sort of looked at askance by the older folks. And he talked a bit too much. And he talked with an intensity. A quite bloodless face, he was so intense. . . . He turned pale as he articulately stated and restated the horrors we were inflicting on Indochinese people. And the older folks, I think, decided he was a little shrill. . . . His persuasive power was overwielded, and overshadowed by his intensity, which made him seem to them on the verge of spooky.[42]

But as Joseph Johnson, president of the Carnegie Endowment for International Peace, informed President Lyndon Johnson afterward, it was the "virtually unanimous" view of the conferees "that the United States must accept a long-term involvement in South Vietnam, and that precipitate or dishonorable withdrawal would be disastrous." The "substantial consensus" was that "United States posture should be one that can be sustained for an indefinite period with reduced risks and increased political benefits until such time as the conflict can be resolved in an honorable and peaceful fashion." There should be no surrender. The goal was to maintain a stalemate until the enemy negotiated a satisfactory settlement, and to preserve a noncommunist government in the South.[43]

Weeks after the conference, the North Vietnamese and NLF launched their famous Tet offensive, which showed starkly that United States and GVN control in South Vietnam was thin indeed, that pacification was a shambles, and that the enemy's resolve was undiminished. The offensive increased Ellsberg's discouragement greatly. "Dan was totally down," Guy Pauker remembers. Two months earlier, Ellsberg had believed that changes in U.S. policy geared toward reforming the GVN and ARVN could produce significant and lasting progress. He now argued in a paper—which he sent everywhere, even to Vietnam—on February 28, 1968, one month after the offensive had begun, that he no longer believed that. Most U.S. objectives in Vietnam were lost, he asserted; in fact, the war would never be won. Pacification was dead, and the situation was going to get even worse: an even bigger round of enemy attacks would be forthcoming soon, he predicted, wrongly, despite his essentially accurate assessment of Tet. (That May, he would still be predicting larger enemy attacks in the cities over the summer.) Ellsberg would still have preferred that ARVN fight aggressively and that the war be won, but he believed that the GVN and ARVN would not meet the challenge of Tet.[44]

In another memo, dated March 12, Ellsberg advocated quickly assuming a military stance in South Vietnam aimed at denying victory to the VC indefinitely at an endurable cost. That would involve the U.S. Marines at Khe Sanh fighting their way out of their besieged base and accepting and causing significant casualties, if needed. Ellsberg also advised saturation military operations in areas bordering populated areas and other offensive actions outside these areas. Bombing in support of such ground operations should be increased, he argued, but other strikes should be decreased sharply to minimize destruction of cities and villages. Also, the South Vietnamese armed forces should be reequipped and provided more air support. Ellsberg once again advised greater U.S. intervention in South Vietnamese affairs, advocating a broadening of the GVN—though not to include the NLF—to make it more viable, and radically reforming its armed forces; he suggested specific candidates for political and military leadership. After all this had been accomplished, the United States should stop the bombing of the North with the goal of bringing about a peace settlement, one that, again, maintained noncommunist leadership in the South. But it should bomb infiltration targets if the enemy exploited the halt.[45]

Ellsberg's friend Tran Ngoc Chau, who was then a member of the National Assembly in South Vietnam, visited the United States during Tet and spent a week or two with Ellsberg in California. Ellsberg was "bending everybody's ear" at RAND about Chau's capacity for exercising viable leadership in South Vietnam by this time, Konrad Kellen remembers. Despite Ellsberg's pessimism, he was still working for a better policy, Chau recalls. As one RAND analyst observes, "He at that point was still looking for a politically viable and cheaper way of prosecuting the war."[46]

Despite his discouragement, then, Ellsberg was for hanging tough following Tet, though he was increasingly doubtful that the United States would ever do what it needed to do. Tet may have reinforced in his mind the tragic consequences of the government's rejection of his ideas.[47]

Ellsberg had written his February 28 memo at the request of Morton Halperin, and he recalls doing "a lot of consulting" for Paul Warnke, Halperin's boss, at this time. But Warnke denies that Ellsberg ever consulted for him. Another man in ISA says that Ellsberg was a consultant to the policy planning section of ISA, not to Warnke himself: "Typical Ellsberg exaggeration," he comments. Warnke did speak with Ellsberg around this time. "He came in to talk to me about Vietnam a couple of times, representing himself as John McNaughton's former special assistant," Warnke recounted. Ellsberg seemed "more concerned about the tactics used to accomplish what he regarded as a legitimate objective [in Vietnam] rather than the legitimacy of the objective."[48]

Ewa Pauker, a former research associate at RAND, remembers an evening at her house probably in 1968 or even early 1969 when she suggested jokingly to Ellsberg that, some night during monsoon season in Vietnam when it was pitch black outside, the United States should pull completely out of Vietnam. "He got so mad at me," she recounts. "He said, 'How can you say a thing like that? . . . ' He *really* tore into me. 'How can you even think such a thing?'"[49]

Ellsberg's February 28 memo left its imprint on a memo drafted in ISA for new Secretary of Defense Clark Clifford to present to President Johnson in early March. ISA's memo was part of a major review of U.S. policy in Vietnam sparked by a request by General Earle Wheeler, the chairman of the JCS, and General William Westmoreland for 206,000 more troops. Ellsberg opposed granting the request.[50]

Robert Komer, Lyndon Johnson's pacification chief in Vietnam, received a copy of Ellsberg's memo from Westmoreland. "I blew a fuse," Komer remembers. "I was very irritated that Dan Ellsberg, who had been very pro-GVN, much in favor of many of the things I was doing, was writing memos saying we were in sad shape. . . . But I did not write Dan," who "was very good at paper wars."[51]

One person in ISA who was extensively involved in the U.S. policy review after Tet, a well-respected and fairly dovish man, remembers that Ellsberg "wanted to put in a paper that victory of the Viet Cong was inevitable." This person was not fond of Ellsberg, whose ego and indiscretion bothered him. He came to believe that Ellsberg couldn't be trusted with anything. He stopped returning Ellsberg's phone calls. He did not wish to be allied with him; it would undermine his own credibility. "Dan would express his views in a way that was not calculated to bring about change in the opinions of others who didn't agree with you," he recalls. A small study group of people from outside the Pentagon was put together by ISA after Tet. Somebody wanted to put Ellsberg on the team. "I vetoed it," this man recounts. "I felt that Ellsberg's membership on the team would have definitely tainted the result"—hurt its credibility. "He was personal, and thought to be extreme in his views."[52]

Albert Williams was a low-level White House staffer working on Vietnamese matters at this time. He walked into his office one morning and found his secretary typing away furiously. Williams knew that he had not given her anything pressing to do. "She said that somebody had come in and said that whatever she was doing wasn't as important as what he was going to give her,"

Williams remembers. That somebody was Ellsberg. Williams, who later had contact with Ellsberg at RAND, where they disagreed on Vietnam, adds, "He took himself very seriously."[53]

Ellsberg also distributed other of his writings, asking some people to share them with others. "He sent everybody papers," Adam Yarmolinsky recalled. "He was broadcasting. He was not narrow-casting."[54]

———— ❈ ————

In his indignation at U.S. policies in Vietnam and deceptively optimistic official propaganda on the war, Ellsberg began leaking inside information after Tet. He probably hoped it would help discredit U.S. policies and provide support for his own prescriptions. Leaking also likely made him feel important, on the inside, and something of a political player. According to Ellsberg, he informed Senator Robert Kennedy about Wheeler and Westmoreland's request for 206,000 additional troops. If true, this was Ellsberg's first major leak, though Halperin doesn't believe Ellsberg even knew about the troop request. Assuming Ellsberg did leak to Kennedy, he was probably hoping to both undermine the request and promote himself with Kennedy, whose power and charisma attracted him; he would attach himself to Kennedy's fortunes. But he later claimed, "It was for a good cause, the best, but by doing so I knew I was ruling myself out of a job with Kennedy." (The latter is unlikely.) The *New York Times* broke the story of the troop request—one of the most explosive stories of the entire Vietnam War—on March 10. Its sources were not from the Kennedy camp.[55]

But Ellsberg thought he might have indirectly been the source for the story, he would recall, and he was inspired by it. "When I saw the impact it had after the press got it, I said, 'How crazy. I've been a fool. I should have been affecting policy this way.'" One could really get something done through leaks. Ellsberg leaked more inside information to the *Times*'s Neil Sheehan, one of the authors of the March 10 story. "I ended up giving Sheehan a leak a day," Ellsberg said. "I gave him a lot of stuff that got Westmoreland fired." Ellsberg provided Sheehan information on a deceptive year-end report on the war by Westmoreland and on a CIA estimate of actual VC and North Vietnamese troop strength before Tet. Ellsberg gave Sheehan material from classified documents.[56]

Ellsberg also passed Sheehan documents on a PR campaign that the Johnson administration had conducted in the fall of 1967 claiming progress in Vietnam. He apparently provided an exchange of cables between the U.S. embassy in Saigon and Washington. Sheehan had told Tom Wicker, the *Times*'s Washington bureau chief, that he knew someone who would be willing to provide the cables and had brought Ellsberg into Wicker's office. Wicker vaguely remembered Ellsberg as the hawkish former marine he had met in Vietnam and was a little surprised that this same man was now ready to take this step. Ellsberg told Wicker in some detail about the exchange of cables and showed Wicker one of them. "I told him that this one cable wasn't sufficient in itself," Wicker recounts, but that "if he could produce the [other] cables, we'd go with the story. . . . Well, he protested that I was asking him to take all the risk. That these were classified cables and that he could get into a lot of trouble." Ellsberg could potentially lose his security clearance and his job. He could even go to jail, he worried. "I gave him a newspaperman's spiel about patriotism and all that stuff," Wicker recalls. "At the same time, I told him that if he really wanted the story out, then he had to take the risk." Ellsberg seemed surprised that the *Times* wouldn't go with the story without more documentation. He "thought a 'leak' of this magnitude would produce immediate headlines," Wicker perceived.[57]

Ellsberg was quite cautious when dealing with Sheehan. But Sheehan was even more cautious, and Ellsberg thought he was paranoid. The newspaper columnist Joseph Kraft observed Ellsberg's own vigilance. They both attended a lunch at Senator Edward Kennedy's home in the spring of 1968. "To the considerable embarrassment of everybody at lunch he talked at great length of how wrong he had been" on Vietnam earlier, Kraft wrote. "After lunch I drove him back to Washington. As we drove he kept glancing nervously over his shoulder. When we finally reached town he directed me first to one hotel, then to a second, then to a third, where he finally got out. He was taking precautions, he said, to avoid being followed by agents of the FBI or the Pentagon." Robert and Mary Ellsberg asked their father about Kraft's article after it appeared in 1971. Ellsberg explained to them that he had had reason to be nervous, as he had recently made a leak.[58]

Ellsberg revered Robert Kennedy. Like many other Americans, "he thought he was the savior," Jan Butler recalls. Ellsberg had been impressed by Kennedy during a discussion they had had about Vietnam at a forum in the fall of 1967. According to Ellsberg, Frank Mankiewicz had approached him at the forum and said that Kennedy wanted to meet with him. William Kaufmann, who helped organize the forum, remembers that Ellsberg was extremely anxious to talk to Kennedy there. During their meeting, Kennedy told Ellsberg that "we ought to get together in the future" to talk more about Vietnam, Ellsberg recounted. "I told him of the study I was doing"—the Pentagon Papers—"and he said he would be glad to let me go over his own files on Vietnam, his papers, which I never got around to doing. . . . But I did see him quite a bit in the spring of '68," after spending "a week" discussing Wheeler and Westmoreland's troop request with him. Ellsberg remembered working quite closely with Kennedy's campaign, mainly on Vietnam. "I was working a lot on Bobby's speeches. . . . I was providing the policy line for most of the speeches on Vietnam. . . . I felt I was Bobby's man." At the least, Ellsberg was an extremely knowledgeable source on the war for the Kennedy camp. Peter Edelman, a top Kennedy aide, says he was "very helpful in giving us a very good feel for what was actually happening" in Vietnam.[59]

Ellsberg claimed later that Kennedy asked him to leave RAND and "work for him full time as his central man on Vietnam, collecting information and feeding it to the speech writers." But Edelman doubts that. "It might be that Kennedy asked for his help, and that Dan thought that that was more than he said," Edelman theorizes. "It might be that he was talking about coming and volunteering to do things." Ellsberg said he turned down Kennedy's offer, partly because he'd just started undergoing psychoanalysis in Los Angeles, and because "I wanted to be able to talk to all the different candidates" for president.[60]

Ellsberg did want to work for Kennedy. "He actually wanted to quit [RAND] and go to work full time for Kennedy," Seymour Martin Lipset, who consulted at RAND the summer of 1968, remembers. But Harry Rowen and Albert Wohlstetter "talked him out of it. . . . They pressed him to stay."[61]

Ellsberg claims that Hubert Humphrey offered him a job as well. "I was adviser to Humphrey. He had asked me to join his campaign . . . at a lunch the day he announced in New York his campaign. . . . I was the only one that was offered a job at that lunch." Ellsberg said he was asked to be "the researcher and speech writer" for the campaign. He claims that John E. Rielly, Humphrey's foreign policy assistant, offered him the job, and that Humphrey's people asked him more than once to help out. But he didn't take the job, partly because he was "already feeling much more on Kennedy's side." But he "consulted twice with Humphrey" after Kennedy's death, he recalled. "I spoke a good deal several times to Humphrey and his assistants." He also gave advice to Republican presidential candidate Nelson Rockefeller through Henry Kissinger, in his retelling, and spoke to "[George] Romney's person."[62]

In reality, the lunch Ellsberg spoke of took place the month after Humphrey announced his candidacy, which he did in Washington, not in New York. "The whole idea was to start collecting a team of foreign policy experts who could help us in the campaign," John E. Rielly recounts. Humphrey's men wanted a variety of views at the lunch, and Ellsberg was an articulate critic on Vietnam. Asked if he offered Ellsberg a job, Rielly, who was sitting next to Ellsberg at the lunch, responded, "No. Definitely not. No one was offered a job at that lunch." But "I may have said to Dan—or to a half dozen other people—'If we need help on this issue, I hope we can call on you.'" Rielly also says he never asked Ellsberg to work on the campaign at any other time, and "I would be highly skeptical whether anyone else asked him to do this."[63]

Rielly has one distinct memory of Ellsberg at the lunch. "The wine served was a Chateau Haut-Brion. I think it was 1949, which was a great year, or a great wine. And of course a number of people commented on this. But the guy who seemed most taken with this, and seemed most impressed by it, was Dan Ellsberg," Rielly chuckles. "I don't remember exactly what he said, but I remember he was *really* impressed by that. . . . Dan obviously was up on wines, and he knew a lot about good wine, and he recognized it. And he commented at some length."[64]

Early the following month, June 1968, Ellsberg participated in another conference on Vietnam, this one in Chicago. He was critical of the failure of the United States to learn from its past mistakes and to make reforms in South Vietnam—he was "building an argument for even more intervention," another conferee thought—and of U.S. bombing. "It is simply not acceptable, in the eyes of many people, to kill as many people as we are doing in Vietnam, or even a much smaller number, when the process of violence offers as little promise of success in any terms as it does there," Ellsberg said. (That statement is quoted from a paper he had compiled "in response to several requests," he noted, on his comments at the conference.) But, Ellsberg observed, and here he paraphrased the black militant H. Rap Brown, *"bombing is as American as cherry pie."* He was "very, very emotional" at the conference, Stanley Hoffmann remembers. "Very, very passionate." Ellsberg predicted that "Saigon, to my mind, is unlikely to survive this year and, indeed, perhaps even unlikely to survive the summer." (Ellsberg has a penchant for making such bold yet erroneous political predictions. Besides his questionable judgment, reasons for this may include a desire for attention—they get your attention.) Ellsberg also asserted that "it is worth enormous resources to prevent the Viet Cong from getting into Saigon at all, in large numbers. This means a redeployment of our forces." He was still trying to win, or at least not to lose.[65]

During the conference, Robert Kennedy was assassinated in Los Angeles. "I had just given the policy lines, stayed up all night with Adam Walinsky and Peter Edelman helping on a speech for Robert Kennedy which proved to be his last speech given in San Francisco," Ellsberg recounted. (Edelman doesn't remember working with Ellsberg on any speech during the campaign.) When Ellsberg heard about the assassination, he sobbed uncontrollably. He felt hopeless about Vietnam, and any personal ambitions he had attached to Kennedy were dead.[66]

The assassination apparently made Ellsberg more cynical about American politics (as it did others). According to Seymour Martin Lipset, he was talking "in very radical terms—in relation to the war, to Johnson, and so on"—the summer of 1968 at RAND. "He wasn't inhibited. . . . He was very, very bitterly antiwar, or very strongly antiwar. And very cynical about the government and about national policy. In fact, it raised issues, I remember thinking, so to speak, 'What's he doing here? . . . And secondly, why are they keeping him?'" At RAND, "there was talk of incongruities."[67]

Ellsberg attended his 20-year reunion at Cranbrook that June. "He was turning against the war," Ken Wright recounted. "We'd try to pin him down. He'd always cop out—say we'd agree with him if we knew the facts. But he'd say he couldn't give us the facts because they were classified."[68]

By that fall Ellsberg no longer judged Vietnam hopeless, however. Anticommunists had shown some resilience, he thought, although the GVN and ARVN were still incapable of making much progress in the war. If the United States could endure the stalemate in Vietnam for a significant time, partly by reducing substantially the number of U.S. troops there, Ellsberg believed, it might force a negotiated settlement. Yet, he remained pessimistic that the United States would do what it needed to do.[69]

* * *

Meanwhile, Ellsberg was working on a big study at RAND entitled "Lessons of Vietnam." He planned to write a book, issuing a series of RMs—RAND memoranda—along the way. "I was, again, to draw conclusions for the help of the executive branch and of the president at the highest level," Ellsberg later testified, "to understand, really, what had gone wrong in Vietnam" so that the U.S. government "could avoid failures of this sort in the future." He was "the only man at RAND—actually, in the country—who was on government funds, spending full time doing research drawing lessons from our Vietnam experience."[70]

But 1968 was a pretty fallow year for Ellsberg. "I didn't give RAND a lot of work [on] 'Lessons from Vietnam' that summer," he would acknowledge. "Work on how to have made pacification more effective just didn't seem a very relevant way to be spending the summer while the bombing went on." In fact, "I didn't do any work to speak of," he told me. That whole year, "I did not write much. The summer of '68 was spent *fucking*. Because of total depression about the situation" around Vietnam. Ellsberg didn't begin putting out Ds, or internal drafts at RAND, on his study until June 1969.[71] That is well over a year after he began work on it.

And his Ds, as Ellsberg granted, were rough and incomplete collections of thoughts that he had recorded in his notebooks, now grouped by subject. Some were apparently early drafts of book chapters, but many were notes rather than essays. Some were rambling and written in an almost stream-of-consciousness style. More than once, Ellsberg referred to other papers he planned to write, but never did. Several Ds consisted of his notes on comments by RAND consultants Vu Van Thai or Hoang Van Chi. Themes included the failure of the United States to exert sufficient pressure on the GVN and the need for more effective U.S. policies in the global fight against communists. Ellsberg expressed his desire to thwart or contain communism in Vietnam as late as that August, only one month before he would begin copying the Pentagon Papers. "As late as that summer, the question, 'How *could* we have won in Vietnam?' still held an intellectual attraction for me," he later acknowledged. And a *political* attraction, he might have added. Ellsberg did not criticize the war on moral grounds in his Ds. "They couldn't say how deeply I felt about the war," he explains. "They all had to be in the context of, 'How do you win a war like this?'" because of his hawkish boss, Charles Wolf, who was in charge of his study. And "I could only go so far . . . in a RAND-type report in criticizing the war."[72]

Ellsberg wrote "kind of a book-length manuscript," he remembers. He turned out "these fat Ds . . . at a rate that I never had. . . . I had a couple of secretaries, actually, working at simply transcribing those notes." He was working at home, "and I would ship this stuff to RAND, and transcribe it, and then I could patch this stuff together. So I was able to do it very fast, and I churned out these fast Ds. Which were really quite good." Helen Kwake transcribed some tapes for Ellsberg when his secretary was unavailable. She found them disorganized—like "fruit salad"—and virtually "all one run-on sentence." Further, "he never allowed enough time to get anything done on time," wasn't in his office a lot, and generally "didn't seem to do much," she remembers.[73]

Charles Wolf grew increasingly unhappy with Ellsberg's work. A highly organized, efficient, and methodical man, with high standards and conservative politics, Wolf remembers that Ellsberg had been

> subsidized by RAND to do a book that would be very critical of U.S. policy. And we knew that, and that was fine. But it had to be solid. Nathan Leites . . . and I were asked by Harry Rowen to oversee this project. And we did, and we spent hours reviewing his drafts and going over them with him. With commitments

that he would do thus and so and another draft by such and such a time. And his increasing inability to meet those criticisms and take the time to respond to them [was a problem]. . . . The promises to do second drafts and respond to criticism were breached. Were breached. When someone says to you, "I will get back to you, I will do this," and a week goes by, a month goes by, three months go by, and by which time you've given more comments on another chapter, then the credibility of subsequent promises erodes to nil.

Wolf believed Ellsberg was being dishonest with him.[74]

Others at RAND were aware of Ellsberg's problems with the study. "He had taken it upon himself to do a big thing, and it wasn't getting done," Albert Williams recalls. "He had not delivered. And there was grumbling about the fact he hadn't delivered: 'Is Dan ever going to do something? He's supposed to be doing the great piece.' . . . I think people were looking at those Ds and saying, 'Oh? What's this?' . . . I mean, here's somebody who made his name doing something with the Savage axioms, for Christ sakes, and they were rambling, they weren't sharply focused."[75]

Wolf concluded that Ellsberg simply wasn't getting anywhere. Moreover, whatever his problem was, it seemed to be getting worse. But "I thought, 'Tough shit. What do I care what Charlie Wolf [thinks],'" Ellsberg remembers. "He happened to be department chairman. But my status in this thing did not depend on him at all." As far as status went at RAND, "Charlie Wolf was not even comparable to me at that point." And "I wouldn't bother to tell Wolf what I was doing."[76]

Ellsberg spent a lot of time appraising Wolf's own work, a book manuscript Wolf and Leites had written on political rebellions. He made strong criticisms that may have fueled Wolf's criticisms of him. But, in Wolf's mind, Ellsberg took "the easy way out" by failing to complete his study and, instead, xeroxing the Pentagon Papers to "make a splash—'that will give me the recognition that will make me feel good.'" Ellsberg, Wolf thought, had "a fundamental character flaw . . . of wanting to shine all the time. And that shining being an essential part of his self-esteem." Others would also conclude that Ellsberg released the Papers in part because he couldn't finish his own Vietnam study.[77]

Ellsberg had problems completing other work at RAND at this time, too. Colleagues were asking, "When was he going to produce stuff?," Williams remembers. "People were talking at that point about how little he had produced." "RAND was very upset, because there were a couple of rather important reports that he had begun to write and hadn't finished," Jan Butler recalls. "They were major deliverables and he didn't make them. . . . He wasn't meeting his deadlines. It was clear he really wasn't going to complete these documents" (one surely being part of his Vietnam study).[78]

Much work at RAND was done collectively. A person could produce by contributing at meetings and being an intellectual spark plug. Talk was a valued commodity. Partly as a result, some at RAND still found Ellsberg a truly impressive intellectual force. Ben Bagdikian, who was writing a book at RAND at this time, was struck by Ellsberg's tremendous capacity for "acquiring information and analyzing it and then coming out with a position or with a set of positions. He sort of plunged into all of these things. . . . He would pursue almost anything that came up." Ellsberg was not someone who would shrink at meetings. "He was a presence at social gatherings, and he was a presence at meetings," Bagdikian recounts. "He would enter conversations and very quickly become a dominant element—in questioning, pursuing, bringing information that had not been brought into the conversation before." Long the brightest person in the room, "he had enormous self-confidence," Bagdikian thought. "He was not modest at all. But he didn't have pomposity. He just had aggressive intellectuality that tended to dominate whatever he was in." Bagdikian was amazed at how much Ellsberg knew and how quickly he would educate himself about something. He acquired information at an extremely rapid rate, and while he was opinionated and zealous, he was highly informed and "not immune to information that could change his mind. . . . Unless he was convinced of something, and then you had to have pretty good arguments against his questions."[79]

But in the eyes of others at RAND, the young genius was not flowering. Faith in his gift was declining. "After all these years of experience, I had come to the conclusion that there was probably less there than meets the eye," Gus Shubert recounts. "Yet his attitude always was one of, 'I can talk to this one, I can talk to that one, I'm the great white father. And if you don't believe me, ask Rowen.'"[80]

Harry Rowen was Ellsberg's big protector and defender at RAND. He continued to think Ellsberg a man of great potential. He enjoyed having him around (as much as he was around) and valued him considerably. Albert Williams co-wrote a paper with Rowen, "and Harry went out of his way to get input from Dan," Williams recalls. "He really clearly respected Dan highly for his intellect." Rowen was patient and tolerant of Ellsberg; he advised and listened to him, and welcomed him into his office. He invited Ellsberg to official RAND dinners. Rowen gave Ellsberg a "long lead" and "a lot of slack" on his Vietnam study, David McGarvey reminisces:

I think Rowen stuck his neck out for Dan during the period before the Pentagon Papers. Everyone knew that Dan was a pretty erratic person. They knew he had strong anti-Vietnam War feelings. They also knew it was hard for him to finish up something. And so they [Rowen and others] didn't really have to do this. I think they were really taking a chance. . . . They didn't have to keep him on this project for an extended period of time, and supporting him to do this. So I thought they were really extending him a lot of favors, so to speak. Kind of putting themselves out for him.

Rowen believed that, despite all of Ellsberg's problems, "this mystic of potential was going to suddenly blossom," Shubert remembers, although Rowen may have been getting a bit disenchanted himself by this point, as "this 'I'm going to have it tomorrow, tomorrow, tomorrow' had gone on now for many years, and there wasn't much."[81]

Rowen's friendship with Ellsberg inhibited criticism of him at RAND. "You don't go to Harry and say, 'Ellsberg's no good. Why doesn't RAND get rid of him?'" Robert Komer, who took a position at RAND in 1969, comments. "Or, 'He hasn't written a RAND project in three years.'" Charles Wolf had his hands tied by Rowen. Meanwhile, Ellsberg was issuing papers at RAND that were reprints of his past writings, lectures, and conference comments, and one book review.[82] He probably hoped they showed evidence of productivity.

Ellsberg's growing internal conflict over Vietnam surely contributed to his problems finishing work at this time. There were different minds in him contending with each other. What's more, the pressures he felt to produce must have been substantial. He knew that he knew more about Vietnam than virtually anyone; he was obsessed with the war; he had all the intellectual tools and more; expectations at RAND were high; and he realized he was disappointing people. Yet he still wasn't getting it done. His frustration was undoubtedly immense and growing. His head was a pressure cooker, building up steam.

Ellsberg's problem writing was one reason ("close to the only reason," he says) that he entered psychoanalysis in March of 1968. He and others at RAND hoped the analysis would unlock all that material inside him. When FBI agents came to RAND in the spring of 1970 to investigate an allegation that Ellsberg had been copying top-secret documents, Richard Best recalls, Rowen told the agents, in Best's presence, "Dan has been quite disturbed about the situation in Vietnam since he came back, and it occupies all his thought. He has not been productive. And we've been concerned about [it]. He was advised to consult a psychiatrist to see if he can clear up whatever blockage he has. He can't write anything." Ellsberg remembers that Bernard Brodie, Nathan Leites, and Roberta Wohlstetter had all suffered writing problems and advised him to seek help. "They all said, 'I was just like you. I had the same problem. I was psychoanalyzed. . . . It's a great process. You'll love it. You'll learn so much intellectually. It will change your view of the world. And you'll learn about yourself. . . . *And* it's the best thing you can do . . . for a writing problem.'" Brodie, in particular, was a major fan of psychoanalysis and very proud of how it had freed up his pen.[83]

But Ellsberg's difficulty writing was not the only reason he entered analysis. There was also his disturbing suicidal impulse in Vietnam; he later told an interviewer that he discussed it with his analyst. And there was his depression over Vietnam and his romantic failures. Perhaps larger self-doubts—social, career, accomplishment—also played a role. Who knows all the factors that were feeding his inner turmoil, though his difficult childhood was surely part of the mix, and probably in ways that were not obvious. It's impossible to determine the amalgam of motivations, and Ellsberg's explanations may not be accurate. He would later tell a journalist, "I just had always wanted to undergo psychoanalysis."[84] That is unconvincing.

Bernard Brodie put Ellsberg in touch with Dr. Ralph "Romy" Greenson, who was known for treating Hollywood celebrities. (William Kaufmann remembers "one dreadful dinner" where Greenson was being "extremely indiscreet" about his former patient Marilyn Monroe.) Greenson was also a consulting analyst and a conduit for people from RAND who sought treatment; he referred them to other analysts, including Drs. Lewis Fielding and Alfred Goldberg. Ellsberg recalls seeing Greenson "once or twice," and that Greenson steered him to Fielding.[85]

Fielding was not cheap. Ellsberg saw him four days a week, he says, for either one-and-a-half years or two-and-a-half years (his memory has varied on that). An informed guess would put Fielding's typical fee at around fifty dollars an hour then. In a statement she provided the FBI, Carol Ellsberg indicated that Dan paid $6,000 yearly for the treatment. RAND may have paid part of the cost of his analysis.[86]

Guy Pauker believes RAND subsidized Ellsberg's treatment in another way. "The rumor was—and probably true—that Harry Rowen increased Dan's salary when he came back to RAND after Vietnam to what turned out to be the highest salary paid to any staff member in RAND, in order to make it possible for Dan to get psychiatric treatment," Pauker recalls. "It was distinctly intended to make it possible for him to get intensive psychiatric treatment, which otherwise he would not have been able to afford." If that's true, Rowen was taking a personal interest in Ellsberg beyond that paid to most RAND employees. Ellsberg told me—more than once—that he had the highest salary of anyone at RAND outside the physics department, and was making $39,000 a year. (RAND's records show his top salary was actually $34,000.) Pauker believes one reason for Ellsberg's treatment was a "drug problem that worried Harry Rowen and RAND very, very much. They didn't want to lose him." Others from RAND also remember talk of Ellsberg and drugs. "A lot of people thought he was a lightweight," Anthony Russo reminisces, and according to one story "he had gotten into drugs and that had ruined him." Helen Kwake suspected Ellsberg was "on drugs." Once, Kwake recalls with a laugh, Carleen Abel, Ellsberg's secretary, "came over to me and she says, 'Now he's trying peyote.'"[87]

Ellsberg was initially quite excited by his psychoanalysis. But it ultimately proved disappointing to him. Lying on Fielding's couch, he talked about the car accident that had killed his mother, in particular about his reaction to word of his mother's death and his failure to grieve. But he "never got any insight" into his response, he recalls, other than that he must have felt unconscious resentment toward his mother. Fielding wasn't interested in the car accident or its implications, Ellsberg remembers. "After all, he was a strict Freudian. And he wasn't very interested in things as late as [age] fifteen. We only talked about childhood." Ellsberg says he never got any indication that Fielding considered the accident significant. He later thought this "outrageous." He told a friend that, in addition, Fielding would not put his writing problem at the center of their attention, as requested, and that it was not resolved. But both Dr. Roger Gould and Dr. Alfred Goldberg doubt Fielding would have only wanted to talk to Ellsberg about his early childhood. "I find that surprising, knowing Fielding," Goldberg comments. "In his discussions with me about psychoanalysis, that limitation, that you only talk about the first five years of a person's life, just did not exist as a governing principle in how Fielding saw his work and how he understood people's development." And it's "inconceivable" to Goldberg that Fielding would have overlooked the car accident or paid no attention to Ellsberg's writing problem. Fielding may have probed that problem in a roundabout way, leading Ellsberg to believe he wasn't focusing on it enough.[88]

Ellsberg's psychological troubles were evident to some of his co-workers. "I found him to be jumpy and erratic and bouncing around," Helen Kwake remembers. "He was a wild man." Ellsberg seemed perpetually wired to Kwake. "He would always talk in a staccato type of [voice]. And, 'Do this!' 'I've got to do this!' 'Oh!! I've got to do this!' It was always this very nervous [behavior]. And then he'd leap up on his chinning bar that he had installed across the main entrance of our little office, and do one arm [laughs]." Ellsberg "was acting so strange," Kwake thought, always "frenetic" and "so out of control":

> I was worried about Dan. Because he was so kooky. I mean, he would dictate a letter or something. He'd say, "I want to write a memo to so-and-so." And he'd say, "Now say, '[So-and-so] and Westmoreland said this. It was very important. Give that five exclamation points. *Dot dot dot. Dash dash.* Underline that! Oh, go back up and put that all in caps!'" So you had this thing that had things all over it, and after it was done, I'd say, "Oh, there's Dan's fruit salad."
>
> . . . He gave me a tape for a briefing he gave to the people at RAND who were in on the Vietnam studies. . . . And this one man asked him a question, and he started to answer it, and he would interrupt himself with a subthought all the way through, so that he never got back to the original [question]. For two pages. He just wandered. . . . And then he finally wound down after about five minutes. And then he said, "Does that answer your question?" And everybody snickered. And then the man said, "Well, I guess it's going to have to do." Dan was incapable of completing thoughts at that time.

Of course, one can be restless, wired, and ramble without being unduly disturbed. But when Kwake later saw Ellsberg on television during his trial, "he was so calm," she laughs. "I looked, I said, 'Who's that? . . . They must have him tranquilized.'"[89]

It was Ellsberg's erratic behavior, combined with his outspoken criticism of the war and growing antiwar associations, that led Kwake to perceive he was a security risk. "I just didn't think he was the type of person that should have a TS [top-secret] safe in his office," she says. Kwake told her supervisor of her concern, probably in 1970. "I said, 'You know, there is something going on, I think.' And then the lady said, 'Well, we'll handle it. Don't worry about it.'"[90]

To Konrad Kellen, Ellsberg's jumpiness, his frequently poor judgment, the tendency of his mind to run away from him, his wilder exaggerations and untruths that "come out of God knows where," suggested a man with some underlying difficulties. "He couldn't connect with reality in a strange sort of way," Kellen remembers. For example, "one minute he overestimates, and one minute he underestimates, what can or cannot be done" about Vietnam. "Things just ran away with him."[91]

Kellen and Ellsberg enjoyed each other's company, but the RAND analyst Ellsberg socialized with most was Anthony Russo. They were good friends whose offices were across the hall from each other. Andrew and Mary Marshall would tell the FBI in 1971 that "in recent years Ellsberg's only close male friend was Anthony Russo, and he seems to associate otherwise only with women. The past two years he has had little or no close relationship, either social or business, with any of his fellow RAND employees."[92] Russo and Ellsberg would strike some as an odd couple, though.

Russo was a likable person, fun and humorous, also brilliant, though his intelligence was sometimes underestimated. He had studied engineering in college, then worked for NASA in its magnetohydrodynamics division and published a paper on "the physics of electromagnetic waves in ionized gas," or, in other words, "the absorption of radio waves by a hot flow field." After studying physics and then foreign policy, econometrics, and game theory as a graduate student at Princeton, he had joined RAND. Like Ellsberg, he had begun to turn off on the war when he was in Vietnam, where he had supervised interviewers in RAND's infamous "Viet Cong Motivation and Morale Project," a grossly flawed study Russo recognized as such and criticized openly. By 1967, he felt the United States should quit Vietnam, he recalls. The following year, when Russo and Ellsberg became close, they were both quite critical of the destruction the United States was wreaking in Vietnam, but Russo was more inclined to question the cold war underpinnings of U.S. policy and to see the struggle of the NLF as a just one.[93]

Citing "budgetary problems," Charles Wolf fired Russo in May of 1968, forcing him to leave RAND at the end of the year. "Now, I know you're going to say this is political, but it's not," Wolf told Russo. Ellsberg protested Russo's firing.[94]

Ellsberg and Russo had begun spending time together at RAND after Joan Roberts, a friend of Russo, came into Russo's office one day and said that Ellsberg wanted to meet him. "I said, 'Well, I've already met him,'" Russo recounts. When Roberts brought Ellsberg by, Ellsberg acted as if he didn't remember meeting Russo in Vietnam. Russo thought that odd. "Dan is funny," Russo observes. "He's got the pose of an absent-minded professor that he goes into when he doesn't want to acknowledge something. He doesn't remember or he can't understand." (That's consistent with my own experience with him.) Russo told a journalist that Ellsberg had told Roberts "he wanted to meet some hippies. So she turned him on to me. People had warned me away from him, saying that he was a terrible climber and opportunist, cold, calculating, that whole rap. But he didn't strike me that way at first."[95]

Ellsberg asked Russo to brief him on the Viet Cong morale study. According to Russo, he briefed Ellsberg on it and related matters "just about every day" in

1968. Ellsberg was seeking information for his "lessons learned" study. "He pumped the hell out of my brain," Russo recalls. Russo also gave Ellsberg material from the morale study and loaned him books on Vietnam. "A box of books, he never gave back to me," Russo remembers. "Stuff that I told him I wanted back. You know how he is. . . . He's in such a lofty area that to come down to earth to remember to give somebody a book back" is not a high priority. Russo came to believe that he exerted a significant influence on Ellsberg's turnaround on the war.[96]

Ellsberg told Russo about the Pentagon Papers study. "I said, 'Dan, you've got to leak that stuff,'" Russo recalls. "We talked about leaking every day, all the time." Ellsberg showed Russo "a few things" from the Papers. Russo urged Ellsberg more than once to get the Papers out. "I remember he rolled his eyes at the ceiling" at first, Russo recounts. "It seemed like he felt that that was a big task." Indeed it was. Ellsberg then "kept trying to figure out *what* should be leaked, and maybe the whole thing should be leaked," Russo remembers. "He seemed to be thinking of how to leak it. . . . It occupied his mind a great deal." Russo believes his pushing was pivotal to Ellsberg's release of the Papers.[97]

Talking Vietnam at the office was the lifeblood of Ellsberg and Russo's relationship. Their social life was secondary. "Socially, Dan is kind of strange," Russo says. "You seem to be able to sense the insecurity, and that there was a shtick that he ginned up to cover that insecurity. . . . People always say he's intense. But there's something more to it. It's just an insecurity and working really hard to overcome and establish some image that he wants to establish to cover that insecurity." Even women were "sort of after the fact," Russo recalls. But Ellsberg "wanted to meet some hippie girls. . . . He had a fascination with hippie girls." Russo took him to a commune in Santa Monica known as the Idaho house. Ellsberg did indeed meet some hippie girls there, and he also spent some time with Kimberly Rosenberg, a beautiful 26-year-old divorced "hard-core Topanga Canyon hippie woman," the owner of a vegetarian café, who would later play a bit part in the Pentagon Papers affair.[98]

Ellsberg's unending pursuit of women was, once again, on display at RAND. "He had a special relationship with the girls," Konrad Kellen remembers. "The girls were interested in him. . . . And he always apparently had a lot going." Ellsberg was "cutting a swath through womanhood at RAND," Al Williams understood. One woman at RAND remarked to David McGarvey, "I stopped to chat with him in the hall, and he made a point of sort of looking me up and down." When McGarvey informed Albert Wohlstetter that Ellsberg was acting as a courier to take a classified paper from Santa Monica to Washington, "Albert's eyes kind of widened, and he said, 'Well, I hope he didn't find some tail and chase it to MIT or some place.'" Lynda Resnick, who would play

a key role in the copying of the Pentagon Papers, points out, "You have to understand, here was a really movie-star-handsome guy who women threw themselves at. . . . He was amazingly attractive and magnetic in every way."[99]

Ellsberg liked to squire attractive women to RAND parties. "I remember
my about-to-be-ex-wife disliked him intensely, because he was clearly a great
womanizer," Ben Bagdikian recounts. "Because he had different women every
time, and because he was so aggressive in his talking and his analysis and so
forth." Ellsberg also "had that reputation of all kinds of permutations" sexually,
Bagdikian recalls, "of loving every permutation of heterosexual sex that there
was. That he liked to do it in front of mirrors, he liked to do all sorts of . . . permutations of positions and all the sexual games and so forth. . . . He was re-
puted to have in his apartment a mirrored ceiling. . . . He was like a little
boy. . . . It was like playing with sex."[100]

Helen Kwake, who shared an outer office with Carleen Abel, got a glimpse
of Ellsberg's extracurricular activity at work. "We were sitting there typing one
day," Kwake recounts, "and some blond girl, a very pretty girl that worked at
RAND, came in. And he closed the door. She came out about two hours later. I
don't think they were talking about a serious [subject]. Because her clothing
was a mess. . . . It looked like he was trying out some karate holds or wrestling
holds. . . . And Carleen was ignoring [her]. I'm going, 'Carleen, did you see
that?'" But Abel kept typing. Another time, Kwake remembers, "I went into his
office, and for some reason he made a point of closing the door. And on the
back of the door was this big photograph of a woman—nude—swimming,
taken from underneath. He had taken the photo, so he'd let you know that."
Ellsberg "thought he was hot stuff" with women, Kwake perceived. "And it
wouldn't matter who the woman was. He wasn't that selective."[101]

Jan Butler concurs with some amusement:

> He was interested in sex like he was interested in anything. I mean, it was just
> one of his little hobbies. It was one of the things he was enthusiastic about. . . .
> He would not go out with a married person, but there was no single woman who
> was safe. And I mean nobody. He was just interested, and he just knew that
> everybody was different, and if he had the time he was going to sleep with every-
> body. . . . Homely and old would not have stopped Dan. That would have been
> interesting to him. . . . Crippled. I mean, it didn't matter. He was interested. And
> he was completely nondiscriminating. Completely. Except for the marriage
> thing. I didn't feel exclusive at all. I was not flattered by his attention.[102]

Ellsberg was fascinated by pornography. "He had a big collection of it" and
"his apartment was full of the stuff," recalled the journalist Peter Schrag, who

covered his trial. "He had a little bit of Danish pornography," Butler remembers. "A couple magazines. . . . And he showed it to me one time. . . . He made a comment about [how] he thought that the pictures were not very interesting, because it was obvious that the men were homosexuals. And I said, 'What makes you think so?' And he said, 'Because none of them have an erection.'" One woman who later worked for Ellsberg recounts, "One day I was sorting through stuff and there was this large box, and I opened it up, and it was this box full of really pretty sleazy pornographic stuff." It was "the stuff you get at those pornographic bookstores. . . . It was pretty straight, like 'Sally does,' but it was a whole box of hard-core stuff." (In the 1980s, Ellsberg and his friend Jeffrey Masson, the Freudian apostate and writer, had arguments about pornography that threatened to end their relationship, remembers one person who spoke to Masson about it: "And I had a discussion with Ellsberg trying to at least get him to acknowledge that there was some sexism in pornography. . . . And he was reluctant even to see that. He was reluctant to see that at all. And he was defending it as this great wonderful thing. Sort of saying, 'Maybe Hugh Hefner is a great sexual liberator of his generation, as someone who'd said sex was okay.' And not seeing that women walking about with bunny suits maybe is not such a positive view of women, [that] maybe there was a sexist side to *Playboy*."[103] Once, when Ellsberg opened a chest at his house in search of some notes he wanted to give me, he appeared to try to quickly conceal some pornography in the chest.)

Ellsberg continued to talk openly with others about sex. One RAND colleague recalls hearing "off-the-wall sexual stories." Seymour Martin Lipset got a heavy dose of Ellsberg's tales the summer of 1968. Ellsberg was forever telling Lipset about the new and different things he'd experienced and about the action he'd enjoyed the night before—"trying to show now that he was a real man," Lipset remembers. "Showing off." Ellsberg also talked sex with some women, including Roberta Wohlstetter and Mary Marshall, both of whom were married. Marshall recounts:

> He did it a couple of times when I'm sitting in my living room in a chair, and he's over on the couch and ruminating about what his future attitude would be toward Patricia [Marx] if he married her, and how often he would have sex with her. In other words, he was going to forswear any of his philandering. . . . That was the implication. I mean, he was going to settle down, and, oh, he'd probably only have sex a couple times a week. I'm trying hard not to show my amazement. Not disapproval, because I also liked Dan . . . so I wasn't sitting there clucking. It's just that I'm sitting there thinking, "Why are you telling me this?"[104]

There was a lot for Ellsberg to tell the summer of 1968. "I spent the summer swinging," he remembers. He saw a "succession of girls," "one girl after another," "for the first time in my life really a lot of girls. . . . Promiscuity is not even the word for it. . . . There isn't a good word for what I was doing that summer." Perhaps desperate or out of control would do. Ellsberg sometimes swung with just one woman, but usually he engaged with two, three, or four other people, he recalls. The men in these group-sex sessions never touched each other, he says. But the women made love to each other. The age range of the swingers stretched from the late 20s to the 60s. Ellsberg later told a close friend that he was one of the favorites of swingers who held parties, as all the women wanted him, "although at that time I think he would have probably thrown up at the idea of swinging with a man," the friend says. But "his whole attitude toward bisexuality" later began "shifting very radically."[105]

Ellsberg frequented, among other places, The Swing, a swingers' bar run by a former actor named Greg McClure and his wife, Joyce. "Luv Thy Neighbor," its marquee read. Ellsberg represented himself as "Don Hunter" at The Swing. He did not want his real name listed in the address books of people he did not know well—what if they were arrested and their books were seized?—and worried that "RAND wouldn't have been too pleased." He could lose his security clearance for this, too. (RAND had immediately jerked the clearances of two of its men who were picked up by the vice squad in gay bars. "They didn't even come back into the building," Jan Butler remembers.) Don Hunter was a modification of Andrew Hunt, the pseudonym that Ellsberg and others had used on the *Harvard Advocate*. For a time, Ellsberg had used Andrew Hunt when swinging, "but then I thought, well, I shouldn't appropriate it for these purposes," he recalled. Later, after Ellsberg became famous, one man whom he had met at an orgy and who now suspected that Don Hunter was really Daniel Ellsberg approached him at a rally and told him "how proud he was to have known him," a journalist recounted. "Ellsberg was horror-stricken and asked [the man] to forget about Don Hunter."[106]

"But aside from the pseudonym," Gay Talese wrote, Ellsberg "was hardly cautious about the people he associated with in the bar, or the places he later went for sex parties; he was open to suggestions, was as comfortable in large crowds as in threesomes, and he took pride in his energy and style as a lover. Even after he had made copies of the Pentagon Papers, and might have assumed that the FBI would soon be tapping his telephone and tailing him by car, Ellsberg made no attempt to conceal his nocturnal carousing, traveling from swing bar to orgy—and also to Sandstone [a sexual retreat]—as casually as if he were attending a reunion of Harvard alumni." If true, those are acts of a risk taker, a reckless man, perhaps one who gets high on danger, or an obsessive man. "I never went back to that life of kind of desperate searching around from one person to another," he would say later. It was "sort of a lost summer for me." But "I've never regretted spending the summer that way . . . compared to anything else that was available." Ellsberg denied swinging after he started copying the Pentagon Papers, however, claiming that he stopped the same day President Johnson stopped the bombing of North Vietnam in the fall of 1968. But Talese would put him at Sandstone with Russo and girls from a commune three times the summer of 1970 (nine or ten months after they had begun copying, and after Ellsberg had become engaged again to Patricia Marx).[107]

Ellsberg got Jan Butler out to The Swing one night. "He had car trouble and he called me up and needed a ride back to his place," Butler recounts:

> And so I went out to the [San Fernando] Valley. It was about nine o'clock. And he was sitting on a curb reading the *Wall Street Journal*. . . . He said in order to pay me back for this great service, because he knew I'd been ready for bed when he called, he wanted to take me out for a drink. Well, I knew he didn't drink, because he'd had hepatitis and couldn't. And I said it wasn't necessary. And he really pushed it. Which was unlike him. Well, we end up at this place called The Swing. And when we walked in, you had to put a name tag on. And he said, "Don't use your real name." . . . So I was Joyce.
>
> And we went in, and he introduced me to the bartender, who apparently is the person who passes on whether or not you'll be invited to orgies. . . . He told Dan to bring me to his parties anytime you want. But I still didn't catch on. . . . And then we were sitting having a drink, and a man came up and asked me to dance. And I said, "No thank you," I was with somebody. And he looked a little taken aback. And Dan said, "No, go ahead. Go with him." . . . I mean, it really was extremely peculiar. Anyway, I guess I did dance with this guy, and he wanted me to go home with him to Pasadena. And I said, " . . . I'm with somebody, and I don't know you." And he said, "He won't mind. Believe me."

Butler declined the man's offer.[108]

On at least one occasion, Ellsberg tried to get Butler to join him at a "private party." "He said, 'You don't have to participate. There are rooms where you can pretend like you don't even know what's going on in this mansion,'" Butler recounts. "'But,' he said, 'I need a date. I can't go by myself.' And I said, 'Find one somewhere else.' He called me back then ten minutes later just to make sure I hadn't changed my mind after he got off [the phone]."[109]

Ellsberg did some of his swinging with another girlfriend, an adventurous sort whom, like Butler, he lived with on and off in Malibu. "She was my main rival," Butler remembers. Butler was in Ellsberg's beach house one morning only to notice her rival jogging by—not a pleasant sight for her.[110]

Three or four times, Ellsberg says (six or seven, Talese said), he ventured to Sandstone, a secluded nudist lapland on 15 acres, high up narrow, dangerous, zigzagging roads in the hills of Topanga Canyon. At parties there, members were typically greeted by a woman at a registration desk wearing only glasses; she turned away unwanted arrivals. Some people might be making it on a couch in the reception room; at buffet dinners, the convention was to eat naked. Downstairs was a large semidark room with a fireplace, mats, and pillows. This was where most of the action took place. Ellsberg's friend John Sack, who visited Sandstone a number of times, never thought people were having a lot of fun or showing much passion there, however. "It was just very quiet, steady sex," Sack remembers. "It was almost like a moral obligation, some sort of ritual that you had to do because this was the new thing."[111]

Ellsberg was a card-carrying member of Sandstone. According to Talese, he "adjusted more quickly to the place" than did Anthony Russo. "That's a lot of shit," Russo responds. After the Pentagon Papers came out, one woman at Sandstone who took a liking to Don Hunter saw his picture in the media, and she, too, realized that Don Hunter was really Daniel Ellsberg. She had thought Don Hunter was a good lover.[112]

Russo's dominant memory of Ellsberg at Sandstone is of an episode where his self-doubts seemed to show. "There was one couple there going away at it. And he said, 'That's how I do it.' I'm good, too [laughs]. . . . 'I can fuck like that.'" Ellsberg made the remark "just as seriously as anything," Russo recalls. Russo's memory triggered another one he had of Ellsberg years later: "He asked me, 'When you travel, do girls come on to you?' He said, 'Everywhere I go, they don't come on to me.' He said, 'I haven't had an affair yet.' . . . He was the big hero, and he had to be like Mick Jagger. There had to be all these groupies after him. And he was disturbed that there were not." Sally Binford, who had introduced both Russo and Ellsberg to Sandstone, made what Russo considered a telling observation of Ellsberg after the Pentagon Papers were published and she saw him on television. "She was laughing and saying, 'Look, he looks so good on TV. In person, he's a putz.' That kind of gets to it. He worked real hard to structure himself and to get himself all looking really good. And he brings it off." But "it's like some people would look at [him] and say, 'Oh, what a handsome dude. He really comes off good on TV.' And other people would say, 'This guy's a putz.' I think that's how he looked at himself. I think he really went to the limit to impress people as to how strong he was, what a lover he was, how smart he was—the whole thing. And it gets back to that insecurity."[113]

Ellsberg also visited Elysium, a "pleasure-oriented" nudist "growth center" in Topanga Canyon, as well as the Esalen Institute in northern California, another personal growth center. He enjoyed sunbathing in the nude at his home, too. He wasn't concerned about what other people thought. One of Ellsberg's neighbors was a friend of Albert Williams, and the neighbor would tell Williams about seeing Ellsberg sunning himself naked on his deck where other people could see him. "These neighbors were kind of embarrassed to be jogging along the beach and having Dan lying out there naked," Williams remembers. (Years later, when Leslie Henriques knocked on Ellsberg's door to report to work for him and meet him for the first time, Ellsberg appeared with only a towel on. Though Ellsberg had just gotten out of the shower, "I thought it was a little strange," Henriques recalls.)[114]

Some at RAND envied Ellsberg's lifestyle. Harry Rowen "said that he thought we ought to use Dan's life as a recruiting poster to get summer people out to RAND," Jan Butler remembers. "He was living with Miss Moneypenny [the name of James Bond's secretary]—that's what he called me." And Ellsberg "had a sports car. He lived on the beach. I mean, he was talking about this ideal little life that Dan had. And you could tell that there was tremendous . . . envy. . . . He just thought Dan was terrific and had this wonderful life."[115]

Albert Wohlstetter, Rowen, and others had a theory about Ellsberg's recent life changes. "As they perceived it, he had moved from being sort of square, the military, RAND guy to being hippie-ish, drugs, women . . . the whole shtick," Seymour Martin Lipset recounts. "And with this was politics. . . . They had the sense that he'd changed 180 degrees" and "went overboard." Their interpretation of this, recalls Lipset, who felt it made a certain amount of sense, "was that he had gotten married when he was very, very young, and he had never had a sort of youth, adolescence. So now he splits and he becomes single again. So this is his catching up, and, of course, in a cultural period when you could do this more easily than in the earlier period." They felt Ellsberg had not sown his wild oats, and now that he'd gotten free he was making up for it. But, they believed, Ellsberg would outgrow this phase and come back to battery. He'd be back in shape again.[116]

In the spring of 1968, Ellsberg met someone who would propel him further away from Rowen's and Wohlstetter's views. Much further—like into another universe. He was attending a conference on revolution at Princeton University, co-sponsored by the American Friends Service Committee. The conference had brought together people on both sides of the Vietnam issue. Ellsberg hoped to learn more about how to counter revolutions. At the conference he met a number of peace activists, whom he likely questioned at some length. But one in particular attracted his attention. She was a striking woman of some 27 years. Antiwar activist Randy Kehler found her almost "breathtaking" at a later conference in August 1969. "I think some part of me fell immediately in love with her," Kehler recalls. "She was vivacious and outgoing, and obviously very attractive physically. And engaging in conversation; clearly very bright. . . . She just had a magnetism that was unbelievable. . . . She laughed a lot. She had tremendous energy. She was just this sort of infectious personality."[117]

The woman's name was Janaki Tschannerl, and she was Indian. Her parents were Gandhians. A graduate student at Harvard, she was married to an Austrian pacifist whom she had met in the Gandhian movement. She was a committed Gandhian and pacifist, serious about her politics. She wore a sari and a bindi on her forehead. "I was sitting at the table with her," Ellsberg recounts. "And I was both attracted by her *and* very interested in what she was saying, which had to do with Gandhian thinking. And I began talking to her about it. And we ended up, really, spending all of our time together for the next several days." Tschannerl, who says she was not at the conference that long, remembers saying a few words to the participants about nonviolence in India and the United States, and "Dan coming up to me, and asking me, 'Well, how come you're wearing a leather coat?' . . . Pinpointing a certain contradiction. . . . So we started talking right there. And we spent several hours talking right at the conference site. And so I talked about Martin Luther King and India and . . . the whole philosophy of nonviolence." Ellsberg's questions about nonviolence were probing. He wanted to know how it might be applied to Vietnam and other situations of realpolitik. "It was very intense," Tschannerl recalls. "We covered the whole gamut of nonviolence in history. . . . He wouldn't let go of ideas once he got hold of them. He'd want to look at it and examine it." Ellsberg's arguments were not unfamiliar to Tschannerl, but she (like many others over the years) found her encounter with him exhausting.[118]

Tschannerl piqued Ellsberg's interest in Gandhian thought and suggested books for him to read. They stayed in touch after the conference, talking over the phone a good deal, and getting together in several places. They had "a personal relationship," Ellsberg told me. "I saw living a life with her possibly, which had the limitation that I was never erotically close to her; she was a very austere, unsensual person or woman," he told another interviewer. "It was really a spiritual relationship, where I thought of her as someone who inspired me and taught me. . . . I thought of her a lot in this period, the fact that we

1. Ellsberg (far left, front row) and other members of his entering seventh-grade class at Cranbrook prep school, 1943. His classmate Richard Townsend is at far right. (Courtesy Richard Townsend)

2. Ellsberg (holding basketball) with his seventh-grade intramural basketball team at Cranbrook. His classmate Charles Maxwell is to his immediate right. (Courtesy Cranbrook Archives)

3. Ellsberg (front center) and other members of the debate team at Cranbrook in 1945. Jim Prowse, brother of Juliet Prowse, is behind Ellsberg's left shoulder. (Courtesy Cranbrook Archives)

4. Ellsberg playing the piano in Cranbrook's Amateur Night competition in 1948. (Courtesy Cranbrook Archives)

5. Daniel and Carol Ellsberg holding the purloined ibis at Harvard. (Courtesy Carol Cummings)

6. Kirby Hall with Daniel and Carol Ellsberg. (Courtesy Kirby Hall)

8. Ellsberg and Donald Hall punting in Cambridge, England, in 1953. (Courtesy Kirby Hall)

9. Ellsberg in his Marine officer dress. (Courtesy Kirby Hall)

Left 7. Donald and Kirby Hall. (Courtesy Kirby Hall)

10. Ellsberg with his son Robert. (Courtesy Carol Cummings)

11. Ellsberg (center) playing a war game at the RAND Corporation in the late 1950s. His RAND colleague David McGarvey is to his right. (Leonard McCombe/Time Pix)

12. The RAND Corporation. (Author photo, 1995)

13. Daniel and Carol Ellsberg's home in Los Angeles in the early 1960s. (Author photo, 1995)

15. John Paul Vann (center) and Ellsberg (right) in Vietnam. (Library of Congress)

Left 14. Daniel and Carol Ellsberg at a Kennedy inaugural ball in Washington, D.C., in January 1961. (Courtesy Carol Cummings)

16. Anthony Russo (right) with a rice farmer who had become a refugee in Vietnam. (Courtesy Anthony Russo)

17–18. Daniel Ellsberg in the late 1960s. (Courtesy Jan Butler)

19. Ellsberg in Bedouin garb. (Courtesy Jan Butler)

20. Jan Butler, RAND's Top Secret Control officer and one of Ellsberg's girlfriends. (Courtesy Jan Butler)

21. Robert and Mary Ellsberg at ages 12 and 9, a year before they would help their father copy the Pentagon Papers. (Courtesy Carol Cummings)

22. Robert and Mary two or three years later. (Courtesy Carol Cummings)

23. 10 Hilliard Street in Cambridge, Massachusetts. Daniel and Patricia Ellsberg occupied the third-floor flat in the early 1970s. (Author photo, 1996)

24. Ellsberg and Anthony Russo outside the Los Angeles courthouse in August 1971 before Russo entered jail for refusing to testify before the grand jury. (Courtesy Anthony Russo)

25. (From left) Peter Schrag, Daniel Ellsberg, Anthony Russo, and Stanley Sheinbaum during Ellsberg and Russo's trial. (Courtesy Stanley Sheinbaum)

26. 450 N. Bedford Drive in Beverly Hills, site of the 1971 burglary of Dr. Lewis Fielding's office. (Author photo, 1996)

27. Daniel and Patricia Ellsberg outside the Los Angeles courthouse after the government's case against Ellsberg was dismissed on May 11, 1973. © Bettman/CORBIS.

28. Ellsbeg and his son Michael at an antinuclear rally in 1979. © Roger Ressmeyer/CORBIS

might live her kind of life around the world." He was "romantically involved" with her, Carol Ellsberg later reported to the FBI. He has often spoken of Tschannerl in glowing terms. "Certainly people have misinterpreted his tone sometimes," Tschannerl told me. "Certainly I was in a happy marriage."[119]

Tschannerl had a profound influence on Ellsberg's political thinking. At the conference, she had said, "The concept of enemy has no meaning in my life." No enemies? The idea intrigued Ellsberg. He had considered communists enemies for years. His career had focused to a large degree on combating them. He had even shot at some in Vietnam. It came as a revelation to him that there was a coherent philosophy of nonviolence; he was taken with the Gandhian emphases on truth-telling, openness, and honesty (despite his own dishonesties, or perhaps partly because of them).[120]

Ellsberg's education continued as he read a lot of pacifist and Gandhian literature back at RAND. The literature had a steady influence on him. In one book that influenced him, Barbara Deming's *Revolution and Equilibrium*, Ellsberg tellingly noted, twice, the concept of narcissistic rage next to passages on the need to exercise control over one's actions and life. He also talked to other pacifists, though Tschannerl is "the one who had the strongest influence on my life," he remembers.[121]

Meanwhile, Ellsberg and Patricia Marx had begun seeing each other again on occasion. "I was pretty reserved" at first, Patricia recalls. But they began to talk things out over the phone. "I told him I was pretty angry and upset, for him just kind of not communicating with me, and then calling out of the blue [from Europe] and saying, 'Come join me,'" she recounts. "But we began to clear things up." According to a later friend of Ellsberg, Patricia surprised Ellsberg during this period when she phoned him and indicated that she was now ready to take LSD with him, which she had declined to do earlier.[122] Like Ellsberg, Marx was open to countercultural experiences and experimentation.

When Marx visited Ellsberg in California in around the spring of 1969, she found that the "same old spark was there." Their relationship was on again, so to speak. That fall, Patricia flew out to California again to be with Ellsberg. "That was the beginning of when we really got back together," she reminisces. "Now we were agreeing totally" on Vietnam.[123]

G. Gordon Liddy would later report to the CIA's Dr. Bernard Malloy an incident that occurred around this time: "A very reliable source advised that while the subject [Ellsberg] was residing at his California oceanfront home, the subject telephoned the source who was in Denver at the time. The subject said to the source, 'You'll never guess who I've got in the sack beside me,' and apparently held the phone to the ear of his companion. The source, thinking he was replying to the subject answered, 'The Swede.' Back came a response, 'No, you son-of-a-bitch, it's Pat Marx.'"[124] One may speculate that Liddy's source could have been John Vann, who was betraying Ellsberg at the time of Liddy's report.

Ellsberg broke the news of his reunion with Patricia to the Swede, Yvonne Svenle, who would later confide to one person that he had told her, in effect, he was choosing Patricia over her partly because Patricia was smarter and better educated. "She was very hurt by it," the person remembers, adding, "It had the ring of truth. Because he always used to say that so-and-so's not very bright, or he's very bright." Ellsberg would still see Yvonne after he married Patricia, however. "I think he still liked Yvonne after he was married," Anthony Russo recalls. "He came to see me a couple of times when I was in jail [in 1971], and one day he said that he and Pat had taken acid, and he was bummed out because Pat looked very wizened and wrinkled."[125]

Patricia informed John Simon of her reunion with Ellsberg. "I was very, very fond of her," Simon remembers. "As I still am. And I'm sure that for quite a while I was very upset and shaken by the end of this thing." "The Eddie Fisher of the Pentagon Papers," one writer would call Simon, referring to the man Elizabeth Taylor left for Richard Burton. When the critic Frank Rich became friendly with him in the mid-1970s, Simon "frequently brought up the subject of Pat Marx," Rich recalls. "John Simon always struck me as being somewhat devastated about having [lost her]." But Simon and Patricia still saw each other occasionally "in a friendly way" and talked over the phone after she married Ellsberg. "And until recently—I made a point of this—I would call her up on her birthday," Simon told me in late 1995. And "I remember her writing to me that she was worried that her son [Michael] would have the same birthday as mine, which she didn't want" but which occurred. Eventually relations waned. But "I remember her very warmly, and I will to my dying day," Simon says.[126]

Simon is not fond of Ellsberg. "He hates him," one person who knows both men says. "I was very amused when a woman friend who was quite close to Pat described Ellsberg's looks in a kind of comic way, as looking like a goat or something of that sort," Simon remembers. And "he's a competitive sort of fellow; apparently there was a phase when he decided that he could be as good a film critic as anybody, and certainly as good as I. He was sort of trying to set himself up as a film critic for a while . . . to prove that he could be as good or better at that."[127]

Ellsberg proposed to Patricia on the beach in Malibu in late 1969. It was "something she was not really ready to accept for some time," he recounted, and "something I had not expected to do." His proposal came two days after hearing that Janaki Tschannerl had died, according to his retelling. He was "still shell-shocked from this experience." Randy Kehler had given him the news about Janaki, not knowing that the Janaki who had died was actually a *different* Janaki. "Dan went into a tailspin," Kehler recalls. "A total tailspin. He told me afterward that he went out on the beach . . . and he just walked up and down the beach, crying and weeping and sobbing. . . . He said he felt that the light of his world had gone out." Ellsberg would remember "feeling that there were a few individuals in my life who sort of kept out the dark," and "that my life was suddenly getting very constricted." He walked the beach "all that night," he said. "The notion of reincarnation recurred to me, the fact that she was present somehow in the light, in the birds, in the gulls." Moved by that thought, Ellsberg wrote a poem entitled "Janaki" that included images of darkness, the ocean, a rising red sun, "a disc of red dust on the sky's forehead," and "one dark gull" that "shines in no ordinary light."[128]

When Tschannerl read the poem later, she was completely bowled over by it. "It was about somebody else rather than me," she recalls. "I just find it all very difficult to take, these kind of large feelings."[129]

Meanwhile, Ellsberg's career had, for a time, been looking up. In December 1968, incoming National Security Adviser Henry Kissinger had requested a study of U.S. policy options in Vietnam from RAND. Kissinger contacted his friend Guy Pauker, who flew out to meet with him at the headquarters of the shadow Nixon team at the Hotel Pierre in New York. "I need a study from you on how to extricate from Vietnam," he told Pauker. The extrication would have to occur "honorably," of course; Richard Nixon's would not be the first administration to lose a war. Pauker went to Harry Rowen, who "immediately pulled Dan into this," Pauker remembers. Credit another Rowen assist to Ellsberg. In Ellsberg's recounting, he was the "head" of the study: "I was totally in charge of writing, of organizing the work, on the options paper." Actually, Rowen supervised work on it.[130]

Kissinger agreed to Ellsberg's involvement, but, according to Ellsberg, expressed concern about his discretion. It was "the first time in my life that someone had raised a question of my discretion," Ellsberg claims, which is, of course, far from the case. "Because discretion was my profession." Ellsberg was "startled to hear it." In fact, "I was amazed. . . . I said, 'How could he possibly have raised a question like that? Nobody has ever raised a question like that before.'" But he assured Kissinger he'd be discreet, "as I always had been." According to Ellsberg, Kissinger raised the question of his discretion with Fred Iklé (who also worked on the study), but Iklé has no memory of that, and Morton Halperin says, "In fact, if he [Kissinger] would have objected, it [Ellsberg's participation] wouldn't have happened."[131]

Ellsberg was thrilled to be tabbed for this prestigious assignment. After working on the options study with others at RAND, he flew to New York with Rowen and Iklé on Christmas day, he recounted. Some Kissinger recruits were surprised to see him at the Pierre. "I'd heard of Ellsberg," one said later. "He was a wild man." At the hotel, Ellsberg worked with Halperin, Iklé, and Rowen on the study; he sat down with Kissinger several times, he said. Iklé and Halperin both remember Ellsberg's work as one of his targeted efforts. "That was a situation in which Dan was really very focused," Halperin recalls. Ellsberg has often claimed that *he* wrote the options paper, but, here again, it was a joint effort, and Iklé did the final drafting. Ellsberg departed the Pierre before the study was actually completed. "He had to leave early and see his girlfriend or whatever," Iklé remembers. "He was going to see a date."[132]

Ellsberg did another consulting job for Kissinger right afterward, developing a list of questions on Vietnam—known internally as National Security Study Memorandum 1 or NSSM-1—to put to U.S. government agencies and helping to summarize the answers. "It was my idea to send those questions out," he recounted. (In fact, a rash of questionnaires was sent out to U.S. agencies at this time.) Also, "I wrote all the questions, all but one, strictly speaking." And he was the only person to read all the reports, Ellsberg said. Halperin remembers that, again, Ellsberg was very focused and produced on schedule. Ellsberg also claims that he wrote "the bulk of" the paper summarizing the answers with help from Winston Lord, but the fact is Lord wrote most of it.[133]

The paper showed Ellsberg's enormous knowledge of the war and critical skills: the questions were searching, penetrating, pointed. It was brilliant work that few people could have pulled off.[134]

Ellsberg remembers his work on the options paper and NSSM-1 as "the first piece of staff work that RAND had ever done for the president of the United States." It was "the highest level work that RAND has ever done. . . . Nobody at RAND had written anything that big before." RAND had moved from influencing the secretary of defense to influencing the White House, "and *I* was the one who had done that." Actually, other RAND analysts were then doing other studies for Kissinger.[135]

Ellsberg expressed interest in doing additional studies for Kissinger, but Kissinger said that wouldn't be necessary. Ellsberg was probably envious of Kissinger's career rise. Though smarter and equally ambitious, Ellsberg was not as adroit at smoothing and manipulating others as Kissinger (partly because he couldn't control himself, listen, or respond to other people's moods as well as Kissinger). It undoubtedly frustrated and disheartened Ellsberg when it became clear that Kissinger would not be taking his advice on Vietnam; the Nixon administration largely disregarded the lessons of NSSM-1. Another shot at getting his ideas implemented had come to naught. He subsequently expressed anger at Kissinger to Sam Popkin. "Fury," Popkin remembers. "White fury." Because Kissinger *"didn't listen to Dan. . . .* It really, really bothered him that Henry wasn't listening to him. He was really pissed off. Henry was under his skin. Henry was really under his skin. . . . Kissinger wasn't letting him be his strategist."[136]

Ellsberg's frustration and anger likely pushed him further into opposition on Vietnam.

———

So did reading the Pentagon Papers. The study—called by Leslie Gelb the OSD Vietnam Task Force studies—had been growing steadily since Ellsberg had initially come into contact with it. Its team of researchers—from the military, State, Defense, academia, RAND and other think tanks—had multiplied sixfold. The pages had been growing at a dizzying pace. The thing had taken on a life of its own. It was almost out of control. When completed in January 1969, it totaled 47 volumes, or 7,000 pages "about four feet long," Gelb wrote.[137]

Under Paul Warnke's authority, copies had gone out to about a half dozen Johnson administration officials, Henry Kissinger, and several official repositories. Those repositories included RAND, because, Warnke recalls, "we wanted to have access to them [the Papers]. I was sent a copy after I left the Pentagon, and I didn't have any secure storage of my own." RAND would be a safe place, Warnke reasoned, and obtaining ready access from Defense or another government department might be more difficult. At RAND, one could control them more easily. But Ellsberg says that Halperin later told him "it had nothing to do with that. They had plenty of other places they could store it. They were trying to get it off the books . . . so that Walt Rostow would not find that copy and destroy it. They were afraid that Walt Rostow would track down every copy of this thing and destroy it." Halperin, Gelb, and Warnke were indeed concerned about the study's survival, and Halperin for one had worried that if Rostow or Lyndon Johnson learned about the study as it was being done, they would put an end to it.[138]

RAND did keep the study off the books. At the instruction of Halperin or Gelb, Rowen directed that it not be logged into RAND's normal Top Secret Control system. Jan Butler and her Top Secret Control counterpart in RAND's Washington office were not informed of it. "We were circumvented completely," Butler says. The move was probably meant to facilitate the access of Warnke, Halperin, and Gelb, and to limit the access of others. Rowen would later deny under oath that he had even been aware that the study was stored outside of RAND's system. "Harry was a liar," Richard Best told me, three times for emphasis. Under an agreement with Rowen, access to either of RAND's two copies would be subject to the approval of two people from the triad of Warnke, Halperin, and Gelb.[139]

Carrying two locked briefcases, Ellsberg had brought ten volumes of the study back to RAND Santa Monica from RAND Washington after completing his work on NSSM-1 in early March 1969. The blue-covered volumes were double wrapped in brown paper. Ellsberg deposited them in his top-secret safe at RAND, which had a combination lock on the front. He brought eight more volumes of the study back from Washington that August. This time he forgot to bring his courier designation with him from Santa Monica, so RAND had to make a copy for him. Again, Ellsberg placed the volumes in his safe.[140]

He had obtained the documents with another big assist from Rowen. Before his first trip, Ellsberg had had "quite a dispute" with Gelb about taking the volumes to Santa Monica. He had then phoned Rowen, who had called Halperin to secure permission. "Rowen called me and asked if Ellsberg could get access," Halperin recounts:

> I talked to Gelb and Warnke, because the understanding was that you needed two of the three. And I remember Gelb saying to me, "Do you really think he can be trusted with them?" And I said, "No." . . . And so I went back to Rowen and said, "No." Then he came back to me and said, "Look. Dan Ellsberg has a top-secret clearance. He is working for the Defense Department under contract with RAND on the lessons of the Vietnam War. And the Defense Department knows that he's working on this study. They are giving him access to very sensitive documents in the Defense Department on Vietnam. How can you guys make an independent judgment that he should not be trusted with these documents?" He said basically that he'd agreed to have them stored at RAND with the understanding that RAND would benefit from them. And that we were putting him in this awkward position, that he was sitting on a document of very great relevance to what Ellsberg was doing *officially* for the government. And that he didn't see the basis for us interposing our own judgment.

> So I went back to Gelb and said that while I still had some doubts, that seemed right to me. And he agreed. And we decided not to go to Warnke. . . . We decided not to burden him with that decision. And we were pretty sure he would say no anyway. So we gave permission for Ellsberg to have access to the documents.

Warnke confirms he would have said no, but not because of any concern about Ellsberg specifically. "I basically was very much opposed to giving access. I thought that that was a decision that McNamara ought to make. . . . I turned down everybody." As for Gelb's and Halperin's doubts, "We knew that Dan was feeling very strongly about the war, and therefore he would be tempted to release these documents," Halperin recalls.[141] It was only because Rowen stuck his neck out for Ellsberg, then, that he obtained access to them.

But Ellsberg will have none of this. Anybody who remembers worrying that he would release the study "is remembering it wrongly," he asserts. "It was unthinkable that anybody would do anything with it who had access to it. . . . I wasn't getting access to all this stuff despite fear that I might leak it. . . . There's something very odd about their memory." Halperin, who was working for the Clinton White House when I interviewed him, "cannot speak that frankly" about this, Ellsberg argues, because he might contradict his earlier testimony to the FBI on the Pentagon Papers and thus "he'd be in trouble right now." Moreover, the argument Rowen made for granting him access "wouldn't make any sense," Ellsberg maintains.[142]

Rowen twice kept Ellsberg's volumes of the study in one of his own top-secret safes at RAND when Jan Butler was checking Ellsberg's safe during her inventories. That was to make sure they stayed out of RAND's system. Butler believes Ellsberg also sometimes kept documents at his home.[143]

Ellsberg was supposed to be secretive with colleagues at RAND about possessing the Papers. Hans Heymann had a memorable encounter with him that summer. "I went to see him for something," Heymann recounts. "And somehow his secretary said, 'Oh, he's in there. Why don't you just walk in?' Well, I opened the door, and he was standing at his safe. And as soon as he saw me, he slammed the safe door and he looked absolutely crestfallen. And I said, 'My, you're jumpy. Why are you so nervous?'"[144]

Ellsberg's reading of his second batch of the Pentagon Papers had quite an impact on him. It included the study's early volumes that showed that U.S. officials had been warned of the risks and costs in Vietnam from the very beginning, yet they chose to disregard them. Ellsberg also began to see the war as a case of American aggression and, hence, illegitimate.[145]

He was a wealth of information on the war by this time. He was one of the first people David Halberstam interviewed for his book *The Best and the Brightest.* "Dan was extremely valuable," Halberstam remembers. "Because he had access to the documents . . . he knew something about the planning, about the decision making, that the rest of us didn't know. So that gave him an added insight on certain questions. . . . While I and my friends knew a lot about what had happened on the ground [in Vietnam], we didn't know what had happened on the ground in Washington in the period before '65. And clearly he did." Halberstam never really hit it off with Ellsberg personally, however. "What interests him interests him and nothing else interests him," Halberstam says. "When we had a friendship, it was really driven by Vietnam, not by personal connection."[146]

But it was not simply Ellsberg's intellectual journey on Vietnam, his exposure to new ideas and new politics, the influence of Janaki Tschannerl (powerful as it was), and his growing distaste for the death and destruction that brought about his transformation on the war. Increasingly, the war had seemed to him unwinnable the way it was being fought. But he had been unable to get his ideas implemented by those at the top and was increasingly pessimistic that they ever would be. His frustration over his inability to influence events, to move the levers of power, and his anger at the rejection of his ideas (perhaps, one might say, narcissistic rage), were probably pivotal to his transformation. His frustration also likely contributed to his growing perception that the war was simply wrong; the violence, he concluded, "was senseless and therefore immoral," Neil Sheehan observed. The United States didn't have a right to kill people if there was no prospect of success, Ellsberg thought. Whether he would have switched sides had the war been prosecuted successfully or his advice been taken is an open question. "He became terribly critical, I think, out of frustration," Robert Komer argues. "Nobody seemed to listen a great deal to his ideas. . . . I think frustration is a very important factor in what happened to Dan." By releasing the Pentagon Papers, Komer adds, "he finally found himself listened to." "At some point Dan decided, 'They're never going to do it my way,'" Sam Popkin recalls. "I always felt like he turned against the war because they weren't going to do it his way." There was "a sense of, 'If you're not going to do it my way, fuck you.'"[147]

In the late summer of 1969, Ellsberg had more reason to believe that the government was not going to do it his way. According to Ellsberg, Halperin informed him that President Nixon was threatening major escalation in Vietnam (though Halperin has no memory of telling him that). And John Vann, Ellsberg remembers, told him that Nixon was planning on withdrawing U.S. troops incrementally, slower than Vann and Ellsberg wanted (Vann thought major troop reductions could take place without loss of military effectiveness), and on maintaining a large U.S. residual force.[148]

Meanwhile, there was the pull of Patricia Marx, which many came to believe was key to Ellsberg's turnaround on Vietnam. Ellsberg has usually denied that Patricia's opposition to the war affected him, noting that his shift took place largely when they were separated. One wonders what Patricia thinks of his denials, particularly with all his talk of Tschannerl's tremendous impact on him. "I was one of many influences on Dan," Patricia remarked to one interviewer. When I mentioned to her that many people have said she influenced his views, Patricia responded,

> I love that opinion. And I actually had it [laughs]. And then I expressed it to Dan, and he said it wasn't true. I think he's probably right. Certainly I was the person against the war that he was very close to. So he listened, and he heard what I was saying. But from what he says, and it's consistent with his behavior, he wasn't convinced. Witness that we continued to disagree. He didn't convince me, I didn't convince him. . . .
>
> It's something that I would be very proud of if it were true. And I like to think it's true. And I would have said so. If you just asked me, I would have said, "Well, I had an influence on Dan. I mean, he fell in love with me. I was against the war. I must have had an influence." But I'm afraid to say that probably it was quite minimal, if any.

One gets the sense that Patricia believes she had a bigger influence on Dan than she will say publicly (out of concern for contradicting him, which she is hesitant to do publicly), and some who know them think she was quite influential. She was "probably the most important" person, Don Hall says. "If he'd never met Patricia, he might have changed, but he wouldn't have done 180 degrees," Doug Dowd believes. "I think Patricia did it."[149] Certainly she nourished his shift.

His head on the verge of exploding under all these influences, Ellsberg attended the August 1969 antiwar conference in Haverford, Pennsylvania. It was the first triennial conference of the War Resisters International held in the

United States. Janaki Tschannerl was one of the organizers and had invited Ellsberg to attend. "I knew he was moving in this direction, so I really wanted him to be part of it," she recalls. Tschannerl spent a lot of time with him at the conference, introducing him to other activists. Ellsberg was again an outsider, but with his probing, unrelenting questions. He argued with others at length about the absolutes of pacifism. He was impressed by the intellectual tenor of the conference.[150] During the meeting, his life took another major turn.

He'd been reading Gandhian literature for over a year, and now he was surrounded by pacifists from all over the world, including some of considerable stature and depth, like the Reverend Martin Niemoeller who had spent years in Nazi prisons for opposing Hitler. Ellsberg was moved by his conversation with Niemoeller. Ellsberg also met other Germans who had resisted Hitler. "He hadn't really been aware that there were Germans who were not Jews who had protested and lost their lives," Tschannerl recalls. "I remember his kind of feeling of surprise and being moved by this position that they had taken."[151]

But it was Randy Kehler's speech at the final plenary session that really sent Ellsberg reeling. He had been taken with Kehler upon meeting him earlier. "I thought he was a very likable, attractive person," Ellsberg remembers. "And that he represented the best of American youth." Kehler had also gone to Harvard; he was good-looking, bright, articulate, with a California counterculture bent. He was a draft resister. He expected to go to prison for that soon. The theme of Kehler's speech was two worlds, the world of the past and the world of the future, which was dawning and represented "a new beginning." Kehler also spoke of his refusal to cooperate with the Selective Service System and his likely jail sentence. He felt honored, he said, to be following in the footsteps of other resisters, including buddies of his now sitting behind bars.[152]

As Kehler spoke, his voice broke and he started to cry. "I had a spate of tears," he recounts. "I could not get through the end of my speech." ("One of the things that Dan and I very much have in common is that we cry all the time," Kehler adds. "I literally don't know another male who has the propensity to weep that comes as close to mine that he has. . . . He wells up with tears often. I don't think I've ever had a visit with him where I haven't seen that happen.") The audience was visibly affected by Kehler's speech; listeners also started to cry. Ellsberg, who has often had a hard time recounting his reaction to Kehler's speech without crying, remembers, "To discover that he found that he had to go to prison as the best thing he could do to end the war just really tore my life in two." Ellsberg, too, started to weep; so powerful was his flood of emotions (and one can only speculate on all the bases of those emotions at this time) that he felt compelled to leave the auditorium. "I went to the men's room—he was still speaking, there was nobody there, just a little men's room—and I sat on the floor and just sobbed hysterically for about an hour, close to an hour," Ellsberg recalls. "I couldn't stop crying. And just almost screaming . . . just shaking with sobbing. . . . And my thoughts were that America was eating its young," both in Vietnam and the United States. "Many of us noticed that Dan was very touched and very moved," Tschannerl reminisces. "No question about that."[153]

Ellsberg told me that "either in that hour or within hours" he asked himself, What could *he* do to stop the war if he was willing to go to prison? "And, of course, the Pentagon Papers suggested themselves very quickly." But he told another interviewer, "I didn't think immediately of the Pentagon Papers," and he testified in his trial that he didn't ponder releasing them at the conference or right afterward.[154] Moreover, his subsequent actions with the Papers would suggest someone intent on avoiding prison.

Ellsberg took a far less risky step before releasing the Papers. And who could blame him? He tried to get some prominent Democrats to speak out against the war. In a letter he sent to Charles Bolté of the Carnegie Endowment for International Peace on September 23, which he intended for wider distribution, he called for notables like those who had participated in the Bermuda conference nearly two years earlier to press publicly for an unconditional U.S. withdrawal from Vietnam. Continued huge losses of American and Vietnamese lives were not acceptable, Ellsberg argued. It was now in the national interest to get out of Vietnam. He proposed that influentials urge Nixon to get out before he irreversibly committed himself to the war. Ellsberg advocated that a broad provisional government in South Vietnam negotiate a ceasefire and settlement with the NLF. The war, he declared, was bloody, hopeless, unnecessary, and thus immoral.[155]

It was a clear antiwar statement, and a watershed piece for Ellsberg, even if it came after most other Americans had turned against the war. Its tone was that of a convert: one of self-evident truths and missionary zeal.[156]

One week later, Ellsberg would take the gargantuan step against the war for which he became famous. But, as would befit a man of his complexity, there was much more to his act than simply a desire to stop the war. His standard explanations—his PR line, one might even say—are wanting.

TEN

FRIEND OR COUNTRY?

SEPTEMBER 30, 1969: "HE CALLED UP AND SAID, 'I WANT TO COME OVER and talk to you about what we've been discussing,'" Anthony Russo recounts. "'I've decided that it's time. . . . I'm going to come right over. I've made a decision.'" Russo knew what decision Ellsberg had taken. Ellsberg would remember going over to Russo's apartment: "I went in and said, 'Tony, can you get ahold of a Xerox machine?' I said I had some studies that I wanted to copy. . . . He didn't know what the Pentagon Papers were," Ellsberg claimed, or at least "he didn't have a very detailed knowledge of [them]." Ellsberg said he went to Russo because "I needed some help." Copying, that is, putting Russo in the position of xerox aide, a characterization that nettles him, given the larger role he believes he played in helping get Ellsberg to this point. But Ellsberg also knew that Russo would be willing to take the risks the job entailed. Then "we walked outside to talk about it," Russo recalls. A safety precaution.[1]

Russo knew he was getting involved in something extremely serious. He thought of the scene in the movie *Dr. Strangelove* where the actor Slim Pickens rides the atomic bomb disgorged from the airplane as if he were a rodeo cowboy. "I had an immediate vision of falling out of an airplane, jumping out of an airplane," Russo reminisces. "At that point, I had jumped." He says Ellsberg told him, "I won't say anything. I'll just take the heat for the whole thing. So you're free and clear." Ellsberg told him that early on, Russo recalls, "and he repeated that several times. And I knew damn well that when something like that goes down, I would be the first one they'd come to. Because people had associated us at RAND."[2]

Photocopiers were neither as accessible nor as fast then as they are now, but Russo knew just where to get hold of one, and where the job might be done clandestinely. The person who possessed the machine, a rented Xerox 914 copier, did not recognize the seriousness of her own involvement. Lynda Sinay, Russo's girlfriend ("nothing serious," he says, though they had a fairly tumultuous relationship), owned an advertising agency in a small brick building on one corner of Melrose Avenue, above a flower shop. At the time, it was quite successful—a "hot little shop" some people called it, with Hollywood hippies wearing more expensive clothes than the usual counterculture attire walking in and out—though Sinay would soon fall on harder economic times. Sinay was 26, petite, highly entrepreneurial, driven, and not always a picture of stability. A divorcee, she was a former child television actress; her father was the motion picture executive Jack Harris, whose claim to fame was the horror movie *The Blob*. Sinay opposed the Vietnam War and had demonstrated against it, but she wasn't as political as Russo. "She was more a businesswoman," he says. "She was always thinking about how to make money." Her agency did some nonprofit political work, but that was not her forte. (Later she married Stewart Resnick and, as owner of the Franklin Mint, Lynda Resnick would buy Jacqueline Kennedy's pearl necklace for $211,500 at a much-publicized Sotheby's auction, then sell reproductions.)[3]

Russo asked Sinay if they could use her copier. "I told her the whole story," Russo recounts. "And she said, 'Ooohhh.' She was all impressed. . . . She was a little nervous, but she was going along with it." But Resnick says it was Ellsberg who spoke to her about using her Xerox. "We went out to lunch, and he asked me. . . . That wouldn't be Dan's character to delegate something like that." And she had her own relationship with him. Sinay let Ellsberg and Russo use her machine partly as a favor to them, but also because Ellsberg told her it would help end the Vietnam War. The documents he planned to copy, Ellsberg told her, "belonged to him. They were in his safe at RAND. And he was merely going to take them out, copy them, and return them," Resnick recalls.[4]

"I was so naive," she reflects. "I wanted to help. I never imagined the consequences would be so grave."[5] She would be named an unindicted co-conspirator.

Ellsberg, who had read an exasperating article in the *Los Angeles Times* the morning of September 30 that had suggested more government lying on Vietnam, took several volumes of the Pentagon Papers out of his top-secret safe at RAND that evening or the next. Getting them out of the RAND building was no big deal. He and Russo then commenced copying. "We went into a very heavy night-and-day operation," Ellsberg recalled. Actually, it was mostly at night—too dangerous during the day. "Night to early morning," Russo recounts. "I remember sometimes getting home when it was dawn." Ellsberg said he sometimes went straight to RAND in the morning without going home; other times he would go home and rest, usually going for a swim in the ocean, thinking it was close to his last time ("and I enjoyed it as much as I could"). Sinay's employees often worked late, and she had to get them out of the office to hide the operation from them. "Everyone wondered why I was so tired," she remembers. "I was working all day and all night." Ellsberg paid her to use her Xerox—about $150, at four to five cents a copy, Sinay would later tell the grand jury, though Ellsberg would recall ten cents a page. "Somehow in his mind that made it okay," Resnick recalls. He told her not to read any of the documents. She, of course, did not have a top-secret security clearance (though neither did Russo by this time). "They were protecting me," Resnick says. "I felt safe with them. . . . They said I would be fine."[6]

Sinay's advertising agency had three rooms: a small reception room with a glass wall in front and a desk where a receptionist sat, a central work room that had several desks, and a back room. The Xerox was in the reception room. The machine was nothing fancy. "Sort of a Model T," Russo remembers. "Just a minimal Xerox machine." It didn't have a collator, which would have been a big help.[7]

Sinay helped with the copying and collating, and sliced the Top Secret markings off the tops of some documents. At first Ellsberg used a scissors to sever the markings, then bought a paper cutter to expedite the operation. Russo came up with the idea (actually, an old maneuver in Washington) of putting pieces of cardboard across the top and bottom of the glass on the Xerox machine and "declassifying" the documents that way. Ellsberg thought he might have to make copies of the Papers at a commercial copying business later and could hardly have Top Secret markings on them. But subsequently he kept finding xeroxed pages with the markings still there.[8]

The copying was far from efficient. Ellsberg was no better organized during this enterprise than he was normally; indeed, his mind was probably particularly unsettled now. And the pace of work was almost leisurely. The scene resembled a pizza party at times. "We took turns xeroxing," Russo remembers. "And when we weren't xeroxing, we'd be reading or talking. It was relaxed . . . having pizza or drinking a Coke or wine. Or reading the Papers." More than a few documents caught Ellsberg's attention again. Usually, those people not working the Xerox would be in the middle room, but on occasion someone might be collating at the front desk. Adding to the low efficiency, it was more laborious to work a Xerox in those days than it is today. Sinay's machine was slow; consequently, they made fewer copies than Ellsberg wanted to. Russo remembers putting down the Xerox's rubber cover when he photocopied, but Ellsberg

would say they didn't have time for that. And they were tired. "We were sort of
bleary-eyed," Resnick remembers. For hours on end, under fluorescent lights,
the Xerox's green light would be flashing in their faces, hypnotically, the machine whooshing back and forth, over and over again, the copies piling up. Ellsberg sometimes wondered if he was going blind.[9] It was tedious work, copying
those thousands of pages, trying to keep them in order and to cover the Top Secret markings without losing page numbers or other information.

There were lapses—plenty of them. Leonard Rodberg, who organized the
Gravel edition of the Pentagon Papers in 1971, found the big pile of documents he had to work with "a puzzle." Not only were the page numbers missing, but the top and bottom lines on the pages were often fuzzy and unreadable
or were simply missing, because the pages had been elevated above the glass by
the cardboard. "Which is why there's a lot of ellipses in the Gravel edition,"
Rodberg points out. "Because I didn't have the top and bottom lines." Without
page numbers—and with many pages, including the table of contents, simply
missing—Rodberg had an unenviable task. "I spent two months organizing
them and trying to fill in the top and bottom lines," he recounts. "It was quite
hilarious."[10]

As Ellsberg worked, he could not get a funny scene from the movie *The
Lavender Hill Mob* out of his mind. It was the one where the three bumbling
gold thieves are described by an ultraserious narrator as "these masterminds of
crime." Perhaps that absurd label would soon be applied to him and his co-
conspirators, Ellsberg thought.[11]

The operation got off to an inauspicious start. The very first night, Russo
recounts, "the cops showed up. I was at the Xerox machine, which was right by
the front door. . . . There's a knock at the door. I looked up, and through the
glass wall I saw this LAPD [officer]. . . . I said, '*Oh, my God.* Those guys are
really on the ball.'" The cops appeared "almost as soon as we started," Ellsberg
remembered. "I thought, 'Fantastic. These people are amazing; they're really
good.'" "So I covered the stuff up real cool," Russo recounts:

> I said, "Cover everything up, guys. There's a cop at the door." So I went to
> the door, and my heart was in my throat. . . . And the guy asked about what
> we were doing. And we said, "We're just doing some late work. We're xerox-
> ing a proposal here." And he was very cordial. He said, "Well, you know
> your burglar alarm's on." So I called Lynda. Lynda came running up. She
> said, "This is my office." Then she showed them all kinds of I.D. That
> seemed to satisfy him. But he said, "Well, can I just take a walk
> through?" . . . He walked into the back room, walked out, and left, and that
> was it. . . . That was a close shave.

Sinay apparently hadn't turned off her burglar alarm. "We've been having some trouble with the burglar alarm," Russo said he told the policeman. "The alarm technician was here earlier. He left his card in case anything happened."[12]

Ellsberg and his cohorts also tripped the alarm on other occasions—"three times a week" Ellsberg would claim that his prosecutor later determined. Indeed, the *second* night, Ellsberg recollected, at around two in the morning, he was working the Xerox only to hear another knock at the door. He waved to the two cops through the glass wall, covered up the Top Secret markings on the documents, and went to the door. Again the officers made a pass through the office. *These masterminds of crime.* "We were too stupid to break into our own office," Resnick recalls. "It was like the Keystone Cops or something. . . . It was just like a comedy of errors."[13]

Other people also showed up, including Kimberly Rosenberg, who helped out (according to Russo, though Ellsberg testified otherwise). Ellsberg "liked to impress his dates" with the copying, Russo remembers. "He brought Kimberly up there and tried to impress her." Rosenberg arrived bearing "refreshments." Later, apparently at a second copying site, Yvonne Svenle showed up. "I was very security conscious," Russo recalls. "I wanted us to go up there by ourselves, wear rubber gloves. Ellsberg wanted to bring his dates, and bring his children," Russo laughs. "He brought Vu Van Thai up there. And I was thinking, 'Oh, my God. This is all she wrote.'" Thai was there to meet Ellsberg for dinner. Characteristically, Ellsberg handed Thai a document to read: "Hey, Thai, look at this." As a result, the FBI would find Thai's fingerprints on the document and he, too, would become an unindicted co-conspirator. So much for protecting others. "I thought, 'Well, I'm on the back of a tiger,'" Russo reminisces. "I knew some shit was going to come down. Because you don't do something like that and let other people in on it without it getting out." (When Carol Ellsberg later told one of Dan's attorneys, Charles Nesson, that it had been quite stupid of Dan to have involved so many people in the copying, Nesson agreed.) But Ellsberg would recall, "I had the impression that I was the only one in real jeopardy."[14]

After each copying session, Ellsberg later testified in his trial, he always returned the Papers to RAND the next working day. That seems unlikely, given his disorganization and the greater risks that would have involved. Ellsberg's testimony was probably designed to help beat the criminal charge he faced that he had "converted" the documents to his use; he had not deprived anybody of the material, he was effectively saying. He told me that he never kept the Papers at his house. That, according to his own trial testimony, is untrue. He has also said he "took charge of" all the photocopies, but Russo told me, "From the very beginning, I had a stack of [them] in my closet. . . . I always had a box in my closet throughout that whole year."[15]

The mission required Ellsberg and Russo to move heavy boxes of documents around, and they sometimes joked about how schlepping the boxes was an albatross around their necks. Transportation did not always go smoothly. "Ellsberg was very careless," Russo remembers. "He had this little sports car, and he'd throw a box in the back and take off. And the stuff one day was all over the coast highway. . . . The Papers just explode[d] out of the back seat."[16]

Most of the Papers Ellsberg ultimately copied came from a full set that Jan Butler put into RAND's Top Secret Control system, one that came into her custody on October 3 evidently as a result of a mailing mistake by Leslie Gelb. Ellsberg found it easier to take the bindings out of this set than the bootleg volumes. But it took Butler many months to log it into RAND's system, given its sheer mass and her other work. "I hated the whole thing long before I knew I had reason to," she remembers. Ellsberg pressured her to pick up the pace. "I wouldn't have gotten it done that fast if Dan hadn't been saying, 'I need that volume. I need it done,'" she recounts. One night, "he came to me and he said, 'I really want that volume.' And I said, 'Well, it would take me an hour to log it in.' And I said, 'I've got to go pick up my cleaning.' I had my laundry done across the street . . . where he also went for his cleaning. And he said, 'Give me your slip. I'll go get your cleaning. You log in the document. . . . ' And that's what we did. I suppose he took it home that night."[17]

Ellsberg did not inform Butler of his copying of the documents. She had earlier made it clear to him

> that if he had something really juicy to tell me that it wouldn't stop with me. . . . And I remember after we stopped dating, I was at the mart one Saturday morning, and he was there with his kids. And we sat and talked for a while. And he said, "What's going on in your life?" And I was telling him about this guy that I was dating. And I said, "What's happening with you?" And he said [in a hushed tone], "The most exciting thing." He said, "Can you keep a secret?" And I said, "Don't you remember? I can if it's not too good, but it sounds like it might be." He said, "Oh, yeah, I forgot about that." And he didn't tell me. But what he wanted to tell me was about copying the Papers, I'm sure.[18]

———※———

Ellsberg put his own children—Robert and Mary, then 13 and 10—in jeopardy. On October 4, a Saturday, at around one o'clock in the afternoon, he drove over to his ex-wife's house. Carol Ellsberg would record several months later:

> Dan came over to the house to pick up the children and asked to speak to me. He asked if I would be able to get along without any money from him for several months. I said that this would not be possible because my only other income was $4,600 from my fellowship [at UCLA].
>
> He said the reason he asked was that he might lose his job at RAND and would have to go "underground" because if he were fired from RAND, he would probably have difficulty getting a job teaching, although he had previously had many offers.[19]
>
> He said that he was going to spend most of his time working in the peace movement from now on. . . . He and 4 or 5 other men at RAND had written a letter to the *NY Times* stating their opposition to the war. Before they sent it, he was going to see Harry Rowen and ask his permission to send it. If Harry said no, he would resign from RAND and send it anyway.

He "told me very dramatically that he was against the war and had written this letter," Carol Cummings remembers. She thought, "Well, if you're only now getting around to opposing the war, you must be the last person on earth to do so." Carol opposed the war and had always been more dovish than Dan.[20]

Ellsberg would later explain his visit with Carol this way: "Almost as soon as I'd begun xeroxing, I felt I should warn my former wife . . . that the alimony was likely to stop very quickly . . . so that she could find alternative income. And she was very dismayed to hear this, [and] felt that I was shirking my obligations to the family. And I explained that in prison I simply wouldn't be able to carry on the payments and I felt I had to do this." Carol remembers no talk of prison. Her written account continues:

> I asked what he was planning to do for money if he left RAND and he said he would live on his savings and maybe borrow money.
>
> I said that it had been my observation in the past that he had always had difficulty living within his income and I wondered if he had thought of what it would be like without his beach house, his $6000/year psychoanalysis and his high standard of living. He said that he would be willing to give it all up, and that he had thought when he looked at the beach that morning that he might be seeing it for the last time. . . .
>
> As he was leaving, he asked if Robert could help him with some work that afternoon. I said it was up to Robert. He said, "You don't mind?" and I said "No."

Ellsberg would recall telling Carol he intended to give some classified documents to the Senate and that he would likely face a criminal charge. "She apparently misunderstood and didn't know, really, what I had in mind" for Robert, however, he said. "I wasn't really paying a lot of attention to what he said," Carol remembers:

> I wanted to get across I wasn't very interested in the details of what his thinking was on the war or what he was planning to do. "If you want to write the letter, write the letter." . . . He may have said, "I'm going to do important things." You know, I didn't care what he did. . . . He told me he was going to do something, but it was all kind of vague. . . . I thought, "So he's against the war. He's sending a letter. And he's doing some stuff." But . . . I didn't know he was copying top-secret documents. . . . He may have thought he was warning me about something, but I didn't catch on that anything significant was happening. . . . He didn't say, "Can my son come along and copy top-secret documents?"

Had Ellsberg been forthright, "I would have started screaming and yelling," Carol points out. "Here you have a mother who wouldn't let the kid go watch him jump out of a plane. You think I'd let him go copy top-secret documents? I mean, I grew up in a military family. I've always taken those things seriously."[21]

Probably the same day, Yvonne Svenle was walking down the beach in front of Ellsberg's home in Malibu and dropped in on him. Ellsberg was getting ready to leave with a "thick" accordion file of papers. He seemed "in a hurry," Svenle later testified in his trial. He told her he was going to "copy those papers." And "it seemed that it was something important." Ellsberg also informed Svenle "he was going to pick up his children and take them with him," she testified. Svenle advised Ellsberg that he should not involve his children in the copying. Ellsberg did not tell her what the papers were, but on another occasion he tried to tell her about them, Carol Ellsberg later informed the FBI. "She told him that she did not want to hear another word—that she was a citizen of Sweden and that it could be treason for him to talk to her," Carol reported. "He said that he trusted her and she told me that showed how stupid and indiscreet he was—to trust a former mistress whom he had treated badly."[22]

Carol Ellsberg also recounted in her written record of October 4:

> When Robert returned that evening, he told me what the "work" had consisted of. They had gone to the office of a woman friend of Dan's who had an advertising agency and had spent the afternoon xeroxing documents. . . . Some of the documents had "Top Secret" on them. . . . Several times, police officers

came to the door. Apparently the people inside the office were accidentally turning on the burglar alarm every time they opened the front door or something of that nature. Dan got upset whenever this happened.

Robert was very impressed that he had been allowed to work the Xerox machine all by himself. He did not realize the seriousness of the events. He had been troubled by the Top Secret designation, but his father had told him it was alright.[23]

This was Robert Ellsberg's debut using a Xerox machine. "Robert came back and said . . . 'I learned how to work a Xerox today,'" Carol Cummings remembers. "And I said, 'Oh, did you, dear? That's nice.' And he said, 'Yes, Daddy was copying all these top-secret documents.'" Robert had asked his father if it was okay to do so. He told his mother about the severing of some of the Top Secret markings (and, subsequently, that his father burned the trimmings). "I don't know if I had a sense of just how momentous this was," Robert told me. "I didn't really know much about what the content of the documents was. But I knew that these were secret documents bearing on the history of the Vietnam War, and that we were doing something risky. . . . I had a sense of being included in something very secret and important" that would help end the war. Plus it was fun just to work a Xerox machine, although "it was kind of a tedious, time-consuming operation. And not especially efficient," Robert attests. He later told his mother that he did all the copying, and that his father was sorting and handing him documents while "the others in the room were reading newspapers." Robert also helped his father with the copying on one or two other occasions. Perhaps a few hundred pages went through his hands, he says.[24]

Ellsberg told Robert that he would probably go to prison for his activity and that he wanted Robert to feel connected to it in some way. He would subsequently say that he hated the thought that Robert would soon read in the newspaper "that his father was in prison and was charged with very heavy crimes" without having explained to him why and shown him that his decision to copy the Papers was "made in a serious, responsible, calculated way, calmly, after reflection. That I hadn't suddenly flipped or done something terribly impulsive. . . . I wanted my son to have that memory of someone that he respected." Ellsberg also claimed that Robert encouraged him to bring him along, but Robert says, "I didn't encourage him to involve me."[25]

Ellsberg's explanation to his son did not fall on deaf ears. Robert was a serious boy, advanced beyond his years politically—due in large part to his father—and interested in the Vietnam War. His father had spoken to him about Gandhian ideas (leading to a lifelong interest in them). Around this time, his father gave him a copy of Thoreau's "On the Duty of Civil Disobedience," which had a big effect on him. He became interested in nonviolence. His father also gave him other books of this nature and "insisted" that he read them. Robert looked up to his father. "I thought that he was brilliant, and that he set a kind of example of moral seriousness," Robert recalls. "And that he had a sense of history and a sense of being kind of engaged in great historical drama, in which what one person thought or did really might make a difference in the world." His father "seemed a kind of larger-than-life person in a lot of ways" to him.[26]

But Robert would come to have mixed feelings about his involvement in copying the Pentagon Papers:

> On the one hand, I feel kind of proud and privileged to have had a sort of small part in something that I feel was important. I don't take special pride in it, because I was too young to take responsibility for that decision. . . . It was more helping my father. He asked for my help, and I helped him and did what he asked me to do. But I believed entirely at the time that what he was doing must be the right thing to do. And I was predisposed from earlier that year and the reading of Thoreau and Gandhi and this sort of thing to understand the kind of rationale and motives that he explained to me. I certainly shared his sense of the seriousness, urgency, of ending the war. . . . If he'd kept it a secret from me, I think I would have felt very left out [later].
>
> That doesn't necessarily mean that I had to be involved in xeroxing the Papers, I suppose. And in retrospect, as a father, I can recognize questions about whether that was a great idea. It certainly involved my family—my sister and my mother and myself—in a way that we wouldn't have been involved materially otherwise. And that caused a great deal of suffering to my mother, which was certainly unnecessary. And her feelings about the whole thing would have been better, and my life in those years would have been happier, if that had not happened.

Asked whether he would involve his own children, at that age, in copying the Papers, Robert said he probably wouldn't.[27]

Carol Ellsberg further recorded in her written account of events: "I was extremely disturbed by what Robert told me and I told him so and that it was wrong of Daddy to copy those documents and that it was wrong of him to have Rob help him. I privately felt that he must have had a psychotic break to do such a thing. I called my lawyer, on Monday I believe, and told him what had happened. . . . I also discussed it with one of my supervisors at work. We all felt that Dan must be seriously mentally disturbed to have shown such poor judgment." Carol was horrified. "I went ballistic," she remembers. "I was *so* upset that a child would be involved in this. I was *beside* myself." She phoned Dan immediately. After several unsuccessful attempts to reach him, she told him, "I need to talk to you right away about these documents." Dan quickly replied, "Don't do it on the phone." "Well, I need to talk to you," Carol responded. "This is very serious." She expressed her anger at him for involving Robert and said that he must be unaware of the implications of his act. Ellsberg told her "I was not to discuss this ever on the phone," Carol recorded. She reached him twice over the phone, and both times he quickly told her not to discuss it.[28]

But Ellsberg agreed to meet with her over dinner at a Chinese restaurant in Pacific Palisades, where she was taking Robert to an orchestra rehearsal, four days later. They rarely met. It was an acrimonious dinner. Carol wrote later that she told Dan:

> 1. . . . Robert was too young to be aware of what he was doing but that he had been disturbed and worried by the events.
>
> 2. Had he informed his analyst about what he had done? I asked this because I had considered calling this doctor myself if he did not know what was going on. I thought perhaps Dan might listen to his advice, if not mine.
>
> 3. That he had committed a serious crime for which he could be sent to prison . . . [and] he had not thought about how much it would hurt Robert and Mary if their father went to prison.
>
> 4. I felt that he was surrounding himself with people who would not mind letting him be a martyr and go to prison. . . . He should listen to advice from someone who does not have any private political motives for profiting from his (Dan's) mistakes.

Ellsberg tried to explain to Carol the importance of his action, but she wasn't interested and told him, "Listen, I don't know what you're copying. I don't want to know . . . I don't want to hear about it." The less she knew, the better. "I didn't want to hear about the heroics," she recalls. "I just wanted him to keep these children out of it. . . . Keep the children out of committing a crime and being part of it. And me, too. . . . If he wants to be a hero, be a hero on his own time." She was "obsessed" with protecting her children.[29]

Ellsberg told Carol that he had thought she understood what Robert would be doing with him, and that "he valued Robert's advice and maturity," Carol wrote later. Further, "his analyst did know all about it." And "he was not breaking any law. . . . People reveal TS material all the time. . . . As for prison, he didn't think that had quite the stigma it once had."[30]

But if Ellsberg did believe he was not breaking any law (a statement he has contradicted in interviews), why did he tell his son he would probably go to prison? Carol believed his action was illegal and told him later, "If they find out about it, Robert will have to testify about it, and he won't lie. And I won't either. We will have to testify in court against you." Ellsberg replied, Carol recalls, "That's alright, because if it ever comes out, I will come forward and tell the truth. So you won't ever have to testify." He would "spare them any further embarrassment," in the words of an FBI document. "And I said again, 'Keep them out of it,'" Carol recounts. "I knew this was *extremely* serious. . . . I knew what was going to happen. I mean, how could *he* not know what was going to happen?" But during the course of their dinner on October 8, "I was somewhat reassured in the sense that I did not see him as psychotic," Carol recorded.[31]

Ellsberg told Carol that he would not involve Robert in copying the documents again. But he did anyway. The "same cast of characters was present" the second go-around, Robert would tell his mother. This session occurred under circumstances that Ellsberg claimed didn't violate her injunction. But Carol felt otherwise. Her ire mushroomed. Ellsberg also involved his daughter after Carol had levied her injunction. Mary Ellsberg told me that her own involvement

> was basically an accident. We had accompanied Dad and Tony Russo to the taping of a TV show on the war where he was interviewed. . . . On the way home from the show, he decided to stop by an office above a flower store. . . . At first I could see that I was in the way. Dad wanted me to stay in the car, but I complained. Then he took me upstairs and left me in an inner waiting room and told me not to enter the xerox room where Robert and he were working. As I remember, Tony was hanging out, smoking a cigarette, that night. I felt left out, and probably to keep me busy, he gave me some papers to chop Top Secret off the top and bottom. . . . That is how my fingerprints ended up on some of the pages. This was the only time I participated in the copying. It was obvious that something secret was going on, and I knew it had to do with ending the war, and that it was dangerous. Dad told us at the time that he might go to jail for a long time for what he was doing. He told us not to talk about it to anyone, including Mom, and I didn't.
>
> Afterward much was made of our role as "unindicted co-conspirators," and Dad often mentioned it in his speeches, maybe to make us feel included in his fame. . . .
>
> Although at some level I felt proud of having been involved, I also felt like a fraud when I heard Dad and others celebrating our participation. It was pretty clear to me that the main reason I had been involved was because it was too much trouble to take me home first, and because I was a pest and couldn't sit still.

Ellsberg would recall bringing Mary "just because she was with us going out to dinner" that night, and that he had not planned to involve her: "I had thought she would stay in the other room, and she didn't." He later forgot he had brought her, hurting Mary's feelings.[32]

As Mary was wielding the paper cutter to sever the Top Secret markings, she asked why they were doing that. Her father explained that it was best that the copies not be so conspicuous. Both Mary and Robert "seemed to be sort of wondering what they were doing," Russo remembers.[33]

Mary also now questions her involvement. "I don't believe that I would have involved my own children in such an action, and certainly, it did cause all of us, and particularly my mother, a lot of pain," she says. Robert argues: "In retrospect, the idea of involving a little child like Mary in something like this, and trusting her to keep her mouth shut, is kind of reckless. And she came home and she was mostly just excited that she had been able to do something as dangerous as chopping off [the markings with the] paper cutter. . . . I would not allow my nine-year-old son near one of those. . . . I think she thought that we were doing something kind of adventurous, and wouldn't have fully comprehended."[34]

Ellsberg's decision to involve his children was a foolish and irrational act. His inner turmoil over the copying may have muddled his thinking, though his bad judgment was not out of character. It was "sort of beyond my comprehension," Thomas Schelling comments. "I thought that was a very selfish thing. As though, 'I'm going to be a martyr, I want my son to identify with me. And I want him to know all about what I'm doing and why I'm doing it, because after I'm assassinated, my son, Robert, will at least know that it was all in a good cause.'" Perhaps Ellsberg hoped to impress Robert with his action. "He just has to show his children how big his penis is," one psychiatrist analyzed. Ellsberg may have also wanted to deepen his bond with Robert and to serve as a political model to him. He would say that he didn't think he was putting his children in danger, however, "because I thought the responsibility was so obviously mine and it was so absurd, really, to think that these others were involved." But "it's obvious to me now that they were in greater danger than I realized," and "this kind of family scene will probably sound somewhat ludicrous or casual when it's described in court. . . . It will sound odd."[35]

Under stressful circumstances, Mary also told her mother about the copying. In April 1970, after the FBI had begun investigating Ellsberg's activity, Carol Cummings recounts, he came over to her house and said,

> "Have you been talking to people about it?" And I said, "No." Which was true; I hadn't. . . . I figured *he* must have been talking. He's such a blabbermouth. But he turned on Mary and said, "Mary, you must have told somebody." And Mary said, "We didn't tell anybody, Daddy. You told us, we didn't

even tell Mommy." That's when I found out that Mary had been copying them, too. . . . He accuses his poor old little child. . . . I assumed he would stop doing it when I told him to stop doing it, but he didn't stop doing it. I didn't know he would have the children do it when I'd made it so very clear. And I didn't know he'd have *Mary*, who *really* was *really* too young to be involved. . . . It's inconceivable . . . just inconceivable. No adult would do that.

Mary remembers:

> In fact, I hadn't told anyone, including my mother, because Dad had told me not to, and [said] that if I told anyone about it I would get him in trouble. It was a pretty big secret for a ten-year-old to keep, and it had taken some effort on my part. (I was known in the family for having a big mouth—one of my famous lines was to a friend Mom had bought a present for: "Guess what? We have a surprise for you and it's a book.") I guess I felt a bit indignant that he would assume it was me. That was the moment at which Mom found out that Robert had gone again and that I had been involved in copying the Papers, and then she really hit the roof. She was upset that I hadn't told her, and furious that Dad had ignored her original entreaty to keep us out of it, and especially for having told us to keep secrets from her. I don't remember Dad discussing it with me directly, although it's possible that he did. I am quite sure that no one ever apologized for having accused me of talking about the copying.[36]

Their mother's alarm was hard on Robert and Mary. "They realized anytime they mentioned this whole subject that I would get hysterical," Carol Cummings recounts. "Here was this big thing, and they admired him, and thought they'd done an exciting thing, and they couldn't talk about it to me, because I'd get hysterical and cry or something. It was a tough situation for everybody. . . . They had this wild mother who couldn't see *any* redeeming social value in it at that time, except how harmful it had been to us."[37]

The person who had been talking about the copying was actually another member of Carol's family. Carol had gone out to Colorado to visit her father (who was then in the hospital) at Christmas in 1969. The copying was "preying on my mind a good deal," she recalls. She thus told her stepmother, Camille, about it. Carol was not close to Camille; they had a strained relationship at times. Her stepmother was difficult and not always honest with her. Camille had earlier been an expatriate in Paris and married to a well-known novelist; she had gone to bullfights with Hemingway and had known other famous writers like Gertrude Stein and James Thurber, she would say. "I was just so anxious to talk to somebody about it," Carol remembers. "And she was in the family. . . . I just figured, 'Who could be safer than your own family?'" Camille asked Carol not to tell her father about the copying, saying that it would only upset him. So Carol didn't, which she later regretted, because, as a lawyer, he would have given her good advice, she thought.[38]

Camille then took a step Carol never dreamed she would take. On January 20, 1970, Camille contacted the FBI office in Denver. "A source with whom insufficient contact has been had to determine reliability" are the words one FBI memo used to identify her. According to the document, she told a special agent that Carol had informed her of Dan's copying and Robert's involvement. Camille would explain years later in a letter to Carol that she felt Dan had done "a terrible thing" and that it had been her "patriotic duty" to go to the FBI, Carol remembers. According to RAND's Richard Best, an FBI official in Los Angeles subsequently told him that Robert had been worried about the copying and had mentioned it to Camille himself, perhaps at dinner. But, most likely, it was Carol who spilled the beans. She would come to judge her disclosure a huge mistake. She was astounded when she found out what Camille had done. "I was just bowled over," Carol recalls. "It was an *amazing* revelation. . . . I was the one that turned him in to the FBI without even knowing it." How could Camille do that to her own family? Carol thought. Camille didn't apprise her husband of what she had done.[39]

During a later Christmas holiday, after the others at her California home had gone to bed, Carol confronted Camille about her deed. "She was *flabbergasted*," Carol recounts. "She was flabbergasted that *I* knew. And she was flabbergasted that the FBI had told anybody that she had told them. . . . She said, 'They said nobody would ever know! They said they had a special file where they kept the names of confidential informants.' And I said, 'Well, it looks as though they lied to you.' . . . She went upstairs, and she came down again. She wanted to explain to me how she'd only done it because she's patriotic." Camille never expressed any regret for it.[40]

Since learning of Dan's copying, Carol had been waiting for the other shoe to drop while hoping and praying that the whole nightmare (and that's what it was for her) would all go away. Her feeling of utter helplessness in the face of impending doom was the worst part of the whole Pentagon Papers affair for her. She knew that something most unpleasant was going to take place, "and I couldn't do anything about it," she recalls. "And no matter how I fussed and fumed and ruminated and cried, it was going to happen. . . . It was on my mind all the time. . . . 'What does this mean for the children?'"[41]

Carol's agitation led her to confide in another person. "She was obviously bothered by the whole thing," Mary Marshall remembers. "I used to go over there in the evenings, maybe once a week. And we'd be sitting there chatting. . . . She began to tell me a little bit about it. But she was very hesitant. . . . Then another time she told me a little more about it. And then a little more." Soon Marshall herself began to get alarmed. Marshall had earlier worked at RAND; she took violations of security even more seriously than Carol did. The two discussed ways to put a stop to Ellsberg's activity. "She was older than I and more experienced, and knew all these RAND people," Carol says. "I didn't know what to do."[42]

Carol wasn't interested in talking to Dan again about the matter. That was a hopeless proposition as far as she was concerned. In fact, she wasn't interested in talking to Dan about *any* matter. She and Marshall discussed going to Harry Rowen. But Carol didn't want to talk to Rowen either. She worried that Rowen would not be sympathetic to her, given his friendship with Dan; he might not even believe her. And if Marshall spoke to Rowen, "he would have just thought that I didn't know what I was talking about," Marshall suspected. "I'm just a woman." But Marshall told Carol she would see what she could do. She felt they needed to speak to someone whom Rowen knew and respected, who would then inform him. "I'm not going to tell you who it was, but I got somebody to do it," Marshall told me. This person, or persons, went to Rowen and told him about the copying. Afterward, Marshall informed Carol that the deed had been done. "We both heave a great sigh of relief: 'It's all under control,'" Marshall recounts. "Well, it wasn't. Harry did *nothing* about it."[43]

Ellsberg and Russo worked the Xerox at Lynda Sinay's office over a dozen sessions, perhaps copying at least 3,000 pages there. They xeroxed intermittently over a period of several months, after which they shifted their operation "almost exclusively" to another site, the Westwood office of two men Russo knew who did "social science consulting." One of them was an architect, the other a political scientist whom Russo had known at Princeton. The authorities never found out about the copying at this site, which had two rooms and looked like an architect's office, with drawing boards and, again, one Xerox. Ellsberg and Russo copied there "numerous times," Russo recounts. "Because after a while I figured it was kind of risky with Lynda being involved, who was kind of flaky." The deterioration of relations between Sinay and Russo was probably a factor in this transition. "And I wanted a little more privacy," Russo says. "I thought that would be a better place. So we did a lot of work up there. . . . We'd go there like at eleven at night and xerox into the wee hours. And one night about midnight, one of the guys [who worked there] came in. He just popped in, and he looked over at what was in the Xerox machine. A big smile broke out on his face. And he didn't say a word. He just went to his desk, got some stuff, and left."[44]

Wary of the FBI, Ellsberg stored copies of the Pentagon Papers in a number of locations. He feared G-men would pounce on him at any time. "He had a couple of girlfriends where he left boxes in their closets," Russo recalls. Starting in late 1969 or early 1970, Ellsberg gave copies to the attorney Martin Garbus, whose legal and political advice he sought. Garbus stored the documents under the eaves of his garage at his house in Woodstock, New York. At one point he kept a carton in the hall closet in his New York apartment, and at another point his sister-in-law stored his set in the back of her own closet in Boston. The FBI would eventually keep an eye on Garbus: "My phones were tapped, strange calls came in to my house, black cars sat outside to let us know the FBI knew," he wrote later. But "part of the deal in getting involved with Dan—from day one—is knowing that the government would know all about you," Garbus told me. Garbus understood that "there was no way that he [Ellsberg] was as circumspect as other people. I knew people who had done other things, whether it be political or otherwise, whom you could trust with your life. Dan wasn't that. . . . And there were many conversations Dan and I had about somehow being more circumspect and not telling this person. I suspect there's a large universe of people who knew."[45]

Indeed there was. Ellsberg was typically indiscreet about the Papers, despite the risks. Without mentioning the study, he hinted to some people that he was up to something big and prepared to go to jail for it. He loved playing with his secret. He explicitly told other people about the Papers and gave parts of the study to a number of people. He probably couldn't help himself. Possessing the Papers was exciting and made him feel important, and he wanted confirmation of their significance. Some memories of his hints and disclosures:

- "Dan told me about all this stuff he'd found at RAND, and that he was xeroxing it," Don Hall remembers. "And I was bored. . . . I wanted to change the subject. . . . He'd talk and talk and talk, and I wouldn't be interested." Back in 1965, "he'd talk on the government's side. Now this time he was [saying] 'the government was a bunch of liars,' and he was going to release it."

- "Dan told me on more than one occasion that he expected to go to prison for what he was doing," Thomas Schelling recalls. "And the first time he said it, I thought he was just grandstanding. . . . By the second or third time, I had the impression he was telling me something. . . .

But I thought he was exaggerating what he would be subject to. . . . But when the Pentagon Papers appeared, it all made instant sense to me."

- "He called me up and . . . said, 'I have to talk to you. I have something very urgent,'" Jerry Goodman recounts. "And he came down on a train and he came and he sat in the living room. . . . He said, 'I *really* have to talk. . . . We have to go out of the house.' I said it was cold out. . . . 'Why do we have to go out of the house?' He said, 'Well, you never know. The place could be bugged.' I said, '*My* house bugged! Bugging an institutional investor?' He said, 'Oh, you don't know.' I lived on the edge of the woods, so we went tromping through the woods. . . . And he said, 'I've got all these papers. . . . I think they ought to come out. . . . I think they're very important to people. . . . I xeroxed them.' I said, 'Well, what are you going to do with them?' He said, 'What do *you* think I should do?'"

- "He came to my office in the Fairbanks Center, the East Asian Center [at Harvard], and closed the door and sat down, and asked me, in very sort of hypothetical terms, what I thought of someone who would re-lease a large number of classified papers that would have the aim of ending the war, that would show that the war had been misguided from the beginning, and so forth," James Thomson recounts. "But that [such] a person would be breaking the law and might be put in court under anything from espionage onward. I sort of sensed, of course, that he had something big up his sleeve. . . . I had no idea what he had up his sleeve, but I knew he had something big up his sleeve. . . . He was, again, revved up. On the verge of something Olympian. . . . But he was so high-strung about the war anyway. . . . He had the convert's burning soul. His soul was on fire with a desire to do great things to kill the devil."

- Ellsberg told Konrad Kellen he was willing to go to jail over the war. "Wouldn't you?" he asked Kellen. "I wouldn't even think of it," replied Kellen, who had a wife and two children. "I come from Nazi Germany." The conversation "depressed me," Kellen says. "Because I felt that, with friends like that, again you don't need any enemies."

- Ellsberg told another friend a study existed that would "blow the lid off" the war.

- At a dinner of Vietnam scholars during a conference of the American Political Science Association, "I suggested that some prestigious and im-portant organization, like this association, should sponsor a study of de-cision making on the Vietnam War," Jeffrey Race recounts. "Dan Ellsberg spoke up and said, 'But the study has already been done. It's in a safe in Washington. All you have to do is get it.'" But "I had no idea, and I think nobody else at the meeting had any idea, what it was that he was referring to," Race says.

- "He told me that he'd got something very exciting and very interesting they were going to be doing in Malibu, and I ought to come out to Malibu and work with them," John Sack remembers. "He said, 'You'll find this very interesting.' . . . It was xeroxing the Pentagon Papers."

- "They had all these papers at the kitchen table and dining room table," Mary Jane Vann recalls. "They were very intense, working on that stuff." Ellsberg and John Vann were at Vann's Littleton, Colorado, home discussing the documents at night. "Dan had a whole bunch of papers," John's son Jesse remembers. "And my father was looking them over. And they were agreeing or nodding on this point or that point." Jesse would later describe the scene to the FBI. "They were engaged in some very spirited and heated discussion," John Allen Vann, another of John Vann's sons, recounts. "The conversation itself had to do with purpose and whether or not—I recall a reference to Machiavelli—whether the ends justified the means. . . . It was obvious to me that the discussion was regarding whether or not the ends justified the means of the approach that was being taken. And more than just hawk versus dove type of conversation." John Allen deduced that the documents were "explosive," although he too didn't know what they were at the time. Both he and his mother would later conclude they were parts of the Pentagon Papers. Ellsberg would say that he told Vann about his copying of the Papers and wanted Vann to read them.

- "He left a copy with me," Richard Falk remembers. Ellsberg had been staying at Falk's home during a teach-in at Princeton. "A heavy, heavy thing," Falk says. "It was xeroxed material, and Xerox paper then was very heavy." Ellsberg wanted Falk to commit himself to reading the Papers, which, of course, was not a trivial commitment, "and they were hard to read," Falk recalls. "The xeroxing wasn't very good." Neither was the organization, and "it was hard to handle that bulk. It wasn't bound in any way." As for their discussions about the study, "I'd say more that I listened to him than talked to him," Falk chuckles. "I think that almost always he's a person that talks rather than listens" and is "very preoccupied with his understanding of things, and slightly missionary about inducing other people to share that understanding." Ellsberg subsequently contacted Falk several times to see what he thought of the Papers. Falk found them interesting, but thought Ellsberg was overestimating their likely public impact and was acting obsessive about them: "I mean, the agenda of the Papers dwarfed in some way a concern with the war."[46]

On at least one occasion, Tony Russo also toyed with the secret of the Papers, though rather innocuously. Gus Shubert and his wife were at Ellsberg's Malibu beach house with Harry and Beverly Rowen, Russo, and perhaps one or two others. Shubert noticed that Russo, whom he felt had been underrated at RAND, was kind of on the edge of the crowd and approached him. "'Well,' I said," Shubert recounts, "'what are you doing to keep yourself busy these days?' And he looked at me with this mysterious look, and he said, 'Oh, I'm managing to find a thing or two to do.' He said, 'I'm keeping pretty active, as a matter of fact.'"[47]

According to Ellsberg, he copied and released the Pentagon Papers solely for political and moral reasons. In a nutshell, he had come to oppose the Vietnam War and felt that releasing the study would discredit the war and heighten the public's disillusionment with it. "I always thought that it might have a very big effect on consciousness," he told me. An explosive and decisive effect, he actually believed. "He thought it would end the war," Marty Garbus recalls. Ellsberg was "always absolutely certain" about that. "I thought his perspective was naive and grandiose," Garbus says. But it's a perspective that fits a recent convert of questionable judgment, apocalyptic visions, and with a large ego. Ellsberg may have even fantasized at times that he would single-handedly stop the war. One person who knows him comments, "He has very little capacity to understand how the same thing can affect different people in very different ways. . . . So he has a capacity to get things wrong. I think he thought that when he did the Pentagon Papers it would end the war immediately. Because he thought everybody would see the same things he did" in the Papers. And Ellsberg believed strongly in the power of information to change attitudes. He "is always searching for the right data and getting the right data to the right person," Morton Halperin says. "I can imagine Dan saying, 'Look, I didn't know this. If everybody knew this, it would change the policy.'"[48]

Ellsberg would claim later that he never thought for one minute releasing the Papers would end the war, however. He is keenly sensitive to the view— widely held by those who knew him—that he overestimated the impact the Papers would have. "It's absurd," he told me. He thought the impact of the Papers "would be low—to zero." But he believed the Nixon administration might overreact dramatically to his disclosure, he says, undermining itself by engaging in just those sorts of criminal activities it ultimately undertook. He was writing at RAND on such "revolutionary judo," he points out.[49]

Ellsberg has always emphasized the roles of Janaki Tschannerl, Randy Kehler, and other opponents of the war in providing him with radically new political perspectives and models for action. And they clearly had a profound effect on him; he was genuinely moved and inspired by them, and taken with the Gandhian emphasis on truth telling. Kehler, a modest man, believes that he was "sort of the straw that broke the camel's back." But Ellsberg has at times handed out credit for his political inspiration pretty widely, leading one to wonder if he has an ex post facto agenda of conveying that he was acting purely out of political impulses rather than personal ones. Anthony Russo remembers with amusement one journalist observing at the time of Ellsberg's trial that at parties Ellsberg would "always tell about what inspired him. And half the time somebody at the party would have inspired him. He had all these stories. It was something." Ellsberg later said that eight Minnesotans who broke into a draft board office in the summer of 1970 had strongly influenced him (this after he had copied most of the Papers); he also said that learning the story of a man who was beheaded for resisting Hitler had inspired him. Ellsberg has even said it was lessons he learned at Sandstone that helped turn him into the kind of man who would release the Papers.[50]

Without question, Ellsberg hoped to end the war by disclosing the study. The human suffering in Vietnam had come to affect him deeply. "What was his motivation?" Patricia Ellsberg asks, rhetorically. "It was the children were burning alive. They were being burned alive. And he felt it."[51]

But most human behavior has multiple roots. It is also often undertaken for reasons the person is not even aware of or fully understands. Ellsberg is an immensely complicated man with considerable psychological needs. He almost certainly made his decision for a complex mix of reasons, feeling the push and pull of different—and sometimes conflicting—impulses, concerns, doubts, and outright fears.

Ellsberg had for years shown a marked desire to be prominent, to stand out, to star. That desire had seemed almost childish at times. He liked being the center of attention and was a habitual self-promoter. He was not known for selfless acts. Ellsberg thought of himself in large, heroic, and romantic terms— he would influence history. He also craved praise and applause; to an inordinate degree, he seemed to need the approval, the admiration, and even the adulation of others. It is virtually certain that a primary reason he released the Pentagon Papers was to achieve greater recognition. Quite likely, he wished to become renowned. He may have even hungered for fame. All that would have fit him to a T. "This is a guy who wanted to make a mark," Charles Nesson, his later lawyer, thought. "What the right wing was saying—he just needed to get his picture in the paper one way or the other," one left-leaning friend at the time argues. At Ellsberg's fortieth birthday party in Cambridge, Massachusetts, in April 1971, "he went around all evening saying, 'I swore I would be famous by the time I was 40, and I didn't make it,'" Sam Popkin remembers. Ellsberg repeatedly bemoaned the fact that he wasn't famous yet, Popkin says. "He said his goal had been to be famous by the time he was 40." "You have to remember that he was approaching a certain age," Jan Butler points out. And "he knew he was brilliant, and that nobody else knew it, except the people in his tight little circle where everything was top secret. But the man on the street did not know Dan Ellsberg. And I think he wanted him to . . . I think that was partly what was bothering Dan."[52]

One member of Ellsberg's defense team, who opposed the Vietnam War before Ellsberg did, explains his act simply: "He's an egomaniac. It was a way to be out there. . . . He was a guy who wanted to make it big. And if he could have made it big with his Q clearances and been secretary of defense, he would have been perfectly happy to be up there, as long as his name was on the marquee. . . . He seemed like somebody who's susceptible to whatever is going to boost his own image, his own presence. So I never had any sense of any sort of deep values or morality. He's basically an opportunist. And this was an opportunity." Peter Young, who was one of Anthony Russo's attorneys during his trial, echoes, "Had it not been the Pentagon Papers, it would have been something else." The member of Ellsberg's defense team quoted above, who thought Ellsberg's release of the Papers extremely important and who admires the act itself, adds, "I don't think he has a threshold of morality. . . . Most people, there's a certain floor, and you're not going to do anything beneath that. I don't think he has one. I think his floor is quicksand."[53]

Ellsberg denies that he released the Papers for publicity. He'd never had any desire for public notice, he says. He was "a backroom boy," an "anonymous bureaucrat," and "happy with that." "I hadn't been nurturing some secret desire for publicity all this time," he told me. And "the fact is, I foresaw nothing but bad publicity in establishment press. . . . Nothing but condemnation." He would be called a "traitor," a "madman," and a "terrible guy," he recalls anticipating, and people on the left "would probably never forgive me for my RAND and government past. They would just say, 'Thanks a lot, Johnny-come-lately.'" He was later "quite surprised when I got this flood of congratulation and thanks."[54]

Ellsberg had also been led to think of himself as special since he was a boy, a superior person destined for important accomplishments. But he had not enjoyed the success that he had anticipated or desired. He had failed to meet other people's expectations of him as well. He had not cut it as a Pentagon aide; he had not been invited back into the government. Now he was having a hard time getting work done at RAND. He was virtually treading water on his Vietnam study. He couldn't write it, so he'd copy and release it, many felt, in essence. He'd make his big contribution, his big splash that way. "In a way, the Pentagon Papers may have been his way of doing [i.e., publishing], instead of the book that he might have wished he had written, but couldn't," Thomas Schelling argues. Ellsberg would remark in the spring of 1971 that perhaps disclosure of the Papers would be a satisfactory substitute for the book he had hoped to write by age 40 but hadn't written. Or at least it would provide some consolation. Releasing the Papers would also relieve him of the burden of his Vietnam study. Overall, it was a way to bounce back. "He was, in some sense, bound for greatness," Charles Nesson observes, "and Dan Ellsberg had kind of come a cropper. And he was going to recover." This "was reflected by the delight he took in being the number one media guy" after the Papers were published, Nesson notes. "And the fact that he could call a news conference. That delighted him. And I think that delighted him because it was consistent with the Ellsberg he wanted to be and thought he would be."[55]

When Sam Popkin got to know Ellsberg in the fall of 1970, he detected considerable concern about accomplishment. "He was really going through a midlife crisis of productivity, fame, and fortune," Popkin remembers. "He certainly saw himself as an underachiever." Yet Ellsberg felt he wasn't appreciated enough. "He hadn't made a success anywhere he'd gone," Popkin says. "He wasn't at peace. . . . He had ambitions of being something—not just the smart kid people kept around." Measured by the standard of his enormous potential, or by his earlier work in decision theory, Ellsberg hadn't accomplished much for some time, Popkin argues: "He'd been really quite fallow. There's no getting around it."[56]

Ellsberg denies feeling that he hadn't realized his potential. "I was at the top of my career" as a consultant to the government, he maintains. "In that career, no one was higher. And I was where I wanted to be. . . . I never felt more successful in my life than I did in the year 1969 from a career point of view." He had just done the Vietnam options paper and NSSM-1 for Henry Kissinger, he pointed out. "So the idea that I wasn't succeeding is just ridiculous."[57]

But, as we've seen, Ellsberg had been frustrated and angered that his advice on Vietnam had not been taken. People would listen to him now. He may have released the Papers partly out of ire or vengeance at those in the establishment who had turned their back on him.

A desire for atonement also probably inspired him. "He was terrifically torn about the whole question of conscience and individual guilt," one person recalled. "He was obsessed about his own personal responsibility." When Tom Oliphant of the *Boston Globe* spoke with Ellsberg in late 1970 and early 1971, he encountered a deeply anguished man. "I remember vividly: 'Am I a war criminal?' 'What is the extent of my responsibility?' 'What is my guilt?' 'Why didn't I speak up [earlier]?'" Oliphant recounts. "And no showboating. Deadly serious emotional business. . . . I mean, every one of these questions—not idle philosophical material for him, but rather the stuff of intense internal turmoil. *Obvious* intense internal turmoil." Ellsberg was unique in the degree to which he felt pain over his earlier complicity, Oliphant thought. "I think it was clear that he was troubled by the fact that he had been part of the war machine," Howard Zinn, who got to know Ellsberg around this time, remembers. "And that in a sense he felt that, by his act, he was trying to make up for that. He wanted to do something to distance himself from his past and from what he had done."[58]

But Ellsberg also denied being motivated by atonement. "The simple fact is that I have not ever felt tortured by guilt," he told one journalist shortly after the Papers were published. But in a lecture he gave shortly *before* the Papers were published (that is, before he was putting out a public line on their release), he stated, "As I look back at my own role in the last eight years, it is with a heavy sense of guilt." (He apparently edited this statement out of the version of his lecture published in his book *Papers on the War*.) One left-leaning scholar, who dealt with Ellsberg over the Pentagon Papers before they were published and who detected an impetus of atonement, observes, "He will talk about his feelings and his history and how he changed, but . . . he is filtering. So he's not somebody who lets it all out."[59]

Ellsberg's act also probably reflected his love of adventure. If he needed an infusion of excitement, drama, and danger in his life, he had it now. His enthusiasm for sharing discoveries and secrets with others was also evident. "It's true of sex, it's true of nuclear command-control, it's gonna be true of the war in Vietnam," Schelling chuckles. And some people noticed Ellsberg's impudent streak. "It was just this sort of outrageously bratty thing he would have done," Joan Cleveland thought when she first heard of publication of the Papers, even before Ellsberg had been identified as the source of the story.[60]

In addition, it is quite possible that Ellsberg was playing to Patricia Marx, or even to Janaki Tschannerl. He would impress them, even win their affections (although Patricia's may already have been won). "I'm very glad he did what he did, but if you're going to try to win over Patricia, how better to do it than with the fucking Pentagon Papers?" his friend Doug Dowd remarks. "To prove it" (that he was now against the war too). "Naturally, he went overboard. Which is what he does. On everything he does, he goes overboard."[61]

Ellsberg's less-flattering motivations may lessen the moral worth of his act in some people's eyes (including mine). Yet a person's behavior can be judged on bases other than motivation. And how many people wouldn't like greater recognition? One's views on the matter are almost inevitably shaped by politics. Mary Ellsberg relates,

> Even as a child, I was amazed by how superficial and naive most adults seemed to be in their judgments of my father. Those who admired him were absolutely blind to his personal flaws, whereas the people who disagreed with him politically felt compelled to vilify him and to attribute his actions to the most doubtful motivations, as if his complex personality undermined his contribution to ending the war. . . . If I have learned anything in my life, it is that very rarely are we guided by single and entirely selfless emotions. I have met a great many heroes in Nicaragua who I would not have liked to be personal friends with. This has given me a bit of perspective on my own father.[62]

Whatever his mix of motivations, so strong were they that Ellsberg copied the Pentagon Papers despite awareness it would harm the career of his best friend, RAND President Harry Rowen, who had aided and supported him in many ways. Ellsberg told his ex-wife on October 4, 1969, that "his only regret was that this would hurt Harry Rowen who had been so good to him," Carol wrote. "That was my main concern," Ellsberg told me. "I knew it would affect him badly. And there was no way around that. . . . There was no way to avoid it and do what I felt had to be done to help end the war." He admits he betrayed Rowen by releasing the Papers. "I took an action that was certain to have a bad effect on his career. . . . And it was fairly likely to be a factor in [the RAND board of trustees later] kicking him out of RAND." Also, "I knew I was going to hurt RAND by putting out the Pentagon Papers. I hated to do it. It wasn't just Harry I was worried about. . . . I liked or loved lots of people there. . . . But I knew the one who would mainly be damaged by this was Harry." That anguished him, Ellsberg says. But his cause was bigger than Rowen, bigger than RAND. E. M. Forster once said, "If I had to choose between betraying my country and betraying my friend, I hope I should have the guts to betray my country." Ellsberg said his choice was not that simple: thousands of people, some his friends, would suffer if the Vietnam War continued.[63] Of course, it's possible that he didn't really think through how his action would affect Rowen and others at RAND.

Ellsberg's betrayal of Rowen would later be one reason for his unpopularity at RAND. "He double-crossed Harry," Jim Digby says. "He double-crossed the whole institution, but he particularly double-crossed Harry," and "that's why most of us have reservations about Dan as a person." "Dan literally—but I mean literally—stabbed Harry Rowen in the back," Guy Pauker asserts. "If he had taken a knife and stabbed it in Rowen's back, he couldn't have done much more than what he did with the Pentagon Papers."[64]

Ellsberg is troubled by this aspect of the affair. But he seems most troubled by how it hurt his image among his former colleagues. "Look, I did something that these people will never forgive me for," he once remarked to me, out of nowhere. "I betrayed a promise. But above all, I hurt my best friend." Ellsberg says his anguish over hurting Rowen was attenuated by the expectation that he would be going to prison, however. "It was very much easier to do that given that I was going to suffer a lot more than anybody else." Ellsberg has frequently claimed that he expected to go to prison "for the rest of my life," or "forever," for releasing the Papers. It was effectively "a suicide mission," he told me.[65]

This is Ellsberg-the-poseur. He recognized the danger he was in and probably derived some satisfaction out of that. But, as we shall see, his first plan for disclosing the Papers was designed, in significant part, to provide him legal cover. He strove to avoid jail. He wanted martyrdom without suffering—"an upper-class martyrdom," Marty Garbus observes. "Martyrdom in velvet," another person put it. Ellsberg's posing is probably partly to convince others, and perhaps even himself, that he had purely political motives; far from looking for fame, he was sacrificing himself for a larger cause. Yet, at the same time, martyrdom may have appealed to him on some levels. His attorney Leonard Boudin and others would perceive that an element of Ellsberg was drifting toward martyrdom during his trial. Ellsberg may have even fantasized about jail while fearing it and doing everything he could to avoid it. Prison would help expiate his guilt over betraying Rowen and RAND, and over his own role in the war. Prison could also serve as validation or redemption. "I think Dan is one of those people who perhaps feels that, in some sense or another, he's affirmed himself if he does get punished," Doug Dowd says.[66]

———◈———

Meanwhile, Ellsberg and others at RAND were giving Harry Rowen another form of trouble. This one Rowen was aware of: the antiwar letter to the *New York*

Times. Ellsberg and five other analysts who wished to express their opposition to the war had considered various means, including a study report—Ellsberg's first choice—before settling on the letter, which was a departure from RAND norms. Until then, dissent on Vietnam had been kept largely behind closed doors there and within appropriate tactical limits. To write a public letter, however tame that might seem to other opponents of the war, was virtually leaving the reservation at RAND. Ellsberg was nervous about it, remembered Neil Sheehan, who helped him obtain coverage of the letter in the *Times,* as it risked his position in the national security establishment. His nervousness about this risk at the same time he was copying the Pentagon Papers is more reason to believe that he didn't really expect a lifetime behind bars for releasing them.[67]

The six analysts asked Rowen if they would be fired if they released the letter. They said they were prepared to resign (or be dismissed) if he forbade it. Rowen was in a bind. He worried about how the letter would affect RAND. He didn't want any trouble with the Pentagon. "But he didn't hesitate—he wasn't going to accept our resignations," one of the signatories recounts. Rowen said it was okay to release the letter if they made it clear they were not speaking for RAND.[68] Besides Ellsberg, the signers included Paul Langer, Melvin Gurtov, Konrad Kellen, Oleg Hoeffding, and Arnold Horelick.

The six analysts considered how to appeal to newspapers. They asked the media analyst Ben Bagdikian for advice. "The others were just interested in which paper to send it to, where would it have the most effect, and how do they go about it," Bagdikian recounts. "But Dan pursued it beyond the others. He'd come to my office afterward. . . . He asked everything: 'Which paper has the most influence?' 'How do editors make decisions?' 'How does the *New York Times* make decisions?' 'On what basis do they make it?'" Bagdikian stressed to Ellsberg that the "paper of record" was the *New York Times.* That seemed to be an important thing to Ellsberg.[69]

The *Times* quoted extensively from the letter on October 9. The *Washington Post* ran it in full three days later. The letter called for the United States to unilaterally withdraw all its forces from Vietnam within one year "at the most." "Short of destroying the entire country and its people," the letter argued, "we cannot eliminate the enemy forces in Vietnam by military means." Further, "the importance to the U.S. national interest of the future political complexion of South Vietnam has been greatly exaggerated. . . . Above all, the human, political, and material costs of continuing our part in the war far outweigh any prospective benefits."[70]

This was Ellsberg's first public antiwar statement, which went somewhat beyond his earlier letter to Charles Bolté. He was a fairly recent—some would say late—arrival to the position of unilateral withdrawal; he was the last of the six signers to get there. He'd recently argued for negotiations and then mutual withdrawal. Ellsberg was also the only one of the six who had previously been a hawk. Paul Langer says that at one point Ellsberg "held up the drafting of the letter because he wanted to change the wording in the direction of . . . toning it down."[71] It's curious that the last of the six to advocate unilateral withdrawal was the one copying the Pentagon Papers. Either there was more going on with him than politics or he was simply prepared to take greater risks to stop the war.

The letter was released at a time of mounting public opposition to the war. Unilateral withdrawal had become "respectable," as one of the six pointed out. But the letter upset others at RAND. Angry communications were exchanged. Some worried that it would harm RAND, even blow it up; the letter risked their jobs, they contended. Ellsberg's boss, Charles Wolf, one of four analysts who wrote a response published in the *Washington Post*, later refused to shake Langer's hand because of the letter. But "I pushed and pushed it through," Ellsberg remembers. He told Rowen afterward, "This RAND letter isn't the end. I'm going to create more trouble for you." But "I don't count that as a real warning."[72]

Albert Wohlstetter later told others that he began to worry that Ellsberg was "getting dangerous" at this time. Ellsberg was a security risk and might stray further off the reservation, Wohlstetter believed. He told Rowen to watch out for Ellsberg. "He never talked to me again," Ellsberg recalls.[73]

Others also approached Rowen about Ellsberg around this time. Several told Rowen, in effect, "Look, there is a real problem here," Hans Heymann remembers. "I don't know exactly how it was put, but there was ample notification to Harry . . . that this guy was not to be trusted, or that we have serious misgivings about his discretion." But "Harry wouldn't listen."[74] (Of course, some of this talk of issuing warnings about Ellsberg may get overstated in the retelling.)

Heymann himself had had discomforting encounters with Ellsberg. Besides the occasion when Ellsberg had nervously slammed his safe door shut, he had once remarked to Heymann, "By the way, that was a great chapter you wrote for the Vietnam task force"—the Pentagon Papers, Heymann recounts; "it really ought to be published." Heymann laughed and said, "'You're very funny. Not in our lifetimes, Dan. That stuff is loaded with the most highly classified stuff you ever encountered. And nobody will ever let that out.' He said, 'Well, you don't know how these things get out. They have a tendency to get out. Don't rule it out.' I thought, 'My God, the guy's gone nuts.'"[75]

Ellsberg reveled in the publicity that the RAND antiwar letter received. He sent copies of it, the *Times* article on it, and other mentions everywhere. He sought maximum attention for the letter, indeed, seemed to crave it. "He had millions of copies made," remembers Helen Kwake, whom he had copy them. "He'd have us . . . go back and xerox some more, go back and xerox. And then I'd send them to this one and that one. . . . He just thought that was the greatest." It was, "Look, we're in the *New York Times*," Kwake recalls. "He had them hanging around. And everybody that came in had to see *the letter*."[76]

Meanwhile, Ellsberg was continuing his efforts to build establishment opposition to the war. He circulated his letter to Charles Bolté widely. He spoke with former members of the Johnson administration and pressed them to take a stand against the war. He urged them, as Democrats, to publicly share or assume responsibility for the war with Nixon, and to tell Nixon not to make the same mistakes they did. He was rebuffed.[77]

More reason to get the Papers out.

———◦◉◦———

That same October Ellsberg began making his move. He spoke with James Lowenstein, an aide to Senator J. William Fulbright whom he had earlier met in Vietnam. Ellsberg indicated that he had a classified government study on Vietnam that "he thought would be useful to us," Lowenstein later recounted to another Fulbright aide. Ellsberg wanted to release the Pentagon Papers through hearings sponsored by Fulbright's Senate Foreign Relations Committee (FRC). That would gain the Papers national attention and enhance their political impact. Ellsberg wished to star in the hearings; he performed well on stage. The FRC had a cloak of respectability, and release through it would also allow Ellsberg to remain part of the establishment, still something of an insider (though an outsider among the real insiders), despite the rebuffs he'd recently suffered. Ellsberg did not want to be a political pariah. He told Noam Chomsky that he still expected to be accepted by the establishment after his disclosure. "Because he wanted to be," Chomsky recalls. Not least important, release through the FRC would provide Ellsberg protection against prosecution. That consideration was probably uppermost in his thinking. "I thought I was much safer . . . if they came out in a hearing," he remembers. Fulbright had the clearances legally required to receive the Papers, and members of Congress had legislative immunity. The chances of imprisonment went way up if he gave them to a newspaper, Ellsberg understood. He had seen Neil Sheehan of the *New York Times* recently, and although Ellsberg had already leaked to Sheehan and had confidence in his discretion, he had not said anything to Sheehan about the Papers. Testifying before Congress would allow Ellsberg to take center stage, but discreetly leaking would not. And taking credit for the leak would risk political rejection and jail.[78]

In mid-October, Fulbright invited Ellsberg to testify later that month as a signatory to the RAND antiwar letter. Charles Wolf told Ellsberg he should resign from RAND if he testified. But Ellsberg refused, and Harry Rowen didn't want him to resign. On October 21, however, Fulbright announced that he was postponing the hearings "as a matter of courtesy" to President Nixon, who had scheduled a Vietnam address for November 3.[79] Ellsberg's hopes for a quick release of the Papers had been dashed.

On November 2, a Sunday, Patricia Marx arrived at Ellsberg's Malibu home. "The phone rang within an hour," Ellsberg recounted. Sam Brown of the Vietnam Moratorium Committee, which had organized unprecedented nationwide protests against the war on October 15 and was planning more for November 15, was inviting him to fly to Washington to answer Nixon's speech, Ellsberg recalled. So he and Patricia jetted off to Washington. "I came out, and then the next day I was going back east with him," Patricia remembers, though she had flown out west at his invitation to be with him.[80]

Before getting on the plane, Ellsberg checked a suitcase full of the Pentagon Papers. It included parts on the 1964 Gulf of Tonkin affair, an illuminating case of official deception on the war. (Ellsberg would often transport the Papers as regular check-in luggage.) Ellsberg's suitcase also held notes he had taken in the Pentagon on a Defense Department "command and control" study of Tonkin, also classified top secret. Patricia did not know what he was carrying to Washington.[81] Ellsberg believed the documents would get Fulbright's attention. President Lyndon Johnson had lied to Fulbright about Tonkin, and Fulbright was not happy about it.

On November 4, Ellsberg wrote a critical response to Nixon's speech. A group of Democratic congressional representatives used his essay to fashion an antiwar resolution advocating that U.S. forces in Vietnam "be systematically withdrawn on an orderly and fixed schedule—neither precipitate nor contingent on factors beyond our control." Ellsberg also consulted for Republican Senator Charles Goodell, who introduced legislation calling for a complete U.S. withdrawal by December 1970. Robert Sachs was a young intern to Goodell and believes Ellsberg had earlier shaped Goodell's position on Vietnam. "He was helping educate him," Sachs recalls. "He provided a lot of the substance of what became Goodell's position."[82]

Ellsberg gained a 45-minute meeting with Senator Fulbright on November 6 attended by Fulbright aides Norvill Jones, Carl Marcy, and James Lowenstein. Ellsberg had requested to see Fulbright "for guidance on what he should do" with the Pentagon Papers, recorded Jones, who met with Ellsberg before the meeting (when Ellsberg expressed concern about his legal risks). During the meeting, Ellsberg spoke about how Congress and the American people had been deceived on the war. He offered to provide documentation. He stated that he could get hold of a classified Defense Department history of U.S. decision making in Vietnam, and he briefly described it. "He thought it would be dynamite" if it was released, Norvill Jones recounts. "That it would cause Congress to take strong action to end the war." Jones was skeptical. He had worked in Congress for years. "I just knew it was not going to happen," he remembers, "even without knowing what was in what he said he had." This would be a major difference of opinion between Ellsberg and Jones, whom Fulbright appointed his point man on the Pentagon Papers, throughout the entire affair. "I never thought that they would have a significant impact on either Congress or the public," Jones recalls. And after reading some of the study, "I knew that he was grossly overexaggerating the impact it would have." Ellsberg seemed "greatly misguided" to Jones. (Jones came to believe events confirmed his sentiments: In 1971, several weeks after the Nixon administration had turned over a set of the Papers to both the House and the Senate, Jones discovered that only one senator had even bothered to look at the Senate's set and for only a few minutes at that. Also, a Senate vote on the McGovern-Hatfield antiwar amendment shortly after the Papers were published yielded essentially the same results as a vote the year before.)[83]

Feeding Jones's doubts was uncertainty about exactly what Fulbright's office would be getting from Ellsberg. "We had no way of knowing what the potential might be, other than that it just was not going to be any kind of dynamite," Jones remembers. And "I didn't know where in the hell he got the Papers at the time. This was all a mystery."[84]

Jones also had questions about Ellsberg himself. "In the first meeting he was articulate, but nervous and worried," Jones recalled. "He spoke fast and made jerky movements. He seemed to be a harried man." He was "clearly agitated about the war, and somewhat overwrought, I'd say. Which just sent up caution flags to me. I didn't know how stable a person he was. I didn't know who he was talking to about his contacts with us either." Ellsberg had "this rather pent-up energy," Lowenstein chuckles.[85]

Jones came to have another reason to wonder about Ellsberg. Jones's secretary told him, "You'd better be wary of that fellow. He came in one day when I was alone and tried to put the make on me." Jones notes, "My secretary was most unattractive. She's a great person, I loved her dearly, but she was most unattractive, and not the kind that the ordinary person would try to put the make on.

Anyway, she just didn't like the guy at all because of that. . . . She said he had bed-room eyes." Jones himself never particularly cared for Ellsberg. "I didn't dislike him. I just was very wary of him."[86]

At the November 6 meeting, Ellsberg handed Fulbright a portion of the Papers on Tonkin, and a manila envelope containing his notes on the command and control study (which Fulbright had earlier attempted to pry loose from the Defense Department without success). Fulbright turned the documents over to Jones and told Ellsberg to work with him. Among Fulbright's aides, Jones alone would have access to the Papers, and Fulbright would rely largely on him for advice on them. Jones locked the documents in his safe. He would treat classi-fied information the way it was supposed to be treated.[87]

Fulbright was interested in what he heard from Ellsberg and said that the best approach might be for Ellsberg to testify in an executive session of his committee. Fulbright thought Ellsberg's motives were lofty and respected what he was trying to do, but the senator was a politically cautious man who "be-lieved in playing things by the book," Jones recalls. He was not inclined to re-lease top-secret documents. Fulbright later told Senator George McGovern that "he'd never done that and that he wasn't about to start now," McGovern remembers. Among other things, it might injure and split his committee, which he might not be able to carry on this issue anyway. Nixon and his lieu-tenants would have even more reason to attack him. "We knew we were playing hardball with some tough people," Jones reminisces. "It was war."[88]

Fulbright had Jones draft a letter to Secretary of Defense Melvin Laird ask-ing for the Defense Department history on an official basis. Thus began a long—and unsuccessful—effort by Fulbright to get the Papers through that channel.[89]

On November 7, Jones passed to Fulbright Ellsberg's notes on the com-mand and control study of Tonkin, along with a note saying that "it makes very interesting reading" but "there is nothing of significance new as to the details of the attack." That afternoon Ellsberg brought Jones a copy of NSSM-1 (or por-tions of it). He was now handing out material on the Nixon administration as well. Maybe that would help get their attention. Jones subsequently gave NSSM-1 to Lowenstein and Richard Moose, another Fulbright aide. (Moose later attempted to get the Vietnam options study out of Ellsberg as well but failed de-spite making a trip to California.) The same afternoon, Ellsberg also handed Jones "a number of sealed manila envelopes which he asked me to keep in the safe for him, without revealing what was in them," recorded Jones, who provided me his complete file on Ellsberg and the Pentagon Papers. "I never did know and he eventually took them away." Ellsberg also gave Jones an envelope containing a volume of the Papers. He told Jones he should "feel free to read" it.[90]

After these meetings, Ellsberg waited for his opportunity, hoping for hearings, believing they would come soon, while trying to keep in touch with Jones. "He was a big phone caller," Jones remembers. Jones, who did not always take Ellsberg's calls, believes he never gave Ellsberg any encouragement that the FRC was going to move on the Papers.[91]

———

Around ten days after meeting with Fulbright, Ellsberg spoke with Randy Kehler in an Italian restaurant in San Francisco. Speaking in hushed tones, Ellsberg told Kehler about the Papers and his intentions. He also said that "he had all of this top-secret information about U.S. nuclear war plans" in the early 1960s, including contingency plans for an all-out nuclear war, Kehler recalls. Ellsberg told Kehler that he had been the first civilian ever admitted to one war room in which he'd seen some nuclear plans. "My impression is he had gotten unprecedented access," Kehler remembers. "And that he therefore carried this burden that no other civilian in the world, let alone our country, could possibly carry, including the president of the United States. . . . Because no other civilian knew, including the president." Ellsberg was considering releasing the nuclear information too, he told Kehler. But he worried that if he disclosed both sets of material, they would detract from each other in the media, plus he might be accused of showboating. And since bombs were falling in Vietnam, that was the most pressing issue—though he would "certainly" release the nuclear stuff later, Ellsberg said.[92]

Kehler was not excited about the Pentagon Papers. "My attitude was, 'So what's new? They've been lying to the people,'" Kehler recounts. "But I was in shock about the nuclear war stuff." *That's* what Ellsberg should release, Kehler told him. "He thought that putting out the Pentagon Papers would have no effect," Ellsberg recalls.[93]

Patricia Marx also had her doubts. Sometime after their flight to Washington on November 3, Ellsberg told her about his copying of the Papers. She had even helped with that "a little . . . just by chance . . . one or two times," she remembers. "But I didn't really know the full implications of how dangerous it was to be doing [it]. . . . He said that there's nothing in there that would compromise the nation's security. So I didn't worry about it that much. . . . I trusted him pretty well in his judgment there." Ellsberg is "a man of very thoughtful judgment," Patricia would say. But, for a time, she was in something of a fog, as "he was not telling me the full implications of what he was doing."[94]

As Patricia came to learn more about the Papers and the risks Ellsberg was taking, however, and after it became clear that he was having trouble getting Fulbright and other senators to play ball with him, Patricia had serious questions. If others weren't running with the Papers, what made Dan so sure they would have a big impact? "I just would ask what he thought was the likelihood of it making a difference, since nobody else seemed to be thinking it was so urgent to get out, including Fulbright, who was against the war," Patricia remembers. "And why he thought it would or could make such a difference. And whether it was worth it."[95]

Patricia went to Marty Garbus for legal advice. More than once. "I understood that she was terrified," Garbus recounts. "Pat had very deep-seated fears." For one thing, "she had a wild horse by a bit, in a way. And she understood that Dan's attractiveness was that energy and passion. She also understood that it ought to be second-guessed." Patricia worried that Ellsberg would suffer ignominy and imprisonment. Moreover, she didn't want to suffer a breach with her family, whom she knew would not look favorably on his release of the Papers. "She was not jumping off a cliff," Garbus says. "Pat is someone who tries to accommodate."[96]

At her request, Garbus researched the criminal problems Ellsberg might face. He thought there was a good chance Ellsberg would be convicted of espionage, and that anyone who aided him could also face the death penalty. That must have been sobering news. Garbus spoke with people he respected (including Leonard Boudin at great length) about the Papers' likely political impact. The "nearly universal judgment" of these people, he recalls, was that release of the documents would not have great impact, and perhaps even no impact. That made Garbus himself wonder whether it was worth the risk.[97]

Ellsberg's obsession with the Papers sometimes caused problems in his relationship with Patricia. But she was probably a steadying and tempering influence on him. Assuming he could be tempered. "My suspicion is that nothing tempers Dan," Garbus comments. "That he cared for her a great deal, but I think that their relationship was that she had to accommodate to his underlying needs and desires. And in exchange for that, she got what Dan had to give her." Anthony Russo worried that Patricia was holding Ellsberg back; he was a bit suspicious of her. He wondered if the Papers would ever see the light of day.[98]

Meanwhile, Ellsberg continued his explorations of the peace movement. In January 1970, at his initiative, he met twice with Donna and Alber Wilson, former RAND scientists who had protested the war from day one. Ellsberg was interested in their thinking and in an earlier dialogue they had organized at RAND with Quaker peace activists. "I think he was trying to affirm himself" on Vietnam, Donna Wilson says.[99]

The same winter, the peace activist Joan Libby had a long conversation with Ellsberg at an antiwar conference about the war and how to end it. "He was making the rounds of different conferences," Libby recounts. "I think he was really sort of getting a look at who these antiwar folk were. He was just a kind of oddball intellectual at that point, I think, to a lot of people, who thought he was very interesting. And he knew so much about the policy and decision making, and the facts behind the decisions, or the fallacies. If you take a look at how the war was being played in the press at that point, he could really sort of take that stuff apart, and this statement or that statement by a government official. Because he knew them all, practically."[100]

That winter Ellsberg also spoke at a conference in Washington sponsored by ten U.S. congressmen on U.S. war crimes in Vietnam. He alluded to inside knowledge he possessed of U.S. policies in Vietnam. He declared that, as "a former official of the Defense Department and the State Department," he was "a possible defendant in a future war crimes trial." Ellsberg told some legal scholars at the conference that "papers did exist which corresponded to the Nuremberg documents." He wanted to get the Pentagon Papers into the courts, thinking that would also give him some legal protection. But the scholars were discouraging about getting them into the courts. "So I kept checking with the Fulbright committee," he remembered.[101]

On February 25, the Thieu regime in Saigon sentenced Ellsberg's friend Tran Ngoc Chau to 20 years in prison (later changed to ten, of which he served four and a half). Chau was charged with having liaison with a person dangerous to the security of South Vietnam—one of his brothers, Tran Ngoc Hien, a high-level North Vietnamese intelligence officer. Through their contacts, Hien had first hoped to convert Chau, then, failing that, to establish a back channel for peace negotiations with the United States. Ellsberg was outraged at Chau's railroading and the U.S. embassy's tacit approval of it. Before Chau was sentenced, Ellsberg had leaked incriminating, highly classified cables of U.S. Ambassador Ellsworth Bunker, who he felt had acted terribly on the matter. The State Department investigated Ellsberg for the leaks after he was apparently fingered by an accomplice in State. Ellsberg also spoke on the record about Chau's plight and passed information to the FRC. The *New York Times Magazine* asked him to write an article on Chau and his case, but he failed to get it done.[102]

Chau's plight propelled Ellsberg further down the antiwar path, fueling his anger and disillusionment with the U.S. government. He had long linked Chau with his own cause on Vietnam. Chau's arrest represented, in part, a rejection of his own ideas. He debated whether he could continue working within the system. He would say later that the case was one of his turning points on Vietnam.[103] It, too, fed his desire to get the Pentagon Papers out.

The month Chau was jailed, Ellsberg asked Richard Moose if he thought Senator Fulbright or the FRC would be interested in receiving more of the classified Defense Department history. "I said I was sure they would be," Moose recorded. Ellsberg visited Norvill Jones again in Washington and asked if he would like a full copy of the study (or at least a good deal more of it). Ellsberg was trying to get the FRC to get off the dime on it. Jones told Ellsberg he would like a copy as an individual but not on behalf of the FRC. He "did not want the committee involved in something with such sensitive overtones," Jones said.[104] That could not have been a good sign to Ellsberg.

In late February or March, Ellsberg air-expressed Jones two bundles of documents. "They're on the way," he informed Jones over the phone. Jones put the documents in his safe. He apprised Fulbright that he had received them "from the person who gave us the portions last year," also noting, "They are extremely voluminous." Jones felt somewhat overwhelmed by their size. The FRC now had 20 to 25 volumes of the Papers, some 3,000 pages worth, nearly half the total, and probably "the bulk of the most significant material," Jones wrote.[105]

But Jones found the bundles of documents in disarray. "There was some duplication with as many as three copies of some sections," he wrote later. Some pages, though stapled together, were out of sequence, and there were gaps. "A few volumes are either not complete or are in draft form," he wrote. Some pages had "Top Secret" on them, others did not. "It was a big jumbled mess," Jones told me:

> I had no idea what they were, because they were not in any order. And right away, at the beginning, I did not find any index or anything that would help me assemble them in any kind of order. So all I knew is I had a big stack of papers on various assorted topics relating to the history of the war. But making heads or tails of it was very, very difficult. And I didn't have the time to do it. I used to bring a packet home some nights and use it as bedside reading to put me to sleep at night. But in terms of being able to sit down and methodically go through and sort it into some order, I just didn't do it. I didn't have the time to do it, and I didn't find them interesting enough or useful enough in any way to do it. I saw them as things for historical purposes, but nothing that really would be useful in terms of doing what Ellsberg thought that they would do.[106]

On March 12 at 3:30 in the afternoon, Ellsberg met with Fulbright alone. There is no record of what was said. But things were not going the way Ellsberg wanted them to. Jones found many of the documents "dull and boring," he subsequently recounted to Fulbright, and "was unable to see how the papers would reveal anything of significance to the committee that would have a bearing on the current situation in Congress relating to the war, even if they could have been made public, and told you so at some point not long thereafter." Jones said he informed Ellsberg that he did not, "as a practical matter," see how they could be used productively short of obtaining them officially.[107]

———————

Meanwhile, the other shoe was starting to drop on Carol Ellsberg. On the morning of February 18, at the direction of FBI headquarters, a special agent from the FBI's Los Angeles office by name of William McDermott informed her over the phone that the FBI wished to "make an appointment to discuss a matter with her," an FBI document records. "Mrs. Ellsberg stated that she desired to know the nature of the inquiry. It was explained to her that the matter concerned her former husband and possibly some documents." Carol's heart must have been racing. Her fears, it was now clear, had been well founded. Carol had "no idea" why *she* was being contacted or how the FBI had found out about Dan's copying, but "they know something, and they know that I know something," she thought. She didn't think of her stepmother; perhaps Mary Marshall came to mind. She was furious at Dan anew. "Mrs. Ellsberg stated that she desired that the interview be conducted away from her residence and she made an appointment to visit the Los Angeles Office at 11 A.M. on February 18, 1970," the FBI recorded. In other words, immediately and away from her children (whom she did not tell about the FBI's call) and neighbors. Carol phoned an attorney first, however, evidently the one who had handled her divorce, and he then called the FBI and declared that any interview would have to be done in his office. What's more, he and Carol would have to know in advance the matters to be discussed. The FBI would only tell her attorney that its inquiry involved a security matter Carol might be able to clear up. The FBI elected not to interview her under her attorney's conditions.[108]

Around a week after the FBI phoned Carol, "the thought occurred to me that Dan might have given the documents to Robert for safekeeping," Carol recounted in a statement she prepared for her attorney on April 2 (one already quoted from in these pages). "I looked in his room, but did not see them."[109]

Was she thinking about turning them over to the FBI? Later events suggest that she might have been.

FBI agents subsequently called on Carol at her house. "It was funny," Robert Ellsberg remembers. "They came to the door, and they were so suspicious. Of course, they're trying to be inconspicuous, but there was something so odd about these two men, kind of in gray suits and nice government cars, coming to the door. And they were very polite. But there was something so odd about it that I think I even took down their license numbers. They were very embarrassed and thought that was very funny when my mother told them that they'd made such an odd impression." Carol says she declined to talk to the agents.[110]

Carol did not inform Dan about the FBI's phone calls, according to her April 2 statement, but she did let him know about the FBI's visit to her house. That was "probably as much of a complaint as anything," she laughs. Her report "alarmed him a little bit"—probably more than a little. The State Department had investigated him for the Chau leaks, and now the FBI was coming around. His goose might be cooked. But Carol told him that she had advised the agents she wasn't going to talk to them. Thus, she had done all she could to protect him, and out of concern for their children. Dan asked Carol "if there was some other reason I was angry at him," she recorded—some other reason besides involving their children in copying top-secret documents, that is. Carol did not note her response. She advised their children not to discuss the documents with their father again. Later, Dan asked her on more than one occasion if she had heard from the FBI again.[111]

The FBI contacted RAND about Ellsberg's reported copying in late April. Harry Rowen told two FBI agents, in Richard Best's presence, "We have in here some very sensitive papers on the U.S.-Vietnam situation," Best recounts. "And if it were anything, I think it might be that." Rowen "knew damn well what it was," Best says. "He knew right away. . . . He knew in the spring of 1970 that it was the Pentagon Papers." But according to Ellsberg (and he apparently bases this on FBI documents he later saw), Rowen downplayed the sensitivity of the papers, said Fulbright had a right to them, and pointed out that Ellsberg was leaving RAND anyway. In Best's retelling, the FBI agents said to Rowen, "Can we have the titles?," and then Rowen "turned to me and said, 'Dick, will you give them the titles?' And I said, 'Yes. . . . I'll have it put together and bring it down to your office tomorrow.'" Which Best did. But the FBI couldn't get any trace of Ellsberg's copying at RAND.[112]

Rowen, it appears, did not take the FBI investigation all that seriously. The FBI's allegation was unproven; the bureau itself could not yet act. Rowen did not alert Defense Department security officials of the investigation (that would later infuriate those officials), nor did he direct that RAND undertake its own investigation. Further, Rowen didn't speak to Ellsberg about the FBI's visits, nor did he move to get Ellsberg's security clearance revoked (a drastic step). In the meantime, Ellsberg kept copying, including "a lot of the hottest stuff," he recalls.[113] Rowen's inaction—in part a product of his friendship with Ellsberg—would prove costly to him.

Ellsberg said later that he obtained a September CIA memo indicating that the FBI was providing the CIA information on him at this time, and that the CIA had directed that he not receive any security clearances. Moreover, that August or September, he said, at the Los Angeles airport, someone stole his briefcase from an Avis counter when he went to the bathroom or to a pay phone. He believed the FBI did it. The FBI was good at stealing briefcases, he said.[114]

The FBI dropped its investigation of Ellsberg in the fall of 1970 after the Justice Department and the FBI decided that it did not merit continuation. "The FBI had a solid case but did nothing with it," the White House's Charles Colson later heard to his dismay. According to Ellsberg, he saw an FBI document indicating that it dropped the probe because it might prove embarrassing to have investigated Fulbright, who "could have made a stink." But that seems an unlikely cause; the FBI had not shown fear of Fulbright before (as Norvill Jones can attest). Ellsberg also claimed that it was "inconceivable that the president was not told about this case at that time," and that Henry Kissinger was also informed. When he met with Kissinger that September, Ellsberg recalled, Kissinger "acted oddly."[115]

On April 15, Ellsberg resigned from RAND. He did so "immediately, in a day," he remembered, after hearing from Carol about the FBI's visits, "on the assumption that the FBI would certainly be coming, and it would be very hard on Rand to be associated with me." He didn't want to "embarrass" RAND, he said. But the FBI didn't come after him, and "then Rand seemed interested in having me come back and finish a paper I'd been writing"—on revolutionary judo—so he stayed on at RAND as a consultant until September. But "only to finish work on [his] manuscript," Rowen would tell the FBI.[116]

Actually, Ellsberg's resignation was not born out of an impulse to protect RAND. "Ellsberg had been encouraged to look for another position," Rowen told the FBI. "It was agreed he should leave in April." That was partly because Ellsberg had said he felt "inhibited" while employed at RAND. His criticisms of the war and the U.S. government, he would explain later, had caused "great apprehension among all of my colleagues," and he felt that "it was unfair of me to keep subjecting them indefinitely to that kind of apprehension"—this from the same man whose release of the Pentagon Papers caused them far greater apprehension. In particular, Ellsberg said, he wanted to speak out against U.S. complicity in Chau's imprisonment.[117]

The Chau affair did hasten Ellsberg's departure from RAND. But it was not a completely voluntary departure. His problems completing work also fed into it. "Frankly, Ellsberg was pressured to move on," one high-ranking RAND official later revealed. "He had been very unproductive and had not delivered on some of his promises. . . . He was good at a first draft, but never followed through; his department head was increasingly unhappy with him from mid-1969 on." That department head, Charlie Wolf, brought his displeasure to the attention of Rowen, who didn't fire people easily but who would have been the one to encourage Ellsberg to seek another position. "Charlie probably made his case, which was pretty strong, and said, 'We're never going to get this [Vietnam study from Ellsberg], and we ought to get somebody else,'" Gus Shubert says. When I asked Wolf if Ellsberg had been pressured to leave RAND because he wasn't getting his work done, Wolf responded, "The performance evaluations for him, as part of the standard process, did involve comments of that sort." Wolf thinks the evaluations hastened Ellsberg's departure. "He wasn't forced to leave," Wolf says, and he himself didn't suggest that Ellsberg do so, but "if the evaluation is saying it's not getting anywhere, and there were commitments and promises and they still haven't been complied with, that can be viewed by the recipient as pressure. . . . I would have said to him, 'Look, you've got to do these things that you promised to do.' And he just was not getting anywhere. Now, from that process, one could very well infer—he could very well infer—that this isn't the place." "There was certainly a nudge," RAND's Albert Williams believes: "You know, 'Dan, for Christ sakes, when are you going to [do it]? You've got all this stuff, but it's not coming together.'"[118] Like copying the Papers, leaving RAND would also afford Ellsberg a way out of his study.

But there were other brilliant people at RAND who had difficulty writing, so it is unlikely that that was the only factor in Ellsberg's departure. His politics also probably shaped it. He may have experienced a chill among some of his colleagues. "People at RAND were just opposed to him," Konrad Kellen remembers. "Because he was a very vocal dove." And "his whole way of doing things was too flamboyant for RAND."[119]

Ellsberg denies feeling pressured to move on because he wasn't getting his work done. "I was one of the most valuable and distinguished people . . . that RAND had," he claims. "I was a terrific asset, whether I produced for them this month or that month. . . . So Charlie couldn't fire me because I wasn't producing or something. Nor did Rowen have the slightest desire to fire me."[120]

Ellsberg resigned in an unsettled frame of mind. "He says, 'What am I going to do with my life?'" Kellen recounts. "He wanted to write something. [But] he didn't know what to do. So I said, 'Why don't you go and lecture at the universities about the Vietnam War?' . . . But he didn't want to do that."[121]

Ellsberg had indicated to Rowen that he could obtain an appointment as a research associate at MIT. He had a "standing" offer from MIT, he claimed later. Everett Hagen, the acting director of MIT's Center for International Studies, felt the center had an overly establishment bent and wanted to bring in someone with a more critical orientation. Ellsberg would "write a book or two" while there, Hagen envisioned when MIT signed him up that April. He would also offset the center's William Bundy, who recalls nominating Ellsberg himself: "They said they wanted somebody with a different viewpoint toward the war than mine" to make it "a balanced ticket," and "I thought he was an extremely able guy" and "would have something to offer." Ellsberg took a steep pay cut, down to $20,000—"their top salary," he says—to join the center.[122]

On May 13, at the request of Rowen and Wolf, Richard Best moved to clear all top-secret material from Ellsberg's safe at RAND. It was time to get his bootleg copies of the Pentagon Papers into the system. In the midst of the FBI investigation, Rowen did not have to tell Best why. Best was irritated that he, RAND's security officer, had not been told about these bootleg copies before. He instructed Jan Butler to clear out Ellsberg's safe. Butler, who was not aware of the FBI probe and who thought that Best's instruction reflected his "longtime dislike" of Ellsberg and a desire to "get" him, could not reach Ellsberg and wanted to wait until she did. "Nobody ever knew where Dan was or when he'd be in or when he'd be out," Best remembers. The FBI would later determine that Ellsberg rented a car in Jamaica on May 17.[123]

On May 20, Rowen informed Best that Richard Moorsteen, another RAND analyst who had been granted access to the Papers, now had the volumes in question and that he should pick them up from him. Ellsberg, perhaps out of concern for the FBI investigation, or simply because he didn't need them anymore, had earlier turned the volumes over to Moorsteen. Best directed Butler to pick them up from Moorsteen, and she subsequently logged them into RAND's system. Butler also removed top-secret documents from Ellsberg's safe on May 20.[124]

Meanwhile, Senator J. William Fulbright had invited Ellsberg to testify before the Senate Foreign Relations Committee on May 13. Ellsberg flew to St. Louis, Missouri, to speak at a teach-in at Washington University on May 8—"my first public speech against the war," he remembered. It occurred in the wake of the U.S. invasion of Cambodia and the Kent State shootings, which had sparked a powerful firestorm of protest across the country. Ellsberg was among the many outraged. He may not have had an easy time getting out of Los Angeles, however. Helen Kwake remembers him "flying in" to his RAND office one day around this time and saying that he's going to testify at some committee hearings in Washington: "He comes running into the office, and he's saying, 'Pat's down in front of the front door with the car and the motor running. Here—I've got to have all this stuff xeroxed. Carleen, run and get this xeroxed right away.' So she took off. And he's pacing back and forth. And he's going, 'I can't wait! I can't wait! I'm going to miss my plane. . . . ' And then he looks at me and he says, 'When she gets back, have her get a RAND car and meet me at the airport.' . . . And he takes off." After Carleen Abel returned from the copying machine, Kwake informed her of Ellsberg's instructions:

> So she runs out. She's gone. About an hour or so later, the phone rings, and it's Dan. He and Pat had gotten a speeding ticket going to the airport, and he missed the plane. And he didn't see Carleen. So he's in the bar at the airport. And I said, "Well, I guess Carleen will be coming back, since she didn't find you." He says, "Yeah, but when she gets back, have her come back again, because I'm on the next flight."
>
> So then she comes back in about another hour. And by then it's going to be hard [for her] to catch the next [flight]. And she had a blowout on the way to the airport, and had to get a mechanic. . . . She says, "I can't do it again. I can't!" . . . And so I said, " . . . I'll drive you to the airport."
>
> We get to the airport, she leaps out. . . . She had to run the half a mile. Everybody's loaded on the plane. And they had to put the telescoping thing back out to the plane for her to get on. Everybody's bolted to the seat. She had to walk up to him and hand [the material she had xeroxed] to him.
>
> By the time we got back to the office, we're both shot. I said, "And we got Dan on his plane again. . . ."

It was vintage Ellsberg, Kwake thought: the chronic lateness, and first running into the office and then charging off to go somewhere else.[125]

Before the Foreign Relations Committee, Ellsberg predicted that if the war continued, "a change in our society as radical and ominous as could be brought about by our occupation by a foreign power" might take place. Though also characteristic of Ellsberg in its hyperbole, that statement accurately reflected the drama and tension of the times. Many Americans thought the country was falling apart. Ellsberg alluded to the Pentagon Papers in his testimony, but did not rise to the occasion as much as Fulbright and his aides had hoped—despite prompting by Fulbright "on three occasions," Richard

Moose would later note. "He had the opportunity then, if he had chosen to do it, to say, 'I've got all these papers and I'd like to turn them over to the committee in a formal way,'" Norvill Jones remembers. Ellsberg did not do so, although he had led Fulbright and his aides to believe he would. They had viewed his testimony "as a forum for Ellsberg to talk about what he had," Jones recalls. "Not all of it, necessarily, but at least some of the juiciest parts." But "he wasn't as forthcoming as we had hoped that he would be. . . . He just was not willing to go for broke at that point." Ellsberg would explain later that he thought the FRC planned to hold hearings using the Papers *afterward,* and "since I wanted to preserve my availability as consultant and possible witness for these more comprehensive hearings, I did not rise fully to Senator Fulbright's invitation to add some comments" on the Gulf of Tonkin affair.[126]

Ellsberg continued to press Fulbright's aides after the hearings. Again Jones told him that he didn't think the documents were of use to the FRC. Moose avoided some of the many long-distance phone calls Ellsberg placed to him in 1970. "He was pressing me very hard to get the committee to do something with the papers," Moose recalled. Ellsberg asked Moose if the FRC would release a memo he might write incorporating some classified material, "thereby getting some new information out while at the same time affording him some protection," Moose wrote Jones. "I also recall discussing Ellsberg's desire to 'do something' with Norvill." Ellsberg had come to see Jones as an obstacle. "As time went on, the phone calls became more and more urgent—put it that way—to try to get something done officially with the committee in terms of hearings," Jones recounts. "And I kept steering him off in other ways to get the material made public. You know, going to other senators and congressmen, [and] through the press."[127]

At RAND, Ellsberg was bumped up to a small fourth-floor office to finish his revolutionary judo paper. He was in only occasionally that summer, at the end of which RAND terminated his consultancy. Despite repeated requests by Best and his assistant, Ellsberg refused to sign RAND and Defense's "Security Termination Statements" certifying that he was not retaining any classified information and would not disclose any to those not cleared for it.[128]

ELEVEN

"WE'RE ALL WAR CRIMINALS"

ELLSBERG EXPLORED OTHER WAYS OF RELEASING THE PENTAGON PAPERS that summer of 1970. Or at least some of the Papers. Ralph Stavins, Marcus Raskin, and Richard Barnet, all of the left-leaning Institute for Policy Studies (IPS) in Washington, were then writing a two-volume study on U.S. planning of the Vietnam War, and Stavins had interviewed Ellsberg for it in California. Ellsberg apparently told Stavins about the Papers. Stavins and his colleagues wanted them. "They knew it was important material and that it was central to the project they were doing," Leonard Rodberg, one of their colleagues at IPS, recalls. They also felt Ellsberg had a responsibility to make the Papers available to the public. They wanted to stop the war and thought release of the Papers could help do that. They also sought to document U.S. war crimes in Vietnam. They believed U.S. officials should be held accountable for those crimes. "Marc and Dick wanted [the Papers] out once they understood what was in them, which was early on," Rodberg says. "I had no doubt that this was very important," Raskin remembers. "No question about it."[1]

Stavins was the right person to try to pry the Papers from Ellsberg. Tough, arrogant, and steely, at least in his outward manner, he was good at getting information out of people who were reluctant to give it. Stavins was known for browbeating people; he had a certain talent that way. He also had a kind of charm and flattered people when it served his purposes. Ellsberg was acting as if he owned the Papers. "He was very possessive about [them]," Anthony Russo recounts. "He would tell people that they could read the stuff, they could use it, but they had to check with him. What they used, they had to check with him. . . . That was always the line he told me that he told people."[2]

Stavins visited Ellsberg several times in California. Raskin accompanied him on at least one trip. Stavins and Ellsberg developed an intimacy, though they were never really friends. Their mutual interest in sex and women had a lot to do with their relationship. But Ellsberg was reluctant to give Stavins or his IPS colleagues the Papers. Publication in their book would probably not make a big bang—at least not under Ellsberg's name—and he wanted control of them. "He wanted the decision to be his," Barnet remembers. Ellsberg agonized about whether to give IPS the Papers for a long time. He wanted to release them "through some official channel," Barnet recalls. "Both because of the effect and because it would provide him more [legal] protection. . . . I think he wanted cover, and I think he also wanted the achievement and the fame." Ellsberg seemed quite conflicted to Barnet. "On the one hand, I think he probably wanted in some way to be pushed. But he also didn't. . . . He was extremely ambivalent and difficult to deal with. Because he'd go back and forth." Ellsberg would play cat and mouse with you, Stavins would tell Neil Sheehan. He would dangle the Papers in front of you, but he wouldn't let you have them, as he enjoyed the feeling of power that possessing them gave him.[3]

In response to Stavins' requests for documentation on U.S. decision making in Vietnam, however, Ellsberg turned over bits of the Papers to the IPS scholars. "They got little pieces from him," Rodberg recalls. Then they got more pieces. "They were pressing Dan," Rodberg remembers, and it "took a certain number of trips to get what they got." The scholars spoke with lawyers about the criminal risks of holding the documents.[4]

Behind Ellsberg's back, the scholars were disparaging of his possessiveness with the Papers. They thought that Ellsberg wasn't making a strong enough effort to get them out. And they were disdainful of his previous involvement with the war (and his earlier nuclear hawkishness). "They felt he was a hawk who was complicit," Rodberg recounts. "I mean, to Marc Raskin he was a war criminal. . . . At the time, they viewed Dan as one of the worst of the worst. Right up there with Bundy and McNamara." They wondered if Ellsberg might be seeking penance. "There was no doubt that he was totally undoing that war," one person close to the situation says.[5]

Personality conflicts further strained relations between Ellsberg and the scholars. Relations between Barnet and Ellsberg "were never all that good," Barnet remembers. "I'm not sure that our personalities mesh." Though friendly, Ellsberg struck Barnet as "relatively humorless. Sober. There wasn't much levity to lighten [the discussions]. And they were rather intense sessions." One of the IPS scholars recounts, "He'd always focus on what he's saying—often repeated it. I wondered what's going on in his mind." Ellsberg would talk sex at some length.[6]

That same summer of 1970, Louis Lomax, a writer and professor, also emerged as a candidate for publishing some of the Papers. Lomax was a friend of Sally Binford, who was a friend of Russo. "Sally called me up one day, and she says, 'Come on over here now. I've got somebody I want you to meet,'" Russo recounts. Lomax and Russo then "just got into it and talked all afternoon, all night long, all the next day, over a bottle of wine," Russo recalls. "And I told him about the RAND project"—the Viet Cong Motivation and Morale study—"and he was just really excited about that." Lomax said he wanted to speak with William Attwood, the editor in chief of *Look* magazine, about doing an exposé on it. Russo took Lomax out to see Ellsberg in Malibu, where they spoke over lunch at the Sea Lion restaurant. Ellsberg and Russo talked in general terms about the Papers to Lomax, without mentioning a specific study. But "as far as I could see, this was a going relationship," Russo says. And Lomax *"was ready to go."*[7]

But Lomax died only days later. According to one story, Lomax, who was black, stopped in a bar frequented by racists in New Mexico and was ambushed down the road. Whatever the cause, "he lost control of his car," which "skidded across the highway" and "overturned three times," his obituary in the *New York Times* stated on August 1. Attwood, who met once with Russo, decided he didn't want to pursue the story. A former U.S. ambassador, Attwood was turned off by Russo's countercultural ways and probably disinclined to publish classified material.[8] Ellsberg may have been reticent as well: there was no legal cover here, and *Look* could not put out all of the Papers.

But Ellsberg leaked parts of the study to Richard Dudman, the Washington bureau chief of the *St. Louis Post-Dispatch*. "I used to call him up in Malibu," Dudman recounts. "He'd say, 'I've got a document on this,' and he'd read me a lot of top-secret stuff. And I met him once in New York and he had a briefcase full of stuff. It didn't occur to me that this was a cache that ought to be disclosed wholesale. . . . I told him I would like any information he could give me, and I kept going after it. . . . I was a little surprised he was so loose with the stuff." After leaving a restaurant together on one occasion, Ellsberg and Dudman walked several blocks, then Ellsberg stopped and exclaimed, "Oh, I forgot my briefcase," Dudman humorously remembers. The briefcase contained some classified documents.[9]

Russo and Ellsberg threw around other ideas for getting the Papers out. Ellsberg considered hiring someone to print them, then giving a copy to every member of Congress. "We talked about the fact that most newspapers, even alternative newspapers, were infiltrated, and the question would be how to get it done [i.e., leak it] without somebody ratting on us," Russo recalls. "And I said,

'Well, you know, if it comes to it, we could just stage a "happening" and drop them out of helicopters.'" The idea was offered "half serious[ly]," Russo says. "It was like a working model [laughs]." It was entertained "in a desperate mood," Ellsberg would remember. The Papers, he pointed out, "would be rather difficult to police up entirely."[10]

Ellsberg and Patricia Marx were married on August 8. According to Ellsberg, they had earlier put off their wedding out of concern the FBI was going to call on him at any time for copying those top-secret documents. It would not be good to get married only to be led away. Ellsberg was now overjoyed to be marrying Patricia.[11]

Patricia was then working on a book of interviews of biological scientists. She never completed it.[12] For some time to come, her career would be Dan's career.

Their wedding was held at the grassy country estate of Patricia's brother, Louis Marx, Jr., in New York. It attracted coverage in the *New York Times* society pages: "The bride wore a white silk chiffon gown and a floor-length headdress crowned with fresh stephanotis blossoms." Though Jewish, Dan and Patricia had a Presbyterian ceremony. "It was just a fairy tale," Patricia remembers. "Everybody I loved in the whole world [was there]—lesser of Dan's friends, I'm afraid."[13]

Louis Marx, Sr., thought well of his new son-in-law. After all, Ellsberg was a former marine officer and Pentagon aide who had carried a civil service rank equivalent to lieutenant general, and Marx knew the value of generals. "He didn't like any of his sons-in-law very much, but, of them, I was the most popular because I was a lieutenant general," Ellsberg later said with a smile. "He visited me in Vietnam, and I had a better house than his friend, the head of the air force." Patricia's brother "was delighted about the marriage," Patricia recalls. He "had thought I should marry Dan. He thought he was by far the most attractive man I had considered getting married to. And so they were all for it. But they didn't know about the Pentagon Papers."[14]

A time bomb was ticking close to the Marx family.

Vince Davis sent John Vann the *Times* article on the wedding, and with memories of the Dan Ellsberg he had known in the Pentagon in mind, commented, "I hope he has matured enough to make this second marriage a stable and happy one."[15]

After their wedding, Dan and Patricia boarded a helicopter on her brother's lawn and flew off to New York for the night: a gift from her brother, and not the standard stuff of antiwarriors. (After the Papers were published,

Time magazine ran a photo of Dan and Patricia running off hand-in-hand to the helicopter. The photo did not play well with former colleagues already angry at Ellsberg over the Papers. Their jobs had been threatened, and here he was living like royalty, and famous.)[16]

Patricia and Dan then flew to Hawaii for their honeymoon. "Which we interrupted to come back for an interview with Henry Kissinger," Ellsberg recounted later. "I cut my honeymoon in half," he said. But Patricia has no memory of that—nor did Dan himself when she asked him about it before speaking with me. "So I don't think Kissinger interrupted the honeymoon," Patricia says. "Dan had a paper that he was working on or had to submit or something, so there was some pressure to get back to finish the paper," which was for a conference of the American Political Science Association (APSA) in Los Angeles in September. "They had a deadline, so that was kind of impinging" on the honeymoon.[17]

Ellsberg made a splash at the APSA convention. Letting out more bits of the Pentagon Papers—he had "official access," he pointed out, without acknowledging the existence of the study—he presented a paper entitled "Escalating in a Quagmire" that assailed the "quagmire" theory of U.S. involvement in Vietnam. In the paper, he went after other people while making a large statement (as he had done in his other major work, "Risk, Ambiguity, and the Savage Axioms"). Ellsberg directed his attack, in particular, at the former Kennedy aide and historian Arthur Schlesinger, Jr. That was a bold move (just as going after Leonard J. Savage had been a bold move). Schlesinger's version of the quagmire theory argued, in short, that the deepening of U.S. involvement in Vietnam had occurred incrementally as a result of optimistic, yet ill-founded, internal advice promising success with each new step. After pointing out the strengths of Schlesinger's theory, Ellsberg went in for the kill with a short, swift stroke. As an explanation of the major U.S. decisions, he asserted in a version of his paper published the following spring in *Public Policy*, Schlesinger's thesis "is marred only by being totally wrong for each one of those decisions over the last twenty years." "Not one" of the important time periods "fits Schlesinger's generalization to the slightest degree," he contended. This is the Dan Ellsberg who had honed the art of sticking in the knife under Albert Wohlstetter. Ellsberg argued that U.S. intelligence had been persistently pessimistic about long-term U.S. prospects in Vietnam. Policies that had increased U.S. involvement were "holding actions, adequate to avoid defeat in the short run but long shots so far as ultimate success was concerned." Politically, American presidents could not afford to lose in Vietnam, and they postponed defeat. New U.S. commitments "reflected desperation more than hope," Ellsberg wrote.[18]

Ellsberg failed to budge Schlesinger from his quagmire thesis. But his presentation at the APSA convention attracted considerable attention. "There was a lot of buzzing in the hallways: 'Did you hear Dan Ellsberg?,'" Herbert Kelman, a Harvard psychologist, remembers. It was "like something historic had happened. I mean, some kind of electricity" was in the air. Ellsberg's "was an unusual kind of talk for these professional meetings," Kelman notes. That was not only because of what Ellsberg was saying, its provocativeness and arresting effect, its grand sweep, and what some undoubtedly saw as its sheer brilliance (Adam Yarmolinsky would call Ellsberg's paper the best he had ever seen on why the United States had become involved in Vietnam), but also because of who was saying it: a former government and RAND man. "He was an establishment figure," Kelman points out. "I mean, if this had come from a left-wing critic, it wouldn't have attracted much attention. But that it was coming from him—that attracted the attention." Ellsberg won an award for the best paper at the convention. He circulated his draft and the published version widely. Recipients included Robert McNamara and Henry Kissinger.[19]

Some at the convention found Ellsberg a bit odd, though. John Coldwell, who had studied and worked for the U.S. government on counterrevolution in Southeast Asia, and who had classified access, thought Ellsberg seemed untethered and overwrought. Ellsberg was "rambling on" about classified matters Coldwell thought he shouldn't be discussing, as well as "making vague allusions to smoking pot," Coldwell recalls. He remarked to his friend Jeffrey Race, "Look, this guy is a little too tightly wrapped. It amazes me that he has access to the kind of material he has." Coldwell told Ellsberg he could get in trouble for talking about classified matters in the wrong forum, but "I think he felt what I was saying was irrelevant," Coldwell remembers.[20]

Speaking on the same panel as Ellsberg at the APSA convention was Leslie Gelb, who, it will be recalled, had chaired the Pentagon Papers study task force. Gelb was then a fellow at the Brookings Institution. He also argued against the quagmire theory. The analyses Gelb and Ellsberg presented "showed (naturally) some strong similarities," Ellsberg wrote later. By "naturally" he presumably meant they had both been informed by a reading of the Papers. Gelb felt those similarities were too strong, however. And that they were not simply a product of the Papers. Gelb believed firmly that Ellsberg had plagiarized his work. He was quite angry about it. "He was pissed," Len Ackland, who was Gelb's research assistant, remembers. "It was quite clear." Ackland, who would later work on Ellsberg's defense team, and who applauded his release of the Papers, was also convinced that Ellsberg had plagiarized Gelb. "That's clearly what happened," he told me. "I remember reading Ellsberg's paper and [thinking], 'I've read this before.'" (That was the same reaction I had when I read a published version of Gelb's paper after reading Ellsberg's piece. The similarities in their main theses are striking, though that in itself is not evidence of plagiarism in either direction.) "And then when he misspelled 'Sorensen' in one of his endnotes, and I had misspelled 'Sorensen' when I was doing the footnotes [for Gelb's study]," Ackland recalls, "that was kind of the clincher: 'Wow.'" Ackland, who was a journalism professor at the University of Colorado when I interviewed him, was, of course, intimately familiar with Gelb's study, "and I certainly went over Dan's paper quite carefully, in doing comparisons and contrasts." Ackland concluded that "it was either a miracle of simultaneous invention, or he had borrowed ideas from Les's work. . . . It was either a miracle or plagiarism."[21]

Ellsberg and Gelb had exchanged papers before the conference and discussed their ideas. Gelb believed that Ellsberg had then changed his paper to incorporate Gelb's thesis as its main theme. He felt betrayed by Ellsberg. (After the Pentagon Papers were published—which only increased Gelb's anger at him—Ellsberg would have the temerity to refer to "my friend Leslie Gelb" in his book *Papers on the War.*) "Dan had a lot of facts and figures in his head, and he's a very smart guy, and he glommed onto it [Gelb's thesis]," Ackland argues. "It was a way to structure" his paper. "And the thing he failed to do was to credit Gelb with being the source of the ideas, or the organization."[22]

Actually, in two footnotes in the paper he presented at the conference, Ellsberg seemed to go out of his way to praise and credit Gelb's work—while simultaneously drawing attention to their differences. In the published version of his piece, "The Quagmire Myth and the Stalemate Machine," Ellsberg expressed his "particular debt to Leslie Gelb" this way: "I am happy to acknowledge great stimulation from discussions with Gelb . . . whose studies of the earlier periods [of U.S. involvement in Vietnam] preceded my own and who in particular pointed out that the propositions emerging from my study of 1961 and my experience in 1964–1965 applied as well to decisions going back to the 1940s and 1950s." One wonders if that was meant to appease Gelb. (After the Papers were published, Ellsberg phoned Gelb and asked him if he wanted his name mentioned in footnotes in *Papers on the War.* Gelb thought that the real purpose of the call, however—as he reported to the FBI—was to learn how he and others felt about Ellsberg's release of the Papers.)[23]

Others would also come to believe that Ellsberg was guilty of plagiarism, including David Halberstam, Neil Sheehan, and Anthony Lake, who looked into the matter with skepticism only to conclude that Gelb was right. The *New York Times*'s Marty Arnold, who heard about Ellsberg's alleged plagiarism during his Pentagon Papers trial, remembers that "the whole Halperin-Gelb-Warnke clique of people" were "pissed off about it."[24]

If Ellsberg did appropriate Gelb's thesis or other ideas, it is a major mark on both his character and record of intellectual achievement. "The Quagmire Myth and the Stalemate Machine" is the crown jewel of his Vietnam writing.

Ellsberg's problems completing his paper in time for the APSA conference may have contributed to any plagiarism. He was up against it and, as Ackland concluded, may have found that using Gelb's framework was a way to pull it together. "Ellsberg was just looking for a quick way out," Ackland believes. More speculatively (and here we may be going out on a limb), another incident may have contributed to Ellsberg's plight: his briefcase that he said was stolen from the Avis counter at the Los Angeles airport contained all his notes for his paper and possibly the text itself. That must have thrown him for a loop (though he presumably could have obtained another copy of his paper).[25]

Gelb confronted Ellsberg. "They came to some kind of an agreement, but it was hot and heavy there for a while," Ackland remembers. During his trial, Ellsberg and Ackland were not at all close. "Dan was always rather standoffish with me," Ackland recalls. "And I figured it was because I had worked for Gelb" and "he knew that I knew" about the alleged plagiarism. "But he never said anything to me. And we've never talked about it." Ackland doubts Ellsberg's fundamental integrity.[26]

———◦———

Meanwhile, Henry Kissinger had not been eager to meet with Ellsberg. But journalist Lloyd Shearer, who was friendly with Ellsberg, had an appointment to interview Kissinger and, at Ellsberg's urging, Shearer took him along. At San Clemente, the Western White House, Kissinger evaded Ellsberg, however. When Shearer tried to get him to talk about Vietnam, Kissinger "looked at me quite nervously and made it clear he didn't want to talk in front of me," Ellsberg recounted. He passed Ellsberg off to his aide Alexander Haig.[27]

"I went to San Clemente again, and again wasn't able to see him," Ellsberg remembered. "But on one last visit I did see him. I was kept waiting, and when I finally got in he said he could only see me for half an hour." Ellsberg apprised Kissinger of his understanding of the Nixon administration's Vietnam strategy, he recalled, and urged Kissinger to read the Pentagon Papers or at least the summaries in them. "But do we really have anything to learn from this study?" Kissinger asked. That disheartened Ellsberg. Kissinger told him as they parted that he was "very anxious" to see him again, however, indeed that it was "very important" that he see him, Ellsberg recounted. But Kissinger then canceled three straight appointments.[28]

———◦———

In Cambridge, Massachusetts, Dan and Pat Ellsberg moved into a desirable third-floor flat at 10 Hilliard Street, several blocks from Harvard Square. They hung a chair from the ceiling of their living room, almost like a swing. But more eye-grabbing to those invited to see them were the mirrors the Ellsbergs had installed in their bedroom. They lined the slanted walls, and a huge mirror was attached to the ceiling. "The whole thing was lined with mirrors," Hind Sadek Kooros, an archaeologist who owned the house with her husband, Jamshid, remembers. "Mirrors were all over the place." "The bedroom was completely plated," recalls Jeremy Larner, who first got to know Ellsberg in Cambridge and who, when he saw the mirrors, "immediately thought, 'This is Dan's doing, not Pat's.'" "Pay no attention to them" Patricia remarked to visitors on one occasion. "It's just a fantasy that Dan has had since childhood." One person who spent time in the Ellsbergs' apartment but who didn't want to be quoted by name remembers that there was also more erotica around than he'd ever seen before. "That was kind of part of their life," he says. "An interest in erotica." He also noticed a commissioned, full-length Picasso charcoal sketch of Patricia on the wall. Nude, of course. Patricia had participated in nudism with Ellsberg and would soon (or perhaps already had) come to share his ability to engage in talk about sex.[29]

The Ellsbergs did not associate much with their neighbors. They were "very taken up with their own lives," the author Priscilla McMillan, who lived next door, recalls. "We never really were related to them, connected to them, in any way," remembers Stewart Perry, who lived with his wife, Helen, directly underneath the Ellsbergs in the second-floor flat at 10 Hilliard Street. Stewart Perry, a friendly, modest man who struck me as charitable yet discerning, and not the type who criticizes people readily, ran a small nonprofit group working for low-income community economic development; he and Helen, a writer, had backgrounds in applied psychiatry, and had long protested the Vietnam War. They thus had common ground with the Ellsbergs. But Dan showed no interest in them. "He was a very arrogant person," Stewart recalls. "He was not particularly forthcoming at all." Helen thought Ellsberg "a spoiled brat. From the moment I first had contact with him, he was arrogant. And it was like a little boy." McMillan noticed then and later that Dan used people. It is not an uncommon observation of him. He "let other people be his handmaidens," she says, adding with a chuckle, "And you do get the feeling from him that he's doing it in the name of a higher cause. That it's worth it, and they'll enjoy it, because they'll know it's in a good cause." McMillan adds, "Dan isn't interested in what other people do. . . . He was interested in what he was doing."[30]

The house at 10 Hilliard Street was a remodeled one, with internal apartments that made for a close living situation. But "he didn't make it easy," Stewart Perry recounts. "Even when we were trying to be helpful to him at the point when he was in trouble [after the Pentagon Papers were published], he was not appreciative in the slightest." And "if it hadn't been that we were politically sympathetic to his plight, we wouldn't have had anything to do with him." The Perrys wondered what Patricia saw in Dan. In the Ellsbergs' marriage, "you certainly felt as if the softness was on Pat's side, the warmth," Stewart recalls. "And his was very cold and nonrelated." Some people would come to see Patricia as Dan's handmaiden. She appeared to McMillan to serve Dan's interests—"that he was the brilliant one and she might be a little bit enslaved, or at least certainly a very willing helpmate."[31]

The Perrys and the Ellsbergs had not gotten off to the best of starts at 10 Hilliard Street. Soon after they had moved in in December of 1970, the Perrys noticed that whenever someone came to visit the Ellsbergs, the buzzer rang in their apartment. The buttons for the buzzers were on the tenants' mailboxes, and it turned out that the Ellsbergs had earlier taken over the mailbox whose buzzer sounded in the Perrys' apartment because the mailbox for their apartment had a broken lock. "We had to ask them to change it back," Helen Perry recalls. They did, but Dan "wasn't giving" about it. The Perrys suspected the Ellsbergs had known about the problem before they spoke to them. More aggravating, the Ellsbergs were night owls, and "they were very loud walkers," Stewart recounts, "because they had no carpeting down." The Perrys asked them, Could they please put some rugs down or something of the sort? "Pat was just a lovely person, so you could say anything to her in a courteous way, and she was very responsive," Stewart says. "So she eventually got carpeting put down—a *lot* of wall-to-wall carpeting put down, more than was necessary—to handle our needs. But Dan was very unpleasant about it." Ellsberg, whose typewriting into the wee hours of the morning—and his response to their complaint about it—also bothered the Perrys, told me: "Just after they moved in down below us, I get a phone call at night. . . . 'You're walking around in your apartment.' And I said, 'Yes, I am.' They said, 'With *shoes* on.' I said, 'Yes, I guess that's true.' 'Well, we can't *sleep* down here.' . . . She was really hysterical. That's been a joke ever since: With *shoes* on. You're walking with *shoes* on."[32]

The door to the Perrys' apartment was on the landing of the stairway the Ellsbergs descended when leaving the house. Sometimes the Ellsbergs would take off at night. "They would go out for a ski vacation or something and leave quite late," Stewart recalls. "You can see somebody coming back late, but they would *leave* late"—"and be very noisy about it," Helen interjects. "They would wake up the household." The tenant downstairs, who was the director of the Loeb Drama Center at Harvard, would complain to the Perrys about it: What in the world were those people doing leaving late at night and banging their stuff around? The Perrys later wondered whether one or more of these late-night excursions involved moving the Papers rather than skiing. "One reason that we felt off about them was that they were not considerate or sophisticated," Helen Perry reminisces. "You don't take over somebody's mailbox. They were like high school kids in that way. It was sort of playing with life." Dan "was not a good neighbor," Stewart says.[33]

At MIT's Center for International Studies, Ellsberg was "moving in about seven different directions," William Bundy, his colleague there, remembers. "He never showed up at the center." "I don't think he did much," another colleague, Edwin Diamond, recalls. "I mean, I at least put on a seminar. I don't know if he even did that."[34]

Diamond, a former editor at *Newsweek*, had one memorable conversation with Ellsberg. After Diamond had given his seminar on the media or perhaps at a social gathering, Ellsberg approached him and intently began pumping him. "He wasn't very curious about *Newsweek*," Diamond recounts. "He particularly wanted to know what I knew about the power structure—or who was doing what to whom—at the *New York Times*." More specifically, Ellsberg wished to know what Diamond knew about the relationship between the *Times*'s Washington bureau and its editors in New York. He seemed "awfully curious about the *New York Times*," Diamond says.[35]

Bundy, whose presence at the center may have attracted the bomb that exploded there, was writing his memoir on Vietnam. He was emotionally drained at the time from Vietnam and career and family difficulties, and generally not in good spirits. "I was very low in those Cambridge years," Bundy recalls. "I was just kind of numb, frankly. A lot of this period I was numb. I wanted to get on with something else." He and Ellsberg didn't talk about Vietnam. "I put on a couple of presentations, but he didn't show up," Bundy remembers. Bundy never published his Vietnam book: Ellsberg's release of the Papers undercut it.

"I thought I'd been overtaken by a mass of material," Bundy says, even though he had read the Papers and had a copy. (Bundy and David Halberstam had a heated exchange after Halberstam asked him for a set. "I got this whiny, bullshit answer back from him," Halberstam recounts. "You know, snively. About, 'If Bob gives you a set,' as if McNamara would be the keeper of the truth. . . . I was quite pissed.") Bundy had not been able to cite the Papers in his writing, and when they were published the truth was out—one couldn't finesse the truth any more, or say, as officials were prone to do, "If you only knew what we knew." Publication of the Papers destroyed the ability of former war architects to write the memoirs they might have wanted to write.[36]

Ellsberg didn't get a lot of work done on the Vietnam book he had planned to write at MIT. "I remember all of us at both Harvard and MIT became convinced that poor Dan would never get anything finished," Thomas Schelling remembers. "He was just incapable." "He was supposed to be doing research and writing, but we never talked about that," Howard Zinn, who was at Boston University at the time, recalls. Schelling, who taught at Harvard, had lunch with Ellsberg several times during this period. "I found him becoming very tedious," Schelling recounts. "He was developing what might be called 'revisionist' views of all kinds of things in history. And we'd sit down to lunch and I'd make some idle remark, and Dan would start talking, and he wouldn't stop talking for an hour and fifteen minutes. And I got to where just getting rid of him was what I had to do at lunchtime. . . . He was full of conspiracy theories that I was afraid were true, but I didn't really want to hear about them," Schelling laughs.[37]

Schelling participated in a Vietnam discussion group at Harvard with Ellsberg. "By this time he's very angry," Sam Popkin, another participant, recounts. "His attitude this time is, 'Nothing's going to work.' And anytime somebody said something's going to work, he'd go after them." In a review he wrote for the *Washington Post* that November, Ellsberg savaged a collection of essays on Vietnam and the hopes they expressed by the journalist Robert Shaplen, whose views he had once shared.[38]

Ellsberg may have spent more time at Harvard than at MIT. (Twice in one interview with me, he recalled being at Harvard during this period, only to correct himself, "I mean MIT.") He began hanging around the newsroom of the *Harvard Crimson*. Frank Rich, who was editorial chairman of the *Crimson*, didn't know who Ellsberg was when he introduced himself to Rich and others on the newspaper and indicated that "he knew a lot about what was going on in the Vietnam War," Rich remembers. "He was eager to tell us some of this information." Ellsberg had "an obsessed quality that was unusual," Rich thought. "It was striking. We all found it striking. We may have shared his politics, but there was this kind of evangelical quality that was different."[39]

Many former *Crimson* writers visited its newsroom, but Ellsberg was a somewhat rare bird there. The newspaper was a locus of antiwar activism, even radicalism, and Ellsberg had previously been in on the war. He was "sort of a celebrity to us even before the Pentagon Papers," another former *Crimson* editor remembers. "There weren't many grown-ups who had actually been in Vietnam who hung around the *Crimson*. And he was repentant for his sins. So he was a very interesting figure to us." Ellsberg's hushed tones added to his insider aura. "He'd have all these theories about the Vietnam War," Scott Jacobs, an executive editor of the *Crimson*, recalls. "When he'd interject something into the conversation, he seemed to speak with some authority."[40]

Ellsberg appeared eager to fit in with the young *Crimson* crowd and to be looking for a new community to join after leaving RAND. He acted almost as if he wanted to be one of the boys at the *Crimson*. Again, there was talk of sex. Another former *Crimson* editor comments, "He was a fish out of water. He'd left his whole life, everything he was about to betray in a certain sense, everything he'd ever done. He was looking for family.... On the one hand, we thought he was sort of cool. And on the other hand, you felt sort of sorry for him. Because he was this fish out of water. And it seemed slightly inappropriate for him to be hanging out and taking drugs like he was 22 or 20.... It really seemed to me that he no longer fit anywhere." Ellsberg would often eat with Rich and Jacobs, lunching at the Signet Society. Some editors visited his apartment, and he partied with them at their homes. "I smoked dope with Dan Ellsberg," Jacobs laughs. "He liked hanging out with us," Rich says. "As did his wife," who was quite curious about how to buy marijuana. One former *Crimson* editor remembers that Dan was also interested in how to buy marijuana, "which was not the most difficult thing to do at Harvard at that time. But he seemed kind of naive about it." This person recalls a *Crimson* colleague telling him that Dan and Pat wanted to buy some pot, so the colleague "scraped together an ounce of marijuana somewhere, and brought it to Pat, not to Dan. And she said, 'Oh, my God. A whole pound.' And he thought this was hilarious, that they really didn't know much about [it], that they would mistake an ounce for a pound."[41]

Ellsberg helped one *Crimson* editor out of a jam. This person was taking a class taught by Doris Kearns on national security in the spring of 1971. He rarely attended her lectures and never went to the discussion sections; indeed, he never even bothered to sign up for a discussion section. Consequently, when the time came for the final exam, an open-book essay exam that asked students to advise the president on some situation of international conflict, "I didn't have a clue," he recounts. "And I was very much from the antiwar mindset and not into thinking in strategic imperatives. So I didn't have any idea what to say. So I went to Dan. . . . Well, of course, to him, this was mother's milk. And he reeled it off. He reeled off an answer about the various considerations and the different balances of power you had to consider and so on. And I nodded and I wrote it all down. And I got an A in the course."[42]

Ellsberg's introduction to most *Crimson* editors had followed an escalation of the Vietnam War in November 1970. President Richard Nixon had ordered two days of intense bombing of North Vietnam, including cities, and a commando raid on Son Tay prison west of Hanoi. Ellsberg, who learned about the bombing from a sign spray-painted on a wall as he walked to the *Crimson* for a post-football-game party, feared that an invasion of North Vietnam and a complete renewal of U.S. bombing might be coming next: "I thought, 'These are the final hours. We're going to be escalating any time now.'" The "final chapter was on us." Ellsberg warned of such possibilities in a piece in the *Washington Post* co-written with two MIT colleagues, including Noam Chomsky. The editors who were gathered at the *Crimson* office thought his reaction to the escalation "somewhat hyperbolic," however. So, apparently, did Harvard professor Stanley Hoffmann, who remembers Ellsberg warning at this time that the United States was likely to use nuclear weapons in Vietnam. Ellsberg said he knew that the Pentagon had such a plan on the books. "Frankly, he made no sense," Hoffmann recalls; "the Pentagon had plans for everything." James Thomson, another Harvard professor then, remembers Ellsberg warning about the possible use of nuclear weapons after the allied invasion of Laos three months later too. While Ellsberg always seemed extremely well documented, says Jeremy Larner, who was at Harvard's Institute of Politics at this time, "I didn't trust Dan's apocalyptic kind of mood," which went beyond Vietnam.[43]

Nixon's escalation of the war intensified Ellsberg's desire to get the Pentagon Papers out. This is apparently when he fully apprised Patricia of his mission. When Patricia read the Papers, she thought it very important to release them. She found them powerful reading: the manipulation, the lies, the callous disregard for human life—it all stunned and horrified her. She was now "the only other person" copying them, she remembers. But it was a painful, agonizing situation for her, partly because of the risks and uncertainties, but also because she was "completely alone in it, because I couldn't tell my family, I couldn't tell my friends," she recalls. "You couldn't tell anyone, really. . . . I'm very close to my sisters; I couldn't talk it over with them. There was nobody I could turn to. Except my own conscience."[44]

At the *Harvard Crimson*, Ellsberg began making phone calls to try to organize opposition to the bombing. Before ducking into the managing editor's office, "he said something about calling Cyrus Vance and Senator Charles Goodell to arrange a Senate antiwar filibuster," Rich wrote afterward. Two editors invited Ellsberg to address an evening *Crimson* editorial board meeting to develop a statement on the bombing. In the dimly lit conference room, Ellsberg began by telling the editors in some detail about his establishment past. "He was enthusiastic about that," Rich recounts. "He was almost in a kind of confessional mode. He was energized about it. It was not something that he was bashful or reluctant about. And, in fact, I remember that because it was such a novelty. Given our politics and our perspective at the time, you'd think perhaps he would be sheepish about presenting these things. . . . He was a mesmerizing talker. We were kind of blown away by him when he spoke to us at the meeting." But Ellsberg characteristically went on too long: "At a certain point he would exhaust you. And we'd like to go on to the next activity. It wasn't so easy."[45]

<hr />

That year Ellsberg also hung out a lot with Sam Popkin, an assistant professor of government at Harvard some eleven years younger than him. "We spent huge amounts of time inhaling together and going to movies together and talking about Vietnam," Popkin remembers. Also an intense man, Popkin was a moderate war critic and antileft. He found Ellsberg one of the smartest people he'd ever met, if overly advertising of his accomplishments and knowledge. "He certainly made sure you knew," Popkin laughs. "He made sure I knew that he knew everything there was to know about nuclear targeting. . . . He certainly felt full of special information." ("He does it in quiet little ways," his friend Doug Dowd comments. "Always in the top of the class, always this, always that. . . . He lets you know.") Popkin's time with Ellsberg was not laidback. "You don't ever really relax with Dan," he points out. "Because there's always some turf he's defending, or [he's] interrogating you to prove his principles are right." Ellsberg's voice would change as he prepared to pounce.[46]

As for his standard sex talk, "there was a lot of wink and nudges to it," Popkin recounts. In a nutshell, the message Popkin heard from Ellsberg was: "I did really well at Harvard. I know a lot of things you don't know. And I'm fucking a lot of things you're not fucking." When it came to stories of him and Patricia, "he just sort of [said], 'Oh, we went off for the afternoon. Went off in the country. . . . And a lot of amazing things happened,'" Popkin remembers. Pat was present when Ellsberg said this. "That's what was so funny," Popkin says. "That's part of the reason I didn't say, 'Oh? And what did you do?'" But Pat "just sort of smiled. . . . I always wondered why Pat wasn't more embarrassed." Again, there were photos, including of a nude Patricia under a waterfall or the like. Patricia was also present when Ellsberg showed these photos.[47]

As for Ellsberg's womanizing, he was often "all over women . . . in the most inappropriate settings," Popkin remembers. One man who knew Ellsberg in Cambridge at this time recalls that, sometime after the Papers were published, Ellsberg began rubbing the back and shoulders and touching the hand of this man's fiancée as the three of them were sitting in the grass on the bank of the Charles River. "We said, 'What's going on?'" he recounts. "What are you supposed to say? . . . Nobody knew what to say or do! . . . 'Is this the stress of a man under indictment?' But then we realized there is this part of him that is just always out of control and . . . looking for sex. . . . It was like it was unconscious! Like he's talking, and like he's coming on to her." (Told this account, Doug Dowd remarked, "Completely plausible. I don't think there's any doubt at all. That's *exactly* what he does. I've seen him do it.")[48]

<hr />

It was during his time at MIT that Ellsberg became friends with both Noam Chomsky and Howard Zinn, two radical critics of the war. Chomsky had earlier met Ellsberg when Ellsberg had approached him after one of his many talks on the war. At Ellsberg's request, they had then gone out for a cup of coffee to talk. "He told me his background and who he was," Chomsky remembers. Also, "he had heard my talk and he thought it was basically on target, and he had personal background which could much enrich it, both from personal experience from the inside and from documents that he had. And then we went ahead and explored that. But he didn't know me and he wasn't going to tell me too much. . . . But it was enough for me to be interested. . . . And after that we saw quite a lot of each other." Ellsberg showed Chomsky parts of the Pentagon Papers, and they discussed them. Ellsberg asked Chomsky not to talk about them with others, and Chomsky didn't. Between themselves, Ellsberg and Chomsky talked about how to interpret the Papers and the light they shed on the planning of the war. By the time the Papers were published in June of 1971, Chomsky had already read all of them. He was not optimistic about what impact their release would have, however. Indeed, he thought there would be essentially no impact.[49] (How many people must have told Ellsberg that? Their talk could not have been reassuring.)

Ellsberg's conversations with Chomsky, laserlike in their intensity, were something to observe. "I remember once I was having lunch with Dan and Noam," Howard Zinn recounts. "Now, when Dan and Noam got together, it was like a fusillade of facts and information going back and forth. You know: 'Yes, it was on November 22.' 'I think it was November 23.' . . . And Dan and Noam were going back and forth with this stuff. And then when we walked out of the MIT building where we had lunch, Dan suddenly turned to me and said, 'Howard, I noticed you didn't have much to say.'" Chomsky's writings had a big impact on Ellsberg. They had earlier led Ellsberg to question whether the United States had any right to be in Vietnam, and suggested that U.S. involvement was a crime.[50]

After Zinn met Ellsberg at an antiwar meeting, he and his wife, Roslyn, began seeing Dan and Patricia socially. "It was good to have the two women around, because then things got lighter," Zinn recalls. Patricia was more easygoing than Dan and "willing to talk about other things than the war. Dan zeroes in on a subject and holds onto it and won't let go." The two couples went to the movies together, as Ellsberg liked to see lots of movies and still does, including action movies most intellectuals would not choose to see. "He sees himself as a man of action and physical courage and all of that," Zinn observes. ("It's like an addiction," a close friend of Ellsberg told me in the 1990s. Ellsberg normally goes to movies "two or three times a week," as a way of "participating in hugely dramatic events" and to escape his problems—"and a lot bothers him.")[51]

One evening in the winter or spring of 1971, Ellsberg told the Zinns he had something to tell them in "strict confidence." He apprised them of the Pentagon Papers. Would they like to see some of them? Indeed they would. Ellsberg disappeared into his bedroom and came back with a stack of them. (During my visit to the Ellsbergs' former Hilliard Street apartment, I noticed huge crawl spaces in the bedroom—possible storage sites.) Howard Zinn took the Papers down to his car. "Then I brought them to my office here at Boston University," he recounts. "And I kept them under my desk . . . and read them whenever I got a chance. In between meetings with students, I would pick up part of the Pentagon Papers and read them." Ellsberg asked Zinn what he thought of them. Zinn said it would be absolutely terrific if the public could have them. "I think he wanted confirmation that this was really an important thing to do," Zinn recalls.[52]

Ellsberg made more copies of the Papers in Cambridge, including at the Gnomon Copy Service near MIT. According to Harrison Salisbury's book *Without Fear or Favor*, Ellsberg asked for "a rush job on a box of secret documents he was using, he said, in a history of the Vietnam war." If true, that was

taking a chance. Ellsberg paid with personal checks, another risk. The economist James Galbraith was then an undergraduate student at Harvard, and a
roommate of his in Quincy House worked at Gnomon and handled the documents. Galbraith said he'd like to see them, so the roommate brought some of
them over. Once, when copying at some place in Cambridge, Ellsberg again
tripped a burglar alarm, bringing police to the scene. He also did some copying
commercially in New York.[53]

Among those who stored documents for Ellsberg in Cambridge was one of
Patricia's half brothers, Spencer "Rainbow" Marx, a "schizzy" hippie type
known to opt for sleeping out under the trees, doing yoga in the nude, and
meditating surrounded by candles—all while a guest at other people's homes.
Patricia's stepmother, Idella, who had an apartment near the Ellsbergs, may
have also helped out. Both Spencer and Idella would later be called before
grand juries. The Justice Department's Robert Mardian stated that Idella had
reportedly been "observed" in an apartment containing "numerous cutting
boards which could be used to trim xerox copies."[54] If Idella was involved, her
husband would not have been pleased had he known.

Jeffrey Race, who was then a graduate student at Harvard, also stored
copies of the Papers for Ellsberg. One day probably in the spring of 1971, Race
recounts, he was riding his bike from Harvard Square to his parents' house
(where he kept most of his possessions). "I was stopping at a gas station. . . . I
was putting air in my tire. . . . And Dan pulled up. I think he had a BMW. He
said, 'I was just going over to see you at your house. . . . Could I leave some
things in your basement? I have some cardboard boxes.'" Race pedaled over to
his parents' house as Ellsberg drove his car. They then carried some boxes
down to the basement. Race says he did not know what was in the boxes and
didn't ask. They were sealed.[55]

Someone would subsequently come by the home of Race's parents and
pick up one or more of the boxes. "I had no idea what they were," Race's
mother would remember.[56]

———⊕———

Meanwhile, Ellsberg had sought psychiatric help again. The stress of the Papers surely contributed to his disquiet. Sometime between December 30,
1970, and January 4, 1971, Ellsberg placed a call to Dr. Lewis Fielding from a
room he was occupying at the upscale Bel Air Hotel in Los Angeles, Howard
Hunt later determined. On January 29, a Friday, back in Cambridge, Ellsberg
saw a psychiatrist by the name of Dr. Arthur Valenstein. He saw Valenstein

again on Tuesday, February 2, Hunt noted. Patricia Ellsberg also saw a psychiatrist that spring.[57]

The evening of January 29, after seeing Valenstein, Ellsberg attended an off-the-record conference at MIT's Endicott House outside Boston where Henry Kissinger was speaking. This was, of course, the same Henry Kissinger who had just been jerking him around on appointments. After Kissinger spoke in a manner typically designed to pacify his listeners and seem sympathetic to their concerns, and following other questions, Ellsberg rose to speak. Had the Nixon administration made any estimates of the likely number of Indochinese casualties in the Vietnam War in the next year? Ellsberg asked. Could Kissinger provide those figures? A rather pointed query. "Cleverly worded," Kissinger called it. According to Ellsberg, Kissinger was "completely stunned" and "it was the first time he'd shown any break in his poise at all" during the evening. Ellsberg told Kissinger he was not trying to be clever and pressed him again, even more bluntly. Kissinger said Ellsberg was accusing the administration of being racist. (Kissinger later told Nixon, John Ehrlichman, and H.R. Haldeman that Ellsberg had "heckled" him.) The moderator called the proceedings to a close.[58] Not many people had confronted Kissinger in quite *that* way in such gentlemanly settings.

As Kissinger was speaking that evening, U.S. B-52s were bombing enemy positions in Laos to "soften" them up for the allied invasion of Laos. Eleven days later, ARVN troops crossed the border. At Harvard, James Thomson and other liberal critics organized a teach-in. Ellsberg "wanted to be one of the panelists, but the student leaders who met with him beforehand thought he was too intensely far out and would not be very persuasive," Thomson recalls. Ellsberg's talk about the Nixon administration going to nukes seemed extreme, and his manner disconcerted them. "They were turned off," Thomson says. Ellsberg believed Thomson had kept him out of the teach-in. "He thought that he should have been on the panel, and temporarily was very suspicious," Thomson remembers. "Ellsberg gets very suspicious."[59]

Yet Ellsberg was more moderate in his views than many student protesters (some of whom had doubts about him because his conversion was recent), and he looked more the government-professor type, with his tweedy suit coats and shorter hair—"not a hippie," Scott Jacobs remembers. "He was definitely into nonviolence. I think Dan Ellsberg believed that if the true story of Vietnam came out, reasonable men would stop this war. And I think the mood of students at that time was, 'There's not time for reasonable men to consider the issue. Let's just get out of there.' . . . Dan was probably in the conservative camp among the protesters. . . . He needed an argument. He needed to have a constructed argument that supported a position." Both culturally and politically, recalls Tom Oliphant of the *Boston Globe*, "clearly he'd changed. But on the other hand, he hadn't changed all that much."[60]

To a veteran activist, Ellsberg could seem naive. Herbert Kelman spoke at a meeting at one of the Harvard student houses on his experiences with nonviolent direct action in the civil rights movement going back over 20 years. Kelman may have also talked about his resistance to the Korean War. He did not know Ellsberg when Ellsberg responded to his remarks. "It was kind of an odd reaction, of saying, 'My God, did people do that this long ago?'" Kelman recounts. "It was a newly discovered thing for him." Ellsberg seemed "really impressed with the fact that there were people who have been thinking about these kinds of things, and this whole resistance, and acting on it in one way or another for such a long time." He also seemed to be "searching for people who had thought about this before" and "seriously thinking about going this way in his own life."[61]

Ellsberg's behavior during the May Day civil disobedience in Washington in early May of 1971 amused Howard Zinn and Noam Chomsky, who were in the same affinity group with him. The objective of May Day, a largely youthful protest, was to shut down Washington by blocking streets and bridges. "It was very funny," Chomsky recounts:

> He was sort of leading us around as if we were his platoon and he was a marine commander. You know, "Let's race over here. They won't see us over here." He was *very* excited. To me, it was just a horrible war. I just wanted to get done with [the protest] and get out of there. And I think everybody in the group felt that. That kind of quizzical view: What the hell are we doing here? . . . But he was just having a ball. I remember once he got Maced [from] about two feet away. And, oh god, he was just ecstatic. I mean, it was so out of character with the group that he was in. But . . . he likes drama, he likes excitement, he's very courageous, and he'll try all sorts of things. . . . I remember . . . feeling that, "Look, here's a guy who thinks he's out in the jungle in Saigon, and the best he can do for a platoon is us old guys." We were trailing around after him, but he's trying as best he can, and . . . the more dangerous it got, the more . . . he'd be delighted. Which struck me as really weird. I'd much rather have been home. . . . He was more at ease with the kids on May Day than I was.[62]

Zinn also remembers Ellsberg taking charge of their affinity group "like the platoon sergeant or the lieutenant":

> Dan felt that was his job. That he was the only person. Well, I had been in the military, but I was in the air force. That didn't count, right? He was a marine. As though we were playing this sort of funny game with the cops, where we

would sit down in the middle of a street and block it . . . and when the tear gas came, we fled the tear gas and reassembled, and Dan would tell us where to go next [laughs]. . . . And we'd do this three or four times. And then at one point we were huddled together on a street corner . . . and that's when this policeman came up to us and sprayed Mace into my eyes and Dan's eyes. And the two of us were temporarily blinded. . . .

Dan liked to be in the center of things. Even at the expense of being Maced. There was something heroic about being Maced.

Ellsberg was also showing the enthusiasm of the novice. After returning to Cambridge, he proudly displayed to young people at the *Crimson* a photograph of himself, Chomsky, and Zinn taken during the protest.[63]

Not everyone found Ellsberg's behavior during May Day amusing, though. Len Ackland and his future wife were also in his affinity group, and in the Washington Mall, Ackland recalls,

he was just beside himself with wanting to lead the charge. And so he took a couple of trash cans and dumped them in the street. And my wife, then a friend, just balled him out and said, "What are you *doing?*" You know, she didn't know who he was at all. And she said later that if she had known she probably would have been a little bit more reticent. But she just rode him up one side and down the other for how stupid this was. You know, trashing the Mall—what kind of political statement is that going to make? But that was the way he [was]. . . . He always wanted to be out there, wanting to be seen, wanting to be engaged, and wasn't always thoughtful about it.[64]

After Ellsberg saw that the battle was diminishing, he flew to New York, and that afternoon, at his and Patricia's stylish East Side apartment, he showered, "got the tear gas out of my hair, put on a new suit, and went to the Council on Foreign Relations to hear McGeorge Bundy give the first of his scheduled lectures on lessons of Vietnam," he remembers.[65] That's quite a transition. Ellsberg still wanted to be a member of the foreign policy establishment.

Two days later, he attended a large rally on the Boston Common at which Howard Zinn spoke. Afterward, he came up to Zinn and said—in a low, emotional voice—"Howard, that was the best speech I've ever heard in my life."[66]

Ellsberg joined another civil disobedience protest the next day at the federal building in Boston. He seemed uncomfortable sitting there, one among many people waiting to get dispersed or arrested. "I don't think that he was used to being just a cipher," Hilde Hein, another participant in the demonstration, aptly remarks, and "one is at a demonstration like that." After several hours, the cops moved in, roughing up some of the protesters. "Dan was very upset by the sudden outbreak of violence," Hein recounts. "I mean, it wasn't terribly violent, but Dan wanted to protect the women, which we all thought was pretty funny, because we were more experienced than he was. . . . The women were all kind of astonished at this gladiatorial, chivalric thing that he exuded. It was kind of inappropriate in the circumstances. And he was sort of cute and sweet, but not terribly effective."[67]

When police moved on Ellsberg, he put his hands over his head. "This four-foot baton smashed my Rolex watch" and "drove glass into my wrist, and the watch into my wrist," he recalls. "So my wrist was rather badly cut, and I was bleeding a lot and had to go have it bandaged." To his surprise, however, Ellsberg noticed that, just like in the television commercials that showed watches emerging unscathed from sharks' stomachs and surviving other ordeals, his watch was still running. He subsequently attended an arms control seminar with establishment types wearing a bandage conspicuously on his wrist.[68]

Ellsberg expressed disappointment to friends that he had not been arrested at the federal building or during May Day. "We must be willing to put our bodies on the line," he told Tom Oliphant.[69]

Ellsberg spoke in the language of the protesters: words like murder, for instance. Greg Wierzynski was *Time* magazine's Boston bureau chief and got together two or three times with the Ellsbergs in Cambridge. He found it odd that a man with a coat and tie on, and a nice apartment, who had worked in the Pentagon, would be using such words. He was also struck by the intensity with which Ellsberg used them. "I thought he was kind of a strange guy," Wierzynski remembers. "He was not a relaxed dude. . . . He wasn't very relaxed in anything." But Ellsberg fascinated Wierzynski. Here was a guy who had served in Washington and Vietnam, "he seemed to be a great authority on the subject, and yet he seemed to be so totally alienated from the government, from the policy of the government. And I had never before seen a guy who had served the government and become alienated."[70] Or at least *that* alienated.

"Murder in Laos" was the title the *New York Review of Books* put on its front page for an article Ellsberg wrote following the invasion. In the piece, Ellsberg perceptively described the Nixon administration's threat strategy in Vietnam and accurately predicted future escalations. He wrote with some emotion of murder in Laos. The angry tone of the article contrasts starkly with the enjoyment he had derived earlier from hunting the enemy in Vietnam. He circulated the article in draft, including to Tom Wicker, who then wrote a piece bearing its imprint, which condemned Nixon's "policy of escalation" and the "slaughter of innocents" in Indochina.[71]

Ellsberg, who had read many of the Nuremberg documents, spoke out increasingly against U.S. war crimes in Vietnam. He attacked those who had been connected with the war as war criminals, and those who did not protest it as "good Germans." Some, of course, thought his tone self-righteous. He had turned; those who had not were immoral, or worse. "It wasn't that he just talked about the war—he had narrowed it down to war crimes and war criminals," one dovish friend remembered. In late 1970 or early 1971, Len Ackland attended a meeting at the Brookings Institution on the Vietnam study then being directed by Leslie Gelb. (Gelb's study was eventually published as a book entitled *The Irony of Vietnam: The System Worked.*) Ellsberg, who was on the study's outside advisory board, was at the meeting. "Out of nowhere," Ackland recounts, during a discussion of Gelb's first two chapters, Ellsberg "said, in effect, 'Gentlemen, we have to realize that we're all war criminals.'" "I remember the statement so vividly, and just kind of the dropped mouths, the sort of, 'Huh? What's going on here?'" Ackland says. "I was so stunned. . . . And I just remember that the subject was changed. It didn't go into a discussion of war crimes. . . . It fairly quickly got back, quote, on track, to talk about the chapters that were under discussion by the committee. But there was certainly that sense of, 'Whoa. Something's going on with Dan here.'"[72]

Ellsberg did not call John Vann a war criminal, however. Vann was still waging the war in Vietnam, and perhaps more effectively than most Americans there. Other people whom Ellsberg attacked as war criminals were considerably less harmful to Vietnamese. Ellsberg had remained good friends with Vann, despite their differences; they continued to respect each other.[73]

Vann was trying to put some distance between them, though. One night in early March of 1971, when Vann was home on leave, Ellsberg waited at Vann's hotel in Washington until the morning hours for him to return, only to finally give up and go over to the home of Neil Sheehan (who worked late) to spend the night. John Allen Vann remembers his father telling him afterward that he had deliberately stood Ellsberg up. "He wanted to avoid him," John Allen recalls. "My father said that there were differences, and he just didn't want to be close to Dan at that point. I remember distinctly talking about it." John Allen believes the reason was the Pentagon Papers. It would not benefit Vann's career to get too close to that situation. "I have a clear belief that my father knew what Dan was up to. I really do," John Allen says.[74]

Ellsberg read Albert Speer's memoir, deepening his sense of his own complicity in war crimes in Vietnam. If one chooses not to know, but *can* know, the consequences of policies with which one is involved, Speer had written, one is still responsible for those consequences. "I come before you as a war criminal,"

Ellsberg told campus audiences. One writer would recall "the glazed-eyed, Martin Lutherish manner" in which Ellsberg would begin speeches by confessing to being a war criminal. "I was participating in a criminal conspiracy to wage aggressive war," he remarked quietly to Tom Oliphant. But "it would be pretentious to suggest that I'm a very important war criminal," he said later.[75]

Oliphant was a young journalist covering politics, including antiwar politics, for the *Boston Globe* at the time, and he saw Noam Chomsky regularly. One day over lunch at Joyce Chen's restaurant in Cambridge in late 1970, Chomsky advised him, "There's a new guy in town. And you ought to go see him." Chomsky told Oliphant about Ellsberg. Oliphant, who called Ellsberg almost immediately, came to see their talks as a coming-out of sorts for Ellsberg in the press. "This was the initial stages of pouring out all these accumulated feelings, going back 15 years," Oliphant remembers. "So he would talk about nuclear weapons decision making with the same Pauline fervor that he would talk of Vietnam." Oliphant found Ellsberg completely unguarded. "The idea of in any way shielding what he had to say with 'background' or 'deep background' or 'off the record' or anything—Dan was totally open," Oliphant recalls. "Totally."[76]

It was in these talks that Ellsberg expressed his pain and anguish to Oliphant over whether he was a war criminal. His anguish made him fascinating to Oliphant. Their discussions were not short. "To take his life story, even in a short one-day version, was a long talk," Oliphant recounts. "To talk about Nixon was a long talk. To gradually understand what he was up to took a long talk. . . . And the way Dan talks it tends to be a lot longer than that. . . . You'd have lunch, and then sooner or later you'd wander back to that apartment in Cambridge. . . . And you'd be lucky if you were gone at six. . . . There wouldn't be a light on in the apartment. The sun would be setting, and down it would go. And he's going on."[77] (Exactly the scene I would later experience when interviewing Ellsberg for this book. His face would change with the light, but his intensity and powers of concentration would show no decline; indeed, they seemed to pick up steam.)

In their very first conversation, Ellsberg mentioned "the Gelb study" to Oliphant. "In the fall of 1967, Robert S. McNamara . . . ordered a secret review of the entire history of the war," Oliphant wrote in the first sentence of a front-page article in the *Boston Globe* on March 7, 1971. Oliphant disclosed that only three men (Gelb, Ellsberg, and Morton Halperin) had read all of the study, and noted that all three now advocated swift U.S. withdrawal from Vietnam. Oliphant was probably the first newspaperman to write more than fleetingly about the Pentagon Papers, although Lloyd Shearer, a.k.a. Walter Scott of *Parade* magazine, had revealed its existence in *Parade* several months earlier in response to a query from a Mr. "B.T. Clancy." "Will it be made available to the public so that we may finally learn the truth about the origin of the war?" Clancy had asked Scott. (One wonders if Ellsberg was, in effect, Clancy. This may have been another way of playing with his secret. Shearer denied it.) "There are no plans to make it public," Walter Scott had said.[78]

Oliphant visited Gelb after speaking with Ellsberg. "He was just appalled," Oliphant remembers—appalled that Ellsberg had talked to a reporter about the study. "Les was just terrified. . . . It was his study and it was out." After "just endless attempts, he would barely confirm its existence."[79]

Ellsberg also told Oliphant about his contacts with J. William Fulbright over the Papers. "And then he asked me how things surfaced," Oliphant reminisces: "What is this system like? What do people do?" Ellsberg was obviously eager to get the Papers out, but Oliphant had no illusions he would get them. That didn't keep him from asking, though. "I said, 'Where is it?'" Oliphant laughs. "He said he didn't have it." Ellsberg gave Oliphant no indication that he had xeroxed the Papers. "I got a distinct signal from him that either he didn't have it, or 'Don't bother me with getting it here. That that's not what this is about,'" Oliphant recounts. Ellsberg led Oliphant to believe the Papers were still locked up in a government vault somewhere, "and the whole idea was, 'How do you unearth it?'"[80]

Ellsberg found Oliphant's March 7 story inspiring. Charles Nesson, his later attorney, would tell Oliphant that it pushed him to go to the *New York Times* with the Papers, Oliphant recalls:

> He said Dan had gotten to the point where he thought that this [the Papers] was almost like a magic potion, and that all you had to do was to sit down with it and you'd understand. And that the piece that I ended up doing fed directly into that mind-set that Dan had . . . what it looked like on the front page of the paper and everything: "My God, look at what happened to these people who worked on this project and read all this material. It changed them forever." And he already had this inkling, believe me. But after the thing appeared, it was like we're talking about a magic potion.[81]

Oliphant's article attracted little, if any, attention from the rest of the media. But others noticed it, including Henry Kissinger. "Kissinger went nuts," Oliphant remembers. "He called the office the next day. Wanted copies." When Oliphant informed Ellsberg of that, Ellsberg quickly began making more copies of the Papers. For safekeeping.[82]

Kissinger would not be the only one disturbed by Oliphant's piece.

Around the time of his first conversation with Oliphant, Ellsberg had been invited to Minnesota to testify in the trial of eight protesters who had broken into a draft office—those he later said had influenced him to release the Papers. "I immediately flew out with a bunch of the Pentagon Papers in my suitcase," he recalled. He hoped to introduce them in the trial and thereby gain legal protection. But he was unable to do so. He also spoke with Charles Nesson about using them in a Harvard Law School function such as moot court. "I couldn't really figure out a way to do it so that it would make sense in terms of our function here," Nesson remembers.[83]

In January or February 1971, Ellsberg paid another visit to Senator Fulbright's aide Norvill Jones in Washington. Again Jones tried to steer Ellsberg away. "I had a long session with him about alternative ways of getting the material made public, such as through leaks to the press or getting a congressman or senator to put the papers into the Congressional Record," Jones would recall. "He was seeking guidance from me as to who might be of potential for using them in some way on an official basis. . . . I was actively urging him to pursue various other options." Ellsberg was already thinking about leaking the Papers to a newspaper, Jones recounted, but seemed worried that he would face criminal charges if he went that route, whereas disclosure through a member of Congress would provide him some protection. Ellsberg still "seemed convinced that public release of the papers was the key to getting Congress to cut off funds for the war," Jones recorded. Ellsberg subsequently spoke again with Fulbright aide Richard Moose, telling Moose that he wanted to speak with other senators who might consider releasing the Papers. "We discussed various names," Moose recalled. Ellsberg asked Moose if he thought disclosure of the Papers "would have any impact and I said that I doubted it," Moose wrote.[84]

After testing out both Eugene McCarthy and Charles Goodell and finding the prospects in these quarters unpromising, Ellsberg would remember, he arranged a meeting with Senator George McGovern. A likely candidate. Ellsberg recalled speaking with McGovern "quite a bit in the course of one day." But McGovern says of their meeting, "I think you'd be amazed how brief it was," which was "just a few minutes." Ellsberg told McGovern about the Papers. He thought releasing them "would have a staggering impact," McGovern recounts:

> I told him I thought that [releasing them] was illegal, and that if there was any illegality that he is the one that should risk the illegal action, since he'd been a longtime supporter of the war and I had been a longtime critic. I thought that

now that he had gotten religion on the war, he should confess and take whatever legal rap there was in releasing the Papers. . . . I wasn't about to break the law as a United States senator. I felt that that was his responsibility; since he had control of the Papers, that he should take whatever risk was involved. . . . I was somewhat indignant that he would suggest that it was fine for a United States senator to break the law, but not for him.

McGovern suggested to Ellsberg that he give the Papers to the *New York Times.*[85]

"A total fucking lie," Ellsberg calls McGovern's memory of their meeting. "What he said was, 'I want it, I want it, I want it. I'll put it out.'" But "'let me think about this for a week.'" ("I have no recollection of that," McGovern chuckles.) Ellsberg also remembers, "He takes a copy of the Constitution off the wall . . . and he opens it up . . . says, 'Look, I as a senator cannot be questioned about anything that I say on the floor of the Senate.'" Reading McGovern's account of their meeting in one book, Ellsberg told me, "my heart was pounding. . . . My impulse is to pick up the phone and say, 'You motherfucker.' I was really outraged. And I may still do that."[86]

McGovern did not particularly care for Ellsberg. "There was a certain arrogance that I saw in him that turned me off," McGovern remembers. "And a kind of an implication, 'Well, now that I have decided that the war doesn't make sense, everybody else ought to immediately turn off on it.' You know, I'd turned off on it years before then. I just kind of resented the lack of appreciation for people who had been opposing him and other advocates of the war all those years." (In a later piece by the *Washington Post*'s Nicholas von Hoffman—which noted "how strange" Ellsberg was and likened him to Albert Speer—McGovern is quoted as saying that Ellsberg "suffers from the sin of self-righteousness.") As he was talking to Ellsberg, the thought crossed McGovern's mind that Ellsberg might have a guilty conscience: "I had the feeling that it was a kind of a confessional on his part. . . . He seemed embarrassed about his previous support of the war effort." But McGovern was not exactly sure who Daniel Ellsberg really *was.* "I had no idea what he had, and I didn't know if his judgment was good or bad. I didn't even know whether he was rational."[87]

McGovern says he never seriously considered releasing the Papers. "I thought it was a breach of government regulations, and I didn't want to be a part of that." It would have caused him all kinds of problems, particularly as a presidential candidate. Also, "I thought that from what I was told was in the Papers that I'd made most of those points on the Senate floor over and over prior to that, as had Frank Church and Senator Fulbright and [Mike] Mansfield and others over the years."[88]

Ellsberg thought that at last he'd found his man, however, he would recall. Then he didn't hear from McGovern, so he called him up. "Dan, I can't do it," McGovern told him, in Ellsberg's retelling. McGovern related that he had solicited the advice of his friend Senator Gaylord Nelson, and that Nelson had counseled against it. Ellsberg had just talked to Nelson. He had alienated him. Ellsberg had "tried him out" by suggesting some "lesser measures" against the war, and concluded that Nelson would never release the Papers. Ellsberg had lit into Nelson, which probably hurt his standing with McGovern.[89]

Ellsberg attempted to meet with McGovern a second time, but McGovern's office directed him to John Holum, McGovern's legislative assistant, who told Ellsberg the documents would not be of use to McGovern.[90]

Ellsberg spoke with the veteran progressive journalist I. F. Stone after meeting with McGovern, and told Stone that he was trying to get some secret papers on the war out. His friend Janaki Tschannerl had urged him to give the Papers to Stone. "That always was my advice," she remembers. "Give it to the people." But Ellsberg wanted a wider readership. According to Ellsberg, Stone told him that McGovern was the best bet, applauded his effort, and cried as they parted.[91]

Ellsberg put out some feelers to people from *Time* magazine at a memorable dinner on February 7, the eve of the invasion of Laos. The dinner was at the beautiful home of *Time*'s David Greenway on the Charles River in Needham, Massachusetts. *Time* had become discredited in some circles over its prowar Vietnam coverage, and Henry Grunwald, its new managing editor, wanted to increase the sophistication of its coverage partly by tapping intellectuals at gatherings like this one. Greg Wierzynski, who organized the dinner, recalls inviting Ellsberg because he was an articulate critic on Vietnam and because he had earlier had an odd conversation with Ellsberg in which Ellsberg had talked, in hypothetical terms, about some study that could show that U.S. policy in Vietnam "was all a big lie," Wierzynski recounts. "That what we were saying and what we were doing were two different things." With Wierzynski, Ellsberg didn't actually say that the study existed. Rather, it was, "What if there was such a study?" Ellsberg intimated that he had it, though, or "that he could get hold of it very quickly," Wierzynski recalls. "It was pretty obvious that he was trying to pick my brain on how to get this thing out" and "fishing around on whether I would bite at this, or [whether he would] let me have this."[92]

Wierzynski didn't pick up all of Ellsberg's signals at the time, however, and the whole idea struck him as monstrous. "The idea that a guy would walk away from the Pentagon or from any government [office] with a suitcase full of classified documents was absolutely mind-boggling to me," Wierzynski recounts. "I'd served in army intelligence, and the whole business of security and 'lock your safes' and all that had been drummed into me. I just couldn't fathom that very well." And the more Ellsberg hyped the study, the more skeptical Wierzynski became: "He talked of it in such apocalyptic terms that I thought he'd be exaggerating and grossly overstating."[93]

According to a July 1971 *Boston Globe* account of the dinner at Greenway's house, Ellsberg "dominated" the discussion "with his concern that it was 1964 all over again in Vietnam," and talked about "American insensitivity to bombing Asians and about Kissinger's unwillingness to answer to this point" at the background session the week before. "He was extremely hyper," Greenway recalls. "Very outspoken and talkative. He kind of amazed everybody. . . . He was boring in about the war, about this, about that." But Ellsberg apparently made less of an impression during the dinner than he did afterward, when the guests had repaired for brandy and cigars. Ellsberg and two or three of the *Time* men were talking off to one side; Patricia was with them. (Ellsberg had "insisted on bringing her" to the dinner, Wierzynski remembers.) Ellsberg "was intense as hell," Murray Gart, who was *Time*'s chief of correspondents, reminisces. "All keyed up. . . . He really came on strong." Ellsberg repeatedly referred to classified documents that he said he had worked on and had access to, and asked how one might best release them publicly. "He started doing the same routine with Grunwald as he had done with me," Wierzynski recalls. "Except he was even more obvious. . . . 'Well, what would you do if you'—and Grunwald started saying, as I recall, 'Well, we don't take articles by outsiders.'" It was "like an Ionesco conversation," Wierzynski reflects. "People are talking at each other at somewhat different levels. And this went on for a while."[94]

Ellsberg talked for quite some time, Wierzynski recounts: "And then he became kind of tiresome, actually. He started having beads of sweat on his forehead. Which was sort of out of character. He hadn't had anything to drink, whereas everybody else was, you know [chuckles]. It was late in the evening, and it was a good dinner, it was a very elegant house, and the river was right at your feet there, and this guy is relentlessly pushing his idea. You know, this kind of monstrous concept of exposing the state's secrets."[95]

Around midnight, as the evening drew to a close, Wierzynski drove Grunwald, Gart, and the Ellsbergs back to their places. It was a cold night, snowy, with ice on the ground, "after a fair number of drinks, and nobody's head was terribly clear," Gart recalls. Dan was in the front seat with Wierzynski, Patricia in the back with Grunwald and Gart. Ellsberg talked more about secret studies. He "was rattling on and on some more in the car," Wierzynski remembers. "Grunwald by this time had lost all interest in Ellsberg and was trying to flirt with Patricia. He was sort of a little bit of a dirty old Viennese. . . . And I think

Gart was trying to flirt with Patricia, too, but he sort of was responding to Ells-berg. It was strange. So we went on like this for half an hour or so." They pulled up in front of the Ellsbergs' Hilliard Street flat, where they talked some more in the car. "By this time Henry's eyes were rolling in the back of his head," Greenway says. Ellsberg told the *Time* men he had something that might interest them. Perhaps after running upstairs to his apartment, he handed them a large manila envelope.[96]

Grunwald thought it might contain some of those secret documents Ells-berg had been talking about. But it was merely a draft of an essay Ellsberg had written (apparently his Laos piece). It was "a kind of dog-eared manuscript," Gart remembers. "Something that looked pretty shopworn.... We weren't particularly interested, and we told him we weren't interested." "We thought he was just making a pitch for writing in the magazine, and tended to dismiss the whole thing," Wierzynski recounted. "After all this very highly hyped talk of studies, he gave us this. . . . It looked like he was submitting a manuscript to *Time*. And we sort of concluded that all this highly classified information that he was talking about was . . . his own study. We just didn't think there was any-thing more than that. . . . He had talked in such grand terms about this thing, and then he produced a whimper."[97]

———※———

Under pressure and cajoling from Ralph Stavins, Ellsberg gave more of the Pa-pers to the IPS scholars. Leonard Rodberg estimates that Ellsberg gave them half the study, though he held back the best material, Neil Sheehan would later deduce. Sorely testing Stavins' patience, Ellsberg tantalized him with the prospect of receiving more documents.[98]

Ellsberg soon came to perceive that the IPS scholars were not being care-ful enough with the Papers. They were making copies of them and even show-ing them to others, he suspected. And indeed, "I remember spending nights xeroxing," Rodberg recalls. Ellsberg worried that things could spiral out of his control. He made Stavins turn over tapes that Stavins had made of some docu-ments. He eventually asked for the documents back. But, as he suspected, the scholars kept at least one copy—though Marcus Raskin and Richard Barnet swore to him that they did not, he would say later. Anthony Russo sensed from a distance that "there were a lot of spats going on" between Ellsberg and the scholars. Ellsberg and Stavins would have a falling out. Barnet believes it was over whether Stavins "did exactly what Dan understood he was going to do, or what they agreed he would do" with the documents. Stavins was mad that Ellsberg was jacking him around, playing his games, while Ellsberg probably thought Stavins was untrustworthy and trying to force his hand. Stavins told Ellsberg that IPS was moving ahead with publication of their book—with quotations from the Papers—whether he liked it or not. Well, then he was going to be punished, Ellsberg replied.[99]

A major source of the ill feelings was a questionable move by Marcus Raskin, one he would come to regret. In late December 1970, the *New York Times Book Review* had published a piece by Neil Sheehan that had called for an inquiry into U.S. war crimes in Vietnam. It had caught the IPS scholars' attention. The piece was moving and important—"essentially a break with what the *Times* had been writing," Raskin thought. Sheehan might be just the man for getting the study out, the scholars thought. "We had gotten at that point to the idea that a newspaper person should take the lead in trying to get it published, and certainly somebody connected," Barnet remembers. "And that was the newspaper everybody wanted."[100]

If Ellsberg wasn't going to release the Papers, the IPS scholars decided, they would have to move for him. "We wanted it out," Rodberg stresses. And they were tired of dealing with Ellsberg and his power trips. Maybe Sheehan could pry more of the documents from him.[101]

Neil Sheehan was a handsome man, highly intelligent, driven, sensitive, a dedicated journalist. He was extraordinarily thorough and aggressive in his pursuit of his sources, but very slow when it came to the writing. "It was very difficult to get him to write anything," Tom Wicker remembers. Sheehan's career was not going particularly well. A workaholic and former alcoholic, and an insomniac, Sheehan had his share of personal demons. Even after the Papers were published and that had been added high on his list of accomplishments, Sheehan was dour and morose. Like many writers, he desired a Pulitzer Prize. He believed that he should have won one in 1964 for his Vietnam reporting for UPI. He felt slighted again when he didn't win a Pulitzer for publication of the Papers. He was also bothered that other journalists questioned how much legwork actually went into his acquiring them. Sanford Ungar wrote that they "had been virtually dropped in his lap, rather than ferreted out on his own initiative." (The *Times* used the phrase "investigative reporting" to describe Sheehan's role in obtaining the Papers, which he also felt didn't give him enough credit.)[102]

At Raskin's initiative, he and Stavins met with Sheehan over lunch. They told him about the Papers. Barnet joined in subsequent discussions with Sheehan about the documents. Raskin gave Sheehan portions of the study. That was his questionable move. The scholars did not tell Sheehan who their source was initially. Sheehan was, of course, more than a little interested, though he did not yet know the full scope of the Papers. Raskin recalls coming to an "agreement" with Sheehan "that he'd be sure they'd be printed if they were given to them [the *Times*] but also that they had to write an article about war crimes." It was important to Raskin that the Papers were played in the *Times* as evidence of war crimes. "Mr. Sheehan made no such proposal to me," A. M. Rosenthal, then the *Times*'s managing editor, remembers. "Nor did anybody else." Raskin says he also had a "deal" with Sheehan that he would be able to write a piece in the *New York Times Book Review* on the making of the IPS book on the war. But that agreement fell by the wayside too, he says.[103]

Later, after Sheehan learned that Ellsberg was the source of the documents, Stavins advised him of the difficulty of dealing with Ellsberg and his ego trips and said that Sheehan would eventually tell him off. Sheehan responded that he had plenty of patience.[104]

Ellsberg was, of course, furious when he found out about IPS's contacts with Sheehan over the Papers. He and Raskin had a short but "frank exchange of views," Raskin recalls. "There's no question that relations were not great after that," Barnet remembers. "I think he felt that either Ralph or Marc had overstepped."[105]

Raskin and Barnet had encouraged Ellsberg to meet with Sheehan himself, more than once, and strongly. Raskin was extremely reluctant to talk about his involvement in the Pentagon Papers affair with me, but after being prodded, he did disclose that

> I wanted him to have his own relationship to Sheehan as early as possible. . . . I was very concerned in March of that year of 1971 that I had gone beyond what was a morally sound thing to have done by giving the Papers that I had to Sheehan. And that was the fundamental reason that I urged him to take up his own relationship with Sheehan. So that I could recapture my own soul. . . . Because I was putting him, or so it seemed, and so he felt . . . in a dangerous position. That even though it was the case that he had been shopping the Papers, the reality was that *he* was shopping them, he was doing it. Now, all of a sudden, I was the one who was doing it—who, in effect, had cut the deal with the *Times* . . . when I gave them to Neil.

Raskin concluded that he had helped put Ellsberg "through a very great deal of pain. So there is a bit of shame on my part." Rodberg was surprised when told this. This was not the Raskin he remembered. Raskin, Barnet, and Stavins "were so disparaging of Ellsberg for hanging back," Rodberg says. "They were very upset at that point."[106]

Ellsberg met with Sheehan, but he didn't tell him about the Papers at first. They discussed, among other things, war crimes. Sheehan showed Ellsberg a draft of another essay he had written for the *New York Times Book Review* that called for an inquiry into U.S. war crimes. The piece impressed Ellsberg.[107] Then, that night in early March when Ellsberg went over to Sheehan's home after waiting in futility for John Vann to return to his hotel, they had a fateful discussion.

Ellsberg was agitated over his failure to find the right outlet for the Papers, Sheehan would remember. He told Sheehan about the study. This was the moment that Sheehan realized Ellsberg was the source of the documents. He questioned Ellsberg about it, and Ellsberg acknowledged it. Sheehan also attempted to calm Ellsberg and to get him to think more clearly. Ellsberg expressed fear that the FBI was tailing him and would confiscate the only copy of the Papers he had in Cambridge. He made a hard decision, under great internal tension. According to Sheehan, he agreed to let the *New York Times* publish the Papers if the *Times* would subsequently publish the entire study in book form. Ellsberg said later he set two conditions before Sheehan: that the *Times* publish a great portion of the Papers, and that it print actual documents. But he wanted serious consideration given to printing the whole study. Ellsberg desired congressional cover before the *Times* published the Papers, however, he told Sheehan later. He even entertained the hope of prior coordination between a member of Congress and the *Times*. But Sheehan told Ellsberg that he couldn't make any commitment before he and those in power at the *Times* had read the study, and to return to Cambridge and wait for him to come up after he had talked to them.[108]

Soon thereafter, Sheehan asked Robert Phelps, the news editor of the *Times*'s Washington bureau, to step out of the bureau's newsroom into its reception lobby. He worried about being bugged in the newsroom. Sheehan told Phelps about the Papers and Ellsberg's condition that the *Times* publish the entire study. Sheehan also went to see Tom Wicker, then a *Times* columnist. "Sheehan came in and he told me that he had something very confidential to talk about," Wicker remembers. At Sheehan's insistence, they stepped out of Wicker's office, too, then proceeded to walk in a square pattern in the corridors of the *Times*'s Washington bureau, Wicker recounts, "through the newsroom and around private offices and back. . . . Neil and I walked around that route for, I would say, five minutes. . . . I remember he was extremely cautious about the thing. . . . I had no reason to think that my office was bugged. But he didn't want to take any chances. This whole thing was very secretive. . . . The main thing I remember is how insistent he was on secrecy and confidentiality." Sheehan described the Papers to Wicker and said he could get hold of them. He asked Wicker if he thought the *Times* would publish them. "I said, 'Neil, I think so, but I can't guarantee that,'" Wicker recounts. "'The *Times* will publish those papers if James Reston says they should, and if he says they should not, they won't. Reston has got that kind of clout.'" Wicker assumed from Sheehan's extreme air of secrecy that the documents were more than a little explosive. Sheehan himself believed they were "like a thermonuclear vial."[109]

Reston, a *Times* vice president, columnist, and friend of the powerful, told Sheehan that the *Times* would have to see the Papers before consenting to publish all of them, but that he had the green light. Sheehan then phoned Ellsberg and, under an alias, went up to Cambridge to meet with him.[110]

Sheehan was shocked at the Ellsberg he encountered there: frenzied, emotional, and out of control. Patricia Ellsberg appeared to Sheehan to fear that her husband was on the edge of a nervous breakdown. Sheehan was only now beginning to understand the full scope of Ellsberg's personality. As he would observe later, Ellsberg's frenzy probably reflected not only fear of prison, but guilt over betraying Harry Rowen, RAND, and the national security system as a whole, and the prospect of ending up a pariah. Sheehan was disconcerted to learn that, since their late-night talk at his home in Washington a week earlier, Ellsberg had been having the Papers microfilmed at his apartment and xeroxed at a commercial site in Cambridge, paying with personal checks. There would be no saving Ellsberg's hide when the Papers were published, Sheehan thought. While in Cambridge, Sheehan was also alarmed to read Tom Oliphant's piece in the *Boston Globe* in which Ellsberg had spoken openly of the Papers. He was disturbed as well to learn that Ellsberg had almost turned over the Papers to a defense attorney in the trial in Minnesota, and that he might do so in another trial in the future. Such amazing indiscretion, Sheehan thought. At the suggestion of Patricia, who was eager for Sheehan to calm Ellsberg, and who was advising caution with the Papers to Dan, Sheehan encouraged him to be more discreet. But Ellsberg resented that, thinking it condescending. Sheehan helped Ellsberg preserve and disperse the microfilm copies of the Papers. (Ellsberg's lawyers would later be alarmed at his microfilming, with its hint of Whittaker Chambers' microfilmed Pumpkin Papers and his accusations of espionage against Alger Hiss.) Fearful of going to prison, Ellsberg reneged on his agreement with Sheehan on publication of the Papers by the *Times*. He harangued Sheehan that he was the only person taking any risks and spoke of the years behind bars that he faced. But Ellsberg agreed to let Sheehan read the Papers at Spencer "Rainbow" Marx's apartment. He gave Sheehan a key to the apartment. He told Sheehan to read the volume on Tonkin first—and not to copy the Papers. "If I give it to you then I lose control over it," he reportedly told Sheehan. He did not provide Sheehan a copy of the negotiations volumes though Sheehan requested them. He said later he did not want to be seen as trying to undermine U.S. peace negotiations.[111]

Ellsberg and Sheehan's relationship was rife with distrust. Ellsberg "teased and tortured Neil," recalled Max Frankel, who was then the *Times*'s Washington bureau chief, "dangling" the stuff in front of him as well without wanting to give it up. Ellsberg treated Sheehan as an instrument for getting the Papers out. Sheehan, too, got disgusted with him. Sheehan would later tell Ellsberg that he started to distrust him when Ellsberg claimed he had the documents under his control and Sheehan knew he did not. Sheehan thought Ellsberg was lying to him and playing a con game, Ellsberg concluded from a subsequent discussion between them. Ellsberg had told Sheehan that he had asked the IPS scholars to return all copies of the Papers to him and had received them, but the scholars had told Sheehan that Ellsberg had authorized them to retain copies. Sheehan also feared that Ellsberg would give the Papers to a competitor behind his back; he knew that Ellsberg was looking for congressional cover. He further worried that the IPS scholars would get parts of the Papers out first. "The atmosphere was paranoid, almost psychopathic," Harrison Salisbury wrote. Sheehan's own nerves were "close to break-point." Ellsberg later seemed annoyed that Sheehan had doubted his integrity. Ellsberg claimed that "if he'd fully leveled with me and told me how important he thought it was" that the *Times* publish the Papers before a member of Congress released them, "I would have deferred to him."*[112]

Sheehan believed the Papers were invaluable and had to be published. He felt the American and Indochinese people were owed this record for their blood. But he also wanted the glory, the credit for obtaining and publishing the study. He chose to deceive Ellsberg and copy the Papers behind his back. "Neil

---

* Relations between the two men would continue to be strained after publication of the Papers. Sheehan found Ellsberg's egocentricity, inconsiderateness, and lecturing of him exasperating and off-putting. Ellsberg was rude to him at an airport. Sheehan thought Ellsberg painted himself as a much bigger hero in the Pentagon Papers affair than he really was. Sheehan expressed reticence about appearing with him at the same awards ceremony. Sheehan deposited papers in the Library of Congress from his book on John Vann for use by researchers, and some of them suggest strongly that he came to dislike Ellsberg, indeed, was contemptuous of him. "I know there's not entirely good feeling out there all the way around," Sheehan's friend David Halberstam told me (Sheehan notes on Ellsberg interviews, undated [SP, box 121]; Sheehan, "DE Interview Notebooks" and "DE Tape Summaries" [SP, box 64]; Sheehan to "Abe," January 3, 1972, incorrectly dated 1971 [SP, box 161]; other SP documents; Halberstam interview).

Sheehan ripped him off," Anthony Russo observes. "It only happened because Neil Sheehan ripped him off. Had it been left to him, he would have fuzzed around continually." In effect, Sheehan did to Ellsberg what Ellsberg had done to the RAND Corporation. Ellsberg later told Sheehan he could have made the case (apparently in a lawsuit) that the *Times* had copied and published the Papers without his permission, and damaged him.[113]

In mid- to late March, from a pay phone outside the Cambridge motel where he was staying under an assumed name, Sheehan called his wife, Susan, and asked her to come up secretly and register under an alias in a hotel nearby. He needed her help copying. Harrison Salisbury would place them both at the Treadway Motor Inn, under the aliases Mr. and Mrs. Thompson, but the FBI came to believe Neil Sheehan may have used the name Samuel Johnson (which would have been appropriate—Johnson was a famous English man of letters) at the Treadway, and that Susan Sheehan may have used the alias Susan Dowling at the Continental Hotel. Samuel Johnson, the FBI found, made phone calls to Daniel Ellsberg and Spencer Marx. The FBI also determined that Samuel Johnson told the Treadway he was with the Control Data Corporation at 25 Broadway in New York, but that the Control Data Corporation did not have an address there nor any employee by name of Samuel Johnson.[114]

Sheehan also phoned Bill Kovach, the *Times*'s correspondent in Boston. "He didn't say a lot on the phone," Kovach recounts. "He said he was in town, he needed some help, and could I meet him in Cambridge." Sheehan wanted to say as little as possible over the phone; he didn't even want his name spoken. "He gave me his room number," Kovach recalls. "I went up to the second floor." There Sheehan told Kovach he needed to copy some documents on a high-speed machine at a place that would work through the weekend, including nights. He was in a rush. "He didn't tell me who he got them from and I didn't ask him," Kovach remembers. (Kovach came to think they were being kept in an office at MIT, but the FBI found that the Sheehans taxied between Spencer Marx's apartment and a copying business.) Sheehan further informed Kovach that "they were a study of the Vietnam War and they were classified," and that they "had to be back in the hands of the people from whom he had gotten them by Monday morning," three days later. "He also said he needed to do it somewhere outside of Cambridge, where it would not be so easy to trace," Kovach recounts. Sheehan indicated that he and others at the *Times* were trying to keep the operation quiet at the newspaper. "He was very nervous . . . and anxious to get his work done," Kovach reminisces. "He was onto something. That was clear." Sheehan wanted Kovach's involvement in the operation limited: "I offered to help copy the things, but he didn't want me to. He said he and Susan would take care of it."[115]

Kovach told Sheehan he knew of a place where the copying might be done. By happenstance, Kovach had noticed that in the town of Bedford, near Carlisle where he lived, a new print shop with a high-speed Xerox had opened. The machine was brand new. Kovach told the shop's owner that he had a manuscript that needed to be turned in on Monday morning. The owner said he would need the money up front for such a big job. But Sheehan didn't have the money, so Kovach had to call the national desk of the *Times* in New York and ask them to send him some money. The *Times* wired $600 via Western Union. Kovach paid the proprietor by check, which later earned him a visit from FBI agents. "I was standing at the door in my underwear: 'If you guys want to come into the house, you're welcome to come in. But I don't know what you're talking about.' And they said, 'No, we're not coming in.'"[116]

Sheehan encountered other problems. Someone in Samuel Johnson's room made no less than six phone calls to locksmiths after 7 P.M. on Sunday, March 21 (the first date of the Sheehans' three-day copying siege), the FBI later determined. Had the Sheehans or someone else lost the key to Spencer Marx's apartment? Had someone changed the lock? In any case, the locksmiths were then closed. Further, unbeknown to Kovach, the shop owner in Bedford was a retired military officer. He wondered about those Top Secret markings. But Sheehan displayed his White House press pass and assured him that everything was proper, that the documents were part of the manuscript and had been declassified. Subsequently, the copier broke down, another, perhaps even more stressful, development.[117]

At some point, probably during this three-day period, Sheehan phoned his friend K. Dun Gifford late one night, rousing Gifford out of bed. "He just said it was really important, and would I help him?" Gifford recounts. "Neil was very agitated. . . . I didn't know what he wanted. I thought he might have been in trouble." What Sheehan wanted was a copier, and right away. He expressed "lots of urgency," Gifford says. "He had to get the documents back by six or seven the next morning." Gifford believes this was so Ellsberg wouldn't find out he'd made copies of them. "He had the study for a limited number of hours. And it was a *lot* of papers." Gifford took Sheehan to his office, the real estate investment firm Cabot Cabot & Forbes. They had a copier.[118]

Sheehan may have felt a pang of guilt about copying the Papers behind Ellsberg's back. In late May he visited Ellsberg at the Ellsbergs' apartment in New York. Sheehan asked to borrow a set of the Papers to work on them. Ellsberg agreed, although he had always told Sheehan that he could not take a copy out of the apartment unless the *Times* had decided to publish them. Ellsberg claimed later that he was by this act giving Sheehan his permission to publish the Papers.

Sheehan would explain his request as seeking moral release from his deception of Ellsberg. But David Halberstam says, "I never knew Neil to agonize over it."[119]

In late March, Sheehan succinctly described to Max Frankel the classified history of the Vietnam War he had obtained and provided Frankel a sample from the 1964 period. Sheehan indicated to Frankel that the *Times* now had perhaps 6,000 pages of the history. He declared it a gold mine and again urged secrecy. He stored a copy at his mother-in-law's home.[120]

That same month, through Richard Moose, Ellsberg requested another meeting with Senator J. William Fulbright, and on March 31 he spoke with Fulbright and Norvill Jones in the senator's office. Ellsberg was still looking for a member of Congress to put the Papers in the *Congressional Record* "in order to lessen the risk of possible legal action against him," Jones recorded. But Ellsberg "emphasized that he was prepared to go to jail if necessary." He also declared "that he had already shown some of the material to someone at the *Times* who was very much interested in it," Jones wrote. Ellsberg sought Fulbright's advice on ways to get the Papers out. Fulbright was pessimistic about their likely impact on his colleagues in Congress but wanted to take a look at a sample again. The next day, Jones sent him a highlighted section of the Papers on events prior to the Gulf of Tonkin affair and a memo stating: "I am very leery about Dan Ellsberg and believe that we should keep him at arm's length. I have repeatedly warned him about not getting the committee's name involved in any way in his efforts to do something with the material he wants to get out, but I fear that for his own purposes sometime he may let it be known that he has supplied the committee with a copy. I had gone through an exercise with him a couple of months ago about what he might do with the material and had assumed that he was either pursuing some of those suggestions or had given up on the idea."[121]

On April 7, Ellsberg celebrated his fortieth birthday at his flat in Cambridge, taking the occasion, as we have seen, to bemoan repeatedly to Sam Popkin that he wasn't famous yet. At the party, K. Dun Gifford was talking to a woman whom Ellsberg had evidently shown some of the Papers on Tonkin. Gifford, a former aide to Senator Edward Kennedy, had earlier read some material on the affair. The woman began questioning Gifford about Tonkin. "She knew a lot about it," Gifford remembers. "I was surprised." Tiring of her queries, he told her that "the whole goddamn thing" was going to be published soon anyway. The woman subsequently informed Ellsberg what Gifford had said. Enraged, Ellsberg went over to Gifford's house. "He was agitated," Gifford recalls. "That the stuff was going to be published, and how did I know, and what did I know about it? And I just said I'd heard rumors about it." Ellsberg then confronted Sheehan.[122] More reason for distrust.

In mid-April, Ellsberg phoned Norvill Jones and asked if Fulbright had any more advice for him. Jones said he had not heard from Fulbright on the subject and assumed he did not. Jones told Ellsberg he thought he was pursuing the approaches they had discussed earlier. "He said that he was but did not want to go too far if you had any further thoughts for him," Jones recounted for Fulbright later. "I made it clear to him that I did not want to be involved any further in his plans and that he should not let it be known that he had made available a copy to me. After talking to me he apparently tried to call you and I advised you not to return his call." Ellsberg was again trying to circumvent Jones, his roadblock to Fulbright. "I just thought [Fulbright] was getting into dangerous water," Jones recalls. "Further, that [Ellsberg] was a character [whom] we didn't know what he was doing, where he got the Papers, or exactly what games he might be playing. I just thought [Fulbright] ought to keep him at arm's length. . . . And at this point my view of his personality did enter into my urging Fulbright not to have contacts with him. . . . It was an important factor in trying to keep him at a distance." For "he was getting very nervous," Jones remembers. "And sometimes on the phone he appeared to be almost frantic. And clearly he felt in danger, and he was looking for some way to protect himself." Ellsberg told Jones, too, that the FBI was following him, and that he was sure he would be going to jail. "I remember his voice breaking fairly consistently in those last conversations," Jones says. "Just a nervous voice . . . a nervous crack."[123]

On April 19, Ellsberg attempted to shop the Papers to Representative Paul (Pete) McCloskey. They were both panelists at a teach-in on Vietnam at Princeton University. McCloskey and Ellsberg each spoke for a long time at the teach-in, particularly Ellsberg ("it was almost impossible to stop him," remembers Richard Falk, who as a Princeton professor helped arrange the teach-in), and consequently, although the event ran until after midnight, Falk and a couple of others on the agenda were unable to speak. "There was a man down at the end of the table that I didn't know what his name was and never heard of him," McCloskey recounts. "I said I'd just come back from Vietnam and that the government was flat out lying. . . . And the man at the end of the table passed a note down to me. He says, 'You're absolutely right. Can I talk to you afterward? Dan Ellsberg.' . . . He wanted to give me information to back up what I was saying."[124]

McCloskey reportedly turned down Ellsberg's offer of documents initially (as did, or so Falk understood, Senator Vance Hartke, who also spoke at the teach-in). McCloskey, a maverick Republican, was thinking about challenging President Nixon for the presidency and worried that releasing the material would hurt his crusade. And like Fulbright, he didn't believe that he had a right to disclose top-secret data. But he agreed to take "a whole sheaf of documents" that Ellsberg brought to his office in Washington shortly thereafter. Mc-Closkey locked the documents in his safe. "My commitment to him, when he gave them to me, was to try to get the Defense Department to release them and make them public, or to try to get my subcommittee on government informa-tion to hold hearings on them," McCloskey remembers. McCloskey, who was only a junior member of his subcommittee, wrote Secretary of Defense Melvin Laird requesting that Laird make the documents public and stating that if Laird did not, he would put them in front of his subcommittee.[125]

Ellsberg arranged to join McCloskey on a flight to California in early May. This was the only time McCloskey would give Ellsberg. "He met me at Dulles airport," McCloskey recounts. "We had seats together. And all the way back to California—about a five-hour flight—he kept handing me papers out of a brief-case. And some of these he would be clipping something off the top, which I learned was a Top Secret designation. . . . It was fascinating reading. And three days later, when I came back from California . . . he got on the plane on the way back, and another set of papers. So that by the time that I'd gotten back to Washington, I'm going to say I had roughly a quarter or a third of what later turned out to be the Pentagon Papers. . . . I mean, these were huge things." Mc-Closkey had the impression during the flight that Ellsberg had given the Papers to the *New York Times* but believed he was in a position to tell the *Times* when it could publish them.[126] Ellsberg's belief could not have been further off base.

McCloskey again put the documents in his safe. "For the next several weeks I would take them home at night from my office," he recalls. "I had a big stack by my bed, and I'd read some every night."[127]

Ellsberg also called on another Republican member of Congress that spring. The former Senator Charles Mathias told me that Ellsberg gave him "a stack" of the Papers "maybe a foot high." Mathias subsequently took them to Senate leaders Mike Mansfield and Hugh Scott, who "directed that we lock them up in the Foreign Relations Committee safe," Mathias recounts. "We were going to see what they were. But we didn't want them just kicking around." That would have put them next to the collection of Papers that Ells-berg had provided Norvill Jones. Mathias told Ellsberg the Papers were "just history," however, Ellsberg recounted, "and that it was essential to have any documentation on the Nixon administration." So Ellsberg went upstairs to the FRC offices and retrieved a copy of NSSM-1—the compilation of questions and answers on Vietnam from the first days of the Nixon administration—that he had earlier given the FRC. "Mathias assured me that very shortly he would be reading it aloud on the Senate floor and reading it into the record that way,"

Ellsberg recalled. Mathias doubts that, however. Ellsberg then didn't hear from Mathias.[128]

—————◆—————

Ellsberg was a deeply worried and unsettled man that spring. It was exhilarating to be running around with the Papers. "It made him a personality, it put him in a loop," Marty Garbus comments. "It made him excited about parts of his life. It was a thrilling thing to do. And the fear that other people had of touching this hot stuff also made the whole thing more dangerous and more precarious"—and thus more exciting. But combined with that excitement was extraordinary frustration, anxiety, and fear. One member of Congress after another had turned Ellsberg down. The chance of attaining a respectable form of stardom and legal protection looked increasingly slim. Ellsberg had to confront the specter of prison head on. He told Howard and Roslyn Zinn that he had given the Papers to the *Times* and members of Congress, but "they hadn't done anything with them," Howard Zinn remembers. "And he was very troubled about that. . . . None of them had done anything with it, although they had promised that maybe they would." "It was terribly frustrating," Ellsberg would say later. "As I found out these various people were unwilling to help, I began to feel that the FBI might already know something about it and might pick me up at any time, swoop in and take everything before I got it out. My main fear was that the whole thing would be aborted." Ellsberg was convinced he was being watched closely.[129]

Anthony Austin, an editor for the *Times*, spoke with Ellsberg for a book Austin was writing on the Tonkin Gulf affair. During their first discussion, Austin phoned his wife in New York from Ellsberg's Cambridge flat to tell her that he'd be back that evening and mentioned that he had some "terrific material." "Dan's face changed, he grew agitated and went 'Shh!' with a finger to his lips," Austin remembers. "So I cut the phone call short."[130]

Ellsberg himself wondered if his mission was really worth all the risk. Was he the only person who felt the Papers were that important? When he told his friend Jerry Goodman, during the aforementioned walk in the woods outside Goodman's home, that no one was biting on the Papers and that he was thinking about taking them to the *New York Times*, "I said, 'Are you out of your mind?'" Goodman recounts. "'You're gonna be in deep shit if you do this. . . . And it's gonna come out on page 48 of the *New York Times*. It'll be there one day and it'll be forgotten, and you'll still be in trouble. . . . Nobody's gonna even read them.'"[131]

Adding to Ellsberg's disquiet enormously, Neil Sheehan was stiff-arming him. Sheehan was keeping him in the dark on the state of deliberations over the Papers at the *Times*. In fact, Sheehan was lying to him about it in an effort to mislead and manipulate him while simultaneously pretending to be open and trustful, Ellsberg came to perceive. Sheehan was still telling him in May that there was no hope the *Times* would come to a decision on publishing the Papers in the next month or two—although the *Times*, fearful of being scooped, was actually moving full steam ahead, albeit cautiously, nervously, conflictedly, and with uncertainty about the final decision. Sheehan also told Ellsberg he was working on a book on another subject but wanted to study the Papers some in the evenings. Study them, indeed! Sheehan worried that if he told Ellsberg the *Times* was going forward with the Papers, Ellsberg later deduced, Ellsberg might get cold feet with the *Times* and preempt the newspaper by taking the Papers elsewhere or by increasing his pressure on McCloskey (whose possible plans for the Papers worried Sheehan). Sheehan showed no concern for his legal vulnerabilities, Ellsberg complained afterward, with some justification, though one has to believe that Sheehan would have given Ellsberg greater protection than Ellsberg would have given Sheehan. Ellsberg recalled that his last phone conversation with Sheehan during this period was several weeks before publication. Others at the *Times* were also keeping him at a distance. "For a period of time he didn't know what was going on," Garbus remembers. "He couldn't get information from them. He wanted to blow it up. I mean, he just wanted to say, 'Screw it.' . . . His frustration level was very high." Meanwhile, of course, he was also being stiff-armed by Norvill Jones. Ellsberg was angered by these slights. He would claim that when he subsequently told the painful story of Sheehan's deception and betrayal of him to A. M. Rosenthal of the *Times*, Rosenthal was moved to tears.[132] That is highly unlikely.

Others were also frustrated that the Papers had not yet seen the light of day. "One time I felt like, 'Maybe I should rip him off,'" Anthony Russo recounts with a laugh. "'It seems like he's not getting anywhere. . . . ' And that's what a lot of people were thinking." Russo remembers Lynda Sinay once "denouncing Dan, saying, 'We went through all these changes to use my Xerox machine to do this number, and he's not doing anything.'"[133]

The men at IPS were set to move in the days immediately preceding publication of the Papers. "Up until they were released," Leonard Rodberg recounts, it was the impression of the scholars that Ellsberg wasn't sure he wanted to release them. "During that critical few days" before the *Times* published the Papers on June 13, Rodberg says, Barnet, Raskin, and Stavins were ready to give their copies to the *Washington Post* if Ellsberg didn't act. "I mean, they were pressing." The scholars, who worried that Sheehan and the *Times* might also be wavering, had connections to the *Post*. There is "no question" in Rodberg's mind that Barnet or Raskin told Ben Bradlee, the executive editor of the *Post* (whom they knew) or someone else at the *Post* about the Papers before the *Times* printed them. The scholars may have even passed portions of the Papers to Bradlee or others, Rodberg believes. (Raskin denies giving any Papers to Bradlee.) "By the time that you get to June 13," Rodberg recalls, "they were going to see that the Papers came out whether Ellsberg gave the go-ahead or not. Now, Marc may feel badly about that now. But in that time there was no stopping it. I mean, once we had the political agenda we had. And it was going to happen fast. I just remember that . . . three- or four-day period as being very, very tense. . . . There was no waiting anymore."[134]

Meanwhile, Ellsberg had attempted to get a better sense of life behind bars. He visited Randy Kehler in an Arizona prison, where Kehler had been sent for resisting the draft. "I think Dan was very curious about prison, and that we talked a lot about what it was like for me," Kehler reminisces. Also, "he was trying to be attentive to my needs, and 'what did I have?' and 'would I like to get the *New York Times*?'" Ellsberg purchased Kehler a subscription to the *Times*. "But he didn't tell me what I was going to read," Kehler says.[135]

———◆———

In the days before publication of the Pentagon Papers, word began trickling out. Hedrick Smith of the *New York Times* phoned Leslie Gelb to question him about the study. Gelb deduced, to his horror, that the *Times* had it and was going to publish a story on it. This had to be Dan Ellsberg, Gelb thought. "He was certain," a good friend of his at the time recalls. Gelb worried that the eye of suspicion might be cast on him, or that he would be held partially responsible for Ellsberg's act. When the *Times* began publishing several days later, Gelb recounted, "I was nearly paralyzed. . . . My anxiety was very personal. Rather than thinking about the fate of the nation, I was thinking about the fate of Leslie Gelb." His career in government might be ruined. "He was so upset about it," his friend says. He thought Ellsberg's act atrocious. "Gelb felt that, to some extent, he had been betrayed," Paul Warnke remembers.[136]

After hearing from Hedrick Smith, Gelb visited Morton Halperin, who was also at the Brookings Institution. "He walked into my office and said, 'A reporter from the *New York Times* has called, and they seem to have the study . . . and they're planning to publish it,'" Halperin recounts. Neither Halperin nor Gelb had the slightest doubt where the *Times* had obtained it,

Halperin says. "I was certainly upset." Halperin thought Ellsberg "clearly had violated the trust we had placed in him."[137]

Gelb also contacted Warnke, who had been tipped off about the *Times*'s plans by a reporter from the *Washington Post*, who had wanted to know, "And did I have a copy, and could they have it?" Warnke remembers. Warnke did not suspect Ellsberg since he did not know him well. But he was also upset. "I thought that whoever had leaked it had certainly breached their commitment," he says. Warnke contacted Robert McNamara and McNamara's successor as defense secretary, Clark Clifford, who had never liked the idea of compiling the Papers in the first place. The three men met at McNamara's house. McNamara "didn't seem distraught," Warnke recalls. "You know, he obviously thought it was something that Ellsberg should not have done. . . . Again, that he had made a commitment—that was the confidentiality—and he breached it." Yet McNamara "wasn't frantic." But, according to Carl Kaysen, McNamara was extraordinarily angry at Ellsberg and felt he'd been betrayed. When McNamara came to realize everything that was now out there, he had to have felt devastated. He probably regretted ordering the study. "McNamara hates me," Ellsberg says. "He won't talk to me."[138]

On the morning of June 12, the day before publication, Ben Bagdikian, then an assistant managing editor at the *Washington Post*, phoned Harry Rowen. The two men had lived about a block apart in Washington in the early 1960s. The *Post* had known for a while that the *Times* had "some secret operation" going, Bagdikian remembers, and Ben Bradlee was "almost manic" about finding out what it was. Bagdikian told Rowen, "We hear that the *Times* has something that's supposed to be very hot, and it's something to do with a RAND report," one, it was rumored, bearing on Cuba. Rowen said "he knew nothing about that," Bagdikian recounts. "I said, 'Well, do you know anything about any other subject matter?' He said no." Rowen wanted to know what Bagdikian knew.[139]

Late that afternoon at the White House, officials learned that the *Times* would be running a story on a "Vietnam archive" the next day. If Richard Nixon was informed, it didn't disturb his good mood. He was uncharacteristically merry as he mingled with guests at his daughter Tricia's wedding. Aware of photographers, Nixon even danced, a first for him in the White House (he made it clear to his cabinet afterwards that it was "not my nature"). But in the basement, Al Haig was concerned. He was trying to find out what he could about the Papers. Haig called Walt Rostow, the former national security adviser, in Austin, Texas. "Who leaked them?" Rostow asked. "We think it is a guy named Ellsberg," Haig replied. "I gave him a reply that he never expected," Rostow recalls.

"I said, 'That son-of-a-bitch still owes me a term paper.'" Rostow was referring to Ellsberg's unfinished study of crises in 1964.[140]

David Halberstam also received an upsetting phone call that day. Susan Sheehan told him about the *Times*'s impending publication, and he was angry. Halberstam was almost finished with his book *The Best and the Brightest* and worried that release of the Papers might force him into some substantial rewriting. (Ellsberg would claim that the Papers "thoroughly demolished his initial thesis.") Halberstam thought Neil Sheehan should have forewarned him. "I was slightly irritated, only because Neil was a friend," Halberstam remembers. "I'd found out from other people what the *Times* was going to do a couple weeks in advance, and I wish I'd found out from Neil." Ellsberg later told Harrison Salisbury that he had not given Halberstam a copy of the Papers because they had not hit it off, and Ellsberg once told me that Patricia had not fully trusted Halberstam with them. "I wouldn't have wanted the documents," Halberstam claims. "It wouldn't have been good for my book."[141]

Anthony Austin was in agony on June 12. Late that morning, another editor in the *Times*'s "Week in Review" section, John Desmond, "called me into his office, and he says, 'You know, Tony, I know that you're writing a book on the Tonkin Gulf affair. And you ought to know that the *Times* is coming out with a front-page story on the Tonkin Gulf. Kind of the inside story,'" Austin recounts. "And he says, 'I don't know what it's all about, but I understand it's based on what they call the McNamara papers.'" Desmond's disclosure came out of the blue, Austin says. "I had not the slightest suspicion that the *Times* was working on this story." Although Austin had obtained secret intercepts recorded during Tonkin that he doubted would be appearing in the *Times*, he was distressed that much else of what he had thought would be new in his book might be scooped. Shaken, Austin returned to his desk and called Ellsberg immediately. He would probably know something about the McNamara papers.[142]

Austin told Ellsberg what he'd learned. "Dan said, 'Oh?'" Austin recounts. "He didn't say much." Mostly just "Ah ha. Ah ha. Okay." That sort of thing. It was the guarded Dan Ellsberg. But he wanted to know if Austin was sure the *Times* was publishing the Papers. "He was perked up," Austin remembers. "It wasn't a very extended conversation. I had a sort of feeling that he was glad to know and that maybe he wanted to do something."[143]

This was the first wind Ellsberg received of publication of the Papers, and he was ready to explode. He had not given anybody at the *Times* the green light (he would still be complaining about that weeks later, and to his decidedly unsympathetic ex-wife, no less). He had not even authorized copying of the Papers. He had not heard from the *Times* on whether they would print all of them or a great portion of them. Now, they had apparently stolen the documents from him. He had been left vulnerable to an FBI raid without warning. Ellsberg realized that Sheehan had been dishonest with him. And he didn't know what the *Times's* plans were. He was heading into the spotlight he sought, but not in the manner he sought. Patricia would tell Sheehan sometime in the next few days that Ellsberg was wild with anger about his deception of him.[144]

In his rage, Ellsberg tried to stop publication, Sheehan would record (without revealing whom Ellsberg contacted for that purpose). Ellsberg also called Sheehan. Another *Times* man took the call. Sheehan asked for Ellsberg's number and told his colleague to inform him when 100,000 copies of the paper had rolled off the press. By then it would be too late for Ellsberg to do anything about it. Sheehan was playing hardball. From a pay phone later, he called Ellsberg's apartment but to no avail. When he reached Patricia, he told her it was a complicated story and that Dan should do whatever he could to protect himself. Sheehan said he would remain silent. The next contact between Ellsberg and Sheehan would not be until 1972; it was an accidental encounter at that, and one Sheehan probably had not wanted.[145]

After failing to reach Sheehan, Ellsberg called K. Dun Gifford. He was quite upset, Gifford remembers, and "looking to see if I knew anything. And I didn't."[146]

Ellsberg also tried to contact A. M. Rosenthal. But Rosenthal told his secretary (who took the call) that he didn't want to speak to anybody. "I didn't know what he wanted to say, but I didn't want to hear it," Rosenthal would recall. Ellsberg also tried to reach Tony Russo, but again he failed to make contact.[147]

That evening, the Ellsbergs had dinner at the Zinns' home. When Dan arrived, he was still quite perturbed, Howard Zinn remembers. Zinn asked him what was wrong. Ellsberg related that he had just learned of the *Times's* impending publication. "Dan was pissed because they hadn't told him about it," Zinn recounts. "And I thought, 'What are you pissed about? You wanted them published. And here they are doing it. And you're angry because you weren't told.'" Ellsberg's mood "was the opposite of what I expected," Zinn says.[148]

"But he calmed down," Zinn recalls, "and then suddenly began to feel good about the fact that it was finally going to be printed." The Ellsbergs and the Zinns smoked some marijuana (perhaps one reason Ellsberg calmed down). The Ellsbergs had brought the marijuana over, wanting to get it out of their apartment—this was no time to have illegal drugs around. The two couples smoked as much of it as they could, then flushed the rest down the toilet. They then went to see the movie *Butch Cassidy and the Sundance Kid*, which Dan "was seeing for about the fourth time, and which we were seeing for the first time," Zinn humorously remembers. The movie's elements of adventure, danger, and excitement, the camaraderie on display, and the heroic figures all would have appealed to Ellsberg. "He *loved* that movie," Zinn says. "And he wanted us to see it."[149]

In Harvard Square, after the movie, the two couples found themselves in an odd scene. Some stocky men who appeared to be from another country, perhaps a South American one, approached them. "They were dressed outlandishly," Zinn recounts. "In some strange way." One of the men thrust his hand forward and asked the Zinns and Ellsbergs to stop. The Zinns and Ellsbergs were still a bit high. "How do we get to the Combat Zone?" the man asked, in a foreign accent. The Combat Zone was a strip joint in Boston.[150]

When they arrived home, the Zinns' 22-year-old son was there. The smell of marijuana was still in the air. What was going on? the son wanted to know. His parents had advised him when he was in high school not to smoke marijuana.[151]

Later that evening, the Ellsbergs decided to get some more things out of their apartment. Helen and Stewart Perry remember being awakened by the Ellsbergs late that night and hearing something being dragged down the steps. The Ellsbergs were "quite noisy," Stewart recalls. "Taking some stuff out. And we looked out the window, and they were loading the car. . . . We thought, 'Oh, they've gone for another of their trips. And it'll be quiet for a few days.'" The Perrys were disappointed when the Ellsbergs returned, laughing.[152]

Quiet was not what was in store for the Perrys.

TWELVE

BATTLE MODE

THE *NEW YORK TIMES* STORY ON SUNDAY, JUNE 13, 1971, CARRIED THE understated headline "Vietnam Archive: Pentagon Study Traces 3 Decades of Growing U.S. Involvement." To its left was a photo, more eye-catching to many readers, of a smiling Richard Nixon with his daughter Tricia at her wedding.[1] Yet the story marked the beginning of the greatest leak of government secrets in U.S. history. And with a war going on, no less.

After, one suspects, little sleep, Dan Ellsberg headed into Harvard Square to purchase extra copies of the *Times* before the local supply ran dry. He liked to have extra copies of writings bearing his name, and this was no different—Ellsberg would be attached to this story soon enough. Afterward, more than one person would remember seeing Ellsberg lugging a stack of newspapers with a big smile on his face. Frank Rich ran into him at the Harvard Square newsstand buying multiple copies of the *Times*. "I sort of said, 'Well, gosh. What's going on?'" Rich recounts. "And he sort of gave me a sly smile and . . . some vague answer . . . like, 'I may be going out of town for a while.' He said something slightly conspiratorial." Rich thought it made a certain amount of sense for Ellsberg to buy more than one copy, as he was obsessed with Vietnam. But it was far-fetched for Rich to imagine that someone he knew had set such a major news story into play. However, as Rich and others at the *Harvard Crimson* read more about the Pentagon study in the *Times*, they began to notice similarities with things Ellsberg had told them. "And we began to wonder very quickly if Dan might be the source," Rich remembers.[2]

Many people, in fact, suspected that Ellsberg was the source. Some, as we've seen, were certain of it. There were those on the inside who were aware that he was among only a handful of people who had access to the Papers. Others knew he simply had a lot of documents. There were also all those hints that he was up to something big, his playing with his secret, and his open talk of it. And Ellsberg was now fervently opposed to the war, many knew, and a man who liked to share his discoveries with others. Not least telling, he would have loved the limelight. "When the Pentagon Papers appeared, it all made instant sense to me," Thomas Schelling remembers. "This has got to have been Dan Ellsberg," William Bundy thought.[3]

Roman Kolkowicz and Bernard Brodie discussed the publication of the Papers at length over dinner. "We pretty much agreed, 'That's typical Dan,'" Kolkowicz recounts. "It has to be dramatic. It has to be kind of cosmic. And he has to be the hero."[4]

Tom Oliphant, of course, knew immediately who was responsible when he saw the *Times* stories the morning of June 13. He had gone out to get the Sunday papers at around 7:30 and was sitting in his car. "I started laughing," he recounts. "I just remember laughing for about fifteen minutes. And then getting a cup of coffee and sitting in the car and chuckling some more as I realized how extensive the publication was in the paper and obviously what was coming. And I immediately dropped everything to begin to try to reach him." He failed. Ellsberg, Oliphant concluded, was not at his home and had slipped out of sight. (But Ellsberg would recall being at home all day on June 13 and 14. Perhaps he wasn't answering the phone.) Oliphant then called Noam Chomsky, who said "not much, but enough," Oliphant remembers. Then "I just started immediately putting out the word" that he wanted to locate Ellsberg. "It didn't take two hours to realize that he was underground, that he'd disappeared. . . . He was around, but he was not available. I mean, he wasn't hiding, but he made himself pretty scarce almost immediately." Oliphant tried to get a message to Ellsberg: Call him. "Once I realized the sensitivity around the mention of Dan's name, that made it even more apparent that at least he had had a role in this," Oliphant recalls.[5]

Like most everyone else, Janaki Tschannerl was taken by surprise at publication of the Papers. "Everybody was really astonished," she remembers: "'What is this? Where did it come from?'" Tschannerl didn't realize at first that this was the same top-secret study Ellsberg had told her about. But "as I read this, I said, 'Wait a minute,'" she recounts. "'What is this? *Yes*, indeed. Yes.'" Tschannerl, too, got on the phone. "I called Dan: 'Is this what I [think]?' And nobody answered. It just rang, rang, rang. . . . It was actually funny. . . . Within the day it was clear that something was going on. I couldn't reach Dan or Pat." Tschannerl decided not to leave a message with their answering service. Government wiretapping of dissenters in those days required that one be careful. But the Ellsbergs, who had recently attended Tschannerl's thirtieth birthday party in Cambridge, called her later that day. "They didn't say who they were," she recalls. "Something like, 'This is a surprise, isn't it? Were you surprised?'"[6]

That evening, the Ellsbergs had dinner at Peter and Marian Wright Edelman's home in Newton, outside Boston. (Here we know he left his apartment.) Philip and Ann Heymann were also there. Several years earlier, the Heymanns had fixed up Patricia with Ann's brother. The couples discussed the morning's stories in the *Times*. Dan seemed "terribly excited" about them, Philip Heymann recalls. Ellsberg acted as if he were sitting on pins and needles. "My wife and I both remember Dan saying, 'Did you see the newspaper? Did you see the newspaper?'" Heymann recounts. "He was sort of excitedly and maybe with some frustration trying to figure out whether we had, in fact, seen the story. . . . People weren't paying as much attention to it as Dan seemed to think was warranted." Ellsberg kept trying to steer the conversation back to the Papers. "He didn't say that he had done it, but you could sort of infer that he wasn't saying he didn't do it either," Peter Edelman reminisces. He "intimated that he knew more than you could possibly know unless you really had been there." Ann Heymann remarked at one point that a lot of what was in the *Times*'s articles was not new—hardly what Ellsberg wanted to hear. At the end of the evening, Peter Edelman mused to himself, "The way Dan is talking about this—hum, what's going on here?"[7]

Anthony Russo was unaware of publication of the Papers most of that Sunday. He usually purchased a copy of Sunday's *New York Times*, but it was a sunny day, and he and others had been out in the park in Santa Monica. When he got home, Russo turned on his radio and heard the story around 6 P.M. "I said, '*Oh, my God*. It has *hit*,'" he recounts. Russo tried to reach Ellsberg, to no avail, then and in subsequent days. It was not a good sign. In the meantime, he waited to hear from the FBI or the police. He knew it would only be a matter of time. It was a lonely wait.[8]

Robert Ellsberg had almost forgotten about those top-secret documents that he had helped his father copy—and which his mother had said not to discuss with his father—though Robert had been depressed and concerned, when he saw a *Los Angeles Times* article on a "vast collection" of "secret government documents" on the Vietnam War on Monday, June 14. "Instantly I knew what it was," he recalls. "I just remember just cheering and just yelping [with] excitement. . . . I was very excited. Of course, I couldn't tell anybody about it."[9]

Except his sister and mother, of course, who also instantly knew. So *this* was what Dan had been copying, Carol Ellsberg now realized. Her reaction was one of anxiety and dread. "I'd been waiting for two years for the other shoe to drop," she remembers, her agitation over the affair still evident 25 years later. "And then one day it happened. . . . 'Oh! God! Oh, no.'" Mother and son, with their contrasting sentiments and emotions, went out to get a copy of the *New York Times*.[10]

When Mary Marshall read about the Vietnam archive in her morning newspaper, she was also perturbed. Marshall now understood that her and Carol's scheme to derail Dan by reporting his copying to Harry Rowen through another party had come to naught, that "nothing had been done about it." Marshall thought, "This never should have happened." She had believed it was all under control, but now it was clear that it had never been under control, that Rowen had not acted. Marshall received a phone call that morning from an official in Washington, a friend of hers and her husband, Andrew. The man had never liked Ellsberg. In a laconic way, "he said, 'Am I right in assessing that it's our friend who did this?'" Marshall recounts. "He didn't even mention his name. He didn't have to. And I said, 'Yes, it looks like that to me.'"[11]

Upon reading a story in the *Los Angeles Times* on the Vietnam study, Lynda Sinay started feeling nervous. She wasn't sure the story pertained to the copying of the documents that had been done at her advertising agency, "but there was something vaguely familiar about all this," she remembers.[12]

Early the same week in Cambridge, Jeremy Larner was walking down a street,

> and all of a sudden here comes Dan with two guys I'd never seen before. . . . These guys have big overcoats and hats. They're serious looking guys. And the moment I saw him, it suddenly occurred to me that it could have been Dan. And I said, "Dan, was that *you?!*" And his face lit up. And then he [put a finger across his lips]. And he walked on. I was puzzled. . . .
>
> Later on he said to me, with great glee, "I'm sorry I didn't stop to talk to you, Jeremy. But those were FBI agents who were questioning me." But it was kind of farcical, because in a way Dan was only too glad to be known. He was very happy that I had come to this realization.[13]

On June 14, Ellsberg phoned his son from Cambridge to see if Robert had heard the news, and if he had not, to point it out to him. "Dad, was that you?" Robert asked him, Carol Ellsberg would report to the FBI. His father replied that they could not talk about it on the phone.[14]

In the RAND building in Santa Monica, there were a lot of worried and angry faces. Nerves were on edge. The air, at least in many quarters, was electric. "We all knew in our gut that it was Dan who did it," Gus Shubert, who was then a RAND vice president, recalls. That Sunday or Monday morning, Shubert recounts, he was sitting in the office of RAND President Harry Rowen, who was well aware that this spelled nothing but trouble for both him and RAND, and who was under other pressures:

> The phone was ringing . . . and his secretary would [say], "It's so and so." And he'd put it through and put it through. And all these people were calling him and saying, "It has to be Dan." . . . From all over the country. And during the middle of that barrage of calls, I remember him taking the phone and slamming it down in a huff, and he said, "I don't need this. I *just* don't need this."
>
> . . . Harry always thought that Dan was capable of doing it. . . . So he was not surprised. From the beginning, he thought it had to be Dan. So I kept saying, "Give him a chance. Give him a chance." And he kept saying, "Come on. Come on, Gus. You know damn well it was Dan. . . . I always was uneasy that he would do something like this, and now he's done it."

"Nobody had to tell Harry that morning that it was Dan," Richard Best attests.[15]

George Tanham spoke with Rowen in his office that Monday morning. Rowen was then with RAND Senior Vice President J. Richard ("Goldie") Goldstein. Tanham had flown in from Washington and had not yet seen the newspaper. "They were glum," he recounts. "They were in a state of shock and knew it was goddamn serious."[16]

Rowen probably feared from the start that his job was in jeopardy (he knew that the chairman of RAND's board of trustees, Newton Minow, was not a fan). He appeared uncommunicative, withdrawn, numb to Best during this period: "He was there and that was all." Rowen was "extremely angry and anxious about it," Patrick Sullivan, who was a RAND psychologist, recalls. "Desperate to try to fend off the most dire consequences, and totally engaged in that battle." Yet Rowen seemed, on the whole, calm and admirably in control of himself, even while his mind was racing to determine what he should do next, how he should comport himself—he knew that he would be speaking with the board of trustees soon—and, not least significant, how he would explain his past actions vis-à-vis Ellsberg and the Papers. He knew that he had some explaining to do. On a personal level, an emotional and psychological one, Rowen was quite hurt. "He was absolutely crushed," Shubert remembers—"crushed to think that someone as close to him, someone he knew as well as Dan, would do that. . . . He was really down. Done in by one of his very best friends." Rowen "felt betrayed in every possible way," another RAND analyst says. "Stunned."[17]

It could not have failed to occur to Rowen that he had aided Ellsberg's career significantly. He had given him important consulting assignments in the

Pentagon. He had shaped John McNaughton's hiring of him. He had brought Ellsberg back to RAND after Ellsberg had returned from Vietnam, and possibly even raised his salary. He had been Ellsberg's chief defender and protector at RAND, sticking his neck out for him, even extolling him. He had been patient with Ellsberg in the midst of his horrendous work problems. He had also involved him in a prestigious consulting job for Henry Kissinger. He had then played a pivotal role in Ellsberg's gaining access to the Pentagon Papers at RAND. On top of all this, they had been very good friends. "A fair number of people felt they'd been made fools of in trust and sponsorship of Dan, but in Harry's case it was a ruinous thing," William Kaufmann comments. Rowen, who does not like to talk about this whole affair even with former RAND colleagues, and who declined my interview requests, came to detest Ellsberg. "What he did was a really lousy thing," Rowen told me during a short conversation at Stanford University in 1995.[18]

During Shubert's meeting with Rowen, Albert Wohlstetter walked in. He also knew this had to be Ellsberg, and he, too, was angry about it. Wohlstetter thought Ellsberg was a traitor who had committed a despicable act and was thus now a despicable person. He also came to detest Ellsberg and felt betrayed. He had taken Ellsberg under his wing at RAND, virtually hired him, then trained him, welcomed him into his home almost like a member of his family, and talked him up among other people. Now this is what he got in return? Wohlstetter may have worried about how this debacle would affect his own reputation and influence at RAND. He was the gray eminence behind Rowen's throne and controlled many of the important decisions. In essence, Rowen was always second in command behind Wohlstetter, who had an almost Svengali-like influence on him. If Rowen's position at RAND was in jeopardy, so was Wohlstetter's.[19]

Wohlstetter remarked to Rowen and Shubert, "Listen, fellows. The only way Dan could have gotten greater satisfaction out of this is to have released the Papers in one fell swoop while hanging naked upside down from a very tall tree."[20] Wohlstetter knew Ellsberg.

As was his custom, Richard Best arrived at his RAND office at around 7:30 the morning of June 14. He was single, a recent widower, and RAND Washington liked to call him early, so he got in early. Also per his custom, Best began his morning by reading the newspaper; it was a way to get used to being at work. "I opened the paper: Christ, here's the headline in the *Los Angeles Times*," he recounts. As RAND's security officer, he picked up the phone and called the FBI office in Los Angeles. He asked to speak to Neil McGinnis of the internal security division. "I said, 'Neil, do you remember the investigation you were doing on Dan Ellsberg last year on top-secret information?'" Best remembers. "'The headlines of the morning's *Los Angeles Times* are it.' . . . He said, 'Can you prove it?' And I said, 'I can't prove it at the moment, but there's no possibility it's anything else.'" Best also remarked to McGinnis, who seemed overly relaxed about the matter, "I think you'd better get hot on it, because you're going to have Washington crawling up your drawers any moment now."[21]

As soon as Best put down the phone, Harry Rowen was on the line. Could Best please come down to his office? Larry Henderson, RAND's vice president in Washington, was there when Best arrived. "Damage control has started," Best notes. Like Rowen, Henderson had been intimately involved in the storing of the Pentagon Papers outside RAND's Top Secret Control system, and in allowing Ellsberg access to them. He, too, knew that he had some explaining to do before the board of trustees. Best did not care for Henderson. "I couldn't trust the son-of-a-bitch," he says. "I didn't want any part of him." Rowen and Henderson wanted information from Best—lots of it—and for him to gather material on the antecedents of this disaster. They wanted him to collect all copies of the Papers. "And it had to be very quickly," Best remembers. He believed they had their eyes out for scapegoats. "When I got down to Rowen's office, I realized they were looking for somebody to put it on," he says. He thought, "Those sons-of-bitches, I'll give you straight answers, but that's all you'll get." Best learned shortly that at least one RAND official wanted to fire him. "If they fired me, I was going to blow the front office apart," he says with a laugh. "I would have scorched Larry Henderson's ass and Harry's ass."[22]

———※———

Across the country in Washington, Marcus Raskin and Ralph Stavins were having breakfast with Ben Bradlee of the *Washington Post*. The mood at the *Post* was not good, given the *Post*'s clobbering by the *Times*. Raskin had phoned Bradlee at his country home in West Virginia the day before. He had been "hush-hush and secret," Bradlee recalled. According to one account, Raskin was "shaken" that the Papers were coming out at this moment, right before the IPS book on the war was being released. IPS had been preempted. But Raskin says his concern was otherwise. When he read the Sunday *New York Times* articles on the Papers, he remembers, "I assumed they came from us" since he had given Neil Sheehan portions of the Papers. But Raskin noticed that the *Times* had not run an accompanying article on U.S. war crimes, as Sheehan had agreed that the *Times* would. And there was no mention of the IPS book. "I was upset," Raskin recounts. "They did not play them in the way that I thought we had agreed they would." Hence he called Bradlee, who was rabid about getting his hands on a set of the Papers. "Of course, it was Ben who was very shaken," Raskin laughs. He recalls telling Bradlee, "You can have some of these papers. . . . You can have what we have," but that the *Post* had to play them "in the context of war crimes." Bradlee would not agree to that. "His concern was not to put it out in such a way that it would appear on the front pages of the *Washington Post* that they had taken sides against the war," Raskin says. Raskin and Stavins offered Bradlee the manuscript of their IPS book, which quoted from the Papers, but Bradlee turned it down, finding it "a polemic against the war."[23]

Many journalists wished to speak to Dan Ellsberg at this time. *Time* magazine's Greg Wierzynski knew exactly what this was all about when he heard about publication of the Papers over the radio. He called the Ellsbergs' Cambridge flat. "I left a pile of messages . . . a ton of messages," he remembers. Another writer from *Time* went up to Cambridge the afternoon of June 14 and spoke with Ellsberg shortly thereafter. "He wasn't real happy about seeing me at that point," the journalist recounts. "He was both exhilarated by all the publicity and impact of this thing, and he was also somewhat apprehensive about his own personal position and just what threat it might be posing to him. So he was torn at that point. . . . We didn't talk for real long—not as long as I would have liked. And he did not lay a set of the Papers on me, which I would have also liked, since we didn't have them at that point." Soon Wierzynski received a brief message from Patricia Ellsberg on his answering machine confirming, in effect, Dan's responsibility. *Time* was working on a story on the Papers, and "there was a question at *Time* whether we would use 'allegedly Daniel Ellsberg' or 'reportedly,'" Wierzynski recalls. "And I remember telling people, 'Don't worry about this. Because we know for sure it was Ellsberg.'"[24]

Two journalists from *Newsweek* also spoke with Ellsberg early that week. He refused to comment on whether he was the *New York Times*'s source, but, "his bony face taut with tension," he proved to be "almost a compulsive talker," a *Newsweek* article recounted. The three-hour interview began in a French bistro and ended in Ellsberg's office at MIT. Ellsberg seemed delighted that the *Times* had published the Papers. "I'm glad it's out," he said with a smile. And with another smile: "I am flattered to be suspected of having leaked it."[25]

On Tuesday, June 15, the Justice Department obtained a temporary injunction in federal court ordering the *Times* to stop publishing the Papers. Justice contended that publication violated a provision of the espionage laws. For the first time, the U.S. government was suing the press to stop it from revealing information for reasons of "national security." Ellsberg was angry when the *Times* elected to obey the court injunction. After all his trials and tribulations getting the Papers out, their release had been halted after only three days. He would now have to pursue other outlets. "I hadn't expected to give them to any more than one paper," he said later.[26]

The next day, Wednesday, June 16, there was another disturbing development. After, to Ellsberg's astonishment, a reporter from the *Times* had called him to ask if he was the source of the Papers ("*You're* asking *me?*" he responded), and after Ellsberg had called the *Washington Post* from a pay phone—saying he believed he was under surveillance—and refused to confirm or deny that he was the source, the journalist Sidney Zion phoned a radio talk show late that evening to identify him as the leaker. Zion, who knew that other journalists as well as the FBI had Ellsberg's name, had originally picked Ellsberg from a list of people who had access to the Papers. Then "I went around town" questioning people, Zion remembers. "I knew right away a bunch of people knew, because just the way their eyes looked." Zion could not get ahold of Ellsberg on the phone either, despite trying fervently. "Finally the answering service lady told me, 'You know, everybody's been calling him,'" Zion recalls. He was widely denounced for his disclosure. "The next thing I know the whole world came tumbling down on my head," Zion recounts. "Every hypocrite in the world. . . . They decided that I was a rat. I was an informer. All kinds of shit. . . . They were cutting me dead. . . . I had to go back and practice law. . . . They really ruined me." But "all I did was break a story. It was coming out anyway. Everybody was trying to get it." Zion was not unaware that identifying Ellsberg could cause Ellsberg trouble, but he had talked to "a mutual friend," he says, who had said, "No, no. By no means. He wants it out. Don't even worry about that." Marty Garbus, who met with Ellsberg shortly afterward, remembers that Ellsberg was angry at Zion but also elated about being identified. Zion's disclosure hastened Ellsberg's move underground.[27]

When Lynda Sinay got up that Friday morning and saw Ellsberg's picture on the front page of the *Los Angeles Times*, she thought, "Oh, my God. What am I going to do now?" She started shaking. She was terrified. "I just knew I was in big trouble," she recalls.[28]

By this time the FBI was onto Ellsberg—the bureau had pinpointed him as the "prime suspect" on June 15—but he was not interested in talking to them. When two agents knocked on his door in Cambridge the morning of June 17, only hours after Zion's disclosure, no one answered. The agents refused to comment on their activity to a small group of newspeople who had gathered.[29]

The Ellsbergs had taken cover.

Early that morning they would have been found in a run-down motel in the Boston area. The weather was hot, and the air conditioner in their "dismal" room wasn't working, the *Washington Post*'s Ben Bagdikian learned when he met with them there at around 2 A.M. "The room was stifling," Bagdikian recalled.[30] Dan was not in the best of moods.

Bagdikian had arrived at the room through a route marked by rigmarole. The previous afternoon, he had received a perplexing message at the *Post:* "Call Mr. Boston from a secure phone." The only Mr. Boston Bagdikian knew was in Great Britain. He suspected "Mr. Boston" was a fake name and that the message involved the Pentagon Papers. Bagdikian walked across the street to a hotel that had a row of pay phones. A voice on the other end of the line told him "an old friend had an important message for me, but I had to give the number of a public phone where the friend could call me in a few minutes," Bagdikian recounted. "I gave the number of the phone next to mine." Soon Dan Ellsberg was on the line. Bagdikian was not especially surprised to hear from him, although he had not suspected Ellsberg was the source of the Papers until this point, he says. (But Don Oberdorfer, who was then also with the *Post*, recalls asking Bagdikian, after seeing the first of the *Times*'s stories on the Papers, "Do you know how to get hold of Dan Ellsberg?") Ellsberg asked Bagdikian if he could "commit the *Post*" to publishing the Papers. Bagdikian said he would have to call him back. Ellsberg gave him another number that had an answering machine. If Bagdikian could get the *Post*'s commitment, he should leave a cryptic message. Bagdikian chose the code words: "Mr. Medford from Providence will wait for you at the hotel." (Bagdikian had earlier written for the *Providence Journal.*) Ellsberg enjoyed this sort of cloak-and-dagger intrigue, and both men had to be careful. The specter of the FBI moving in and stopping them in their tracks at any moment was now very real. "*I* was afraid of intervention," Bagdikian remembers. "Because we always assumed at the *Post* it was always possible that there was an informant from the FBI. And I think the FBI made sure they could have an informant on every paper they're concerned with, either in the switchboard or something like that. So that there was reason for me to be concerned." Ellsberg told Bagdikian he should bring a large suitcase with him if he came up to Boston.[31]

After getting a commitment from Ben Bradlee over the phone from the airport, Bagdikian flew to Boston and checked in at the motel under the name "Medford," only to hear the young man behind the desk say: "I got a message for a 'Mr. Bagdikian' who's expected tonight. Is that anything to do with you?" A slip-up, apparently. Bagdikian was forced to break his cover. This would not help his chances with the FBI. As soon as Bagdikian got to his room, the phone rang. Ellsberg again. Things were clicking now. Bagdikian was to go to a residence in Cambridge to get the "material" and to leave word with the desk clerk to let some friends into the room while he was gone. Did Bagdikian have back trouble? Ellsberg asked him. "This stuff is very heavy," Ellsberg said. Bagdikian did have back trouble. He feared ending up on the ground, out of commission, writhing in agony, the whole operation aborted. That would be all he needed; he was then going through a difficult divorce.[32]

After passing through Cambridge's Porter Square and finding the residence with a little difficulty—his taxi driver had to walk up to dark porches and light matches to determine the street numbers—Bagdikian got out. He was greeted in the house by, among others, a woman in her thirties or forties. "I said, 'Dan Ellsberg said I could pick up some things here,'" he recounts. "They knew exactly what I was talking about. And they showed me the boxes, and I took one." The box, one of two, had heavy twine around it, which made it easier to carry.[33]

"As I dragged the box off the motel elevator into the third-floor corridor, there was Daniel Ellsberg, a plastic bucket in hand, returning from the motel ice machine," Bagdikian recalled. "He was haggard and complained of a terrible headache." "I got a feeling he was under great stress," Bagdikian says. "I got a feeling he was tired. He hadn't slept much. He had that whole demeanor. And he *looked* tired. . . . But very controlled. It was clear how he wanted [the Papers] handled. . . . He hadn't gotten sloppy in his thinking." Ellsberg showed a great desire to get the Papers into the *Post* now that the *Times* had been enjoined. "I think that just dominated his thinking: Get them published, get them published, get them published," Bagdikian recalls. "He had a way of concentrating his energies."[34]

In the motel room with Patricia was another man who seemed to be a lawyer and a friend of Patricia. His role, it was apparent to Bagdikian, was to protect Patricia legally. The man was quiet but "obviously monitoring everything very carefully," Bagdikian remembers. He made Bagdikian uneasy. Patricia, whom Bagdikian liked ("in contrast to Dan, she was quiet and modest in manner"), did not say much but was keenly focused on events. "Where's the other box?" Ellsberg asked Bagdikian. Bagdikian said he thought this one had everything. Ellsberg then picked up the phone, and subsequently a young man knocked on the door. "Dan opened the door just wide enough to drag the second box into the room and quickly shut the door to hide the messy scene inside," Bagdikian recounted. Bagdikian got only a glimpse of the man. After Ellsberg told Bagdikian he had some conditions, Patricia's friend told her, "I think we should leave now," and those two departed.[35]

Ellsberg specified that the *Post* could not publish material that would compromise secret U.S. code. That could mean a much shorter prison sentence.

"He had that very well researched," Bagdikian recalls. Ellsberg also demanded that Bagdikian not reveal his identity, and that Bagdikian secretly deliver the other box of Papers to a member of Congress. With bitterness that surprised Bagdikian, Ellsberg told him about his experience with Neil Sheehan and others at the *New York Times*. "He was angry and hurt that he was cut off by the *Times*," Bagdikian recounts. "He thought they were not going to publish it, or at least the three months went by and nothing happened, and he couldn't get hold of Sheehan, he couldn't get through to anybody. They wouldn't talk to him. They just cut him off."[36]

Bagdikian agreed to Ellsberg's conditions, and the two men went to work "cutting and sorting." It did not go smoothly. Bagdikian ended up with "a disorganized mass of photocopied sheets completely out of sequence and with very few page numbers." "The whole thing was a big undifferentiated mess when we got it," Don Oberdorfer recalls. "I remember it taking us a while to get it into some kind of order so we could begin to see what we had." After lying down for an hour or so, Bagdikian called a cab and headed for the airport with his two heavy boxes.[37]

The *Post* had its set of the Papers, or at least most of one, and began publishing them the next day, Friday, June 18. But it was also quickly halted by a court order.

On June 17, Jacqueline Barnett, sister of Patricia Ellsberg, phoned Robert Ellsberg. She advised him that "she had heard from Dan and Pat and they were well and happy," Carol Ellsberg would report to the FBI. The same day, according to Richard Salant, who was then president of CBS News, someone offered CBS portions of the Papers "on an immediate release basis from sources who were in a terrible rush to get these things published." Also through third parties, Ellsberg approached NBC and ABC. But they too turned down the Papers.[38]

Aware that the FBI was watching their apartment, Dan and Pat Ellsberg chose not to return home after completing their mission with Bagdikian. The FBI stepped up its effort to find Ellsberg, media ringed their apartment, and a horde of reporters and cameramen scoured MIT in search of Ellsberg. He called an MIT staff person the next morning and told her not to be alarmed by his disappearance. He asked that the director of MIT's Center for International Studies, Everett Hagen, distribute copies of his writings to the media or "anyone who wanted them." Ellsberg also suggested that one of his neighbors distribute copies to people surrounding his home. MIT disclosed the phone call against Ellsberg's wishes. Journalists tracked down John Simon at a film seminar in Wisconsin in the vain hope that he would know Patricia's whereabouts ("I was quite amazed by the whole thing," Simon says). "I've been holding my breath for several days since I heard about this thing," Harry Ellsberg, Dan's father, told the press. "I thought it could have been him." But "I'd back him up 100 percent. . . . I believe we have to get the hell out of Vietnam." As for his son's legal jeopardy, Harry Ellsberg said, "He's been through worse than this, skydiving and scuba diving and skiing."[39]

Marty Garbus met with the Ellsbergs around this time at another motel, this one on the banks of the Charles River in Cambridge. In fact, Garbus remembers, it was the Treadway Motor Inn, the same place Neil Sheehan had stayed on the weekend he had taken the Papers from Ellsberg. Dan or Pat had called up Garbus. "They wanted to figure out what was going on" legally, Garbus recalls. "I told them about indictments." Their thoughts were on "a potential criminal process," and "I had an advantage in that I had been thinking about these problems for a long time [and] had done the 'research.' So I was more knowledgeable than anybody they knew." Though Ellsberg probably expected an indictment, his mood at the time was one of "exultation. Not fear," Garbus remembers. "Finally that this thing he had been living with for so long had exploded. And also it was a vindication of him. He was *right*. He was right in that it was worth enough to be on the front page of the newspapers."[40]

Charles Nesson and Leonard Boudin also met with Ellsberg that week. Ellsberg had spoken to Boudin, a friend of Garbus and a renowned civil liberties attorney who was then teaching a course at Harvard with Nesson, about representing him. "Dan realized that he wanted and needed a lawyer pretty early on," Nesson remembers. Boudin asked Nesson, who had aided him recently on another antiwar case, to help him on this one. The two "went through with Dan all the ins and outs, as we would understand them, of what it would mean if he went underground," Nesson recounts. Ellsberg "went underground because he wanted to get the rest of the Papers out," Nesson says. "And he felt that if he did not go underground, he would be arrested right away and that would be the end of it." Ellsberg claimed later that he did so to avoid "exposing people who were helping me." Nesson thought the move astute:

> Because he was trying to bring attention to the Pentagon Papers. . . . And the Papers themselves are not fascinating. . . . Had the administration just ignored them when they were published in the *New York Times*, they would have sunk like a brick. I can't believe anybody would have read them. But the fact that Dan was a particular goad to Nixon, and that [Attorney General John] Mitchell was so willing to be provoked, gave Dan the opportunity to focus attention in a quite amazing way. And the fact that he went underground, and then during the period while he was underground succeeded not only in evading all of the efforts to find him, but at the same time salting the Papers

around to major papers all over the country, so that they were popping up, it put tremendous focus on what he was doing, gave tremendous interest to these Papers, made the FBI look as if they didn't know what they were doing, made Dan basically look like he was running an army rather than just a little individual effort. So it was pretty well executed.[41]

Ellsberg, Nesson recounts,

was in a battle mode. He was like on a campaign. There was no sense of fear or trepidation or anything. . . . He had an objective in mind. And it was always his most amazing quality that he could focus on something maniacally. You know, just be on it. And during that period what he was *on* was getting these Papers out. He'd been trying to get them out for years. . . . They'd begun to come out through the *New York Times*, and now he had this window, and he was going to get them out.

. . . He loved battle. He loved battle. And he was a tactician. You're moving things around with him. The fact that he could make the Pentagon Papers pop up in different papers around the country, and that the government didn't have a clue what was happening, and that he could do a newscast [while underground] and he could somehow screw [the government]—he loved all that stuff. He has a very tactical mind.

"Dan has two modes," Garbus comments. "He has a battle mode, and then this other mode, which is this vulnerable, crying mode. And I'm not so sure that he has many other modes."[42]

The *Boston Globe* was the next place the Papers popped up. Tom Oliphant had been knocking on doors, making phone calls, and leaving messages everywhere in his drive to reach Ellsberg. He had even called Ellsberg's father and brother, receiving "very polite and curt" responses from both men, who didn't know Dan's whereabouts and who didn't want to talk much. The night of Zion's disclosure, Oliphant had received an anonymous call from a youngish male who said he had been asked by Ellsberg to call him, that Ellsberg was about to be named, and that Ellsberg "wanted you to know that," Oliphant recounts. The gist of this and other calls Oliphant received during the week (also from unnamed intermediaries, whom he believes were mainly graduate-student types, including graduate assistants of Noam Chomsky) was, "We'll be in contact. Just be patient" and "Let's see how it goes" with the court injunction against the *Times*. "The message that I got through third parties that week was just, 'Cool it,'" Oliphant remembers. "'We know where you are. Just relax.'" Oliphant knew "that it was just going to be a matter of a day or two until they got in touch with me to begin the arrangements for the *Globe* to get some" of the Papers. "Because of my relationship and the work that I'd done with Dan, I had no doubt he'd take care of me." Also, the *Globe* had long opposed the Vietnam War. "The reason we at least got third whack at them was we were probably the most anti-Vietnam newspaper in the U.S. at that time," Tom Winship, then the *Globe*'s editor, told me. And "I always thought Chomsky really put in a good word for us. . . . He and I had a very good relationship."[43]

As long planned, Oliphant flew to San Diego on Friday, June 18, to visit his parents, who were ill. As it turned out, he decided it was better to be in San Diego anyway, as it would confuse the FBI and other journalists about where Ellsberg was. The dateline on his articles would be San Diego, leading people to think Ellsberg might be in California. "I know I said something to the effect that this is really going to fuck up the search," Oliphant reminisces. And, indeed, "for about 48 hours it completely fucked up the search for him."[44]

As soon as Oliphant arrived at his parents' house that evening, before he had even had a chance to unpack, the phone rang. It was the first of a series of collect calls that weekend from people who were, again, speaking for Ellsberg. One caller asked Oliphant to look into the state of the FBI's search for Ellsberg. A couple of times the callers "could not go beyond the literal words of a message they were passing on," Oliphant remembers. His conversations became strictly "phone booth to phone booth. . . . By Sunday I wasn't talking from my parents' house even. I was taking phone calls in a pay phone right by my favorite surfing beach." Delivery to the *Globe* was the most dangerous pass-off for Ellsberg and his accomplices. He was now being hunted in earnest. It wasn't a game. "There were two things clearly coming from them," Oliphant recounts. "First is, would we refuse to obey an injunction? Unlike the *Times* and the *Post*. . . . They were very serious in asking whether we would consider disobeying an injunction." But all Oliphant could say was he'd pass the request up the food chain.[45]

Then came a second request: Could the *Globe* write that Ellsberg wanted his two children and his father to know that he was okay and was thinking of them, and that he was deeply grateful for his father's support? This request came from James Thomson, Oliphant remembers, though Thomson did not identify himself on the phone. Oliphant recognized his voice. Thomson and his family were then staying in the Flamingo Motel in Palo Alto, California, where they were visiting relatives. Thomson was one of those people who had suspected Ellsberg from the start; the FBI, in turn, wondered if Thomson was sheltering him. Thomson was uncomfortable in his clandestine role. "He asked if I'd keep his name out of it," Oliphant recalls. Thomson remembers this episode somewhat differently. At his motel he received "a mysterious call" from Oliphant, he recounts:

> He asked me to go to a pay phone, because he had a message for me. So I went out of the motel [laughs]. . . . Went to the pay phone, dialed the magic number, which was Oliphant. And he told me that he had a message for me to convey to Ellsberg's father in Michigan, and to Ellsberg's children, who were in California . . . that he was alright, that he would be in touch with them soon. . . . And I pondered the request. I thought it was peculiar. But I talked to my wife about it [laughs] . . . and made those two calls. I didn't say who I was. But I just said I'd been asked to convey this message to each of these phone numbers. And they were grateful.

Robert Ellsberg recalls receiving a phone call from someone who identified himself as "a friend of your father's" and who said, "I have heard from your father and I just want to let you know he's okay."[46]

Oliphant requested from Ellsberg's intermediaries the section of the Papers on the Kennedy administration. It would be digestible, focused, and appeal to Boston-area readers.[47]

At 10:30 A.M. on the morning of Monday, June 21, by prearrangement, someone who identified himself as "Bosbin"—a code name used earlier by more than one person with Oliphant—phoned Tom Winship. Winship rejected Bosbin's demand that the *Globe* promise to disobey any court injunction but agreed to another condition. "He asked us to xerox a huge number of copies" of the Papers, Winship recalls, though "I'm not so sure we ever did." Three hours later, in another phone call, "Bosbin spoke very mysteriously and outlined to me his rather circuitous method for us to get our hands on the Papers," Winship recounts. One person from the *Globe* was to go to a pay phone in Cambridge, another to a pay phone in Newton. They were to report their numbers to Winship, who would then receive another call from Bosbin to get those numbers. Bosbin would then phone one of the two *Globe* people to indicate that the Papers were coming his way. "He asked me to describe what the two people looked like," Winship remembers. The *Globe* man in Cambridge heard nothing, while Tom Ryan, whom, like his counterpart, no one would have reason to recognize, got the call in Newton. ("It was as safe as we could think of to make it from everybody's point of view," Oliphant says.) Ryan ultimately returned to the *Globe* with "a large brown package enclosed in a zippered plastic bag."[48]

After other intrigues, that is. A historian who was in touch with Ellsberg when he was underground had earlier phoned Howard Zinn and asked him to go to a pay phone. The historian had given Zinn a number at which to call him. The two had then arranged to meet at a park on the Charles River, where the historian had passed Zinn a "very bulky" package containing a large chunk of the Papers. Zinn then took the Papers over to the home of a friend, Hilde Hein, who lived a few blocks from him and who had helped him shelter Daniel Berrigan when Berrigan had been on the lam the year before. "He just came into my backyard one day with this package," Hein reminisces. "We were outdoors, which is the safest place to be." Hein didn't want to know too much about the transaction. It was another situation where the less one knew, the better. The historian had told Zinn that he could call Winship and give him an address without saying what the address was all about, that "Winship would know what I was talking about," Zinn recounts. Zinn gave Winship Hein's address. Then, one day, after keeping the Papers at her house for a short time, Hein recalls, a stranger appeared at her door. "He was an older man. He was quite amazingly dressed. He was wearing a straw hat and a short-sleeved shirt with suspenders. And he was comfortable in himself." The man, who may have identified himself as Tom (and was probably Tom Ryan), picked up the Papers from Hein. "They were badly mimeographed," Winship remembers.[49]

After the *Globe* began publishing stories based on the documents the next day, June 22, Winship swiftly received a phone call from John Mitchell. The attorney general called Winship "Tom," even though "I'd never met the bastard," Winship recalls. "He was very chummy, but he didn't mince any words." If the *Globe* did not cease running the stories, Mitchell declared, the government would move against the newspaper. "We intend to go forward," Winship replied. "I found saying no to the attorney general was one of the most thrilling moments of my life," he says. During the call, Winship's secretary came into his office and told him, "Your friend Bosbin is on the line." But before Winship could get to him, Bosbin hung up.[50] The *Globe* was also quickly enjoined from further publication.

But stories based on the Papers appeared in the *Chicago Sun-Times* within hours. James Hoge, that newspaper's managing editor, had earlier tried without success to reach Ellsberg, then directed reporters in the *Sun-Times*'s Washington bureau to "check all the usual ports of call," particularly in Congress, "to see if we couldn't get in on the game," he remembers. Just as the *Post* was being shut down, the *Sun-Times* had obtained access to parts of the Papers through its congressional contacts, a friend of Hoge in particular. "But we were not able to develop much beyond that initial burst" of stories, Hoge recalls. His source "felt that he couldn't continue to make it available to us. . . . I suppose he didn't want to run the additional risk of exposure."[51]

The *St. Louis Post-Dispatch* obtained its Papers through another cloak-and-dagger route. Richard Dudman, its Washington bureau chief, had called everybody he could think of in a desperate effort to get his hands on the documents after the *Times* had begun publishing them. At I. F. Stone's suggestion, he contacted Leonard Boudin. "He said something like he wished he could help me," Dudman recounts. "Something noncommittal. But not too long after that, I got an anonymous call, saying that if I wanted to send somebody up to Cambridge, up to a public phone there, they would receive a call." Dudman sent his deputy bureau chief, Tom Ottenad. "Then they sent him to another phone, then possibly to even a third one. Then, finally, he got instructions to go to the upstairs back porch of a kind of a row house in Cambridge, and to look under the newspapers on top of a table on the back porch. And he found quite a stack of the Pentagon Papers there. And he raced back, and we worked all night, and we got them out."[52]

Other newspapers that gained access to parts of the Papers included the *Los Angeles Times*, the Knight newspapers, the *Christian Science Monitor*, and *Newsday*. "I must say that I exercised a certain personal taste," Ellsberg explained afterward. "I was anxious to give it to the newspapers that I thought had told me the truth in the past." In what sense, he did not say. Patricia helped him distribute the Papers. She probably imposed some organization on what must have been a highly demanding task and calmed Dan when needed. "My fingerprints were all over the Papers," she recalls. "She's my partner in crime," Ellsberg remarks.[53]

The antiwar journalist David Obst crisscrossed the country retrieving copies of the Papers for Ellsberg. It was not an easy job. "Dan wasn't sure where he'd left all of the copies," Obst revealed later. Noam Chomsky, who was also in touch with Ellsberg when he was underground ("I sort of knew what town he was in, where he was likely to be, who he was likely to be with," Chomsky says), played a key role in distributing the Papers to journalists. "I was one of the press contacts," he recounts. "Dan had several people who were press contacts. . . . Everybody wanted a piece of it. . . . Everybody knew that this stuff was coming out and that there's some source where it's coming out from. So journalists were looking around to find out how they could get some documents. . . . People were contacting me and I told them how they could get a copy." Other accomplices in Cambridge stored parts of the Papers for Ellsberg. (When Leonard Rodberg subsequently collected missing segments for the Gravel edition, Ellsberg sent him to the homes of several younger antiwar types who had chapters tucked away in their basements.) Derek Shearer, son of Lloyd Shearer and later U.S. ambassador to Finland under Bill Clinton, was among those who assisted Ellsberg's effort. "There were a bunch of people who helped out," Ellsberg would remember. "Some of them were people I knew slightly, some I knew very well. Some I never met. . . . They were all in the movement." Ellsberg broke down in sobs when recounting their help.[54]

Ellsberg had not relinquished his goal of getting a member of Congress to release the Papers and thereby provide him legal cover. On June 18, someone phoned Democratic Senator Mike Gravel of Alaska and asked him if he would be interested in using the Papers in a filibuster that he was planning against the draft. "From all evidence known to me, he was simply the only person in the Senate willing to do it," Ellsberg recalled. The 41-year-old Gravel said he would; he planned to read all of the Papers on the Senate floor in the longest filibuster in U.S. history. Ellsberg arranged for Ben Bagdikian to give Gravel his second box of the Papers, and on June 24 Bagdikian drove over to Washington's Mayflower Hotel, where he found Gravel waiting on the sidewalk; they put the box in the trunk of Gravel's car. Gravel stored the Papers under his bed at home.[55] (How many people had copies of this thing under their beds?)

For his marathon session, Gravel planned to have a urine bag under his pants, supports for his legs, and a back brace. That afternoon, June 29, he also had an enema "so that I would be completely cleaned out." But Gravel was thwarted by a Republican colleague that evening, leading him to announce a special session of his Senate subcommittee. As he read on the war's horrors from a prepared statement in that forum at 1 A.M., he began to cry, his body shaking. He could not continue. Leonard Rodberg, who had received a phone call that morning from Gravel's office asking if he knew anything about the Papers and if he would be willing to help Gravel, and who had then spent the day trying to organize them, thought it was the tension and stress that caused Gravel to break down. Gravel placed the Papers in the subcommittee record, and his office distributed copies to the press.[56]

The Ellsbergs, who had just surfaced from underground at this time, had gone to the movies with Howard and Roslyn Zinn that evening. Afterward, they stopped in Harvard Square, and Howard Zinn flipped on the radio in the car as Gravel was doing his reading. "Dan got very excited," Zinn recounts. "He was exultant that it was being read into the *Congressional Record*."[57]

———◆———

Ellsberg would recall staying in five places while underground eluding the FBI—which, he said, was undertaking what the press called "the biggest FBI manhunt since the Lindbergh kidnapping." "Four, six, I don't know," Patricia said when asked to confirm the number. One was, of course, the motel on the banks of the Charles. Rumor would later circulate that Ellsberg stayed at the Sandstone Retreat in California (the FBI would turn up there), but that is almost certainly untrue. Ellsberg probably did not leave New England and spent most of his time in Cambridge. He told the press when he surfaced that he had never left the Boston area and had moved from home to home, at times staying with "friends we didn't know." "I was spirited from apartment to apartment," he said later. Howard Zinn believes the Ellsbergs stayed for a time with Janaki Tschannerl, who saw Ellsberg's disappearance as an act of nonviolence and may have encouraged it. Tschannerl, who did not want to talk about this topic with me, suggested that she had helped arrange housing for them, though "they never stayed with me." The Ellsbergs' neighbor Priscilla McMillan heard that they stayed at first with friends on Brattle Street in Cambridge, not far from their apartment. Certainly they needed relatively invisible people to shelter them (though one friend of Ellsberg told me that two "well-known people in Cambridge" hid him and asked him never to tell).[58]

Charles Nesson, who was in contact with Ellsberg when he was underground, says "he was living in an apartment . . . right around here"—here being Harvard Law School. "He didn't go to Canada and he didn't go to Colorado and he didn't go any[where]," Nesson recalls. "He basically stayed in Cambridge. . . . He borrowed a friend's apartment." Nesson and Leonard Boudin visited Ellsberg there:

> We were under pretty intense surveillance. And basically what we'd do is, Leonard and I would meet here. We both rode bicycles. This law school is completely linked together with underground tunnels in a network that nobody who doesn't live and work in the law school could understand very well. And so, basically, Leonard and I would take our bikes in at some point and walk them through to some other point, come up, and then ride them the wrong way down one-way streets and in pathways through buildings til we were convinced that nobody could possibly be connected with us. And then we'd go to Dan's apartment. We'd sit and meet with him.[59]

Nesson and Boudin assumed their phones were tapped and used pay phones to call Ellsberg to arrange the meetings. Their assumption led to a humorous incident. At Boudin's house the weekend before Ellsberg surfaced, they were negotiating over the phone with the U.S. attorney over the terms of Ellsberg's surrender. "We wanted them to promise that we could walk him in and surrender him . . . as opposed to them grabbing him and handcuffing him and taking photographs and all that kind of stuff, like they would want to do," Nesson recounts. "Basically they would want to make him out to be somebody that the FBI *caught:* 'Here is the fugitive.' . . . We wanted him to be able to voluntarily surrender and make it perfectly clear that he was walking in of his own accord." The U.S. attorney "was saying that he'd like to be able to do that, but he was basically being told he couldn't do that. And he said something about how he thought that was silly. At which point there was this crackling on the line," Nesson laughs. "It was really funny. And he said, 'What's that?' And I said, 'Well, we assume the line's been tapped.' And there was silence on his end for like 30 seconds. And he said, 'Do you really think so?'"[60]

Jeffrey Race had recently returned from a trip to Canada and New York State when Dan and Pat Ellsberg appeared at his Cambridge apartment one afternoon, probably on a Saturday. Race had been pretty sure Ellsberg was the source of the Papers when his mother had informed him over the phone of their publication while he was on vacation. "I connected it with the boxes in my cellar," Race recalls. Then "Dan showed up one day at my apartment and asked if he could stay with me. And I said, 'Sure.'" Ellsberg had arrived before Race had returned to his apartment from his Army Reserve training. "He saw me in the army uniform, and I think he may have thought it was somebody else coming for him," Race recounts. "As I recall, we had a chuckle over that." Race's apartment was in Harvard Square, no more than a 15-minute walk from Hilliard Street (and not far from Harvard Law School). He understood perfectly well why Ellsberg had sought him out. "I knew many people were looking for him and wanted to talk to him. . . . He needed a place to crash."[61]

The Ellsbergs stayed with Race and his fiancée for around three days. "We had a good time together," Race reminisces. "There was no tension. . . . We just relaxed and watched television and had a good time. . . . It was like a little party. We went out and got food, and prepared food. And we had a few chuckles and watched the news." By mutual agreement, they chose not to discuss the Papers and Ellsberg's legal situation much. Dan and Pat did not leave the apartment, Race recalls, though Dan made phone calls (and asked Race to make and take some calls for him). One incident stands out in Race's mind. He and his fiancée and Patricia were watching the news while Dan was asleep on the floor. The newscaster was talking about the large FBI dragnet for Ellsberg, the fact that they were looking everywhere for him. "The three of us just chuckled and said, 'Well, he's right here sleeping on the floor in front of us in Harvard Square,'" Race remembers. "We just thought it was a really amusing, ironic situation."[62]

Another place the Ellsbergs took cover while underground was a cabin at a ski resort in New Hampshire. The resort was run by a friend of David Greenway of *Time* magazine. "I arranged that," Greenway recalls. "I thought that it would be in my interest to have him hidden away from other reporters [laughs]. So I called up the friend of mine who ran the ski resort in New Hampshire and said, 'Can I hide Daniel Ellsberg up there in one of your houses?' He was looking for a place to hide."[63]

The Ellsbergs' second-floor neighbors at 10 Hilliard Street also had contact with them when they were on the run. "A couple of days or so after he disappeared, we got a telephone call," Stewart Perry recounts. Dan, of course, had rarely spoken to them before. "They were asking for some personal effects. She wanted her hair dryer and a certain belt . . . and maybe another item or two. And then . . . 'Please, can you also pick up certain items that would be embarrassing if they were found publicly.'" Those items included erotic Indian statues and *Kama Sutra*, the classic Indian sex manual. The Perrys had to get the key to the Ellsbergs' flat from the landlord, Jamshid Kooros (whom the Ellsbergs asked to remove some other books for them). The Perrys had never been in the Ellsbergs' apartment before. The Ellsbergs told them that somebody would be calling to pick up the stuff. The go-between turned out to be an old friend of the Perrys, Herb Kelman, the Harvard psychologist.[64]

The Ellsbergs also asked the Perrys to take down the mirrors in their bedroom. Those, too, could prove embarrassing. The leaker of the Pentagon Papers might be described in the media as an exhibitionist or a narcissist, among other things. Stewart had to ask Kooros to help him with that one. "We looked at it, and it was just too big a job," Stewart recalls. "It required big people and stepladders and whatever. It was really hard to manage. It was a *huge* mirror on the ceiling. . . . So Jamshid and I, we can't do anything about this. So I went down and told Helen about it, and she said, 'Well, why don't you just tack an India print over it?' So we went up and put an India print on the frame." Word of Ellsberg's mirrors later circulated. "He was obviously the talk of the town," Kelman says.[65]

In addition, the Ellsbergs asked the Perrys to take in their mail. "So periodically he'd come by the apartment," Helen Perry recounts. "And, of course, he had a key to the house, so he'd come right up to the floor and knock on the door. And I didn't know who it was, because normally people introduced themselves by buzzing." After identifying himself, "he'd say, 'I want my mail.' So I'd go and get his mail. . . . He'd say, 'Is this all?' I said, 'Yes.' And he'd walk off. I mean, I never heard him say thank you. . . . He felt he was the most important person in the world at that point." Patricia "would sort of explain, Well, you know, he's very tense and . . . under pressure."[66]

Helen Perry had recently broken her leg and was mostly in bed and had to use a walker. It was not an easy trip to the door. On top of that, journalists were camped with their equipment outside 10 Hilliard Street; some were stepping on the Perrys' rose bushes, going through their trash bins, and phoning them. "That experience with the press was awful," Stewart remembers. "They were just absolutely ruthless in their need to make their story." Once, Helen had to be carried out of their apartment on a stretcher and taken to the hospital in an ambulance under the scrutiny of the press; journalists bombarded her with questions even as she was being carried to the ambulance. Moreover, FBI agents were coming by the Perrys' apartment and knocking on their door, even sitting on their second-floor landing and waiting for them to emerge (they refused to talk). The Perrys suspected their phone was tapped. That summer, Stewart would also suffer the shock of being called before the grand jury, forcing him to hire a lawyer at a time when he had limited financial means. Adding insult to injury, Ellsberg told him, in a condescending manner, that people were raising money for his own legal expenses, and although they hadn't raised much, they could allocate some to Stewart. "I said, 'Thank you. I'll manage by myself,'" Stewart recounts. "I was really insulted, the way he said it, and the fact that I knew his wife was either a millionaire or going to be a millionaire." Ellsberg's tone was "very, very patronizing: 'We'll take care of you.' . . . But at the same time telling me he didn't have much money." Also, there were assorted gawkers outside the Perrys' apartment to deal with. (Hind Sadek Kooros, Jamshid's wife, the archaeologist, remembers a young Radcliffe girl ringing her doorbell and asking which garbage can was Daniel Ellsberg's and could she look in it? "I said, 'Well, you're welcome. Before they collect the garbage, go ahead and look.'")[67]

The upshot of all this was that the Perrys were in trying circumstances themselves. And yet Ellsberg was making demands on them and not offering anything in the way of thanks. Contributing to their resentments, the Perrys questioned Ellsberg's motives for releasing the Papers. "I always felt that he did it because he thought the time was ripe and he could make a big splash with it," Helen says. "He was just looking for prestige and recognition." Says Stewart, "I think most people around here, many of whom were writers themselves, kind of had an ironic feeling about the Pentagon Papers controversy, as being a way for Dan to somehow finesse the fact he wasn't writing." Although most people on Hilliard Street were also against the war, applauded his act, and refused to talk to the FBI, "there wasn't much sympathy for him," Helen remembers. Kelman recalls hearing "criticisms having to do with self-centeredness."[68]

<hr />

Ellsberg wanted to have some public visibility while underground (hardly unique among political fugitives), and he surfaced in an interview with Walter

Cronkite. Broadcast the evening of June 23, the interview was arranged through a series of clandestine and shadowy contacts, another cat-and-mouse game. "It was laborious and highly secret and almost juvenile in its complexities," Cronkite told me, somewhat irritatedly. There were "a lot of mysterious phone calls back and forth. . . . It was all very cloak-and-dagger."[69]

Gordon Manning, a vice president of CBS News who oversaw Cronkite's show, had earlier suggested that Cronkite, who knew Louis Marx, Sr., and his brother, David (particularly David, a good friend), call the Marx brothers to see if they could reach Ellsberg to arrange an interview. Cronkite said he'd call David, but that he was going to be "out of pocket all weekend" at Lake Placid in upstate New York. "So I said, 'Well, give him my number,'" Manning recalls. After Cronkite left a message with David Marx, he received a message back saying "that perhaps something could be arranged, but that . . . they were afraid that my phone would be bugged on this matter," Cronkite remembers with a chuckle. "That they needed to talk to somebody else. That they couldn't call me." So, Cronkite says, he passed them Manning's number. (Manning scoffs at this part of Cronkite's retelling, saying, "Cronkite was going off on a holiday in Lake Placid and he didn't want to be bothered up there.")[70]

Late one afternoon shortly thereafter at Manning's Westport, Connecticut, home, "my wife answered the telephone and she said, 'Hey, there's a guy named Mr. Boston . . . on the phone,'" Manning recounts. "She thought it was a funny name. He said, 'Just call me Mr. Boston. . . . That's my code name. . . . I understand that Cronkite wants to interview Daniel Ellsberg. . . . I'm a friend of Daniel Ellsberg.'" Boston also told Manning he was a graduate student at Harvard, and possibly that he was doing some teaching there. "He said, 'Ellsberg has high regard for Cronkite,'" Manning recalls. "And I said, 'Fine. . . . How can we arrange this?' He said, 'Can you be on the Harvard campus tonight at eight o'clock?'" Manning said he could, so they arranged to meet in front of one of Harvard's libraries.[71]

Manning had only about three hours to get to Cambridge, so he chartered a plane to Boston. After getting lost coming out of the Sumner Tunnel and ending up in the Back Bay area across the Charles River from Cambridge, he arrived at Harvard and was standing in front of the library when "suddenly a guy leaped out of the bushes," he recounts. "It was a bearded guy. Not an unattractive guy. . . . Dark hair, dark beard." The man would turn out to be very intelligent and interesting to talk to. "But he scared the hell out of me," Manning remembers:

> He said, "Mr. Manning? . . . I'm Mr. Boston. . . . Follow me at a quick pace."
> So I followed him. We went down to the Yard; we came to a car. He said,

"Jump in." Then we started a back and forth [route]. We drove down streets in Cambridge, and we drove back. I said, "What's going on? I thought we were going to see Ellsberg." He said, "Well, people are always following us." They were very security minded and very paranoid about the fact that he was a fugitive from the law. Finally, we came down a street, not far from Harvard Square, and he said, "Jump out and go up to the third floor."[72]

It was a wooden structure with flats. A triple-decker. Manning went up to the third floor and knocked on the door. Inside was Ellsberg. And "there they are, stacked up to the ceiling: the Pentagon Papers. All wrapped," Manning remembers. There were also some other people there, younger people, and Patricia, who again would be very quiet as she listened and got coffee for Manning and Ellsberg. "I said, 'Well, I know your father and I know your uncle,'" Manning recounts.

> And she introduced me to Ellsberg. And there's Ellsberg with the zealot eyes of his. He's very intense. And he says, "We want CBS News to publish the next set of Papers." And we've got to do them tomorrow night. I said, "Well, now, Mr. Ellsberg, television's not a linear medium. What we want to do is have Walter come up here and interview you. You know, there's criticism of you—about your lack of patriotism, and about your being a fugitive from the law—and you'll have a chance to justify your actions. . . . But it has to be an interview." He said, "No, they have to be put on television." He kept saying, "You've got to put these Papers on television." . . . I said, "Can't I persuade you that Cronkite should interview you and you'll make a case?" "No, no. You must put the Pentagon Papers on television."

"The entire Pentagon Papers had to be read over the air," Cronkite recalls with another chuckle. "It started out with that"—later Ellsberg stipulated that the interview had to be restricted to a discussion of his views on the war and the Papers—"and obviously that was impossible." But Manning finally said, Okay, some Papers might be read over the air, providing that Ellsberg gave them material that had not yet been published, and that Manning and his superiors approved it. "So he pulled out about six bundles of these things," Manning remembers.[73]

By this time it was around one in the morning. Manning emerged from the flat buzzed up on coffee and carrying his six bundles wrapped in paper and twine. A light rain had begun to fall. He started to walk over to the Commander Sheraton Hotel to call his boss, Richard Salant, in New York. "Suddenly a cop car drives up," Manning recounts. "He said, 'Having a walk in the rain? You've got heavy bundles there.' And I said, 'Yeah, but I'm young and I'm able to walk.' He said, 'Hey, get in. It's going to rain hard.' . . . So I sit next to this cop and on my lap was the Papers."[74] The policeman missed a golden opportunity.

After the cop dropped him off at the Commander Sheraton Hotel, Manning phoned Salant, who agreed that, of course, they couldn't put these things on the air.[75]

Manning eventually arrived at his own hotel, the Ritz-Carlton in downtown Boston, that morning and read the Papers there. To his disappointment, they were disjointed. In a conference call with Salant and Frank Stanton, the president of CBS, Manning proposed that they try to get Ellsberg to agree to an interview without CBS quoting from the Papers. Salant and Stanton were skittish about being a party to Ellsberg's apparent violation of the law. "They were afraid of the law cracking down . . . on CBS," Manning says.

> But I finally persuaded them. . . . So I called Mr. Boston. Again, I was using my contact. And he said, "Why can't you put the Papers on the air?" And I explained to him. He, of course, understood that television is not a linear medium. And I said, "Cronkite can fly up, and we can interview [Ellsberg]." He said, "We're going to be at another flat. We're going to be in a house. I'll give you the address later if I can persuade Dan to be interviewed by Cronkite." He called me back in an hour and said, "Yes, there'll be an interview," and I should go to another house in Cambridge. They had moved . . . packages of the fucking Pentagon Papers all night long, I guess.[76]

Cronkite's plane was grounded in Providence owing to fog, so he had to rent a car and drive up to Cambridge. "I said, 'Meet me at the Commander Hotel,'" Manning recalls. "'Go to this first phone booth.' I mean, we were getting involved in this, too." Cronkite recounts:

> I was supposed to go to the Commodore [sic] Hotel and await a phone call. Well, it turned out that the phone booth in the Commodore Hotel was down by the men's room in the basement. And the foolishness of trying to—a network anchorperson doesn't go anywhere incognito. It was ridiculous. I got into the lobby and I no sooner started looking around the place when the manager came out and said, "Mr. Cronkite, what can I do for you?" . . . He was urging me to use the phone in his office. He said I didn't have to use the pay phone. And [I was] trying to make excuses for this. And hanging around the men's room was not conducive to my reputation.
>   . . . They were supposed to call, but I hadn't heard anything. . . . I kept going down and back. It was just incredibly awkward. People were coming up for my autograph. And the manager kept saying, "I don't know why you won't

wait in my office, Mr. Cronkite. I'll get you out of this crowd." That kind of thing. It was just ridiculous.

Finally, Cronkite remembers, "I was about to give the whole thing up, when I saw a guy approaching the door of the lobby of the hotel who looked conspiratorial. A young man. These were all young people, students, I think, and that's why it was so cloak-and-daggerish. But I saw one of them approaching, and he saw me and kind of gave a nod of recognition and turned to walk back toward a car waiting at the curb. And I followed him. And that's the way we made contact." The young man and the driver of the "broken-down sedan" apologized to Cronkite for being late, but said that they had had to lose a car that had been tailing them. They then did "the circuitous routing bit" and, upon reaching their destination, drove around the block three times.[77]

Manning and a CBS producer had in the meantime gone to the house where Ellsberg and his accomplices were now gathered. It was a small, gray, single-family dwelling—"a cottage," Cronkite calls it—in Cambridge. "Not terribly well kept up," Manning points out. Ellsberg would say years later that he still didn't know where it was. Janaki Tschannerl had had a hand in arrangements (or so I distinctly gathered from our interview). It was early afternoon, the weather was hot, and "it's really very jumpy over there," Manning recounts.

> Suddenly a car drives up, and a guy with a clipboard looks up, and he's scrawling things down. And Ellsberg said, "That's the FBI. . . . Listen. Here's how we're going to do it. We're all going to run out the back door." They had an escape plan. I said, "Listen. Let me go down. They don't know me. Let me go down and talk to this guy." So I go down and the guy is sitting there. And he says, "Hey, do you live here?" And I said, "Yeah." He said, "You know, we have a difficult time finding your gas meter. Can you show me your gas meter so I can take a reading?" I pretend I know where it is. I go in the back—that's where those things usually are—and it was behind a bulkhead door. So we got it. I said, "Hey, it's only a gas meter."[78]

In the interview, Ellsberg was at the peak of his game. Dressed in a conservative, dark pin-striped suit, with a black-and-gray tie, sitting in a white chair, a curtain behind his left shoulder, he spoke calmly, self-confidently, deliberately, more slowly than usual, pausing often. He disagreed diplomatically with Cronkite at one point. Some of his answers sounded rehearsed, however, and a number of times he appeared distinctly to look at notes, off screen, to his right. His face, particularly above his lips, perspired a bit—shades of Richard Nixon (which Ellsberg might have found amusing later). The Papers, Ellsberg told

Cronkite, "raise questions of whether we have been playing follow the leader a little too long. . . . It must be painful for the American people now to read these papers—and there's a lot more to come—and to discover that the men whom they gave so much respect and trust, as well as power, regarded them as contemptuously as they regarded our Vietnamese allies." Ellsberg took a shot at his former colleagues; his antiwar activities, he said, were "simply very baffling" to them, "none of whom had read the study," but who could be counted on to refer in the future to "some strange things about my intensity."[79]

As might have befitted a politician, Ellsberg concluded the interview with a reference to his father and religion (though he says he hadn't planned it). "My father had a favorite line from the Bible, which I used to hear a great deal when I was a kid: 'The truth shall make you free,'" he remarked. "And I hope that the truth that's out now . . . it is out of the safes, and there is *no way*—no way—to get it back into the safes, I hope that truth will free us of this war." Years later, Ellsberg broke down a bit when recounting these remarks.[80]

After the interview, Manning told Ellsberg it was going to run the following night on the *CBS Evening News*, and that they'd also probably do a late-night special. "He said, 'I want that on the air tonight,'" Manning recounts. "Again with those fiery eyes. I always remember those eyes burning a hole in you." Manning explained to Ellsberg that the only way they could broadcast the interview that night was for him, Manning, to go to CBS's affiliate in Boston and process and edit the film there. "As soon as it gets into that station, everybody in the world is going to know that Ellsberg is in Boston, in Cambridge," Manning told Ellsberg. "And the FBI will find out, and your cover is going to be blown." But Ellsberg replied, "I want it on the air tonight. Do that. I'll take that risk." So Manning agreed, and he then had the pleasure of watching both ABC and NBC news report that evening that Ellsberg remained a fugitive while Cronkite was simultaneously interviewing him on a third TV screen. Ellsberg left the home in which the interview was conducted after it was over and "before we were permitted to leave," Cronkite recalled.[81]

Meanwhile, *Time* magazine had been attempting to interview Ellsberg for a cover story it was preparing on him. Greg Wierzynski had been phoning all over the place, placing his own calls to the Marxes, in an effort to locate Ellsberg. "A lot of people pretended that they knew where he was," Wierzynski remembers. Marty Garbus led Wierzynski to suspect that he was sheltering him, so Wierzynski drove—unannounced—to Garbus's vacation house on the shore somewhere in New York. It was a Friday evening, and Garbus had just arrived for the weekend. Garbus "played games with me," Wierzynski recounts. "Sort of rhetorical games." So, no luck there. *Time* chased Ellsberg for a while, but then his trail turned cold.[82] (One is led to conclude that either David Greenway wasn't speaking openly with other *Time* people about his sheltering of Ellsberg, or that that came late in the game.)

According to Ellsberg, he turned down *Time*'s requests to interview him. Through his lawyers, he told *Time* he was too busy, he says. "So the word came back: 'Well, then there's no cover story. Because we've never done a cover story without an interview. That's a rule.'" Ellsberg remembers being told it would be the first time since Adolf Hitler graced the cover of *Time* that the cover subject would not be interviewed. "I'm in good company," he told me, referring to Hitler. "That's world historic company."[83] This is a prime example of how Ellsberg's ego can lead him to be his own worst enemy.

The *Time* cover story was predictably critical of Ellsberg and his release of the Papers (a "dangerous" act), and contained glaring errors of fact. (One whopper: a picture of 10 Hilliard Street with the caption, "Ellsberg's Cambridge home: Beyond the wildest radical dream." The Ellsbergs, of course, rented only the top unit, a fact that was known to *Time*.) The story also included Ellsberg's response to his mother's death—"Now I don't have to play the piano again." He said he called his father after the piece came out and said, "Brace yourself, that's only the beginning." (Remembering his father's supportive response, Ellsberg sobbed for two or three minutes.) But Ellsberg told me, "That was the only really good magazine piece ever done on me. . . . I'd give that one to anybody." And he did. "He was so thrilled when he was on the cover of *Time*," Marva Shearer, Lloyd's wife, remembers. "He carried copies around with him, in case you hadn't seen it." Shearer adds, "This was really one of his driving interests, his notoriety. Even today. When he comes by, he shows us a speech he just gave, and would like Skip [Lloyd] to write about it."[84]

———— ◉ ————

Meanwhile, Carol Ellsberg's nightmare had gone from bad to worse. After Dan had been identified as the source of the Papers, the press began to focus attention on her, too. His decision to slip out of sight had made her a juicier target. He was not available, and they wanted to know where he was. He had not stepped forward and told the truth as he had told Carol he would. "She was furious with Dan all over again, because of [his] bringing the notoriety onto the family," Mary Marshall recalls. "She was really mad at him at this point. Probably more angry than she had ever been at him before." He had really gotten her family into a mess now, and she had known this was going to happen. (Charles Nesson told Neil Sheehan several months later that she was angry at Dan because she was a scorned woman; Nesson even expressed to Carol his belief that Dan had left her. Had Ellsberg told Nesson this?)[85]

June 17, the day after Sidney Zion's disclosure, was "the worst day" yet, Carol wrote her father and stepmother two days later. "The phone didn't stop ringing from morning (7 A.M.) until night. In addition, there were mysterious vans which took turns being parked outside the house, moving a few feet from time to time. Also, although I know this sounds paranoid, for a period of hours in the afternoon, a General Telephone truck drove slowly by the house every few minutes until about six P.M." "We were besieged by all kinds of reporters and everybody immediately," Robert Ellsberg recalls. "Journalists and TV and whatnot were camped out in front of our house. So we really felt you couldn't get in and out of the house." "All the newspapers were calling me up. . . . 'Where is Dan?'" Carol remembers. "That was what everybody wanted to know." But Carol had no idea where he was. "I haven't heard from him in some time," she told a reporter after he disappeared.[86]

Eleanor Hoover, a stringer for *Time* magazine, lived down the street from Carol; her son had played with Robert and Mary Ellsberg when he was younger. Hoover, whom Carol had not talked to in quite a while, had the gall to call up Carol and try to be nonchalant about it. "Well, how have you been? How are the children?" Hoover asked. "I was very annoyed," Carol recalls. "I said something pretty cool," but then "she called me a few days later and said, 'Carol, I won't bother you again, but they want to know what color his eyes are.' And I said, 'Eleanor, they're blue-green like the Mediterranean.' Of course, she didn't know whether to believe me or not," Carol smiles. Dan later accused Carol of sending Hoover around to see his friends.[87]

Also on June 17, the FBI paid its first visit to Carol since agents had come by her house in the spring of 1970. "Around noon, a couple of FBI agents came to the house," she wrote her father and stepmother. "They were extremely polite and kind. I asked them in and told them that while I wished to be cooperative, I had to think of my children." Carol told them she was willing to talk about Dan, but that she would have to call her lawyer. Her attorney then arranged for an interview at the FBI office the next day. During a meeting with her attorney the evening before, "I told him that I had talked it over with the children, and decided that I wanted to cooperate fully with the FBI," she wrote afterward. In the FBI's interview room, two agents "again presented their FBI credentials for our inspection. I told them I was impressed by their scrupulosity!" Carol's attorney requested total immunity for her. When the agents asked when she would be willing to talk if she got immunity, Carol said "any time, today." This is when she told the FBI that she thought Dan should be in jail if he had released classified material. The FBI wanted to know where he was, but she couldn't help them. "We parted with expressions of mutual esteem and much bowing and shaking of hands," Carol recounted. The FBI agents she dealt with "were very decent men," Carol told me. "They were so much nicer than Dan's lawyers to me. Of course, I was their witness. They treated me always with very great respect. . . . I think they really felt for me." "She had trust for a couple of these agents who were in charge of the case," Robert Ellsberg remembers.[88] They befriended her, and, one might reasonably theorize, played her some.

On Sunday, June 20, the FBI served Carol with a subpoena to testify before the grand jury the next morning. This was another highly upsetting development. Once again, exactly what she had feared would happen was happening. "I remember very vividly his [Dan] saying, 'You'll never have to testify. I'll come forward,'" she says. "He didn't do that." Carol thought she shouldn't have to be in this position. Now she would have to testify about her children, whose names would appear in the newspapers. "It just killed me," she recounts. "I was beside myself." And quite scared. She drove down to the courthouse by herself, then wandered around downtown Los Angeles waiting for her turn to testify. "It was awful," she says. "I was really alone. . . . I was walking the streets *praying* until it was time to go in." She spent some time sitting nervously in the waiting room. It was a small room, and there was Jan Butler. Butler appeared to be surrounded by people supporting her, like RAND lawyers. "I went over there and I said, 'Hi, Jan . . . I'm Carol Ellsberg. I think we've met sometime in the past,'" Carol recounts. "She was very cold. Of course, she was probably nervous as a cat too. . . . But I remember thinking, 'Gee, nobody will even speak to me.'"[89]

Before the grand jury, on the advice of her lawyer, Carol took the fifth. "That was about the lowest day of my life," she remembers. She felt humiliated taking the fifth. It was a "horrible, horrible" experience. Her emotions were raw, her loneliness stark. "It was *very*, very painful to refuse to answer a lawful question." (Years later, whenever he spoke with her about it, Dan would act surprised that she had taken the fifth.) Carol was then brought before a federal judge and granted immunity. She testified, as required. "I could have gone to jail, but I didn't think I should have to go to jail," she says with a laugh. "That seemed unfair. . . . I told them the answer to any questions they asked me."[90]

Her testimony was damaging to Dan. He would later tell her that she should have called him before she testified (but, of course, she didn't know where he was, as if that mattered to her). He also said that he would not be on trial were it not for her testimony. (Carol told Nesson it was "a 3rd or 4th order cause at best," that he would not be on trial had he not involved their children and "insisted on confiding in me—against my wishes.")[91]

The morning after her testimony, Carol phoned the Los Angeles FBI office and related that, during her conversations with the lead U.S. attorney on the case the day before, "she had withheld the name of an individual whom she considered as innocent and whom she did not want to involve," an FBI document records. "She said that this person is Yvonne Svenle who came to her home last night and told her that she (Svenle) had been interviewed by the FBI. Svenle advised that she had refused to answer some of the questions posed by the interviewing agents because she knew that Mrs. Ellsberg's children were involved and she did not want to bring them into this matter. . . . Mrs. Ellsberg stated that Yvonne Svenle is now ready to answer any questions posed." Another angry ex-lover ready to talk. Svenle's next interview was that very day.[92]

The next day, June 23, Carol had no less than three conversations with the FBI. Two were over the phone, one was in person. Carol passed along information that Robert had given her about Kimberly Rosenberg and about the two rounds of copying Robert had joined. Carol also provided the FBI the April 1970 statement she had prepared for her attorney on the events of October 1969, a document most damaging to Dan, and from which the FBI first learned that he had seen a psychoanalyst. Further, Carol provided the bureau information on Mary's involvement in the copying. Based on Robert's and Mary's reports to her, Carol named names—Sinay, Russo, "a South Vietnamese gentleman." On top of all this, and among various other pieces of information, Carol reported that Dan had spent some time with Yvonne Svenle in California that May, and that he had also planned to visit the Elysium nudist retreat.[93]

The next day, Carol phoned the FBI office and relayed additional information that she had elicited from Mary that day on events and participants the evening Mary had helped with the Papers.[94] The FBI agents either had her in the palm of their hands, or she was out for revenge, or simply eager to talk to sympathetic ears, or all three.

Carol subsequently told Nesson she had refused to talk to the FBI. "I didn't really know enough to tell them anything much," she told me. "I told them everything that I knew about the Pentagon Papers, which was nothing." But Mary Marshall, whom the FBI also visited, recalls, "They saw her almost like two or three times a week . . . to really get anything and everything that she might have forgotten or there might be a clue [on]. They were desperately looking for the cache of Papers that he [Dan] had. . . . She would suggest various places that she knew that he'd been at or that he might have hidden the stuff. . . . And they would take her for a ride and chitchat with her."[95]

On June 25, the FBI asked Carol to sign a short affidavit based on her grand jury testimony; her April 1970 statement may have also informed this affidavit. She didn't know exactly what she was signing or the possible consequences. The FBI agents, who told her they were making the request for the U.S. attorney, advised her to speak to her lawyer before signing it. Carol's attorney told her, erroneously, that she had to sign it. He was not a criminal lawyer. (Dan, who thought that her lawyer was an absolute disaster at this time and probably still resented him from the divorce, would more than once refer to him in a condescending tone to Carol as "your divorce lawyer.") Even after Carol drove down to sign the affidavit, "the FBI man kept saying, 'You know, if you want to change your mind, it's okay with us,'" she recounts. "They were doing everything they could do except say, 'You idiot, don't sign this. It's going to cause you a lot of pain.'" Dan would claim later that Carol signed it mainly to keep their children out of the case, but Carol denies that.[96]

The affidavit provided a basis for a criminal charge against Ellsberg. It and three others were attached to a warrant for his arrest that was issued that evening, making Ellsberg officially a fugitive. He was charged with unauthorized possession of top-secret government documents. Carol's affidavit, which hit the media almost immediately, brought her even more press attention; it led many to think she had turned Dan in. She and her children went out for dinner that evening with friends from their church. By the time they got home, their phone was ringing off the hook. "I was getting calls from all over the country, and all the local reporters," Carol recalls. "It was *wild.* . . . I didn't realize that this thing was going to be spread all over the papers the next day." Carol told the reporters she was sorry, but she had nothing to say. In the middle of the night, she got a call from a reporter from one of the Chicago papers who advised her to take her phone off the hook and move out for a few days. "I said, 'Thank you very much. That's good advice.' And sure enough, first thing in the morning, there were reporters all over the lawn." At 7 A.M., she told the FBI afterward, a group of them knocked on her door and attempted to interview her with photographers at the ready. Reporters were also knocking on her neighbors' doors to ask them questions about her. Carol phoned Mary Marshall that morning and reported that she and her children couldn't get out of the house.[97]

Within hours, Lloyd Shearer paid Carol a visit. She didn't know him. Nor did she know that he was the editor of *Parade* magazine and "Walter Scott." "He called and said he was a friend of Dan's, and he realized that I was in a very bad situation, and, 'Would you like to get the children out of there?'" she recalls. "And I said, 'Yes, I would.' . . . He was going to help me." According to an FBI document on an interview the bureau did with Carol two days later, Shearer "told her that although he was a friend of Daniel Ellsberg, he felt that what he had done was wrong and he stated that Daniel had picked the wrong type of attorneys to defend him." He offered to shelter Carol and her children at his house, which was just down Sunset Boulevard. Marva Shearer, who was a writer herself, says the idea was "just to give her a little haven, where the children wouldn't be frightened." Robert and Mary did seem a little frightened, Marva says.[98]

The Ellsbergs escaped through their backyard over a neighbor's fence. The Shearers aided their escape. "Mom had left the house and couldn't get back in because of the press camped out on the front lawn," Mary Ellsberg recounts. "She called us from the neighbors and told us to climb over the back fence. I believe she was waiting with the Shearers already." Robert and Mary spent the afternoon at the Shearers; Carol also spent some time there. Carol thought Lloyd Shearer might have ulterior motives, but he seemed nice and offered moral support, and "we were pretty alone and didn't have many options," Mary Ellsberg says. "I was so desperate that day that any kind person I would tell them whatever they wanted to hear," Carol recalls. It was Mary's impression that Lloyd was in contact with her father and had come to get them at her father's request.[99]

When Carol phoned Mary Marshall that evening after returning from the Shearers, she related that this nice man from their neighborhood had rescued her family, been very good to them, wonderful in fact, very solicitous, asking her all kinds of questions, with his wife tending to the kids. Marshall asked Carol who this nice man was. Told it was Lloyd Shearer, "I just almost died," Marshall recounts. "I said to her, 'Oh, my God, Carol!' I said, 'He's a *newspaperman.*'" Marshall got the impression from Carol that she and her children had "spilled their guts" to the Shearers, that Marva "took the kids aside and pumped them in an adroit way." Carol informed the FBI two days later that Lloyd Shearer had plied her for information on her grand jury testimony and affidavit. "She now suspects that Shearer may have been prompted in his solicitude for her by motives that are not in her best behalf," an FBI document records. "She now realizes that she never wanted to talk to the press concerning her or her children's involvement in the past actions of her former husband, but through the professed friendship of Shearer she had done just that." Carol complained to Dan a week later that, while the FBI had not interviewed Robert and Mary, "his friend Lloyd Shearer had thoroughly questioned them in a devious manner." Speaking of Carol, Marshall told two FBI agents, "That girl needs to be on a leash." One of the agents responded, "A short leash."[100]

Shearer invited Carol and her children to have dinner at his house two days after sheltering them. He was not through. He said that Dan would be calling his children there. But Carol informed the FBI that "she now intends to tell Shearer that she does not wish to be contacted by him in the future, will not come to his house for dinner on June 28, 1971, and will tell him that if her former husband telephones their children at Shearer's home she will give him the number of a friend where they can be reached during the evening," the FBI recorded.[101]

Carol's stepsister, whom she hadn't seen in many years, was in town the day the Shearers pumped her, and that evening she and Carol sat and talked in Carol's house in the dark so that the media wouldn't bother them. When Carol was at work during the week, Robert and Mary locked themselves in the house and were told not to open the door or answer the phone.[102]

All this was happening just as Carol was about to run her psychology experiment for her Ph.D. at UCLA. Reporters came looking for her there, too. "I couldn't go into the lab, because they were showing up at the psychology department," she remembers. "I became alarmed and stayed away."[103]

The Ellsbergs didn't have that many friends at the time, but some offered their help, including some from church and Mary and Andrew Marshall. Though Mary Marshall was very kind to Carol, "it was clear to me that she had a lot of animosity toward my father," Robert remembers. "Not just enough that he was wrong, but it was evil what he had done . . . a terrible betrayal. . . . And she said, 'The reason he probably did this was because he has never really gotten the recognition that he deserves. He didn't advance. Everybody thought he'd be a golden boy, but he has not really gone as far as they thought.' . . . I remember sort of thinking, 'Is that possibly true?' And then I thought, 'That's not [true]. She's describing a different person.'"[104]

Carol Ellsberg was then getting phone calls from people she hadn't heard from in years. Kirby Hall called to see if she could visit during a trip out to California. Carol said fine, but "then a little while later I got a phone call from her saying not to come, that she had moved to the neighbors," Hall remembers. "She told me later that she thought probably I wanted to come just because Dan was famous."[105] Carol had gotten more cynical about other people's motives.

Carol's paramount concern remained her children. "My mother had a deep, deep mother-lioness kind of sense of protection of us," Robert Ellsberg recalls. She did *not* want them in the spotlight or caught up in the criminal investigation. "I wanted to keep my family out of it," she says. "And it was hard to do. . . . I was very fierce about trying to keep them away from the press." Robert began to internalize his mother's fears. "I was very concerned about just how angry she was and how upset she was," he remembers. For many years afterward, Robert would recoil almost instinctively whenever anybody asked him about this whole period: "Watch out. Danger zone. Lights flash, and then something bad's going to happen if you talk about this," as he'd been led to believe there'd be "horrible consequences" if he and Mary got sucked into the media's glare.[106]

Robert also feared other horrible consequences. "After the Pentagon Papers came out, I really believed that it was very likely that my father would be assassinated," he recounts. "That was a kind of constant dread and fantasy that I had. That I was going to pick up the paper one day or turn on the news and hear that he had been shot or something." Thus, while it was an exciting period for him, it was profoundly unsettling as well. "I was frightened about my father, I was a little stressed with my mother, unsure about what was going to happen, a little giddy about all the excitement—it really seemed as if this was having the desired effect that he had wanted," Robert recalls. "But it was stressful. . . . I don't miss those days at all."[107]

To Carol's distress, the Justice Department directed the FBI to interview Robert. Her lawyer advised her to grant her consent, arguing that if she refused the government would call Robert before the grand jury, which would be much more traumatic for him. But her father disagreed, thinking the U.S. attorney would be reluctant to ask a minor to testify against his father before the grand jury. So Carol withheld her consent. But Robert was called to testify that fall. Dan was furious; Robert was an eyewitness. (Charles Nesson would deem Robert's testimony quite harmful, saying he provided some very damaging information on which the prosecution built its case, that Robert had named everybody involved and described how the copying was done.) They were going to use his own son against him, Ellsberg fumed. He blamed Carol and her lawyer while also believing that Justice had reneged on an agreement with her not to call Robert if she signed the affidavit.[108]

The morning of Robert's testimony, the journalist Joe McGinniss was with Ellsberg, who was running typically late. McGinniss recounted: "He races out the door of the apartment. Slaps the elevator button. Realizes he's forgotten important papers. Races back to the door of the apartment. Realizes he's locked himself out, forgotten his key. 'Have you ever been married?!' he asks. 'Have you ever been divorced?!' He turns away, muttering expletives about his ex-wife's attorney. 'Asshole!' His fists are clenched and trembling with rage." Over the phone that morning, Dan told Carol to fire her lawyer, hire one from his camp, Arthur Berman, and refuse to let Robert testify. She declined on all counts. Nesson urged her to "call a press conference and denounce them," Carol remembers. She refused. She found Nesson, who was also playing up to her, too smooth and "a little on the slick side," and she didn't trust him. She told him, dryly, that it was really not in Dan's interest for her to give a press conference. It was *Dan* who was making Robert testify, she seethed.[109]

Down at the courthouse, Carol's ire mushroomed. Arthur Berman tried to get the judge to fire her attorney, appoint a new one, and *take custody of Robert.* When she learned of that last astonishing move—perhaps a tactical one designed to delay and then keep Robert from testifying—Carol's anger at Dan and his lawyers was positively white-hot. (Years later, when Robert tried to get his father to understand why his mother was still mad at him over the Pentagon Papers affair, Robert asked his father, How do you think it made her feel when one of your attorneys asked that custody of me be taken away from her?) At the courthouse, Robert met the new lead U.S. prosecutor in the case, David Nissen, and had his finger and palm prints taken. Before the grand jury, "I pretty much just told the story of what had happened," he remembers.[110]

The night after Robert's testimony, both Dan and Charles Nesson called Carol and expressed their anger at her for not doing what they had wanted her to do.[111]

Lynda Sinay had been right: she was in big trouble. On the late afternoon of June 22, FBI agents knocked on her door and handed her a subpoena to appear before the grand jury the next morning. "I said, 'For what?'" Sinay (later Lynda Resnick) recounts. "They said, 'We think you know.'" Sinay's entire life passed before her.[112] Her own nightmare was beginning.

On the advice of her attorney, Luke McKissack, a prominent criminal lawyer, Sinay took the fifth before the grand jury. After being granted immunity, she testified about the copying of the Papers. Afterward, Anthony Russo accused her of betraying him. "He said, 'How could you do this to me?'" Resnick recalls. Russo claimed that she had turned him in. She disputed that, "and then we found out later it was Robert that told everybody . . . about us," she says. Sinay told a reporter who contacted her at home after her testimony, "I just want to be left alone."[113]

But she was not left alone. The press camped out in front of her home as well, and she kept getting dragged back into the grand jury room. "My whole life was ruined," Resnick remembers. "It was horrible." The FBI was on her tail too, and they weren't as friendly as they were with Carol Ellsberg. "I was followed everywhere," she says. Sinay told her psychiatrist, "They're going to break into your office. They're going to steal your files." (Her psychiatrist, it would turn out, was in the same building as Lewis Fielding.) One day, when

Sinay was wearing a white, long-sleeved, Victorian-style dress ("I wore a lot of white," she laughs), David Nissen, whom she came to despise, "sent me into a drunk tank to be fingerprinted. . . . I was in a cell to scare me . . . a round cell with all these drug addicts, drunken people. I'd never seen anything like this in my life. And they took me in the center of this round cell . . . and they finger-printed not only my hands but all the way up my arms with black ink, with this white dress on. And I'm crying. And these people are screaming. . . . And then another time he took me by the back of the neck. . . . He said, 'I am going to get you if I die doing it.'"[114]

Sinay was frightened. She found the government ruthless, yet she could find no sanctuary in her own camp. She was having problems with her attorney, Luke McKissack, who appeared a bit high strung and wasn't always available. Ellsberg phoned Sinay and told her, in effect, "Lynda, you are going to be indicted for perjury. . . . You've got to drop this guy. I'm going to give you a list of six names of attorneys. You choose the one you like the best." But the attorney Sinay chose presented other problems. Meanwhile she feared a perjury indictment.[115]

Sinay neared the point of psychological collapse. "I was a wreck," Resnick recounts. "For months I was in a state of panic. At times I couldn't speak. My vocal chords would go. And I had a tightness in my chest. I was worried about my children. I thought I might go to jail. Who would raise my kids?"[116]

On Friday, June 18, Tony Russo received his expected visit from the law. The FBI knocked on the door of his apartment in Santa Monica Canyon shortly after he had arrived home from his job with the Los Angeles County Probation Department. They wanted to talk to him about Daniel Ellsberg. "I said, 'I don't want to talk to you,'" Russo remembers. "And they said, 'Have you got a lawyer?' I said, 'That's no business of yours.' And they said, 'Well, okay. Grassy ass.'" And "sure enough, my ass was grass."[117]

Russo knew he had to move quickly. He called Lloyd Shearer, whom he figured would know what was happening with Ellsberg. "Oh yeah, he was ready to talk," Russo recounts. "He wanted to get together." Russo and Shearer talked quite a bit for about two weeks, then somebody advised Russo to watch out for Shearer, so he cut him off.[118]

But not before Shearer had made contact with Ellsberg for Russo through his son Derek in Cambridge. Russo then received an odd call from Charles Nesson. Nesson told him, "A client of mine says that you'll recognize the following poem," Russo recalls. "And he recited a poem that I had written, 'Trip City,' which was kind of a code name for the Pentagon Papers," Russo laughs. "He recited that, and he says, 'So you'll know who I am.' I said, 'Oh yeah.'

And we had a laugh. That was the first contact." To Ellsberg. Indirect. Russo then made arrangements to travel quietly to Cambridge to see Ellsberg. The two co-conspirators had to get their stories straight. Russo thought they were in it together.[119]

On June 22, two FBI agents subpoenaed Russo to appear before the grand jury. Justice wanted to turn him into a witness. But Russo refused to testify even after being offered full immunity. "How could I be a fink?" he says. "From the beginning, there's no question . . . I was not going to testify. . . . If I were to testify against Ellsberg, I don't see how I could ever live with it." He would be "ratting on a friend" while he was protected. Had he testified, Russo concluded, Ellsberg would have been dead meat.[120]

Ellsberg was not happy about Russo's decision. He wanted him to testify. He told Russo they had nothing to hide. Ellsberg knew that Russo's refusal risked Russo getting indicted too. (Russo's attorney had, in fact, told Russo it would get him indicted.) Ellsberg did not want Russo indicted. He wanted to stand alone—in the courtroom, on stage, in the press. His trial was to be "*the* media event . . . of the season . . . maybe of the decade*," Russo's later attorney Peter Young comments. "And, definitely, Tony Russo's indictment threatened to spoil all of that." Ellsberg still hoped to maintain some political respectability and ties to the establishment. He also wanted to win his case. If he was paired with Russo, it would hurt him on all counts. Ellsberg thought "I was horning in on his thing," Russo recalls. "He even told people that. . . . By refusing to testify, I had injected myself into this thing." The Ellsbergs "saw me as a wild-eyed radical, and I was going to blow it for Dan," Russo says. But "the truth is, that comes totally from Ellsberg's ego position. . . . It was always focused on him. There was no identity to me." That infuriated Russo. Asked if he didn't, in fact, want to get indicted, Russo responded, "No, heavens, no [laughs]. But if that was the price I had to pay, I was willing to pay any price not to go against my conscience."[121]

Russo spent a month and a half in jail for refusing to testify. "Goodbye, brother," he told Ellsberg, grasping him, before entering jail.[122]

When Louis Marx, Sr., learned that his son-in-law was responsible for releasing the Pentagon Papers, he was outraged. This was not the man he thought his daughter had married. He had not been aware that his daughter had married a man who was planning on committing treason. "My father was apoplectic," Patricia Ellsberg, who mainly learned about it later, remembers. "Absolutely apoplectic. And just ranting and raving. More than I realized. But I realized it plenty. . . . He would talk about nothing else. . . . He admired Nixon. . . . He was very anticommunist. So he just thought it was a betrayal of

the country, of his family, that Dan would subject me to this. He never expressed that much anger at me. It all went to Dan. . . . But then, of course, Dad
is such a patriarch that that would follow. You know, the wife doesn't have
much to say about it. So he wouldn't have held me very responsible." When
Patricia's father spoke ill of Dan to her and said he should be in jail, "I just said,
'I don't want to talk about it,'" Patricia recalls. "I said, 'Dad, I love you . . . and
I don't want this to come between us. But if you insist on talking about my husband or this in this way, I don't want to see you.'" So Louis Marx vented his
rage mainly toward others.[123] He didn't want to lose his daughter.

Patricia's cousin Marlene Twaddell, daughter of David Marx, remembers
that her parents and Patricia's father thought that Ellsberg had committed an
atrocious act of disloyalty and simply couldn't grasp it. They didn't like the
"stigma" it had brought onto the Marx family; it had besmirched their good
name. They also felt Ellsberg hadn't been considerate of Patricia: he had
foisted her into the spotlight and the middle of a controversy.[124]

The episode became the tragedy of Louis Marx's life. He never talked to
Ellsberg again. "He wouldn't speak to him," Patricia recalls. Nor would her
brother, Louis, Jr., who was also outraged. "He just thinks Dan did the wrong
thing," Patricia says. "And he's, I think, loyal to Dad. . . . He feels that somehow Dan didn't act in a way that was considerate of my father or me. Which,"
she laughs, "was true."[125]

The split in her family pained Patricia. Her father and brother "didn't
admire [Dan] in the way that I feel was totally appropriate," she remembers.
"I would have loved if they'd said, 'I disagree with him, but he's a brave and
wonderful man,' or something like that. But they didn't. They just thought it
was a betrayal all the way around. So it was very painful. And it's continued to
be painful." Patricia longed for the three men she loved most in the world to
get along, but two of them now detested the third. "They hated Dan," Stanley Sheinbaum, who would administer Ellsberg's legal defense effort, understood. "I suspect they hated Dan beforehand. He's not the most lovable guy
in the world."[126]

Patricia also paid a financial price: her inheritance suffered. "I got a portion," she told me. "And I would have gotten more if this hadn't happened. . . . I
think I would have gotten substantially more money. But it was his [her father's]
to give. And I look at it as a gift. . . . He wanted to give money to me, I think,
but he didn't want it to go to Dan. So he was in a bind." (One friend of Ellsberg
told me that, according to Ellsberg, Patricia's father or brother demanded that
he sign a contract preventing him from benefiting from the Marx family's
money after the Papers came out, and that Dan and Patricia, who wanted him to

sign it, fought sharply when he hesitated.) Patricia's brother, who is quite wealthy, also doesn't want Ellsberg to get any of the family's money.[127]

But the younger generation in the Marx family overwhelmingly applauded Ellsberg's act. "My sisters were supportive," Patricia recalls. "My younger half brothers were supportive." "Everyone in our generation supported Dan," Twaddell says. "We thought it was a very brave and heroic thing that he had done."[128]

———◉———

At RAND, reaction tilted heavily in one direction. "It was a very, very sharp and bloody division, and I would say it was 97 percent 'hang him from the highest tree in town,' and there were about 2 percent 'I'm not so sure,'" Gus Shubert recounts. "If he had one defender in that organization, I wasn't aware of it," Patrick Sullivan says. More than one RAND employee said something about killing Ellsberg. His action had hurt RAND's relationship with the Pentagon badly (the air force had practically wet its pants), and people at RAND feared it might cost the think tank influence and some of its contracts. They worried about RAND's future: the institution could go right down the tubes. Were the feds now going to come in and close the RAND Corporation down? The Pentagon might cut it off completely, take all of its flesh, and RAND might have to try to survive on unclassified business (a frightening prospect). RAND employees feared they might lose their jobs, their pensions, their livelihoods. All because of Ellsberg's grandstanding. Work almost came to a halt. "Nobody was untouched by this in the organization emotionally," Sullivan remembers. People exhibited the most extreme kinds of emotions. There was panic and "such paranoia," Jan Butler recalls. "We all were so stunned." The mood at RAND "became more and more paranoid and fearful and angry. And people were accusing people of things; not necessarily overtly, but friendships were broken. It was a very sad time." Some suspected that the five analysts who had signed the antiwar letter with Ellsberg in the fall of 1969 had conspired with him again.[129]

Most at RAND considered Ellsberg a loathsome traitor. A few thought that they had been right, he was not to be trusted. "I hope they hang the son-of-a-bitch," Richard Best remarked to Harry Rowen and Richard Goldstein. Many felt Ellsberg had done quite a number on Rowen. "I thought it was really kind of like biting the hand that feeds you," David McGarvey remembers. "The general opinion of those RANDsters who were in-the-know was that Ellsberg had done a terrible thing to his good friend," Robert Komer recalls. There was immediate concern for the fate of Rowen, who commented to the press, "There can be no excuse or proper reason for the violation of trust and confidence by any person who has received a high security clearance from the government." Sullivan heard that Rowen "really dumped on Ellsberg" through some form of communication to him, but Ellsberg says they had no contact. (Ellsberg once told me that he doesn't know whether Rowen was mad at him, then, evidently aware of the absurdity of that statement, quickly said, "Yes, I have to assume that he was very angry." In a subsequent interview, he claimed, "I've never known to what degree Harry felt badly . . . how much he held that really against me.")[130]

Secretary of Defense Melvin Laird, never a big fan of RAND and now feeling somewhat red-faced over it, accused the think tank of "lax security practices" and ordered that air force personnel take custody of all classified documents there. Top-secret material would now have to be perused in a special room. RAND also lost access to some particularly sensitive data, and Pentagon investigators roamed the halls conducting an inventory of its classified material to reevaluate RAND's requirements. To those analysts who worked with classified material—almost all of them—these developments were a pain in the ass, an indignity, and an embarrassment. And what did they have in their safes that they shouldn't have? Some nervously cleaned out their safes, cramming material into the classified waste disposal bins in the hallways at RAND, filling them up. Analysts now had to make damn sure their inventory was in order. FBI agents and other investigators were conducting interviews at RAND, asking about specific documents: Could we please see that one? "It was very intimidating," recalls Hans Heymann of the visit he received from five investigators. When Heymann volunteered that he had technically violated security regulations when traveling, "they all looked at me like I was crazy," he recounts. "And they said, 'We're not interested in stupid security violations. We want to get Ellsberg.'"[131]

But the air force's control of RAND's classified material was nominal, a face-saving move (the air force's men "sat in there and played poker all day," Jan Butler recalls), and many at RAND were relieved that the restrictions were not greater. Fast footwork in Washington had apparently limited the damage. Yet, who knew what stringent measures might be imposed in the future?[132]

Best and Rowen rode downtown together to testify before the grand jury; Butler headed down the same morning. Rowen feigned unawareness to Best that the Pentagon Papers had been stored off the books at RAND, outside its Top Secret Control system, least of all that he had approved that unusual arrangement. As they walked out of RAND to get in a company car, Best recounts, "I said, 'Harry, how did you know that Dan had another set of them?

Where did you get that information?' . . . Got a very vague [response]. He's under a lot of pain. 'Uh huh.' He just didn't know. Twice more within the next week I had a chance to ask him that: 'Harry, have you been able to think of how you knew that Dan had a set?' The son-of-a-bitch" again said little. "He was afraid if he told me too much, [his] whole involvement in this would come out," Best says. "Harry was really withholding all along."[133]

Best and Butler also signed affidavits that were attached to Ellsberg's arrest warrant. Butler, who was "stunned" to learn that Ellsberg was responsible for the release of the Papers, and who then spent months doing "around-the-clock surveys to find out what Dan had seen, what he hadn't seen, what he'd signed off on" at RAND, had mixed sentiments about his act. Although she, too, hadn't been aware that her affidavit would be used as a basis for a criminal charge against him, when she heard over her car radio one morning that a warrant had gone out for his arrest, "it didn't bother me at all," she remembers. "I felt no guilt about it. . . . My feeling about it was Dan . . . broke faith with RAND, with his colleagues, and with the security system. . . . He did it knowing what the consequences would probably be. . . . I felt no compunction about making statements that might get him arrested. It just didn't trouble me at all."[134]

Butler's earlier relationship with Ellsberg now came under heightened scrutiny at RAND. Some saw it as "an additional sordid component added to the already sufficiently sordid picture," Sullivan chuckles. Best was summoned to the RAND front office, a side room there, for a meeting with Rowen and Goldstein. "The first question Goldie asked me [was], 'Do you know that your Top Secret Control officer was sleeping with Dan Ellsberg?'" Best recounts. "And I said, 'Yes, I knew that.' And he said, 'You're not concerned that she was sleeping [with him]?' And I said, 'Now, wait a minute. . . . I knew that she was *dating* Dan Ellsberg. I didn't know whether she was or whether she was not sleeping with him. And it's none of my business.' Well, they were a little bit appalled that I hadn't looked into this, I think." Of course, Rowen had already known about Butler's relationship with Ellsberg, and Goldstein was no lily of purity. "Everybody in the front office lost their head, except Gus Shubert," Best says. "He was the only sane head in the whole place."[135]

Butler was the scarlet woman at RAND. Many thought she supported Ellsberg's release of the Papers. Some suspected that she had even collaborated with him, or at least that she knew a lot more than she was letting on. "There was always a suspicion that somehow I was in a conspiracy with Dan," Butler recounts. "And I simply wasn't. But I think that Harry Rowen believed it." The White House's Charles Colson would recall seeing reports that Ellsberg's relationship with "a security officer at RAND" had allowed him access to nuclear secrets. People "had fantasies about us that simply weren't true," Butler says. And some people "didn't know what to say to me. They didn't know whose side I was on. It was extremely uncomfortable, and it went on for two and a half years." One day in the hallway, a woman ducked into an unused office and closed the door until Butler passed; another woman grabbed Butler by the arm and threw her down the stairs. "It was very strange, because I kept thinking, 'Why is this person reacting this way, and this one reacting that way?'" Butler remembers.[136]

Butler was moved out of her job as RAND's Top Secret Control officer. "You've got to shoot everybody who had any taint," Sullivan comments. "I think it was that simple." Clear the decks. "The board of trustees gave RAND an order to find me a job that was clearly a promotion and clearly not a demotion, so that I couldn't sue them," Butler recalls. "But they wanted me out of the TS office. . . . So they got me this funny little job, which was clearly a demotion." Butler thought it unfair, that it made her look guilty. She came across a memo in the RAND front office recommending to management and the board of trustees that the new Top Secret Control officer be "an older woman and somebody rather plain. . . . Somebody homely and old." Butler thought, "Aren't they stupid." *That* wouldn't have stopped Dan Ellsberg.[137]

When Rowen was tossed overboard, it was announced in newspapers: "Firing of Rand Chief Tied to Pentagon Leak," the *Washington Post* declared. Rowen suffered a public humiliation. He was scared and worried about his future.[138]

Ellsberg was not the only reason that Rowen walked the plank. Rowen had long been a thorn in the side of the air force, and his interest in expanding domestic projects at RAND had not helped their relationship. More important, Rowen was widely considered a poor manager and administrator. "He couldn't manage his way out of a wet paper bag," one RAND trustee complained on more than one occasion. Rowen was not a man to make crisp, tough decisions, some felt. His days as RAND's president may have been numbered anyway. But Ellsberg's release of the Papers and "the whole Rowen and Ellsberg relationship" was "certainly the trigger" behind Rowen's firing, discloses Gus Shubert, who attended the emergency RAND board meeting that decided Rowen's fate and who was in frequent contact with a "very, very disappointed and very anxious and worried" board chairman Newton Minow during this period. "There was the feeling that Rowen had been of supreme bad judgment in relating to Dan this way," Shubert recalls. The board could not have been pleased to learn that Rowen had not acted after the FBI had informed him of Ellsberg's copying of top-secret documents over a year earlier. When I asked Rowen during our short conversation in 1995 if he thought Ellsberg's action had pushed him out at RAND, he replied, "Oh, *sure*. I don't think there's any doubt about it." "It was the last straw," another RAND man remarked. He had been involved in the whole Pentagon Papers debacle too heavily. The Pentagon and RAND's board of trustees were both most unhappy about the affair (though some RAND trustees stressed that Rowen's canning had to be done right, decently, and one cautioned, "You're going to ruin this man's life"). Again, it was time to clear the decks, if only to cleanse RAND, to remove the taint, and to appease Washington. "The board of trustees said, 'He's got to be out of here before the [Ellsberg] court sessions start,'" Best remembers. But RAND released a statement to the press claiming that both Minow and Rowen "have made it clear that the Pentagon papers matter bears no relationship whatsoever" to Rowen's departure. "Change," Rowen said, was a force for "maintaining vitality in institutions and in people."[139] In other words, the standard PR babble.

Years later, Ellsberg would ask one RAND man how his release of the Papers had affected Rowen. The man told him it got Rowen fired. Ellsberg acted surprised to hear that (though he could not have been surprised). He told me that he "felt bad" about hurting Rowen, but said "anyone who knew the situation would say I was just one factor in his losing his job, and not even the most important factor. . . . He was just too liberal."[140]

John Vann was also upset by Ellsberg's release of the Papers. Vann was "enraged at Ellsberg," Neil Sheehan wrote, "cursing him to mutual acquaintances and shouting that Ellsberg . . . ought to be thrown into jail." "He felt it was a treasonous act," his son John Allen Vann recalls. "He thought it was a cowardly act." And a despicable one. Vann, too, felt he'd been stabbed in the back by a friend. But despite "an obvious strain" and some heated arguments between them, John Allen says, his father and Ellsberg remained friends. "We remain in agreement about many things," Vann wrote Ellsberg that September.[141]

Edward Lansdale was also mad at Ellsberg. He, too, thought his disclosure treasonous, an act of thievery. "I feel strongly that he broke a trust," Lansdale wrote Ellsberg's former colleagues on his counterinsurgency team in Vietnam. He believed Ellsberg sought public acclaim and had "a martyr complex." But he had mixed sentiments. He still felt affection for Ellsberg. "Lansdale still seemed to think rather highly of Dan, and did not, as far as I could determine, hold this against him," Joe Redick says.[142]

Lou Conein was less charitable. His involvement in the U.S.-backed coup that had killed Ngo Dinh Diem in 1963 and in other clandestine activity in

Vietnam had been held up to the light with publication of the Papers. Journalists were hounding him (as they were Lansdale), forcing him to change his phone number. He hadn't known Ellsberg had the courage to do something like this. He felt Ellsberg should go to prison.[143]

Lyndon Johnson declared that release of the Papers was "close to treason." He saw "the ghostly hand of Robert Kennedy" on the documents. Robert McNamara was "a Kennedy man," Johnson thought. Johnson had surrounded himself at his ranch in Texas with "at least a million" classified documents—possibly "the biggest collection of classified papers ever assembled by one man," the columnist Jack Anderson wrote—for use in writing his memoir. But no one would put out an arrest warrant for Lyndon Baines Johnson. Indeed, he would be over a million dollars richer from his book.[144]

THIRTEEN

BOOMERANG

RICHARD NIXON SAW THE *NEW YORK TIMES*'S STORIES ON THE VIETNAM archive on Sunday, June 13, 1971. His initial reaction was muted. It was "criminally traitorous," White House Chief of Staff H. R. Haldeman wrote in his diary, echoing Nixon, that classified documents had been passed to the *Times*. And it would not help Nixon's Vietnam policy. But "no skin off us," John Ehrlichman recorded in his notes during a meeting with Nixon. "Papers of two Democratic presidents," although it "splashes on us," since their administration was part of the same establishment that the Papers showed had been deceptive. "The key now is for us to keep out of it and let the people that are affected cut each other up on it," Haldeman wrote.[1]

Charles Colson also urged restraint. "We must be exceedingly careful not to overreact," he wrote Haldeman, with considerable irony in retrospect. Colson agreed that the Papers touched the Nixon administration; a poll conducted on June 21 found that 41 percent of the American people felt that the administration was deceiving the public about its conduct of the war. But when those surveyed were asked who was "*most* guilty of doing something wrong," 39 percent said it was the person who had released the Papers, 30 percent said it was the Johnson administration, and only 10 percent said the Nixon administration. And while the Papers helped the antiwar movement, Colson understood as well as anyone, they had not hurt Nixon's approval ratings. (Ellsberg would later claim that "Nixon's lowest ebb in popularity, the actual bottom, was caused by Daniel Ellsberg and the Pentagon Papers.") "The Democrats are being hurt much more severely than the Republicans," Colson wrote. Yet only a modest 51 percent of Americans were even aware of the Papers' publication. "To the extent that the public is aware of it, they do not understand the issues very well," Colson noted. "The heartland isn't really aroused over this issue. . . . As for the credibility of government, a case can be made that it has already reached its low point. This incident simply confirms what many people think anyway." And Nixon could always set the public straight on things: "According to Lou Harris' theory . . . 50 percent of the American people at least will always believe what any president tells them because they want to believe what any president tells them." And Americans will quickly tire of the issue.[2]

Yet panic spread in the White House. While hardly out of form, the overreaction was tremendous with fateful consequences for the Nixon administration. National Security Adviser Henry Kissinger flew into a rage, fanning Nixon's own burgeoning ire. "Dr. Kissinger was even more alarmed over the leaks than the president," Colson testified afterward. "He believed that the leaks must be stopped at all costs, that Ellsberg must be stopped from making further disclosures of classified information." Kissinger and Nixon had both been complaining about leaks since taking office (on June 14 Nixon blamed the leaking on intellectuals who "will lie, cheat, anything" and "have no morals"). Kissinger worried that the release of the Papers would hurt secret negotiations that he was then undertaking with the North Vietnamese and Chinese, and that his past ties to Ellsberg would harm his standing with Nixon (who would tell other aides that "virtually every one of these people" involved in the release were either students or associates of Kissinger). Kissinger moved to distance himself from Ellsberg. Before Nixon and other officials, he described Ellsberg in unflattering and disquieting terms. Although Ellsberg was a "genius" and the brightest student he'd ever had at Harvard, said Kissinger (who'd never taught Ellsberg), he was "always a little unbalanced" and had "shot at peasants" from helicopters in Vietnam. "Henry made a big point of Ellsberg's psychiatric imbalance," Haldeman recalled. Upon abusing drugs he'd "flipped," Kissinger related, and switched "from hawk to peacenik." His actions were not those of an ideologue, Kissinger said, but rather those of an opportunist. What's more, Ellsberg was a sexual pervert who had sexual relations with his wealthy wife in front of his children, Kissinger claimed. Ellsberg wasn't your typical disgruntled mainstream bureaucrat, Kissinger implied; he was more dangerous. "The picture was very murky and very alarming," one official who was present said. By the end of this meeting, Nixon was as mad as Kissinger. They ought to "kill" Ellsberg, Kissinger reportedly told Nixon, speaking figuratively, one has to presume. After Kissinger left one meeting with Nixon, "the president was very upset and was pounding his desk and using colorful language," Colson recalled.[3]

Kissinger was probably less concerned with disclosure of the Papers than with the possibility that Ellsberg might release other classified material. Ellsberg might have copies of NSSM-1 and the Vietnam options paper that he had helped write earlier, Kissinger worried with good reason. Current and former National Security Council staffers might have given him other material. Perhaps most troubling, Ellsberg might have information on U.S. nuclear targeting (which, of course, he did). The possibilities were ominous.[4]

Nixon would have worked himself into a lather over publication of the Papers without Kissinger's assistance, as the release involved several predictable triggers—a major leak, an apparent attempt by Nixon's enemies to undermine him, and the collusion of the press. He was a pugnacious man inclined toward vengeance. Plus, Colson despised Ellsberg and fed Nixon's anger. But Kissinger aroused the president and fueled the White House's response.

Nixon was swiftly raving himself. The situation was grave, perilous, he angrily told aides. Release of the Papers undermined U.S. foreign policy across the board and compromised the system for keeping government secrets. And it would embolden other leakers. Nixon was angry at the *Times* for publishing the documents. "Until further notice under *no circumstances* is anyone connected with the White House to give any interview to a member of the staff of the *New York Times* without my express permission," he directed Haldeman on June 15.[5]

Feeding the alarm of Nixon and his aides were two key unanswered questions: who, exactly, was a party to this treasonous act, and what else did the perpetrators have? The White House did not believe that Ellsberg had acted alone. In fact, the first "suspected villain" had been Leslie Gelb (just as Gelb had worried). Morton Halperin and Paul Warnke were also suspect. On July 2, Nixon noticed a newspaper story in which Ellsberg—one of the many "little people who love to be heroes," he observed—said he'd had help. "I'm not so interested in Ellsberg, but we have got to go after everybody who's a member of this conspiracy," he told Haldeman and Colson. When Colson pointed out that Ellsberg had said he'd leave it up to those who had helped him to decide whether to reveal themselves, Nixon replied, "He must be a rat. What a rat. . . . I got to say for [Alger] Hiss. He never ratted on anybody else." Commented Haldeman, "Well, Hiss was a more dedicated-type spy than Ellsberg is. Ellsberg—he's going on a totally different basis. . . . Hiss knew exactly what he was doing and why. Ellsberg probably doesn't." Nixon wondered how Ellsberg had looked on television the night before.[6]

The list of possible conspirators was long and stretched wide politically. Even the staunch cold warrior Paul Nitze attracted suspicion. "He's a co-conspirator with Gelb and Halperin," Ehrlichman reported to Nixon on September 10. "Paul

Nitze is?" Nixon responded, incredulously. "I'm quite sure. Quite sure that he's the guy," replied Ehrlichman, who may have confused Nitze with Warnke. William Kaufmann also merited "a hard look," Colson felt. Kissinger's aides may have been involved too. Charles Cooke, a State Department aide whom the administration believed had given Ellsberg classified material on the railroading of Tran Ngoc Chau that Ellsberg had leaked to the press, was also probably "in on it." "This Cooke, I'm going to get him killed," a livid Nixon told Kissinger, who responded, "I frankly think he ought to be fired, Mr. President."[7]

Colson thought the Papers themselves might be the stuff of a conspiracy. "There is a school of thought which is gaining momentum that the Pentagon papers were initiated by Bobby Kennedy forces to be used in the '68 campaign to throw over LBJ," he wrote to an aide on July 1, in accord with Lyndon Johnson. David Young of the Plumbers reported another theory that the study "was a surreptitious operation from the beginning. McNamara simply wanted all documents collected."[8] Neither theory held water.

The White House believed that Neil Sheehan was a member of the conspiracy. FBI reports suggested that Sheehan had stolen the Papers from Ellsberg, possibly even bag-jobbed him. "That was a big rumor, a big thing," G. Gordon Liddy remembers. "And the FBI was quite into that. They didn't know what part Neil Sheehan had had. . . . They suspected the hell out of it, and they had a lot of stuff. . . . It wasn't necessarily just Ellsberg: maybe Ellsberg's trying to take all the credit. . . . There was a whole lot of talk about it in the FBI." The bureau was aware that Sheehan had xeroxed the Papers. That the *Times* was writing that Ellsberg *said* he gave the Papers to the press also suggested to the White House that the *Times* had not simply received them on a silver platter from Ellsberg. Officials correctly suspected that Sheehan had another source. "It's possible that Sheehan stole that stuff from a source different than Ellsberg's sources," Colson or Nixon offered in a meeting on September 18. "I think he probably had two sources," Attorney General John Mitchell opined. Fred Buzhardt, the general counsel of the Defense Department, told Liddy that "the more Defense investigates, the closer they come to proving that it was not the Ellsberg documents which were published by the *New York Times*." Buzhardt speculated, in Liddy's words: "Ellsberg had a copy of the McNamara study. Others had copies of the McNamara study. Copies varied in form. . . . An equivalent of the Ellsberg holdings was possessed by IPS. Sheehan stole portions of the IPS holdings without the knowledge of IPS, Ellsberg having told Sheehan of the existence of the IPS holdings and how to steal them."[9] That last part is fairly wild stuff.

Liddy subsequently reported to Egil Krogh and David Young that Buzhardt apparently had "the results of certain computer analyses which will be the basis of an opinion (probably correct) that Ellsberg was not the person who transmitted the McNamara Study to the *New York Times*." "The key to the McNamara Study problem," Buzhardt argued, again off course, "lies in Gelb and Halperin, not in Ellsberg." Krogh offered that "Ellsberg actually had nothing to do with the release of the Pentagon Papers but was trying to take all the public credit to make himself a hero."[10]

Nixon wanted Sheehan's involvement in the conspiracy known. "Bob, you haven't followed the instructions I've given," he sternly told Haldeman on July 5 in a taped White House conversation. "I want it leaked now. Goddamnit." Nixon felt Sheehan was "guilty as hell," but recognized that if "you prosecute a newspaperman, you're in a difficult position." Mitchell directed that Sheehan not be prosecuted without his specific approval.[11] Sheehan was not indicted.

A conspiracy of dovish Democrats and the liberal press was bad enough, but Nixon and his aides feared communists were also involved. Ellsberg had cavorted with domestic communists in Minnesota, according to intelligence. Even more alarming were his possible foreign communist ties; they raised the stakes dramatically. A Soviet double agent working under cover at the United Nations reported to the FBI that, several days after the *Times* began publishing the Papers, a man bearing a letter signed with an alias and stating his reasons had handed over a full set of the Papers—"the whole shooting match," in Liddy's words—to the Soviet embassy in Washington. The Soviet agent, a short chunky man with a doctorate in chemistry code-named FEDORA—Fatso, some FBI agents called him—had been feeding information to the FBI since 1962. It seemed "logical" to Liddy that the man who had reportedly delivered the Papers to the Soviet embassy "might very well be Ellsberg. . . . But we didn't know that for a fact." The FBI, Liddy points out, "didn't give us the identity. They claimed they didn't have it." Krogh said later it was "a working hypothesis" that "there had been direct foreign involvement in the disclosure of the Pentagon Papers" and that this report "reinforced" that hypothesis. According to sources of Seymour Hersh, "no one questioned the authenticity of the agent's report," as "he was believed to be one of the important informers in the national security establishment."[12]

The White House worried that Ellsberg might be a Soviet intelligence informer. Kissinger had intimated earlier that Ellsberg could be an agent. If true, his cache of state secrets—some more damaging than the Papers—might be going straight to the enemy. That was profoundly disturbing. There was also a report that the North Vietnamese had received a copy of the Papers. The

Plumbers asked the FBI to check with MI-5, the British intelligence agency, to see whether Ellsberg had had any contact with Soviet officials when he studied at Cambridge University in the early 1950s. MI-5 said no. FBI agents questioned Carol Ellsberg about their contacts. "They wanted to know about what happened when we were in England, who we saw," Carol Cummings remembers. "Was I aware of any communists that we knew or that we'd had any contact with?" (Carol told the FBI of their meeting one friendly Russian with whom they'd lunched and gone to an event at the Russian embassy, but that "Dan had gotten kind of nervous about it. . . . So we didn't go to their next embassy affair.") When Carol heard that the Papers had been passed to the Soviets, she was also alarmed: "I thought, 'My God, maybe he's really done something that's harmful to the United States of America.'"[13]

But, most likely, no one delivered the Papers to the Russian embassy. "That's just ludicrous," one former CIA official said when told about FEDORA's report. "This guy is in the category of a really washed-out character." CIA Director Richard Helms told David Young that he doubted the report, and the CIA was never asked to investigate Soviet involvement with the Papers. A member of the Watergate Special Prosecution Force (WSPF), who read all the material the FBI provided it on the FBI's contacts with the White House about Ellsberg, observed in one of many WSPF memos I obtained through a Freedom of Information Act request, "None of the FBI material mentions or even alludes to the delivery of the papers to the Russian Embassy. Nor is there anything in the material to suggest that Ellsberg had foreign or subversive contacts and, equally as significant, there is nothing to suggest that the Bureau suspected or theorized along those lines. The simple fact is that the investigation was thorough without revealing any evidence to indicate Ellsberg had any foreign connections."[14]

After the *Washington Post* wrote about the alleged delivery in June 1973, the Soviets dismissed it as "a fabrication" and "absolutely groundless." Ellsberg angrily denied it and aptly pointed out that during his trial "the government made no such allegations—which would have strengthened their case immeasurably." David Nissen, Ellsberg's lead prosecutor, recalled that although he had been informed early on that the Papers might have been passed to the Soviet embassy, he never heard that Ellsberg himself had been responsible, and hence the matter was not investigated.[15]

One wonders if the White House had a hand in concocting this story. Charles Colson, among others, was fairly imaginative about dirty tricks and a real pro at fostering disinformation. He would later vaguely attribute the report to "various government agencies." Ellsberg hypothesized that the White

House orchestrated an actual delivery of documents to the Soviet embassy, but that is much less likely. He told the Watergate prosecutors that the White House had also produced a picture of someone alleged to be him leaving the Soviet embassy.[16] That's not so far-fetched.

The White House, of course, used the report to smear Ellsberg. In official hands by at least June 25, 1971, a Friday, the story was promptly leaked over the weekend by Colson to Victor Lasky, a conservative journalist and well-fed conduit of White House propaganda ("our man," Colson told a colleague). Lasky wrote about the alleged delivery in articles published on June 29 and July 10. The leak may have been intended not only to tarnish Ellsberg's image but also to influence an impending Supreme Court decision on whether to allow newspapers to continue publishing the Papers. If so, it didn't work on the second count, as on June 30 the court ruled that newspapers could resume publication. Colson also reported the delivery to another "very loyal friend," the *Detroit News*'s Jerald terHorst, a neighbor of his in Washington who was "not the best journalist in the world," he told White House Press Secretary Ronald Ziegler.[17]

———◆———

The White House would have liked to paint Ellsberg as not only a subversive with foreign communist ties but a homosexual to boot, and the following year a wild story floated around that made both claims. In 1972 a man we'll call Robert Russell told the FBI that in 1971 a friend of his, whom we'll call Charles Masterson, had informed him that he had gone to bed with Ellsberg on several occasions. Now, according to Russell, Masterson told him he wanted to extort money from Ellsberg by threatening to reveal his homosexual activities. Russell and Masterson, who had been sexual partners at times, decided that Masterson would attempt to obtain some of the Pentagon Papers from Ellsberg since they were allegedly salable. According to Russell's story, Masterson managed to get around a hundred papers from Ellsberg that had never been published. They had the "usual top secret-confidential type markings on the cover sheets," Russell told the FBI. The two men thought they might be able to sell them to the Soviets for $5,000, then swindle the Soviets for another $100,000 by claiming to have "the 3,900 remaining pages of the Pentagon Papers." Russell felt they would probably have to use force to obtain the $100,000, however, so he purchased a snub-nosed five-shot Smith and Wesson. A friend of Russell told him their plot "would be a good way to 'screw' the Russians for the way the Jews were being treated in Russia."[18]

One day in late June 1971, according to Russell, he entered the Soviet consulate in New York (not Washington) and stated that he had some stolen government documents. After "getting nowhere," he made it known that the documents were the Pentagon Papers, at which point he was "taken up a back stairwell to an office that overlooked the street and which had a padded door." A man he spoke with there did not seem too interested until Russell threatened to "go to Ottawa, Canada, to sell the papers to the Chinese," he told the FBI. A week later, he purportedly rendezvoused with a Soviet representative at the Plaza Hotel in New York. The man gave him $2,500 for the hundred pages, saying that's all they were worth, but that he would buy the remaining 3,900 pages for $50,000 in a few weeks.[19]

According to Russell's account, he reported to Masterson that, unfortunately, he had been unable to make contact with the Soviets at the Plaza Hotel. Masterson did not have the "competence" to carry out the next stage of their scheme, he believed, so he was going to leave Masterson out of it. Shortly thereafter, Russell told the FBI, Masterson came to his apartment "stoned on acid" and accused him of pocketing the money. A violent confrontation ensued. Masterson retrieved a butcher knife from the kitchen, and Russell grabbed his gun. He then shot Masterson, who "stumbled out of the apartment and down the stairs." Russell called his mother, then an ambulance and the police.[20]

"Implausible" and "inconsistent with data previously developed" was the FBI's evaluation of Russell's story. An associate of Russell's attorneys told the FBI that Russell was in need of a psychiatrist (that seems fairly obvious). Charles Nesson investigated the story and also found it false, but was reluctant to put it down on paper for fear it would damage Ellsberg's reputation. Russell had evidently hoped to trade his story for dismissal of criminal charges against him. Ellsberg began receiving calls from reporters about it. He denied it.[21]

———— ◎ ————

The White House worried about what was coming next. Would more top-secret documents soon be appearing in newspapers? "I don't give a damn how it is done, do whatever has to be done to stop these leaks and prevent further unauthorized disclosures," Nixon ordered Colson and Haldeman. "I don't want excuses, I want results." Egil Krogh would recall being "repeatedly" informed of the "extreme threat" of "further unauthorized disclosures." Ellsberg had declared publicly that he had other state secrets. Intelligence reported that he had shown a penchant for collecting documents as a Pentagon staffer, and that Jan Butler had found classified documents at his home in Malibu. Krogh understood that Ellsberg "probably had access to a number of subjects of great sensitivity which, if disclosed, could prove very embarrassing," including on U.S. atrocities in Vietnam. Robert Mardian, who was then an assistant U.S. attorney general, would remember "the pervasive feeling" that "the Administration was unaware of exactly how much information Ellsberg had," and that both State and Defense had been "extremely interested in seeing that Ellsberg was indicted as soon as possible" because that would deter him from releasing other classified material. "We knew he had a lot of stuff," Liddy recalls. "But the FBI and anybody else didn't know what," exactly, partly because RAND "had been particularly lax in the keeping of the logs as to what went in, what went out, and what have you." And nobody knew where Ellsberg kept his cache of material.[22]

Officials were disturbed by RAND's "malpractices" (to use Liddy's word). Fred Buzhardt could not understand "why we continue to do business with Rand, knowing all that we do about them." Both Buzhardt and the Justice Department believed that Harry Rowen and others at RAND were now lying to or withholding from investigators. RAND had apparently prepared a paper setting out its account of the Pentagon Papers affair, but "no one would agree to sign it," Buzhardt reported. During a conversation on August 11, Liddy recorded, Buzhardt predicted that "the president is going to be very upset when he receives the DOD report on Rand. . . . I know he is going to say 'wipe it out.'" In fact, Nixon had already said that. "We've got to get our enemies out of the clearance business. I mean, Rand," he told Haldeman on July 5. Nixon applauded the Pentagon's crackdown at RAND: "Let them squeal."[23]

Release of the Papers reawakened Nixon's earlier desire to seize some classified material on Vietnam that Leslie Gelb had reportedly taken to Brookings. On June 17, Nixon gruffly ordered Haldeman, in another taped conversation, "Goddamnit, get in and *get those files.* Blow the safe." Two weeks later, Nixon again directed Haldeman, "Break into their files and get that stuff out. And let them scream." After Haldeman remarked, "I don't have any problem with breaking in," Nixon suggested undertaking the burglary at "around eight or nine o'clock . . . and *clean it out.*" "Do they understand how we want to play the game?" Nixon asked Haldeman, speaking of aides. "Do they know how tough it has to be played?" The next morning, Nixon was still hyped on a break-in. "We're up against an enemy, a conspiracy, that are using any means," he harshly lectured Haldeman and Kissinger, banging his hand on his Oval Office desk for emphasis. "We are going to use any means. Is that clear? Did they get the Brookings Institute raided last night? No. Get it done! I want it done!" And the next morning: "I really meant it when [I said] I want to go in and crack that safe. . . .

Brookings is the real enemy here." Nixon said he wanted men available for burglaries at Brookings and RAND whenever necessary and "at all costs."[24]

Nixon's desire to break into Brookings grew even stronger when Colson reported that a Brookings study was then underway on Vietnam using more recent classified material—Gelb's study. "It looks to me like we may soon expect another installment in the Pentagon Papers written by the same authors but doubtless more up to date," Colson wrote John Ehrlichman on July 6. Nixon erupted at Haldeman when informed: "Goddamnit, Bob, haven't we got that capability in place?"[25]

But White House operative Jack Caulfield reported to Colson that there was no way to crack Brookings. "Start a fire if you need to!" Colson directed. "You can go in behind the firemen." Colson would claim later to the Watergate prosecutors that he "certainly wasn't serious" about this, but Caulfield recalled that "there could be no mistake about the fact that Colson was dead serious." Caulfield's attorney told the prosecutors that Caulfield never told him "it was considered a joke then or is considered a joke now."[26]

G. Gordon Liddy and Howard Hunt didn't consider it a joke. They developed their infamous plan to firebomb Brookings. Hunt received their marching orders from Colson, Liddy believes, though Hunt never referred to Colson by name in such matters. "True to his training . . . he always said, 'My principal,'" Liddy recalls. Hunt and Liddy planned to buy a used fire engine, repaint it to look like the real thing, purchase firemen's uniforms, and train a squad of Cubans in fire fighting. The bomb would be set off with a timing mechanism. "The fire alarm would have been pulled, there would have been smoke, and they would [say] 'Yeah,' and out of there," Liddy remembers envisioning. "Our guys would be like around the corner—whish, they're there first. And they go in, do what they have to do, go out. And they were told to then just abandon the equipment and everything else: just leave it there. Just donate it to the D.C. fire department," he laughs. But the plan "went up, and Hunt said, 'It's no good.' And I said, 'Why?' He says, 'They're too cheap to pop for the fire engine.' That was the objection, the money."[27]

But Nixon's angry orders had shown his men his desire and willingness to engage in burglaries to combat his enemies. The lessons they drew encouraged planning of the break-in at Dr. Lewis Fielding's office in early September, which was followed by more tough talk about pulling off another bag job. A week later, Ehrlichman informed Nixon that Halperin, Warnke, and Gelb had deposited other classified material on the war in the National Archives. "There's a lot of hanky-panky with secret documents," Ehrlichman related. "And on the eve of the publication of the Pentagon Papers, those three guys made a deposit . . . of a whole lot of papers. Now, I would steal those documents out of the National Archives . . . and photograph them, and find out what the hell is up." Nixon approved the caper. "Nobody can tell we've been in there," Ehrlichman said. But this penetration became unnecessary when a Pentagon official gained access to the documents. Liddy felt "a more forceful approach" to the archivist could have secured access to them sooner.[28]

Shortly before 10 A.M. on Monday, June 28, Dan Ellsberg, appearing nervous to one reporter, and with Patricia close by his side, ended his time on the lam and turned himself in to the U.S. attorney's office in Boston. "I think I've done a good job as a citizen," he said as he entered the building, mobbed by the press and supporters. He took full responsibility for releasing the Papers. His deliberate manner suggested to another journalist that "he had been thinking for some time about what he would say when this moment arrived." That is undoubtedly true. Ellsberg's attorneys had devised a diversionary maneuver to avoid a premature capture before his surrender. "It worked absolutely perfectly," Charles Nesson remembers:

> This was down at the federal courthouse. There was a big crowd. . . . And we sent [Leonard] Boudin, with somebody in the car with him, into the main area. And of course, as soon as anybody saw it was Boudin, all the press started running, so everything focused there, like, "Here he's coming." And in the meantime . . . Dan and I went in a different car and just kind of came in on the side. And while all the hubbub was going on over here, we just zipped in the door and went up and got to the U.S. attorney's office without anybody even seeing us. And he surrendered voluntarily.[29]

Actually, Ellsberg was being observed as he walked into the courthouse—by Richard Best. The government had flown in Best to take a look at him. Best recounts:

> The FBI for some reason had gotten the idea that they might shove in a ringer as Ellsberg, that maybe Ellsberg wasn't going to appear. So they came to RAND and asked if somebody from RAND who knew Ellsberg would identify him. They selected me. . . . So I went to Boston, and that morning we met in the FBI office in the courthouse, and we went up a back elevator so we wouldn't encounter any of the Ellsberg party on the way in. And I was seated off to one side when Ellsberg came in. And it was the strangest thing. He looked at me and he stared. And I was sure he was trying to fix me in his

mind, this guy sitting over there with the FBI, the government people. I don't think he knew who it was. . . . And he watched me quite puzzled for a while. Then he looked back to see.[30]

After police whisked him upstairs, Ellsberg was photographed and finger-printed by the U.S. marshal's office. The record of his fingerprinting indicates he weighed in at 165 pounds and stood five feet, ten-and-a-half inches tall. Fighting shape. "Scar to the left of the left eyebrow," the record reads.[31] From the car accident that killed his mother.

After signing himself out on $50,000 bond, Ellsberg held a short informal press conference outside the courthouse. The large crowd cheered him. Ells-berg was speaking to the world at last. He loved it, his serious demeanor aside. "My dream is to have someone follow me around with a microphone," he later told Anthony Russo.[32]

That afternoon, Ellsberg stood barefoot on his front porch at 10 Hilliard Street talking to several journalists. His neighbor Stewart Perry remembers with a laugh that, shortly after Ellsberg surfaced, he and Patricia once went back into the house and emerged only moments later for the benefit of televi-sion cameras, even though "they hadn't been there at all. They just went inside and then came out again. . . . I was going out myself at that point and I had to get out of the way while this was being done."[33]

On June 28 in Los Angeles, a federal grand jury handed up a two-count in-dictment charging Ellsberg with "unauthorized possession" of "documents and writings related to the national defense"—a violation of the Espionage Act—and with converting those documents "to his own use"—theft. The maximum sentence on each count: ten years in prison. Ellsberg was the first person in U.S. history to face criminal charges for leaking government secrets to a news-paper, and the first to be charged with espionage without being formally ac-cused of passing official secrets to a foreign power. It was a political indictment. The U.S. attorney in Los Angeles refused to sign it. "The theory will be to prosecute primarily for unauthorized possession and willful retention, rather than for transmitting the data to the *Times*, since it is anticipated that the news-papers would inhibit prosecution on the latter basis," White House Counsel John Dean wrote John Ehrlichman that day.[34]

That evening, Ellsberg placed a long-distance phone call to his children at the home of Andrew and Mary Marshall in Los Angeles. Carol Ellsberg telephoned the FBI the next day and reported that Dan had criticized her to their children for testifying against him. Robert had tried to defend his mother.[35]

After his indictment, Ellsberg closeted himself with his lawyers and advisers. Journalists followed his every move when he appeared on Hilliard Street. "There was really almost a stakeout there," his neighbor Priscilla McMillan remembers. "If he just wanted to take his cleaning to the laundry down the street, they photographed him. Pat knew how to sneak out; they didn't always recognize her. . . . But they always photographed him. . . . Sometimes he would stop and there would be a microphone out there and he would speak into it. He never was ungracious to them."[36]

In the White House, Richard Nixon was then plotting strategy for going after Ellsberg and his co-conspirators. He wanted to destroy them, and he knew just how to do it. "I have a feeling that we have a hell of an opportunity here . . . to leak out all these nasty stories that'll kill these bastards," he told Haldeman on July 1. "All evidence that we find with regard to the conspiracy is going to be leaked to columnists . . . and we'll kill these sons-of-bitches," he lectured Kissinger. Nixon wasn't worried about obstructing justice in Ellsberg's trial. "Don't worry about his trial," he told Kissinger and John Mitchell. "Just get everything out and try him in the press. . . . I want to destroy him in the press. Is that clear?" Nixon likened this opportunity to his campaign against Alger Hiss many years earlier. "We won the Hiss case in the papers. We leaked stuff all over the place. . . . I played it in the press like a master. . . . I leaked out everything that I could." Nixon had also helped lead a congressional investigation of Hiss. That approach would be useful here, too. "Far better than having these people indicted and so forth is really to call them before a committee," Nixon told another aide. "Hell, yes, we'll call them up. Give them lie detector tests." Nixon directed aides to consult his writing on the Hiss case. That way "you'll see how it was done," he told Haldeman. "It wasn't done through the goddamn courts or the attorney general or the FBI."[37]

To Nixon, Ellsberg was Hiss.

The president wanted one person in charge of this campaign. But the man would work under his leadership. "I'll direct it myself," Nixon said. "I know how to play this game." He would call the man (even in the middle of the night, if needed—Nixon often woke up then) "and tell him what the cops and robbers games are." The man had to be ruthless. "I can't have a high-minded lawyer like John Ehrlichman," who was "above some crap," Nixon told aides, or John Dean, for that matter. "I want somebody that's as tough as I am, for a change. Just as tough as I was, I should say, in the Hiss case." The "goddamn lawyers" like Ehrlichman, Dean, and Mitchell had "no understanding how tough it is" and were "always worried, 'Is it technically correct?'" Nixon complained. It was "the Colson type of man" he needed, Nixon told Haldeman. In other words, someone with some balls. But Colson had been "hot previously" and was "doing too much" already, Nixon mused.[38]

Departing White House aide Tom Huston, an ultraconservative with a taste for intelligence work, might be right for the job, Nixon thought. After Colson pointed out that Huston could be difficult, Nixon said, "We'll order the son-of-a-bitch to do what needs to be done. You can order him, can't you?" "Not very well," replied Haldeman. "He's an arrogant little bastard," Nixon said. "I don't want some guy who's going to try to second-guess my judgment on this. Because I forgot more than any of them have ever learned."[39]

Officials believed the combative White House speechwriter Pat Buchanan might also be a good commander. But Buchanan claimed strongly that he was the wrong man. He thought trying to smear Ellsberg through leaks to the press "a losing strategy." Perhaps the devious Mel Laird might help out, Nixon pondered: "Tell Laird that here's a chance for Laird to be the strong man. Let him be the guy that breaks this spy ring."[40]

"It would be very good if we had somebody who knew the subject," Nixon remarked to Haldeman. "I mean, what you really need is an Ellsberg. An Ellsberg who's on our side. In other words, an intellectual who knows the history of the times, who knows what he's looking for."[41]

Colson told Nixon there was a man "on the outside" who had the right skills and ideological orientation for the job. "He's hard as nails," Colson reported. "He's a brilliant writer. He's written forty books under pseudonyms." "What's his name?" Nixon asked. Howard Hunt, Colson replied. "Ideologically, he already is convinced this is a big conspiracy." (Hunt told Colson over the phone that day that he believed "the eastern establishment" had "certainly aided and abetted" Ellsberg, and that "the whole thing was all mapped out well in advance.") Hunt was then working for a Washington public relations firm that was a CIA front. "The beauty of this guy" was that "he's working outside," Haldeman observed to Nixon. "We can just hire him as a consultant." Nixon could see the beauty in that.[42] Distance. Deniability.

Colson arranged for Hunt to meet with Ehrlichman. The day of their meeting, July 7, Hunt was hired. "You should consider he has pretty much carte blanche," Ehrlichman told a CIA man over the phone that day.[43]

But Nixon decided to have Ehrlichman supervise the Plumbers unit. That job required someone close at hand, though the outside asset could still be used. Ehrlichman selected Egil Krogh and David Young to serve as cochairmen of the unit (an "awkward" arrangement, Krogh thought); Krogh brought Liddy in. Ehrlichman told Krogh that "the entire resources of the executive branch were to be brought to bear" on their task.[44]

The FBI would later investigate another wild allegation that one William Terry was also a Plumber. A man named Vernon Hebel reported to both the FBI and Senate Watergate investigators that Terry had discussed the Fielding break-in with him in advance, saying that "someone from the East would do the job and that it would be a 'crude' job." Hebel said Terry had also referred to other assignments given to the Plumbers by "the pipe" (John Mitchell, who smoked one) and "the brush" (H. R. Haldeman, who had a crew cut). But the FBI found no evidence that Terry, whom probation officers had earlier described as "a bright young man but 'very much in need of psychiatric treatment,'" was a Plumber. Terry could not be questioned about the allegation: in May 1973 he was found shot to death in the California desert with seven bullet wounds in his body and numerous empty beer cans and several gay pornographic magazines nearby. "Naturally, I am worried that I may be shot and left in the desert also," Hebel wrote Senator Sam Ervin.[45]

Spurring the formation of the Plumbers were perceptions inside the White House that J. Edgar Hoover's FBI was not carrying out its own Ellsberg investigation with sufficient speed, energy, or rigor. "Hoover is not going after this case as strong as I'd like," Nixon told Haldeman and Colson on July 2. "There's something dragging him." After Haldeman phoned Hoover four days later, the FBI began providing the White House with weekly reports on its probe. But they were deemed unsatisfactory. Some officials believed Hoover's advanced age or the FBI's internal divisions might be holding it back, but more felt the main restraint was Hoover's purportedly close friendship with Louis Marx, Sr. "Marx's daughter was married to that son-of-a-bitch Ellsberg," Nixon later remarked, and thus Hoover "just couldn't bring himself to get into it."[46]

In fact, while Louis Marx was a big fan of the FBI, admired Hoover, and had sent him toys to distribute to others, the two men were not buddies. "I know Dad was not a close friend of Hoover's," Patricia Ellsberg remembers. "Whether they ever met or not is in question." And Marx wanted to see the FBI investigation proceed. But there was evidence of foot-dragging. When Charles "Chick" Brennan, an FBI official, recommended to Hoover that Marx be interviewed, Hoover wrote "NO" on Brennan's memo. Brennan either misread Hoover's notation or received it too late, as he directed the New York FBI office to interview Marx. Hoover was angry. According to Ehrlichman's meeting notes of June 29, Hoover gave Brennan 48 hours to decide whether he wanted to quit the FBI or accept a transfer. Brennan accepted a transfer. After

Mitchell asked Hoover to rescind it, Hoover agreed, but demoted and censured Brennan.[47]

The FBI's interview of Louis Marx took place on June 23 when Ellsberg was still eluding the FBI. Marx "was unable to furnish any information concerning Ellsberg's whereabouts or his possible relationship with the 'Pentagon Papers' disclosure," an FBI memo records. Patricia Ellsberg recalls that her father "would have cooperated with the FBI totally if he'd known anything. He was on the FBI's side, not Dan's side," she laughs. "But he didn't know anything. He would have been delighted to tell them anything he knew."[48]

Officials later exaggerated the FBI's foot-dragging to justify the Plumbers' activities. The FBI strongly defended its work. "It was an extensive and exhaustive investigation and we had no indication whatsoever in any way that the White House was not satisfied with what we were doing," a top FBI official told the press. "The problem was that we wouldn't burglarize," a high-level official remarked.[49]

The Plumbers unit would operate under "super-secret conditions" in the basement of the Executive Office Building. Its offices had elaborate security systems, including a ceiling device that projected ultrasonic waves, and sterile telephones; a KYX scrambler phone reached the CIA. "It sounded as if we were speaking to each other from opposite ends of a long drainpipe," Liddy wrote later. Ehrlichman told Krogh that the unit's activities were to be kept secret even inside the White House. Liddy wanted to call the unit "ODESSA" after the organization of former Nazi SS members, and even had a rubber "ODESSA" stamp made and marked his memos with it until Ehrlichman deemed that unwise.[50]

The Plumbers' work was given additional impetus on July 23 when another major leak to the *New York Times* disclosed the U.S. negotiating position at the U.S.-Soviet SALT talks. Nixon was beside himself. Who were these traitors? Was this Ellsberg? The next day, a deeply troubled Nixon summoned Krogh and Ehrlichman to his office and ordered extensive lie detector tests to "immediately scare the bastards." "Listen," Nixon said, "I don't know anything about polygraphs and I don't know how accurate they are, but I know they'll scare the hell out of people." "Cancel all their tennis games and trips to Bermuda and order them all back in, line 'em up and run 'em through the lie detector," Nixon instructed Ehrlichman. He directed Krogh to move "with the greatest urgency" to determine the source of the leaks.[51]

The Plumbers launched a sweeping investigation of the Pentagon Papers affair. They probed the history of the study, its participants, and who had access to it. Ellsberg was, of course, their prime focus, since he clearly had that access along with lots of other classified material, he had copied the study, evidence linked him to its release, and "he was taking the rap for it at any rate," Liddy recalls. "He has made a number of admissions against interest," Liddy reported to Krogh and Young on August 18. The Plumbers investigated Ellsberg's past, lifestyle, motives, and capabilities. "What Ellsberg Knows" became the title of one of Young's folders. Liddy recommended that the Plumbers read Ellsberg's Ph.D. thesis, "Risk, Ambiguity, and Decision," "as it may provide insight into Ellsberg's decision to violate the law and subject himself to the risks involved." The Plumbers collected newspaper and magazine articles on Ellsberg and the Papers—"overt materials," in Hunt's spy lexicon—and video footage of Ellsberg. The Plumbers also investigated Ellsberg's associates. "If there is no conspiracy," Young asked, "what are the motives which bring together the individuals involved? Is it that they want to get control or exercise power? Do they have any nefarious motives?"[52]

Though Hunt floated into the office with his own tidbits from time to time, the Plumbers received most of their information from the FBI. Their secretary's first task was organizing stacks of FBI reports. Ehrlichman's receptionist would remember "a flurry" of these reports coming into Ehrlichman's office. Liddy attempted to coordinate and energize the FBI's efforts. "The FBI investigation has been characterized by a lack of a sense of urgency, substandard lead setting and the stifling effect of internecine administrative bickering," he wrote Krogh and Young. "What ought to have been a classic example of the all-out 'Bureau Special' investigation, in the tradition of the great kidnapping cases of the past, has failed to materialize." ("Bureau Special" denoted prompt attention and high priority.) "I made every effort to get it moved up to Bureau Special," Liddy recalls. "And they promised that it would." On August 10, Hoover reported that it had been, but officials continued to be disappointed. "Old, stale material" was Ehrlichman's characterization of one large batch of FBI documents.[53]

But the FBI threw its net widely. Agents approached a multitude of people. Sam Popkin found two G-men at the door of his Harvard office upon returning from a trip overseas. "I was scared, but I talked," Popkin remembers. "They asked me a whole lot of weird questions about Ellsberg. . . . Like, 'Is he still beating his wife? Is he still preoccupied with sex? Is he still crazy about this?' They were very, very leading questions. 'What kinds of emotional troubles is he having? What kinds of wild things is he doing? What kinds of stresses is he under? . . . Does he masturbate in Times Square at noon?' . . . They were really looking for dirt." And "it was like somebody told them to look for it." The FBI agents also seemed to be trying to determine Ellsberg's motives, and suggested money and glory.[54]

The FBI interviewed many of Ellsberg's former co-workers, including Jan Butler "endlessly." Andrew Marshall reported to the bureau in July that during a social gathering of people from MIT and Harvard that he had recently attended, "people laughingly termed Ellsberg as a 'hippie hypocrite' in that prior to Ellsberg's recent public appearances, he had been unkempt, featured long hair, open sandals and the usual hippie apparel," the FBI recorded. "He now makes his appearance as well dressed and neatly shorn. By way of background, the Marshalls stated that Ellsberg drinks sparingly, does not smoke, is a non-user of drugs although he had one controlled experiment at UCLA with LSD to which he reacted unfavorably, and is believed by people that have known him for years to have latent homosexual tendencies to which he has never given apparent rein." Of those "latent homosexual tendencies," Mary Marshall says, "There's an awful lot of homoerotic aspects to Dan. . . . He made no bones about the fact that he's tried everything." Roberta Wohlstetter, Marshall recalls, believed that Ellsberg was attracted to her husband, Albert, and to Andrew Marshall, "and Roberta always had the feeling that his freedom in talking about sex with her, but also with me . . . was . . . some way of involving us in his sexual fantasies." (Ellsberg later denied ever having a "homosexual affair.") The Marshalls told the FBI that Albert Wohlstetter had informed them he "would welcome the opportunity to talk to the FBI concerning Ellsberg." The bureau planned to interview him the next day.[55]

The FBI continued to interview Carol Ellsberg, who, in turn, continued to phone the bureau. Carol reported on, among other matters, her acrimonious conversations with Dan after he had surfaced from underground, his travel plans, political views ("she believes him to have been basically apolitical" when they were married, the FBI noted), bank accounts, and past income. Carol continued to provide names, including those of Dan's former girlfriends, some of whom the FBI tracked down. The bureau interviewed Yvonne Svenle at least five times. Justice's coordinator of its Ellsberg probe would recall that "the names of Yvonne Svenle and Carol Ellsberg were constantly being mentioned in discussions of the case as potential witnesses against Ellsberg." In late July, Carol related that she'd heard Dan and Patricia had visited Sandstone recently; she described what she'd heard about Sandstone and said Dan was reported to be a member.[56]

Ellsberg later told the Watergate prosecutors that the FBI "was going to all former girlfriends and always asked drug and sex questions," although he may not have been aware that his ex-wife was providing names, and he speculated that the *Time* magazine cover story on him, not Carol, had tipped off the Plumbers that he had seen a psychoanalyst. He didn't think Carol knew Lewis Fielding's name.[57]

Kimberly Rosenberg was also sought by the FBI, but she had fled the country. "As soon as the story broke, she headed for Canada," Anthony Russo remembers. "An Immigration and Naturalization Service lookout notice has been placed against her possible return," the Los Angeles FBI office reported on July 20. The FBI contacted friends and relatives of Rosenberg, and her ex-husband provided information on her. The FBI tracked Janaki Tschannerl to Africa.[58] She was probably one of the "females of foreign birth and extraction" in Ellsberg's life who had caught Howard Hunt's attention.

Frank Rich had just completed a piece on Ellsberg for *Esquire* when, to his amazement, two FBI agents visited him in London. The agents knocked on his apartment door and invited him down to the American embassy, where he was led down a hall to "a room that was out of a parody of the FBI," he recounts. "It looked like they were going to shake you down. Full of framed photographs of J. Edgar Hoover, with guns mounted on the wall. . . . And I was asked a series of the stupidest questions that I'd ever heard."[59]

Two FBI agents showed up at the office of Dr. Robert Akeret, a psychotherapist, in New York on June 14, only one day after publication of the Papers began. Akeret's significance: he treated Patricia Ellsberg. The date is according to him; a record in the Watergate Special Prosecution Force files indicates he was interviewed on June 17. Either date indicates how quickly the FBI was targeting Ellsberg. "They arrived first thing in the morning before I started working," Akeret told me. "Caught me before my first person." The FBI agents "suspected that I was part of a conspiracy having to do with the Pentagon Papers," he recalls. "That's what they kept pushing for. . . . They wanted to know where they were, and who had them, and all kinds of things, all centered on the Pentagon Papers. And they were trying to somehow implicate me in this thing. Which I thought was kind of amusing. Although at the time I was scared." That's partly because Patricia had talked to Akeret about the Papers; she'd expressed her worries and sought advice. "They wanted to know, 'Was she involved?,' and 'How was she involved?,' and all kinds of things like that," Akeret remembers.[60]

Akeret says he refused to talk to the FBI. "I simply said that I knew nothing and even if I did know something I wouldn't say, because it's confidential. . . . They were there about a half an hour, and then they left." Akeret was not called before the grand jury; David Nissen disclosed afterward that he had thought it would be "bad PR," though "fruitful," to do so.[61]

Come November 11, Akeret had more reason to be concerned. On that day, burglars broke into his penthouse office. The burglars were apparently not scared of heights, as (or so Akeret surmises) they walked along an outside wall, climbed a fence, and entered through an unlocked door on his terrace. They then searched his office and left it in disarray. "It just looked like people had gone through my drawers and stuff, and pushed things around, and gone into the file," Akeret remembers. But there was "no way of knowing which file they'd gone through. . . . They could have gone into any file." Akeret noticed that the burglars took only some blank checks; the drawer in which he kept his checks was open. He didn't report the burglary to police. "My feeling was, if I reported it to the police, they would want to know who did I suspect doing it, and that would get into confidentiality," he explains. Akeret suspected the burglars had targeted his Patricia Ellsberg file. He theorized that they took his checks to make it look like a garden-variety robbery. He still suspects Patricia Ellsberg was their target, though "I have no proof."[62]

Akeret informed Patricia of the break-in at their next session. Patricia and Dan also suspected it was a Plumbers job. Justice looked into the burglary, but its records are unavailable; a note on one Justice Department memo said an interview of Akeret was "not necessary," however, suggesting it didn't believe the Plumbers were involved. Other Watergate Special Prosecution Force records indicate that the prosecutors suspected that Bernard Barker, Eugenio Martinez, and Felipe DeDiego had ties to several burglaries in addition to the Fielding and Watergate jobs, but these records do not mention the Akeret entry. Hunt denied being aware of any covert entries targeting Ellsberg or his relatives besides the Fielding break-in. When I asked Liddy about the Akeret burglary, he said, matter-of-factly, "Not our op." Asked if he had any knowledge of the break-in at all, he said, again, "Not our op." Liddy told me he was unaware of any White House links to it and knew nothing about it. Akeret offers another possibility: "I also did some work with some drug dealers that no one else would work with, in trying to get them out of their business. . . . It's conceivable that someone could have gone in there looking for that kind of material."[63]

The FBI also approached other people whose services Patricia Ellsberg had purchased. A dentist who had treated her only once was asked "what he knew about me and what his relationship with me was," Patricia testified in an affidavit. She told a journalist that agents had asked to see some X rays of her teeth, but that her dentist had refused to provide them. A woman Patricia bought some clothing from was asked about the purchase and "whether she knew anything else about me," Patricia testified.[64]

The FBI probed the Ellsbergs' financial records. "Microfilm records of Daniel Ellsberg's Carte Blanche credit card account were obtained and are being analyzed," the Los Angeles FBI office reported on July 20. "A check . . . concerning Daniel Ellsberg's Bank Americard account determined that his is a very active account and that Ellsberg is in arrears in payment." (Nothing had changed in that department since Carol had lived with him.) The Los Angeles FBI office reported six days later on the dates, destinations, and plane fares of numerous trips Ellsberg had taken as evidenced on his Carte Blanche account. The FBI also examined his hotel stays and phone calls that he'd placed from the hotels; Howard Hunt's safe was later found to contain records of calls Ellsberg had made to Yvonne Svenle from his Cambridge home and from the Bel Air Hotel in Los Angeles. The government subpoenaed some of Ellsberg's "old telephone records," but those "were not available since the records were not kept back that far," Krogh and Young reported to Ehrlichman. Other records showed Ellsberg had made "a series of calls" to Dr. Fielding just before publication of the Papers. Some friends with whom the Ellsbergs spoke over the phone were visited by the FBI afterward, Patricia said.[65]

Polly and Philip Cronin, who had known Dan at Harvard, discovered that their home phone was tapped after Polly was quoted in the *Boston Globe* about him. "You'd hear breathing, you'd hearing clicking on and off," Polly remembers.[66]

The FBI would later deny that it wiretapped Ellsberg himself or members of his family. While that is quite possible, it is still a bit difficult to believe. "I'm sure they had that guy covered six ways from Sunday, finally, electronically," Liddy argues. "You know, if the bureau is going to tap you, they would do more than just tap your phone. They would want your room conversations, too. I mean, I remember listening to Sam Giancana and Phyllis McGuire making love. You could even hear the bed springs squeak." The Plumbers' secretary would recall reading an FBI report on a phone conversation of Ellsberg's that she felt was "quite obviously the report of a wiretap on Ellsberg," though the conversation took place before the Papers were released, when a tap on Ellsberg would have been less likely. Robert Mardian's files on Ellsberg were later found to include one folder on "Electronic Surveillance Information." Ehrlichman's receptionist remembered reading an FBI report on Ellsberg based on a wiretap that included "something about his sex life," though she thought he was a friend of the person being tapped; she also read another long report on Ellsberg and it was clear to her that he had been overheard. But Ellsberg's lawyers never found any proof that he'd been tapped.[67]

Ellsberg was overheard numerous times on a White House wiretap of Morton Halperin's home telephone. That tap began in 1969. FBI logs of Ellsberg's conversations on Halperin's phone undoubtedly informed some government reports on him. In these conversations, Ellsberg characteristically "talked openly about drug use and sex," Seymour Hersh wrote. In one conversation in late August 1969, Ellsberg asked his half brother, Harry, if he wished to take "a trip" on some mescaline he had, and advised Harry not to do it at the same time as his wife. Ellsberg told another person "he had left a satchel filled with 'stuff' at his friend's house," the FBI recorded. On July 6, 1971, Nixon and aides discussed the need to review wiretap records to determine whether damaging information on Ellsberg or his co-conspirators could be found.[68]

The FBI also denied wiretapping Lewis Fielding. Yet John Mitchell ordered surveillance of Fielding, and Fielding's attorney told his client it was best to "assume that my office might be bugged," Fielding testified. Ellsberg, who saw Fielding "weekly" during his trial ("just to talk," he said), recalled Fielding telling him that he couldn't guarantee his office was secure.[69]

The Plumbers themselves did not tap Ellsberg. "We don't know that there was any wiretapping by these bums," Nixon remarked to Ehrlichman. After Ehrlichman reported that David Young had told him "flatly there was not," Nixon said, "What the hell did they do then? What did we pay them [for]?" "There was no bugging, I found," Nixon told another aide. "They had the FBI do bugging once it got into the case, let me assure you."[70]

Ellsberg continued to worry he was being tapped. During several conversations with his ex-wife in early July, he "made frequent references to the fact that his telephone is tapped," Carol Ellsberg told the FBI. "As proof of this he stated that while he was in hiding, an associate of his left his place of seclusion and made a telephone call from a public phone booth to Lloyd Shearer. Shortly after the call was placed Daniel stated that plainclothesmen immediately descended upon the phone booth and staked it out for twenty-four hours." Again Dan would not talk with Carol over the phone. "He always felt the FBI was listening on the phone," Carol remembers. But Charles Nesson told her that summer that he didn't think so—"too big a case." Patricia Ellsberg thought her New York apartment might be bugged. Dan later theorized to the Watergate prosecutors that a "secret agency was wiretapping him." Surely he was under surveillance. Jeremy Larner got the impression that Ellsberg enjoyed the thought of being wiretapped: it confirmed the importance of his act.[71]

During the summer of 1971 Ellsberg had his mail at MIT picked up by taxi and brought to his home. He testified in an affidavit that one of the taxi drivers told him that all drivers with their company "had been instructed that when they picked up my mail at MIT they were to stop by their dispatcher's office on the way to my home so that he could check the mail." The driver, Ellsberg testified, said the dispatcher had recently stated while checking his mail that it was being done at the direction of the FBI, and that "all pick-ups of persons from my home were to be reported, with details as to where these persons were taken."[72]

The FBI thought Ellsberg might have stored his cache of classified documents—"ELLSBERG'S HOARD," the *Los Angeles Times* would call it in a gigantic front-page headline—at a Bekins storage facility in Beverly Hills. He might also have "photographic films of documents" there, the FBI believed. By the time the bureau moved on Bekins, David Obst had removed a large footlocker that a Bekins employee told the FBI contained "a large quantity of Instamatic film magazines" that could be used with a camera and another device to copy documents. Following discussions in the White House at the highest level, and after Bekins had alerted the FBI of plans by Ellsberg to remove them, the bureau confiscated 28 of Ellsberg's other parcels.[73]

The FBI pursued leads on Ellsberg's past, personality, and lifestyle. On August 3, at Nixon's request, the bureau provided Krogh a "comprehensive background paper" on Ellsberg. The FBI hoped a memo it sent to Haldeman and Mitchell on Ellsberg's "character" would illuminate his motivation for releasing the Papers and his "desire to dramatize his activities in this regard." Ellsberg's drug use, including his participation in LSD experiments in the early 1960s, attracted the bureau's interest, as did other aspects of his "rather peculiar background" (to use Hunt's words). Only two days after Carol Ellsberg had spoken of Sandstone, Robert Mardian sent Mitchell an FBI "daily summary" of its Ellsberg investigation (apparently for the first time) that noted "Ellsberg and his wife's visit to the 'Sandstone Club' for sexual orgies." The FBI investigated Sandstone. Two agents may have even joined the fun. Carol Ellsberg reported that a friend who had recently visited Sandstone had told her that the operator of the club had stated "that two male persons had come to this location just subsequent to Daniel Ellsberg's departure and although they did not identify themselves, it was the consensus of opinion that these two individuals were FBI agents," the Los Angeles FBI office recorded. "These two individuals were also in a naked state."[74]

Of course, the Plumbers were reading all this stuff. Liddy reported the Ellsbergs' visit to Sandstone to Dr. Bernard Malloy, the chief of the CIA's psychiatric staff, for the CIA's work on a second psychological profile of Ellsberg. "The club caters to individuals interested in sexual orgies," Liddy informed Malloy, virtually quoting from an FBI teletype on Carol Ellsberg's report. "According to information developed by the reporting agency, persons present at the club are in a complete state of undress and perform various forms of sexual activity in front of each other. We will continue to keep you advised of additional information on this subject as it is received."[75]

Richard Nixon, who had developed an unhealthy fixation on Ellsberg and his co-conspirators, was kept closely apprised of the Plumbers' investigation.

According to Watergate prosecutors' notes on an interview with an aide to Ehrlichman, "Ellsberg and Fielding stuff went directly to president. Priority (urgent, imminent)."[76]

The White House continued to debate when, and even whether, to prosecute Ellsberg. "I don't want that fellow Ellsberg to be brought up until after the election," Nixon remarked to Haldeman on July 1. "Convict the son-of-a-bitch *in the press. That's the way it's done.*" But Charles Colson argued that prosecuting the "son-of-a-bitch" could rally "our natural constituency." "He is a natural villain to the extent that he can be painted evil," Colson wrote Haldeman. Moreover, they could use Ellsberg to tarnish other enemies, like Democrats. But Colson worried, as did Nixon and Hunt, that Ellsberg could become a martyr. "It seems to me indispensable that he be prosecuted," Hunt told Colson. "Viscerally I want to see this guy hung. My more cautious and reflective self says 'let's not do it unless we can do it to the profit of the Administration.'"[77]

There might also be problems winning a conviction, officials worried. Hunt and Liddy, who wanted to "nail Ellsberg in a vindictive sense," felt the indictment had been drawn up hastily and was unsatisfactory. To convict Ellsberg on the espionage count, the government had to show (among other things) that release of the Papers had damaged the national defense. But the White House was having problems gathering evidence on such damage. Fred Buzhardt worried that the government was likely to lose the case "because we cannot prove sufficient damage." He and others felt that "it would be better to have the case dismissed on a technicality (e.g., refusal to produce documents) than have Ellsberg go to trial and be acquitted."[78]

Officials also didn't like the idea of giving Ellsberg a podium. Who knew what he might say about war atrocities or stupid policies?[79]

John Vann confided to Alexander Haig that Ellsberg hoped to "make his trial a political circus—in short, an attack on the Administration's Vietnam policy" (in Haig's words). Vann was now betraying Ellsberg. He had considered Ellsberg's release of the Papers a stab in the back; now he was doing his own number. Vann had apparently cooperated in Vietnam with investigators who had questioned him about Ellsberg and the Papers (though he told Ellsberg that none of the investigators "made his trip worthwhile"). He had also advised Henry Kissinger on how the government should proceed against Ellsberg. And after Ellsberg had confided his defense strategy to him during a phone conversation, Vann reported it to Buzhardt. Vann continued to try to distance himself from Ellsberg. He avoided talking about the Papers. He told at least one person that Ellsberg was crazy and a drug addict. In January 1972, Vann told Ellsberg that he shouldn't take it seriously when he heard that he was making derogatory remarks about him, however, that he was just trying to create distance. Vann also told Ellsberg he would testify on his behalf at his trial and would say anything that he wanted, Ellsberg recounted. The distance, Vann said, would make his testimony more effective. But Vann told his son Peter that he did not want to testify.[80]

Vann was playing a double game. When I told his widow, Mary Jane Vann, about it, it didn't surprise her. "That sounds like something he'd do," she said. "And it was to protect him. Whatever he thought was good for him, he did." Her husband "was an opportunist," she said. "He was not a loyal person. He had no loyalty to anyone but himself. . . . He would always go on to protect himself . . . or to get what he wanted." And by then, she thought, he had changed for the worse. "He had come to hate Americans and America" and to believe that the Vietnamese "were the most beautiful, intelligent people in the world, and that we were all idiots and morons and ugly and all of that," she recalls. "And that meant our children and me. He just thought we were all useless idiots. . . . He didn't even want his children anymore. I mean, he just had nothing to do with the kids. . . . He was terrible to my kids, just terrible to them."[81]

At Ehrlichman's instruction, Krogh and Young advised Mardian to "take steps" to delay the start of Ellsberg's trial until March of 1972. Haig, like Nixon, thought it would be best to wait until after the November elections. But when the trial did come, the White House took an "active interest" in Ellsberg's prosecution and "tried to make it as vigorous and far-reaching as possible," one Watergate investigator would note. It acted to "spur them on."[82]

———◦◉◦———

Meanwhile, Howard Hunt was hard at work gathering information geared toward destroying Ellsberg's public image. Hunt's White House safe, which he later warned Colson's secretary was "loaded," would soon hold a thick "Ellsberg" folder containing three copies of a 28-page chronology of Ellsberg's life (one was a working copy); 31 pages concerning Yvonne Svenle, including her FBI interviews; copies of FBI reports on its interviews of Carol Ellsberg; and press clippings on Daniel Ellsberg. Hunt talked to John Vann about Ellsberg. He wished to interview Germaine, Ellsberg's Eurasian lover in Vietnam, too. At Colson's request, Hunt interviewed Lou Conein, but during a boozy conversation that "became more disjointed and garbled" as time passed, a tape recorder that had been placed in a cushion of a sofa malfunctioned under Hunt and Conein's weight. Hunt tape-recorded a phone conversation with Conein the next day in order to recover the lost material; Colson participated under the alias "Fred Charles," White House security man. "Charles" asked Conein if Ellsberg or Vann "had any connections with the drug trafficking" in Vietnam. Conein said no.[83]

With Nixon barking orders, Colson spearheaded the White House's campaign to smear Ellsberg—"the dirty tricks business on getting stuff out," in the words of Ehrlichman, who would later deny under oath knowledge of any such business. Colson told Krogh that Nixon was "breathing down his neck" to get out damaging information on Ellsberg. Both Colson and Hunt wanted to "nail the guy cold." "I think there is a fertile field here," Colson told Hunt.[84] Although Colson was the only official later imprisoned for gathering and disseminating derogatory information on Ellsberg, the other principals, including Nixon, Ehrlichman, and his fellow Plumbers, were knee deep in the mud.

To help nail Ellsberg, and after Colson had discussed the matter with Nixon, Hunt prepared a "scurrilous, libelous" essay (in the words of a Watergate prosecutor) on Leonard Boudin, Ellsberg's lead attorney. "Devil's Advocate—The Strange Affinities of Attorney Leonard Boudin" detailed Boudin's "remarkably extensive" "left-wing and Communist associations" and "career-long defense of the Communist Party, Castro Cuba, assorted spies, perjurers, fellow travelers, conspirators, agitators and violent revolutionaries," in Hunt's words. "The art of espionage, of course, is seldom conducted in the open," wrote Hunt, an author of spy novels. "Nevertheless, it has been said with some certainty that over the years Leonard Boudin has been a contact of both the Czech and Soviet espionage organizations." Hunt noted that Boudin had been required to register as an agent of Cuba and had even "once cut sugar cane to help Castro meet Cuba's export commitments to the Soviet Union." Now, "as Castro's lawyer, he travels frequently to Cuba where he enjoys the revolutionary amenities of the 'Havana Libre' (formerly Hilton) Hotel, as an honored guest." Hunt's essay continued:

> And what of Boudin's client, Daniel Ellsberg?
>
> Most of what Daniel Ellsberg has said in public since he acknowledged stealing the Pentagon Papers seems calculated to position him as having responded to an order of morality higher than his onetime solemn undertakings to his country. This rationale, let it be remembered, was earlier employed by atomic spies Klaus Fuchs, David Greenglass, Morton Sobell and Bruno Pontecorvo.
>
> And although there is as yet no conclusive evidence that Daniel Ellsberg acted on specific instructions of the Soviet Union—as did those earlier informants—the distinct possibility remains that Ellsberg's "higher order" will one day be revealed as the Soviet Fatherland. . . .

> Turning again to history, one wonders whether, as the date of his trial approaches, Ellsberg will lose his nerve and flee to Communist asylum.[85]

Hardly, though Hunt obviously loved writing this kind of stuff.

David Young sent Hunt's hit piece up to Ehrlichman. The next day, August 24, the day before Hunt and Liddy embarked on their reconnaissance mission to case Dr. Lewis Fielding's office, Ehrlichman passed it to Colson with a cover note stating that it "should be useful in connection with the recent request that we get something out on Ellsberg." The "recent request," the Watergate Special Prosecutor Leon Jaworski would later note, referred to Nixon's request to leak derogatory information on Boudin. Ehrlichman informed Nixon two weeks later, "We planted a bunch of stuff with columnists . . . about some of this group, about Ellsberg's lawyers, about the Bay of Pigs. Some of this stuff is . . . going to start surfacing." "Good," Nixon responded. On August 26, Colson passed Hunt's piece to Jerald terHorst of the *Detroit News*. TerHorst said later that Colson gave him the impression that Nixon had approved dissemination of the piece (though terHorst added that "in almost every conversation with Colson he always had the impression that Colson wanted him to believe that whatever he was doing was with the knowledge and direction of the president"). Colson told the Watergate prosecutors that he cautioned terHorst "to check it carefully because the source (Hunt) was a novelist and might overstate things." Hunt would claim his piece formed the second half of an article terHorst wrote on Ellsberg's defense team in January 1972. While that is a slight exaggeration, the last third of the article did unmistakably bear Hunt's imprint.[86]

It is impossible to know how much other harmful information Colson and friends disseminated about Ellsberg, who later said that he knew they were collecting dirt on him and was surprised they didn't seem to be using it. He believed they were gathering it to blackmail him into silence and into keeping those other classified documents to himself. But he would say after his trial, "There really is nothing true that I've been able to think of which would embarrass me at this point."[87]

"With the recent article on Ellsberg's lawyer, Boudin, we have already started on a negative press image for Ellsberg," Young wrote Ehrlichman on August 26. But, Young advised, "the point of Buchanan's memorandum on attacking Ellsberg through the press should be borne in mind; namely, that the situation being attacked is too big to be undermined by planted leaks among the friendly press. If there is to be any damaging of Ellsberg's image and those associated with him, it will therefore be necessary to fold in the press planting with the congressional investigation" of the Pentagon Papers affair, which would hopefully present "a very negative picture" and "identify Ellsberg's associates and supporters on the new left with this negative image." Colson passed material on Ellsberg to members of Congress and tried to get the hearings started; when one congressman told him it might require a call from Nixon, Colson was apprehensive unless the president "could cover it in such terms that it would never come back to haunt him." Legislators were unexcited about holding the hearings. Yet, by pushing them, "it seems to me that we have a good bit to gain politically and with very little risk," Colson wrote Ehrlichman. But Ehrlichman directed Young and Krogh to "turn him (Colson) off."[88]

Two days later, after Nixon spoke of the difficulty of getting "that issue of the Pentagon Papers up front and center again," Ehrlichman observed, in yet another taped conversation, "We have an ally in this, and that is Ellsberg, who still has quite a lot of visibility, and who's very distressed with what's happening. Because they are covering it up. And he's going around the country on television, screaming and hollering about it. . . . You see, that was his great sacrifice for the nation, right."[89] (Ehrlichman was apparently referring to Ellsberg's frustration that the press was not focusing enough on the revelations of the Papers.)

Colson was meanwhile scheming about other ways to "make a little public hay" from Ellsberg's release of the documents. "To paint Ellsberg black is probably a good thing; to link him into a conspiracy which suggests treasonous conduct is also a good thing; but the real political payoff will come only if we can establish that there is what the *National Review* has called a 'counter-government' which is deliberately trying to undermine U.S. foreign policy and the U.S. position in the world and that it is the president who stands against this 'counter-government,' who conquers them and who rescues the nation from the subversion of these unsavory characters," Colson wrote Ehrlichman. The *National Review* article that caught Colson's eye argued that "it has been in one after another of the leading anti-Nixon newspapers that the Papers have appeared. . . . It is anti-Nixon CBS-Establishmentarian Walter Cronkite who got the interview with Ellsberg." Such opposition to the Nixon administration "constitutes an embryonic 'counter-government'" that "makes its own decisions about peace and war, friend and enemy, classifying or declassifying documents." Colson thought the article "one of the most effective explanations of what is really happening in our society that I have yet seen," he told Haldeman. "The 'counter-government' can be a very effective natural enemy for us to exploit. It also ties in perfectly to the Ellsberg conspiracy concept and is exactly the kind of thing I think that the majority of the American people would support the president in fighting and opposing."[90]

But "there is a second objective," Colson apprised Ehrlichman, where "I think the political payoff is even more significant": to "nail our prospective Democratic opponents." That could be done by publicizing revelations of the Papers, including those on the Kennedy administration's involvement in the 1963 Diem coup—"certain pay dirt," Colson called it. "Each of the prospective Democratic opponents next year can be vulnerable if we can tie them or their advisers into gross misjudgments committed during this period," wrote Colson, whose office drafted articles on such ties and fed them to another favorite conduit in the press, Nick Thimmesch. Senator Edmund Muskie, the likely Democratic presidential candidate, was "sort of the prime prospect in this whole thing," Ehrlichman commented. Colson believed they also had the Democrats "on a marvelous hook" since "most of them have defended the release of the documents." "Keep it stuck into the Democrats, so that they squabble about it," Nixon said.[91]

But "Round #1 of the Democrats civil war" (to use Colson's words) did not go as planned. The White House asked Lyndon Johnson to publicly denounce publication of the Papers. But it learned late the evening of June 18 "that Johnson had completely collapsed, was in a state of being totally unstrung, feels that the country is lost, that the president can't rule and that they're out to destroy him, etc.," Haldeman recorded in his diary. "So that ended any participation by him." Johnson bitterly claimed that the *New York Times* and *Washington Post* were trying to "re-execute" him.[92] Also, the congressional hearings on the Papers were never held.

The Plumbers were meanwhile pushing the CIA to develop a decent psychiatric profile of Ellsberg. After receiving the initial, disappointing effort, David Young asked that "we try again," one CIA official recalled. Young told Dr. Bernard Malloy that "the Ellsberg study had the highest priority" and had been requested by Ehrlichman and Kissinger. "I was informed that more biographic material was available," Malloy remembered. "I was requested to give examples of the kind of information needed. I pointed out that . . . data from early life from nurses or close relatives would be useful. I agreed with 'Mr. Linney' [Liddy] that school progress, including testing, would be helpful." Hunt told Malloy that "it would be useful for Dr. Ellsberg's first wife to be interviewed and he felt, 'You can easily arrange that under an operational alias.' It was pointed out that the first Mrs. Ellsberg would be cooperative." Hunt also indicated that Malloy "had been helpful in the medical management of one of his daughters." Malloy recalled that the Plumbers were intent on "undercutting Ellsberg."[93]

Malloy was uneasy about the Plumbers. They seemed to him and the CIA's other psychiatrists "to put an undue store on what psychiatry might do and what we might produce." Hunt's "enthusiasm" was worrisome to Malloy. "He seemed uncomfortable," Liddy remembers. "He seemed to be [feeling], 'Look, I have to be here, I have to do this. But I'm not in familiar surroundings.'"[94]

The Plumbers fed Malloy more data on Ellsberg—"poorly xeroxed classified FBI reports and Department of State documents," Malloy would remember. "While the additional information furnished further suggested that Ellsberg was under emotional pressure it was not possible to arrive at any firm conclusions or comprehensive understanding of the man's personality."[95]

Malloy and his colleagues remained skittish about the whole enterprise. Interviewing Carol Ellsberg would only be done with "the greatest reluctance," they agreed. Malloy simply wouldn't do it. After discussing their findings with the Plumbers, the CIA's psychiatrists hoped, another written profile would not be necessary. "We attempted to fend off a second paper by advising the White House participants that the new material did not add much to our previous information and that no study in depth would be forthcoming," one CIA psychiatrist testified. "It was hoped that this would put an end to the situation," Malloy recalled. It would be risky to have another paper floating around, one based on work that violated the CIA's charter, whose ultimate use they had no control over, and about a man soon to be on trial.[96]

But CIA Director Richard Helms overruled Malloy and his colleagues, and after a "hiatus" owing in part to the Fielding break-in, the Plumbers began leaning on the psychiatrists again, passing them more material on Ellsberg. The Plumbers pressured Malloy in particular, who told a CIA official that his worries did not involve "professional ethics" but legal issues; he desired "that the Agency's connection with this matter must never surface." "When do you deliver?" Hunt pressed Malloy on October 8. That month "Young put a big rush on everything," Malloy remembered.[97]

On October 27, Malloy presented the CIA's findings to the Plumbers orally, but Young, Hunt, and Liddy pressed him to produce a written profile "within a week and they specified that the paper was to bear no signature, no watermark and no subject's name. Interest was expressed in the subject's sexual proclivities and in how he might be manipulated." In an interview with Watergate prosecutors, Malloy recalled that "at this meeting Hunt was asking for Malloy's suggestion as to how Hunt could get 'leverage' on Ellsberg and suggested that someone might want to try to get Ellsberg to defect and go to Algeria before the Ellsberg trial. Hunt also pressed Malloy on how Ellsberg's sexual background could be used as a point of leverage against Ellsberg."[98]

The CIA's second psychological profile of Ellsberg, which Malloy presented to the Plumbers on November 12, was preceded by a note from Richard Helms to Young emphasizing that CIA "involvement in this matter should not be revealed in any context, formal or informal." Helms was slipping: he should have known better than to put that down on paper. The profile was twice as long as its predecessor and more speculative (the Plumbers had demanded a fuller "read-out" on Ellsberg). It was "highly impressionistic," the CIA's psychiatrists stressed, whereas "the *sine qua non* of the psychiatric approach is to obtain information directly from the person himself." Moreover, "these ideas have not been subjected to the usual leavening effect of time, nor has it been possible because of time pressures to subject these concepts to the time-tested procedure of peer review." And "unusually candid" public remarks by Ellsberg, which "may seem at first blush very helpful," the psychiatrists noted, might be "all the more distorted" given "the Subject's propensity to seemingly abrupt about-faces." The profile is worth quoting at length:

A very intelligent man, the Subject also seems to be a person with very strong, although fluctuant, emotional attachments. There is, however, no available evidence to indicate that he is emotionally disturbed in a psychotic or gross manner. Very little is available about his early background, but at 15 he did an about-switch when he gave up the piano at which he had been very proficient, and by his senior high school year he was captain of the basketball team. The loss of interest in the piano, and the subsequent concentration on a sport were associated with an automobile accident. . . . His father was driving and his mother and sister were killed. His father subsequently remarried. *It is possible that strong feelings of resentment and rage and frustration stirred up by death and personal illness or injury are associated with his apparently sudden and extreme shifts in loyalty and enthusiasm.*

In April 1967, the Subject was ill with hepatitis in Bangkok. . . . He had vigorously favored and participated in the pacification efforts of the Vietnam countryside as espoused by General Lansdale, and he had not been ostensibly distressed at that time by taking part in search and destroy missions in which it is quite possible that he actually killed the enemy himself. In 1967, John McNaughton . . . was killed in an airplane accident. It was in these circumstances, and on returning to the United States, that he retrospectively first speaks of feeling more and more that the U.S. should get out of Vietnam. It is possible that the anger and frustration engendered by his hepatitis (and immobilization by bedrest) combined with the loss by an accident of an erstwhile mentor (McNaughton) mobilized a shift in his views. (There may also have been disappointment in his relationship with General Lansdale.)

But if the Subject were this sensitive to these not uncommon stresses of life, what would account for the sudden shifts in his ideals, and in their emotional underpinnings? His central theme for leaking the Pentagon Papers has been that "the Executive" should not alone have so much unshared power as to plunge the country into war and the misery and death that it brings. It is probable that the Subject is not only referring here to the various presidents, but also to his own father whom, after all, he saw as responsible for the death of his mother and sister, injuring him to boot. . . . Whether this intense anger toward his father arose out of resentment toward him for taking the mother from him by death, or whether out of resentment at the father for not accepting him in her place and for marrying another woman, cannot be discerned from the material available. However, the writer would incline toward the latter because of his recurring disappointment in men whom he looks up to and tries to please. Through the years his intense resentment of his father and later those in authority over him was probably to some degree masked by his intellectual gifts which enabled him to differ, to contend, and to disagree in a rather useful way. It is even likely that important men were attracted and interested in this brilliant young man. But the relationships never seem to have been lasting ones, probably because at close range his essentially destructive resentment toward these men was sensed. (He was nudged out of the McNamara Study because his supervisors were uneasy with him.)

And yet, there is also an element of desiring to please, to be influenced by, and to placate an important man, through the use of his natural gifts. . . . But he always moved on. . . . It is probable that an important element in his moving on is associated with his dislike of these submissive qualities in himself. It is also probable that his blatant sexual activities with different women served as reassurance that he was his own man. It is possible that the very variety of women (Swedish to East Indian) was in itself an added assurance, but one cannot say further as to his choice of particular women based on the available material.

In the opinion of the writer, the intense injury to his pride, the rage and murderous anger which is stirred up when his gifts and abilities are not given proper recognition as he wishes is the motivating force for his shifting enthusiasms and for his search for another who will give him his proper due. . . . This Subject's intelligence and ability to carry out his revenge is of special note. Certainly there is evidence that the Subject was reacting with intensity when he called his analyst in the spring of 1971 after leaking the Pentagon Papers to say, "I'm free." It is quite true that in the highly competent kind of analysis with which it can be said with certainty that he was treated, that the non-responsiveness of the analyst *in the manner that gives proper recognition as the patient wishes it* for the gifts that are brought (in the Subject's case probably a dazzling intelligence and security information about the Pentagon) and for the work which is done in the analysis can mobilize intense anger and rage so compelling that the patient must leave the treatment situation to avoid actual physical violence to the analyst. The Subject did leave the analysis after two years (whether terminated by the analyst because of such potentials or by the patient matters little here), and to an important degree the leaking of the Pentagon Papers was also an act of aggression at his analyst, as well as at the president and his father. . . .

It is possible that the Subject is imbued with a certain degree of guilt at the strength of his murderous impulses, the results of which in this instance of the Pentagon Papers are harder for him to ignore. He has made statements that he expected to go to prison, even that he should go to prison for participating in murder (of Vietnamese). However, his sense of conscience has never been severe enough to lead to any such clear punishment-seeking behavior in the past, and it seems likely that on balance he will actively seek to avoid such an end.

It is of course possible that the Subject has more documents with which he will seek to continue to pursue his odyssey of being appreciated (and disappointed) by a senior personage. He has been somewhat active in various antiwar appearances which provide some small, cold measure of what he seeks. More importantly, however, he must also contend with the fact that in spite of the tumult and turmoil engendered by his disclosures, that he has been essentially unsuccessful in gaining his vengeful primary objective—diluting the power of "the Executive." Rather, Vietnam is fading somewhat as the foreign affairs focus of the country shifts to the president's upcoming trips to Moscow and Peking.

It is probable that the Subject, left to his own devices, will continue to play out his pattern of seeking to gain and failing to find the appreciation of important and senior people. Such recurring hopes of course offer the possibility that an important and senior person to whom he would bring gifts would for a time have great leverage and influence with him. Another point of leverage is suggested by his reaction to the disappointment when he is not given his proper due by a senior person for whom he has previously felt respect and admiration. At such times he seems especially prone to change his physical location. His abilities and his experiences (since June 1971) have combined to enable him to expect (and to some degree receive) a special kind of treatment and attention, but personally his pursuit is doomed to failure, for what he seeks is a close, intimate relation of a boy to his father, and that he can no longer have. He could possibly change this pattern if he were to return to psychiatric treatment; perhaps a modification of analysis. If he were to return and participate wholeheartedly, it is possible that his destructive energy could be contained and even used to affect some change in his repetitious behavior.[99]

Although the profile contains several errors (not all included here) and in places is obviously reductionist (particularly where it tries to tie Ellsberg's anger at his father or analyst to his politics and release of the Papers), one is inclined to say "Not bad," given the shortage of information available to the CIA's psychiatrists and the pressures on them to speculate. Their discussions of Ellsberg's narcissistic rage and need for appreciation are largely on the mark. But the Plumbers did not find this profile much better than its predecessor. "It was my impression that the material and information provided were not of direct interest or usefulness to Hunt, Liddy, or Young," Malloy recalled. "These men were interested in obtaining information which could be used to defame or manipulate Ellsberg." "At least we received no other requests," another CIA psychiatrist noted. When I asked Liddy what help the two profiles were to the Plumbers, he responded, "They were of no use. . . . And Hunt was complaining about it."[100]

After the profiles were revealed publicly in 1973, some of Malloy's worries proved valid. His attorney wrote to a member of the Watergate Special Prosecution Force:

> Dr. Malloy is engaged in the private practice of psychiatry in addition to his services to the Central Intelligence Agency. Public notoriety associating Dr. Malloy with the Watergate matter has proved harmful to his practice. . . . We would like to request that the documents which will be forwarded to you by the Central Intelligence Agency be handled in a confidential manner and that no release of Dr. Malloy's name be made to the press. If any public reference to Dr. Malloy is necessary, we request that it be by some description as "a member of the medical staff of the Central Intelligence Agency" or by some similar phrase.[101]

Though the Plumbers shut down their operation in late 1971, Liddy and Hunt were recruited for another mission involving Ellsberg in May of 1972. It, too, was a White House blunder, one whose story is rife with the low comedy characteristic of the seamy side of the Nixon administration.

———— ◈ ————

When Charles Colson got wind of an antiwar protest scheduled for the Capitol steps in Washington the evening of May 3, 1972, he began plotting to turn it to the White House's political advantage. A memo he sent to Jeb Magruder of the Committee to Re-elect the President (CREEP) reads in full: "Attached is an announcement of a rally upcoming this week at which I am sure our friends who would like to send more SAMs to North Vietnam to shoot down U.S. pilots will be present. Now that we have a little warning, let's orchestrate this one perfectly. I think without any doubt we can get a couple of Viet Cong flags, several posters and perhaps one or two scalps. Would you put your troops into this and let me know how it is set up in advance so that we can perhaps turn the publicity our way for a change."[102]

Colson hoped a counterdemonstration would generate publicity harmful to the antiwar movement and embarrass the notables scheduled to speak, including Ellsberg, the radical lawyer William Kunstler, the singer Judy Collins, and some "ass-hole" liberal congressmen. Colson informed Magruder "the craziest of the crazies" would be there. When J. Edgar Hoover was found dead on an Oriental rug next to his bed on May 2 and arrangements were made for his body to lie in state in the Capitol Rotunda the day of the demonstration, Colson's political hopes grew. The protesters would now appear disrespectful to the late, great FBI director, he envisioned. Colson also had narrower objectives. He was eager to obtain a National Liberation Front flag to present to President Nixon, whom in all likelihood Colson informed of his plans for the protest, Watergate prosecutors concluded. Colson "said that the boss—meaning the president—was upset" about the protest and directed, "I want that flag so I can present it as a trophy to the boss," Liddy remembers. It was to be presented like a "head on a platter." Though Colson later denied any knowledge of the operation (he was "sick and tired of smear reports," he said), he admitted to an aide, William Rhatican, that "he had talked a good deal around the White House about his interest in getting a Viet Cong flag." (One Nixon advance man recalled that some kind of award was given for capturing a Viet Cong flag at demonstrations on the road.)[103]

Colson also sought a physical confrontation. "If heads are knocked, that's alright. That's Ellsberg's problem," he told aides, according to notes in the prosecutors' files. "Good for us—hurt Ellsberg." Colson had a vendetta against Ellsberg, one of the prosecutors concluded. Rhatican would remember Colson "bitching about Ellsberg traveling all over the country," speaking and raising money for his defense. Colson kept close track of Ellsberg's activities. John Lofton, a Republican National Committee person involved in organizing the counterdemonstration, said Colson "was particularly interested in Ellsberg." Colson seemed to Rhatican to hate Ellsberg almost as much as he hated Ted Kennedy. That said a lot. Further upsetting Colson and others in the White House, Ellsberg had just released another top-secret document—NSSM-1. Parts of it were published by Jack Anderson, the *New York Times*, the *Washington Post*, and *Newsweek*.[104]

Colson directed Magruder and Rhatican to have CREEP round up some young Nixon supporters for the counterdemonstration. Colson, who'd had a hand in a violent attack on antiwar protesters by construction workers in New York two years earlier, asked Magruder to get some toughs to protect the young Nixon supporters when things got rough. Colson emphasized to Magruder the importance of getting the toughs. Magruder was apprehensive; this was another dubious scheme by "that goddamn Colson," and the two men, who didn't get along well, went through "the usual hassle." But Colson told Magruder that Nixon wanted this done. Ken Rietz, CREEP's youth director, refused to put his troops into a potentially violent situation, however. Going after an NLF flag would "cause trouble," Rietz believed. When Rhatican informed Colson of this reaction at CREEP, Colson directed, "Tell those clowns over there this is something I want done and they better be responsive." He would take care of it, Colson told Rhatican. He'd get Howard Hunt and "his boys" from Miami to handle it. They knew how to deal with demonstrators. The Cubans "were to be disrupters," Rhatican testified later.[105]

Magruder had an assistant summon Liddy to his office. These two men also didn't like each other. Two months earlier, Liddy had threatened to rip Magruder's arm off and beat him to death with it. Magruder asked Liddy to recruit some men to get the flag and protect the others. Liddy told CREEP's Bart Porter he needed $10,000 for the mission. Magruder deemed this "ridiculous." Liddy launched into "a tirade against Magruder." He and Hunt came back with a request for $5,300, which was approved. Liddy returned $2,000 after the operation. "The way it worked with Porter was he would give me the money, and I would receipt it, and then I'd come back to him with an envelope full of receipts," Liddy remembers. "And anything that was left over, there it is, and there's the receipts to match what's not there. And it all would go in an envelope, and that would go in the safe. And at the end"—with the Watergate arrests—"he said, 'You know, you'd better get rid of all that stuff.'"[106]

Liddy spoke to Hunt, telling him that he had "a high-level requirement to level" on him. Liddy asked Hunt to bring up his men from Miami. Hunt promptly called Bernard Barker and asked him to recruit around ten good men. Hunt would speak to Barker over the phone at least a dozen times between May 1 and May 4. He likely received direct instructions from Colson, Watergate prosecutors believed. With the help of Eugenio Martinez, veteran of the Fielding job, Barker recruited eight others, including Felipe DeDiego, another Fielding break-in veteran. Again Barker was in charge, although by the end of this operation one recruit "did not think that anyone was particularly in charge."[107]

The eight recruits were told different purposes of their mission: to attend Hoover's funeral and pay their respects to "this outstanding fighter against communism"; to protect Hoover's casket; to demonstrate against the "hippies and communists" ("It doesn't take much, really, to get me started into something that's against communists," one said later); to confront the protesters; to meet with U.S. officials to discuss "liberating Cuba;" and to "bring us closer together as a team." When one asked a comrade about their purpose, he was told "that he should not worry, that they were staying inside the country." Some felt the CIA was behind the trip; they knew Barker had worked for the CIA. According to one, Pablo Fernandez, a community college student who had a reputation as "a hippie fighter" as well as "a hustler with a loose mouth who was given to boasting," some Cubans were leery of Barker because they felt he might "turn them in to the authorities" if he found a reason, and that Barker had "the reputation of liking money." Barker told at least one of the men there would be future operations. Barker, who wasn't telling the recruits all he knew about this operation but wasn't yet fully informed himself, purchased ten airline tickets on May 2 with "crisp new $100 bills." (His travel agent would shortly sell Martinez tickets to fly to Washington for the Watergate break-ins.) When one of the Cubans offered Barker $100 for his plane fare, Barker accepted it, though he was receiving cash and instructions from Hunt in large white envelopes.[108] Yes, he did like money.

Before the Cubans boarded their flight to Washington at noon on May 3, Barker or Martinez told them "they should leave any weapons behind." Even a penknife would set off the metal detectors, one warned a comrade. Sitting on the same flight with them was the actor Donald Sutherland, who was scheduled to speak at the antiwar rally; he was the enemy. Barker and his men traveled under aliases. Barker explained that this was in case the plane was hijacked to Cuba (though he subsequently apprised one recruit there might be trouble and thus he wanted their identities concealed). On the flight the men were uncertain about their real purpose in Washington. When Fernandez told Martinez that he did not like three of the other recruits as they had "bad reputations" and were considered "unstable and unreliable," Martinez told him "he should not worry about it."[109]

Upon landing in Washington, Barker left the group to phone Hunt for instructions, then the men took a limousine to a hotel, where one noticed that there was a fictitious name on his airline ticket. He approached Barker, who told him "not to worry about it, that everything was under control." Another tried to register at the hotel desk, only to forget his alias; he was forced to consult his airline ticket. One wonders what the hotel desk clerk thought. Because of booking problems, some of the men had to stay at another hotel. According to Fernandez, Barker and Martinez did not stay at either hotel that night; Barker left the first name and two telephone numbers of a woman through whom they could be reached.[110]

As his men engaged in some sightseeing before the evening rally, Barker went to Hunt's office. Hunt instructed Barker to have his men heckle and yell "traitor" when Ellsberg spoke, and to approach the speaker's platform. Hunt also gave Barker xeroxed newspaper photographs of Ellsberg and Kunstler. Hunt directed Barker to show them to his men so they would recognize Ellsberg and Kunstler. (Charles Colson's secretary had earlier made copies of such photographs.) Hunt probably also told Barker to capture an NLF flag if one was displayed and to have his men beat up Ellsberg, Kunstler, and other protesters, Watergate prosecutors concluded.[111]

Hunt claimed later that Liddy gave all these instructions to Barker, but the Watergate prosecutors saw through that. "Hunt was the person who would give the orders to the Cubans," Liddy recalls. "They practically worshipped Hunt. They didn't know me from Adam." Actually, Barker and DeDiego knew Liddy as "George Leonard" from the Fielding job. He was still George Leonard.[112]

Barker briefed his men back at the hotel. He reported that he'd been advised there was going to be a demonstration at Hoover's funeral and that the demonstrators would be raising a Viet Cong flag. They were to seize the flag and prevent it from being raised. Barker passed around the pictures of Ellsberg and Kunstler as well as leaflets announcing the rally. He told his men they should look for Ellsberg ("a traitor") and Kunstler. They should also attempt to break up the demonstration, to terminate it, and to prevent Ellsberg and Kunstler from speaking. According to *Time* magazine, Barker said of Ellsberg, "Our mission is to hit him—to call him a traitor and punch him in the nose. Hit him and run." Watergate prosecutors concluded that Ellsberg and Kunstler were both specifically targeted for attack. Barker informed his men that they would receive no trouble from police, but gave them a phone number to call if they were arrested; Pablo Fernandez assumed it was for "some influential person in the CIA who would help them." There were also higher-level people he could call, conveyed Barker, who planned to phone his wife in Miami at various intervals; if he failed to call, she was to phone a lawyer. Barker also told his men that if they beat up some of the hippies, the U.S. government would be more amenable to liberating Cuba. When Fernandez remarked that the men had no weapons, Barker said, "Just use your hands." One of the men expressed concern to Fernandez about fighting the hippies, since he had recently had hernia surgery. Fernandez said he would "watch out for him."[113]

After viewing Hoover's casket, Barker and his troops, their anticommunist sentiments freshly stimulated, searched for the location of the antiwar rally, which they found only after some difficulty. They then gathered on a balcony and watched the protesters set up their stage, sound system, and a canvas tent to protect speakers from the rain that had been falling throughout much of the day. Barker was sizing up the situation. Some of his men recognized Kunstler and Ellsberg after they appeared; Barker recognized Sutherland from the plane. Martinez told Fernandez he was going to try to get close to Kunstler and possibly pull out the tent's supports, dropping it on Kunstler. That would throw a wrench into things. The men, including Barker, were surprised at the situation they faced—the protesters, who totaled over 500, far outnumbered them. Barker told his troops that when they received a signal from the balcony, Frank Fiorini—better known as Frank Sturgis—was to start an argument with Ellsberg and thereby provoke a fight. Barker didn't say who would give the signal. Sturgis was given this key assignment because he could speak the best English of the group, one member would testify. When Sturgis attacked Ellsberg, Barker instructed, the other men should attack other demonstrators, including Kunstler. Barker said that "the heads at the top" wanted the demonstration terminated "at any cost."[114]

Also on the scene were FBI agents. One of them later testified that two men may have been solely responsible for tracking Ellsberg and Kunstler, respectively.[115]

Barker directed his men to spread out among the protesters in pairs. They did not blend well into the crowd, however. They were notably well dressed in suit coats and sport jackets—appropriate attire, they felt, for paying their respects to Hoover. Some wore dark clothing, others "light, tropical suits" that made them quite conspicuous, one witness remembered. They were "really not dressed in clothing that would allow them to engage in any fighting or struggles," Fernandez said later. Barker himself had donned a leather jacket, though. He was ready to rumble. One of the FBI agents noticed that some of the Cubans were "fairly large."[116]

As the men looked for opportunities to disrupt the rally, Angel Ferrer, a U.S. Army veteran, "especially was looking for the Viet Cong flag." After mingling among the protesters for at least an hour, the men grew restless and hungry for action. "There were a lot of hippies there, screaming, enjoying Hoover's death, and that excited us," DeDiego recounted. Ferrer told the FBI "they observed a group of hippies on the grass playing guitars and acting in a disrespectful manner," and that he and the others "became very upset at these hippies and their disrespectful attitude." Barker angrily told me years later, "These guys were saying we were bombing innocent people, and we weren't bombing the communists. We were bombing innocent people and children and all of that bullshit." They "were *professional* demonstrators," he charged. "Communist paid and inspired professionals. Or leftist inspired and paid. We don't care."[117]

Meanwhile, young counterdemonstrators from the College Republicans, Young Republicans and other conservative groups had appeared on the scene, compliments of the Nixon White House. They were clean cut and well dressed. They heckled the protesters and demanded that Kunstler be disbarred. "We have some sickies with us tonight," Kunstler said.[118]

To the disappointment of the Cubans, the Viet Cong flag was nowhere to be seen. That is not surprising; only a small minority of antiwar protesters ever carried a Viet Cong flag. The Cubans also did not receive a signal from the balcony. Barker directed them to move in and start an argument near the speaker's platform. Sturgis yelled "traitor" at a speaker while making his way through the crowd, but without attracting much attention. Sturgis "was generally ignored," Fernandez recounted. Sturgis shouted "traitor" and other choice words ("communist" was undoubtedly among them) for some fifteen minutes. Judy Collins recalled that one of the men screaming at the antiwar speakers was a "heavy-set, dark male" in a suit with "a cigar in his hand." That would have been conspicuous. Two FBI agents said that this shouting was initially directed at Kunstler, and that the Cubans had moved alongside the stage while Kunstler was speaking. Ted Lieverman, one of the protesters, noticed that there were around seven to ten Cubans lined up along a rope behind the speaker's platform before Ellsberg's speech. They began whispering to each other. Then they started shouting "traitor" and "what do you people think you are doing?" But these efforts to provoke the protesters failed.[119]

"I kept telling the guys to get started, and they wouldn't start," Barker recounts. "So I came over there and I took the leadership. And I told Ellsberg he was nothing but a goddamn traitor, and that he was a disgrace to the Jewish people." Barker was also Jewish; after volunteering to serve in the U.S. Army Air Corps during World War II, he'd been shot down over Nazi Germany and survived 16 months as a prisoner of war ("Tell me something that will scare me," he later told U.S. Attorney Earl Silbert). A tape recording of Ellsberg's speech, which Ellsberg was "quite anxious" to get a copy of, contained shouts of "traitor." "I don't think I was terribly conscious [of it] while I was speaking," Ellsberg remembers. "But I was aware that there were people fighting at the fringe of the crowd, after I had spoken. I went over and watched that."[120]

The Cubans tried to break through a line of marshals at the stage to get to Ellsberg. But despite a good deal of pushing and shoving, they could not get their hands on their quarry.[121]

Ted Lieverman approached Barker and Reinaldo Pico, another Bay of Pigs veteran, who was standing and yelling next to Barker. Lieverman wished to engage them in "some kind of dialogue" and to calm them down. But "almost instantaneously," an FBI agent recalled, Pico, a burly man with long, thick, dark sideburns, threw a punch at Lieverman. "I thought he was going to hit Macho, who's an older man, so I slugged him on the head," Pico recounted. "I gave him a fist." But Lieverman said Pico's punches never landed, that he kept backpedaling. Mike Segal, who was in charge of the protesters' sound and lighting systems (it was after 8 P.M. and dark), remembered that there was again "a lot of pushing and shoving" and that he tried to pull Lieverman out of harm's way. But a man Segal later identified as Sturgis sucker-punched him. "Segal was hit in the back of the head several times, was spun around, and got a fist right in the face," a Watergate prosecutor recorded. "Segal's glasses were thrown off, and he was spun down to the ground." Segal was helped to the side by a fellow protester, who was also roughed up. An FBI agent would remember seeing one of the demonstrators (possibly Segal) grabbed from behind by a Cuban, at which point "Frank Sturgis punched him in the crotch." But "this particular demonstrator was not badly injured because he shielded himself with a clipboard which was broken by Sturgis's punch," the agent testified. Hiram Gonzalez, another of Barker's men, recounted that when Sturgis hit one demonstrator (again possibly Segal), the demonstrator yelled, "Peace, don't hit me!" The hippies were using "a 'communist tactic': they didn't fight back," Pico told a journalist.[122]

Meanwhile, according to Felipe DeDiego, Eugenio Martinez and a comrade had managed to get the tent down on Kunstler and to commandeer the protesters' sound system, which they used "to upbraid the demonstrators." Perhaps Mike Segal, who was now lying or sitting crumpled on the ground, should not have left his post. "The minute the fight started, all they cried was, 'Watch the equipment! Watch the equipment!'" Barker recalls. "You know, it was to safeguard their goddamn equipment." Barker also recounts, "We were supposed to break up their radio little thing, which we *did*."[123]

By now other Cubans had also climbed over the rope behind the stage, and they tore down some "anti-American" signs and started more scuffles. One demonstrator would remember two of the Cubans "shoving, pushing, throwing punches with no provocation." Recalls Barker, "The hippies started coming up with their long hairs. But I had selected an area in the staircase where you couldn't get more than twenty people in, and ten of us was us. . . . So we slugged it out with them there." Barker injured at least one of his hands. Pablo Fernandez told a newspaper reporter that he had been "very disgusted" at being thrown into "the middle of a fight," felt Barker had "betrayed" him, and that he "couldn't hit" a hippie that approached him yelling "Peace." But he told the FBI and the prosecutors a different story: he threw a punch at the hippie and hit another demonstrator in the stomach. "Well done," a policeman allegedly said. Fernandez also grabbed some papers from someone standing near Ellsberg, then passed them to a comrade as the cops moved in.[124]

None of the protesters were seriously hurt. "The whole thing was over almost as fast as it started," Ferrer remembered. It lasted "three minutes at the most" and "received very little attention and caused very little stir," Gonzalez said. As police carted them away, two of the Cubans continued to make derogatory remarks about the protesters. Barker told a woman that he'd started the fight.[125]

Three Capitol Police officers briefly detained Sturgis, Pico, and Ferrer, who "were screaming for the police to let them go and kept telling the officers that they were loyal Americans," Dennis Thompson, one of the cops, recalled. Two men approached the officers; "one identified himself as a Secret Service agent and the other identified himself as an FBI agent," Thompson recounted. These two men, whom Thompson took to be plainclothesmen, were wearing suits and lapel pins; one of the pins was red, white, and blue. Another of the police officers recalled being approached by a dark-haired man in a gray suit who flashed "an ID of some kind." The two men Thompson described took custody of Sturgis, Pico, and Ferrer and escorted them away, Thompson said. But Pico said they were released when a man in a gray trench coat and hat gave "a signal" to the policemen. To Sturgis, their release was another sign that they had been involved in "an approved government intelligence operation." Curiously, a Capitol Police report on the demonstration states, "There were no reported incidents."[126]

Watergate prosecutors considered it a "distinct possibility" that Hunt and Liddy were the two apparent plainclothesmen. Both denied being at the demonstration or impersonating federal agents, however. "Maybe Hunt did. I didn't," says Liddy, who believes sympathetic police let the Cubans go. Yet Magruder suspected that the man who gave "a signal" to release them was Hunt, and Liddy's secretary would recall Liddy telling her that he had been at the demonstration and that "one of his people almost got caught by police."[127]

After the demonstration, Barker phoned Hunt and Liddy at Hunt's office and reported that his men had been unable to get a flag and that there had been some fighting but no arrests; he himself had landed a punch, Barker related. Hunt and Liddy then drove over to Barker's hotel, and the three men and Martinez drove around (better than risking being overheard) while Barker briefed them at greater length on what had gone down. "Liddy was particularly interested if there had been any physical violence at the demonstration," Hunt told the prosecutors. "Barker stated that DeDiego hadn't stood up very well during the demonstration and had been unwilling to follow Barker's orders." That could not have helped relations at the real estate office. Barker apparently felt Angel Ferrer *had* stood up well, though: Ferrer told the FBI that, following the operation, Barker became a customer at his gas station. Hunt also testified that "Barker stated that Ellsberg was well guarded, and, as a result, it was impossible for the group to get close to Ellsberg." After Barker spoke of Sturgis's actions, Liddy commented, "Sturgis is my kind of guy."[128]

Later that evening, Barker praised and thanked his men. But he also informed several that he had been disappointed in events, that their efforts had been ineffective. He gave each of them a new $50 bill for expenses, however (this was the second set of $50 bills he had passed out), and said he was proud of them. On the plane flight home the next morning, Gonzalez told Fernandez he thought that "'they' were probably going to do more of this type of operation in the future." Indeed, when six of the men returned to Washington for the first Watergate break-in three weeks later, some were told they were going to disrupt "more hippie demonstrations against the war where Vietcong flags would be flown."[129]

Inside the White House, Charles Colson was also disappointed. His aide Richard Howard told Bart Porter that "Colson was 'pissed off' because he wanted a flag from the demonstration for the boss." But Howard showed William Rhatican some flyers and said, "We didn't get him (Colson) his flag this time, but we did get these." Howard also said it would be useful to have more such operations. Colson told Rhatican and Howard that Sturgis was "a stand up guy," the kind of American "we need." Indeed, that Sturgis had "iron balls" and "should be presented with a medal."[130]

The action attracted less publicity than the White House had anticipated. Media coverage of the counterdemonstrators was slight, and only one article mentioned the fighting. "I didn't see that the operation accomplished anything," Magruder wrote in his memoir.[131]

Far worse for the principals involved, it became a part of the Watergate scandal. The prosecutors considered the White House's involvement in it a "strong candidate for prosecution." They did not indict Colson (who became "the prime target" of their investigation) for perjury or other crimes "simply because there was not enough evidence linking him to a direct order to assault the demonstrators," one of the Watergate attorneys wrote. Hunt would not clearly implicate him, and Liddy would not talk. When Colson copped a plea to smearing Ellsberg, the prosecutors apparently lost interest in him.[132]

Typically, Ellsberg later blew the operation out of proportion. Nixon had the Cubans brought up to "incapacitate me totally," he claimed. In fact, their orders were "to kill me," he dramatically declared in a public forum; the impetus, he said, was his release of NSSM-1. Ellsberg told me that officials believed he had documents on a plan for a major escalation of the war and wanted to stop him from releasing them. He twice claimed in one interview with me that the Cubans had tried to kill him, and he has made that claim frequently to others. He said that the reason the Cubans didn't murder him is because they noticed the crowd was friendly to him and "they smelled that they were being set up, à la Oswald, to be patsies. . . . So they decided to throw the operation, and they got into fistfights with people in the crowd."[133]

When I told Barker that Ellsberg claimed he and his men were sent to incapacitate or perhaps even to kill him, Barker responded, "Unfortunately, this wasn't true." He believes "the main objective was to break up their demonstration" and stimulate adverse press coverage. He and his men didn't travel to Washington specifically to go after Ellsberg? "No, no. We went up there to break up a demonstration," Barker replied. "Their main job was to go out there and get the flag," Liddy says with a laugh. "They were definitely to create a disturbance and to beat up the bad guys. But, you know, 'Get the flag.' 'Get the damn flag.'" At a public forum later, Ellsberg accused Liddy of attempting to kill him. "He said, 'You tried to kill me,'" Liddy recounts. "And I didn't know what the hell he was talking about. I think he *thinks* that that was [the goal]. . . . No, the main thing was, 'Get the flag.'"[134]

<hr />

By releasing the Pentagon Papers, then, Ellsberg had set in motion a series of abuses of governmental power: the establishment of the Plumbers; their illegal acts, including the Fielding break-in and spreading derogatory information about him; the CIA's two psychiatric profiles of him and help on the Fielding break-in; the White House's plots to burglarize Brookings and penetrate the National Archives; the attempted attack on Ellsberg and other protesters just described; the White House's efforts to cover up these acts and to obstruct justice. Ellsberg's release had provoked abuses that would play key roles in undoing Nixon. All except the National Archives plot were considerations in the Watergate inquiries. The Plumbers and their acts were major factors in not only the Senate Watergate hearings and the Watergate Special Prosecution Force investigations but also the House Judiciary Committee's impeachment proceedings. The Watergate cover-up, which was undertaken partly to keep a lid on these abuses, was also, of course, a major element in the impeachment proceedings.

The Fielding break-in had marked a turning point in the Nixon administration's use of illegalities to combat its enemies. Egil Krogh would come to judge it far more significant than the Watergate break-ins for showing the administration's commitment to illegal acts, and indeed it was. John Ehrlichman deemed it "the seminal Watergate episode."[135] In fact, one can make a case that the Watergate scandal would not have occurred without Ellsberg's release of the Papers. The White House's reaction had boomeranged.

Ellsberg's act also had other effects. It fed public questioning of the war, if not nearly as much as Ellsberg had envisioned. While the *story* of the Papers, the high drama of it, including on television, had greater impact than their content, and although the Papers had little effect on Congress and none directly on the war itself, they showed that the government had systematically misled the public on Vietnam—indeed, that it was even more manipulative and mendacious than most people had realized. (The Nixon administration's George Romney told the press that publication of the documents "confirms his accusation six years ago that the American people were brainwashed about the war," a statement Colson called "most unfortunate.") While there may have been little in the Papers not already known or suspected by many antiwar critics, they constituted fresh, authoritative ammunition. The Bantam edition of *New York Times* articles on the Papers and selected documents was a hot seller, ultimately to the tune of over a million-and-a-half copies, though in all likelihood few people actually read it, and the subsequent Gravel edition sold poorly.[136]

In addition, the public's heightened distrust of government nourished the Watergate scandal that undermined Nixon's authority in Congress and thus his ability to continue waging the war. Nixon could have carried the public and Congress longer on Vietnam without Watergate, which cut him off at the knees. Ellsberg would revel in this, claiming that without the Papers and thus Watergate "there would—flatly—have been major escalation in the air that would have gone on indefinitely, and the ultimate use of nuclear weapons was likely. . . . Had he not hired the Plumbers to get me, had he not gone that route, I think the war would have continued for years."[137]

FOURTEEN

ON STAGE

ELLSBERG STOOD IN THE SPOTLIGHT WITH A CERTAIN EASE AFTER HIS indictment. He had sought stardom, perhaps even needed it. He had stage presence, an actor in him, and great confidence in his abilities. He liked being in the public eye and generally didn't get nervous there; indeed, he seemed to thrive in the limelight. "Zsa Zsa," Lloyd Shearer called him. "My impression was Dan was prepared for this role all his life," Leonard Weinglass, who would become Anthony Russo's lead attorney, recalls. "This, I think, was where Dan felt he ought to be. And this is where he really fit in well. . . . Some people just move into that with a degree of skill and confidence that indicates that they've always had this talent. Dan did." It pleased Ellsberg when he was recognized in public. "*Twice* in Broadway shows, during the show, in curtain time, they announced the fact for this audience that Daniel Ellsberg was in the audience," Ellsberg reminisces. "And the audience gave a standing ovation. . . . On one occasion they *stopped* the performance. The performance for the show stopped, and they said, 'We've just been informed that Daniel Ellsberg is in the audience.' And the *cast* applauded. And the audience rose and applauded." "I thought Dan was fucking unambiguously delighted to be vaulted into celebrity," Jeremy Larner comments.[1]

Ellsberg was also intrigued, bemused, by the whole experience of fame. Who wouldn't be in its initial firestorm? So great was his sense of astonishment that it seemed almost childlike. He pondered what he could do with his fame, which also added drama and excitement to his life. He was "like a kid with a new toy," Russo recalls. Ellsberg could now meet people he would not have otherwise. More women found him interesting; that was no small benefit. (But Anthony Lukas would notice that when a young male employee at a car rental counter in Los Angeles recognized Ellsberg and asked to shake his hand, "the rather stunning blonde behind the counter gave no indication that she knew or cared, and I thought I detected in Dan a slight disappointment that she didn't.")[2]

Tom Winship of the *Boston Globe* had Dan and Pat Ellsberg over to his house for dinner after the Pentagon Papers were published. "His chest was stuck out as far as it could go," Winship remembers. "He was feeling very cocky and smug and very proud of himself." Ellsberg told others he was President Nixon's number one worry. Most discounted such talk, "partly because Ellsberg was so self-indulgent: 'This is just Dan bullshitting again,'" the journalist Peter Schrag recalls. "Everybody at the time said, 'Oh, god, he's just aggrandizing,'" Charles Nesson remembers. "But then, lo and behold, it comes out two years later"—with the Watergate revelations—that "he was absolutely right" Nesson laughs. Sam Popkin, Ellsberg's friend in Cambridge, recalls that "Dan was obsessed with his fame. . . . He loved it. Oh, god, he needed that adulation. . . . There should have been a certain humility there that wasn't there. . . . I felt sad that this man who had these brilliant analytic capacities was just being carried aloft on this adulation. And it was the adulation that mattered, it was celebrity that mattered. . . . There was always a preening quality to Dan. But now it was out of control." After Popkin's fiancée, Susan Shirk, returned from a trip to China the summer of 1971, she and Popkin got together with the Ellsbergs for dinner. "The first question Dan asked her was, 'When you got to China, were the Chinese talking about what I had done?'" Popkin recounts. "And, 'Were they concerned with protecting me and trying to get me free? . . . What were they saying about me?'" Ellsberg fantasized about the Chinese waving signs saying "Free Ellsberg." He later told a reporter that a friend in China had informed him, "I was very big at the time of the Pentagon Papers." He also suggested that Nixon's visit to China in February 1972 might prompt demonstrations of support for him there, like "700 million banners all saying, 'Free Ellsberg.'"[3]

RAND's Paul Langer was reading on the sun deck of his beach cottage in Malibu when Ellsberg approached him and asked, "Paul, what are they saying about me [at RAND]?" These were virtually the first words out of Ellsberg's mouth. When David Halberstam saw Ellsberg for the first time after publication of the Papers, Ellsberg asked Halberstam what Robert McNamara was saying about him.[4]

Ellsberg had begun to refer to himself in the third person. At an informal meeting of his supporters in Cambridge that summer, he asked each person in the room to state their opinion on his likely legal fate. "As I remember it, he phrased the question, 'How long do you think Ellsberg will go to jail?'" Princeton professor Richard Falk, one of his supporters, recalls. "So he had already sort of historicized himself."[5]

Some on Ellsberg's own defense team found him to be an egomaniac. He struck Dolores Donovan as the most egocentric person she'd ever met. Ellsberg seemed to Robert Sachs, who was then a spokesperson to the media for the defense, to become consumed by his fame. "I think it overtook him," Sachs reminisces. "It almost destroyed him," as Ellsberg appeared to get "hooked" on it. Once, when Ellsberg's and Anthony Russo's two defense teams sat down for a meeting, Russo recounts,

> the television was still on, and on came this really weird advertisement spot. Somebody had taken the opportunity to make a statement. It was nothing overtly related to Ellsberg, but they had a guy who looked just like Ellsberg. . . . And he was dangling a watch like a hypnotist. And he had eyes painted on his eyelids. Looked real bizarre. And he started to twitch his eyes, and he's saying, "I am famous!" Dangling the watch. And then—poof—it was gone. And people were sitting there looking at that, and they said, "Ooohhh. God." And then we went on with the meeting. . . . People made the connection and nobody said anything. . . . So there was a lot of the king dancing around with no clothes and nobody saying anything.[6]

Ellsberg would later downplay his affinity for celebrity. "My time as a public figure certainly wasn't unpleasant, and it was interesting for a while; but it's nothing I have a taste for, neither the notoriety, nor the public life," he told *Rolling Stone*. Ellsberg told me, perhaps more frankly, "It was enjoyable. . . . There was no real negative aspect to it. . . . It was often a lot of interruptions—*always*. You couldn't eat out without having a meal interrupted several times for autographs or congratulations or something. . . . I didn't mind. I always gave autographs. . . . Over time, there are a lot of persistent problems with relationships," which Ellsberg didn't want to go into with me, but overall "fame was good," partly because "it was a tremendous boost to my antiwar activity. It gave me a platform." And "I'm glad I had it. Lots of people would envy it. And essentially they're right to envy it." Also, "I ask myself, 'Would I rather be recognized on the street than not by somebody?' On the whole, yes." Same for having his name known. "But it did not give me much sustenance. I didn't get much from it. In other words, it was nice, it was pleasant, but on a rather low level. . . . And I would never have dreamed of doing something for applause."[7]

═══◼═══

On July 13, 1971, Ellsberg appeared on the *Dick Cavett Show*. By releasing the Papers, he told Cavett, he had decided "to stop lying." Watching his friend on television, Sam Popkin thought a certain amount of PR went into his remarks. "There are so many layers of him watching himself . . . saying things," Popkin recalls. "I just could see the layers of calculation in ways I'd never seen them before. . . . Nothing was just what he thinks. It's always both what he thinks and what he thinks he should say to get you to understand what he wants you to believe he thinks."[8]

At a breakfast interview with journalists at the National Press Club in Washington the same month, Ellsberg declared that the Defense Department's top-secret command-and-control study of the 1964 Tonkin Gulf incidents showed that Robert McNamara had deceived Congress on the episode. Ellsberg again denounced official lying on Vietnam at a conference on Capitol Hill later that month; he advocated impeachment proceedings against some Nixon administration officials. "He *loved* kicking the shit out of the government," Charles Nesson remembers. And "he was amazingly good at that."[9]

In early August, Ellsberg was the featured attraction at a Hiroshima Day event on the dunes on Cape Cod. He delivered a long speech in an "unemotional, almost monotone" style (according to the writer Anne Bernays) about the political journey that had led him to release the Papers. Ellsberg spent the night at James Thomson's small vacation house on the Cape; Doris Kearns and Gregory Craig (later counsel to President Clinton) were also there. Ellsberg was "full of himself," Thomson recalls. And he "sort of shocked a few people by going around with his underwear open, with the thing hanging out," on a late-night trip to the refrigerator. "He just happened to walk out, and it was flopping out," Thomson says. But, he laughs, "my friend Gregory Craig thought it was exhibitionism."[10] The irony is rich.

Referring to the Papers, Thomson remarked to Ellsberg, "Dan, that's going to be a hard act to follow, what you've done." "You wait and see," Ellsberg replied. "I've got a much bigger thing up my sleeve." Ellsberg was still thinking about releasing that highly classified information he had collected on U.S. nuclear war planning. He stated at a news conference in Colorado later in August that he possessed secret information on U.S. involvement in crises. He spoke about his inside knowledge of the U-2 crisis in an interview with *Look* magazine.[11]

Ellsberg was not through revealing secrets. He took tremendous pleasure in it.

On August 16, Ellsberg was arraigned in Los Angeles. He pled not guilty to both criminal counts he faced. "Everyone was stunned by several things," Linda Deutsch, who was on the scene for the Associated Press, recounts. "One was that he was so good looking. He was stunning. . . . It was almost like he glowed with this fervor. And Pat was just gorgeous. They were a beautiful couple. They seemed to be out of place in this radical milieu. And he was so articulate. And everything about him seemed to me to be unlike anyone you would expect to be charged as a traitor. I mean, the man had been a hawk. Everybody knew that. . . . And that made it such an incredible story." At a sidewalk news conference, Ellsberg pointed out to reporters that the United States had dropped more bombs on Indochina in the last two years than it had in all theaters during World War II. He then looked sharply at them and said, "Did you know that?"[12]

On September 23, in a packed Washington ballroom, Ellsberg received an award from the Federal Employees for Peace. Before the event, he had fantasized about seeing "posters with my picture on them all over the Pentagon: 'Come hear Dan Ellsberg speak for peace.'" Anthony Lukas, who was writing a piece on him for the *New York Times Magazine*, was sitting next to Richard Strout of the *Christian Science Monitor* that evening. Strout mentioned to Lukas that Ellsberg had called him in July to complain about an article he'd written about him. "He doesn't like to be described as intense," Strout told Lukas. "He doesn't want people to think he's a nut." The audience gave Ellsberg a prolonged standing ovation. He had earlier been unable to find his notes for his speech, but he told the audience that he had "made notes for a very depressed crowd" and decided to discard them after noticing the crowd's upbeat mood.[13]

The White House hoped to take advantage of Ellsberg's appearance that evening to dirty him further. At Charles Colson's request, Howard Hunt and G. Gordon Liddy planned to give Ellsberg LSD to make him appear "incoherent" and "a near burnt-out drug case." "That was Hunt's thing," Liddy recalls. "Hunt always wanted to give LSD to people." They would again use the Cuban asset by infiltrating Cubans from Miami into the dinner. "We'll make waiters out of them," Hunt said. One of them would serve Ellsberg. "One of the earliest dishes on the menu was soup," Liddy wrote later. "A warm liquid is ideal for the rapid absorption and wide dispersal of a drug, and the taste would mask its presence." Hunt went to the CIA for the LSD. "The agency doctors said, 'That isn't going to work, for a lot of different reasons,'" Liddy remembers. "'One of which is absorption rates on skin and things like that.' But they said, 'You never know which way somebody is going to bounce when you give them lysergic acid diethylamide 25. It can be a good trip, a bad trip. You don't know what's going to happen. It's unpredictable.' And you don't do things unless you know what the end result's going to be." An experienced man like Ellsberg might have bounced well—"actually, it might have made me a much better after-dinner speaker," he later joked—but when the plan was finally approved, Hunt informed Liddy it was too late to get the Cubans up and inserted among the waiters. The scheme was "put into abeyance pending another opportunity," Liddy wrote.[14]

A week later, Ellsberg was set to fly to Chicago to receive another award, only to call Lukas (who was still accompanying him) at the last minute to say he'd decided to fly first to Los Angeles that day in order to attend a hearing for Anthony Russo. So he and Lukas jetted off to LA, where Ellsberg rented a Mustang convertible. "He promptly hauls down the top, slings his jacket in back, flicks on the radio and wheels the little car onto the road," Lukas recounted. "Suddenly, it's a different Dan—a freer, jauntier, more exuberant man." After midnight, Ellsberg visited his children, Robert and Mary, then ages 15 and 12.[15]

The next day, the 34-year-old Russo was released from prison, where he had been confined for refusing to testify before the grand jury. Although he had purportedly been on a hunger strike, "Tony was not looking any leaner, and it was a public relations problem," Leonard Weinglass humorously remembers. Russo's attorney at the time had smuggled pastrami sandwiches into the jail. Russo was "maybe the only person in history to gain weight on a hunger strike," Weinglass says. "I am proud to have a friend like Tony," Ellsberg told reporters. But he then did something Russo came to believe a true friend would not do: he convinced Russo to just pick up and fly to Chicago with him. Russo, who had been beaten by prison guards before entering the courtroom that morning and who was not in good shape generally, recounts, "I walked out of jail, Ellsberg put me into a convertible. We rode out to the airport and got on a plane. And there I was going to Chicago, and still with my jail skivvies on. And when I look back on it, it was the goddamnest thing to do to somebody when they get out of jail and they'd been on a 23-day hunger strike. And to me, the whole thing was bizarre. It was just a bizarre cultural shock to go from jail to an airliner. And we're sitting there [in] first class, and they're serving all this delicious food. And I'm saying, 'I'm on a hunger strike, baby [laughs]. I ain't eating.'" Ellsberg questioned Russo "voraciously" about his prison experience.[16]

The American Peace Awards ceremony in Chicago, sponsored by the Business Executives Move for Vietnam Peace, was a garish affair. But from his red-velvet box, Ellsberg, who had been joined by Patricia in Chicago, seemed "to enjoy every minute of it," Lukas wrote afterward. Joan Baez, another award winner, fractured the decorum when she laid two American flags on their sides, adding insult to injury to the organizers of the event. "She insisted on a first-class ticket to come to Chicago, and then didn't accept the prize when she got here," recalls Al Booth, one of the event's main organizers. After speaking, Ellsberg brought Russo out to address the crowd. "I was up there on the stage and they pushed me out to go speak," Russo recounts. "And all I remember is these bright lights—I couldn't see *anything*. . . . And I just started to ramble on." Ellsberg eventually cut him off, but in an affectionate way. "He was really a mercurial personality," Lukas told me, reflecting on this incident. "He could go from enormous self-involvement to enormous generosity and quite beautiful friendship."[17]

After the ceremony, the award winners and some others went over to the Playboy mansion for a late dinner. Hugh Hefner was, of course, the host. "He was all lounged back, drinking Pepsi-Cola," Russo remembers. "He'd pick up the phone and sort of grunt something into the phone—'Limo.' . . . He was the prince." Some women were on hand, including an arresting Playmate, and champagne flowed. Not everyone took to the scene, though. Former senator Wayne Morse, another of the award winners, acted quite uncomfortable. Russo sat with Morse on a sofa. "We talked about the Playboy mansion as a morgue," Russo recalls. "It was all playful and cheerful, but . . . just really phony." Yet Ellsberg seemed to be having an immensely good time. He was the first person in his party to enter the downstairs pool, which resembled an aquarium; people at an adjacent bar peered straight into its blue water through a big window. Ellsberg made "fish eyes" at Patricia through the glass. Two naked women also swam by. "I remember looking at Morse, and his eyes glazed over," Paul Mc-Closkey, who was also on the scene, laughs. "He couldn't believe that he was looking at a naked girl, swimming about four feet away."[18]

At 3:30 A.M., only the Ellsbergs, Russo, Lukas, and Hefner were still sitting at the long dinner table. "Like to see my private quarters?" Hefner asked. "Dan and Patricia nod enthusiastically," Lukas wrote, "and Hefner leads on through his bedroom, with its famous revolving bed, down a spiral staircase to the 'Roman Baths' and their control panel which can set off a spectacular panorama of showers, sprays and neon lights." Afterward, Ellsberg and the other guests were chauffeured to the Executive House in Hefner's limo.[19]

Two days later, Ellsberg and Russo attended a brunch at Al Booth's home in Chicago. Booth found Ellsberg quite congenial and easy to talk to, but his wife, Gisela, a psychologist, was less taken by him. "He's not a particularly warm person," she thought. "He's kind of distant, and not terribly forthcoming. . . . He didn't really seem to care terribly much about who somebody else was, or what they were thinking or doing. . . . He was here several hours and he was much made of, and I felt that there wasn't any way he extended himself. And he sort of treated it [her house] like it was a public place, like a hotel or whatever. I usually am able to establish some kind of rapport with almost anyone. And I found that we sort of remained strangers." Ellsberg treated Russo like a junior partner or even an aide, Gisela noticed. Ellsberg also seemed to be trying to take care of Russo in some way, or to make up for what Russo had just gone through.[20]

Ellsberg called Russo "my closest friend" in a speech he delivered in Los Angeles that November. There were over 15,000 people in the audience—the biggest crowd yet—and some were proclaiming, "Ellsberg for president." Ellsberg's father had flown out from Michigan, and his son, Robert, was also there. But Ellsberg again had speech problems. That morning, after emerging from the Ambassador Hotel's massage room, he excitedly told Patricia, who was sunning herself by the pool, that he had finally come up with a theme for his talk. "That's wonderful, darling," Patricia replied. "Wonderful." The theme came from Thoreau's line, "Cast your whole vote." But in the dressing room before his speech, Ellsberg couldn't pull it together. "I didn't have a clue as to what I was going to say," he recalls. "He was terrible," the writer Joe McGinniss recounted. After his opening remarks, "he trailed off rapidly" and "wandered lamely across much of the hour that followed." He became repetitive. Ellsberg castigated members of Congress for not taking stronger action against the war. ("When I first came to Congress, he said he was very disappointed that I wasn't going to chain myself to the White House gate," Bella Abzug told me. "So I said to him, 'We did that already. We did that fifty years ago'"—to get women the vote. Abzug was offended, and somewhat amused, by Ellsberg's criticism. She was a leading antiwar activist in Congress and had even helped get the Pentagon Papers before the House.)[21]

The next morning, Ellsberg went to a fund raiser for his legal defense at a home in affluent Bel Air. One man enraged him when he remarked, "Now really, Dan, you simply can't try to turn your trial into a major political event. In a presidential-election year, that, very simply, is pissing into the wind." Ellsberg took that as an affront. His hands trembled. "Pissing into the wind," he said, his voice close to a hiss. "*That's why I'm covered with piss!*" It bothered Ellsberg when people didn't take his trial as seriously as he thought they should. "He just doesn't understand that people don't see things the way he does," Richard Falk comments. "He was very concentrated on the trial, and he was trying to persuade others to write about the trial. . . . He would try to stimulate or induce people like me to express in our work what he felt was important."[22]

This was another period of great frustration, anxiety, and stress for Ellsberg. What was going to happen to him now? He was in uncharted territory and felt an enormous amount of angst. Ellsberg was not, as some thought, simply floating on his celebrity. Peace had never come easy to him, and now moments of glory and exhilaration, sometimes many hours of them, mixed with eons of agony. The stakes were high. Prison remained an all-too-clear possibility in his mind; he talked about it a lot. He could go to jail for a long time, he told others. "He was scared," Linda Deutsch noticed. But Ellsberg's expectations would fluctuate over the course of his trial. "I think at the beginning he expected to go to jail," Charles Nesson reminisces. "And I think as the trial went on, he kind of got onto the idea that we could win this thing." But "he was a fighter right from the get-go." Nesson and Ellsberg's other defense lawyers were confident that they could win the case, though a hung jury, or even a conviction, on the theft count was not out of the realm of possibility. (Ellsberg claims, dubiously, "my lawyers told me *to the end* that I would go to prison.") As the end of his trial was approaching in 1973, Ellsberg was quite worried about going to jail. But there was still a martyr in him, which Leonard Boudin had to try to control. Some thought Ellsberg wanted to go to prison. He even looked the part of the martyr to Peter Schrag, who covered his trial: fragile, slender, boyish, vulnerable, frightened, "those big blue eyes, and that voice." ("I can see how he's literally a lady killer," Schrag reflects. "He was both attractive and vulnerable. . . . That's part of his seduction.") Reporters attending his trial believed Ellsberg would never go to jail. That incensed him.[23]

Also troubling Ellsberg in the summer of 1971, his ex-wife remained uncooperative. When he visited Carol in early July in California, he criticized her for signing the affidavit and testifying before the grand jury; her affidavit was "inconsistent and out of context," he said. He told their children that she'd acted stupidly. But he was friendly toward Carol overall. This would be a bad time to anger her any more than he already had. During several other conversations between them at this time, some of which became highly acrimonious, Carol again asked Dan what in the world he had been thinking when he had involved their children in copying the Papers. Dan said that they should be proud of what they had done. "When Carol pointed out the possibility that the children could be called for a court appearance, Daniel stated that it might be good for them and make them better persons," the FBI recorded. "Mrs. Ellsberg stated that Daniel seems to actually want the children to appear either for or against him." Ellsberg seemed to want Carol's approbation, even applause, for what he had done. He asked her if she would mind being photographed with him and their children as a show of solidarity. Carol refused. She also stated that she did not wish to speak to his attorneys, who, of course, eagerly wanted to get her account of events. She didn't want to have anything to do with them. That steamed Dan. "You're not being a good team player," he would tell her, in effect. "I'm not on the team," she replied. "It was dawning on him that I wasn't being friendly with him," Carol recalls. "Dan would have liked to have sat down and chatted and gone over the whole thing with me." Ellsberg's fear of prison brought out an ugly side of him in his discussions with Carol.[24]

Charles Nesson tried a more sympathetic approach with Carol when he visited her that summer. According to her notes of their first meeting, Nesson related that he, too, had been "divorced—difficult to talk to [ex-]wife." He further commiserated with Carol about how difficult *Dan* was. (Robert told his mother, who of course didn't need to be told this, that Nesson was playing up to her.) Like Dan, Nesson tried to convince Carol to hire Arthur Berman, one of their defense lawyers. Most significant in Carol's mind, then and for long afterward, he stated that he could assure her that the defense would never call Robert to testify.[25]

Ellsberg's mood did not improve much when he thought about what impact the Papers had had in the country. He was disappointed that newspapers had published only "a very tiny fraction" of the study. He charged in early August that the press was "now in the business of withholding it from the American public, just as the Defense Department was for so long in that business." The country had not turned around, the walls had not come tumbling down. "I don't think Dan could figure out why the war didn't end when these Papers came out," Mark Rosenbaum, who was a young member of his defense team, remembers. "I think that was a constant thesis. . . . A source of discouragement, but also a source of bafflement. . . . Dan felt that he had delivered the truth, at considerable personal peril. . . . And I think he felt that at that point the war should be over." Ellsberg seemed to Marty Arnold of the *New York Times* to torture himself with the thought that the Papers had not had greater impact, and to seek assurance that his action was important. During the selection of the first jury in his trial, only one of about a hundred people questioned said they had read parts of the Papers. "Dan turned to me and said, 'For this I'm going to do 99 years?'" Leonard Weinglass recounts.[26]

Members of the press were proving annoying to Ellsberg. Journalists whom he had thought were sympathetic to him were writing some unflattering things about him. Michael Kinsley pointed to Ellsberg's situation as an example of the painless martyrdom sought by Harvard men. Ellsberg "still has his high-paying, no-work job at MIT, a beautiful rich wife, star appeal around Cambridge and places like it, the best lawyers at Harvard Law School defending him," Kinsley wrote. "I don't think he much cared for the work of anybody who was writing about him," Anthony Lukas recalled. And those writing magazine pieces "all heard from him about it. He criticized each of us, in turn, to the others. . . . What I'm tempted to say is that anybody who wasn't a thousand percent in his camp was against him." Ellsberg felt reporters should be on his side. He seemed utterly obsessed with his own place in life "and I don't think that he could ever feel that people appreciated it enough or did enough to take note of his contributions," Sanford Ungar, who covered his trial for the *Washington Post*, remembers. "We were clearly seen as impediments to his path to glory." And "he hated us. He thought we were there covering his trial to serve his purposes. He couldn't really imagine anything else. . . . I don't think he saw that anybody else had anything at stake in this case besides himself. I think he really thought that the media were kind of vehicles for his heroic measures . . . tools toward this apotheosis he was going to achieve. . . . Instruments." But while "obviously we were all on his side," Ungar says, "I don't think we were ready to become his mouthpieces. . . . We thought we had some other job to do besides glorifying Dan Ellsberg." "He never really understood why the press was not his ally and partner in this," Robert Sachs recalls. There was a "disconnect. Here you have somebody who was intellectually very bright, high IQ, and yet on some common-sense things would miss."[27]

Ellsberg thought many of those "former friends" providing quotes to reporters—saying that he had done it for publicity and supplying other material for those "hatchet jobs that were done on me"—were trying to somehow absolve themselves of guilt for not having taken a similar step to end the war. "They have to find a reason for my having done it that will not apply to them," he argues.[28]

Ellsberg followed his press closely. "He was obsessed with his media coverage," Frank Rich recalls. "In a way that I would say is not entirely attractive." "He's always been quite preoccupied with how the media portrays him," Richard Falk observes. "And in this period when he was quite prominent, he would want to hear *all* the programs, at the different [times], and whether they repeated [themselves]—you know, the ten o'clock news, what was on at nine o'clock, and so on. He was very preoccupied with that presentation of himself through the media."[29]

Rich's *Esquire* piece on Ellsberg was among the most sympathetic ones, but it still angered him. At the end of it, Rich described a somewhat frenetic and shaky Ellsberg launching into "a near monologue that lasted for close to two hours" over the phone. "It was in the vein of, 'Here are the latest updates on what I'm doing, and this is where I'm speaking,' and so on," Rich remembers.

"And then he just sort of talked and talked and talked." Ellsberg, who said he'd been encountering land mines in his past, "free-associated over the course of his whole life"; he began to cry several times. At one point he had to put down the receiver for two or three minutes. He thought the piece made him appear emotionally unstable.[30]

But it was Lukas's piece that really set him off. It was another rather favorable and gentle profile written by someone who admired his act. But Ellsberg did not care for Lukas's account of the scene in the Playboy mansion, which Rich found ironic given Ellsberg's great and unabashed interest in sex. The scene "sounded totally in character," Rich recalls. "But then it also sounded in character, I guess, that Ellsberg didn't want this presented to the world." As we've seen, Ellsberg was especially upset by Lukas's description of his reaction to his mother's death. At a party later, he was "quite emphatic" about that, Lukas remembers. (But Ellsberg told me he didn't talk to Lukas afterward: "Just the thought of talking to him appalled me. . . . This guy was supernaturally vicious or vindictive." He told me he hated Lukas.) Ellsberg claims that "at the very least, every paragraph of that story has a major misstatement or extremely misleading statement. Most of them—most of them—deliberate. Well, I won't say most of them. Half of them." Ellsberg thought Lukas had made him out to be "a rich jet-setter, arrogant, egotistical, really to the point of megalomania." He claims that it forced Stanley Sheinbaum, who was the chief fund raiser for his defense, to cancel two big events because it undermined support for him. But Sheinbaum has no memory of that. "Anything that focuses on him, there are going to be distortions," Sheinbaum notes. "I know that."[31]

Ironically, Ellsberg came to feel he wasn't receiving enough press. He phoned Sidney Zion to ask him to help get the *New York Times* to devote more coverage to his pretrial proceedings in 1972. "I thought that was hilarious," recalls Zion, who had angered people at the *Times* by naming Ellsberg as the source of the Papers. "Somehow he thought that I still had influence when I couldn't even walk in the building! . . . I was flabbergasted." That year or the next, Ellsberg complained with some vehemence to A. M. Rosenthal that the *Times* was not devoting enough attention to his legal situation. "He seemed to feel let down," Rosenthal recounts. "He had a feeling of being deserted."[32]

During his pretrial process and trial, Ellsberg complained to reporters that they weren't interviewing him enough. "He asked why I didn't interview him more and why other people didn't," Sanford Ungar remembers. He did this "*all the time.*" Ungar got the sense that he was giving all reporters a hard time about it. "He wanted people to seek his perspective on everything, on every aspect of the case," Ungar recalls. "It was as if he wanted a kind of a little polemical shot every day." Ellsberg enjoyed speaking to the press after coming out of court. Sometimes Robert Sachs would ask him, Why don't we have one of the lawyers talk to the reporters this time? But Ellsberg wanted to. It annoyed him when journalists congregated around his lawyers and ignored him. Sheinbaum recounts: "Ellsberg, every afternoon, wanted to gather the press together and explain to them the events of the day. Well, the fucking press wanted to go home [laughs]. And he would go nuts. He would go nuts. And I would have to calm him. Because I didn't want him getting hostile to the press. . . . Anger was rising to too high a level. . . . He felt this was the most important trial in the world, the most important thing that was going on."[33]

Marty Arnold recalls:

> He used to come up to the newsroom all the time, to the press room. And he was always annoying me. He always wanted me to interview him. He always wanted to tell me his take on the day's proceedings. And, you know, he hated me. He never liked me. And I never liked him. And . . . I didn't have time to bullshit with Dan Ellsberg. And I didn't need him. I'd sat through court all day; I knew what their side of the story was. He always wanted an interview. . . . He would whine about it. He didn't understand it. Somehow he thought that the *Times* and he were . . . historically . . . locked together . . . [and] therefore we should do more with him somehow.

Ellsberg told his half brother to read the *New York Daily News*, not the *Times*, on the trial. Theo Wilson of the *News*, he knew, was sympathetic to him.[34]

Reporters certainly saw plenty of Ellsberg. Many lived in the same chic apartment complex, Bunker Hill Towers, three blocks from the courthouse in downtown Los Angeles. They ran into him almost every day. But "I don't think this is a man who was ever satisfied by anybody," Peter Schrag observes. "Nobody was ever quite deeply enough devoted to whatever it is he wanted you to be devoted to."[35]

Many reporters simply found Ellsberg difficult to be around. He was combative, suspicious, pedantic, and condescending with them. He seemed to enjoy sparring with them. "He was very prickly," Linda Deutsch says. Ungar recalls "brushing past him a lot of the time . . . and he would always seem annoyed and distracted . . . talking with that kind of dismissive, condescending tone of his." It was "a funny feeling to run into him. He was really quite dismissive." Ellsberg thought most reporters did not understand him, and most did not, in a sense. They had become quite cynical about him. "I think everything he did, we thought, was for image, PR, for effect," Arnold remembers. "The Self-Effacing Megalomaniac," some called him. And it seemed that all

Ellsberg could talk about was the trial and the Vietnam War. Theo Wilson says: "Some reporters got a little bored with him. Because they'd say, 'How are you, Dan?' . . . And he'd tell them in excruciating detail how he was affected by this and that. . . . Even when he's trying to be one of the guys with the reporters, he never could be. . . . The reporters didn't want to listen to these intellectual dissertations forever. And it got to the point where they'd say, 'God, duck into the bushes. Here he comes.' . . . You could just only hear so much." Even sympathetic reporters would see him in the elevator and head the other way. "There was this avoidance phenomenon, where he would wear thin on people," Sachs recalls. Peter Young, one of Russo's attorneys, puts the problem this way: "The thing about Dan that I think people didn't like was that they never felt any personal connection with Dan. Dan operates on a very cerebral level, and it's all intellectual. It's not a personal interaction somehow. There's some[thing] there that's missing."[36]

Ellsberg also often acted self-righteous with the press, as if he was imparting the truth, something quite important, and more important than what others might have to say (as he did in several press conferences I viewed on videotape, including one 20 years later where the song was the same). Ellsberg lectured reporters. Few had tolerance for that; most learned not to argue with him. And Ellsberg's ego was, once again, off-putting. Carl Bernstein would say later that of all the people he had been predisposed to view favorably, Ellsberg was the one who had most turned him off; Bernstein discerned a gigantic ego. "I can't think of anybody who really liked him personally," Ungar remembers. "I think that his lawyers and the staff of the defense team saw him as this sort of impossible guy. . . . I didn't even think his wife liked him. I mean, I didn't think anybody liked him. . . . The people working on the defense team used to make fun of him all the time."[37]

One journalist who covered Ellsberg's trial, and who wrote some adulatory stuff about him, recalls that when it was over, "I was so sick of Ellsberg. And I think most of the journalists were. When I got into it, I admired him; I thought he was a very courageous guy . . . and I thought he did an incredibly important thing. And then . . . we all got to know him better. . . . He used to . . . try to tell us about the First Amendment," the writer says incredulously. "Sort of, 'Did you guys know about the First Amendment? About free speech?' . . . And everybody is sort of saying, 'Oh, my God.' . . . I think we all had the same feeling about Dan." During the pretrial process, Peter Schrag recounts,

> one night a few of us had gone to a Dodgers game. And we came back from the Dodgers game . . . and we're standing in the garage sort of talking about it.

And Dan had arrived from somewhere at the same time in this garage of this building. And he came over, and he wanted to talk to us about something [else]. . . . And he kept trying to get a word in. And he couldn't get into the conversation about the game, because he had no interest. . . . And there was never a conversation. . . . Whenever you were there with him alone, or if you were in that situation, the only thing he could talk about is what *he* wanted to talk about.

Ellsberg seemed somewhat naive about how to relate to other people. Amid the stress of his trial, his charm had apparently left him. He seemed lacking in humor. "His sense of humor had to do with mocking people who were very wrong," Ungar remembers. Also, "he was always quick to fly off the handle. . . . I always thought of him as being stretched very tight." Dolores Donovan, a young lawyer on his defense team, often got the sense that Ellsberg was on the verge of a nervous breakdown. But a large part of him seemed to thrive on stress and living on the edge. "There was this sort of compulsive excessiveness about him," Schrag thought. (Once over dinner at a Chinese restaurant during the trial, Ellsberg asked Howard Zinn, "Do you like it hot? Do you like your Chinese food hot?" "Well, yeah. Well, sure, we could have one of the dishes we order be hot," Zinn replied. As it turned out, "*Every* dish was super hot," Zinn laughs. "Over the top. Everything is over the top, you know. So I thought it was so characteristic." Another time, on the beach in Malibu early one evening, Ellsberg was the only person in a large party to strip down to his shorts and dive into the cold ocean.)[38]

Under the constraints of television news, Ellsberg could speak concisely with reporters. He seemed to revel in the attention he received and in his access to a podium. But his facial expression was typically grave, with frown-lined intensity. And he could go off. "What I would try to do is make a quick, short statement," Russo remembers. "Then Ellsberg would just logorrhea. He would get fascinated with an idea he had, and he'd go into that. I was *embarrassed*. . . . I remember one press conference we had in the defense office where he went *on and on*. And it was sort of Jesuitical. You know, it was like how many angels will dance on the head of this pin. He'd get fascinated with his own ideas, and he'd say, 'Oh, that's interesting. It's fascinating. . . . What I just said was very interesting.'" Russo came to think that Ellsberg was putting on an act to cover up his insecurities. "And as he improvises, he just gets further and further off into it. And that's what he would do at these press conferences."[39]

One can imagine how frustrating all this must have been for Ellsberg. Here he was on stage at last, widely applauded, and yet many members of the media—his link to the public—didn't even want to hear what he had to say, indeed, were running away from him.

———— ❈ ————

Compounding his disquiet immeasurably, Ellsberg had become a pariah to his former associates. "I lost all my friends in one day," he recalls. "They just vanished." This included literally "*all* my friends," he emphasizes. "Every person I knew in the world. Except my wife and my family," and antiwar comrades he had met since the late 1960s. "But my friends from ten and fifteen years earlier, *all* of them vanished."[40]

An inordinately sensitive man, Ellsberg was wounded quite severely. "It was obviously very painful to him," his friend Randy Kehler reminisces. "And I could feel his deep, deep hurt over that. People that he thought were friends and colleagues . . . just sort of treated him like the plague." (Over the years Ellsberg would often tell Kehler when he had been snubbed by somebody.)[41]

Harry Harris, Ellsberg's former Pentagon colleague, did contact him and received quite an emotional reception. "I called him on the phone," Harris recounts. "He says, '*Harry!* . . . Come right over.' So I went over to his home. . . . When he greeted me, he hugged me. . . . He was very physical . . . very emotional. And he says, 'Harry, you're the only guy that has come to see me. . . . ' He was a leper. . . . Everybody just severed their connections. . . . He was so elated to see me." Also in an emotional manner, Ellsberg would later tell Thomas Schelling's son Andrew that Andrew's father and mother were the only people from his previous world who didn't break relations with him and who still welcomed him into their home after the Pentagon Papers were published. He talked about how Andrew's father had thus been his best friend over the years. Andrew was surprised by that and wondered if his father had reciprocal feelings.[42]

Most people who disowned Ellsberg were angry at him or detested what he had done. Some were also undoubtedly jealous of his fame. Perhaps more than some. And there was another consideration—the potential cost to their own careers of associating with him. At a public event in 1991, Ellsberg recalled that his former RAND colleague Konrad Kellen told him about ten years after the Papers were published, "Dan, my clearance is like my penis. I cannot take any chances with it."[43]

According to Ellsberg, he deliberately stayed away from former colleagues to avoid causing them more trouble. But more likely, he was nervous about the reception he'd receive. He paid no attention to Kellen's concerns. "He would call and this and that," Kellen remembers. "I said to him finally one day, 'You know, I love you dearly, but I can't lose my job. If I lose my clearance . . . I lose my job.'" Ellsberg "scared Konrad Kellen to death," RAND's Richard Best recalls. Kellen "didn't know whether he ought to see him." When Ellsberg arranged to meet with Kellen in the early 1990s, he told Kellen that he was the first person from RAND he'd seen since the Papers were published. Ellsberg asked Kellen about the reaction at RAND to his release of the Papers. "I think he had this fantasy" that people had applauded him, Kellen recounts. "I said, 'But Dan, how naive can you get? You think the people at RAND are going to cheer? . . . You mystify me.'"[44]

Some of Ellsberg's former colleagues would barely be in the same room with him. At some meetings, people from RAND wouldn't recognize him. Both Adam Yarmolinsky and Helmut Sonnenfeldt would "almost comically" try to evade him in the years ahead, Ellsberg recounts. Yarmolinsky, who "cannot be close to McNamara and be very friendly to Daniel Ellsberg," Ellsberg told me, did this at two conferences. When he approached Yarmolinsky at one,

> he wouldn't look me in the eye and was trying to run away from me. And I didn't realize it at first; I sort of thought he was running to a car. And so I sort of ran along with him, and then realized that the guy is doing everything he can to get away from me, lest he be seen in my company. . . . It was quite painful to me. . . .
>
> When I went up to see [Sonnenfeldt], literally I'm talking to him, and there are only two of us in the room, and I was asking him questions—he wouldn't look me in the eye, or acknowledge that he knew who I was. It was incredible. That was an unusual physical experience. Then I saw him another time—similar, wouldn't look at me, wouldn't acknowledge my presence.

Ellsberg says this happened several times with Sonnenfeldt. "I guess it shows a sensitivity, in a way," Sonnenfeldt responds. "Beneath the assurance and the certitudes that he projects, there's probably a very sensitive core." Yarmolinsky told me that Ellsberg approached him "in his usual enthusiastic way" some years after the Papers were published and said that he'd like to come talk to an organization Yarmolinsky was with. Ellsberg also asked Yarmolinsky why his friends wouldn't see him. Yarmolinsky heard "a long monologue" about Ellsberg's marriage on a later occasion. "He's all over you like a puppy," Yarmolinsky recounted. "Whenever I see him, he gives me the big hello."[45]

Equally strikingly, Harry Rowen also refused to acknowledge Ellsberg's presence on one occasion. This occurred in the mid- or late 1970s as Ellsberg and Patricia were walking in a tunnel in the Los Angeles airport late one night. "There is nobody else in this tunnel," Ellsberg recounts. "But then I see a tall figure. As he comes somewhat closer, I realize . . . 'God, it's Harry Rowen. I haven't seen him for years.' So my first thought was, 'Wow. Harry. Great!' . . . My second thought was, 'Shit!'" Ellsberg remembered some things Rowen had testified to in his trial:

> And then my third thought was, "Oh, well, what the hell. It was years ago. . . ."
> All these thoughts are going through my mind fast. And then as we get maybe
> ten yards away or something, I realize that he's not going to look at me, and
> we're going to pass just side by side. So he looked straight ahead, eyes straight
> ahead, not looking slightly. And here we are, the only people in this little nar-
> row tunnel. And he looks straight ahead and walks by. Without having seen
> me. . . . Oooo, it wasn't good. It was not good. . . . He had to have seen me far
> away. And Patricia too. . . . I wanted to be friendly.

But Ellsberg told me that Rowen "cannot be friendly" if Rowen expects to continue consulting. (Ellsberg also ran into Andrew Marshall in a tunnel in the Los
Angeles airport, but they had a different sort of encounter: after exchanging
hellos, Ellsberg asked to "borrow" money for cab fare.)[46]

Ellsberg was surprised to end up *persona non grata*. He felt that, in some
ways, he hadn't really changed all that much. His analysis had simply taken him
in a different direction—the right direction. Now he was a traitor? Noam
Chomsky recalls: "He was shocked to see how people . . . in his close circles reacted. Which I thought was pretty naive. I think he had real illusions about
what these people are like, and what their interests are and concerns are. . . . I
think it was quite a psychological blow for him to see that, after having done
what from their point of view is treachery, they somehow didn't want to have
anything to do with him. . . . I think what he thought is he would be greeted as
sort of a hero and then they would all accept him back."[47]

Ellsberg approached some of his ex-colleagues in search of approval and
reconciliation. He phoned Rufus Phillips, his former associate in Vietnam, and
asked, "Did I understand why he had done this?" Phillips recounts. "And almost
asking that I forgive him, in a way. And I said, 'No, Dan, I can't do that. And
here's why.' . . . He wanted, I think, to have either some understanding or some
forgiveness." Ellsberg also went by Lou Conein's house. "He wanted to see if
what he had done had upset me," Conein remembers. "And I told him, Yes!"[48]

Some of Ellsberg's antiwar friends felt he was too sensitive to what his
former colleagues thought. "There's still a part of Dan that wanted their approval," Howard Zinn recalls. "Dan wants admiration and respect, even from
people who shouldn't matter that much to him. . . . Everybody matters to
Dan. Everybody's attitude matters to him. . . . It's not a healthy way to be. It

just opens you up to too many blows. . . . It's odd, because on the one hand, he breaks with them in such a dramatic fashion by what he does. But on the other hand, there's something in him which is still connected with that old life of his."[49]

Ellsberg was also unpopular with many other Americans. Indeed, broad segments of the public. His act had unleashed a torrent of hostility at him. He received hate mail. "He seemed very upset about it," Jerry Goodman remembers. Though most of it was of the nutty, anti-Semitic variety, some letters were scary, such as those threatening assassination. Like Robert Ellsberg, Patricia worried about him getting shot, rubbed out, perhaps in a crowd.[50]

Meanwhile, Ellsberg had to feel his way through the antiwar movement. Many antiwar activists considered him a hero, and he loved that, of course; Todd Gitlin, an early SDS leader, called him an example of the "new heroism," which "consists in conspicuously throwing one's own complicity back in the face of power." It was gratifying to Ellsberg to be part of a large movement; that may have fueled his later activism after the war ended. "I think that recognition that it's wonderful to be part of a great movement has led him in the years since to be involved in all of those antinuclear protests," Zinn offers.[51]

But other protesters didn't take to Ellsberg. Many distrusted him, given his past complicity, slowness to come around, pragmatic impetus, and egocentricity. "He was very important, even though nobody liked him," Leonard Rodberg remembers. "None of the movement people liked him. And they all thought, 'How did this guy get to be in this position?' . . . He played his role well for that year, but he was never a movement person before, and I don't think since, in terms of organizing any events or working with people or creating. He would just be there as the one the media would focus on."[52]

Robert Sachs arranged a meeting of Ellsberg and the Catholic war resister Philip Berrigan. "It was very odd, because here you had Phil Berrigan, this big hearty Irishman, very warm kind of person, a bear-hug type person, and very comfortable with himself, and Dan not fully comfortable with himself," Sachs recounts. "And I'm not sure they ever clicked."[53]

Though moving leftward, Ellsberg thought some radicals were naive, simplistic, and insensitive to the powers of the state. And it was unclear whom he could trust in the antiwar movement. "Everybody was calling him up," Joan Libby, who worked for him, remembers. "Everybody wanted something from him." Dan and Patricia were open to meeting virtually all the players. "They were so funny, because they thought everybody was terrific," Libby recalls. "I think they both really liked—him more than Pat—the diverse people and what they brought. . . . He was just as interested in meeting Abbie Hoffman as in meeting anybody else." A dinner with Hoffman generated "a lot of animated conversation."[54]

One longtime friend of Ellsberg commented on his associating with radical leaders: "I can remember when he was first applying games theory to defense strategy. He was very proud of the top Washington officials he had dinner with. Now he loves to dine with the big names in radicalism. In both cases, he needed a legitimizing audience, a community which accepted him."[55]

———◆———

Adding to Ellsberg's difficulties, he was then feeling the pressure of a quickie book he had agreed to do. His publisher, Dell, announced in late July 1971 that he was preparing a paperback collection of his Vietnam writings and public statements. Ellsberg planned to donate his $150,000 advance to help war-wounded Indochinese children. But Dell soon canceled his contract when he failed to provide a 20,000-word introduction; part of the book had already been set in type. Ellsberg had to return an unspecified sum of advance money.[56]

Simon & Schuster quickly stepped in, signing Ellsberg up for a book to be issued in November. But that deadline also proved impossible. For Ellsberg was "very, very distracted and distractible," his editor, Ted Solotaroff, remembers. "It was very hard for me to get him to sit down and work on the book. I remember going over to Pat Marx's apartment on Sutton Place and kind of looking out at the East River hour after hour while he fielded phone calls. I think at one point early on I said, 'You know, we really have to get this project going if it's going to work.' . . . I wanted to go over my editing with him. . . . And Pat said, 'Well, you know, we have a war to stop.'" That comment struck Solotaroff as somewhat hyperbolic and "fairly characteristic of their attitude. They were very important figures and the book was . . . not as significant as what they were doing in the public arena. . . . Because it pulled him, even for an hour or two at a time, out of the sort of spotlight. . . . There was an awful lot of them running around." Solotaroff noticed that Dan loved being courted and feted. "Every time the phone rang, he would take the call. And obviously the phone was ringing almost all the time. So he did very little editorial work, consultation." At one point, Solotaroff picked up the phone and Sidney Zion was on the line. Solotaroff thought Ellsberg would not be eager to talk to Zion since Zion had fingered him. "On the contrary, he said, 'No, let me talk to him,'" Solotaroff recounts. "So it was hard to think of anyone whom he wouldn't have rather talked to than work on the book."[57]

Solotaroff became quite frustrated. He didn't have a lot of expendable time, and he was feeling pressure from his boss, the demanding Dick Snyder, whom he knew would not be happy if they failed to take advantage of Ellsberg's fifteen minutes of fame. A certain tension consequently developed between Solotaroff and Ellsberg fairly quickly and was to last throughout their relationship.[58]

It didn't help matters that both Dan and Patricia treated Solotaroff, a well-regarded editor and writer, almost like a secretary who would be used or not used at their convenience. "I had the feeling with Dan that people were kind of disposable," Solotaroff remembers. "You know, you were there for a function. When you performed it, that was that. I would think that his wake is so littered with the rubble of his relationships." That is probably true. "He was very surprised about being edited," Solotaroff recounts. "I think that he felt that he was already an accomplished writer. And he wasn't. There was a fair amount of jargon and imprecision in those papers that was edited out. He became quite friendly with me on the basis of the improvement that was made in the pieces." Solotaroff found Ellsberg to be a narcissist driven by a great sense of insecurity—which seemed to hold him back on the book—with an "almost adolescent hero self-worship."[59]

Ellsberg once suggested that Solotaroff, who often found himself simply cooling his heels at the Ellsbergs' apartment, take advantage of some down time to read his entry in the Harvard alumni magazine. Solotaroff noticed that the entries of other alumni were much shorter than Ellsberg's: "Dan's was about two full pages, and was like a huge, long publicity release. . . . Very little that he had done . . . escaped mention. And when I read that, I realized that I had my hands full. This was someone who was very, very much a person who took himself very seriously and who wanted the world to know about him right away. . . . He's a mythomaniac, and he very much needed to present himself as more than life-sized." Ellsberg was much different than Solotaroff had envisioned. "I had expected someone who was much less publicity minded. . . . It was sort of like suddenly working on a book with Norman Mailer."[60]

Joan Libby also worked extensively with Ellsberg on his book, waging her own struggle to keep him moving. "There was so much of his identity on the line," she points out. "It wasn't a relaxed approach." Ellsberg was attempting to explain his change on the war—in essence, why he had released the Pentagon Papers—and the book had to live up to his reputation for brilliance. He probably feared falling short. And he was working under harrowing time constraints. Libby, her boyfriend David Hawk, Dan, and Patricia ultimately holed up at the mansion of Patricia's father (who was then out of town) in order to force Dan to complete the book. It was an enormously ironic setting. "He needed a place that would be quiet," Libby remembers. "But I think he thought, 'My God, if her family knows we're here. . . . ' That's sort of where we finished it. That's really where we got [a manuscript completed]. We sort of put him away in a room and kept checking on how it was going. . . . Because there was so much going on in his head, it was so easy at a comma to take the wrong [direction] . . . which would take you down to a totally different book. . . . But I kept thinking he was very close." At one point Libby, indeed, discovered that Ellsberg was writing a different book than the one planned. "Dan could never write anything without qualifying every comma," Stanley Sheinbaum recalls. "Everything had to be qualified. And a sentence like this suddenly becomes a paragraph. And it was madness. It was madness." (The first thing Sheinbaum said when I asked him about Ellsberg's effort to write the book was a Yiddish term for woebegone.)[61]

Jan Butler understands that Ellsberg's book, *Papers on the War*, was compiled in large part by Patricia. "She was certainly always there kind of urging him forward and trying . . . to keep it all going," Libby remembers. "We all were . . . marshaling our forces around this guy to see if we couldn't relieve enough things around him so that he could get this done."[62]

Papers on the War was not released until July 1972. Solotaroff had hoped to meld Ellsberg's essays into a cohesive narrative showing the evolution of his views and the reasons behind it, perhaps also making a larger statement about the American turnaround as a whole. But Ellsberg didn't devote enough time to the book, and his writings were not as numerous as Solotaroff had thought. The result was not what he had envisioned. Ellsberg had also hoped for a better book. "But it is this book or nothing for quite a long time, as I have at last come to acknowledge," he wrote in his unpolished and boastful introduction. "Events in my life since June, 1971, have not been conducive to the production of new, finished essays." Godfrey Hodgson observed in a review of *Papers on the War* in the *Washington Post Book World*, "It is not in all respects a satisfactory book. It is stitched together . . . disjointed," the bulk of it "taken up with a miscellany," although "Ellsberg emerge[s] from these pages as a man of courage, and intelligence." "Surprisingly impersonal," Murray Kempton noted in the *New York Times Book Review*. It "bears the cold stamp of the think tank," *Time* observed. Repetitive, "stiff," though at times "moving," *Newsweek*'s reviewer commented. "A series of disjointed papers," Ellsberg himself would later call it. Edward Lansdale, to whom Ellsberg sent a copy, told Ellsberg in a letter that he had been moved by it. Ellsberg claimed later that it changed Lansdale's views on Vietnam and made him cry, though Lansdale's letter said neither.[63]

Solotaroff came to feel considerable pathos about Ellsberg. "He was going to write the history of America's involvement in Vietnam," too, Solotaroff remembers. "It was going to be his life's work. And there was no one in a better position to do it. . . . And I remember thinking to myself at the time that it was, at best, a fifty-fifty shot whether he was going to do this." Solotaroff thought Ellsberg's frequent presence at demonstrations later "was all perhaps a way of running away from writing that book."[64] There is probably some truth to that.

Ellsberg had another nagging problem at the time, a Tony Russo problem, one that threatened to screw up his trial and, by extension, his whole life. That July, aware he was likely to face criminal charges too, Russo had traveled to Cambridge to meet with Ellsberg. "I got there, and David Hawk [who like Libby worked for Ellsberg] had Dan going here, there, and everywhere, one public appearance after another," Russo recounts. "And I was sitting there saying, 'Hey, man, let's get organized.' And he didn't seem to want to say anything. . . . I couldn't corner him," Russo laughs. "He was running off and doing spots and speeches and whatnot. . . . I was just mad as hell, because I couldn't pin him down. I couldn't get him to sit down and talk." Ellsberg was like "a greased pig," Russo thought.[65]

At lunch one day with Dan, Patricia, and others, Russo recalls, he told Ellsberg, "'Well, we've got to have a defense committee.' And Dan said, 'Oh, no. We don't need a defense committee. Pat will pay the lawyers.' And I tell you, I almost lost it in my gut. . . . I thought, '*My God.* I'm on my own.'" To Russo's way of thinking, he and Ellsberg were on the same side, working together for common political goals. But with Ellsberg, "it was like being on the back of a tiger," Russo says. "You had no control. Because here this guy was single-minded and thought only of himself."[66]

Russo felt a bit frantic. "I said, 'Dan, please keep me informed. Because I will be at some point involved in this. I'm already subpoenaed.'"[67]

While back east that summer, Russo joined the Ellsbergs for a visit to Howard and Roslyn Zinns' vacation house on Cape Cod. They went to a nude beach nearby, though the Zinns had never been there before. The Ellsbergs would later invite Howard Zinn into their hot tub in California. "It was typical," Zinn laughs.[68]

In appearance, manner, and lifestyle, Russo might have seemed to the average observer more inclined toward such activities than Ellsberg. That was also part of Ellsberg's Tony Russo problem. Ellsberg worried that his prosecutors could, in effect, sully him with Russo. For Russo was now distinctly part of the counterculture, with his long, fuzzy sideburns, that stringy hair flowing from the sides of his balding head, and his hippie-ish attire. "He didn't like the way I dressed," Russo remembers. "He didn't like my caps." Ellsberg was far more buttoned up; he wore expensive suits to court. And Russo's talk was sprinkled with the language of the sixties. A person probably wouldn't know from talking to him that he had master's degrees in both aeronautical engineering and public affairs from Princeton, or that he had published that paper on electromagnetic waves in ionized gas. Russo was an outspoken political radical. He spoke of U.S. imperialism and revolution. That made Dan and Pat Ellsberg nervous. Russo was already talking about mounting a militant defense. What's more, the Ellsbergs had questions about his psychological stability. They worried that he might go off in some damaging or embarrassing way.[69]

Ellsberg already had enough in the way of image problems without having to worry about Russo, too. And he knew that he had skeletons in his closet. His lawyers and Patricia (who probably worried that some of those skeletons would not play well in her own family and might embarrass her as well) also knew. The fear of damaging sexual disclosures was always in the background during Ellsberg's trial, Robert Sachs remembers. "Because you'd hear various rumors." There was "this undercurrent of stories" on "this other side of his life," which reporters enjoyed kidding Sachs about. But Ellsberg spoke with some openness about his sexual interests with the journalist Peter Schrag and told Schrag about his fascination with pornography. "I don't think he ever made a secret of the pornography," Schrag remembers, and "he talked about his sexual obsessions." Ellsberg's talk led Schrag to wonder about Patricia's sex life, too. "The manner was always sort of vaguely a little bit seductive," he recalls. "She came on to you in some funny way." One journalist would note the contrast between Patricia's prim appearance and her interest in sex.[70]

Ellsberg's concern for his image extended to his physical appearance. During the pretrial and trial, he swam regularly and at impressive length at Bunker Hill Towers. "He'd go down to the swimming pool at six in the morning and swim some astonishing number of laps," Sanford Ungar remembers. "He was in fanatically good physical shape," Charles Nesson recalls. "It just seemed like for hours he was just going up and down in the pool in a kind of steady crawl." Ellsberg presented a striking image of solitude from the towers above. He told Joe McGinniss one day, "I just swam fifty laps in the pool here, and I've got a chinning bar set up. I've been training for this like Bobby Fischer." Ellsberg also dieted; he seemed to Russo to be quite concerned with his appearance. "He liked to shine in the eyes of women," Marty Arnold remembers. "To bask . . . in adoring women."[71]

On December 30, 1971, Russo became officially an albatross around Ellsberg's neck. A federal grand jury handed up a new, much more severe, 15-count indictment that added conspiracy to the mounting list of criminal charges against Ellsberg. He now faced a maximum of 115 years in prison (later reduced to 105). His lawyers had not expected *that* much (nor did they think a sentence of that length remotely possible). Russo was also charged with conspiracy and three counts of theft and espionage. He faced a maximum of 35 years behind bars (later reduced to 25).[72]

Russo's inclusion in the indictment strengthened the conspiracy charge and may have also been a response to his refusal to testify before the grand jury. There was also the possible motive of hurting Ellsberg. "I think it was part of the government's strategy to screw up the defense by pairing them together," Nesson says. "Because Ellsberg as a single defendant looked mighty clean." Moreover, the prosecutors may have anticipated a split defense, one that would become evident in the courtroom.[73]

Ellsberg's frustration at being paired with Russo was astronomical. "The idea, I think, to Ellsberg that Tony Russo would even have 10 percent billing compared to Ellsberg must have driven him nuts," Ungar comments. "I think Dan was offended that he had to share the indictment with Russo." And Russo knew it.[74]

Further aggravating Ellsberg, Russo's name was listed first in the indictment. "The United States vs. Anthony J. Russo, Jr., Daniel Ellsberg," the case was called. Sometimes the clerk would say in court, "The United States versus Anthony J. Russo et al." Under ordinary legal practice, the names of defendants are listed alphabetically. Many believed the government had listed Ellsberg second to snub him, to take him down a notch. "That was done on purpose," Richard Best heard from the FBI. Carol Ellsberg mentioned it to David Nissen. "He kind of smiled," she remembers. "It was meant to annoy Dan." But it may also have been intended to avoid confusion between this indictment and the preceding one.[75]

Shortly after the second indictment, another person entered the picture who would nettle Ellsberg, indeed, would send both him and Patricia completely up the wall. Catherine Barkley, Russo's new wife, was a 24-year-old graduate student at Stanford. She, too, was a radical, though her politics were shallow. She and Russo met at Stanford shortly before marrying. "She proposed that we should get married," Russo recounts. "She said, 'You know, I'll be liable to the grand jury. . . .' And I thought she was really neat. She was pretty, she was smart. And, to me, marriage then didn't mean all that much. I thought of it as a bourgeois institution that had to be struggled against," Russo laughs. To some, Barkley seemed on the make. "Talk about star fucking," Stanley Sheinbaum remarks. "She wanted to be in the middle of everything. . . . I think Catherine Barkley marries one of the stars to be a little more than coequal with all the others."[76]

Barkley constantly poked fun at the Ellsbergs, though mostly behind their backs. She became anathema to them, both politically and personally. "It is *impossible* to imagine the four of them sitting down to dinner together and passing a kind of social evening," Ungar says. "It is utterly impossible to imagine that. I think to Catherine Barkley there would have been a very short distance between Daniel Ellsberg and Alexander Haig." Patricia found Barkley "unjudiciously radical." Barkley further jeopardized Dan's defense, the Ellsbergs feared. They knew her influence on Russo was considerable.[77]

Barkley and Russo had their own tensions. Theirs was a very difficult and trying marriage, Leonard Weinglass remembers. "Lennie played a role in that," Russo says. "Lennie hit on my wife. . . . When I was out of town. . . . And I think she rejected him." Russo began to notice that Barkley wasn't getting a lot of work done on his case. "She lost heart about halfway through the trial and started staying home a lot," he recalls. Their marriage ended right after the trial ended. Barkley became a follower of the 15-year-old Guru Maharaj Ji. After that transition, Russo questioned her sincerity from the beginning: Had she been a plant? Patricia and Dan had earlier wondered about that.[78]

Not long after the second indictment, Russo and Ellsberg had a tempestuous fight one night in front of Russo's apartment. They almost came to blows. A split defense indeed. Ellsberg told Russo that the Pentagon Papers were "his thing, and my thing was the interviews" from RAND's Viet Cong Motivation and Morale study, Russo recounts. "He said, 'You should be working on getting those interviews out.'" It was as if Ellsberg was saying, "Get off my case."[79]

Around this same time, "a *horrible, horrible* meeting" (in Peter Young's words) took place at the Ambassador Hotel in Los Angeles, further straining relations between the two co-defendants. Russo informed the Ellsberg camp that he planned to hire not only Weinglass, a veteran of the Chicago 8 conspiracy trial whose unruly reputation masked extraordinary trial skills, a smooth personality, and a dignified style, but also Young, a radical lawyer who lived in a commune, and another young left-wing attorney named Jeffrey Kupers. The Ellsbergs were quite upset. "They just wouldn't buy it," Russo recounts. "Ellsberg and Pat were just going up the wall. . . . They kept saying that to bring Weinglass in would be to bring in a circus atmosphere and Chicago and all that." But Russo hired all three lawyers against the Ellsbergs' wishes, and the Ellsberg side of the defense soon warmed to Young and Weinglass, who would prove to be the real star among the defense lawyers.[80]

Ellsberg and Russo's relationship deteriorated further during the trial. The tension was great and became almost unbearable on both sides. Another formerly close relationship of Ellsberg's was headed for the trash heap. Partly out of fear and a sense of superiority, Ellsberg handled Russo in the "worst possible way," Richard Falk observed. Ellsberg continued to wall off Russo and wanted to have little to do with him. Ellsberg "didn't want to talk to Russo even," Ungar often thought. "You know, didn't want him around. Just viewed him as this kind of competition for attention." The two co-defendants didn't speak much to each other, and when they did Ellsberg treated Russo "very haughtily, condescendingly," Ungar noticed, or affected a paternal attitude. Russo deeply resented it. Others in Ellsberg's camp were also always blowing him off or patronizing him, Russo perceived. Ellsberg got all the best speaking engagements. And when it came time to schedule fund-raising parties, Russo wasn't consulted. Sometimes Barkley would ask her husband, "How can you let them do this to you?" Russo didn't get much of the spotlight. Rather than feeling famous, he felt ignored. "Tony became the forgotten person in the case," Mark Rosenbaum recalls. "Sort of a footnote to a footnote." The humble number two man, and far back at number two. Ellsberg made it clear to Russo that he was the star of the show. (Years later, during a twentieth anniversary program on the publication of the Pentagon Papers, Ellsberg resisted attempts by Russo to interject comments several times, and monopolized the question-and-answer session, though Russo looked pretty much resigned to it, as if he'd seen it all before.)[81]

Most of the time, Russo bit his tongue with Ellsberg. But sometimes harsh words were exchanged. "He just abandoned me," Russo says. "He betrayed me."[82]

Their differences were sharply evident in their approaches to the trial. Russo viewed it as a confrontation and political theater; he saw himself as part Yippie. He chased after Alexander Haig as Haig was leaving the courthouse and threw a digest of the Papers at him. Russo would have preferred more such fracturing of the decorum. But Ellsberg would angrily ask him, Had it occurred to Tony Russo what all this could do to Daniel Ellsberg? Isn't that exactly what the prosecutor *wants* us to do? Russo felt it wouldn't be such a terrible thing if they did go to jail, though. To his dismay, Ellsberg seemed to be doing everything he could to avoid it. Before the Papers were published, "there's all this talk about going to jail and everything, and then the trial comes along and he's trying to get off," Russo remembers. "He didn't want to go to jail then." And "it seemed to me that it [the trial] was mostly, on his part, ego satisfaction. It was like the war was extraneous."[83]

Russo identified with Vietnam veterans, and on the first day of the trial he marched into the courthouse with a group of vets, who then noisily protested the prosecution's use of a large screen that blocked the view of many in the audience. Russo loved it, but Patricia and Dan did not. "Dan

Ellsberg did not accept Tony Russo's politics and he didn't accept Tony Russo's friends," Peter Young comments. "And Tony Russo's friends were very important to Tony."[84]

Russo also advocated calling radical witnesses—Chomsky, Zinn, Tom Hayden, Robert Scheer. Ellsberg and his lawyers thought that risky, though they allowed it. Tears came to Ellsberg's eyes during Zinn's testimony. "I was talking about the Atlantic Charter, and how the Atlantic Charter had promised self-determination for colonial peoples," Zinn recounts. "And I wouldn't have guessed that at that particular point that Dan would suddenly become overwhelmed with emotion. But he did. Because he suddenly, I guess, became overwhelmed with the thought, 'My God, these promises that were made to the world, and here they're violated.'"[85]

It was the establishment witnesses who mattered to Ellsberg: the Bundys, the Galbraiths, the Schlesingers. Ellsberg seemed to Marty Arnold envious of those establishment types who had done better in Washington than he. In contrast to Russo, he shook the hand of Alexander Haig and informed reporters that he had lunched with Haig at San Clemente.[86]

The day before Russo testified, Ellsberg committed another indignity. "He came up to my room with this phony statement of support, saying that he didn't know of anybody he'd rather be on trial with, and blah blah blah," Russo recounts. "It was all just artificial. Trying to buck me up before the testimony."[87]

Russo's relationship with Patricia was even worse. She came to loathe Russo. "She very much resented Tony," Richard Falk recalls. "And Tony, I think, teased her and sort of baited her a bit. So that they had a very unfortunate chemistry. It was as much that as the substantive issues."[88]

Other pressures were also taking a toll on Russo at this time, and by the end of the trial he had pulled noticeably into himself. He responded to Ellsberg's wall and his dashed political hopes by keeping his own distance. Whereas Young had found him gregarious and outgoing when they had first met in early 1972, when the trial resumed a year later, Young recounts,

> my impression was that Tony had decided that he was going to come to the trial, and that was it. . . . He came to some meetings, but he put in the minimal amount of time necessary to the defense, and devoted himself to his political pursuits elsewhere. . . . He became quite withdrawn. . . . He harbored a lot of resentment. I think if the trial damaged any one person, it was Tony Russo. It made him unemployable in his chosen field. And he suffered a great deal. I don't think Dan suffered in the same way—at all. . . . [Russo] felt very much out of the decision-making process that went on around the trial. . . . He was never asked to give statements to the press. Dan was. Dan reveled in it, and

profited from it. Not monetarily, but certainly in terms of the things he wanted out of life, Dan profited from it.

Russo pointedly placed a bright red book on the defense table that charged Ellsberg with being a former CIA agent who may have been doing the CIA's bidding by releasing the Papers.[89]

After the trial, Russo completely fell apart. "He became somewhat irrational," Weinglass remembers. "He was lashing out at Dan, lashing out at myself. Marriage breaking up. It all began to fall apart for Tony." Another person who knew him recalls: "I thought Tony was losing it. And he lost a tremendous amount of weight. He was skin and bones. And he was exhibiting some signs of paranoia. And he wasn't sleeping. It was purely because he had no job. He had no money. He had nothing."[90]

Russo looks back on the trial and his pairing with Ellsberg and shudders. "It's been a cross to bear, up until now," he told me. "It was a time of anguish. . . . It was horrendous from beginning to end. It was *horrendous*. . . . Every day I was just sitting on my anger." Toward the end, Russo remarked to a journalist about Ellsberg, "To tell you the truth, I really don't want to ever see him again."[91]

———◦———

Meanwhile, Ellsberg had lost another close friendship, this one through violent death. John Paul Vann died in a helicopter crash over the Central Highlands in Vietnam one rainy and foggy night in June 1972. Cruising along a dangerous route, his chopper hit a grove of trees at full speed and exploded into flames. He was 47 years old. Ellsberg cried when he heard the news. "He was just stunned," John Allen Vann, who spoke with him over the phone, remembers. "I could tell that he was emotionally crushed."[92]

At Vann's funeral, Ellsberg was not a popular man among the many war makers and war apologists, past and present, who were gathered. The only one who came up and shook his hand, he would recall, was William Colby. He felt estranged, isolated. Jesse Vann got the feeling from him "that he was being treated like an outsider," and he surely was. Scorned, even. Ellsberg looked much the way his detractors did, however, dressed as he was in his conservative suit. "He was very quiet and respectful," Tom Oliphant remembers. Ellsberg appeared quite worried to one of Vann's half brothers. He had rocked many boats, he told Gene Vann.[93]

Ellsberg sat just behind the Vann family. They appreciated his presence. "He was very kind to my children at the funeral," Mary Jane Vann reminisces. "He meant a great deal to them. Because Dan really went out of his way to talk to them and be kind to them." "He was with us constantly," John Allen recalls. "Literally." Ellsberg took three of the four Vann boys for a tour of the FBI building; agents followed them. He took Mary Jane out for a drink. "He really made it easier," she says. "He was exuding warmth and concern and care for the family."[94]

Ellsberg had earlier been something of an intermediary between Jesse Vann and his father, who hadn't gotten along with each other. Jesse and Ellsberg had discussed his father, Vietnam, nonviolence, drugs (which Jesse was doing—he thought LSD had influenced his decision not to join the army and go to Vietnam, which Ellsberg found quite interesting).[95]

His long hair cascading down below his shoulders, Jesse made a peace sign during his father's funeral. He also ripped his draft card in half and placed one half on his father's coffin. The Vann family was going to the White House after the funeral for an award ceremony, and Jesse planned to give the other half to President Nixon. "To me, Nixon was the enemy at the time," he recalls. But his scheme leaked out, and after family members pleaded with him not to go through with it, Jesse relented. During the award ceremony, Mary Jane noticed, Nixon "ignored me. He looked straight ahead. . . . We filed out, and he shook hands with everybody. When it came to me, I'm standing there with my hand out, and he just looked straight over my head. He wouldn't acknowledge me at all." Mary Jane later deduced it was because she had committed the breach of visiting the South Vietnamese embassy before coming to the White House.[96]

Two months after John Paul Vann's funeral, at the Republican national convention in Miami, Ellsberg gave a press conference in which he charged Nixon with secretly planning to escalate the Vietnam War all along. (Nixon had mined North Vietnam's ports and intensified the U.S. bombing of the North that May.) Ellsberg hoped to build support for George McGovern's presidential candidacy. Before flying to Miami, he had tried to convince a handful of former Kissinger aides and consultants to lend authority to his claim by joining him at the press conference. But they turned him down, and his press conference, which was sponsored by Representative Paul McCloskey, who had gone ahead with his plan to challenge Nixon for the Republican nomination, was something of a dud. He attracted little attention in Miami. Ellsberg charged the former Kissinger aides with putting their career concerns ahead of stopping the war; he pointed out to the four of them who had resigned quietly after the U.S. invasion of Cambodia in 1970 that Nixon had dropped two million tons of bombs since then. One of these men was Morton Halperin, who was aiding Ellsberg's defense. Ellsberg told another of the men, Anthony Lake, right before the convention that he was responsible for all the deaths that had occurred in Indochina since he had resigned, as Lake had not spoken out. Lake was astonished at that statement. He thought it showed tremendous moral arrogance and a lack of touch with reality.[97]

That fall, Ellsberg and Patricia vacationed in Puerto Vallarta, Mexico, where they got themselves into some hot water by giving free rein to the "other side" of their life. "They were just on some beach, and I guess in the buff and making love, and some guys come across them with their gun belts and take them in to the local police station," Robert Sachs recounts. The way Doug Dowd later heard the tale from Ellsberg was that he and Patricia were engaged in "some kind of a galloping funfest, fuckfest . . . just as naked as you can possibly be, and doing everything you can possibly do, according to Dan's story, which he told pridefully. And all of a sudden the feds arrived, the Mexican feds. And there they were, you know, in this Catholic country doing all kinds of naughty things. . . . And they were bundled off to jail, and had one hell of a time getting out of jail. Nobody knew who the hell they were. . . . It was sort of nip and tuck there for a while, apparently, in terms of the legalities of the whole thing. And somebody had to . . . get them out." Sachs heard that one of the Mexican police authorities recognized Ellsberg, at which point he and Patricia feared the episode was going to be splashed all over the media. But the authority was sympathetic to the release of the Pentagon Papers and let them go.[98] One suspects that one of Ellsberg's lawyers had to intervene.

———⊶⊙⊷———

Meanwhile, Carol Ellsberg had her own problems. She was receiving subpoenas from the prosecution mandating her testimony in Dan's trial and attracting more calls from Charles Nesson, who wanted to go over her statements to the government and her pending trial testimony in detail. So did Dan, Carol informed Nesson, but she had refused; she had exchanged angry words with Dan. He was still mad that she wasn't cooperating. Nesson told Carol that he had asked Dan repeatedly not to get in fights with her. If she appeared hostile on the witness stand, it would not do the defense any good. Nesson told her in one meeting that he was going to phone Dan immediately and chew him out for talking to her the way he had. Nesson wanted Dan to apologize to her, but Carol said that wouldn't mean anything. She stressed to Nesson that she didn't want to talk to Dan at all, despite the fact that he had suggested strongly to her that it would not go well for her in court if she contradicted his testimony. Dan was the one who was initiating all their contacts, Carol noted. She also pointed out that he had been inconsiderate of her: besides calling her up and abusing her over the phone, he would stroll uninvited into her house and watch television, and he wasn't keeping up his child support payments. Further, he was leaking inaccurate information to the press. Nesson repeatedly expressed to Carol in one meeting how worried he was about her upcoming trial testimony and the effect any ill will she showed would have on the jury. But what was she supposed to do, Carol remarked at one point—give him a little wink when she got on the stand? Nesson worried that *she* might tarnish Dan, undercut his integrity. For example, the prosecution would love to hear her tell the jury that he had released the Papers because he was approaching middle age and wanted to make a name for himself.[99]

Carol told Nesson there would be no press conferences, no photos or anything of that sort with the children. She didn't want her children exploited by the defense. "I wanted them to be *out* of it," she remembers. "I didn't mind their seeing him [their father] privately. But I didn't want them to be taken to fund raisers. I didn't want them being up on the platform when he gave speeches. . . . I didn't think it was wholesome for children to be part of a media event like that."[100]

If Robert or Mary testified in the trial, Carol told Nesson in effect, it would be over her dead body. When Robert mentioned to her one day that his father had called him up and asked him to testify, Carol hit the roof. "She'd gotten to the point of feeling . . . that would be disastrous," Robert recounts. "She had the sense that her children—her babies—were in just drastic danger." Carol phoned Dan in a rage. "I was *frantic*," she remembers. She couldn't reach Dan, but she got Nesson on the line; he would have to do. Nesson told her that Robert's testimony was "a possibility," her notes of their conversation read. Carol said she was "unalterably opposed" to it, that it might damage Robert by leading him to conclude later that he had helped send his father to jail. She made a veiled threat to Nesson. "I said, 'If you do this, I will have to do something that you won't like,'" Carol recounts. "And he was sort of saying, 'Well, what would that be?' And I said, 'Well, I'm not going to go into that now. But I promise it won't be pleasant.'" Carol didn't have the slightest idea what she was going to do. But she felt better having made the threat. "I feel you have gone back on what you told me two summers ago when you said you would not call Robert," she told Nesson. "I do not remember saying that," Nesson replied.[101] Robert was never called to testify.

In polar contrast to Carol, Dan wanted his children to attend the trial and be "very, very involved in the whole thing," Robert remembers. "To be at his side." Carol only permitted them to attend a few times, however, and with someone she knew. "My mother let us be present with the condition that we would not talk to any reporters," Robert recounts. "If we talked to any reporters, we would never go back again." It took some ingenuity to avoid reporters. Robert and Mary wished to support their father, Robert in particular. "I very much identified with my father and I would have liked to have been involved," Robert recalls. But he worried that if he exceeded his mother's limits of involvement, she would tighten the reins. He and Mary were also acutely aware that their desire to be involved upset their mother. It was hard being caught in their parents' crossfire. While she was sympathetic to her mother's concerns, Mary Ellsberg remembers,

> she was so worried about the fame hurting us, and in some way ruining our character . . . that it made it difficult to enjoy anything at all about the experience, and if we had a good time at an event it felt disloyal, and even like a sign of a potential character flaw. It meant that we crossed back and forth into two different dimensions of time and space, where we tried to fit in as best we could, and kept the two worlds pretty much separate, to avoid hurting or annoying either parent.
>
> Ironically, the only people who seemed sympathetic to the difficulties we faced as children were people who despised him [her father] politically. People who admired him often told us how lucky and privileged we were to be related to such a great man. Very few adults seemed to have any sensitivity at all to the wide gaps which often exist between public and private lives, and to the ambivalence that we might feel about our situation. On a political basis I agreed with my father's actions and was proud of them. . . . That, however, does not mean that he was an easy person to be around.

It was "just a terrible experience," Robert says of this whole period. He jumped at a chance to study in England for the 1972–73 academic year (his senior year in high school). "It was largely a feeling that it was better to be away from that whole scene," he remembers. "And an aspect of that was the tension between my mother and my father. I [didn't want] to be in the middle of that."[102]

Robert, who returned to the United States over spring vacation against his mother's wishes, also found it difficult to gain time with his father. "He was pretty preoccupied," Robert recalls. "It was hard to have just sort of direct access to my father at the time. . . . I don't have a whole lot of memories of just time alone with him during a lot of that period." When I told Robert that I'd heard his father worried about how events were affecting his children, he responded, almost irritatedly, "My father was concerned?" He remembers no signs. "My basic feeling is that my mother was more concerned about how the situation was affecting us than my father," Mary Ellsberg recounts. Moreover,

I don't remember him ever asking us how we felt about it. I think he expected us to find it all very exciting, and sometimes was disappointed when we didn't. On a few occasions I made a point of not being impressed by the glamour, and refusing, for example, to go to a Hollywood fund raiser for his birthday, because I had made plans with my mother and he invited me at the last minute. It turned out that the Beatles, Joni Mitchell, and Barbra Streisand were there, and someone paid her thousands of dollars to sing a song on the telephone. Dad asked her to call me, and was pretty annoyed when I wasn't home (we were having dinner with some friends from church). Of course, it was secretly painful for me to find out what I'd missed, but I guess for me it was more important to try to show him that I didn't want to be taken for granted. I think the only point he got out of this was that I was aligned with my mother, and no matter how hard he tried to impress me, I was impossible to please.

As an adult I tried to explain a few times how difficult this period was and how alone we felt during this time, but it is such a contrast from his own experience that I don't think he really gets it.[103]

Meanwhile, people were asking Carol about Dan far too often. "I couldn't meet any new person without being asked what my relationship was to Daniel Ellsberg," she recalls. "People would come up to me and tell me, 'Congratulations. You must be so proud.'" That kind of thing would press a buzzer in her, Robert remembers. "Almost any reminder or connection with the whole thing became an intrusion and an offense."[104]

——◦◉◦——

Ellsberg thought he had a "good judge," "a secret friend," an ally in W. Matthew Byrne, and that therefore his lawyers should treat Byrne a bit gently. Son of another federal judge and part of a judicial dynasty with all the breeding, Byrne, a Democrat, was in his early 40s, blondish, good looking, the golden prince; the female jurors loved him ("he'd hitch his chair over close to the jury, and all the women in the jury box would just faint," Theo Wilson remembers). A bachelor, Byrne was known as a ladies' man, companion of society women and stewardesses (about which there were jokes, such as, of course he knew the airline schedules), as well as of journalist Elizabeth Drew. Byrne was personable, hard working, legally astute, well prepared, "determined not to make a mistake," certainly not one that could affect his career; he exercised a cool, firm hand in the courtroom. He was always correcting Charles Nesson, who had problems phrasing his questions. Byrne had served as executive director of the Scranton Commission on campus disorders in 1970. He had liked it in Washington; he had a case of Potomac fever. Matt Byrne was ambitious. He was on the rise, way up, his future was all ahead of him. He was being talked up as a future U.S. Supreme Court justice, a U.S. attorney general, or the FBI director.[105]

Byrne didn't particularly care for Ellsberg. "The judge didn't like Ellsberg," Marty Arnold thought. "There was no love lost." One man who spoke with Byrne about the trial over dinner years later thought he found Ellsberg distasteful.[106]

Not surprisingly, Ellsberg's prosecutor David Nissen didn't care for him either, and here the feeling was mutual. Ellsberg hated Nissen. A short man who wore his slicked-down black hair in a razor-sharp part, his shoes shined, and his suits pressed, Nissen was unemotional, unsmiling, coldly methodical, and compulsively neat. A machine, in other words. He and his two colleagues, Warren Reese and Richard Barry, marched into court together "like a football team." Nissen had a studied hostility to reporters. He wouldn't speak to them. They were the enemy. Nissen was an impressive legal technician, but one willing to use any means. "He was playing to win, and . . . I think he fucked with the judge, and fucked with the defense," Peter Schrag recalls. But Nissen had a difficult case, and he knew it. He and his colleagues presented a weak case to the jury; at the end of it, Nissen thought he was going to lose, he would tell Watergate prosecutors. And after the defense had presented its case, he believed there was "no chance."[107]

Ellsberg was not loved in his own camp either. There was considerable tension between him and Leonard Boudin. "The impression I was given by Leonard was that Dan was very difficult for Leonard to work with," Leonard Weinglass remembers. Boudin simply didn't like Ellsberg. He would later be quite open about that with Jamie Kalvin, who interviewed him at length for an aborted biography. "He just didn't like him," Kalvin recalls. "I think Boudin began to hate Ellsberg," Stanley Sheinbaum says. "Really detest him." Certainly, Ellsberg drove Boudin nuts. That's one reason Boudin spent most weekends at Sheinbaum's home in Santa Barbara. "I think Leonard at times felt Dan was a pain in the ass," Robert Sachs says. "And he was."[108]

Boudin, 60, was a charming, engaging, rumpled-looking liberal attorney. "An able Communist lawyer," G. Gordon Liddy called him ("I was never a radical, and I'm still not," Boudin would say). He was perhaps the most well-known civil liberties lawyer in the country. He was a great appeals lawyer; he had argued successfully before the U.S. Supreme Court numerous times. He was a highly intellectual attorney, but with a casual, folksy style in the courtroom. He had limited trial skills, yet a sharp sense for the jugular. He was not into accumulating details. "I'm not interested in facts," he told Howard Zinn. That sometimes left him unprepared in court. Boudin had enormous energy and loved the good life. His daughter, a member of the ultraleft group the Weathermen, was a political fugitive whose situation pained him.[109]

The Ellsbergs had had questions about Boudin before hiring him. "I thought we should have a very, very good trial lawyer," Patricia remembers. "But we never found a lawyer that I thought was better." Patricia's brother had advised her to hire the best trial lawyer possible. Patricia had also worried about Boudin's ties to the left.[110]

The Ellsbergs found Boudin disappointing. Dan came to feel Boudin was letting him down. He told Russo at one point that the outcome of the trial, which began in January 1973 after all sorts of pretrial maneuvers and false starts, would depend on the two of them since their lawyers had done such a poor job. But Boudin found Ellsberg overly controlling. Like many defendants, Ellsberg wanted to be his own lawyer. He did a lot of second-guessing. He would remind his attorneys how Boudin had been wrong previously. Ellsberg seemed to Dolores Donovan to be very preoccupied with relatively minor points, and in court he may have taken more notes than anybody; he wrote everything down furiously. He was obsessed with details "and constantly interfering in the defense planning process," Donovan recalls. "Dan did not understand the legal issues very well. And he didn't understand how to try a case very well. So he was indeed out of synch with Leonard. . . . One of the things that a trial lawyer does is to build issues into the record, so that you have grounds for appeal, and for taking writs and all of that. And that's Leonard's strong point. . . . And so he was doing that." But "Dan didn't understand what he was doing. Dan was more focused on these little facts." And in meetings, "every point was gone over," Mark Rosenbaum remembers. "It was often difficult to get resolution on points. There was not a lot of closure. There was often revisiting of strategic decisions. And I sometimes thought that Leonard's best oral arguments were the ones he delivered to Dan, in terms of really explaining what was taking place." But Ellsberg thought Boudin too casual in court. He wanted more of a script. He was dissatisfied with how Boudin was cross-examining witnesses. Charles Nesson thought Ellsberg sometimes was missing the forest for the trees:

> But I came to respect him. Because the hit rate of what he focused on was so high. If Ellsberg said, "Look at this," it was always worth looking at. There were times when you didn't particularly like it, because you're in a group where everybody thinks they're smart. . . . And he had a way of—probably still does—of kind of grabbing you by the lapels and forcing your attention to something, when maybe you wanted to think about something else. And he was not about to give you a choice of thinking about anything but what he

wanted you to focus on. And it can drive you nuts. But the payoff of taking him seriously was worth it. He would not typically focus on silly things. He might be kind of puffed up in the way he would do it, but when you got past that and you said, "Here, let me just actually pay attention to what it is he's excited about," it always turned out it was worth being excited about.

. . . You don't have a sense that he's open to being persuaded. But it turned out that he was. On matters of the defense, if Leonard or I laid something out, he was a quick study. He could take it in, and he could say, "Oh," and then he'd go in a different direction. He was not wooden by any means. Now, you get into *his* territory, and you definitely get a sense that he's a tough guy to persuade.

Boudin thought Ellsberg could be manipulative. And he was in Boudin's ear all the time. Ellsberg tried to lecture Boudin, hammering home his points until Boudin had to make his escape (then Nesson would get it from Ellsberg). "He would ask you a question," Peter Young recalls, "and it would be some time before you realized it really wasn't a question, it was a comment. And usually a negative one."[111]

But no lawyer would have satisfied Ellsberg. "It isn't a matter of competence," Sheinbaum argues. "No lawyer would have seen eye-to-eye with him on how the trial ought to be going. He's got to have it his way."[112]

Yet Boudin was no angel either. He had his own ego problem. "Boudin's a star in his own right," Sheinbaum points out. But "Boudin's successful over the decades, Dan for the last half hour," and "I could see Boudin saying, 'Where was this son-of-a-bitch when we were really fighting the political wars?'"[113]

The Ellsbergs consulted with other attorneys during the trial. They considered retiring Boudin. They thought maybe he should just plan the appeal. Dan approached Neil Sheehan's attorney, Mitchell Rogovin, about replacing Boudin with Rogovin and his law firm, Arnold and Porter. After Rogovin turned him down, Ellsberg approached another member of Rogovin's firm.[114]

Many on the young defense team staff were not fond of Ellsberg either. "They admired what he had done and were devoted to his legal cause, but few of them liked him as a person," Marty Arnold wrote afterward. "Ellsberg would walk through the defense offices . . . and he would never say hello to them. Indeed, until he finally gave a dinner party for his defense team about a week after the trial ended, he never said thank you to them. . . . All of them made cynical, bitter jokes the next day about Ellsberg's ten-minute 'thank you' speech." But Rosenbaum told me, "I think all of us developed a loyalty to Dan. . . . He was always very kind to me."[115]

Ellsberg's relationship with Morton Halperin, whom he had brought onto the defense team, would also suffer during the trial. Halperin "had some of the same problems with Dan that we all had," Donovan recalls. Halperin was an intriguing, even odd, member of the defense. A man of the establishment, he had been upset by Ellsberg's release of the Pentagon Papers. But as he thought more about the issues involved, he came to believe that the government's efforts to halt publication and prosecute Ellsberg were "inappropriate," and that it was important to win the case to keep such power from the government. Some thought Halperin was drifting a bit with the wind (but if so, he was nonetheless taking a courageous career step). His personal life may have also provided impetus to his joining the defense; he was having marital problems. "I'll never forget Morty sitting with a girl on his lap at a party in the Pentagon Papers trial offices," one member of the defense team recounts. "And I doubt he'd ever done that before in his life. And he was having the greatest time of his life." "He went Hollywood," Linda Deutsch remembers. "He wore bell-bottom pants and he had a purse"—actually, a leather satchel—grew his hair longer, and wore sandals. Halperin, who says he never discussed his views on Ellsberg's release of the Papers with Ellsberg, became an invaluable strategist and tactician for the defense.[116]

Like Halperin, Ellsberg enjoyed the Hollywood flavor of the trial. Much more so. He showed a "small boy's pride" in associating with other famous people. They confirmed his own celebrity. The photographer Jill Krementz later noticed that Ellsberg's eyes would always dart around a room when talking to her at a gathering, sometimes looking to spot some celebrity. And during his trial "he was almost a glamorous figure" in Los Angeles, Deutsch recalls. "A lot of the Hollywood set was attracted to him." He savored that.[117]

Barbra Streisand sang for the glittery Hollywood fund raiser on Ellsberg's birthday in April 1973. Streisand had not performed in public for a while; she feared assassination and critics. To some, Streisand appeared intrigued by Ellsberg. "I was a good-looking young man in those days," one member of the defense remembers. "Barbra Streisand was making eyes at me that night. And I'm sure she would have been making eyes at Dan. . . . Barbra Streisand has an eye for young dark men. So I wouldn't be surprised at all." The Beatles attended the fund raiser, mingling with guests. "I had a discussion with John Lennon and Yoko Ono," Peter Young recounts. "Not with Yoko—she didn't say a word—but with John, standing at the wine bar." (Young gave Lennon legal advice on his threatened deportation for marijuana possession.) All the Beatles except Paul McCartney stood in line to get Ellsberg's autograph.[118]

Yet despite all his admirers and his team of supporters, Ellsberg was something of a loner during the trial. Close friends were absent. Other than Patricia. But she was no small solace. She was Dan's steadfast and total supporter, his protector, counselor, a source of tremendous strength and sound advice. Dan asked for her judgment on everything. She was very much a player. "Pat sat in on our legal meetings and took notes," Weinglass remembers. "I was very impressed with how she was dealing with all that. She wasn't the supportive wife and nothing more than that. She was someone who was getting on top of the case." Patricia always wanted to learn more. She also helped organize Dan's life, coached him on the press, mediated with others, and was a conciliatory force. She was almost a center of serenity and (like Carol Ellsberg before her) in some ways a motherly figure to Dan. More than anybody, she kept him together. Patricia was into yoga, Zen, and exploring the Arica spiritual path to self-realization, all of which contributed to her serenity. Her stepmother, Idella, who came to the trial, was also into Arica: over lunch one day, Idella would tell a priest from Carol Ellsberg's church about her guru, Oscar. "Just as you probably think your God is with you all the time," Idella remarked, "I know that Oscar is with me."[119]

A dominant memory of many from the trial is Patricia standing loyally by Dan's side, bending her knees and looking adoringly, even worshipfully, up at him. She was "starry-eyed," Peter Schrag recalls. "You know, 'My hero.' . . . Later when I saw Nancy [Reagan] do it, she reminded me of Patricia." Journalists joked that the defense should simply place a cardboard cutout of a swooning Patricia next to Dan to save her the trouble. Her adulation of him seemed largely genuine but also partly performance. Patricia says that media portrayals of her as someone content to stand loyally by Dan's side didn't bother her:

> I adored him. It was totally true. Dan was so superb. He was such a hero to me. . . . And the secret was we were always holding hands. . . . And Dan would just hit a home run one after another. I mean, he would speak the truth. It was like something was coming through him. And I *adored* standing next to that, being beside him. Because we were so close, and I was so much his partner, that it was a very powerful experience to be standing there when Dan was so brilliant, so articulate, so eloquent. . . . He was off-the-charts wonderful. . . . You know, there is Gandhi's phrase, the truth force. And there are many ways to interpret that, but there was a power in Dan. . . . And it was a privilege. It was just extraordinary to be present. And we had the whole world watching. It was amazing. . . . He's almost like a prophet. Don't quote that out of context. . . . But there's that moral fervor.

I was struck when interviewing Patricia by her virtual worship of Dan, which again seemed partly authentic and partly put on. "I'm not a fool about people, and I recognize Dan's limitations, which socially in many ways are enormous," she told me. And "he's also impossible at times." But "I don't think I've *ever* seen him do something that was compromising. . . . I just *never, ever* felt a discordant note, in terms of the highest motivation. It's pretty amazing. And that's why I'm completely loyal and devoted to Dan. . . . He is an utterly honorable man. . . . I *really* admire him. . . . He's a rare person. . . . That's why I put up with so much for so many years. . . . He's a large, large person. To this day I feel very privileged and blessed in being married to him." Patricia at one point read to me from her notes on what she wanted to convey about Dan in our interview: "Speaker of the truth. Heroic. Brilliant. . . . Dedicated. Noble. Sexy. Handsome. Passionate. Deeply sensuous. Large in scope. Creative." In Dan's presence, she told me, "The reason I stay in love with a personality as difficult as Dan's is this profound moral integrity of this man. . . . I feel it is a privilege of my life to be a party to someone of this scope and depth and relevance to the world." Dan was moved by that.[120]

But at the trial, observers sensed that Patricia had her hands full. "We all thought that she was quite forbearing," Sanford Ungar remembers. "That she was putting up with a very difficult character of a husband." "Many of us wondered, Why was she with Dan?" Len Ackland, who worked on the defense, recounts. "How could she put up with his shit?" Patricia confided in a female journalist that she wondered if their marriage would survive normal times, that Dan could be tiresome and so self-absorbed that he was not always the greatest company. According to a friend of Dan, Patricia would tell him after the trial, in effect, Alright, now it's my turn, I've been devoting myself to your thing for several years, now I want to do my thing and lead my own life.[121]

Patricia did some fund raising for the defense and sold some property she owned to raise additional money. But her wealth hurt the defense's ability to attract funds. Some people assumed the Marx family would bankroll the defense. But her father refused to help. Many people think Patricia is loaded, but she says that's not true. "My brother is, and I'm not. . . . And Dan really needs to earn every cent he gets. And it makes it much harder. I know one woman who has a foundation who simply will not believe that Dan needs to earn money. And the inheritance I do have is rapidly running out. . . . I don't have a lot of money. I'm spending the capital I do have. And so I'll have very little money in a short number of years." But "I have a *very* wealthy brother, and I don't think he would ever let me go be in the poor house." Her brother would not be generous to Dan, though.[122]

***

Jan Butler was called by the prosecution to testify in Ellsberg's trial, only to suffer the indignity of being questioned about her testimony in advance by Ellsberg's former boss, Charles Wolf, whom she considered a friend. "He was one of the scared people," Butler recounts. "And he asked me if I'd have a drink with him after work. Which was very unusual for Charlie," who was married and strait-laced. Over a drink, "he said to me, 'How are you going to testify? What are you going to say in court?' . . . I was stunned. He was pumping me for management."[123]

When either Richard Moorsteen or Harry Rowen was on the stand, Butler found herself gasping for air. She knew that what Moorsteen and Rowen were saying was untrue in some respects. "It was so disturbing to me that I had to leave the room," she remembers. "I just knew that I could hardly breathe. And I went out and sat in the hall. And after about an hour . . . there was a recess, and one of the press guys came out and said, 'If that's the kind of liars you've got at RAND, our country is in very bad hands.'" Two years later, a depressed Moorsteen would either commit suicide or accidentally ingest a deadly mix of two types of sleeping pills and a drink, according to the two versions of the story. There are those who believe he killed himself in part because Moorsteen, a highly sensitive man, had perjured himself and that had weighed on him. In any event, Moorsteen's testimony—like Rowen's—was evasive and replete with hedging and memory lapses, most notably on the storage and handling of the Papers at RAND. Listening to Moorsteen, "I was out of my mind with rage," Ellsberg recalls. He icily told Moorsteen's and Rowen's lawyer, "There has been perjury on the stand today. Knowing perjury. You tell your clients I am not going to prison on the basis of perjured testimony." Ellsberg felt both Moorsteen and Rowen had now betrayed *him*.[124]

On the stand herself, Butler contradicted the testimony of both Rowen and Moorsteen. To protect them, their lawyer urged that Butler be prosecuted for perjury and conspiracy (among other things) after the trial. But she got a good lawyer who prevented it. "But for two weeks I thought that I was going to be going to jail," she remembers. "And I was pretty miserable." When Butler told Ellsberg about all this later, he started to cry.[125]

Ellsberg's own testimony—or the pressure of it—also brought him to tears. The tension had been building for weeks. This was his time to address the world, at length and in detail, his platform to explain himself, what he had done, and its importance. The media would be there in droves; reporters would have to listen to him now. His father and two children would also be there. His testimony had to be right. And he would be speaking to the all-important jury, which some thought could go either way on the theft counts. The impression he created on the jurors was crucial. Should they give this man the benefit of the doubt?

Ellsberg's preparation was torturous and belabored. "It took forever," Dolores Donovan recalls. Ellsberg and his lawyers went through his testimony "over and over again," Mark Rosenbaum recounts. "And it would constantly change. . . . I remember there were times when Dan just sort of lay down on the ground on his back. . . . There are Broadway plays that don't go through as many rehearsals as did that testimony. . . . There was just an enormous amount of stress and tension. It wasn't clear how that testimony was going to come out. I remember the last night preparing for it, and it did have a rhythm to it by then . . . but one of the lawyers saying, 'Who knows what's going to happen tomorrow.'" That was partly because Ellsberg's answers during rehearsals "would always be longer than had been hoped for," Rosenbaum remembers. "There was an enormous amount of agonizing over what should be said and how it should be said." The tension between Ellsberg and Boudin came to a head. "On the eve of his testifying, he had lost confidence in Boudin," Russo recalls. Again, Ellsberg wanted a more linear, scripted presentation than Boudin had in mind. He also wanted to go into more biographical detail, which he believed would enhance his expertise and help the jurors understand why he had released the Papers. "We made concessions to Dan," Donovan recounts. "I think his position was the jury had to understand his motive for doing it. And so we let him explain why he did it." Ellsberg was sensitive to questions about his motive. Boudin and the other lawyers worried that he would come off as distant and egotistical to the jury.[126]

The tension threatened Boudin's health. "It caused Leonard to have a physical breakdown," Weinglass remembers. "Leonard took ill just before Dan testified, as a result of the intense pressure that was put on him." His heart condition flared up. Feeling "very tired and faint," Boudin asked for a recess the second day of Ellsberg's testimony.[127]

In a packed and hushed courtroom, Ellsberg's testimony got off to a rocky start. Speaking in "a barely audible voice," then in "a manic stream-of-consciousness" style, he suggested that, as a government consultant, he had been ubiquitous in crises, task forces, briefings, war planning, speech writing, nuclear command posts, and the like. "Ellsberg, seemingly, had been everywhere and seen everything," Schrag recalled. But he had problems describing exactly what he had *done*. And there was "too much Harvard," Schrag observed. His testimony "began as pretentious fumbling"; it was "disjointed, an avalanche of unfocused questions and undisciplined, self-serving responses . . . stringing together names and titles and allusions to an endless series of higher-than-secret operations. He had reported to McNamara, Bundy, Katzenbach, Harriman, Nitze, and Vance, drafted questions for Kissinger, selected problems for the personal attention of McNaughton"—you get the picture. As his lawyers had feared, he'd gone off. And his style was "very stiff," Rosenbaum remembers. "Everyone was concerned after the beginning of his testimony that he was coming across as arrogant, removed, and not a terribly warm person." "It was like he had gone over it a billion times in his mind, and then gotten tense when he was actually delivering it," Charles Nesson recalls. Nesson advised Ellsberg that he had to be more lucid, had to cut out what one member of the defense would call "that egocentric shit." Patricia also stepped in with advice.[128]

During the noon recess on the second day of Ellsberg's testimony, after he had described some of his experiences in Vietnam, including witnessing a burning village ("It was a very bad scene," he said quietly), and also less emotional experiences, Ellsberg sat down at the defense table and cried. Patricia came up and comforted him. He had slipped temporarily over the edge. "He broke down just because of the accumulated stress," Donovan thought. And there had been plenty of that. "The tension" caused it, one of the jurors said afterward. But another argued, "He thought he flopped. He thought he messed up. He didn't express what he had really come to express." There was "suspicion that the great performance had not started well," Schrag wrote. Some reporters cynically wondered if Ellsberg was crying partly for effect, though.[129]

But Ellsberg got into a groove, Boudin's questioning became more delimiting, and when it was all over, the defense thought Ellsberg's testimony had been terrific. Yet Ellsberg was disappointed; it had been shorter than he had anticipated. "Lawyer's call," Robert Sachs explains. "I think they established what they wanted to through him and didn't want to open up more areas for cross [examination] than they needed to." Ellsberg "thought he was going to have more of an opportunity to tell the story. And suddenly it was over. And what about all that he had prepared, and all he was going to tell? . . . There was a big letdown." But "I think the feeling on the legal team's part was one of relief. That we kind of got on and got off without lecturing the jury." Ellsberg had sought reassurance along the way. "I remember Dan saying, 'Well, how's it going? What do you think?'" Rosenbaum recalls. "I mean, to almost anybody on the street he'd say that."[130]

———◦———

Meanwhile, events were unfolding that would throw the trial into disarray. In the mid-afternoon of April 26, 1973, eight days after Ellsberg's testimony had concluded, and after court had adjourned that day, Judge Byrne abruptly summoned all attorneys back to the courtroom. He was waving an envelope. Byrne asked David Nissen if the prosecution wished to turn over the contents of the envelope to the defense. Nissen said he would have to check with the Justice

Department. Russo believed the government had some desperate move up its sleeve, one targeting him. "Tony Russo thought that the judge was going to put him in jail or something," Theo Wilson remembers. But that was not the case, and Weinglass sensed as much: he told Russo after leaving court, "That's something that could end the trial."[131]

Inside the envelope was a memorandum revealing that E. Howard Hunt and G. Gordon Liddy had burglarized the office of Ellsberg's psychiatrist. (John Dean had revealed the break-in to the Watergate prosecutor Earl Silbert on April 15.) Byrne chose to disclose this explosive information in court the next morning, first in a low voice at the side bar. Richard Best was in the courtroom, as he was scheduled to testify again that day. He recounts: "They pushed me to one side to have a conference at the side bar. And the government attorneys were up there, and the defense attorneys, and the two defendants. The government attorneys had long faces. The defense attorneys and Russo were elated. But only Dan had a long face. A long, worried face. And I thought, 'What the hell could he be telling them that delights these people, dismays these people, but dismays Dan Ellsberg?' . . . He had a wrinkled brow. He was worried."[132]

Ellsberg was stunned by the disclosure. In a circle with his attorneys, he questioned whether it should be made public. He may have even opposed making it public. He was certainly nervous and agitated. According to Schrag, Ellsberg said that this bombshell would have no impact on the case. "I think he didn't want it revealed," Peter Young recalls. "I don't think he wanted people to know that he was going to see a psychiatrist. . . . He didn't want it out. . . . And I imagine he was willing to use any argument to stop it from being exploited." Sachs sensed "great sensitivity" around the issue. (Many years later, one member of the defense mentioned the break-in at Ellsberg's psychiatrist's office at a press conference with Ellsberg, "and Dan was sitting next to me, and visibly stiffened. So to this day he doesn't like it known that he had a psychiatrist.") Ellsberg was also worried about what the burglars might have pulled from his psychiatrist's files. "I think it was very upsetting to him that not only was the world in touch with the fact that he had spent a lot of time with psychiatrists, but that the office had been burglarized," Nesson reminisces. "And I don't think Ellsberg knew exactly what was going to come out of that. . . . You know, if everything you say to a psychiatrist over the course of a couple years is suddenly going to come public, you have reason to be a little nervous maybe." But Ellsberg would claim later that at the side bar Byrne "looked at me and addressed me directly for the first time" during the trial: "'Mr. Ellsberg, I don't have to release this information in public if you want me to keep this quiet. I can keep it under seal.' I replied, 'Are you kidding? Put it out!'" If that is true, it could only have occurred after intense discussion between Ellsberg and his attorneys, who felt that release of this bombshell was critical. "I thought that it meant the case was over," Nesson recalls. So did Russo.[133]

Ellsberg told the press he was "speechless." Understandably, he declined to identify his psychiatrist (whom he wouldn't have known for sure at this point was Lewis Fielding anyway, and whom in the days ahead he would always refer to as simply his doctor—"I'm not going to get into any discussions that I had with the doctor, or with my wife, frankly, or my son," he told reporters who barraged him with questions about his psychiatrist). Ellsberg phoned Fielding twice that day to learn what he could about the break-in, probably upset that Fielding had not told him about it. When Fielding's name was leaked to the press, Fielding was besieged by reporters. "He wouldn't talk to the press," his friend Dr. Alfred Goldberg remembers. "He wouldn't talk to anybody about it," including his friends. In the defense office, "there was a sense of elation," Rosenbaum recounts. "And I remember Dan . . . sort of being off to the side, and not universally sharing in that elation. . . . 'Shouldn't we let the verdict come down first?' It wasn't that it should be disposed of, this information. But there was a sense that this was not a pure political victory, or a pure personal victory. . . . I just have a visual image of Dan off to the side, questioning whether or not, essentially, Is this the way to bring down the final act? . . . You know, this had been this grand Shakespearean drama, at least to the public, and is this the right ending?"[134]

Watergate west had now joined Watergate east. More specifically, Daniel Ellsberg had been tied to the burgeoning scandal. That may have alleviated some of his distress: his historical significance had grown.

Across the country in the White House, officials were scurrying to contain the damage and cover themselves, and had been since a disgruntled Howard Hunt had threatened in mid-March of 1973 to disclose the "seamy things" he had done for the administration ("I was thinking about the Fielding episode," Hunt later told the grand jury). John Ehrlichman, who didn't need to be told what Hunt was thinking about, had begun weaving a cover story to Richard Nixon—one he'd advanced to Egil Krogh before the break-in—that Hunt had merely been "an investigator" who had gone too far and had to be stopped (when he added that such an admission may let Ellsberg off the hook and get him a mistrial, Nixon interjected, "Isn't it damn near through yet? . . . Isn't that case about finished?"). The next day, March 22, after a frightened Krogh had advised Ehrlichman that he was prepared to inform Justice of the break-in, Ehrlichman told Krogh "that Hunt was stable and Krogh should hang tough." When Ehrlichman informed David Young several days later that he had not known about the break-in in advance, Young corrected him and said, "in fact, his approval of the matter was reflected in a couple of the memos" sitting in the briefcase of files on the Plumbers' investigation that Young had brought over to his office. "And I pointed to the briefcase," Young recounted. Ehrlichman replied that he had "taken those memos out and thought he should keep them because they were a little too sensitive and showed too much forethought." Young subsequently found two especially incriminating memos missing. Ehrlichman later lied voluminously—"repeatedly," the Watergate prosecutors concluded—indeed, perjured himself, about the break-in and related matters. Two among many whoppers: first Ehrlichman claimed he hadn't known before the break-in that Ellsberg even *had* a psychiatrist, then, when one of the incriminating memos surfaced, he claimed that he thought the entry could be performed with Fielding's consent.[135]

Nixon would maintain that he didn't learn about the break-in until March 17, 1973, when John Dean told him about it, or possibly a bit earlier, when the photographs Hunt and Liddy had taken during their reconnaissance mission two years earlier surfaced. "This is the first I ever heard of this," he told Dean in their March 17 conversation, aware that the tape recorder was rolling. But that is highly unlikely. We know that Ehrlichman informed him of that "little operation . . . out in Los Angeles" right after it occurred, without, apparently, being specific then. It was "reasonable to conclude," two members of the Watergate Special Prosecution Force wrote later, that Ehrlichman "consulted with the president on an operation as dramatic as this." Ehrlichman would probably not have shouldered it alone. Nixon later told Haldeman that while he had "no recollection" of Ehrlichman informing him of the break-in until that March, "If I had to know it, I had to know it." He acknowledged to Ehrlichman in another taped conversation released in recent years that Krogh might have told him about it in one of "those long conversations that you had with him about this" (Ehrlichman's words). While it's possible that Ehrlichman preserved some measure of deniability for Nixon, it also seems highly unlikely that Charles Colson, who had secured funds for the break-in, did not speak to Nixon about it. Colson, who feared more damaging disclosures after the break-in was revealed and consequently argued on May 1 that the government should move to get the Ellsberg case "dismissed *immediately*," told the prosecutors it was his "impression" that Nixon had been aware of the break-in right afterward. Ehrlichman would even theorize that Nixon had ordered it in the first place ("That's a suspicion," he told me in an interview for an earlier book. "I can't prove it"). Nixon implied to Haldeman that he had ordered it. And it would be consistent with Nixon's track record for him to have issued general marching orders, along the lines of, "Get that material on Ellsberg. I don't care how you do it. Just get it." Shades of Brookings, in other words. Nixon aide Leonard Garment would "remember very clearly Krogh's coming into my office and saying, in effect, that the instructions came out of the Oval Office." On top of all this, Ehrlichman told Colson that Nixon had authorized the operation, and Ehrlichman told the grand jury that Nixon had "specifically approved" a covert trip to Los Angeles by Liddy and Hunt to get information on Ellsberg.[136]

After the break-in was disclosed, Nixon and his aides often sounded on tapes I listened to like common criminals trying to protect themselves and get their stories in order. Nixon repeatedly stressed that he had no knowledge of the operation—"such a miserable collection of shit," "such a jackass thing," "this strange, strange trip to California"—until March, and blamed others for it, like those "crazy fools" Hunt and Liddy. "Dean was the one that implemented the whole thing," he told U.S. Attorney General Richard Kleindienst on April 25. And "they got nothing. It was a dry hole. . . . Shit, it's the dumbest goddamn thing I ever heard of. . . . What the Christ would you learn from his goddamn psychiatrist?" And "Christ, *I haven't the slightest idea about the Goddamn thing.*" Nixon thought it would "kill" the Ellsberg case. (Kleindienst told David Nissen that day to try to persuade Byrne to let the trial continue.) On May 3, Nixon commiserated with Secretary of State William Rogers, "My God. They're going to screw around now about why did they break into the psychiatrist's office. Everybody's going to think, What the hell a stupid thing was that? *Goddamn.*" The break-in was "the toughest" Watergate revelation "for all of us," Nixon told Ronald Ziegler. But "I think the whole thing right now is to play everything very tough. That everybody else is lying." Also, "the president knows a hell of a lot of things, but does he know what the Christ some dumb assholes are going to do? . . . Goddamn to hell, I didn't tell them to go fuck up the goddamn Ellsberg place." Nixon complained to Haldeman, "Damnit, if they're going to have a grand jury about this stinking little thing, it's unbelievable. . . . Buzhardt was pointing out that, generally speaking, a breaking and entering, which involves no theft or anything, you know what I mean, is in most states only a misdemeanor. Which I hope to Christ is the case. Because it's just a crime to have Bud Krogh kicked around on this damn thing." Especially as "that son-of-a-bitch Ellsberg" will probably have "a monument" built for him "on Harvard Square."[137]

The break-in was one reason that Ehrlichman, at the direction of Nixon and after he could not get Kleindienst to do the job, phoned Judge Byrne from San Clemente on April 4 to ask if Byrne would like to discuss a possible "federal appointment." According to Ehrlichman, he told Byrne that he did not know if this was an "appropriate time" to discuss such a matter, but that Byrne replied, "I see no reason why we couldn't talk right away." The next day, at San

Clemente, strolling out toward the bluff overlooking the Pacific, Ehrlichman asked Byrne if he was interested in becoming the director of the FBI. Dangling that plum in front of Byrne might lead him to handle the disclosure of the break-in and the trial favorably, Nixon and Ehrlichman hoped (in vain), such as by not informing the defense of the break-in and by making sure that Ellsberg did not get off completely. "It seems clear that this was the beginning of an effort by Nixon (through Ehrlichman) to influence Byrne," one Watergate prosecutor wrote. The prosecutors even considered charging Ehrlichman with obstruction of justice or bribery, but did not develop enough evidence. Ehrlichman recalled that Byrne showed "very strong interest" in becoming FBI director, and even offered some thoughts on how the FBI might be improved. Byrne later tried to fob off the meeting, however, claiming to have decided "I could not consider such a proposal at that time but would reflect upon the matter." Nixon exchanged pleasantries with Byrne.[138]

The next day, Byrne made a fatal mistake. Meeting with Ehrlichman once was bad enough, but he phoned Ehrlichman to request *another* meeting (which Ehrlichman took as "a symbol of heightened interest"). In Ehrlichman's retelling, Byrne told him that he had been giving "a lot of thought" to their conversation, "and I would like to talk with you again." Byrne, one suspects, was feeling a little intoxicated by the prospect of heading the FBI and was not thinking as coolly as usual. They met in a park in Santa Monica near the home of Ehrlichman's mother the next day. Byrne again expressed "very strong interest," Ehrlichman recounted. But Byrne claimed he reiterated that he could not consider the offer while the trial was going on.[139]

It was obviously improper conduct by both sides. While some people might have given Byrne the benefit of the doubt had he ventured to San Clemente just once, the second meeting, at his request no less, was indefensible. "Why Byrne doesn't have the decency to resign is beyond me," one lawyer said afterward. "I know I'll never have any respect for him again."[140]

The morning of April 30, before court opened, Charles Nesson got word that Byrne had met with Ehrlichman. Nesson considered it an astonishing breakthrough. He was the only senior lawyer still in the defense office; the others had gone off to court. Nesson's next move would prove controversial: rather than hitting Byrne with this news in open court before he had a chance to come up with an explanation—and without consulting with the other lawyers, at least on Russo's side—Nesson chose to phone Byrne's chambers and state that the defense possessed this information and would open court with a motion for a mistrial based on it. Weinglass was angry when informed minutes later. "He wanted to jump him," Nesson recounts. "He was just worried that somehow they'd weasel out of it. He thought that if we'd just jumped him with it, he wouldn't have time to come up with a counter." Russo thought Nesson had sold him and Ellsberg out. "He just did it as a matter of course," Peter Young remembers. "And I think he did it because he thought it was the gentleman's thing to do. . . . We thought it was not in the best interest of our client." Nesson explains: "On the one hand, I thought we just had him cold. And second, I thought that this guy's career is about to go up in smoke, and he at least deserves some notice [chuckles]. And third . . . it was my sense of what was professional. That when you make a big move, you give the other side notice of it." Besides, he felt the case was over at that point.[141]

When Byrne finally appeared in court that morning to read from a prepared statement, his face was flushed. His emotions were evident as he read from his statement. One member of the defense team, who was sitting closest to Byrne, recalls that as he delivered his statement,

> the judge's face was ashen. . . . His lips were ashen. They were gray. His face was gray. . . . He looked pasty. He looked terrible. He looked like he was dead. And it was because he'd been kicked—he should have known better—but it was because he had been just kicked in the balls by the Nixon administration. Deliberately. Both in, first, the attempt to influence him, and second, the deliberate disclosure [to the press of the meetings]. . . . They had the judge in a horrible, horrible position. . . . He had just been made to look like a gullible fool who was taken in by the Nixon administration, by virtue of his own ambition. . . . I think he just wasn't in control of his faculties.

Byrne said he wanted "no misunderstanding" of the meetings and gave his version of events.[142]

Byrne's career ambitions now lay in ruins. His hopes for a high-level government post, major political advancement, perhaps even the court of appeals, were dead. The trial became the tragedy of his life. "He never recovered from it," Linda Deutsch observes. "And the only reason he's still there"—on the federal bench—"is it was a lifetime appointment." Yet Byrne's mistake was out of character for him, Deutsch believes: "It was like the Shakespearean fatal flaw. Which was ambition. . . . This was too tempting."[143]

The trial was also now a shambles. Agents of the same government that was prosecuting Ellsberg and Russo had not only broken into Ellsberg's psychiatrist's office but flagrantly tampered with the judge, whose conduct was now suspect. "The White House, by initiating this meeting, has irretrievably compromised the court," the defense argued in a motion to dismiss the indictment on May 1. Not for the first time, the defense also cited the attempted assault on Ellsberg by

Bernard Barker and friends a year earlier, along with other governmental impro-
prieties. "From the very beginning, this proceeding has been characterized by
prosecutorial abuse extending all the way to the White House itself, which is un-
paralleled in the history of American jurisprudence," the defense argued. "The
result has been a prosecution which is a travesty on justice."[144]

Byrne did not grant the defense's motion to dismiss, but the case appeared
to be headed for at least a mistrial, and possibly a dismissal as well. The prospect
of passing the case on to the jury could not have been a particularly appealing
one to Byrne after the disclosure of his meetings with Ehrlichman, as there was
no way it would stand up on appeal. "I think he wanted out of this case," Nesson
says. On the other hand, Byrne didn't want to mistry it on the basis of his own
impropriety. Yet he seemed intent on getting part of the case to the jury. Ambition, dislike of Ellsberg, judicial philosophy, and lack of authority for dismissal
based on government misconduct—all may have influenced him.[145]

Neither Russo nor Ellsberg were excited about a dismissal. They wanted
the validation of a verdict and public exoneration. An acquittal would be a
clear-cut victory. A dismissal would leave things hazy, and no legal precedent
would be set for changing laws on government secrecy and the release of classified information. (Convictions, however, would have set strong legal precedent
for bringing criminal charges against leakers of classified information and their
recipients.) Both Russo and Ellsberg had been distinctly unenthused about an
earlier effort by the defense to get the case dismissed in 1972, after it had been
revealed that a member of the defense (Boudin, it turned out) had been overheard on a wiretap. Ellsberg had been "definitely opposed" to a dismissal then,
Young recalls. But the lawyers were now keen on a dismissal, even though the
jury looked good. "I think all of us felt that they would be acquitted," Young remembers. "I think we all felt very, very confident. We were certainly totally
confident there would be no conviction. That at worst it would be a hung jury
perhaps on the theft count." But juries can be fluky: Could this one be trusted?
And they didn't know how Byrne would instruct it.*[146]

---

* Later discussions with the jurors suggested that they would have voted to acquit on the
espionage and conspiracy counts, and possibly on the theft counts as well, but that their
verdict on theft would have depended strongly on Byrne's instructions, and that a hung
jury there was quite possible; even convictions on one or more theft counts were not out
of the realm of possibilities. One juror who was leaning toward acquittal commented on
Ellsberg: "He put a lot of light on himself. I'm sure he will benefit from it some way.
There's more to it than meets the eye." This juror was "not going to accept him just the
way he is" (jury discussion, May 20, 1973, transcript; *LAT*, May 12, 1973).

Following waves of sensational new revelations on the break-in and other White House abuses of power, ones "no novelist could invent," as the *New York Times* put it, Byrne learned on May 10 that Ellsberg had been overheard on a wiretap of Morton Halperin's home telephone. Also, the FBI said the records of the conversations were missing. Byrne was incensed. The government had been under orders to provide him any such records. Byrne fired off a list of terse questions to Justice, but the answers were unsatisfactory. This was the final straw. But it also gave Byrne his out.[147]

Word circulated that he was prepared to grant a dismissal. That evening, Theo Wilson and Linda Deutsch had dinner with the Ellsbergs. (Barbra Streisand was also in the restaurant and joined them for a while.) "I was bullshitting with Dan," Wilson recounts. "I said, 'You know, this is what happens with gangster trials, Dan.'" Mobsters were always getting off on technicalities like wiretaps. Ellsberg was bothered by the comparison, though Wilson was just kidding around. "He didn't want it to end like a Mafia trial," Marty Arnold recalls, and certainly not on the basis of a wiretap alone. After dinner, "Dan calls up Lennie Boudin and Lennie Weinglass," Wilson remembers. "He says, 'Okay, I'm not accepting this. We've got to go until the end of this trial. I don't want a discharge from the jury.'" Boudin, who by then wanted to choke Ellsberg, later chided Wilson for getting Ellsberg worked up. "He said, 'You're the one! You almost made me crazy,'" Wilson recounts. "He said, 'Here I was so happy to get this, and here Dan'—and he said, 'And you know Dan.'" Ellsberg "gave me the worst night of my life because of that crack," Boudin told Wilson. "He had us up all night discussing strategy."[148]

During the noon hour the next day, May 11, President Nixon and Alexander Haig remarked on the trial in the Oval Office. "Of course, it's going to be a mistrial, and we want it to [be] and the quicker the better," Haig said. "That's right," Nixon replied. "Get it over with and forget it." Nixon complained to Haldeman that afternoon how "the sonofabitching thief is made a national hero and is going to get off on a mistrial. And the *New York Times* gets a Pulitzer Prize for stealing documents. . . . They're trying to get at us with thieves. *What in the name of God have we come to?*"[149]

That afternoon, after Ellsberg and his lawyers had gone around some more about a dismissal, in a jam-packed courtroom, Byrne read from another statement. Minutes after he had finished reading and retired to his office, he looked to Schrag "like he was in a state of collapse." Ellsberg and Russo fixed their eyes intently on Byrne as he read from the bench. "His face was flushed, and occasionally he stumbled over words," Schrag recounted. "Governmental agencies have taken an unprecedented series of actions with respect to these defendants," Byrne declared. Those actions included the establishment of the Plumbers, the Fielding break-in, the CIA's two psychological profiles of Ellsberg, the wiretaps, and withholding of information. "The totality of the circumstances of this case which I have only briefly sketched offend 'a sense of justice,'" Byrne stated. "The bizarre events have incurably infected the prosecution of this case. . . . I have decided to declare a mistrial and grant the motion to dismiss."[150]

Cheers, whistles, and applause burst forth from spectators in the courtroom and those in the corridors who had been unable to get in. "Looking back on my career as a journalist—and I've covered some big stories and a lot of dramatic events—it was one of the two most dramatic moments I've seen as a journalist," Arnold reflects, the other being Martin Luther King's "I Have a Dream" speech. "It was an incredible moment to me. The system was working, in some way, finally."[151]

Ellsberg and Russo embraced their lawyers, aides, and wives "in an emotional panoply of hugging, kissing, laughing and crying." Nesson lit up a cigar. Ellsberg, who had practically flown into Patricia's arms, appeared relieved, elated, jubilant. "I think this prosecution was aborted by the White House because we were getting too close to the highest authority—to the president," he said, clutching Patricia outside the courthouse amid a crush of media. Nixon, Ellsberg said, "deserves his day in court."[152]

"Aren't you just as glad it's all over, though?" Nixon remarked to Haig the next morning. "I think it's good to have it over," Haig replied. "This guy ain't going to be the big hero," Nixon said.[153] But they were struggling to see the silver lining.

Back in the courtroom, "there was celebration all around," Nesson remembers. "But I think that shortly afterwards there were second thoughts about it" on both Ellsberg's and Russo's parts. "Both Dan, and Tony in particular, felt that they were being robbed of the people's verdict on this," Young says. "They were robbed of justice without any verdict on the merits of what they had done."[154]

Priscilla McMillan, neighbor of the Ellsbergs in Cambridge, ran into Patricia on the street late that summer. "I asked her if she was disappointed," McMillan recounts. "And she said, 'Oh, no.' And her words were, in effect, that they knew they had brought down the president."[155]

While looking at Patricia, Ellsberg announced when the trial was over his intention to "make love in every climate on earth." "She was sitting there grinning, and 'Oh, sweetie,'" recalls Arnold, who suspected that Ellsberg would carry out his plan. "I remember thinking, 'He's going to be traveling,'" Young laughs.[156]

FIFTEEN

Outcast

Before doing any traveling outside the country, Ellsberg testified on government secrecy, speaking before a joint session of Senate subcommittees chaired by Senator Edmund Muskie on May 16. It was a triumph; members of Congress were treating him with respect. "Dan had a soapbox for a little while," Tom Oliphant remembers. And "this was the day he got his dignity. . . . This was the day when he really was listened to. . . . I could tell it was a big deal for him." In a short but rambling presentation, Ellsberg informed the senators that he had "lived in the world of secrets" during the twelve years he "worked for the president," and thus knew that "secrecy corrupts just as power corrupts." He had explained this to Henry Kissinger, he apprised the senators, in some detail. He described "entire rooms in the Pentagon with safe doors outside, with a guardian, with a computer list up to date hourly and daily as to who is admitted in that room, and unless you know the codeword and are on that list, you cannot enter that room or know of its existence." There were clearances even the president didn't know about, Ellsberg asserted. He called for "wholesale declassification."[1]

It is unlikely he would have done so had his star in Washington not dimmed earlier. Rather, he would have still enjoyed "eating secret honeydew" (as he now termed classified information).[2]

When in Washington, Ellsberg continued to make requests of Leonard Boudin, who was getting ready to leave Los Angeles. Boudin finally told him, "Dan, the trial is over. I'm not your lawyer anymore."[3]

Ellsberg attended the Senate Watergate hearings in Washington. He closely followed the mushrooming revelations, including those on his own part in the scandal. "I am a Watergate junkie," he would say later. Attending the hearings was also a way to remain in the limelight. Ellsberg was "a front-row spectator, a willing provider of a readable quote for any reporter who wanted one," Marty Arnold recounted. Ellsberg told another reporter, "I'm just fascinated by this. . . . We were going to go camping but after our trial we just can't stay away from this and the TV set." He took extensive notes at the hearings. As he watched them, he came to believe that he had been "hunted" by the Nixon administration: "I had this sense that the president was coiling himself for one last attack on me. . . . I'm sitting in front of that television set, all alone, and all I can do is shake my fist at the screen, without being heard. . . . I wait for the senators to say something on my behalf, and they never do." Ellsberg could not get the Senate Select Committee to read a statement rebutting White House accusations against him. He worried about future accusations and felt isolated. He later visited the offices of the *National Lampoon* in New York to purchase 40 copies of an issue featuring a Watergate comic strip he was in. He wanted the original artwork.[4]

On May 20, Ellsberg appeared on *Meet the Press*, where he faced hostile questioning. He handled it impressively. But one exchange went like this: moderator Lawrence Spivak: "You are not quite answering my question." Ellsberg: "But my answer to the question is still very important."[5]

Two days later, Ellsberg phoned the offices of several senators to challenge the nomination of Elliot Richardson as U.S. attorney general. He contended that Richardson had not been completely forthcoming about his awareness of CIA assistance to the break-in at Dr. Lewis Fielding's office. Ellsberg also attended the Richardson hearing.[6] It was hard to pull himself away.

After returning to California, where he and Patricia plunked themselves down in Malibu, Ellsberg testified before a grand jury investigating the Fielding break-in. He told reporters that Fielding's files on him did not include "anything I would be ashamed of or want to hide." But he opposed revealing the contents of their conversations "because that would set a bad precedent for violating the doctor-patient relationship." Fielding himself refused to say one word to reporters as he walked into the grand jury room.[7]

The Ellsbergs then did their traveling—New Zealand, Tahiti, and other spots. Dan met his children, Robert and Mary, in France. "Then Dan left them in Paris," Carol Cummings remembers. "They'd said they wanted to stay on for a few days. So he let them stay on. . . . I didn't know about this ahead of time. I thought they were with him. The first I knew of it was when I went to pick them up at the airport and only Robert got off. And he said, 'Mary decided she wanted to stay a few more days.' . . . She was 15. I said, 'Where is she staying?' 'Well, she met some girls at this bookstore.' 'What are their names?' He couldn't quite remember their names. I was *beside* myself, just *beside* myself." Mary returned three days later.[8]

The Ellsbergs moved to Mill Valley in California's Marin County the following summer, where they rented a secluded, plate-glass-windowed, oak-floored redwood house atop a winding mountain road and overlooking a valley full of streams; a heavy redwood gate with chains and locks afforded some measure of privacy. Japanese wind chimes tinkled in the wind. The Ellsbergs spent two relatively quiet, isolated years there. "I spend a lot of time alone now," Dan said in 1976. One visitor to the Ellsbergs' home found them living in a fairly disorganized manner, and without much furniture in the living room, which had several large pillows covered with prayer rugs. Dan watched the news on two television sets simultaneously.[9]

Sometime between September 28 and October 1 of 1974, an intruder entered their house while the Ellsbergs were away. The intruder made his entry through one of the unlocked windows or simply strolled in through the front door, which had also been left unlocked. "The house had been thoroughly gone through," the police report on the burglary reads. "The perpetrators also searched under the house. The search was very neat." Patricia reported to Mill Valley Police Lieutenant Robert Sisk on October 2 that the following items were missing: an expensive Oriental rug, a Turkish rug, stereo and camera equipment, and two pairs of binoculars. Dan subsequently reported to police that a black briefcase with the gold initials "DE" had also been taken. It contained notes and a paper he had written on decision making in international crises, he said. A "B-4 Air Force type bag" (in the FBI's words), also containing notes, Ellsberg told the police, was missing too. Four briefcases full of papers were missing in all, he later told the press. He did not know all their contents, but they included copies of classified government documents and the notes he had taken years earlier on U.S. nuclear war plans. Ellsberg said the documents should not have been classified and "were acquired during ten years of working for the Defense Department and the State Department." And "the bulk of it is extremely privileged information having to do with communication between my lawyer and myself" over his trial. Thousands of sheets of paper had vanished in all.[10]

A curious handwritten note had been left on Ellsberg's desk. It read:

Sorry Daniel,

    Not a word of this to *anyone*—much trouble will be avoided if you negotiate properly. Don't slip!

                —Soon you'll know[11]

Ellsberg believed the burglary was the work of the Plumbers. He called the Watergate Special Prosecution Force and reported that some of his purloined papers bore on matters that John Ehrlichman claimed had justified the Fielding break-in. They would be helpful to Watergate defendants, he told police. Leonard Boudin thought it unlikely that it was a Plumbers' job, but Ellsberg "believed that these papers would surface during the course of the Watergate trial," one member of the prosecution force recorded.[12]

But Mill Valley police quickly concluded that the burglary was the work of one Kevin Quinn, a 21-year-old Mill Valley resident with a lengthy record for burglary and possession of stolen property. The theft "appears to be just a plain dumb, routine burglary," Mill Valley Police Chief William Walsh stated. "Nothing political about it," said a Marin County assistant district attorney. Police recovered Ellsberg's papers, or at least most of them; some had been buried in a local park. But even after police concluded that Quinn was their man, Ellsberg refused to give up the notion that it had been a Watergate operation. "I want most of all to know who this burglar is and who he was working for," he declared at a press conference. While the burglar "may not have been paid with new $100 bills," he said, the extortion note was suspicious. And "when my private papers get burglarized, the first thought that occurs to me is federal officials and the White House." President Gerald Ford, Ellsberg pointed out, was "the man who was nominated by Mr. Nixon and who gave Mr. Nixon the pardon." The FBI sought to seize the classified papers. The government, Ellsberg said, was attempting "to control and destroy everything I have—that includes everything in my head."[13]

One wonders if he felt somewhat foolish after this episode was over. While he had reason to speculate about government involvement, it was ultimately another episode in self-aggrandizing, overdramatizing, and perhaps attention seeking. Ellsberg said later he could not let the burglary prey on his mind, however, as he had other things to do. "I, for instance, want to spend a lot of time making love to my wife," he told *People* magazine.[14]

⸻

While Ellsberg enjoyed some quiet in Marin, he was never one inclined to sit in one place for very long, and he did a lot of hopping about and traveling as usual. He returned to Washington. He approached Senators Frank Church and Stuart Symington, both of whom were investigating the CIA; in the wake of Watergate and blockbuster revelations by Seymour Hersh on the CIA's abuses, Congress was conducting probes into the agency's activities. Ellsberg wanted to get the full truth out about the CIA's involvement in the Fielding break-in and its psychological profiles of him. He was also attempting to interject himself into the congressional investigations, to remain relevant and important, to continue the ride he was on—the high, the drama, the excitement, the publicity. Ellsberg could not let go. And he still liked talking to men in power. He spoke with journalists about the CIA's involvement in the Fielding break-in, trying to get them to impugn the report of the Ford-appointed Rockefeller Commission, which had concluded that the CIA had not been aware that the disguises and equipment it provided Howard Hunt would be used for "improper activities." The CIA had gone after him too, Ellsberg was telling others, and, of course, there was some truth to that.[15]

But Ellsberg did not find very eager audiences. He flew from Washington to California once to speak with Symington on the plane, as it would be his only opportunity to see him. But when Ellsberg boarded the plane, he discovered that Symington was sitting in first class, and Symington would not come back to sit with him. Also, Church told Ellsberg to provide the details to his staff. And Ellsberg couldn't interest any journalists in going after the Rockefeller Commission. Most likely, many people found him old news, tiresome even, and were put off by his egocentrism and obvious desire for the spotlight. Senator James Abourezk, a strong critic of the CIA's covert operations, Marcus Raskin of the Institute for Policy Studies, and others were turned off by a long, self-promoting talk that Ellsberg gave at a conference on the CIA and covert action on Capitol Hill in September 1974. Abourezk cut him off.[16] Ellsberg's tendency to embellish events and the extreme nature of some of his statements probably hurt his credibility among some congresspeople and journalists.

Ellsberg also attempted to block the confirmation of former Watergate prosecutor Earl Silbert as U.S. attorney for the District of Columbia and to promote an investigation into a possible cover-up of Watergate by the Justice Department. He seemed desperate to draw attention to himself. He still needed a stage.[17]

Ellsberg arranged to get the material he had collected on U.S. nuclear war plans into the hands of two congressional subcommittees around this time. That would provide him legal cover. He hungered for congressional hearings on the nuclear material: he would star in those hearings. It would be another heroic act, and a valuable one, as greater public scrutiny of the war-planning process was long overdue. But the subcommittees turned him down. Ellsberg mused that both he and the subject were too controversial. He was "still looking for dramatic things to do that would make a big difference," Noam Chomsky remembers. And he strove "for years" to get his nuclear documents out, "thinking they would have a dramatic effect. . . . He was never able to get anybody to look at them. . . . It didn't go the way he had hoped. He'd hoped it would be another Pentagon Papers, but on nuclear policy."[18]

Ellsberg had earlier considered making a run for Congress. For the Senate, from New York. That would keep him in the public eye. He had become the Ralph Nader of foreign affairs, he reportedly thought. (Ellsberg still likened himself to Nader 20 years later.) But while he undoubtedly enjoyed listening to any appeals to run, his prospects would have been quite slim. He later denied that he considered mounting a run, but Congresswoman Bella Abzug and others heard otherwise.[19]

Ellsberg even reportedly entertained thoughts about getting back into the government again under a liberal Democratic administration. That was no more likely than becoming a senator. Whistle-blowers of his magnitude don't tend to get rehired (quite apart from his unsatisfactory performance as a Pentagon aide). "I believe that he will be a sad, perhaps bitter man," Marty Arnold wrote in January 1974, as "it is hard to believe that any future Administration . . . will give a position of trust to a man who may not keep its secrets. I would predict that Ellsberg has reached his high point, that although there will be brief sputterings of headlines in the future, Dan Ellsberg will reluctantly fade from the spotlight."[20] That prediction was fairly on the mark.

Ellsberg also envisioned another public role for himself. "When his trial was over, I think Dan saw himself as having a great position as, say, a very fine TV or radio commentator," Theo Wilson recalls. But "he went to Washington and I gather from how he spoke to me—the word is not spurned, the word is he just couldn't get anywhere there. He was nothing to them. . . . I said, 'What happened?' . . . He keeps saying, 'They were not interested.' And that had to be a terrible blow. Not because he's a man of ego; that's not it. It would be to anybody who had been front-page news for so long, big front-page news. And it availed him naught." It was Wilson's impression from talking to Ellsberg that he had approached "everybody," including the television networks, about being a commentator or the like.[21]

In the years ahead, the mainstream media would only infrequently seek out Ellsberg's views. That wounded him. "Once in my life, having tried many times, I was invited to be on *MacNeil-Lehrer*," he told me in 1995. It occurred during the 1991 U.S. bombing of Iraq. "It was all set up." But when Ellsberg called about some arrangements, "they said, 'Oh, we've replaced you,'" he recounts. "And I was replaced with Todd Gitlin," the professor and writer. Ellsberg came to believe it was because *MacNeil-Lehrer* had typecast him as a demonstrator and Gitlin as an analyst. Gitlin had been invited on the show to talk about the Gulf War and American opposition to it in light of the 1960s. "It's false to say that I was his rival, although *MacNeil-Lehrer* may have presented me that way to him," Gitlin recalls. "Insofar as he was going to be on the show, it was not to be the ex-

pert on the antiwar movement of the '60s." Ellsberg was interviewed during the
1990 U.S. military buildup in the gulf for a free weekly newspaper in the Bay
Area; Tim Beneke, his interviewer, had sought him out in part because Ellsberg's friend Jeffrey Masson had told Beneke it would be good for Ellsberg's
morale and self-esteem to be interviewed (both evidently being low). After the
interview came out, Ellsberg ordered a thousand copies of the newspaper to distribute to members of Congress and other influentials. Ellsberg seemed grateful
to Beneke for interviewing him and then basically letting him write the interview up. "He was saying to me how he can start things, but he can never finish
things that he writes," Beneke remembers.[22]

Ellsberg hit the paid-lecture circuit after his trial, speaking mainly before
college audiences on Vietnam, Watergate, the Nixon administration's moves
against him, nuclear weapons, the Pentagon Papers, and other periods in his
odyssey. He typically overstated his importance to Nixon, substantial as it was
(which again raises the question, Why does he need to do this?). People were
already starting to forget and he didn't want to be a footnote to history, Ellsberg told one group of students. He traveled briefly with Jane Fonda in the fall
of 1974 to raise money for the Indochina Peace Campaign. At one fund-raising
cocktail party in Detroit, "he seemed unable to mix with strangers at close
range," a reporter perceived. Paid lecturing would provide essentially Ellsberg's only income for years, but he could make a decent income that way, and
he didn't have to earn a lot, given his marriage to Patricia (although she wanted
him to pull his weight). He took in around $40,000 lecturing in 1975, he told a
journalist, donating $14,000 to various causes. His earning capacity from lec-
turing was then near its height. "My lecturing pays for my secretary and my
phone bill," he would tell an interviewer ten years later. "I've got *some* phone
bills. And all my personal expenses. . . . Pat pays for the house and the children.
And the rest."[23]

Ellsberg drew mixed reactions on the road. Many people found him inspirational and a riveting speaker, a hero, and a brave, admirable man. Others
thought him odd. One, a teacher who took his history class to hear a talk by
Ellsberg in New Haven, Connecticut, in the spring of 1974, and who considered Ellsberg one of his heroes, found him quite strange, a very angry man underneath the smooth, controlled, witty exterior; he could now believe an earlier
report that he had read of Ellsberg picking up an M-16 and leading some soldiers in Vietnam. Ellsberg was an extremist, this listener thought. He noticed
that Ellsberg became incensed with a questioner who said that people wanted
to know if he was mentally ill since he had seen a psychiatrist (perhaps Ellsberg
should have just laughed at that). Ellsberg then regained his self-control, but

this episode and Ellsberg's testy, hostile reaction to his own question about disclosing classified information showed in the mind of this listener how thin that control was. (Some 20 years later, Ellsberg gave a talk in a class taught by Sanford Ungar at American University. "I think some of the people listening to him thought, 'Oh, God, fascinating guy. Interesting. What a privilege to get to hear him.' And some people just thought, 'This guy is really weird. He's really strange,'" Ungar recounts. Ellsberg seemed "zoned out," distracted, and he "pretty much rambled on. He would suddenly think of a point he had meant to make earlier. It was a kind of interrupted stream of consciousness.")[24]

Ellsberg became famous for giving long rambling lectures. Some people over the years would liken him to Fidel Castro of the six-hour speeches. "I don't go as long, but I could," Ellsberg laughs. "I could go as long as Castro if people gave me the time." It would not be unusual for crowds to thin while Ellsberg was still at the podium, moving from issue to issue, trying to get it all in, speaking softly, almost inaudibly in the early going, then building in force and rhythm, his brow frequently furrowed, his head thrusting back and forth to emphasize his points, quickly smiling at his jokes, in part for effect, moving his hands about to enhance the presentation. On at least one occasion, student activists who had invited him to speak at a protest would have to literally wrestle the microphone away from him. Many activists in the 1970s became averse to inviting Ellsberg to speak, given his tendency to talk interminably; there was a lot of rolling of eyes and looking for exits during his speeches. Activists needed him to draw, but could you get him to shut up? Ellsberg's marathon speeches were, at root, another form of self-indulgence, another manifestation of his ego and his lack of self-discipline, of his belief that what he had to say was quite important, something others should know, and the truth. During a rambling three-and-a-half-hour talk at Cranbrook in 1975, Ellsberg played up his role in Watergate to the hilt (he was now steeped in material on himself), talking on and on, ultimately losing his audience, many people departing. But at least one listener told him afterward that he had been sensational. Ellsberg sounded almost like a wild man at times toward the end of this talk (which I listened to on tape), not fully in control, and not a man of great judgment.[25]

Some years later, Ellsberg was invited to participate in a roast at the Playboy mansion. He evidently didn't know what a roast was, and he gave a "*long and serious*" speech about "the state of America and the state of the world," one friend recounts. "He really lost his audience and offended his audience, which wanted to get on with it. He certainly sensed that something was wrong. . . . And afterwards he was really nervous, saying . . . 'Did I screw up? Did I do something wrong? Did I look bad?' . . . And I was telling him, 'Don't worry about it. It's a stupid thing called a roast.' . . . But he was very worried about the perception that people had about him."[26]

Ellsberg would have trouble keeping to a time clock when introducing someone else, too. When Jeffrey Masson spoke in the packed mezzanine of Cody's bookstore in Berkeley, California, after Masson's book *Against Therapy* had come out in 1988, Ellsberg "introduced" Masson for 30 or 40 minutes, "trying to rehabilitate Masson's reputation," Tim Beneke remembers. (Masson had earlier taken a few shots, some quite suspect, some not, from the journalist Janet Malcolm.) "The people in the audience started saying, 'We want to hear Jeffrey Masson talk about therapy. We don't want to hear [you],'" Beneke recounts:

And Ellsberg's saying, "Now, wait a minute, wait a minute. Now, hang on, hear me out. Now, you may have certain preconceptions about this man." And he had transcripts of the Janet Malcolm interviews, and he was being very lawyerly in demonstrating that Malcolm had really screwed Masson over in certain ways. Specifically, that he makes one grandiose statement here, one grandiose statement here, one grandiose statement here, and Malcolm takes them and presents them as if he said them one after another. . . . He was going on and on about this. . . . It was longer than any introduction I'd ever heard. And people started getting impatient.[27]

Lecturing on the college circuit was not the type of academic engagement Ellsberg valued most. He would rather have been engaged with other scholars than giving lectures to largely undergraduate audiences. And he came to loathe all the traveling. "Unfortunately, because I could easily make a living as a speaker, I find the travel aspects of that awful," he told me. "Torture. . . . I'm exhausted most of the time. . . . I have to take sleeping pills when I travel." Sometimes he gets sick. Also, "people want to eat dinner with you, they want to do [other things]. This is one thing that tires you out. And they want a reception afterwards. So you get lots of applause, you get lots of stroking, and so forth. You then go to a lonely hotel room or a dormitory. You can't sleep."[28]

Keeping organized was probably a problem, too. Ellsberg is well known for missing planes, running late, forgetting things. In 1994 he was invited by a former colleague in Vietnam, Frank Scotton, then with the U.S. embassy in China, to speak in China under the auspices of the USIA; he would be an example of an American dissident. Ellsberg phoned me two nights before making the trip and asked if I would be interested in driving him to the San Francisco airport and doing an interview then. When I arrived at his house as scheduled at 11:15 A.M. the day of his flight, he was still packing, trying to pull it together (he'd only slept two hours the night before, he said, as he'd been up most of the night getting ready), and we didn't get out of his house for 40 minutes. "This is all too typical," his longtime assistant Jan Thomas remarked with an amused smile and a roll of her eyes. When Ellsberg finally made it out the front door, lugging his bags, his pants riding low, he didn't have any shoes on. He chuckled when someone brought that to his attention. What would it have been like to arrive in China without any shoes on? he mused aloud. After driving down the road a bit, we had to return to his house to pick up some papers he had forgotten to give me. When told this story, Margaret Brenman-Gibson, a friend and admirer of his, commented, "That's common. I sort of take that for granted. . . . I've said more than once, 'I'm never going to travel with you again,'" for Ellsberg forgets airline tickets and other things and is always late. "He has left his briefcase on the file [cabinet]. Then you get a phone call from the airport: 'Oh God, I've done it again.'"[29]

Ellsberg struck some in the mid-1970s as still living in his past, stuck in it, unable to move beyond the Pentagon Papers and Vietnam. One couldn't talk to him for a minute without being right back there with the Papers, Harrison Salisbury remarked in October 1976. But Ellsberg found it difficult to write about his past. After his trial was over, "my impression was he never wanted to write anything," Anthony Russo remembers. "Because I felt that he had sort of a PR structure to the story and he didn't want to bother it. And he couldn't sit down and write the truth. His block at writing is he wants to portray a certain Ellsberg, which subconsciously he knows is not true. And so he can't write."[30] That is an astute comment. Todd Gitlin spoke earlier about how Ellsberg reveals many smaller secrets about himself while withholding deeper secrets. It is those deeper secrets that Russo's analysis alludes to.

But Ellsberg told journalists after the trial that he planned to return to a life of research and writing. Asked by Jan Wenner of *Rolling Stone* whether he intended to get more involved in "the Movement," he responded, "My own real desires and talents are quite different. They are to do research and analysis—intellectual kinds of pursuits—with some time, I'm sure, spent on immediate political challenges. People will be asking me and things will rise up. But I would like to spend my life reading, reflecting, trying to understand things and trying to write about them." He waxed nostalgic about his time at RAND: "In the future I see myself doing something very similar to that, not for Rand or anything like it, but probably on my own for a year or so, and ultimately in connection with a university or some research institute."[31]

Ellsberg, of course, knew he had talent as a writer. He wanted to write a book on nuclear weapons. It would be on the secret history of U.S. nuclear policy and something of a blockbuster. In the mid-1970s, "he basically invited me, I'm sure many other people, to push him to write the book," Todd Gitlin remembers. "He solicited people assuring him how important it was." But

Alice Mayhew at Simon & Schuster turned the book down (possibly after hearing from Ted Solotaroff about Ellsberg). Still, there was the possibility of a memoir and other books. But Ellsberg found himself unable to write (which probably fueled his kicking about Washington and elsewhere). He remarked to Neil Sheehan in 1975 that he was enjoying doing the research, as usual, but wasn't able to get anything down on paper. He again remarked to Sheehan in 1976 that he hadn't been getting any writing done. Three years later, he told Sheehan that he was going to get started on that book on nuclear weapons.[32] High standards, insecurity, restlessness, impatience, lack of self-discipline, and disorganization all probably remained inhibiting factors.

Leslie Henriques can attest to the last trait. In 1980 Ellsberg wanted her to help organize his filing system. Henriques, who worked for him for about a year, found that there was "no method" to his filing system. Ellsberg was "totally" disorganized, she recalls, and "crazy last-minute" activity was common. "Mundane things, he can't deal with," she says. She doesn't remember any writing. "I don't think that he can focus on that. . . . He is off in another world a lot of the time." Ellsberg traveled a lot. When Henriques and her husband had coffee with Dan and Pat, discussions moved toward the Pentagon Papers. She found Ellsberg unappreciative of her work for him, unhelpful, difficult, and wrapped up in himself.[33] (Ellsberg was still looking for somebody to organize his files, which seemed quite disorganized, when I first met with him for this book in 1994. I offered to do so, but he responded with a smile and remarked, "That would be like letting the fox inside the chicken coop.")

Ellsberg spoke with the literary agent Sterling Lord about representing him. Seymour Hersh, whom Lord represented, had brought the two together. Lord first saw Ellsberg at Hersh's home. When Lord walked in, "Ellsberg was sitting in the living room totally absorbed in the television," Lord recounts. "He barely noticed me as I was walking through the living room. . . . It was sort of like saying hello without taking his eyes off the TV." When Ellsberg subsequently came to see Lord, "it all seemed so tentative," Lord recalls. "It was like, 'On the one hand, on the other hand.' . . . I very quickly began to think that I wasn't going to get anything to represent. . . . The discussions were so nonspecific. It never seemed like anything was going to happen. . . . He would show up in my life every nine months or a year or so." Lord thought Ellsberg's wealth (among other things) was not conducive to making something happen. And nothing ever did happen.[34]

Ellsberg told me that the actor Martin Sheen spoke with him about doing a TV documentary on him for CBS. "I was going to be a producer on it," he remembers. "To assure that I had a full say in who wrote the script, what the script said." Sheen "was *the* producer," Ellsberg says. "Under Norman Lear."

Sterling Lord was his agent, Ellsberg recalls. "He said, 'Don't do this til you have a book. You won't really have control over this til you have a book, or at least a manuscript.' . . . But they kept getting more and more serious about the thing, and saying, 'Look, we'll give you this, we'll give you that.' And Sterling Lord said . . . 'This is getting to be an offer we can't refuse.'" But the deal was killed by new CBS owner Laurence Tisch shortly after he came in in 1986, Ellsberg says; he remembers being ready to fly out to sign the contract the next day. But, told Ellsberg's account, Lord said he had no memory of any of it.[35]

There would be more talk about a book on nuclear weapons later, and more research, even a contract offer for a quickie book. And there would be more research on decision making in crises ("I was about to start writing up research I'd done on the Cuban missile crisis, which I participated in," Ellsberg told an audience in 1991, but then the Gulf War started). And there would be some research funded by the MacArthur Foundation on U.S. threats to use nuclear weapons. But it, too, didn't pan out. One person at MacArthur told me that Ellsberg didn't turn in what was expected of him, and that somebody should have told him, "You didn't do what you said you were going to do. Give us our money back." And there was that talk about getting back into decision theory and writing another article, which also didn't bear fruit. "He wanted to write the great book, which he never was able to do," Richard Falk remembers. "He has had in his mind, for a very long time, one or more books, and the books are always very ambitious books," his friend Doug Dowd says. "It has to be a big splash." But "I've never seen a page of anything, except essays, articles, and that sort of stuff." Ellsberg would also begin drafting a memoir, a project that became extremely important to him, partly because I was writing this biography of him. (He would tell one person that he was writing the memoir because of it.) But he worried that his memoir was loaded with psychological land mines. Howard Zinn noticed in 1995 that Ellsberg was more concerned than he had been in the past "with getting something in writing. After all these years when he hasn't really written." Ellsberg had earlier begun renting an apartment and spending most of his time in Washington, and when Zinn saw him there he told Zinn that Patricia was in California and that he had an "agreement" with her that he would stay in Washington in order to hunker down and write. Ellsberg and Zinn spoke at the opening of a play Zinn had written. "But he came to the play," Zinn chuckles. "And then he was going to go off on the weekend to the Cape to the conference that Bob Lifton has" in Wellfleet. Ellsberg was "obviously looking," Zinn thought, "for excuses not to write."[36]

To Margaret Brenman-Gibson, Ellsberg seemed terrified at the prospect of holing up in Washington to write. But Ellsberg would tell people that, living with Patricia, he can't write the way he has to write—for long stretches, at erratic hours, into and even through the night—because that will ruin his marriage; Patricia won't put up with it. She wants him to write, indeed to earn some money from it, but at reasonable hours. "She hasn't seen it happen here [in California], and it's been my belief . . . for a long time that that was strongly related to my living with her," Ellsberg says. "Because prolonged writing drives her crazy. . . . It's always looked like I either stay in the marriage or I be a writer." But Patricia was skeptical he'd get the memoir done in Washington. Ellsberg's friend Donald Hall, the writer and poet, has urged Ellsberg to write every day at regular hours as he does, but Ellsberg has responded that he can't do it that way and gets a bit irritated with Hall. Tension developed between them. "That came between us for years," Ellsberg recalls. "I just got so tired of his clearly feeling that, if I wasn't writing—which I wasn't—that I wasn't accomplishing anything. That wasn't my self-image. That was his problem."[37]

Ellsberg remained a frustrated, unfulfilled intellectual. According to friends, he is well aware that he has not written much for a person of his talents and is quite sensitive to that observation. In his 1984–85 *Who's Who in America* listing (his last), he described his occupation as "writer, lecturer, former government official, political activist." For publications, he listed his book *Papers on the War* and said he was a contributor of articles to professional journals. But his contributions to the journals he listed were made in 1956 and 1961. (Ellsberg beefed up his *Who's Who* listing noticeably between 1974 and 1984. One wonders if questions about accomplishment played a role.) Ellsberg told me that "publishing is not my profession" and that it was "irrelevant" to criticize him for not publishing much. "It's not my job, it's not my aspiration, it's not my goal. I don't measure my worth or my productivity or my whatever accomplishment in terms of published work."[38]

But his problems writing led him, at least in part, to seek another round of psychoanalysis in the mid-1970s. That round would last for only a year and end disastrously.

———

Ellsberg had remained deeply interested in psychoanalysis and was exploring a range of psychoanalytic thinking, and reading a lot as usual. He was interested in, among other things, narcissism. Dr. Allen Wheelis was a highly regarded psychoanalyst and a writer. Ellsberg read some of Wheelis's work before seeing him ("that's why I went to him," he says) and then during the analysis, typically studying Wheelis's writings in great detail. "I read his books, and he knew I read his books," Ellsberg remembers. "We discussed them a little. Which was a very questionable thing for him to do." Ellsberg acknowledges that he entered analysis again because of his problems writing, but one suspects he also had other motivations. This was another difficult period in his life. "It was hard for a long time," he once said to me, in a very soft voice.[39]

Ellsberg kept notes on his sessions with Wheelis. He began to analyze Wheelis. "For my own protection," he says. "I felt there was something funny going on. . . . I began to feel that there was something that was being totally missed in the analysis." His relations with his father. "We talked about my mother a lot, but he seemed to be very unwilling to talk about my father," Ellsberg recalls. "Uninterested. He'd change the subject all the time." Ellsberg found a clue as to why in one of Wheelis's writings. "And then I went back through the stuff I'd already read, and read it very closely. And found a pattern in his own writing that could explain what the problem was between us." It became "perfectly obvious," Ellsberg says, that Wheelis had "had a relationship with his father that was *very* close to my relation with my mother." In Wheelis's book *The Quest for Identity*, the character who appears to represent his father is, like Ellsberg's mother, highly demanding and exacting. In fact, he is quite cruel to Wheelis. He is deeply religious, too. Ellsberg also discovered that Wheelis "had a relation with his mother that was very close to my relation with my father. And it was very clear. In his books, his mother is simply missing. Except as a wonderful figure. It was very clear that he had reason to be very angry at his mother . . . to feel that his mother had let him down in a serious way . . . had not protected him in certain ways from the father. And nevertheless there is no criticism. But endless bitterness toward the father."[40]

After giving the parallel some thought, and wondering how Wheelis might react if he brought it up, "I said, 'Look, I think I've found what the problem is here,'" Ellsberg recounts. He told Wheelis, he says, "It seems to me that you're very unwilling to talk about my father and my relations with my father. . . . I think I see a reason here. . . . My father was in the role of your mother, and you're very clearly excluding any anger or criticism of your mother. . . . I think if I were to express, or as I have expressed, criticisms of my father, you're going to hear that as criticisms of your mother. . . . And you don't want to hear that." Wheelis was "very unhappy" to hear this, Ellsberg recalls. "He reacted very emotionally, and impulsively." At the next session, Wheelis said, according to Ellsberg's retelling,

> "I agree with you. We should terminate the analysis." And I said, "What!?" Nothing could have been further from my mind. I was trying to cure the analysis. The idea of quitting had not even occurred to me. . . . "Terminate the

analysis." Like that. Out of the blue. So I was so shocked and astounded by this behavior. . . . It was absolutely startling and shocking behavior. . . . So I said, "Well, let's talk about this a little." I thought, "I'm in with a madman."

. . . So we then talked for a week, face to face—me paying for it. . . . We talked daily, but face to face now, which I insisted. And in the course of that he said . . . "Of course, you're right. I was having a countertransference reaction there. You're absolutely right about the relationships here. You hit it on the head. And no question, I do avoid that subject [of] my mother, and so forth. And it probably does create a problem in our analysis."

Ellsberg says he pointed out that Wheelis invited his patients to read his books, that other patients must also comment on them, yet he was so sensitive to such comments. "He said, 'Yes, they do,'" Ellsberg recounts. "He said, 'But let's face it. . . . It's one thing when a neurotic 19-year-old girl makes some comment on you. . . . Whether it's true or not, you can toss it off. . . . But when you say something, it cuts a little deeper. . . . You just can't dismiss it.'"[41]

Also in Ellsberg's retelling, "at the end of the week, he said, 'Well, I'm happy to continue now. . . . Let's go on. Why don't you come tomorrow, and we'll resume on the couch.' And then to *his* astonishment, I said, 'I don't really feel like doing that.' Because what he had revealed in this week . . . cured me of psychoanalysis."[42]

One wonders if Ellsberg's anger at Wheelis at this point (he may have felt rage) wasn't fueled by both Wheelis's seeming rejection of him ("we should terminate the analysis") and his frustration with the analysis, perhaps a feeling that it wasn't getting anywhere, that he wasn't getting what he had come for, that his problems writing, or his other psychological difficulties, weren't being solved, or even approached adequately. And he was paying a lot of money for this. "I got disillusioned with it, so I left," Ellsberg remembers.[43]

After this second bout with psychoanalysis, Ellsberg talked "with *enormous* disparagement" about psychoanalysis, "and with arguments and citations and a bibliography," Donald Hall recalls. "He came to think it was really horseshit. . . . He just spoke with great scorn. Contempt. . . . He had stats about the cure rate and so on. And he was throwing facts at me." He has "a *tremendous* stockpile of resentment" at psychoanalysis, Margaret Brenman-Gibson, a psychotherapist herself, says. "It's a fraud, basically, as a therapy—it just doesn't work," Ellsberg told me. Once, he started to liken classical psychoanalysis to chiropractic, then stopped and laughed, "But chiropractic *does* work. . . . Psychoanalysts just make your life worse or do nothing, or at best don't hurt it." His two analyses "added virtually nothing to my self-understanding" and were a "*total* waste of time," he said, adding, "I've never said that publicly."[44]

Many people have lost faith in psychoanalysis. It's also true that many narcissists prove resistant to psychoanalysis and other forms of psychotherapy. They often exhibit, among other behaviors, defensiveness, devaluation of their analyst, intolerance of dependency, an attempt to defeat the analyst, and rage at the analyst. They may also use the analyst "as an audience for their own independent 'analytic' work." It seems we can put a check mark aside several of those categories in Ellsberg's case. But there would be lots more therapy in his life.[45]

In the 1970s Ellsberg sought another academic position. Or at least he put some feelers out. Intellectual stimulation, exchange, and debate remained at the heart of his life: he was an intellectual without an intellectual home, and he longed for one.

Ellsberg expressed interest in teaching courses at Berkeley and UCLA. "He intimated that he would like to get a gig teaching summers or being a visiting professor in sociology" at Berkeley, Todd Gitlin, who was then teaching at Berkeley, remembers. Ellsberg may have even made a formal request. But he didn't get a position. He was interested in the transition that Gitlin had made into the academy. Ellsberg also expressed interest in other types of university involvements. But it's unclear how systematically he approached his job search. It may have been like talking about writing books. "He was improvisational," Gitlin recalls. "He was writing the script as he went along."[46]

Ellsberg complained to others that he had not been invited to a faculty seminar since the Papers had been published. That was a source of great sorrow and disappointment to him. He felt shut out, blackballed by academia. "He couldn't get a job anywhere," Harvard's Richard Zeckhauser, with whom he would inquire about academic positions, remembers. "The academic community just turned their back to him," his former Cranbrook classmate Jo Isaacson understood. "They wouldn't accept him in any position."[47] But while releasing the Papers had hurt Ellsberg's prospects for a job in many places, including academia, where he was too controversial for most university departments, his problems completing work and other limitations may have also hurt his academic prospects. He'd been out of the game for a while, neither teaching nor publishing (he'd apparently never taught a college course before), and there was the question of what, precisely, he would teach; his background was in economics, but he hadn't been active in that field for some time, and teaching courses on the Vietnam War, peace movements, nuclear weapons, or the like could only take him so far (although he had the intellectual ability to pull together courses on a tremendous variety of subjects). There may have also been questions among some about his personality and desirability as a colleague.

Ellsberg was invited by undergraduates to teach a student-sponsored course on "nuclear weapons and foreign policy" at Stanford in 1979. He probably didn't emerge from it with a great evaluation as a teacher. "It became a problem in the political science department," Alexander George, Ellsberg's former RAND colleague who had since become a Stanford professor, recalls. Members of the department debated whether the course should count toward the requirements for a political science degree. "What I heard later was that the turnout for the course at the beginning was very large, a great deal of interest, and that it dwindled very rapidly," George remembers. Also, that Ellsberg "relied too much on his memory of what he personally was involved in. . . . I guess it was understandable, but these were not written memoirs, you know. . . . He stimulates himself on memories. It may not be as well organized."[48]

From the mid-1970s into the 1980s, Ellsberg participated in a discussion group of antiwar intellectuals that was enormously important to him. "It was his sole institutional place," Gitlin, who was also a member, recalls. "He was a very devoted attender of these meetings." Gitlin saw a lot of Ellsberg in action at the meetings. "He had a way of going off into stories that were personal," Gitlin recounts, echoing George. "I think this became more marked in the time that I knew him. That is, that a meeting would tend to turn to the relaying of a personal experience. Which mainly had the same structure. Namely, 'Here is something I've never said before.'" The stories included "'my encounter with Henry Kissinger, my conversation with John McNaughton.' A lot of it was that. . . . 'Here is something that happened in Vietnam. Here is something that happened when I was in the Society of Fellows at Harvard.' And then sometimes it was personal sagas. I heard a fair amount about his sexual conquests. Unsolicited," including about "some woman he was fucking every afternoon" at Harvard and "some woman he met in a hotel room in Santa Monica," Gitlin recalls. There was "a lot of that."[49]

Margaret Brenman-Gibson was a clinical professor of psychology at the Harvard Medical School when she first met Ellsberg at Robert Lifton's annual intellectual gathering in Wellfleet on Cape Cod in 1982. At the end of the meeting, Ellsberg remarked, "Maybe this can be my new intellectual family." He was still looking for a replacement for RAND. He dreamed more than once of being back at RAND. Ellsberg told Brenman-Gibson and John Mack, who was also at the Harvard Medical School, about his being shut out of academia. They offered to invite him to teach a course at Harvard. "He said, 'If you did that, it would be a first, and I would be very grateful,'" Brenman-Gibson recounts. So she and Mack arranged for Ellsberg to teach a course under a center Mack had set up called the Center for Psychological Studies in the Nuclear Age. As a birthday present, Brenman-Gibson gave Ellsberg tapes of his lectures. "This is, by far, the best birthday present I've ever had," he told her. He became a research associate at Mack's center.[50]

Ellsberg also put out feelers about other academic positions. Could he be a research fellow here? What about teaching a course there? And he attended many seminars. But this was a pale imitation of the intellectual life he sought and had earlier seemed destined for. He had been tabbed for truly extraordinary intellectual achievement and a rich intellectual career. His former Harvard mentor Thomas Schelling, who, it will be remembered, had considered him one of the smartest people he had ever known, came to think Ellsberg was squandering his genius:

> I think he's leading an utterly wasted life. I think he's deluding himself. He doesn't make much of an effort to get involved in anything like academic or intellectual circles. About the only place I see him, except when we've had him to dinner a couple of times . . . was [in] a group organized by one of my colleagues at [the University of] Maryland . . . a lunch meeting where somebody would give a talk on arms control. And Dan would usually show up. Well, I would say that was pretty dull stuff for somebody of Dan's intellectual talents. . . .
>
> I think Dan likes to engage with people who will admire him. And I think if Dan had to come out to the University of Maryland and sit down with six of my smartest colleagues to talk about what he's doing in the field of disarmament, he wouldn't make much of an impression. And I think he may feel that, if he sticks around with [antinuclear activists] . . . Dan can be quite a hero to them. But I don't think in a dozen years he has attempted to present himself to a critical professional audience. . . .
>
> There's really a remarkable contrast between him and Mort Halperin. Mort has the kind of self-confidence that allows him to be willing to risk making a mistake. . . . Mort, I think, doesn't desperately need the approval, let alone the admiration, of an audience. . . .
>
> I think Dan has become something like a charlatan. A little like those . . . couple of basketball teams, professional teams, that used to go around the country taking on college teams and beating them, playing humorously. . . . Dan is a little like that. He can't quite make the professional leagues, but he's clever enough to look as if he can play rings around these college students in basketball. So he picks an audience where he knows that he's glib and experienced. If people challenge him on his views, nobody's going to ask him a question he hasn't heard before; he's been practicing this for 20 years.
>
> But he must occasionally look at himself in the mirror and wonder what he's been doing with his life for the last 20 years.

That is undoubtedly true, even if Schelling places little value on Ellsberg's antinuclear activities. There would also be questions among some about whether

Ellsberg was losing a few steps intellectually and becoming less focused. "He wanders, he rambles," Sam Popkin observed in 1995. "He's not the same person. . . . He's all fuzzy now and spacy. It's like he's preoccupied more than ever." In one recent phone conversation, "there was a kind of losing the connections," Popkin recalled. "Like, 'Where was I?'"[51]

Ellsberg's marriage to Patricia surely had a major effect on the path his life took after his trial ended. Though finances would be a source of strain in their marriage, her wealth allowed him a great deal of leeway. He didn't necessarily have to develop another career. When Todd Gitlin began spending time with Ellsberg in the mid-1970s, Dan and Patricia had by then moved to a gorgeous place off San Francisco's North Beach area with a fabulous view of the San Francisco Bay. "What struck me was that he was living in a world of rich people," Gitlin recalls. "They were San Francisco rich people. . . . It was a world of people who had nothing to do with politics. They were men wearing double-breasted suits at a time when that was not stylish." (In the late 1970s the Ellsbergs would move to Kensington, a desirable spot above Berkeley, where they lived in a modest two-story frame house whose deck afforded a beautiful view across the San Francisco Bay.) Ellsberg would later express displeasure to Gitlin that Patricia was supporting him, however. Many men whose wives support them find that troubling. When Carl Kaysen remarked to Ellsberg that he had married a very rich woman, "with some sharpness, he said that he never lived on her money," Kaysen remembers. "That he earned enough from his lecturing and writing" to support himself. "He reacted very sharply."[52]

Meanwhile, Ellsberg's politics had continued to evolve. In the 1970s he had become something of a radical, more critical of capitalism. His involvement in radical circles had something to do with that, as did, perhaps, the appreciation he received in some of those circles. "I used to think a radical explanation of Vietnam, that we were there for profit, was wrong," he told a reporter in the fall of 1974. "But just recently I'm beginning to think the radicals were always right, that the precedent of losing part of our capitalist empire, the American sphere of influence, is intolerable to our system." Though still steeped in Gandhian thought, Ellsberg devoured Karl Marx's writings. When Neil Sheehan interviewed him in the mid-1970s, Ellsberg launched into monologues about the merits of Marxist analyses in two interviews, though Sheehan had come to talk to him about John Paul Vann; Ellsberg appeared to have become obsessed with the latest truth he'd found.[53]

Ellsberg was impressed with Doug Dowd's book *The Twisted Dream*, a radical economic analysis, and attended a talk by Dowd at some economic association meetings in 1975. Afterward, he came up to Dowd and introduced himself—as "he likes to do," Dowd recounts—"'I'm Dan Ellsberg.' And he sort of expects you to sort of fall backwards." Ellsberg told Dowd he'd read his book and that it had changed his way of thinking about economics. Ellsberg asked Dowd if he'd like to get together. "So we began to have lunch together," Dowd recalls. "And always at his behest. . . . I don't think Dan and I have ever, ever come together at my initiation."[54]

Ellsberg has complained often that friends don't call him more. "That's a constant complaint on Dan's part, with a few highly selected people," one close friend says. "That they don't seek him out. . . . I believe it happens rather routinely, and mostly with men whom, in the beginning, he has a marvelous exchange. And that what happens then, I think quite often, is there's a falling out." Ellsberg has apparently had some difficulty maintaining friendships. "He has, in fact, suggested . . . in effect, 'What is it with you? How come I always have to telephone you?'" Dowd recounts. "He at one point said, 'Well, I haven't seen you for something like six, seven months. And I'd like to see you, but I'm going to leave it up to you to call.' . . . And I never did. But he did. . . . I like to see him very much, once in a while. But really once in a while. Because it's too heavy a diet for me."[55]

Dowd finds Ellsberg an unusually interesting person and highly stimulating company, extraordinarily well informed, but too egotistical and too intense—as do most people—"and needing to be, so to speak, on the high wire all the time." Ellsberg has also ignored some basic social conventions with Dowd. After they started having lunches together, "I began to notice that I was the one who was always paying for the lunch," Dowd remembers. "This is really funny about Dan. I think probably in some unconscious way he probably thought he was in some sense doing me a favor [by having lunch with him]. So why shouldn't I pay for the goddamn lunch? So at some point, I said, 'Dan, it'd be perfectly all right with me if we just always went Dutch on this.'" But the first time Ellsberg was going to pay for his own lunch, he didn't have any money with him. Also, Dowd and his then-wife had Dan and Patricia over for dinner several times, "and never a call back," Dowd recounts. "Finally Patricia asked us to come over for dinner. . . . We got over there and they didn't have any food in the house. It was really remarkable. It was sort of a remarkable pattern. And I finally said something to Dan. I said, 'Let's cut out the horseshit about this.' . . . To make matters worse, one night they invited us out to dinner . . . and I'll be goddamned if he didn't have a penny with him. . . . They invited us to dinner, they didn't have any money with them. So I had to pay for the dinner." Asked how he interpreted

Ellsberg's behavior, Dowd responds, "I thought it was chickenshit. . . . I said, 'Dan, you know, for Christ's sake, if we're going to eat together, we should both pay our own bills.' And it was after *that* that they had us over for dinner in Mill Valley and didn't have any food in the house. And Dan had to go down to the market and buy some food. I think we didn't eat until 10:30 or something like that," Dowd laughs. "Very funny kind of stuff. Really odd." Years later, the Ellsbergs invited Dowd and his subsequent wife over for dinner, and they ended up picking up the food at a restaurant and bringing it back to the house.[56]

Dowd also noticed that during their get-togethers Ellsberg was always guiding their conversations. The fact is, Ellsberg often turns conversations into lectures and dominates them. His father had been prone to lecturing, and Ellsberg likes the stage in social settings too. He finds it hard to sit in the background, again feels that what he has to say is quite important, that others should hear what he has to say, indeed, should *want* to hear it, that it's something they need to know ("I'm didactic," he says). And he lacks the self-discipline to rein himself in: "It's out of my control to some extent," he claims. In one-on-one situations, Ellsberg often clings to people and won't let go, talking on and on until he feels he's convinced them of his point. Often, it's because he's annoyed or angry with them. "I'm a famously good listener when I listen," he says. "I don't listen as much as I should. . . . I can monologue indefinitely." After Ellsberg had met Randy Kehler's wife numerous times and spoken to her over the phone, he asked Kehler, more than once, "What's your wife's name?" But sometimes one gets the sense that Ellsberg is not hearing what you're saying, only to discover later that he captured it all and just didn't react to it, perhaps partly because he was rushing to make a point. And when one lets him talk, he can go down tributaries but still remember where the main stream is, and ultimately return to it; then he's off down another tributary. But people sometimes find his lecturing so grating that they will up and leave the room. That's apparently what Bill Clinton did once. He was attending a small dinner party at Lloyd Shearer's home in Los Angeles in 1975; Ellsberg, a featured guest, dominated the dinner conversation. When Peter Laitin, who was then ten years old, left the table after dessert and headed into the backyard, he was joined by Clinton, who said something like, "I can't stand him either." "He even got up and decided that he'd had about enough," Laitin recounts. "He basically told me, 'I've had enough of that inside. I see you have had enough, too.'"[57]

Ellsberg's lecturing and domination of conversations is "a major social problem for me, and always has been," he acknowledges. "It has limited my acquaintances. . . . It doesn't keep me from having close friends. But it keeps me from being invited to parties, or . . . from having . . . a wide range of social acquaintances outside work. . . . I just don't get invited. And I understand. There's lots of reasons, and that's probably a main one. . . . I've heard lots of complaints that, 'My God. That guy talks and talks and talks.'" Among the complaints have been Patricia's. Sometime after his trial was over, "she just got fed up with it," Ellsberg recalls. "And she's just very sensitive to it. She has an allergy to it. She can't stand it." Her "tolerance for it now is about ninety seconds. If she hears me in a lecture mode, it's over."[58]

Ellsberg also told me, with arresting bluntness, "Listen, I have no social life. Which I can live without. Neither I nor Patricia care too much about social life." No social life? "Zero. I mean, being invited out to dinner? We never get invited out. The exceptions to that would be counted on one hand. . . . That isn't because we don't have friends. We have close friends. . . . But it's only a handful of people." (When Dan informed Patricia in front of me that he had just been telling me that nobody invites them over for dinner and they have no social life, Patricia's facial expression suggested thoughts along the lines of, "I can't believe you're telling him that.") After Ellsberg moved to Washington, "I was very lonely [there]," he told me. Save for dinners at Seymour Hersh's home, "I don't think I ate in another home in the three years [since]. And I don't think I was invited out to dinner in three years. Now, I invited people out to eat with me a handful of times. But normally I'd be alone, and I'd work late at the office or I'd go home and work, or I'd go to a movie. But I was quite lonely. After hours."[59]

Politics are a glue in Ellsberg's relationship with Doug Dowd—as it has been with other friends over the years—and after they'd gotten together a few times, Ellsberg asked Dowd why he had never bought the cold war. Ellsberg found that quite interesting, but Dowd found it more interesting that Ellsberg *had* bought the cold war, and he told Ellsberg why he thought he had bought it: "You're just always going around in some spiral which keeps you around people with power and prestige and so on. . . . For some reason or another, you just have to be around people with power." And "if you're going to be around people with power in this society at this time, they are going to be people who are cold warriors." Ellsberg didn't openly disagree with Dowd. "He was chewing on it," Dowd recalls. "And I had brought it up more than once with him. And I said, 'I think it's a real problem.'"[60]

Todd Gitlin's relationship with Ellsberg was typical of many people's experiences with him. Gitlin was initially enthralled by Ellsberg. Their first conversation lasted some eight hours. "Mostly he talked," Gitlin remembers. Other marathon talks followed. "I found him one of the most, if not the most, seductive people I'd ever met," Gitlin says. "He exuded a magnetic force." But Ellsberg also seemed to need to be riveting. He likes to seduce men as well as women. "He wanted you on his side," Gitlin reminisces. "He wanted you to be his exponent, his supporter, his caregiver, caretaker, sponsor. Many things. This tremendous need to absorb people into his universe." But "I became aware quite early that when he was interested in my life and my preoccupations, he tended to ask the same questions over and over again. So it wasn't too long before it dawned on me that he wasn't really taking in anything. . . . I don't think he was hearing much in one-to-one conversations. . . . When you observe this syndrome playing itself out so many times, then you weary of it, and you realize it's not really a relationship."[61]

When Ellsberg talks about those "persistent problems" he has experienced with relationships, problems that he attributes to his fame, these sorts of things—his self-centeredness, his lecturing and domination of conversations, his failure to hear, his inconsiderateness, his ultraintensity, and his ego—may contribute to them. So might his doing everything at the last minute or at his convenience and expecting others to be available then, his chronic lateness, and his insensitivity or inattentiveness to people in other ways.* "He's not the most socially sensitive person that I've ever been around, or empathetic," Patricia

---

* Ellsberg's inconsideration of others has also rubbed some conference organizers the wrong way. In 1995 Eric Schroeder organized a conference on Vietnam at the University of California, Davis. He found dealing with Ellsberg extremely frustrating. "Ellsberg was initially quite excited about coming to Davis for the conference," Schroeder remembers. "So we proceeded on that assumption, and put his name on the literature." Then Ellsberg neglected to purchase his airline ticket on schedule and acted "spacy" over the phone about the conference. After one of Schroeder's interns outlined the conference to him again, Ellsberg said he wasn't sure he could make it anymore, that he had something else on his calendar now, but that he was not giving the intern a definite no. Then a month before the conference, Schroeder was in Washington and decided to visit Ellsberg at his office at Physicians for Social Responsibility a few blocks from Schroeder's hotel. "I went up to the office, asked the receptionist for him," Schroeder recounts. "She looked at me like I'm crazy. . . . She said, 'He keeps very irregular hours. . . . If he comes in at all, he comes in in the afternoon.'" Schroeder left a message there and at Ellsberg's home. But Ellsberg never called him back. A letter Schroeder sent Ellsberg also went unanswered. Ellsberg finally called Schroeder the *morning* the conference began and left a voice message. "He's sort of cheerful on the phone: 'Well, *Hi*, Eric.' He turns on the charm. And every time I'd talked to him on the phone before then [it was] . . . 'Well, who are you?' . . . But this time it was like, 'Well, Hi, Eric, I'm sorry I haven't talked to you before this. . . . I have some bad news for you. But this hunger strike [that he was then on in support of nuclear disarmament] is going really well here. . . . Unfortunately, I just got examined by my doctor. He said even though I'm really fit and everything, I shouldn't be traveling. And he's prevented any air travel at all. So I was thinking until the last minute I could come and do this.'" But, Schroeder points out, "if he really thought he was coming at the last minute, he didn't follow up on that end and have any kind of plane ticket" (Schroeder interview).

grants. And there's Ellsberg's penchant for talking about himself and his fixation on whatever issue he's fixated on at any given time and inability to relate to other issues. "He's not good at small talk, and he's not good at any issue that does not obsess him," one person who knows him says. "I mean, the things that allow most of us to get through the humdrum and the mundane don't appeal to Dan. He's really brilliant at what he does, but he has no sense of the periphery and how ordinary people get on with each other."[62]

But many people do want to remain friends with Ellsberg—Dowd and others like Howard Zinn, though one gets the sense that Zinn too does not prefer a heavy diet of him. Noam Chomsky also remains a friend, although he and Ellsberg have gone long periods without talking—"life is much too intense to keep up personal contacts," Chomsky explains. Ellsberg calls Seymour Hersh his best friend in Washington. The author Peter Dale Scott, a retired Berkeley English professor, is perhaps his best friend in the Bay Area, though at one point they too suffered some sort of breach ("I'm through with him," Ellsberg told another friend), but one that was repaired. Other friends have included Jeffrey Masson, who shared Ellsberg's disaffection from psychoanalysis, his boyishness, high energy, quickness, brilliance, and some would say narcissism, not to mention his womanizing. (After meeting a friend of Jeremy Larner, "they both called her every single day the rest of the time she was in town," Larner remembers. "It was clear what they wanted, but it's like they didn't take no.") But Masson and Ellsberg would have their fights as well; they had a falling out once over the way Ellsberg had treated a woman. "I do not accept, as Jeffrey Masson does," the need for "absolute openness and absolute honesty . . . in a relationship," Ellsberg told me.[63]

It's easy to see why many people enjoy Ellsberg. He's a fascinating man, he can be very funny and entertaining, even quite caring when inclined. He is enormously intellectually stimulating. His energy can be contagious, his political dedication admirable, his openness and boyishness appealing (certainly his relations with many men over the years have been nourished by his talking about sex, a key reason for his talk). His sensitivity and vulnerability, and the candor he displays at times about his shortcomings, also appeal to people. Boring he is not (except when he monologues). And there is his celebrity, faded as it is, and his legend, faded too, which attract many to him.

———◆———

Insofar as Ellsberg has had any kind of career since the early 1970s, it has been as a freelance political activist, mainly focused against nuclear weapons. Political activism is, in many people's eyes (certainly in mine), a laudable way to spend one's time. But it, too, is not a path Ellsberg would have chosen, not a calling. "I am not an activist," he said in 1976, again pointing to his scholarly bent. "The antiwar stuff had to be done, but it was no kind of life I would have chosen." But there were those barriers he faced in other directions: he had torturous problems writing and thus couldn't be a writer (despite a strong desire and a favorable financial situation); his academic job prospects were poor; and he certainly couldn't go back to his former life as a defense analyst and consultant, as he'd burned his bridges. But because of his fevered and driven character, he had to throw himself into *something*. He also liked the feeling of being part of a movement, though he was not easy in groups, and activism was a way to be out there again, speaking out, in the spotlight at times; he could get plenty of applause, and even be a star in some circles. "He went looking for gurudom," Sam Popkin thought.[64]

There were also chits being called in. When, after not seeing him for years, Jan Butler had breakfast with Ellsberg and asked what he was doing, Ellsberg told her about his antinuclear activities. "I said, 'How did you get interested in that?'" Butler recounts. "'I never knew you were.' He said, 'Frankly, I wasn't.' And he said, 'I'm beginning to be interested in it. . . . I owed so many people so much, with the Ellsberg defense fund [for his trial]. . . . Now they're calling in their markers.'" Asked why he was an activist, Ellsberg replied to a journalist in 1976, "I feel I have to do it. The notoriety I got, thanks to Nixon, means I can raise money for these causes. I can draw a crowd now."[65]

But Ellsberg also had deep, heartfelt political concerns. He wants to make a difference. He'd been interested in nuclear issues for years; he knows almost everything one can know about nuclear weapons. Although he'd earlier been a nuclear hawk, he had a genuine turnaround (though he would claim he's been consistent over the years). His desire to save the world from nuclear annihilation, his sensitivity to human suffering, his emotional reactions to it are very real. (Still, "I think he tries to pass his emotions off sometimes as not being emotions, as being something else, as being analytical statements or something like that," Doug Dowd says. "I think he very much wants to be passionate, in a small circle. But I think through the rest of the time he wants to come on as . . . dispassionate . . . keeping his emotions in some sense or another behind the screen someplace.") Ellsberg became a highly driven antinuclear activist—what other type would he have become?—although his activity has been episodic over the years. "It's not really been very consistent over time in the sense of a sustained engagement," David Cortright, a disarmament leader, observes. Also, "there is a problem of him wanting to be in the front, to be recognized and acknowledged as a great leader and a central figure in all of this. And at times that's been difficult, and it's caused disruption with some people. . . . Among a lot of the mainstream peace groups, he's looked at sometimes as a pain. You know, as someone who steals the show. You never know what he's going to say when he gets up to speak." Argues Dowd, "There is a genuinely honest, serious [political] involvement with him that is not a power trip, at the same time that his power lust fits in nicely with all of that prestige and fame and 'I'm Dan Ellsberg.'"[66]

Ellsberg made a strong impression on many when he participated in protests against the Rocky Flats nuclear weapons plant in Colorado in 1978. Peace and environmental activists, who had organized and demonstrated against the plant for years, were then holding a big national protest. Ellsberg says he joined it because of the neutron bomb; he had learned that Rocky Flats would produce the weapon if President Jimmy Carter gave the green light (which he later did). The neutron bomb was designed to kill people while leaving buildings intact. Ellsberg considered it "the bomb that would be the match that would light thermonuclear war." (Carter himself was "a man whose desire for vast, almost God-like power is extreme, very extreme," he said.) Ellsberg spoke at a neutron bomb forum in Amsterdam in March of 1978 and also traveled elsewhere in Europe.[67]

His activity posed a problem in his marriage. "I started being away a lot in January," he recalls. Patricia had given birth to their son, Michael, on May 12, 1977. "I had promised that I would be very much a partner on this baby, in bringing it up," Ellsberg remembers. But "I was away from home a lot. And when I was back, I was totally preoccupied with what I was doing. Patricia said I was crazy. . . . I wasn't present when I was back." Patricia was getting angry, although she didn't complain a lot at the time, Ellsberg says. "She just resented it, and felt abandoned." Patricia still resents it when she thinks about it. "The scar will never totally heal," Ellsberg says. But "I had to do what I was doing. . . . And it was the right time to do it, to go all out. Even at the cost of my family, I would say."[68]

Ellsberg also angered Rocky Flats organizers. They had planned a sit-in on the railroad tracks at the plant. "We were going to test the government and see what would happen with a one-day sit-in," Judy Danielson, an American Friends Service Committee (AFSC) activist who was one of the early organizers against Rocky Flats, recounts. "No one had ever done a direct action on a nuclear weapons facility like this ever in the United States." Ellsberg let it be known that he was going to float a proposal that protesters stay on the tracks longer than one day—indefinitely, in fact. He then put forward his proposal when huddled with other protesters out on the tracks. "Imagine our surprise when Dan Ellsberg—who felt very strongly about these issues—he decided he wasn't going to leave after the first day," Danielson remembers. "He was going to stay there. And all these college kids decided they'd stay with him. . . . He announced he was going to do this, and then other people could join him." It was "completely unexpected." Ellsberg had not said anything about this at the elaborately planned training sessions for the sit-in.[69]

Wearing a cowboy hat and hiking boots (he would later don full black cowboy regalia at some antinuclear protests), Ellsberg argued that a longer stay would make for a more powerful political statement. But some Rocky Flats organizers thought he was acting rather arrogantly, coming in late on Rocky Flats, then hijacking the leadership of the protest and unilaterally changing its course after they had killed themselves organizing it. Moreover, he was doing it in a way that risked alienating members of the local community while detracting energies from other activities planned. Organizers also felt responsible for the some 35 people who had stayed out on the tracks in the snow and cold. "He certainly didn't ask us anything," Danielson recounts. "The way it appeared to us was that he really didn't care much about this campaign. I'm not even sure he knew how much organizing had gone into this." Says someone who studied the protest extensively: "The local organizers felt completely undermined by what he did. . . . He came in with his own agenda. And the AFSC had been doing a lot of very serious organizing, very solid organizing . . . and trying to really build a base. And Ellsberg essentially came in and couldn't have cared less about any of the local organizers and what they were trying to do. He was here to make his statement and be photographed." Ellsberg's participation was "for him," this person believes. "He didn't give a shit about anybody else."[70]

Robert Sachs worked for Colorado Congressman Tim Wirth, a critic of Rocky Flats, after helping on Ellsberg's Pentagon Papers trial. Sachs consequently knew a lot about the plant "before Dan ever heard of Rocky Flats." Then, one night, Sachs saw Ellsberg on the television news, sitting on a track. To Sachs, it was another sign that Ellsberg had become hooked on fame.[71]

A heated dispute erupted on the tracks. "We were out on the tracks yelling and screaming at Dan Ellsberg," Danielson recounts, with some amusement in retrospect, "and having an argument about, 'We can't support this if we don't have the energy and the backup.'" Emotions were running full throttle. Ellsberg was adamant about the need to remain on the tracks. "He was definitely going to stay there," Danielson remembers. She and others "were furious, just furious. That he wouldn't consider local organizers' viewpoints. . . . He was taking over an organizing job, and we had not invited him to be the organizer. We invited him to be a participant. So we were quite angry about it." They felt the change in tone of the protest had hurt their effort to build a mainstream movement.[72]

What's more, after Ellsberg had decided to stay put, "he didn't have much to do with us," Danielson says. "He certainly never came to us and asked us about how this fit into the campaign, what we would think about it, how we were feeling, how he could support the campaign." (At a 20-year reunion in 1998, "he came up and said, 'You know, it would be good if we could just sit down and talk,'" Danielson remembers. "'There are some things we need to work through.' And it didn't happen. He didn't have time.")[73]

But many people out on the tracks were moved by their experience. One day, under a plastic shelter to protect themselves from sleet, as they were taking turns telling about themselves and what had brought them to Rocky Flats, Ellsberg broke down repeatedly. "I had found my way home to a family," he would recount. "I spent most of the day crying, my face in my hands, as I listened to each story in turn."[74]

Ellsberg was an inspirational figure to some at Rocky Flats. He lent an air of authority. Joining a "Quaker visitation" the week before the sit-in, he spoke to local notables. "I think he really moved some people," Danielson reminisces. "He was very impressive. He knew a *lot* of stuff. . . . He was a great person to take around to these government officials." Ellsberg spoke about his inside knowledge of U.S. nuclear war plans. To the young people out on the tracks, he recounted the briefing that he gave McGeorge Bundy on the Joint Strategic Capabilities Plan. Many of them admired Ellsberg; he was something of an honorary leader to them. "These people who decided they were going to stay on the tracks were really touched by him," Danielson noticed. He was "very outgoing, quite affable, very talkative. . . . And he really liked these kids. . . . He got to be real buddies with them."[75]

Ellsberg was arrested four times at Rocky Flats. James Schlesinger, then U.S. secretary of energy and a former colleague of Ellsberg at RAND, would say later that having Ellsberg arrested was the most satisfying thing he'd ever done. Schlesinger had never liked Ellsberg, and by now he couldn't stand him.[76]

Ellsberg's third arrest came on his son Michael's first birthday. "Patricia was just really furious at me," he remembers. "For still being there, and for having gotten arrested again without telling her, and without any agreement with her." But "I didn't want to talk to her on the phone about what my plan was," which was to keep returning to the tracks after getting out of jail and "build up a huge pile of arrests. . . . Which nobody had ever done before. And that would have sent me away for a long time. . . . Of course, that would have been a terrific betrayal of her." Ellsberg did not tell Patricia about his plan until nearly 20 years later. He may have been acting out his impulse to martyrdom through his plan. But the judge undermined it by raising bail each time.[77]

Robert Ellsberg joined his father on the tracks. He fasted in jail, then read a moving statement at his arraignment. His father wept. Reading Robert's statement during a radio interview two years later, he cried again.[78]

The poet Anne Waldman, who participated in the Rocky Flats protests, remembers that Ellsberg was acting more like a single man than a married one at the time. He spoke with Waldman about celibacy, but "from the Buddhist perspective."[79] If Patricia had reason to believe he was acting like a single man, it may have fed her anger.

Ellsberg also joined antinuclear protests at California's Lawrence Livermore National Laboratory. Again he was largely a celebrity presence and speaker, lending his legend to enhance participation and credibility and attract media. But he was also willing to get arrested, which impressed other protesters not only at Livermore but elsewhere over the years. "They were sort of taken aback that somebody of his stature would be willing to risk arrest like they were, and then go to jail, and sit down for a rather uncomfortable situation in the middle of the sand somewhere, or be roughly treated by cops," Randy Kehler recalls. "He made it a high priority in his life to be out on the sort of front lines. . . . Obviously he enjoyed it too. And I'm sure he liked [the fact] he got a lot of attention. . . . He's not a man of a small ego."[80]

Ellsberg was among 170 busted at Livermore in February 1982. A photo of him, smiling slightly at the camera, made the *New York Times*. Ellsberg and some 1,300 others were arrested at Livermore again in June of the following year. As at Rocky Flats, he was not one of the organizers of the protest, at least until the very end. "He's not a grassroots organizer," his friend David Hartsough observes. "I think he's more a person that does what he believes is right, who speaks out on issues . . . talking with government officials and media people, and to movement groups. But he's not the organizer." Ellsberg seeks in large measure to convince the influential and prominent with rational arguments. Mobilizing people for protests, door-to-door canvassing and the like are not his cup of tea. But he can be a keen political strategist, and he served on the national strategy committee of the Nuclear Weapons Freeze. "I think he is good at sitting down with a small group of people and strategizing," Hartsough says. "But I haven't seen him be kind of part of a group that—over weeks, months—meets to actually carry out the work." Ellsberg, something of a loner as an activist too, may feel he's above that: functioning as simply one among equals can be unappealing to many recognized people. "I think there's a certain patrician air, is what I get sometimes," the activist Ken Butigan, who has worked with Ellsberg some and who admires him, told me. "A certain reserve. . . . As with a number of people I know who have a certain celebrity, I think there's a certain living in another dimension, almost, that comes across. . . . But I've never experienced him as overbearing. . . . I don't think it's even his bent to swagger and throw his weight around."[81]

After the June 1983 bust at Livermore, Ellsberg spent a week or two with some 500 other male protesters in a big circus tent at the Santa Rita Jail (the women were in another tent). He led workshops, imparting his knowledge about nuclear weapons, the lessons of Vietnam, his life. His workshops proved popular and educational to many listeners. Ellsberg was also interviewed on the television show *Nightline* from the jail, but here he was not at his best. He appeared tense and somewhat out of control. His mere appearance on *Nightline* was uplifting to other protesters, though. "We were wondering, 'Does anybody in the world hear or care?'" Hartsough recounts. "And so to have one of our folks be able to get out there, and both tell a story about why we were there— and that we *are* there—and what some of the key issues are, was a tremendous boost to people's morale."[82]

In 1982 Ellsberg went to Leningrad on a Greenpeace ship to demand that the Soviet Union stop nuclear testing. While there he spoke with some Soviet policy advisers on the ship, arguing that if the Soviet Union took the initiative to halt nuclear testing, the U.S. Congress might respond in kind. The Soviet advisers "told me later that my encouragement to them led them all to write memos proposing a six-month moratorium," Ellsberg says. These advisers put forward their ideas again when Mikhail Gorbachev came to power. In 1985, Gorbachev announced a unilateral moratorium on testing (which lasted for 18 months). According to Ellsberg, the Soviet advisers told him, "It's your moratorium." He also claims substantial personal responsibility for a second Russian moratorium. "I am *mainly* responsible for that. Strangely enough. I was in Moscow at exactly the right time talking to exactly the right people. To get them to do something that I do not believe they would have done had I not been there." When the second Russian moratorium was announced, "I thought, 'Well, for what it's worth, *I* did that. *I* did that.' . . . I had to persuade every one of those guys." Moreover, the Russians announced "*my* program. Six points—one, two, three, four, five, six. . . . It was not a coincidence."[83]

In 1992, the U.S. Congress approved a nine-month moratorium of its own. President George Bush reluctantly signed the bill. "Without that chain," Ellsberg contends, referring to the events described above, "there would have been no bill for Bush to sign." He also claims to have been key to getting Bill Clinton to extend the Bush moratorium in 1993: "I had great influence."[84]

Whatever the facts, it is reasonable to conclude that Ellsberg is overstating his influence on both the Russian and U.S. moratoriums. While he probably did speak to influential people at various points, and he was intensely involved in the mobilization in the United States for the U.S. moratorium, in the overall picture he was one among many players—in the halls of power, the broad publics, and peace movements in both Europe and the United States—who influenced those initiatives. (Other Western peace movement leaders also urged the Russians to adopt a moratorium.) But his recollection is characteristic, and again suggests someone whose insecurities (in this case about his accomplishments after the Pentagon Papers, perhaps) compel him to brag.

There would be other acts of civil disobedience against nuclear arms—in Europe, at the Nevada nuclear test site—as Ellsberg continued to speak out against the weapons in other forums, such as interviews, mainly in publications with smaller readerships than he would have preferred. In the interviews, Ellsberg displayed a truly dazzling array of knowledge—of particular weapons, their capabilities, U.S. nuclear strategy past and present, command and control—throwing out facts and figures from a seemingly bottomless supply, albeit with typical exaggerations. For example, "in the last thirty years," he asserted in 1985, "every time U.S. troops have been surrounded or allied troops have been surrounded and in danger of capture, there has been serious military and civilian consideration given to using nuclear weapons to protect those troops." Ellsberg seemed to love dazzling others with his knowledge and having a podium still. He was obviously extraordinarily well read. Whereas Thomas Schelling now saw him as a charlatan of sorts, some of his younger interviewers put him on a pedestal (two interviewers in the *Progressive* wrote of "his brilliant U.S. government career"). Ellsberg made copies of his interviews and writings and distributed them to others.[85]

Ellsberg also protested against U.S. policies in Central America in the 1980s, racking up more arrests. His daughter, Mary, then living in Nicaragua, had something to do with that. Mary testified at his sentencing for one arrest in San Francisco, at which Ellsberg argued that the U.S. mining of Nicaragua's harbors and its aid to the anti-Sandinista Contra rebels were "equal to the planning for the Nazi invasion of Austria and Poland." The afternoon following his arraignment for this arrest or another one over Nicaragua, Ellsberg was busted at the University of California, Berkeley, for committing civil disobedience in a protest against South African apartheid. He had now been arrested at least 25 times, by his count.[86]

David Hartsough once invited Ellsberg to join him on his nine-foot sailboat to attempt to block a U.S. Navy ship carrying arms to El Salvador. Ellsberg did not know much about sailing, which proved unfortunate, as he and Hartsough encountered heavy seas and ultimately capsized. A press boat came rushing over to get photographs, and the person at the controls gunned the engine in reverse to get just the right photo of Daniel Ellsberg bobbing in the water in his life preserver. Ellsberg almost got sucked into the propeller. Hartsough had to grab onto him to keep him from going down.[87]

Ellsberg also did a lot of lobbying against U.S. policies in Central America, talking to people in power and the press. He seemed particularly attracted to other protesters of prominence as well, other former establishment types, ex-CIA, ex-military. "Like they'd all gone to the same school or something," Ken Butigan says. "And they had a certain distinctiveness and notoriety."[88]

Through interviews, Ellsberg acted at times as a wide-ranging political commentator touching on a variety of topics. But one highly regarded left-leaning radio host in the Bay Area told me, "Every time I have him on, I don't know how to introduce him except as the person who released the Pentagon Papers." Ellsberg had never really done anything besides release the Papers, this person thought, and was not really an expert on anything. "We've had him on the show many times, and every time we have him on he acts like he doesn't remember me," this person added. "It's a way of showing he's superior. . . . He's not a man of the people."[89]

In 1992 Ellsberg embarked on Manhattan Project II, an antinuclear campaign whose goal was to "reduce nuclear weapons to near zero" by the end of the century. Margaret Brenman-Gibson worked with him closely, if tumultuously at times, on the project. Ellsberg again focused to a significant degree on talking to policy types in Washington. It's questionable how much effect the project had. "I don't know if it had a great deal of impact," David Cortright says gently. "I think it was primarily a vehicle for Dan to be involved in the issue. I can't say that I'm really clear what the project strategies and tactics were. . . . I don't think there was much that was added to the overall movement for disarmament." Ken Butigan was then on the steering committee of an anti-nuclear testing group. "My impression is he didn't build a base around it," Butigan recalls. "My impression is that it's not a national organization, or [that] he's built constituencies and chapters and all of that."[90]

Ellsberg approached some former colleagues and officials about the project, including prominent nuclear doves from the establishment like Paul Warnke, William Colby, and McGeorge Bundy. But he usually got only their ear for a time, occasionally use of their name on some literature promoting the project. Bundy upbraided Ellsberg at a press conference he held when Ellsberg asked a question that turned into a speech. The problem was, Ellsberg wasn't thought of highly in these circles. These people didn't want to be associated with him. This wasn't the place to go for support. This was a fundamental problem with the Manhattan Project II, and one that has limited Ellsberg's political effectiveness more broadly. One former official he approached, a well-regarded arms control expert and dove, told me that Ellsberg comes off as "a little overeager. Perhaps displaying more self-confidence than, in fact, he has. There's something just a little sort of odd about him." Ellsberg gave out literature on the project at a RAND reunion and asked people to distribute it to others at RAND. "He's always handing you his most recent analysis of whatever, and saying that he's about to place an op-ed piece somewhere," Townsend Hoopes, a former Pentagon deputy and undersecretary of the air force, says. Asked what he thought of Ellsberg's antinuclear activities generally, the arms control expert responded, "They have not been terribly effective. I think it's in part because he is not held in tremendously high esteem."[91]

He meant by other notables. But Ellsberg is not held in high esteem by many people on the left either, and that has also limited his political effectiveness. "Most people don't think highly of Dan," Marty Garbus, the civil liberties lawyer, notes. One professor with a long history of progressive political activism, who, although solicited, chose not to get involved with the Manhattan Project II, thought it "too much of a personal thing."[92]

In 1995 Ellsberg hoped to get world leaders and other prominent people to join him in a fast for the abolition of nuclear weapons in front of the United Nations during deliberations on extension of the Nuclear Non-Proliferation Treaty (NPT). But he again had problems attracting participants. "We didn't get the people we had [sought]," he remembers. "We had reason to hope we would get some big people on it," including the Dalai Lama, Nelson Mandela, and Desmond Tutu. But "we'd announced it, so it was hard to back off of it." Only a paltry few joined Ellsberg in front of the UN; his top recruit was the Reverend William Sloane Coffin. "At times there were just like Bill and Dan sitting out there on their chairs," David Cortright recalls. Ellsberg didn't get any press coverage to speak of, and he again angered other antinuclear activists. As at Rocky Flats, he came in late, after much organizing had been done and many other events planned. "There had been a big effort underway for some months," Cortright recounts. "We had a 'Citizens Assembly' there. And there were dozens of groups present, from all over the world, really. And we had a conference, and there was a demonstration, and a series of workshops. . . . A whole range of activities that were undertaken by lots of different groups." Ellsberg's idea of holding a fast came "toward the tail end," Cortright recalls, not long before the conference began, when "the plans were pretty much in place." (A call for the fast was dated only two weeks before the conference was set to begin.) Once more, Ellsberg seemed insensitive to the existing plans and eager to take the limelight. "There was some tension around it," Cortright re-members. "You know, the notion, 'Where was Dan months ago when we were starting to plan this?'" Some people felt "that he was coming in at the last minute trying to steal the show, and would it be a diversion of interest and en-ergy" from the other activities? Cortright adds, "He comes in so powerful, he comes on so strong, that it is kind of a force of nature that blows a wind through the existing operation, and can shuffle the papers around, and it disor-ganizes things."[93]

Ellsberg was in a state of utter despair after the conference. "He just went into a tailspin," Margaret Brenman-Gibson recalls. He was in "a formidable depression." His vulnerability seemed at a zenith. Ellsberg, who may have gone on antidepressant medication, struck Brenman-Gibson as suicidal. (This was not the first time he had seemed suicidal to her. She had worried for years that he might kill himself, as he'd sometimes expressed the types of thoughts that suicidal people express and been in terrible states of despair.) "I was totally de-spondent," Ellsberg acknowledges. For one thing, the conference was a disap-pointment to all those who had hoped it would result in a firm commitment to nuclear disarmament by a certain date on the part of the nuclear powers. And it looked to Ellsberg as if there would never again be another chance for a nu-clear test ban worldwide. "It was hopeless," he remembers. He remarked to Brenman-Gibson, "Oh, God, I have to keep on doing this for another 30 years." Those do not sound like the words of an activist by nature. There were also awful disputes with her, his most loyal supporter. Not least significant, Ellsberg was painfully disappointed in his ability to draw people. His unpopu-larity in many circles probably hurt him anew. He'd been snubbed often of late, and now he'd stepped on more people's toes. Meanwhile, his funding for the Manhattan Project II was running out.[94]

Ellsberg continued to crave the respect of the establishment. "I think he's very caught up in that," Marty Garbus comments. "He wants acceptance.... And I really always thought that it was very important to him—and is impor-tant to him today—that the establishment recognize him. I'm sure ... he would love to get, if not a Distinguished Service Cross from the army, then a Medal of Honor or something like that for meritorious service to his country. Or short of that, the highest award that Harvard could bestow after whatever it's done for McGeorge Bundy et al. ... I think that's a very deep-seated desire that Daniel has." Archibald Cox, who was fired as Watergate special prosecutor for demanding tapes and documents from Richard Nixon, was widely held in high esteem in the country, "and I think Dan feels, 'Why don't I have that same regard?'" Richard Zeckhauser says. "'What I did was much more courageous than what Archie Cox did. Archie Cox resigned to go back to a Harvard professorship. I gave up my entire career to turn this nation around.'" Most of all, Ellsberg would like Robert McNamara to say to him, You were right, I was wrong.[95] Which, of course, will never happen, though perhaps it should.

Ellsberg had thought his former colleagues would renew relations with him after his trial ended, but, with some exceptions, that never happened. To his great and enduring pain, he remains a pariah. He eagerly wants to be accepted by his ex-RAND colleagues again. At a dinner at Thomas Schelling's home in the 1990s, he acted like "a 65-year-old adolescent," one RAND person who was present thought, "constantly trying to shine the spotlight on himself" and asking if assorted former colleagues *liked* him—as in, "What about *him? Does he* like me?"[96]

Ellsberg harbored hopes that he could reestablish friendly relations with those former colleagues to whom he had been especially close, particularly Albert Wohlstetter and Harry Rowen. "I wouldn't like them to die or me to die without that having happened," he told me. Wohlstetter died in early 1997, but he and Ellsberg did have a friendly phone conversation sometime before then, when Ellsberg had called after Wohlstetter had suffered a heart attack. Ellsberg also talked briefly with Rowen at a seminar Rowen gave at Berkeley in the 1980s. Ellsberg asked Rowen a question, and they spoke afterward. "He was so friendly that it was as though we'd never spent a day apart," Ellsberg recalls. "Just like old times." (But in another interview with me, Ellsberg remembered Rowen was less friendly.)[97]

Years later, Ellsberg was able to arrange a dinner with Rowen, who brought his wife and one or more of their children along "in defense" to "saturate" whatever Ellsberg had to say, according to a person with whom Rowen and his wife spoke about the dinner. By Ellsberg's account to his son Robert afterward, the dinner went well, but the Rowens did not seem to my source to be excited about doing it again. Asked why he was going to meet with Ellsberg, Rowen had told the source, "You know, it was a long time ago. And it is the Christian thing to do." Ellsberg told Robert he had apologized to Rowen for the pain he knew he had caused him, and that Rowen had said, yes, he had caused him pain.[98]

Ellsberg was then going around trying to mend fences and make amends with other former colleagues as well. At least for one, Ellsberg's visit was somewhat awkward. The man didn't quite understand what it was all about, why Ellsberg was there.[99]

Ellsberg says that some people who wouldn't speak to him before "suddenly got very friendly" after the cold war ended. And for that reason. "In the new era, nobody runs away from me, to speak of," he says. Even Robert McNamara didn't run from him when they found themselves in the same room at the Council on Foreign Relations, he recalls. Helmut Sonnenfeldt became quite friendly: "The cold war ends, and he comes up to me at the Council on Foreign Relations, says, 'Dan! It's been so long. Where the hell have you been?'" But Sonnenfeldt denies that the end of the cold war had any effect on their relationship. "We have not really been particularly friendly," he says. And Ellsberg concedes, "None of them are terribly warm and friendly."[100]

All of this was taking place as Ellsberg was suffering torturous marital problems. "The strains have been terrible," Doug Dowd says. Ellsberg's marriage to Patricia has been, by all reports, a strange and seriously erratic one. "Maybe every relationship is odd, but that's a particularly odd relationship," one friend of Ellsberg comments. Ellsberg and Patricia have been on the brink of giving it up numerous times; they've talked divorce. "There were times when it seemed as though we wouldn't stay together," Ellsberg says. They've always spent lots of time apart and done their own things (which may have extended their marriage). They've seen marriage counselors. Friends have perennially expected them to finally part.[101]

They embarked on a long-distance relationship after Ellsberg took up residence in Washington in the early 1990s. In Washington, Ellsberg lived off social security and grant money, some substantial, though Patricia may have helped support him. Ellsberg also obtained an advance to write his memoir, but he worried about his financial future, which looked shaky outside his marriage.[102]

Ellsberg told others that he moved to Washington to be left alone to write, or to further his political goals, and there was some truth to both claims, but his marriage probably also had something to do with the move. He told one person that he and Patricia were undertaking a trial separation.[103]

By both their accounts, Dan has driven Patricia absolutely crazy at times. In fact, many times. She's told him that any woman would find him hard to live with, would find plenty to complain about. Sometimes he's almost "writhing on the floor," he says, so painful are her observations. "I believe I'm quite an expert on Patricia's problems with me," he says, problems they discuss "on a 24-hour cycle, or certainly a weekly cycle." "It's difficult," Patricia told me. "It's not been an easy life. But it's been a life that's meaningful." And "there are all these nice guys I could have married, but they were really boring." Ellsberg's preoccupations are a constant source of strain on their marriage. His frenetic states can also be trying, as can, in all likelihood, his self-centered behavior, his unreliability, his lecturing, and his persistent womanizing. As in many marriages (such as his previous one), there have been sexual tensions. Dan is "always in some sense or another trying to reach new highs," one friend points out. "He just has to always be breaking records."[104]

But he and Patricia apparently agreed at some point to have an open marriage. "They both need to see other people, obviously," another friend comments. "Neither of them is content with a monogamous relationship. I don't know if Dan would respond if Pat said, 'Okay, I'm not going to rove around.' I wonder if Dan would then say the same thing." It seems unlikely his behavior would change at the end of the day. He's had lots of extramarital affairs. Leslie Henriques got in trouble with him once when she mistakenly opened a love letter from a woman in Europe. Ellsberg's need to express himself sexually remains extraordinary. "He likes to make conquests," one friend observes. "Dan has always got an eye out for [women]. . . . And every time he meets another woman, right away his eyes are just magnetized. And he sort of just moves right in there. . . . He acts as though he's in his twenties or thirties. . . . I think if he sees that there's something to conquer, he wants to conquer it." In part, proving himself again, perhaps, and devouring the whole world. "I think the whole sexual thing is a power trip for him ultimately," one friend analyzes. "As I think much of his life has been." Ellsberg will sometimes make it possible for others to meet his girlfriends, who are usually younger.[105]

He has not always behaved admirably with them. At least two women who had affairs with Ellsberg emerged from their experiences "very angry women." They found him to be "a man who's not there" and "a man who does a lot of drugs," a well-known writer who knows both women recounts. ("He was doing a lot of acid in the early '80s," the writer reminisces.) The two women also discovered that Ellsberg had "a very strong sexual drive, and drugs fuel it. And at the same time, he's absent, so he's not a giver. I know there were also very strong feelings of betrayal." The two women, to whom Ellsberg talked about his marriage a lot, emerged with strong sentiments that "having an affair with Dan is a trip. And then it was a trip from which you parachuted out without feelings of respect," the writer recalls.[106]

As the looser 1960s and 1970s gave way to the '80s and '90s, Ellsberg still sought multiple-partner activities. "Three-way stuff is not uncommon," Stanley Sheinbaum points out. One man remembers going to the Ellsbergs' house in the late 1980s, "and we ended up in the hot tub. He was very insistent that we go into the hot tub. With a neighbor." In fact, Ellsberg had "always wanted to go into the hot tub," this man recalls. "From the time I started seeing him in Berkeley, he often wanted to do the hot tub. . . . I was wondering what this was about." And in the late 1980s, "it felt sort of Marin, *Bob and Carol, Ted and Alice.* But also anachronistic." One friend of Ellsberg told me, "More than once, Dan has tried to—and I don't mean this in any nasty way, this is natural for him—but more than once he's invited me—very clear, no question about it—to participate in some kind of a trio, a quadrangle, for all I know a septimo. . . . But always something that has some kind of complications to it." In the many years this man has known Ellsberg, "not a year has gone by that some kind of a ploy that had me getting involved in some kind of a sexual thing with him has not come up," the man recounts. Our interview took place in 1995, when Ellsberg was 64. "It never stops with him," this friend says. "He needs that." The friend thought Ellsberg might have had his eye on his wife. He says he never chose to participate: "I'm not a sexual athlete," which, he thinks, Ellsberg fashions himself to be.[107]

Others have also found Ellsberg too far out on these matters. Once in the early 1990s, he invited Sheinbaum to partake when Sheinbaum was in Washington. "He would talk about it in the abstract," Sheinbaum recalls. "You know, three-way. And then he said, 'Stanley, you're missing something.'"[108]

"I think that Dan sees himself as being fully liberated with respect to sexual questions," Doug Dowd says. "And wants to test it out, in some sense or another, to see how fully liberated he is. Or to find out what liberation means. I think that he has some need to try to push out toward whatever the boundaries are." The poet Allen Ginsberg would recall Ellsberg telling him about one occasion when he was in bed with a woman and another man. Ginsberg related the anecdote to Andrew Schelling. "Dan found that he wasn't that interested [in the man], but it gave him some real insight into fear, I guess, sexual fear, and the relationships of power there," Schelling remembers. "And he told Allen that he was working on a new model of political power based on this experience."[109] Always the intellectual.

The Ellsbergs have remained very different people. Patricia is extensively into metaphysical, spiritual, New Age pursuits; she's practiced lots of meditation, Buddhism, and various offshoots of Eastern thought. ("Enjoy Being" and "Breathe" read two stickers on their refrigerator in California in 1995—probably directed in part to Dan.) She's traveled a good deal to participate in workshops and retreats on personal growth, self-realization, various spiritual paths, meditation and the like, seemingly searching for the right path. She has pointed out to Dan that she's joined him in many of his activities, and at her urging, or possibly insistence, Ellsberg has participated in some of hers. He's tried to get into them, even found some reasonable, but some of her New Age stuff revolts him. "He struggles with that all the time," a friend of his says. "Because he knows that if he refuses to do this, she then backs off."[110]

Friends have often wondered what has kept Patricia in the marriage. "How can anyone really be with Dan?" one asks rhetorically. They could understand what kept Dan in the relationship. Besides being in love with Patricia, it was hard for him to face the prospect of another failed marriage, and there was the benefit of her wealth. "I thought it was her money," Leslie Henriques told me. "She had a lot of it, and he needed a lot of it to do what he was doing. I mean, that's sort of a very cold way of looking at it. . . . I think she really cared for him, and I just think that he was so involved with himself that he didn't care for anybody. I'm sure on one level he cared about her, but. . . ." Some people thought he would never leave Patricia because of her money. Ellsberg also needed Patricia to take care of him in other ways, and how many women that forbearing would he find? For her part, Patricia obviously loved Dan deeply; they've had a truly powerful bond. Also, she had her own vulnerabilities and insecurities to cope with. There was the question, for instance, of what she had done with her own life. "She's a terrified woman," an old friend of hers remarks. "What is her achievement in life? . . . Her achievement was she was married to this man who did this thing," i.e., released the Pentagon Papers. Some people think Patricia needs to believe in a powerful figure.[111] That might help explain her worshipful posture toward Dan. In addition, she probably recognized that he needed her and worried about what would happen to him if they split up.

Ellsberg has talked openly with people about problems in his marriage, but he has sometimes had difficulty acknowledging his own responsibility for them. "He's spoken very intimately to me about his upsetness with Patricia from time to time," Dowd says. "But he's never indicated that *he* might be the one who was in some sense or another the problem. Nothing like that." Ellsberg has seemed to Dowd to be asking for an unequal relationship. "You're asking her to take a lot and give a lot," Dowd has told him. "And you're doing whatever you want to do. You're not really being fair about the whole thing." But Ellsberg's response is "as though he were taking a couple of notes which happened to blow out the window afterward."[112]

Michael Ellsberg has been a strong glue in their marriage. Perhaps as much as anything else, he kept them together for years. Yet Michael had an unpromising childhood. By two accounts, he did not get as much care from his parents as he could have used. When Leslie Henriques worked for Ellsberg, Patricia, whom she liked quite a bit, "spent a lot of time away" attending workshops, Henriques remembers. Dan was also gone a lot (and "they were not away together a lot"). Michael was then three or four years old. "I always wondered what was happening, because they didn't really seem to be there for him," Henriques recalls. "Because even she was doing her own thing."[113]

Michael's bedroom was downstairs, adjacent to his father's office, and away from his parents' bedroom upstairs. It was loaded with toys: this was, after all, a Marx Toys family. His father also brought him stuffed animals from overseas, and Michael had a vast collection of them. It was Henriques's perception that Ellsberg didn't want to deal with Michael much of the time. "He'd come in to talk to his dad, and he'd shoo him away," she recounts. Ellsberg's office "was sort of off-limits for Michael." (But once, when two-year-old Michael arrived home with Patricia, Ellsberg shouted, with apparent delight, in the presence of a journalist who was interviewing him, "Michael's home!," then showered him with kisses. In my presence later, he made a loud display of his disappointment when Patricia informed him that Michael had just phoned and he had not been given a chance to talk with him then.) "I haven't been a perfect father to Michael, for all we know," Ellsberg would muse.[114]

Friends have been curious about what kinds of influences Michael has been exposed to. "We've often wondered, 'What is it like for him?'" one friend says. "It can't be easy. But he seems to be a very nice kid."[115]

To both Henriques and Margaret Brenman-Gibson, who spent a lot of time with Michael, it was clear he was a very lonely young boy. "He wasn't a happy kid," Henriques remembers. "I mean, he wanted his parents. . . . I remember him complain that he wanted to be with them." He complained primarily to his nanny, Elena, who was also the Ellsbergs' maid, and to whom Henriques talked a lot. "She was the caretaker," Henriques recalls. And "she had very strong feelings about him. She really was worried about what was happening to him. . . . It was very sad. I was very fond of him. I like kids, and I really took to him. And I really felt sorry for him. . . . You could tell, even from four years of age, that he was unhappy."[116]

One scene stands out in Brenman-Gibson's mind. She came into the Ellsbergs' house one time, and there was little Michael sitting alone in the kitchen eating his "dinner," which was an egg in an egg cup. It was poignant. One of Michael's caregivers was a disciple of a guru, and dressed the part. Dan "wasn't paying enough attention," a friend of his says.[117]

Elena took good care of Michael, so "I don't think he was neglected," Henriques points out. "But there was very little interaction with his parents. . . . I really didn't feel that they wanted to be around Michael." Henriques saw the situation getting worse toward the end of her work for Ellsberg in 1981. "You know, he had Elena, and I think she felt bad, because he wanted his parents." If Michael "turned out at all sane, it's a great credit to him," Henriques says. "It was really hard for him."[118]

Michael graduated from Deerfield prep school in Massachusetts and then attended Brown University. Meanwhile his father's parenting had evidently improved. Mary Ellsberg offers, "I have the impression that he has been somewhat more attentive with Michael" than he had been with her or Robert. A strong tie developed between father and son. Some thought Michael became a real credit to both his parents. "He kind of got the best qualities in Dan and me," Patricia says. And "he turned himself around."[119]

———

Robert Ellsberg attended Harvard. He felt a calling to fill his father's shoes, to be worthy of him, and his freshman year he notified the Selective Service System that he would refuse to register for the draft (which had just ended, though young men still had to register). "There's no question in my mind that the kind of influences [I felt] from my father, and the kind of lessons that he was trying to impress on me, and the kind of ideas that he exposed me to entered into the whole chemistry of who I became," Robert says. "And through the exposure to other draft resisters I met through him . . . I grew up believing that I too would go to jail for resisting the draft." When Robert was threatened with prosecution, he went to see Harvard's Charles Nesson, his father's former lawyer. "I definitely had a sense that I was in some ways retracing his steps," Robert recalls.[120]

But Robert's draft resistance upset his dad. "He'd certainly wanted to impress his values on his children," Robert remembers:

> But then the idea that the consequences of that was that his son might go to prison because of ideas that he had impressed on me would be upsetting for anyone, especially since he had not gone to prison. So I remember when I finally told him about this, told both my parents, they reacted in different kinds of ways. My mother, of course, thought, "My God. This is my worst nightmare. This is what his father's influence has done to him now. Now his son is going to go to prison." . . . I felt I couldn't really talk to her, I couldn't really explain to her, partly for rational reasons, but partly because it pressed these irrational buttons for her. So that if anything brought up the flag "Daniel Ellsberg," it would drive her crazy. And so I felt that here I was kind of drawn in a lot of ways to follow his path, and admiring that and attracted by that, but I felt that was something she could not respect or comprehend.

But "the irony was that he also was very shocked and worried about this. Of course, ethically he took it very seriously. He didn't think I was just being a copycat. But he really tried to talk me out of it. . . . 'Don't do this unless you really feel there's absolutely no other alternative, [that] this is ethically what you must do.'" Robert eventually registered for the draft, finding little support at Harvard and feeling unready to face prison. (His father would later tell an interviewer that Robert was the only one in his class at Harvard who found draft registration a serious moral issue.)[121]

His draft battle influenced Robert to leave Harvard after two years to work at the *Catholic Worker*, a radical pacifist newspaper in New York. His mother worried about what would become of him. Robert converted to Catholicism, which may have also hurt his mother, an Episcopalian, but "my father actually reacted more strongly," Robert recounts. "Partly because that was at a time when I felt that he was very interested in everything I was doing to protest nuclear weapons and everything, but I felt [that he] didn't have much clue as to what was going on inside of me. And at a time when I don't feel we had a really frank and open relationship. And I think he was just kind of astonished in a way to find out that I was contemplating something so large and [had] not discussed it with him. And it was a sign of how much I was accustomed to just not bringing up with him." One of Robert's neighbors at Leverett House at Harvard, Chuck Stephen, remembers that Robert was disaffected from his father at the time and felt his father "wasn't there," so to speak. He did not seem to think highly of his father, Stephen recalls, and thought his reputation overblown; his father wasn't the man many of his admirers thought he was. Robert spoke disparagingly of his father at times. As for his conversion to Catholicism, "it had not occurred to me to discuss this with him," Robert remembers. "Because I never discussed religion with him. And he was very upset. And he was upset about the Catholic church in particular, which he had all kinds of negative associations with." Did this represent a rejection of him? "He took it very personally," Robert says. "We had a really hard conversation." But his father later apologized, which Robert thought was an important moment in their relationship.[122]

Robert, meanwhile, had been dealing with his own mini-celebrity. Any relation to Daniel Ellsberg? people would all-too-frequently ask him. His mother had warned him about their motivations. "To a certain extent I think she impressed on us this idea that you [should] be very careful about people who seem to be interested in you and pay attention to you but who are really just interested in your father," he recalls. "And then not to trust people who show interest in that." Robert got tired of being asked to lay himself open to those who were curious about his experiences. "People are pretty insensitive to the fact that there might be anything that could have been stressful or difficult about this whole thing," he says. "People tend to think, 'Wow, that must have been a very exciting thing.'" He also wanted to be viewed on his own merits.[123]

Robert returned to Harvard in 1980 and graduated *magna cum laude* two years later. He subsequently earned a master's in theology from Harvard and is now the editor-in-chief of Orbis Books, a small religious publisher. He is married to a lecturer in English at Barnard College and is the father of three children. His relationship with his own father has matured. "In some ways, my older son tells me, I'm a lot easier to deal with," Daniel Ellsberg told me. "He said just the other day, 'You listen better. And you're less judgmental. And you're easier to be around.'" Says Robert,

> I think that he is less obsessive than he was. And he used to have more of a tendency to kind of lecture all the time and have these kind of morbid obsessions with nuclear war and torture and evil or something like that. And he would kind of be trying out ideas on you, and kind of forcing you to talk about deep intellectual topics. . . . And it was hard just to chat with him. Because everything was like a seminar a lot of the time. And he would go on and on and on about nuclear war or whatever insights he had about Marxist theory or whatever. And he was like just a sort of intellectual sponge always kind of soaking up, absorbing huge new topics inside out. . . . And if you knew a little bit about one of these topics, you felt . . . swamped by this high-powered volume of reflections and thoughts he would have about it. . . . I was kind of more intimidated by that and I didn't have any way of saying, "I don't want to talk about that" or "Please stop it." . . . And so there were times when I felt I just couldn't handle that. . . . At some point over the last number of years, he has mellowed just an enormous amount and is much easier to converse with.[124]

Mary Ellsberg has had an especially trying relationship with her father. She became quite resentful of him, finding him (or so I judged from her comments to me) self-centered, unreliable, insufficiently attentive to her and Robert, and hurtful to her mother, among other things. She also felt less included than Robert in his political doings. She attended Yale. "He wanted her to go to Harvard—Carol told me this—and she defied him and decided to go to Yale," Mary Marshall remembers. "She's always been a kind of a halfway defiant [daughter] trying to get out from under the father." Mary developed a strong aversion to living in his shadow. For a time, she tried to be all-American. She traveled to Nicaragua in 1979, shortly after the Sandinistas had taken power, to do her senior thesis on health education. She stayed. "She wanted to get as far away as she possibly could from her father and his reputation," Kirby Hall heard from her mother. "Because everywhere she went: 'Oh, are you Daniel Ellsberg's daughter?'" Mary told me:

Since I was twelve, people have asked everywhere I go whether I'm related to Daniel Ellsberg—at school, writing checks at the drugstore, making plane reservations, etc. Often, people that I was meeting only casually would say, "I'd really like to talk to you about what it was like being Daniel Ellsberg's daughter," as if this was something that they thought I would naturally enjoy discussing as well. It felt voyeuristic and made me mistrust most people's reactions to me. I'm sure that part of the attraction of living in a country where no one knew or cared who my father was is that it gave me an anonymity to meet people on my own terms, which was important for developing my own sense of identity. It was not a conscious gesture, but during the eight years that I worked on the Atlantic Coast of Nicaragua I was known only as "Mary Carroll."[125]

Mary worked on public health and women's issues in Nicaragua. She married a Nicaraguan (whom she later separated from), had two children, and earned a doctorate in epidemiology and public health in Sweden. Her father spoke quite highly of her, but their relationship continued to have its problems. One day in the 1980s, one of Dan's friends remembers, the friend and Ellsberg went into New York for a meeting, and afterward Ellsberg informed his friend that Mary was coming into New York that evening from Nicaragua and consequently he couldn't be with his friend then. Ellsberg's friend was irritated, as she would have planned something else for the evening had she been told about this beforehand. After the friend expressed disappointment to him, Ellsberg called Mary, and the way the friend interpreted what was taking place over the phone, some of Mary's comments were of the flavor of, "What the hell is going on here? I come all the way from Nicaragua. I haven't seen you for this long time. And somehow . . . you always have something more important or more interesting than me."[126]

Ellsberg would later make it one of his missions in life to get back into Mary's good graces. "I think he realizes it's not going so well," Carol Cummings says. "That's a recent mission."[127]

When I asked Mary how her father had changed over the years, she responded, "I haven't seen enough of him in recent years to form much of an opinion about this."[128]

Many people I spoke with in the mid-1990s thought Dan Ellsberg had changed very little. "There is some mellowing in old age, but it's strictly relative," Ben Bagdikian laughs. "He's in some ways changed less than anybody I know," Don Hall says. "And in appearance in lots of ways. The way he moves is not like a

64-year-old [now a 70-year-old]. . . . He talks pretty much in the same way. I think there's a little less ebullience or quick sudden laughter than there was in the 19-year-old that I knew first. But the distance between those two bodies or matters is less by far than it is in the people I can measure him against. . . . There seems to be a tremendous consistency of tone in the way he engages the world." "He's changed remarkably little," Thomas Schelling echoes.[129]

But Ellsberg has become more introspective, more conscious of his personality and his shortcomings. "One thing about Dan, he's honest," Howard Zinn says:

> Very honest about himself and his feelings and his inadequacies, or what other people perceive in him. He's very, very straightforward about that. And I think because he wants to talk about that. He wants to test what other people have said with you. And I saw him just recently. He was apologizing for a conversation he had had with me and Roz. And for what he thought was talking too much. . . . He was sensitive about that. . . . He always wants to know how he is coming across, and whether he's done something wrong or done something to offend you. . . . I think maybe Pat has turned his attention to himself and maybe caused him to look at himself more critically.[130]

As have other people.

Ellsberg has remained a chronically insecure, vulnerable, and highly sensitive man. One person remembers sitting next to him at a party after a book-reading attended by well-known intellectuals in the late 1980s. "Ellsberg was sitting there kind of sulking. He wasn't the center of attention. And I wondered what was wrong. He seemed in real distress. . . . He was frantically trying to contribute something to this whole conversation. . . . He was working feverishly. It was like a mouse or a squirrel gathering nuts. I thought, 'What's driving this guy?'" Ellsberg was "frantically trying to come up with something that nobody's thought of." He seemed desperate, and driven by some sort of self-doubts. "I think he's feeling very insecure these days," Zinn observed in 1995. "And troubled. And doesn't know where he is," having just ended his affiliation with Physicians for Social Responsibility for his Manhattan Project II. "He's sort of on his own. And that must be very, very hard for somebody who was this historic figure to now be, in some ways, obscure." Other people's opinions of him continue to matter greatly to Ellsberg. "I think he's not just sensitive—I think he's rubbed-raw sensitive," Doug Dowd says:

> It's as though he has electrodes on. It's as though he were a radar screen or a radar set looking for signals all the time. I think that's one of his problems. . . .

> I think he's always looking for the signs that are favorable and unfavorable to him. . . . As though out there there's all kinds of good things and bad things, and he wants to know what they are, coming his way. He has to, in some sense, know. And it must be a really difficult way to live. . . . I mean, I can just imagine what it's like with him when he's fucking some woman, in terms of wanting to know, "How has it been for you?" . . . I think he's very receptive to that information. Asking for it. Needing it.[131]

Several times, Ellsberg became enraged when we discussed slights of him. His voice deepened, became rougher, sometimes there was profanity, with spittle forming at the side of his mouth. It was a different Ellsberg and a little unnerving.

Like most of us, Ellsberg can also choose not to see his personal shortcomings. He may hide some of those deeper secrets that he keeps about himself from himself, too. One friend of his remarked, during an interview in which we discussed Ellsberg's sense of specialness, egocentrism, and need for approbation, among other traits,

> As with a lot of very, very bright people, I don't think Dan cottons onto himself about these things at all. I don't think he has a sense of himself. In other words, what seems to be obvious to me, perhaps to you and others, I don't think he sees himself that way. If he were listening to all this, if he could listen to this tape, for example, he would say, "That's not me. No, that's not me at all you're talking about." I don't think he's got that. I don't think he *can* have that. You understand? I think it would destroy him if he had some sense that there's some kind of a systematic problem with the way he approaches his own life. . . . Probably from time to time he is troubled by it. But he's never said anything to me—and he's said a lot of intimate things—but he's never said anything that would indicate that he's troubled by himself at all.[132]

There is a pathos to Ellsberg. He's a tragic figure to a large degree: a man of truly exceptional intellectual promise who never realized his promise, a man whose greatest triumph was accompanied by all sorts of pain, anger, and aggravation, a man who never really had a second act. "This is a guy who blew his mind," Peter Schrag comments. "And it's sad. It's just fucking sad." Sam Popkin likens Ellsberg to "the Heisman trophy winner who never gains a yard in the pros. . . . He didn't quite ever adjust. . . . He never, ever sat down and did what he'd agreed to go somewhere and do." That last comment only slightly overstates it. Unlike many star athletes, Ellsberg had transferable skills. But he's seemingly always in turmoil, always struggling with himself, racked by his failures, never really satisfied with his successes, restlessly jumping from one thing to the next, showing an incorrigible lack of self-discipline, unable to bring most of his projects to completion, always running late ("he caught a lot of air" barreling down his driveway in his car and "came skidding in like in a police raid," one photographer remembers when Ellsberg screeched up late for a photography session at his home). And now his best years are in the past. Several of his former RAND colleagues asked me, in almost the exact same tone of voice, "What does he *do* now?" Some added some variant of the following: "Lay on railroad tracks trying to get arrested all the time?" The last part is, of course, a caricature, but the question is a reasonable one. When Joe Baker and Lou Conein had lunch with Ellsberg and asked him what he had been doing, they found that "you just can't pin him down."[133]

Ellsberg is the type of person who needs structure in his life—requirements, deadlines—to produce. Without a job, he has had little structure in his life. It's not a situation conducive to maximizing his abilities. "Has a lot of time been wasted? Have I used my time efficiently? Certainly not," he told me.[134]

When I said to him, rather insensitively, but not without cause, that I thought his failure to reach his intellectual potential had caused him a fair amount of anguish, he replied, "That's your feeling, that's your feeling." As for what he was doing now, Ellsberg said that his former RAND colleagues should know "I'm doing work that is more useful, more effective, for the [greater] benefit of this country and the world than anything I ever did at RAND, or anything known to me that anyone did at RAND. Except the release of the Pentagon Papers. Which was the best thing that ever came out of RAND. . . . It justified the existence of RAND. For all the bad things they did, it came close to making RAND worthwhile." He added, again speaking of his political activities, "Have I had an impact on anything in, let's say, the last 20 years? Not much, actually. But no bad effects. If I was at RAND, I'd be doing bad things. I'd be making the world worse. Now I'm harmless."[135] Perhaps he had a certain point.

To a significant degree, Ellsberg still lives in the past. One person with whom he's had many discussions has noticed that their talks always revert to Vietnam, the Papers, or maybe some rally at which Ellsberg had spoken several years earlier alongside some other famous people. "With Dan, talking about the present and the future doesn't do very good, because that's the less interesting part of his life," this person notes. "He would like to talk about old things. . . . And I think that what he did was remarkable and courageous and so on and so forth, but I [am] not fascinated by that subject." When meeting others, most people talk about what they're doing in the present or about something that has a future consequence, this person points out. But "when Dan Ellsberg meets people, the most interesting thing about his life is something that happened 25 years ago." It was hard on Ellsberg that many younger people at Physicians for Social Responsibility did not know who he was.[136]

Ellsberg claims that the waning of his celebrity did not bother him. "No problem," he says. "When it was over, I never missed it [for] a moment. At all." But he still relished being noticed. "There is a boyish pride in being recognized," Don Hall has witnessed. "A silly boyish pleasure in being recognized." Hall recounts: "One time I drove him out to Lebanon [New Hampshire] to the airport, and he had to get a ticket. And he handed the guy his card, and the guy said, 'Are you the Daniel Ellsberg?' And Dan just grinned from ear to ear. Like a little boy! I could have punched him: 'Fake humble, Dan. Don't do that.' Because Dan doesn't understand about that. It's strange . . . not knowing enough not to grin at the name recognition. . . . You know, there's something pretty weird when you're a 60-year-old who is like that."[137]

For some egotistical people, the further they get from their successes, the larger their ego seems to get. One person who has known Ellsberg for years has noticed that his has become much more grandiose. "The farther he is from power, the worse it gets," this person points out. "Somehow if he's not successful, then he has to make a bigger thing out of it. . . . I mean, he doesn't even begin to pretend to be interested in me anymore."[138]

Richard Zeckhauser observes that Ellsberg is "very worried about his place in history. We had dinner with him one night. He was with my kids," who were then seven and twelve. "He was very eager to know what they knew about him. Fortunately, they knew about him because . . . before he came for dinner I told them who he was. But I think it would have been a real blow to his ego . . . if he had shown up and then said, 'What do you know about what I did vis-à-vis the Vietnamese war?' and they would [have responded], 'I'm sorry, I really don't know anything.' I think he would have been very hurt."[139]

INTERVIEWS

The following people were interviewed for this book, some more than once, between the dates of September 1994 and January 2000. Other sources asked for anonymity. Most people were interviewed in person, but some were queried over the phone:

Bella Abzug, Len Ackland, Robert Akeret, Martin Arnold, Anthony Austin, Ben Bagdikian, Joe Baker, Gunther Balz, Bernard Barker, Ed Barlow, Richard Barnet, Robert Bates, Francis Bator, Tim Beneke, Richard Best, Robert Beyers, Donald Blackmer, Al Booth, Gisela Booth, Simon Bourgin, Margaret Brenman-Gibson, Ed Brunner, William Bundy, Floyd Bunt, Ken Butigan, Jan Butler, Michael Carey, Noam Chomsky, Joan Cleveland, William Colby, John Coldwell, Merrell Condit, Lou Conein, David Cortright, Philip Cronin, Polly Cronin, Walter Cronkite, Dora Crouch, Carol Cummings, Norman Dalkey, Judy Danielson, Vincent Davis, Arnaud DeBorchgrave, Walt Denison, Linda Deutsch, Edwin Diamond, Jim Digby, Fred Dockstader, Dolores Donovan, Doug Dowd, Richard Dudman, Peter Edelman, Frank Eldridge, Daniel Ellsberg, Mary Ellsberg (via e-mail), Patricia Ellsberg, Robert Ellsberg, Ann Elms, Richard Elms, Richard Falk, Thomas Fennell, Frances FitzGerald, Richard French, Alvin Friedman, John Kenneth Galbraith, Alfred Gannon, George Gannon, Marty Garbus, Murray Gart, Alexander George, K. Dun Gifford, Todd Gitlin, Alfred Goldberg, Jerry Goodman, Sallie Goodman, Roger Gould, Bill Green, David Greenway, David Halberstam, Donald Hall, Kirby Hall, Allen Halper, Morton Halperin, Harry Harris, William Harris, David Hartsough, Fred Haynes, Hilde Hein, Deirdre Henderson, Leslie Henriques, Ann Heymann, Hans Heymann, Philip Heymann, Fred Hoffman, Stanley Hoffmann, James Hoge, Townsend Hoopes, Lowell Hukill, Fred Iklé, Jo Isaacson, Andrew Jackson, Scott Jacobs, J. Norvill Jones, Jamie Kalvin, William Kaufmann, Carl Kaysen, Randy Kehler, Konrad Kellen, Herbert Kelman, Glenn Kent, Leo Keshishian, Roman Kolkowicz, Robert Komer, Hind Sadek Kooros, Bill Kovach, Arnold Kramish, Helen Kwake, Richard Laird, Peter Laitin, Paul Langer, Jeremy Larner, Norma Lawrie, Bob Leister, Wassily Leontief, Joan Libby, G. Gordon Liddy, Seymour Lipkin, Seymour Martin Lipset, Ashley Lipshutz, Sterling Lord, James Lowenstein, J. Anthony Lukas, Robert Lukeman, Gordon Manning, Howard Margolis, Andrew Marshall, Mary Marshall, Charles Mathias, Charles Maxwell, Paul (Pete) McCloskey, Stuart McCombs, George McCoy, David McGarvey, George McGovern, Priscilla McMillan, Bob Miller, Carl Miller, Charlotte Miller, Charles Nesson, Andrew Norman, Don Oberdorfer, Tom Oliphant, David Osnos, Lauren Otis, Bradley Patterson, Ewa Pauker, Guy Pauker, Eugene Paul, Helen Perry, Stewart Perry, Tom Peterson, Rufus Phillips, Douglas Pike, Myron Poe, Sam Popkin, Jeffrey Race, Marcus Raskin, David Ratner, Joe Redick, Lynda Resnick, Frank Rich, John Rielly, Peyton Robertson, Leonard Rodberg, Carl Rogers, Mark Rosenbaum, A. M. Rosenthal, Walt Rostow, Anthony Russo, Robert

Sachs, John Sack, Ned Sack, Alice Schelling, Andrew Schelling, Thomas Schelling, Peter Schrag, Eric Schroeder, Marva Shearer, Stanley Sheinbaum, Gus Shubert, William Simmons, John Simon, Peter Solbert, Ted Solotaroff, Helmut Sonnenfeldt, Bernard Sosner, W. Laird Stabler, Richard Steadman, Thelma Stubbs Smith, Patrick Sullivan, George Tanham, James Thomson, Alice Tipton, Richard Townsend, Tran Ngoc Chau, Frank Trinkl, Janaki Tschannerl, Marlene Twaddell, Sanford Ungar, Jess Vann, John Allen Vann, Mary Jane Vann, Tom Varbedian, Renee Vollen, Anne Waldman, Paul Warnke, Leonard Weinglass, Tom Wicker, Greg Wierzynski, Albert Williams, Donna Wilson, Theo Wilson, Tom Winship, Charles Wolf, Ken Wright, Adam Yarmolinsky, Bernard Yoh, Peter Young, Richard Zeckhauser, Howard Zinn, Sidney Zion, Barry Zorthian.

ABBREVIATIONS

APT	Abuse of Power Tapes
ARVN	Army of South Vietnam
BG	*Boston Globe*
CA	Cranbrook Archives
CP	Carol Cummings Papers
Crimson	*Harvard Crimson*
DE, MV	Daniel Ellsberg, Mill Valley, California, burglary file
DFP	*Detroit Free Press*
DOE	U.S. Department of Energy
Fielding	Fielding break-in investigation records
GVN	Government of South Vietnam
HJC	House Judiciary Committee impeachment investigation
JFK	John F. Kennedy Library
LAT	*Los Angeles Times*
LBJ	Lyndon Baines Johnson Library
LP	Edward G. Lansdale Papers, Hoover Institution Archives
May 3	May 3, 1972, demonstration investigation records
Meiklejohn	Meiklejohn Civil Liberties Library
NA	National Archives
NLF	National Liberation Front
NSC	National Security Council
NSF	National Security Files
NYT	*New York Times*
OSD	Office of the Secretary of Defense
POF	President's Office Files
RS	*Rolling Stone*
Sachs	Robert Sachs Papers
SFC	*San Francisco Chronicle*
SISBPN	Statement of Information Submitted on Behalf of President Nixon
SLO	Senior Liaison Office (Lansdale team)
SP	Neil Sheehan Papers, Library of Congress
SSC	Senate Select Committee on Presidential Campaign Activities investigation
VCF	Vietnam Country File
WHSF	White House Special Files, Nixon Project, National Archives
WP	*Washington Post*
WSPF	Watergate Special Prosecution Force records, National Archives

NOTES

PROLOGUE

1. SSC, Book I, 372; Bernard Barker interview; "Watergate Report," NBC News, April 3, 1974 (WSPF, Fielding, box 2); Charles Colson to John Ehrlichman, July 6, 1971 (WSPF, Fielding, accordion file following box 3); Frank Martin to Files, August 16, 1973 (WSPF, Fielding, box 15); "Summary of Interview with Egil Krogh," April 3, 1974 (WSPF, Fielding, box 20).

2. HJC, Book VII, Part 2, 1103; "EB" to Acting Director, FBI, June 28, 1972 (WSPF, Fielding, box 3); "Watergate Report," NBC News, April 3, 1974 (WSPF, Fielding, box 2); G. Gordon Liddy interview.

3. HJC, Book VII, Part 2, 1106–7; Liddy interview; Krogh affidavit, May 4, 1973 (Sachs).

4. "AC," Memorandum for the Record, July 8, 1972; "AC" affidavit, May 8, 1973; Robert Cushman affidavit, May 11, 1973; "HA" affidavit, May 18, 1973; "HA," Memorandum for the Record, August 23, 1971 (prior five items in WSPF, Fielding, box 3); Nick Akerman to Files, August 1, 1973 (WSPF, Fielding, box 19); William Colby, Memorandum for the Record, December 18, 1972 (WSPF, Fielding, box 3).

5. Liddy travel voucher, August 30, 1971; Liddy request for travel, August 25, 1971 (prior two items in Ehrlichman, WHSF, box 21); David Young to Ehrlichman, August 25, 1971 (WSPF, Fielding, box 2); Hunt, 164.

6. Alfred Goldberg interview; Roger Gould interview.

7. Gould interview; newsletter of Los Angeles Psychoanalytic Society, late 1994 or early 1995; Goldberg interview.

8. Gould interview.

9. Dr. Bernard Malloy, Memorandum for the Record, August 20, 1971 (WSPF, Fielding, box 3); Donald Hall interview.

10. Roman Kolkowicz interview; Liddy to Malloy, October 29, 1971 (WSPF, Fielding, box 3).

11. Henry Kissinger to Richard Nixon, June 1971, no day indicated (WHSF, Dean, box 53); Liddy interview; Phil Bakes to Files, October 16, 1973; Akerman to Files, August 7, 1973 (prior two items in WSPF, Fielding, box 20); Liddy to Krogh and Young, November 4, 1971 (WHSF, Young, box 15); Liddy to Krogh and Young, September 23, 1971 (WHSF, Young, box 13); Nixon and Colson conversation, June 29, 1971 (APT, NA).

12. Charles Nesson interview; Daniel Ellsberg radio interview on "Democracy Now," Pacifica, June 13, 1996.

13. Carol Cummings interviews; FBI documents on Carol Ellsberg interviews, June 25, July 9, 1971 (WSPF, Fielding, box 18); Carol Ellsberg notes on Nesson conversation, July 10, 1972 (CP).

14. Carol Ellsberg notes on Nesson conversation, July 10, 1972 (CP); FBI documents on Carol Ellsberg interviews, June 17, June 22, June 24 (two), June 25 (two), June 29, June 30, July 1, July 9, July 13, 1971; Director, FBI, to Archibald Cox, September 26, 1973; other FBI documents, July 9, July 12, July 19, July 20, July 27, 1971; May 13, May 28, 1974 (prior nineteen items in WSPF, Fielding, box 18).

15. Director, FBI, to LA FBI, July 9, 1971; Director, FBI, to Cox, September 26, 1973; James Wagoner and W. Raymond Wannall statements, May 13, May 28, 1974; FBI document on Carol Ellsberg interview, June 25, 1971 (prior five items in WSPF, Fielding, box 18).

16. Bakes to Files, July 20, 1973 (WSPF, Fielding, box 20).

17. Robert Ellsberg interview.

18. Anthony Russo interview.

19. Sanford Ungar interview; Martin Arnold interview; Leonard Weinglass interview.

20. HJC, Book III, Part 2, 943; Howard Hunt grand jury testimony, May 2, 1973 (Sachs); Liddy, 163.

21. Document on interview of Douglas Hallett, no date (WSPF, Fielding, box 19); Bakes to Files, July 9, 1973 (WSPF, Fielding, box 15).

22. Liddy interview.

23. Director, FBI, to LA FBI, July 9, 19, 1971; FBI document on Donald Moore interview, May 20, 21, 1974; FBI document on Harry Swerdlow conversation, July 28, 1971 (prior five items in WSPF, Fielding, box 18); Goldberg interview; LA FBI to FBI Director, July 27, 1971; LA FBI to Acting Director, May 1, 1973 (prior two items in WSPF, Fielding, box 18).

24. Liddy interview; HJC, Book VII, Part 2, 980; SSC, Book IX, 3736; Hunt grand jury testimony, May 2, 1973 (Sachs); Young memo on March 27, 1973, conversation with Ehrlichman (WSPF, Fielding, box 1).

25. HJC, Book VII, Part 2, 1105; Liddy interview; Krogh and Young to Ehrlichman, August 11, 1971 (WHSF, Ehrlichman, box 21).

26. Maria Martinez affidavit, April 30, 1973 (Meiklejohn); Hunt, 166; Liddy, 164; HJC, Book VII, Part 3, 1279; Hunt grand jury testimony, May 2, 1973 (Sachs).

27. Liddy travel voucher, August 30, 1971 (WHSF, Ehrlichman, box 21); various CIA documents (WSPF, Fielding, box 3); HJC, Book III, Part 2, 941.

28. "Outline of Closing Argument," no date (WSPF, Fielding, box 1); HJC, Book VII, Part 2, 1172–74, 1155, Part 3, 1311; Phil Heymann notes on Krogh interview, June 20, 1974 (WSPF, Fielding, box 3).

29. Hunt grand jury testimony, May 2, 1973 (Sachs).

30. Liddy to Krogh and Young, August 18, 1971 (WSPF, Fielding, box 2); Hunt grand jury testimony, May 2, 1973 (Sachs); Liddy interview; SSC, Book IX, 3782; *LAT*, October 1, 1973; Krogh radio interview, October 28, 1973 (WSPF, Fielding, box 20).

31. Liddy interview; Malloy, Memorandum for the Record, August 13, 1971; Director of Medical Services to Director of Security, CIA, August 10, 1971; CIA personality assessment, August 9, 1971; Malloy affidavit, May 9, 1973; "AF" to Richard Helms, November 9, 1971; "AF" affidavit, May 25, 1973; "AB" affidavit, May 15, 1973 (prior seven items in WSPF, Fielding, box 3).

32. CIA personality assessment, August 9, 1971 (WSPF, Fielding, box 3).

33. Liddy interview; Krogh and Young to Ehrlichman, August 11, 1971 (WHSF, Ehrlichman, box 21); Bakes to Files, July 20, 1973 (WSPF, Fielding, box 20).

34. Liddy interview; Krogh and Young to Ehrlichman, August 11, 1971 (WHSF, Ehrlichman, box 21).

35. SSC, Book IX, 3782, 3886; Strober and Strober, 232; "241-Colson," no date (WSPF, Fielding, boxes 22–23); Leon Jaworski to Edward G. Docekal, July 24, 1974 (WSPF, Fielding, box 2).

36. "Closing Argument," no date (WSPF, Fielding, box 1); "Jeff Shepard," October 25, 1973 (WSPF, Fielding, box 21); "Summary of Interview with Egil Krogh," April 3, 1974 (WSPF, Fielding, box 20); HJC, Book VII, Part 3, 1258; Martin to Files, August 16, 1973 (WSPF, Fielding, box 15).

37. Akerman to Files, August 20, 1973 (WSPF, Fielding, box 15); Bakes to Files, July 11, 1973 (WSPF, Fielding, boxes 22–23); Bakes to Files, July 19, 1973 (WSPF, Fielding, box 19); list of items in Hunt's safe (Meiklejohn); HJC, Book VII, Part 3, 1306–7.

38. Young to Ehrlichman, August 26, 1971; Ehrlichman to Colson, August 27, 1971 (prior two items in WSPF, Fielding, box 2); "Closing Argument," no date (WSPF, Fielding, box 1).

39. Colson to H.R. Haldeman, June 25, 1971 (WHSF, Colson, box 129); three documents on interviews of Joan Hall, July, October 1973 (WSPF, Fielding, box 19); LA FBI to Acting Director, June 18, 1973 (WSPF, Fielding, box 18); Martin to Files, August 16, 1973 (WSPF, Fielding, box 15).

40. "Closing Argument," no date (WSPF, Fielding, box 1); Jaworski to Docekal, July 24, 1974 (WSPF, Fielding, box 2); "Summary of Interview with Egil Krogh," April 3, 1974 (WSPF, Fielding, box 20); HJC, Book VII, Part 3, 1241–43.

41. *Harper's*, "Mission Impossible," October 1974, 52.

42. HJC, Book VII, Part 3, 1258; Liddy, 165; Liddy interview.

43. "Inventory," no date (WSPF, Fielding, box 1); Liddy, 165; *George*, "Time Machine: Watergate," June 1997, 107.

44. "Inventory," no date (WSPF, Fielding, box 1); Liddy interview; HJC, Book VII, Part 3, 1278.

45. Liddy interview; Liddy to Krogh and Young, August 18, 1971 (WSPF, Fielding, box 2); *NYT*, August 25, 1971; *LAT*, October 1, 2, 1973; Hunt grand jury testimony, May 2, 1973 (Sachs).

46. FBI document on interview of Mary Denburg, July 6, 1972 (WSPF, Fielding, box 18).

47. FBI document on interview of Mary Denburg, July 6, 1972 (WSPF, Fielding, box 18); Liddy, 190–91.

48. "Inventory," no date; "Outline of Closing Argument," no date (prior two items in WSPF, Fielding, box 1); Barker interview; Hunt grand jury testimony, May 2, 1973 (Sachs); *Harper's*, "Mission Impossible," October 1974, 51, 52; G. Goldman to File, September 13, 1973 (WSPF, Fielding, box 2); *LAT*, May 11, 1973.

49. HJC, Book VII, Part 3, 1280; *Washington Star*, October 10, 1973.

50. *Harper's*, "Mission Impossible," October 1974, 52; Dolores Donovan affidavit, April 30, 1973 (Meiklejohn); Lewis Fielding affidavit, April 29, 1973 (WSPF, Fielding, box 18); Maria Martinez affidavit, April 30, 1973 (Meiklejohn); Barker interview.

51. Martinez affidavit, April 30, 1973 (Meiklejohn); Donovan interview; Barker interview.

52. HJC, Book VII, Part 3, 1281, Book I, 209.

53. Liddy interview; "Bernard Barker, Montgomery County Detention Center," September 13, 1973 (WSPF, Fielding, box 2); Barker interview.

54. Barker interview.

55. "Draft Closing Argument," no date (WSPF, Fielding, box 1); Liddy, 167; Liddy interview.

56. *Harper's*, "Mission Impossible," October 1974, 52–53; HJC, Book VII, Part 3, 1283, 1306; Beverly Hills Police report, September 4, 1971 (WSPF, Fielding, box 15); Ashley Lipshutz interview; document on Michael Haigwood interview, no date (WSPF, Fielding, box 15); Bernard Sosner interview.

57. Lipshutz interview; Beverly Hills Police report, September 4, 1971 (WSPF, Fielding, box 15); HJC, Book VII, Part 3, 1284–86; Fielding affidavit, April 29, 1973 (WSPF, Fielding, box 18); *Harper's*, "Mission Impossible," October 1974, 52, 53.

58. Hunt, 170–71; Liddy, 167–68; Liddy, Memorandum for the File, August 4, 1971 (WHSF, Young, box 13); Liddy interview.

59. Liddy interview.

60. Fielding affidavit, April 29, 1973 (WSPF, Fielding, box 18); HJC, Book VII, Part 3, 1286–90; SSC, Book I, 376; FBI document on interview of Joan Hall, February 6, 1974 (WSPF, Fielding, box 18); Barker interview; Goldberg interview.

61. Barker interview; *LAT*, May 5, 1973; "Draft Closing Argument," no date (WSPF, Fielding, box 1); HJC, Book VII, Part 3, 1292.

62. HJC, Book VII, Part 3, 1291, 1312, 1321; Barker interview; Beverly Hills Police report, September 4, 1971; document on interview of Clinton Brickley, no date (prior two items in WSPF, Fielding, box 15).

63. Sosner interview; Beverly Hills Police report, September 4, 1971; "Beverly Hills Police," no date (prior two items in WSPF, Fielding, box 15); Lipshutz interview.

64. Sosner interview; Goldberg interview.

65. Beverly Hills Police report, October 25, 1971; Arrest and Booking form; Elmer Davis to Captain Rutherford, November 12, 1971 (prior three items in Meiklejohn); FBI document on Irving Shimer conversation, May 1, 1973 (Sachs).

66. Beverly Hills Police report, September 4, 1971 (WSPF, Fielding, box 15); Maria Martinez affidavit, April 30, 1973 (Meiklejohn); document on Brickley interview, no date; "Beverly Hills Police," no date (prior two items in WSPF, Fielding, box 15); FBI document on B.L. Cork interview, May 1, 1973 (WSPF, Fielding, box 18).

67. Fielding affidavit, April 29, 1973 (WSPF, Fielding, box 18); *LAT*, June 6, 1973; Ellsberg interview; Hall interview; Neil Sheehan, "Vann Book Outline, 1965–67 Period" (SP, box 65).

68. Fielding affidavit, April 29, 1973 (WSPF, Fielding, box 18); FBI document on Shimer conversation, May 1, 1973 (Sachs); *LAT*, April 30, 1973; "Fielding," two documents with same title, no dates (WSPF, Fielding, boxes 1, 18); document on Brickley interview, no date (WSPF, Fielding, box 15); FBI document on Cork interview, May 1, 1973 (WSPF, Fielding, box 18).

69. Bakes to Files, August 7, 1973 (WSPF, Fielding, box 18); HJC, Book IV (SIS-BPN), 100, Book VII, Part 3, 1293–94; Lukas, *Nightmare*, 100; "Closing Argument," no date (WSPF, Fielding, box 1); *LAT*, October 1, 1973.

70. Fielding affidavit, April 29, 1973 (WSPF, Fielding, box 18); Goldberg interview.

71. Fielding affidavit, April 29, 1973; Bakes to Files, August 7, 1973 (prior two items in WSPF, Fielding, box 18); Gould interview; Goldberg interview.

72. Document on interview of Ellsberg and Boudin, May 1, 1974 (WSPF, Fielding, box 18).

73. Gould interview; Bakes to Files, August 7, 1973 (WSPF, Fielding, box 18); Bakes to Merrill and Breyer, September 25, 1973 (WSPF, Fielding, accordion file following box 3); Liddy interview; Liddy, 157; Henry Hecht to Merrill, August 29, 1973 (WSPF, Fielding, box 20); Malloy, Memorandum for the Record, August 20, 1971 (WSPF, Fielding, box 3).

74. *LAT,* April 27, October 1, 1973; Strober and Strober, 221; Goldberg interview; Fielding affidavit, April 29, 1973 (WSPF, Fielding, box 18).

75. Goldberg interview; document on interview of Ellsberg and Boudin, May 1, 1974 (WSPF, Fielding, box 18); Strober and Strober, 220–21.

76. Barker interview; HJC, Book VII, Part 3, 1289–91; Liddy interview.

77. Document on interview of Ellsberg and Boudin, May 1, 1974 (WSPF, Fielding, box 18); *LAT,* June 6, 1973; Ellsberg's 1973 *RS* interview (reprint), 16.

78. Hunt, 172; *Harper's,* "Mission Impossible," October 1974, 53; Liddy, 168; Barker interview; Liddy interview; document on interview of Ellsberg and Boudin, May 1, 1974 (WSPF, Fielding, box 18); FBI document, August 24, 1973 (WSPF, Fielding, box 18).

79. Liddy interview.

80. Liddy interview; Liddy, 168–69; Lukas, *Nightmare,* 101; *NYT,* May 2, 1973.

81. Liddy interview; Bakes to Cox et al., no date (WSPF, Fielding, boxes 22–23).

82. HJC, Book VII, Part 3, 1306, 1312–13; Krogh radio interview, October 28, 1973 (WSPF, Fielding, box 20); Liddy interview.

83. HJC, Book VII, Part 3, 1314–16; Ehrlichman "60 Minutes" interview, June 29, 1973 (WSPF, Fielding, box 16). Nonetheless, after Liddy applied for admission to the District of Columbia bar a few months later, Ehrlichman attested in a letter that "he was a very effective member of the [White House] staff and undertook numerous difficult assignments with great skill. . . . He has approached all problems, even the most sensitive, with the highest sense of integrity" (Ehrlichman to William Morris, June 6, 1972 [WHSF, Ehrlichman, box 21]).

84. Hunt grand jury testimony, May 2, 1973 (Sachs); HJC, Book VII, Part 3, 1304; notes on interview of Colson, March 31, 1973 (WSPF, Fielding, box 15); SSC, Book IX, 3677; three documents on Hall interviews, July, October 1973 (WSPF, Fielding, box 19); Bakes to File, July 9, 1973 (WSPF, Fielding, box 15).

85. Nixon and Ehrlichman conversation, September 8, 1971 (APT, NA).

CHAPTER 1

1. Alfred Gannon interview; Alice Tipton interview; Ellsberg interview; Tom Varbedian interview; Leo Keshishian interview; Norma Lawrie interview; Eugene Paul interview.

2. Ellsberg interviews; Paul interview; Mary Ellsberg interview.

3. Tipton interview; Paul interview.

4. Gannon interview.

5. Tipton interview; Ellsberg interview; Myron Poe interview.

6. Ellsberg interview; Poe interview; Lawrie interview; Paul interview.

7. Lawrie interview; Poe interview; Gannon interview; Varbedian interview.

8. Poe interview; Ellsberg interview; Lawrie interview.

9. Alfred Gannon interview; Varbedian interview; Tipton interview; Merrell Condit interview; Fred Dockstader interviews.

10. Charlotte Miller interviews.

11. Miller interview.

12. Anonymous source.

13. East High School records, Denver; Miller interview; Ellsberg interview.

14. Poe interview; Tipton interview; Miller interviews; Dockstader interview; *Highland Parker*, July 11, 1946; Ellsberg interviews; Tom Peterson interview.

15. Miller interviews.

16. Miller interviews.

17. Miller interview.

18. Harry Ellsberg's death certificate; Miller interview; *Denver Directory*, 1909; Ellsberg interviews; Ellsberg interview with Studs Terkel, 1980 (tape).

19. *Coloradoan*, 1914; Ellsberg interviews; Harry Ellsberg's University of Colorado academic transcript.

20. Ellsberg interviews; *Who's Who in America*, 1958–59; East High School yearbook, 1909, photo; Susan Williamson phone conversation; Poe interview; Miller interviews.

21. Daniel says it was eleven months later, while newspaper articles say Gloria was two years younger than him, and neither her birth nor death records are publicly available. Ellsberg interview; Davenport *Democrat and Leader* and *Detroit News*, July 5, 1946.

22. Miller interviews; Ellsberg interview; Cummings interview.

23. Ellsberg interviews; Poe interview; Margaret Brenman-Gibson interview.

24. Ellsberg interview; Miller interview; *Detroit News*, July 5, 1946; Sylvia Sanders, Deborah Ferris, and Christine Arciniaga phone conversations; Ellsberg interview with Terkel, 1980; Harry Ellsberg's radiation exposure records at Hanford, 1948, 1949 (in my possession); Rhodes, 497–500, 556–57; Angela Lowman, Janice Parthree, and Terri Traub phone conversations. Regarding Willow Run, Ferris, an employee of Albert Kahn's Project Management Department, told me that "chief engineer" was "a strange way to put it," given that engineers from three disciplines were involved in designing the plant, and that the "principal in charge" was not Harry Ellsberg. Sanders, Kahn's head librarian, determined that he was not the "superintendent engineer" on Willow Run either. U.S. Department of Energy records, obtained through a Freedom of Information Act request, show that Harry Ellsberg visited Hanford in 1948 and 1949, after the plant was constructed. He may have been working as a consulting engineer on plant modifications. There are no other DOE records of Harry Ellsberg's presence at Hanford. A book on Hanford's construction by Harry Thayer (see bibliography) does not mention Harry Ellsberg, and Thayer told me Ellsberg's name never came up in his research. And if there was one "chief structural engineer" at Hanford (which two DOE employees who oversee records of Hanford's construction told me is unlikely), this person would have worked for DuPont, and there is no mention of Harry Ellsberg in DuPont's records at Hanford either.

25. Ellsberg interviews; Cummings interviews; Miller interviews.

26. Ellsberg interview; Hall interview.

27. Varbedian interview; Allen Halper interview; Keshishian interview; Poe interview; George Gannon interview.

28. Halper interview; Paul interview; Varbedian interview; Lawrie interview.

29. Miller interview; Ellsberg interview; Cummings interview; Keshishian interview.

30. Miller interview.

31. Lawrie interview; McGinniss, 97.

32. Ellsberg interview; Miller interview.

33. Dockstader interviews; Cummings interviews.

34. Ellsberg interviews; Condit interview.

35. Ellsberg interviews; Varbedian interview; Peterson interview; Poe interview; Robert Bates interview.

36. Ellsberg interviews; Poe interview; Dockstader interview; Bates interview.

37. Poe interview; Ellsberg interview; Halper interview. Halper was later a principal at Barber.

38. Poe interview; *Senior Scholastic,* November 8, 1973, 11; anonymous sources.

39. Paul interview; Poe interview; Lawrie interview.

40. Doug Dowd interview.

41. Miller interview; Freeman, 159–60, 250; McGinniss, 192, 197; Cummings interview; Brenman-Gibson interview; Ellsberg interview; Carl Miller interview.

42. Ellsberg interviews; Joan Cleveland interview.

43. Ellsberg interviews; Sheehan notes on November 17, 1986, Ellsberg conversation (SP, box 63).

44. Brenman-Gibson interview; Sheehan notes on November 17, 1986, Ellsberg conversation (SP, box 63); Ellsberg interview.

45. Ellsberg interviews; *Senior Scholastic,* November 8, 1973, 9; Varbedian interview.

46. Ellsberg interviews.

47. Ellsberg interview.

48. Dowd interview; Brenman-Gibson interview; Freeman, 252; Klein and Tannenbaum, 130; Dockstader interview.

49. Dockstader interviews.

50. Miller interview; Poe interview; Ellsberg interview; Cummings interviews; Haushalter, v, 27.

51. Ellsberg interviews; Poe interview.

52. Condit interview; Bates interview; Ken Wright interview.

53. Miller interview; McGinniss, 197; Mary Ellsberg interview; *Who's Who in America,* 1974–75; Ellsberg interview.

54. My discussion of narcissism is based primarily on Kernberg, Mollon, Fine, Rothstein, Kohut, Lowen, Schwartz-Salant, and several interviews.

55. Kernberg, 235.

56. *Senior Scholastic,* November 8, 1973, 11; Ellsberg interview; anonymous sources.

57. Kolkowicz interview.

58. Brenman-Gibson interviews; Ellsberg interview.

59. Anonymous source; Dowd interview.

60. Hall interview; Lynda Resnick interview.

61. Von Franz, *passim.*

62. Ellsberg interviews.

CHAPTER 2

1. *Crane,* May 23, 1947; September 27, 1946 (CA); Gunther Balz interview; *Cranbrook School,* 1943–44 (CA).

2. Richard Townsend interview; *Crane*, November 8, 1946 (CA); *Crane*, November 5, 1948 (Robert Beyers papers); *Cranbrook School*, 1947–48 (Val Rabe papers).

3. W. Laird Stabler interview; Bradley Patterson interview; *Crane*, September 17, 1943 (CA).

4. Mark Coir conversation; Ellsberg interview; Balz interview; Charles Maxwell interview; Wright interview; *Brook*, 1947, 1948 (CA).

5. *Cranbrook School*, 1943–44 (CA); Townsend interview; *Crane*, May 23, 1947; December 7, 1945 (CA); Bob Leister interview; Walt Denison interview.

6. Townsend interview.

7. Townsend interview; Dora Crouch interview; Denison interview.

8. Balz note to author and interview; Maxwell interview; Crouch interview.

9. Thomas Fennell interview; Dockstader interview; Wright interview; Robert Beyers interview; Stabler interview; Balz interview.

10. Dockstader interview.

11. Maxwell interview; Townsend interview; *Brook*, 1948 (CA).

12. Wright interview; Dockstader interview; Maxwell interview; Fennell interview.

13. Dockstader interview; Floyd Bunt interview; Townsend interview; Stabler interview.

14. Wright interview; David Osnos interview; *Brook*, 1948 (CA)

15. Dockstader interviews; Condit interview; Bates interview; Bunt interview.

16. Dockstader interviews; *Detroit News*, June 18, 1971.

17. Fennell interview; Stabler interview; Jo Isaacson interview.

18. Fennell interview; *Crane*, June 5, 1948 (Beyers papers); Isaacson interview; Peterson interview; Dockstader interview; Maxwell interview.

19. Townsend interview; Ellsberg interview; *Crane*, April 9, 1948 (Beyers papers); Maxwell interview.

20. *Crane*, February 18, 1944 (CA); Townsend interview.

21. Osnos interview; Isaacson interview; *Senior Scholastic*, November 8, 1973, 10; *Crane*, April 9, 1948 (Beyers papers); Maxwell interview; Ellsberg interview.

22. Isaacson interview; Crouch interview; Richard Laird interview; *Brook*, 1948 (CA); Maxwell interview.

23. Ellsberg interview; Ogden and Richards, *passim*; *Crane*, April 9, 1948 (Beyers papers); Ellsberg grade report at Cranbrook, June 1948 (in my possession).

24. *Crane*, December 21, 1945; April 11, 1947 (CA); Osnos interview.

25. Isaacson interview; Wright interview and phone conversation.

26. *Crane*, 1943–48 (CA); Ellsberg interview.

27. Crouch interview; *Senior Scholastic*, November 8, 1973, 11; Sheehan notes on Ellsberg conversation, November 17, 1986 (SP, box 63); *Crane*, April 9, 1948 (Beyers papers); Townsend interview.

28. Crouch interview.

29. Crouch interview.

30. Townsend interview; *Brook*, 1948 (CA); *Crane*, May 5, 1944; May 11, 1945 (CA); Bunt interview.

31. *Brook*, 1944–48 (CA); Ellsberg interviews; Ellsberg's "Civilian Background" Marine Corps form, 1954 (in my possession); Stabler interview.

32. Ellsberg interview; *Time*, July 5, 1971; *NYT*, June 27, 1971; second CIA psychological profile of Ellsberg, November 1971 (WSPF, Fielding, box 3); Wright interview and phone conversation.

33. *Crane*, November 16, December 14, 1945; December 15, 1944 (CA).

34. Maxwell interview.

35. Ellsberg interview; Ise, *passim; Senior Scholastic,* November 8, 1973, 10.

36. *Crane,* April 9, May 14, June 5, 1948 (Beyers papers).

37. Ellsberg grade report at Cranbrook, June 1948.

38. *Crane,* January 24, 1947 (CA); Beyers interview; *Crane,* November 21, 1947 (Beyers papers); Ellsberg essay, December 11, 1995 (in my possession); Ellsberg interview with Terkel, 1980; Patterson interview; Maxwell interview.

39. *Brook,* 1948 (CA); Stabler interview; Townsend interview; *Crane,* April 23, 1948; December 5, October 31, October 3, 1947 (Beyers papers).

40. Townsend interview.

41. *Crane,* February 6, 20, 1948; November 21, 1947 (Beyers papers); *Brook,* 1948 (Townsend papers).

42. Ellsberg interview; Dockstader interview; *Brook,* 1948 (CA).

43. Wright interview; *Crane,* April 30, 1948 (Beyers papers).

44. *Brook,* 1948 (CA); Bates interview.

45. Bates interview.

46. Ellsberg interview; Bates interview.

47. Ellsberg interview.

48. Seymour Lipkin interview; Carl Miller interview; Bates interview.

49. Ellsberg interview.

50. Lipkin interview; Richard French interview.

51. Ellsberg interview; Charlotte Miller interview.

52. Ellsberg interview.

53. Ellsberg interview; Lipkin interview; Charlotte Miller interview; Brenman-Gibson interview.

54. Davenport *Democrat and Leader,* July 5, 1946; Miller interview; *Detroit News,* July 5, 1946; *Rocky Mountain News,* July 5, 1946.

55. Charlotte Miller interview; Ellsberg interview.

56. Ellsberg interview; Charlotte Miller interview; Brenman-Gibson interview.

57. Ellsberg interview.

58. Ellsberg interview.

59. *Democrat and Leader,* July 5, 1946; Ellsberg interview.

60. *Highland Parker,* July 11, 1946.

61. *Highland Parker,* July 11, 1946; *Democrat and Leader,* July 5, 1946; Ellsberg interview.

62. *Democrat and Leader,* July 5, 1946; Ellsberg interview.

63. Ellsberg interview; *Democrat and Leader,* July 5, 1946.

64. *Democrat and Leader,* July 5, 1946; Ellsberg interview.

65. Ellsberg interviews; Andrew Hunt (Ellsberg pseudonym), "Social Call," *Harvard Advocate,* December 1949.

66. Ellsberg interview.

67. Ellsberg interview.

68. Mary Ellsberg interview; Miller interview.

69. Hunt (Ellsberg pseudonym), "Social Call."

70. *Time,* July 5, 1971; Ellsberg interview.

71. Lukas, "Month," 98; Ellsberg interview; Lukas interview; letters column in *New York Times Magazine,* January 16, 1972.

72. *Democrat and Leader,* July 6, 1946; *Rocky Mountain News,* July 9, 1946; *Highland Parker,* July 11, 1946; Ellsberg interview; Miller interview; Cummings interview.

73. Miller interview; Lukas, "Month," 102.

74. Miller interview.

75. Ellsberg interview; *Highland Parker*, July 11, 1946.
76. *Rocky Mountain News*, July 9, 1946; Ellsberg interview.
77. Ellsberg interview.
78. Dowd phone conversation; second CIA psychological profile of Ellsberg, November 1971 (WSPF, Fielding, box 3); Ellsberg interview.
79. Poe interview; Lauren Otis interview.
80. *Senior Scholastic*, November 8, 1973, 10–11; *Crane*, June 5, 1948 (Beyers papers); Otis interview; Dockstader interview.
81. Blauner, xi; Mollon, 60; Ellsberg interviews.
82. Ellsberg interviews; Lifton, *passim*.
83. Pincus, 152, 171–72; Blauner, xi.
84. Ellsberg interview; *Crane*, April 9, June 5, 1948; November 7, 1947 (Beyers papers); Ellsberg grade report at Cranbrook, June 1948; *DFP*, June 18, 1971.
85. *Crane*, 1943–48 (CA); Dockstader interview.
86. Charlotte Miller interview; Bob Miller interview.
87. Rich, 286; Stuart McCombs interview.

CHAPTER 3

1. Ellsberg interviews; McGinniss, 197.
2. Philip Cronin interview; Donald Blackmer interview; Carl Kaysen interview; Andrew Norman interview.
3. Hall interview; Ungar, 44.
4. Bob Miller interview; Ungar, 43; Charlotte Miller interview; Ellsberg interview; Lukas, "Month," 98.
5. Kirby Hall interview.
6. Cummings interviews.
7. Cummings interview; Isaacson interview; Cleveland interview; Townsend interview.
8. Cleveland interview; Blackmer interview.
9. Ellsberg interview; French interview. French looked up Ellsberg's midterm and final grades for me.
10. Cleveland interview.
11. Hall interview; Gooch, 122.
12. Hall interview.
13. Hall interview.
14. Rich, 286; Ellsberg, "The Long Wait," *Harvard Advocate*, September 1949; Ellsberg interview; *Crimson*, Freshmen Registration Issue, September 1949.
15. Ellsberg, "Long Wait."
16. Ellsberg, "Long Wait."
17. Hunt (Ellsberg pseudonym), "Social Call"; Ellsberg interview.
18. Hunt, "Social Call."
19. Ellsberg interview; *Crane*, October 29, 1948 (CA); Cummings interview; Hall interview.
20. Sam Popkin interview.
21. Hall interview; Ellsberg interview; Rich, 286.
22. Ellsberg interview; Cronin interview; Ned Sack interview.
23. Cronin interview; *Crimson*, 1950–52.

24. *Crimson*, May 18, 29, June 2, 20, October 13, 14, 16, 27, 1950; April 10, September 28, October 11, 1951; Rich, 286.
25. Ellsberg interview; Hall interview; William Simmons interview; Cronin interview.
26. *Crimson*, October 24, November 10, 1950; Cronin interview; John Sack interview; Norman interview; Hall interview.
27. Rich, 155.
28. *Crimson*, May 5, 1951; May 23, 1952. See also *Crimson*, December 9, 1950; September 27, October 6, December 3, 1951.
29. *Crimson*, February 28, March 1, 1951.
30. *Crimson*, March 12, 1952; Ellsberg interview with Kai Bird, 1993 (transcript in my possession); John Kenneth Galbraith interview.
31. *Crimson*, March 15, 1951.
32. Ellsberg interview; Philip Cronin interview; *Crimson*, October 25, 1951; Rich, 286.
33. Ellsberg interview.
34. *Crimson*, May 31, 1952.
35. Ellsberg interview.
36. Ellsberg interview; Hall interview.
37. Ellsberg, "The First Two Times We Met," 334; Ellsberg interview; Van de Velde, *passim*; Brenman-Gibson interview.
38. Ellsberg interview.
39. Cummings interview; Ellsberg interview; Cleveland interview.
40. Cleveland interview; Hall interview; Cronin interview.
41. Cummings interviews; Hall interview.
42. Norman interview; Sack interview; Hall interview; Ellsberg interview.
43. Cummings interviews; Hall interview.
44. Don Hall interview; Ellsberg interview; Kirby Hall interview.
45. Hall interview.
46. Don Hall interview; Kirby Hall interview; Ellsberg interview; Cummings interview.
47. Hall interview; Mary Marshall interview; Ellsberg interview.
48. Ellsberg interview; Hall interview; Cummings interview.
49. Cummings interview; Hall interview; Ellsberg interview.
50. Don Hall interview; Ellsberg interview; Kirby Hall interview.
51. Cummings interview; Ellsberg interview.
52. Cummings interview; Hall interview; Sheehan, "DE interview notebooks" (SP, box 64); Cleveland interview.
53. Hall interview; Ellsberg interview; Cummings interview.
54. Ellsberg interview.
55. Cummings interviews; Ellsberg interview.
56. Ellsberg interview; *Crimson*, November 18, 28, 30, December 13, 1950; Hall interview.
57. Cummings interviews.
58. Jerry Goodman interview; Ellsberg interview.
59. Marshall interview; Ellsberg interview.
60. Day, 9; Hall interview; Cummings interview.
61. Ellsberg interview; Cummings interviews; Hall interview.
62. Blackmer interview; Cleveland interview; Don Hall interview; Kirby Hall interview.
63. Kaysen interview; Wassily Leontief interview.
64. Cummings interviews.

65. Kaysen interview; Ellsberg interview with Bird, 1993; Ellsberg interview; Cleveland interview.

66. Kaplan, 63; *Crimson,* April 21, 1951; April 26, 1952; query of Harvard Archives; Ellsberg, "Theory of the Reluctant Duelist," *passim;* Hall interview; Young, 26–27; Jerry Goodman interview; Townsend interview; Ellsberg, "Classic and Current Notions of 'Measurable Utility,'" *passim;* Rich, 288.

67. Cleveland interview; Cummings interview; Ellsberg interview.

68. *NYT,* June 27, 1971; Ellsberg interview with Bird, 1993; Thomas Schelling interview; Hall interview; Kaysen interview.

69. Ellsberg interview with Bird, 1993; Ellsberg interview.

CHAPTER 4

1. Jerry Goodman interview; Cummings interview; Kirby Hall interview.

2. Rich, 288.

3. Don Hall interview; Kirby Hall interview.

4. Cummings interview; Rich, 288; Leontief interview.

5. Ellsberg's military service records (in my possession); Ellsberg interview with Bird, 1993; Grant, 38; Simmons interview; Kaysen interview; Leontief interview.

6. Don Hall interview; Kirby Hall interview; Blackmer interview.

7. Ellsberg speech at Cranbrook, October 1975 (tape in my possession); Ann Elms interview; Kaysen interview; Ellsberg interview.

8. Cummings interview; Goodman interview.

9. Ellsberg interview; Blackmer interview; Grant, 39.

10. Brenman-Gibson interview.

11. Ellsberg's military service records; Cleveland interview; Cummings interview; Ellsberg interview.

12. Cummings interview.

13. Ellsberg interview.

14. Ellsberg interview.

15. Ellsberg interview.

16. Ellsberg interview.

17. Ellsberg interview.

18. Ellsberg interviews.

19. Ellsberg interview.

20. Ellsberg interview.

21. Ellsberg's military service records; Ellsberg interview; *Reason,* June 1973, 5; McGinniss, 197; Richard Elms interview.

22. Elms interview.

23. Elms interview; Hall interview.

24. Elms interview; *Look,* October 5, 1971, 40; Sheehan, "Vann Book Outline" (SP, box 65); Sheehan, "DE Tape Summaries" (SP, box 64).

25. Ann Elms interview; Richard Elms interview.

26. Elms interview.

27. Ellsberg interview; Cummings interview; Elms interview; Peyton Robertson phone conversation.

28. Ellsberg interview; Goodman interview; Kaysen interview; Cleveland interview; Leontief interview.

29. Cummings interview; Kaysen interview; Marshall interview.

30. Ellsberg's military service records; Cummings interviews; Cleveland interview.

31. Cummings interview; Robertson phone conversation; *Life*, July 2, 1971, 31.

32. Ellsberg interviews; Ellsberg's military service records; Sheehan notes on Ellsberg conversation, November 17, 1986 (SP, box 63); Richard Elms interview.

33. Ellsberg interviews; *Time*, July 5, 1971, 10.

34. Ellsberg interview; Don Hall interview; Kirby Hall interview; Simmons interview.

35. Society of Fellows records (phone inquiry); Ellsberg interviews; Rich, 288; Kaysen interview.

36. Ellsberg interview.

37. Polly Cronin interview; Ellsberg interview; Ann Elms interview; Cummings interview.

38. Anonymous source.

39. Ellsberg interviews; Goodman interview.

40. Ellsberg to Adam Yarmolinsky, November 23, 1965 (Yarmolinsky, box 43, JFK); Ellsberg interview; Cummings interview.

41. *Look*, October 5, 1971, 33.

42. Rich, 288; Cummings interview.

43. Leontief interview; Cleveland interview.

44. Simmons interview; Cummings interview.

45. *Time*, July 5, 1971, 9; Cronin interview.

46. Schelling interview.

47. Schelling interview; Ellsberg, "The Psychology of Deterrence," May 7, 1958 (copy in my possession).

48. Schelling interview.

49. Schelling interview; Ellsberg, "The Theory and Practice of Blackmail," iii, 22n, 23n; note to author from unnamed scholar.

50. Schelling interview.

51. Jim Digby interview; Thomas Schelling interview; Andrew Schelling interview.

52. Ellsberg interview; Albert Wohlstetter phone conversation; Ellsberg's 1973 *RS* interview (reprint), 13, 25.

53. Townsend interview.

54. Wohlstetter phone conversation.

55. Ellsberg's 1973 *RS* interview (reprint), 2; Kolkowicz interview; Deirdre Henderson interview.

56. Richard Falk interview.

57. Ellsberg, "Theory and Practice of Blackmail," *passim*; Simmons interview; Rich, 288; Rich interview; Ellsberg interview; Ellsberg presentation of "Theory and Practice of Blackmail," June 28, 1960, David Elliot summary (copy in my possession).

58. Ellsberg, "Theory and Practice of Blackmail," 38; Salisbury, 53–54; Ellsberg "corrections" to Salisbury (in my possession); Popkin interview; Richard Barnet interview; Ellsberg presentation of "Theory and Practice of Blackmail," June 28, 1960.

59. Ellsberg interview; Schelling interview.

60. Kaysen interview; Schelling interview; Simmons interview; Ellsberg interview; Gus Shubert interviews.

61. Ellsberg interview; query of Harvard Archives.

62. Ellsberg interviews; Cummings interview.

63. Ellsberg interviews.

64. Hall interview; Cleveland interview; Cummings interview; anonymous source.

65. Cummings interview; Ellsberg interview.
66. Elms interview; Cronin interview.
67. Cummings interview.

CHAPTER 5

1. Simon Bourgin, "Brains for Hire—The Rand Corporation," September 1958 (copy in my possession); Ellsberg's RAND Employee History Report, April 1970 (Meiklejohn).
2. Bourgin interview.
3. Bourgin, "Brains for Hire"; Alexander George interview.
4. Kolkowicz interview; Kaplan, 86.
5. Kolkowicz interview; Norman Dalkey interview; Schelling interview.
6. David McGarvey interview; Schelling interview; Wohlstetter, 211.
7. Kolkowicz interview; Schelling interview; Ed Barlow phone conversation; Ewa Pauker interview.
8. Frank Trinkl interview.
9. McGarvey interview; Cummings interview; Digby interview; Ellsberg, "The Crude Analysis of Strategic Choices," 6n; Trinkl interview.
10. Ellsberg interviews.
11. George interview; Kolkowicz interview.
12. Arnold Kramish interview; Kolkowicz interview; Guy Pauker interview.
13. Dalkey interview; Shubert interview; Frank Eldridge interview.
14. Schelling interview; Richard Zeckhauser interview.
15. Ellsberg, "Risk, Ambiguity, and the Savage Axioms," *passim;* Zeckhauser interview; Dalkey interview. On Ellsberg's research, see also *Quarterly Journal of Economics,* November 1961, 670–94, May 1963, 327–42; *Econometrica,* July 1961, 454–55, April 1958, 325.
16. Trinkl interview; Dalkey interview.
17. Dalkey interview.
18. Zeckhauser interview.
19. Zeckhauser interview.
20. Kolkowicz interview; Guy Pauker interview; Ewa Pauker interview; Marshall interview; Fred Hoffman interview; Popkin interview.
21. Bourgin interview; McGarvey interview; Zeckhauser interview.
22. Paul Langer interview.
23. Pauker interview.
24. George interview; Kolkowicz interview; Guy Pauker interview.
25. Marshall interview; Schelling interview; Kolkowicz interview.
26. Shubert interviews; Kolkowicz interview.
27. Dalkey interview; Trinkl interview; anonymous source; Kolkowicz interview.
28. William Kaufmann interview; Howard Zinn interview; Popkin interview.
29. Dalkey interview.
30. George interview; Ed Brunner interview; Trinkl interview.
31. Digby interview; Konrad Kellen interview; Hoffman interview; Langer interview; Eldridge interview; Ellsberg interview.
32. Cummings interviews; Ellsberg interview.
33. Marshall interview.

34. Ellsberg interviews; Schelling interview; Ellsberg's 1973 *RS* interview (reprint), 39.

35. Shubert interview; Kolkowicz interview.

36. Cleveland interview.

37. Ellsberg's 1973 *RS* interview (reprint), 26, 27; Ellsberg interview.

38. Ellsberg's 1973 *RS* interview (reprint), 27, 28.

39. Digby interview; Kolkowicz interview; Shubert interview; Yarmolinsky interview; Sheehan notes on David Halberstam lunch, May 23, 1975 (SP, box 67).

40. Schelling interview.

41. Digby interview; Popkin interview.

42. Ellsberg interviews.

43. Todd Gitlin interview; Marty Garbus interview; discussion with Daniel and Patricia Ellsberg.

44. Discussion with Daniel and Patricia Ellsberg.

45. Robert McNamara to John F. Kennedy, October 6, 1961 (POF, box 77, JFK); Trinkl interview; Schelling interview; Ellsberg, "Strategic Objectives and Command Control Problems," August 12, 1960 (copy in my possession).

46. Marshall, Martin, and Rowen (eds.), vii; Kahn, x, xii, 20, 21, 71, 84, 86, 169, 403–7; Ellsberg, "Crude Analysis of Strategic Choices," 8n; Cummings interview; Schelling interview.

47. Kolkowicz interview.

48. Barnet interview; Elms interview.

49. Dalkey interview; Kolkowicz interview.

50. Ellsberg, "Strategic Objectives and Command Control Problems," *passim;* Ellsberg interview.

51. Ball, 37; Ellsberg, "Should Fixed, Primary Command Sites Be Hardened?: Comments on WSEG-50, Enclosure C," *passim* (copy in my possession)

52. Eldridge interview; Digby interview; Yarmolinsky interview.

53. Ellsberg preface to Daniel and Pope, 8; Kaplan, 275–76; Ellsberg interview with Bird, 1993; Kaysen interview. U.S. government documents on Eisenhower's authorization to certain military commanders to use nuclear weapons in specified emergency situations were declassified in 1998 through the efforts of the National Security Archive in Washington. The National Security Archive has those documents, many of which are heavily censored.

54. Kaysen interview.

55. *Aviation Week and Space Technology,* September 11, 18, December 4, 1961; Ellsberg, *Papers on the War,* 15n; Ellsberg interview with Bird, 1993; Kaysen interview; Eldridge interview.

56. Ellsberg, "The First Two Times We Met," 331–35; Andrew Schelling interview.

57. Kaplan, 276–77; Robert Lukeman interview; Ellsberg interview; Glenn Kent phone conversation.

58. Kaplan, 277; Ellsberg interview with Bird, 1993; Ellsberg interview; Lukeman interview; Kent phone conversation.

59. Ellsberg interview; Walt Rostow interview; Ellsberg interview with Bird, 1993.

60. Shubert interview.

61. Sagan, "SIOP-62," 23–24, 41; Kaysen interview; Rosenberg, "The Origins of Overkill," 9, 25; Rosenberg, "Reality and Responsibility," 37, 38; Lukeman interview; Kaufmann interview; Ellsberg interview with Bird, 1993.

62. Kaysen interview.

63. Kolkowicz interview.

64. Trinkl interview; Ellsberg interviews; Ellsberg radio interview on KPFA, Berkeley, August 9, 1999; Ellsberg preface to Daniel and Pope, 8, 12; various published Ellsberg interviews; Ellsberg "corrections" to Herken (in my possession); Herken, 141–43.

65. Marshall interview; McGeorge Bundy to Ted Sorensen, March 13, 1961 (NSF, box 270–73, JFK); Shubert interview.

66. Ellsberg interview with Terkel, 1980; *Catholic Agitator*, June 1995, 4; Ellsberg radio interview on KQED, August 25, 1995; Ellsberg interview.

67. Sagan, "SIOP-62," 22–24, 35–36, 44, 50; Rosenberg, "Origins of Overkill," 6, 61, 64–65, 67; Sagan, "Change and Continuity in U.S. Nuclear Strategy," 290; Kaysen interview; Rostow interview.

68. McNamara to Secretaries of Military Departments et al., March 1, 1961 (POF, box 77, JFK); Ellsberg interviews; Kaplan, 278–79.

69. Ball, 190, 190n; Kaplan, 279, 416n; Trinkl interview.

70. Ellsberg interviews.

71. Ball, 189–91; Lukeman interview; Rowen, 230; Kaysen interview; Kaufmann interview.

72. Trinkl interview; Rowen, 227, 230.

73. Ellsberg interview; Yarmolinsky interview; Trinkl interview.

74. Ellsberg interview; Rostow letter to author.

75. Elms interview; Marshall interview; Ellsberg interview.

76. Butler essay, undated (Butler papers).

77. Henderson interview.

78. Henderson interview.

79. Halberstam, *Best and Brightest*, 31; Henderson interview.

80. Cummings interviews; McGarvey interview; Ellsberg interview.

81. Schelling interview.

82. Ellsberg's 1973 *RS* interview (reprint), 24; Digby interview; Kolkowicz interview.

83. Yarmolinsky interview; Robert Komer interview.

84. Kaufmann interview; Rich, 290; Cleveland interview.

85. Cleveland interview.

86. Digby interview; Ellsberg interviews.

87. Langer interview; Shubert interview; Hans Heymann interview; Richard Best interview; Butler interview; George interview.

88. George interview.

89. Ellsberg interviews; Hoffman interview.

90. Ellsberg's Harvard 15th anniversary report, 1967 (Meiklejohn); Kolkowicz interview.

91. Ellsberg interview; Rostow interview; Kaufmann interview.

92. Kaufmann interview; Beschloss, 527.

93. George interview.

94. Roswell Gilpatric letter to author; copy of Gilpatric speech (in my possession); Gilpatric oral history (JFK); Ellsberg interviews; Beschloss, 331–32, 351, 353, 370.

95. Shapley, 142–45; Yarmolinsky oral history (JFK); Kaufmann interview; Ellsberg interviews; Yarmolinsky interview.

96. Ellsberg Pentagon Papers trial testimony, vol. 109, 19,486–87 (Butler papers); Ellsberg interview; Kaufmann, 300–313.

97. Ellsberg interview; Vincent Davis interview; Davis to John Vann, February 28, 1966 (Davis papers); Ellsberg to Fred Hoffman, May 30, 1966 (SP, box 27).

98. Digby interview; Pauker interview.

99. Kaufmann interview; Kolkowicz interview; Shubert interview.

100. Shubert interview; McGarvey interview; Hoffman interview.

101. Shubert interview; Eldridge interview; Kaufmann interview.

102. Ellsberg, "Crude Analysis of Strategic Choices," "Vagueness and Decision," and "Should Fixed, Primary Command Sites Be Hardened?" Ellsberg's second "P" was published as a "reply" in the *Quarterly Journal of Economics* (May 1963, 336–42).

103. Ellsberg, "Strategic Objectives and Command Control Problems"; Kaufmann interview; Dalkey interview.

104. Ellsberg, "Vagueness and Decision," 2n; Pauker interview; Ellsberg interview.

105. Ellsberg interviews.

106. Dalkey interview; Popkin interview. Though the literature on writer's block is not well developed, the inhibiting effects of perfectionism, grandiosity, and narcissism are considered in Kantor.

107. Schelling interview; Zinn interview.

108. Ellsberg interview.

109. McGarvey interview; Shubert interview; Marshall interview.

110. Ellsberg to Yarmolinsky, November 29, 1965 (Yarmolinsky, box 43, JFK).

111. Shubert interview.

CHAPTER 6

1. Ellsberg interview.

2. Newland, 240; Ellsberg interview; Sallie Goodman interview. Constance Newland was Moss's pseudonym.

3. Newland, 51, 133.

4. Sallie Goodman interview; Jerry Goodman interview.

5. Sallie Goodman interview; Harris, 183, 193.

6. Sallie Goodman interview; Jerry Goodman interview.

7. Ellsberg interview.

8. Cummings interview.

9. Phone conversation with Thelma Moss's daughter; Ellsberg interview.

10. Ellsberg interview; McGlothlin, 13; Shubert interview; Guy Pauker interview; Kramish interview.

11. LA FBI to FBI Director, July 27, 1971 (WSPF, Fielding, box 18); McGlothlin, 4–5; FBI document on contents of Howard Hunt's safe, May 2, 1973 (WSPF, Fielding, box 18).

12. Ellsberg interview; Goodman interview.

13. Ellsberg interviews; Cummings interview; FBI statement of W. Raymond Wannall, May 28, 1974 (WSPF, Fielding, box 18).

14. Ellsberg interviews.

15. Ellsberg interview.

16. Ellsberg interview.

17. Cummings interview; Ellsberg interview.

18. Cleveland interview.

19. Ellsberg interviews; Cummings interview.

20. Cummings interview.

21. Ellsberg interviews.

22. Ellsberg interview.

23. Ellsberg interview; Brenman-Gibson interview; discussion with Daniel and Patricia Ellsberg.

24. Kolkowicz interview.

25. Marshall interviews; Cummings interview; Robert Ellsberg interview.

26. Kolkowicz interview; Marshall interview; Ellsberg interview.

27. Ellsberg interviews; discussion with Daniel and Patricia Ellsberg.

28. Cummings interview; Mary Marshall interviews.

29. Ellsberg interview; Cummings interview.

30. Marshall interview; Kolkowicz interview; Brenman-Gibson interviews; Cummings interview; Hall interview.

31. Andrew Marshall interview; Mary Marshall interview; Yarmolinsky interview; anonymous source; Schelling interview.

32. Don Hall interview; Kirby Hall interview; Heymann interview; Bourgin interview.

33. Kolkowicz interview; Ellsberg interview.

34. Kolkowicz interview; Ellsberg interview; Kaufmann interview; Zeckhauser interview.

35. Andrew Marshall interview; Guy Pauker interview; Heymann interview; Butler interview.

36. Judy Rohloff conversations; Kellen interview; Hall interview; Digby interview.

37. Kolkowicz interview; Ellsberg interview.

38. Mary Marshall interviews.

39. Yvonne Ekman testimony in Ellsberg's trial, vol. 74, 12,858–59 (Butler papers); Goodman interview; Pentagon Papers trial jury discussion, May 20, 1973 (transcript).

40. Kolkowicz interview; Henderson interview; Kaufmann interview.

41. Ellsberg interview; Zeckhauser interview; anonymous source; Cleveland interview.

42. Hall interview; Marshall interviews.

43. Cummings interviews; Shubert interview; Hall interview; Ellsberg interview; Marshall interview.

44. Cummings interviews; Ellsberg interview.

45. Ellsberg interview.

46. Ellsberg interview; Yarmolinsky interview; Yarmolinsky oral history (JFK).

47. Ellsberg interviews.

48. Yarmolinsky interview.

49. Ellsberg interview.

50. Ellsberg interview; Cummings interviews.

51. Marshall interview; Robert Ellsberg interview.

52. Farrell, 92; Schelling interview.

53. Schelling interview.

54. Cummings interview.

55. Cummings interview.

56. Ellsberg interviews; Cummings interviews; Brenman-Gibson interview; Cleveland interview.

57. Ellsberg interview; McGinniss, 197; Cummings interview.

58. Cummings interviews; Don Hall interview.

59. Kirby Hall interview.

60. Ellsberg interview.

61. Ellsberg interview; Cummings interview.

62. Cummings interview.
63. Ellsberg interview; McGarvey interview.
64. Marshall interview; Ellsberg interviews.
65. Shubert interview; Ellsberg interview.
66. Hall interview.
67. Shubert interview; George interview; Barry Steiner phone conversation; Kolkowicz interview; Helmut Sonnenfeldt interview.
68. Marshall interview; FBI document on Carol Ellsberg interview, July 13, 1971 (WSPF, Fielding, box 18).
69. Marshall interview; Cummings interview.
70. Ellsberg interview.
71. Cummings interview.
72. Mary Marshall interview; Robert Ellsberg interview; Mary Ellsberg interview.
73. Brenman-Gibson interview; Robert Ellsberg interview; Mary Ellsberg interview.
74. Divorce records of Daniel and Carol Ellsberg (Los Angeles County Records Center); Cummings interview; Ellsberg interview.
75. Ellsberg interview.

CHAPTER 7

1. Schelling interview.
2. Rostow interview.
3. Rostow interview; Ellsberg, *Papers*, 15n; Ellsberg's trial testimony, vol. 109, 19,494, 19,497 (Butler papers); Ellsberg's 1973 *RS* interview (reprint), 13.
4. Rostow interview.
5. Ellsberg's trial testimony, vol. 109, 19,494–95, 19,497 (Butler papers); George interview; Hersh, 386n; Rostow interview.
6. Sonnenfeldt interview; Fred Iklé interview.
7. Schelling interview; anonymous source; Fred Haynes interview; Ellsberg interview; Ellsberg interview with Suzan Ruth Travis-Cline, 1993 (transcript in my possession).
8. Davis interview.
9. Hoffman interview; Haynes interview; Ellsberg interview.
10. William Bundy interview; anonymous source; Harry Harris interview; Townsend Hoopes interview; Morton Halperin interview.
11. Davis interview; second CIA psychological profile of Ellsberg, November 1971 (WSPF, Fielding, box 3); Ellsberg interview with Travis-Cline, 1993.
12. Anonymous source; Haynes interview.
13. Ellsberg interview; Ellsberg's RAND Employee History Report, April 1970, and RAND Security Termination Statement, October 1964 (Meiklejohn).
14. Ellsberg's trial testimony, vol. 109, 19,520 (Butler papers); Best interview; *The Humanist*, January/February 1973, 20; Ellsberg, *Papers*, 220.
15. Ellsberg preface to Daniel and Pope, 8; Ellsberg's Harvard 15th anniversary report (Meiklejohn); Kolkowicz interview; Ellsberg interview with Travis-Cline, 1993.
16. Harris interview; Davis interview.
17. Ellsberg interview with Travis-Cline, 1993; Ellsberg interview; anonymous source.
18. Ellsberg's trial testimony, vol. 109, 19,500 (Butler papers); Alvin Friedman interview.

19. Ellsberg's trial testimony, vol. 109, 19,509 (Butler papers); Ellsberg, *Papers*, 90; Bundy interview.

20. Ellsberg's trial testimony, vol. 109, 19,500–501 (Butler papers); Harris interview; affidavit for Bekins search warrant, September 1971 (WSPF, Fielding, box 20).

21. Ellsberg's trial testimony, vol. 109, 19,502–3 (Butler papers); Friedman interview.

22. *USA Today*, April 11, 1997; George McGovern interview.

23. James Thomson interview.

24. Ellsberg, *Papers*, 87–88; Peter Solbert interview.

25. Solbert interview.

26. Anonymous source; Harris interview; Schelling interview.

27. Friedman interview.

28. Harris interview; *LAT*, April 19, 1974; Ellsberg briefing to RAND trustees, November 11, 1967 (transcript); *WP*, June 29, 1971.

29. Pauker interview.

30. Ellsberg, *Papers*, 297; transcript of Ellsberg speech at Antioch College, April 1965 (copy in my possession); Ellsberg speech draft, undated, spring 1965 (SP, box 65).

31. Simmons interview; Hall interview.

32. Sallie Goodman interview; Jerry Goodman interview; Leontief interview.

33. J. Anthony Lukas interview; Shubert interview.

34. Ellsberg interview with Travis-Cline, 1993; Ellsberg, *Papers*, 19–20, 90, 303; Vince Davis to John Vann, July 15, 1965 (SP, box 57); Bundy interview; Ellsberg speech draft, undated, spring 1965 (SP, box 65).

35. Rich, 292; Stanley Hoffmann interview.

36. Transcript of Ellsberg speech at Antioch College, April 1965; Ellsberg interview.

37. Ellsberg "corrections" to Herken; Hoffmann interview.

38. Hoffmann interview; Ellsberg "corrections" to Herken.

39. Hoffmann interview.

40. Anonymous source; Haynes interview.

41. Davis interview; Davis to Vann, September 8, 1965; Davis to Paul Schratz, July 24, 1965 (prior two items in Davis papers).

42. Davis interview; Cummings interview; Brenman-Gibson interview; Don Hall interview; Butler interview.

43. Anonymous source; Harris interview; Haynes interview.

44. Haynes interview; Harris interview.

45. Anonymous source; Lowell Hukill interview.

46. Harris interview; Hoopes interview.

47. Harris interview; anonymous source.

48. McGinniss, 97; Ellsberg interview.

49. Harris interview; anonymous sources; Haynes interview; Davis interview.

50. Ellsberg's 1973 *RS* interview (reprint), 27; Ellsberg interview; anonymous source.

51. Davis to Vann, September 8, 1965; Vann to Davis, September 14, 1965 (prior two items in Davis papers); Sheehan notes on Gene Vann interview (SP, box 57).

52. Davis interview.

53. Patrick Sullivan interview.

54. Schelling interview. Schelling's anonymous quote is: "He'd take you aside at every opportunity and tell you how he'd suddenly discovered that it was nice on

the inside of a woman's legs, as though he was the first person to find that out. Of course, that's typical of Dan. Ever since I've known him, he's had this almost evangelistic need to communicate to you the truth he's just discovered" (Lukas, "Month," 104).

55. Anonymous source.

56. Hall interview; Hoffman interview.

57. Zeckhauser interview.

58. Guy Pauker interview; Sonnenfeldt interview; Haynes interview.

59. Marlene Twaddell interview; John Simon interview.

60. Patricia Ellsberg interview; *NYT*, August 20, 1972, February 7, 1982 (SP, box 64); *Time*, November 5, 1951, December 12, 1955; *Reader's Digest*, January 1955; Nixon and Richard Moore conversation excerpt, April 19, 1973 (WSPF, Fielding, box 21).

61. *Reader's Digest*, January 1955; Patricia Ellsberg interview; *Time*, December 12, 1955; Twaddell interview.

62. *Time*, December 12, 1955; Patricia Ellsberg interview.

63. Simon interview; *Time*, December 12, 1955.

64. Patricia Ellsberg interview; *Time*, December 12, 1955.

65. Patricia Ellsberg interview.

66. Patricia Ellsberg interview; *Time*, December 12, 1955.

67. Anonymous source; Simon interview; Greg Wierzynski interview.

68. Patricia Ellsberg interview; *Time*, December 12, 1955; Simon interview; Twaddell interview.

69. Patricia Ellsberg interview.

70. Patricia Ellsberg interview; *WIN*, November 1, 1972, 11; Twaddell interview; anonymous source.

71. Ted Solotaroff interview; Falk interview; Simon interview.

72. Patricia Ellsberg interview; Garbus interview; Twaddell interview; Simon interview.

73. Simon interview.

74. Simon interview; Twaddell interview.

75. Simon interview.

76. Patricia Ellsberg interview; Simon interview.

77. Patricia Ellsberg interview.

78. Patricia Ellsberg interview.

79. Patricia Ellsberg interview; Daniel Ellsberg interview.

80. Patricia Ellsberg interview; Garbus interview; transcript of Ellsberg speech at Antioch College, April 1965.

81. Twaddell interview; anonymous source; Simon interview; Patricia Ellsberg interview; Garbus interview.

82. Solotaroff interview; Russo interview; Sheehan notes on Halberstam lunch, May 23, 1975 (SP, box 67).

83. Harris interview; anonymous source.

84. Harris interview; Schelling interview; Halperin interview.

85. Sheehan, *Bright*, 593; Ellsberg interview.

86. Harris interview; anonymous source.

87. Harris interview; anonymous source; Haynes interview.

88. Davis interview; Davis to Ellsberg, July 23, 1965; Davis to Schratz, July 24, 1965; Davis to Earl Rectanus, June 1, 1972 (prior three items in Davis papers).

89. Ellsberg interview with Travis-Cline, 1993.

90. Harris interview; anonymous source.

91. Davis interview; Davis to Vann, September 8, 1965 (Davis papers).

92. Ellsberg briefing to RAND trustees, November 11, 1967 (transcript); Sheehan notes on Ellsberg interviews, no date (SP, box 121).

93. Sheehan, "DE Interview Notebooks" (SP, box 64); *Look*, October 5, 1971, 33; Pauker interview; Davis interview.

94. Davis to Vann, July 15, 1965 (Davis papers); Davis interview.

95. Davis interview.

96. Davis interview; Davis to Vann, July 15, 1965 (Davis papers); Davis to Bernard Fall, July 16, 1965; Davis to Vann, July 26, 1965 (prior two items in SP, box 26).

97. *Time*, July 5, 1971, 10; Trinkl interview; Pauker interview; Grant, 258–59; Shubert interview; Halperin interview; Pratt, 210n; Pratt conversation; Bernard Yoh interview; Lou Conein interview.

98. *Look*, October 5, 1971, 33; Ellsberg, *Papers*, 247; Ellsberg radio interview, KQED, San Francisco, August 25, 1995.

99. Ellsberg, *Papers*, 140; Ellsberg interview with Peter Davis, 1972 (SP, box 64); Henderson interview.

100. Elms interview; Zeckhauser interview.

CHAPTER 8

1. Conein interview; Hukill interview; *WP*, January 1973 (Indochina Archive); *WP*, September 29, 1968.

2. Edward Lansdale to Ambassador Lodge and U.S. Mission Council Members, November 3, 1966 (LP, box 58); Lansdale oral history (LBJ); Lansdale to Lodge, May 27, 1966 (NSF, VCF, box 32, LBJ); Lansdale to SLO Staff, June 4, 1966 (LP, box 55).

3. Leepson, 84; Komer to Lyndon Johnson, April 19, 1966, special annex (Komer, boxes 1, 2, LBJ); Joe Baker interview; Lansdale to Michael Deutch and Rufus Phillips, April 8, 1966; Lansdale to Deutch, June 8, 1966 (prior two items in LP, box 53).

4. Ellsberg interview with Peter Davis, 1972 (SP, box 64); Ellsberg to Yarmolinsky, November 23, 1965 (Yarmolinsky, box 43, JFK); Hukill interview.

5. Ellsberg, "Vietnam Diary," *passim*; Yarmolinsky to Ellsberg, November 10, 1965; Ellsberg to Yarmolinsky, November 29, 1965 (prior two items in Yarmolinsky, box 43, JFK); Ellsberg to Meg Greenfield, February 15, 1966; Ellsberg to Mrs. Jerry Rose, February 10, 1966 (prior two items in LP, box 55); Ellsberg interview.

6. Ellsberg, "Vietnam Diary," 25–26; Langer interview.

7. Ellsberg, "Vietnam Diary," 27; Ellsberg, "Notes on an insecure city," September 23, 1965 (Yarmolinsky, box 43, JFK); Lansdale to "Old Team," July 1, 1971 (LP, box 59). John Sack, Ellsberg's former colleague on the *Harvard Crimson* who spent time in Vietnam, recalls similar taxi warnings. "You get to Vietnam, and the sergeants have all told you, 'Anyone can kill you, but watch out: Roll the windows up in your taxi or they'll throw a hand grenade in.' I got to Vietnam, and I got in my taxi . . . it's a hundred and something [degrees], and I rolled the windows up, and the taxi driver looked at me and rolled the windows down. I thought, 'Ah ha, we have a VC taxi driver, he wants me to be killed with a grenade.' And I rolled the windows up. And then you get used to Saigon, and

then you start going around with the windows rolled down. . . . It always seems that the dangerous thing is something the next guy is doing" (Sack interview).

8. Ellsberg, "Vietnam Diary," 26; Ellsberg, "Notes on an insecure city," September 23, 1965 (Yarmolinsky, box 43, JFK).

9. Ellsberg, "Vietnam Diary," 26, 27; Ellsberg, *Papers*, 138.

10. Kolkowicz interview.

11. Ellsberg to Greenfield, January 3, 1966 (Yarmolinsky, box 43, JFK); Ellsberg to Greenfield, February 15, 1966; Ellsberg to Yarmolinsky, February 15, 1966 (prior two items in LP, box 55).

12. Hukill interview.

13. Lansdale to "Uncle Peter" Richards, July 23, 1971 (Currey papers); Phillips interview; Lansdale to Phillips, October 11, 1965 (LP, box 54); Joe Redick interview.

14. Phillips interview; Komer interview.

15. Currey, 297; Executive Officer to All Team Members, no date; Deutch to "Boss," December 5, 1965 (prior two items in LP, box 50); Deutch to Lansdale, January 6, 1966 (LP, box 53).

16. Ellsberg to Lansdale team, March 9, 1966 (LP, box 55).

17. Sam Karrick to Earl Churchill, October 13, 1966 (LP, box 50); Redick interview; John Sack interview; Baker interview; Barry Zorthian interview; Currey, 296; Sheehan document on Frank Scotton conversation, June 13, 1977 (SP, box 63).

18. Yoh interview and phone conversation.

19. Conein interview; John Vann to Ellsberg, July 17, 1967 (SP, box 27); Baker interview.

20. Sack interview; Tran Ngoc Chau interview; *San Francisco Focus*, March 1991, 88; Hunt and Conein conversation, no date (WSPF, Fielding, accordion file after box 3); Grant, 268; Conein interview.

21. Sack interview.

22. Hukill interview.

23. Baker interview; Phillips interview.

24. Hukill interview; Redick interview; anonymous source.

25. Yoh interview.

26. Hukill interview; Yoh interview; Deutch to Lansdale, March 31, 1966 (LP, box 53); document listing salaries and benefits of Lansdale team members, July 29, 1966 (LP, box 50).

27. Baker interview; Hukill interview.

28. Redick interview; Baker interview; Phillips interview.

29. Baker interview; Redick interview; Ellsberg interview; Ellsberg, "U.S. Policy and the Politics of Others," July 1969 (LP, box 22); Lansdale to "Old Team," July 1, 1971 (LP, box 59); Currey, 328; Lansdale memo for the record, April 21, 1966 (LP, box 55); Phillips interview; Hukill interview.

30. Shubert to Lansdale, April 4, 1966 (LP, box 51); Shubert interview.

31. Baker interview; Ellsberg's trial testimony, vol. 109, 19,519, 19,520 (Butler papers).

32. Lansdale to Bundy and Unger, September 17, 1965 (LP, box 53); Sheehan, *Bright*, 512; Lansdale to Phillips, October 11, 1965 (LP, box 54); Ellsberg, "GVN Concepts of Rural Construction," January 6, February 21, 1966 (LP, box 55); various Lansdale memos, 1966 (LP, box 51); Currey, 296; Karrick to Deutch, August 2, 1966 (LP, box 56); Baker interview; Tom Wicker interview; Wicker, 8, 161; Don Oberdorfer interview.

33. Thomson interview; Douglas Pike interview.

34. Pike interview; Ellsberg, "GVN Concepts of Rural Construction," February 21, 1966 (LP, box 55); Grant, 287–88; Ellsberg memo for the record, October 26, 1965 (LP, box 55); *Harper's*, February 1972, 57–58.

35. Russo interview; Russo, 51. Marcus Raskin, who came to know Ellsberg later, says, "In the meetings that I've been with him, there is not one meeting where it seems to me he is not taking every conceivable note of what everybody is saying" (Raskin interview).

36. Russo interview.

37. Lansdale to Baker, December 11, 1965 (LP, box 55); Ellsberg's trial testimony, vol. 109, 19,565–68 (Butler papers).

38. Rostow interview; Ellsberg to Rostow, June 8, 1966 (SP, box 27); Hukill interview; Ellsberg's trial testimony, vol. 109, 19,527 (Butler papers).

39. Ellsberg memos for the record, September, October, November 1965 (LP, box 55); Ellsberg, "Visit to an Insecure Province," fall 1965 (Yarmolinsky, box 49, JFK); Ellsberg, "The Day Loc Tien was Pacified," *passim*; Lansdale to Ellsberg, September 15, 1972 (LP, box 3).

40. Ellsberg's trial testimony, vol. 109, 19,530, 19,582–84 (Butler papers); Ellsberg to Lansdale, November 26, 1965 (LP, box 55); Ellsberg letters to McNamara, Rostow and McNaughton, June 8, 1966 (SP, box 27).

41. Sheehan, *Bright*, 593; Davis to Vann, July 15, 1965; Davis to Ellsberg, July 31, 1965 (prior two items in Davis papers); Davis interview; Halberstam interview.

42. Prochnau, 279; Sheehan, *Bright*, 605.

43. Mary Jane Vann interview; Harris interview; Vann to Lt. Gen. Le Nguyen Khang, February 7, 1967 (Komer, boxes 3, 4, LBJ); Tom Oliphant interview.

44. Mary Jane Vann interview.

45. Ellsberg, "Visit to an Insecure Province," part III: "Vann Theses," fall 1965 (Yarmolinsky, box 49, JFK); Mary Jane Vann interview; Sheehan, *Bright*, 512, 527, 542.

46. Vann to Schratz, September 1965 (SP, box 26); Vann to Davis, September 5, 1965 (Davis papers).

47. Ellsberg interview; Shubert interview; Sheehan, "DE Interview Notebooks," "Vann Book Outline" (SP, boxes 64, 65); Popkin interview.

48. Sheehan, "Vann Book Outline" (SP, box 65); Vann to Davis, June 10, 1967 (Davis papers); Halberstam interview.

49. Sheehan, *Bright*, 482, 596; Sheehan notes on Ellsberg interviews, no date (SP, box 121).

50. Ellsberg, "Visit to an Insecure Province," fall 1965 (Yarmolinsky, box 49, JFK); Ellsberg, *Papers*, 143–55; draft portions of "Visit to an Insecure Province" (SP, box 64); Vann to Davis, February 13, 1966 (SP, box 26); Stephen Enke to Lansdale, August 8, 1966 (LP, box 52); Albert Williams interview.

51. Ellsberg, "Visit to an Insecure Province," fall 1965 (Yarmolinsky, box 49, JFK).

52. Ellsberg, "Visit to an Insecure Province," fall 1965 (Yarmolinsky, box 49, JFK).

53. Ellsberg, "Visit to an Insecure Province," fall 1965 (Yarmolinsky, box 49, JFK).

54. Ellsberg interview with Peter Davis, 1972; Sheehan notes on Ellsberg interview, no date (prior two items in SP, box 64); Komer interview; Sheehan, *Bright*, 594–96.

55. Ellsberg interview with Peter Davis, 1972; Sheehan notes on Ellsberg interview, no date (prior two items in SP, box 64).

56. Frances FitzGerald interview; Sheehan notes on Jill Krementz conversation, January 24, 1976 (SP, box 65).

57. Redick interview; Sack interview; FitzGerald interview; Deutch to Lansdale, March 31, 1966 (LP, box 53).
58. FitzGerald interview.
59. Ellsberg interview with Peter Davis, 1972; Sheehan notes on Ellsberg interview, no date (prior two items in SP, box 64); Hukill interview.
60. Ellsberg, *Papers*, 17; Sheehan notes on Ellsberg interviews, no dates (SP, box 64); *Look*, October 5, 1971, 33; Conein interview.
61. Popkin interview; Haynes interview.
62. Sheehan notes on Ellsberg interviews, no dates; Sheehan note to himself (prior two items in SP, box 64); Jess Vann interview; Lansdale to "Uncle Peter," July 23, 1971 (Currey papers); Lansdale to Baker, December 11, 1965 (LP, box 55).
63. *Look*, October 5, 1971, 33; Redick interview; Grant, 268; Yoh interview; Hukill interview; Baker interview.
64. Arnaud de Borchgrave interview; *Time*, July 5, 1971, 9; *BG*, June 29, 1971; Sheehan, "Vann Book Outline" (SP, box 65); Ellsberg's trial testimony, vol. 109, 19,571 (Butler papers).
65. Ellsberg's trial testimony, vol. 109, 19,570–76 (Butler papers); *Look*, October 5, 1971, 33–34; Ellsberg, *Papers*, 250; John Sack interview.
66. *Look*, October 5, 1971, 34; Sheehan notes on Ellsberg interviews, no dates (SP, box 121).
67. *RS*, November 5-December 10, 1987, 224; Ellsberg interview with Peter Davis, 1972 (SP, box 64); *San Francisco Focus*, March 1991, 88.
68. *Look*, October 5, 1971, 34; Ellsberg interview with Peter Davis, 1972 (SP, box 64); second CIA psychological profile of Ellsberg, November 1971 (WSPF, Fielding, box 3).
69. Sack interview.
70. Anonymous source.
71. Ellsberg interview with Peter Davis, 1972; Sheehan, "DE Interview Notebooks" (prior two items in SP, box 64); *San Francisco Focus*, March 1991, 81.
72. Shubert interview and phone conversation; Elms interview.
73. Yoh interview; George Tanham interview; John Clark Pratt conversation; Conein interview; Komer interview; Ellsberg "corrections" to Salisbury.
74. Zeckhauser interview; Hall interview; Schelling interview.
75. Marshall interview; Cummings interviews; Ellsberg to Fred Hoffman, May 30, 1966 (SP, box 27); Mary Jane Vann interview; FBI document on Carol Ellsberg interview, June 25, 1971 (WSPF, Fielding, box 18).
76. Mary Ellsberg interview; Robert Ellsberg interview.
77. Lansdale to "Old Team," July 1, 1971 (Currey papers).
78. Ellsberg interview with Peter Davis, 1972 (SP, box 64); Ellsberg "corrections" to Salisbury; *Look*, October 5, 1971, 33–34; Sheehan notes on Ellsberg interviews, no dates (SP, box 121); Strober and Strober, 203.
79. Beneke interview.
80. *NYT*, June 27, 1971; Ellsberg, "GVN Concepts of Rural Construction," February 21, 1966 (LP, box 55); Ellsberg, *Papers*, 169; Rich, 293; Komer interview; Hukill interview.
81. Ellsberg memo for the record, October 26, 1965 (LP, box 55).
82. Ellsberg memo for the record, September 29, 1965; Lansdale to Ambassador, September 29, 1965 (prior two items in LP, box 55). Ellsberg's authorship of the Lansdale memo is indicated at the bottom of it.

83. Chau interview and phone conversation; Grant, 35.

84. Deutch to Baker, October 11, 1965; Ellsberg to Porter through Lansdale, March 10, 1966; Ellsberg, "GVN Concepts of Rural Construction," January 6, February 21, 1966 (prior four items in LP, box 55); Ellsberg to Lansdale and Karrick, March 30, 1966; Ellsberg memo, 1966, undated (prior two items in SP, box 65).

85. Ellsberg memos for the record, November 1965 (two), February 28, 1966 (LP, box 55); Ellsberg to Porter, March 31, 1966 (Yarmolinsky, box 49, JFK).

86. Ellsberg memo for the record, November 23, 1965 (LP, box 55).

87. Ellsberg memos of conversations with Vann and Ted Serong, September 20, 28, 1965 (LP, box 55); Ellsberg memos for the record, November 2, 1965; 1966, no date; Ellsberg to Lansdale and Karrick, March 30, 1966 (prior three items in SP, boxes 64, 65); Ellsberg to Porter, March 31, 1966 (Yarmolinsky, box 49, JFK).

88. Sheehan, "Vann Book Outline"; Ellsberg memo, October 19, 1966 (prior three items in SP, box 65); Ellsberg, *Papers*, 168–69.

89. Harris interview; Pike interview.

90. Ellsberg, *Papers*, 156–70, 300–301; *Pentagon Papers*, vol. 2, 583–87; Komer interview; Ellsberg to Komer, June 9, 1966 (SP, box 27); Karrick to Lansdale, July 1, 1966 (LP, box 56); Grant, 279; Ellsberg attachment to Roles and Missions study, September 8, 1966 (LP, box 56); Ellsberg to Komer, September 10, 22, 1966 (Komer, boxes 3, 4, LBJ).

91. Komer interview; Komer to Porter, April 12, 1966 (Komer, boxes 3, 4, LBJ).

92. Komer interview; Deutch to Komer, September 15, 1966 (Komer, boxes 3, 4, LBJ).

93. Yarmolinsky interview; Ellsberg letters to Rostow, McNaughton, Hoffman, Mc-Namara, and Komer, May and June 1966 (SP, box 27); Ellsberg letters to Komer and Enthoven, September and December 1966 (Komer, boxes 3, 4, LBJ); Ellsberg papers, 1965–67 (Yarmolinsky, box 49, JFK; Richard Elms papers).

94. Ellsberg memo, September 9, 1966 (LP, box 51); Ellsberg to Komer, September 10, 22, 1966 (Komer, boxes 3, 4, LBJ); Rich, 293; Lansdale to Choate, October 14, 1966 (LP, box 53).

95. Sheehan, *Bright*, 681–82; Ellsberg interview with Travis-Cline, 1993; Halberstam, *Best*, 266–67.

96. Ellsberg interview with Travis-Cline, 1993; McNamara to Johnson, October 14, 1966 (Warnke, box 3, LBJ); Ellsberg, *Papers*, 157; Ellsberg's trial testimony, vol. 109, 19,590 (Butler papers).

97. Karrick to "Boss and Joe," October 30, 1966 (LP, box 53).

98. Lansdale memo for the record, November 29, 1966 (LP, box 56); Ellsberg, "The Day Loc Tien was Pacified," iii; Komer interview; Ellsberg's trial testimony, vol. 109, 19,529, 19,533–34 (Butler papers); Porter to Lodge, April 26, 1966 (LP, box 58); Porter to Komer, May 6, 1966 (Komer, boxes 3, 4, LBJ); Karrick to Lansdale, July 1, 1966 (LP, box 56); Redick interview; Sheehan, *Bright*, 612, 615; Zorthian interview; Ellsberg's Harvard 15th anniversary report (Meiklejohn); Ellsberg to Enthoven, December 19, 1966 (Komer, boxes 3, 4, LBJ).

99. Komer interview.

100. Ellsberg interview with Peter Davis, 1972 (SP, box 64).

101. Patricia Ellsberg interview.

102. Patricia Ellsberg interview.

103. Patricia Ellsberg interview.

104. Patricia Ellsberg interview.

105. Patricia Ellsberg interview; FitzGerald interview; FitzGerald, *passim;* Twaddell interview; *Atlantic,* February 1967, 30.

106. Patricia Ellsberg interview; Daniel Ellsberg interview on "Late Night Line-up," 1971 (SP, box 161); *Look,* October 5, 1971, 40.

107. McGinniss, 197; Ellsberg "corrections" to Salisbury; Sheehan, "Vann Book Outline" (SP, box 65); Patricia Ellsberg interview.

108. Ellsberg, "First Two Times," 336; Patricia Ellsberg interview.

109. Simon interview.

110. Anonymous source.

111. *San Francisco Focus,* March 1991, 88; Ellsberg to Vann, September 15, 1967, May 7, 1968; Vann to Ellsberg, January 19, 1968 (prior three items in SP, box 27); Vann to Ellsberg, August 25, 1968; Sheehan notes on Ellsberg interview, November 19, 1976 (prior two items in SP, box 64).

112. *San Francisco Focus,* March 1991, 88; McGinniss, 197.

113. *San Francisco Focus,* March 1991, 88; McGinniss, 197.

114. Hall interview; Sheehan, "DE Interview Notebooks" (SP, box 64).

115. Anonymous source.

116. Ellsberg interview with Peter Davis, 1972 (SP, box 64); Sheehan notes on Ellsberg interviews (SP, box 121).

117. Cummings interview.

118. Butler interview.

119. *San Francisco Focus,* March 1991, 88; Ellsberg's Harvard 15th anniversary report (Meiklejohn); Komer to Ellsberg, March 31, 1967 (Komer, box 3, LBJ); Komer interview.

120. Ellsberg's Harvard 15th anniversary report (Meiklejohn).

121. *Look,* October 5, 1971, 34; Ellsberg, *Papers,* 304, 305; Ellsberg, "First Two Times," 336; Ellsberg radio interview, "Democracy Now," June 13, 1996; Ellsberg "corrections" to Herken.

122. Ellsberg memo for the record, May 6, 1967 (Yarmolinsky, box 49, JFK).

123. Ellsberg memos for the record, May 6, May 4, 1967 (Yarmolinsky, box 49, JFK).

124. Vann to Davis, June 10, 1967; Davis to Vann, June 24, 1967 (prior two items in SP, box 26).

125. Digby interview; Jardini, 264, 285, 367; George interview.

126. Shubert interviews; Andrew Marshall interview; Best interview; Charles Wolf interview.

127. George interview.

128. Digby interview; Patricia Ellsberg interview. Margaret Brenman-Gibson, who knows Ellsberg very well, says he "does everything" at the "last minute. For instance, if he's giving a lecture in Portland, Oregon . . . and he gets there and someone picks him up at the airport, and he goes to his hotel, he'll then call people that he knows in Portland and say, 'How about dinner tonight?' And then when they're not just there at the phone waiting for his call—when they didn't even know he was going to be there—he's very hurt" (Brenman-Gibson interview).

129. Vann to Davis, June 10, 1967; Davis to Vann, August 3, 1967 (prior two items in Davis papers).

CHAPTER 9

1. Ellsberg's RAND Employee History Report (Meiklejohn); Cronin interview.

2. Phillips interview.

3. Ellsberg's trial testimony, vol. 109, 19,597 (Butler papers); Ellsberg's 1973 *RS* interview (reprint), 36; Rich, 294; Ellsberg interview with Peter Davis, 1972 (SP, box 64); Ellsberg interview.

4. Zeckhauser interview.

5. Ellsberg interview with Peter Davis, 1972 (SP, box 64).

6. Butler interview.

7. Butler notes and essay on her relationship with Ellsberg (Butler papers); Butler interview.

8. Butler interview.

9. Butler notes on her relationship with Ellsberg (Butler papers).

10. Butler interview; affidavit for Bekins search warrant, September 1971 (WSPF, Fielding, box 20).

11. Ellsberg to Vann, March 15, 1968 (SP, box 27); Butler interview; Zeckhauser interview.

12. Langer interviews.

13. Butler interview; *Time*, July 5, 1971, 11; Pauker interview.

14. Ellsberg, *Papers*, 240; Ungar, 53–54; Butler interview.

15. Butler interview; Best interview.

16. Best interview; Butler interview.

17. Butler interview.

18. Valentine's Day card (Butler papers); Butler interview.

19. Butler interview.

20. Helen Kwake interview.

21. Butler interview; Best interview.

22. Ellsberg briefing to RAND trustees, November 11, 1967 (transcript); Langer interview.

23. Schelling interview.

24. Ellsberg notes, December 9, 1967 (SP, box 65).

25. Marshall interview; Cummings interview; Mary Ellsberg interview; Cronin interview; Daniel Ellsberg interview; Robert Ellsberg interview.

26. Robert Ellsberg interview; Mary Ellsberg interview; Kwake interview.

27. Mary Ellsberg interview; Marshall interview; Robert Ellsberg interview.

28. Butler interview.

29. McNamara, 256, 280; Warnke interview; Schelling interview; Leslie Gelb to McNamara, January 15, 1969 (Meiklejohn); Halberstam interview.

30. Ellsberg, *Papers*, 15, 18; Ellsberg interview on "Late Night Line-up," August 1971 (SP, box 161); Ellsberg interview with Harry Kreisler, July 29, 1998 (transcript); Halperin interview.

31. *Look*, October 5, 1971, 34.

32. Warnke interview; Ellsberg's trial testimony, vol. 113, 19,831 (Butler papers); Ungar, 57; Halperin interview.

33. *BG*, June 25, 1971; second CIA psychological profile of Ellsberg, November 1971 (WSPF, Fielding, box 3); Heymann interview and phone conversation.

34. Heymann interview; Liddy to Krogh and Young, August 18, 1971 (WSPF, Fielding, box 2); Howard Margolis interview.

35. Ellsberg's trial testimony, vol. 109, 19,601–3 (Butler papers); *Look*, October 5, 1971, 34; Heymann interview.

36. Ellsberg's trial testimony, vol. 109, 19,604–7 (Butler papers); Ellsberg interview; Ungar, 29; Margolis interview; Ellsberg interview with Harry Kreisler, 1998; Gelb to McNamara, January 15, 1969 (Meiklejohn).

37. Ellsberg's trial testimony, vol. 109, 19,605 (Butler papers); Shubert interview; Halperin interview.

38. Margolis interview. The section of the study in question is entitled "The Kennedy Commitments and Programs, 1961," and leads vol. 2 of the Gravel edition of the Pentagon Papers.

39. Shubert interview.

40. Ellsberg interviews.

41. Sack interview; Hall interview.

42. Memo and schedule on Bermuda conference (Yarmolinsky, box 111, JFK); Thomson interview.

43. Joseph Johnson to President Johnson, December 21, 1967; conference "Memorandum on Vietnam," December 12, 1967 (prior two items in NSF, Rostow, box 6, LBJ); Sheehan, "Vann Book Outline" (SP, box 65).

44. Pauker interview; Ellsberg memo for the record, February 28, 1968 (Yarmolinsky, box 66, JFK); Ellsberg memo for the record, January 31, 1968 (Yarmolinsky, box 49, JFK); Ellsberg to Vann, May 7, 1968 (SP, box 27); Ellsberg, "Effects of the Tet Offensive," March 1968 (SP, box 64).

45. Ellsberg, "What to do now," March 12, 1968 (Yarmolinsky, box 66, JFK).

46. Chau interview; Kellen interview; anonymous source.

47. Ellsberg to Vann, May 7, 1968 (SP, box 27); Sheehan, "Vann Book Outline" (SP, box 65).

48. Ellsberg to Vann, March 15, 1968 (SP, box 27); Ellsberg interview; Warnke interview; anonymous source; Ungar, 54–55.

49. Pauker interview.

50. *Pentagon Papers*, vol. 4, 561–84; Ellsberg interview with Peter Davis, 1972 (SP, box 64).

51. Komer interview.

52. Anonymous source.

53. Williams interview.

54. Yarmolinsky interview.

55. Ellsberg interview with Peter Davis, 1972 (SP, box 64); Halperin interview; *Chicago Sun-Times*, hand-dated August 27, 1972 (WHSF, Young, box 7); Sheehan, "Vann Book Outline" (SP, box 65); anonymous source.

56. Grant, 328; Sheehan, "Vann Book Outline" and notes on conversation with Jack Anderson, September 24, 1975 (SP, box 65); *NYT*, March 19, 21, 1968; Sheehan notes, no date (SP, box 63).

57. Sheehan, "Vann Book Outline" and notes on conversation with Jack Anderson, September 24, 1975 (SP, box 65); *WP*, February 9, 1975; Wicker interview; Wicker, 161–63. Wicker would have many contacts with Ellsberg in later years, but came to find him overly loquacious: "My God, he's a talker. You get him on the phone or he gets you on the phone and it's hard to get off. I'll be perfectly frank, for that reason I haven't sought the man out over the years. . . . A conversation with him is very hard to end" (Wicker interview).

58. Sheehan notes on conversation with Jack Anderson, September 24, 1975 (SP, box 65); Sheehan, "DE Interview Notebooks" (SP, box 64); *WP*, June 29, 1971; FBI document on Carol Ellsberg interview, July 9, 1971 (WSPF, Fielding, box 18).

59. Butler interview; Ellsberg's 1973 *RS* interview (reprint), 36, 37; Kaufmann interview; Ellsberg interview with Peter Davis, 1972 (SP, box 64); Ellsberg interview; Peter Edelman interview.

60. Ellsberg's 1973 *RS* interview (reprint), 37; Edelman interview; Ellsberg interview.

61. Seymour Martin Lipset interview.
62. Ellsberg interview; Ellsberg interview with Peter Davis, 1972 (SP, box 64); *Harper's*, February 1972, 54.
63. John E. Rielly interview.
64. Rielly interview.
65. Ellsberg, "Some Lessons from Failure in Vietnam," *passim;* Hoffmann interview.
66. Ellsberg interview with Peter Davis, 1972 (SP, box 64); Edelman interview; Ellsberg's 1973 *RS* interview (reprint), 37; Ellsberg interview.
67. Lipset interview.
68. *Senior Scholastic*, November 8, 1973, 8.
69. Ellsberg, "Betting on the Third Wave," October 11, 1968 (copy in my possession); Ellsberg, "Kahn on Winning in Vietnam: A Review," 4.
70. Wolf interview; Ellsberg's trial testimony, vol. 109, 19,608–9 (Butler papers); *Look*, October 5, 1971, 34.
71. Ellsberg interview with Peter Davis, 1972 (SP, box 64); Ellsberg interview; Ellsberg's Ds, 1969–70 (copies in my possession; also see LP, box 22); Ellsberg to Vann, July 8, 1969 (SP, box 27).
72. Ellsberg's Ds, 1969–70 (copies in my possession); Ellsberg, *Papers*, 25; Ellsberg interview.
73. Ellsberg interview; Kwake interview.
74. Wolf interview.
75. Williams interview.
76. Wolf interview; Ellsberg interviews.
77. Ellsberg interview; Ellsberg, "Violent Politics: The Role of Popular Attitudes and Action in Rebellion and Counter-Rebellion," June 17, 1968 (Allan Goodman papers, Hoover Institution, box 64); Ellsberg, "Revolutionary Judo," D and RM versions, January, July 24, 1970 (copies in my possession); Wolf interview; McGarvey interview.
78. Williams interview; Butler interview.
79. Ben Bagdikian interview.
80. Shubert interview.
81. Digby interview; Williams interview; McGarvey interview; Shubert interview.
82. Komer interview; Pauker interview; Ellsberg, "The Day Loc Tien was Pacified," "The Theory and Practice of Blackmail," "Kahn on Winning in Vietnam: A Review," "Public Goods and Public Bads: Comments on Mancur Olson's 'The Optimal Institutional Mix,'" "Some Lessons from Failure in Vietnam."
83. Ellsberg interview; Best interview; Digby interview.
84. Sheehan, "Funeral chapter, notes for DE" (SP, box 64); *LAT*, October 2, 1973.
85. Ellsberg interview; Kaufmann interview; Goldberg interview.
86. Ellsberg interview; *Look*, October 5, 1971, 40; Gould interview; FBI document on Carol Ellsberg interview, June 25, 1971 (WSPF, Fielding, box 18).
87. Pauker interview; Ellsberg interviews; Ellsberg's RAND Employee History Report (Meiklejohn); Williams interview; Russo interview; Kwake interview.
88. Thomas Schelling interview; Ellsberg interviews; Brenman-Gibson interview; Gould interview; Goldberg interview.
89. Kwake interview.
90. Kwake interview.
91. Kellen interview.
92. Resnick interview; LA FBI to FBI Director, July 20, 1971 (WSPF, Fielding, box 18).

93. Russo, 47–52; Russo interview.

94. Russo, 53; Russo interview.

95. Russo interview; Farrell, 84.

96. Russo interview.

97. Russo interview.

98. Russo interview; LA FBI to FBI Director, July 27, 1971 (WSPF, Fielding, box 18).

99. Kellen interview; Williams interview; McGarvey interview; Resnick interview.

100. Bagdikian interview.

101. Kwake interview.

102. Butler interview.

103. Schrag interview; Schrag, 44; Butler interview; anonymous sources.

104. Anonymous source; Popkin interview; Lipset interview; Marshall interview.

105. Ellsberg interviews; Schrag, 42–43; Ellsberg interview with Peter Davis, 1972 (SP, box 64); anonymous source.

106. *Newsweek*, June 21, 1971, 99; Talese, 360; Farrell, 92; Butler interview.

107. Talese, 360; Ellsberg interview with Peter Davis, 1972 (SP, box 64); Schrag, 42; Ellsberg interview; Sheehan notes on conversation with Talese, October 30, 1978 (SP, box 63). Ellsberg spoke to Talese about his sex life for Talese's book *Thy Neighbor's Wife*. After Talese mentioned in a magazine interview that he had interviewed Ellsberg, Ellsberg tracked Talese down at a place Talese was then staying and wanted to know what Talese was going to write about him. Most likely, Ellsberg worried that he had said more to Talese than he should have (perhaps a frequent postinterview concern for Ellsberg, since he has so little control over his boasting). Ellsberg may have also worried that he would embarrass or anger his wife, Patricia, who may not have known about some of his activities. Ellsberg apparently taped a phone conversation with Talese in order to trap him in some way. David Halberstam would also find Ellsberg zealous about trying to find out what he was going to write about him (Sheehan notes on conversations with Talese and Halberstam, October 30, 1978, September 18, 1975, SP, box 63).

108. Butler interview.

109. Butler interview.

110. Russo interview; Butler interview.

111. Ellsberg interview; Sheehan notes on Talese conversation, October 30, 1978 (SP, box 63); Talese note to author; Talese, 277–78, 332, 345–46, 348; Russo interview; Sack interview.

112. LA FBI to FBI Director, July 27, 1971 (WSPF, Fielding, box 18); Talese, 360; Russo interview; Sheehan notes on Talese conversation, October 30, 1978 (SP, box 63).

113. Russo interview.

114. Russo interview; Talese, 274–75; Williams interview; Leslie Henriques interview.

115. Butler interview.

116. Lipset interview; Langer interview.

117. Ellsberg interview; Randy Kehler interview.

118. Janaki Tschannerl interview; Ellsberg interview.

119. Ellsberg interview; Tschannerl interview; Ellsberg interview with Peter Davis, 1972 (SP, box 64); LA FBI to FBI Director, July 12, 1971 (WSPF, Fielding, box 18).

120. Ellsberg interview with Peter Davis, 1972 (SP, box 64); Tschannerl interview; Ellsberg interview.

121. Ellsberg interviews; photocopy of Ellsberg's copy of Deming's book.

122. *WIN*, November 1, 1972, 12; Patricia Ellsberg interview; Brenman-Gibson interview.

123. Patricia Ellsberg interview.

124. Liddy to Malloy, October 29, 1971 (WSPF, Fielding, box 3).

125. Anonymous source; Schrag, 107; FBI document on Carol Ellsberg interview, June 25, 1971 (WSPF, Fielding, box 18); Russo interview.

126. Simon interview; Rich interview.

127. Anonymous source; Simon interview.

128. Ellsberg interview with Peter Davis, 1972 (SP, box 64); Kehler interview.

129. Tschannerl interview.

130. Pauker interview; Ellsberg interview; Kellen interview.

131. Ellsberg interviews; Ellsberg interview with Peter Davis, 1972 (SP, box 64); Iklé interview; Halperin interview.

132. Ellsberg interview with Harry Kreisler, 1998; Ellsberg interview with Peter Davis, 1972 (SP, box 64); Hersh, 49; Halperin interview; Iklé interview.

133. *WIN*, November 1, 1972, 6; Ungar, 56; Halperin interview; Ellsberg interview.

134. *Congressional Record*, May 10, 1972, 4,976–81.

135. Ellsberg interviews; Shubert interview.

136. Ellsberg's 1973 *RS* interview (reprint), 4; Popkin interview.

137. Gelb to McNamara, January 15, 1969; Gelb to Rowen, July 14, 1969 (prior two items in Meiklejohn).

138. Gelb memo for the record, January 14, 1969 (copy in my possession); Warnke interview; Ellsberg interview; Rudenstine, 27, 32, 361.

139. Butler interview; Rowen's trial testimony, vol. 124, 21,688–89, 21,698, 21,734–35 (Butler papers); Best interview; Warnke, Halperin, and Gelb to Rowen, no date, probably December 18, 1968 (WHSF, Young, box 7).

140. Ellsberg's trial testimony, vol. 109, 19,623–51, vol. 112, 19,702–32 (Butler papers); Ellsberg's courier designations, February 28, August 22, 1969 (Meiklejohn).

141. Halperin interview; Warnke interview.

142. Ellsberg interview.

143. Ellsberg's trial testimony, vol. 112, 19,732, 19,735–36, vol. 113, 19,862–94 (Butler papers); Butler interview.

144. Ellsberg interview; Heymann interview.

145. Ellsberg, *Papers*, 28–35.

146. Halberstam interview.

147. Sheehan, *Bright*, 13; Ellsberg interview; Komer interview; Popkin interview.

148. Ellsberg interview; Halperin interview; Ellsberg's 1973 *RS* interview (reprint), 10; Ellsberg to Rowen, Wolf, et al., April 9, 1969 (SP, box 27).

149. *WIN*, November 1, 1972, 12; Patricia Ellsberg interview; Hall interview; Dowd interview.

150. Kehler interview; Tschannerl interview; Ellsberg interview.

151. Ellsberg interview; Tschannerl interview.

152. Ellsberg interview; Kehler interview.

153. Kehler interview; Ellsberg interview; Tschannerl interview.

154. Ellsberg interview; Ellsberg interview with Peter Davis, 1972 (SP, box 64); Ellsberg's trial testimony, vol. 114, 20,061 (Butler papers).

155. Ellsberg interview; Ellsberg to Bolté, September 23, 1969 (copy in my possession).

156. Sheehan notes on Ellsberg's letter to Bolté (SP, box 27).

CHAPTER 10

1. Russo interview; Ellsberg's 1973 *RS* interview (reprint), 32; Lukas, "Month," 101.
2. Russo interview.
3. Russo interviews; *LAT,* June 25, 1971; Franklin Mint brochure.
4. Russo interview; Resnick interview.
5. Resnick interview.
6. Ellsberg's 1973 *RS* interview (reprint), 31–32; Russo interview; Ellsberg's trial testimony, vol. 113, 19,920 (Butler papers); Ellsberg interview with Peter Davis, 1972 (SP, box 64); Resnick interview; *WP,* June 25, 1971; Ellsberg interview.
7. Russo interviews.
8. Resnick interview; Ellsberg's 1973 *RS* interview (reprint), 32.
9. Russo interviews; Ellsberg interview with Peter Davis, 1972 (SP, box 64); Resnick interview; Rich, 155.
10. Leonard Rodberg interview.
11. Rich, 155.
12. Russo interview; Ellsberg interview with Peter Davis, 1972 (SP, box 64); *New York Post,* January 4, 1972.
13. Ellsberg interview with Peter Davis, 1972 (SP, box 64); Resnick interview.
14. Russo interviews; Ellsberg's trial testimony, vol. 113, 19,923, 19,925 (Butler papers); Schrag, 47; Carol Ellsberg notes on phone conversation with Nesson, January 16, 1972 (CP); Ellsberg interview with Peter Davis, 1972 (SP, box 64).
15. Ellsberg's trial testimony, vol. 112, 19,748–50, vol. 113, 19,921 (Butler papers); Ellsberg interview; Ellsberg interview with Peter Davis, 1972 (SP, box 64); Russo interview.
16. Russo interviews.
17. Ellsberg interview; Butler interview.
18. Butler interview.
19. Russo remembered Ellsberg would "sit around his pad out in Malibu and get stoned and listen to Joan Baez on the record player and say far-out things like, 'Well, I guess I'll have to lead a life of poverty now.' He was very hung up on poverty" (Farrell, 84).
20. FBI document on Carol Ellsberg interview, June 25, 1971 (WSPF, Fielding, box 18); Cummings interview; Robert Ellsberg interview. Carol's written record, dated April 2, 1970, is included in the FBI document.
21. Ellsberg interview with Peter Davis, 1972 (SP, box 64); Cummings interview; FBI document on Carol Ellsberg interview, June 25, 1971 (WSPF, Fielding, box 18).
22. Yvonne Ekman trial testimony, vol. 74, 12,865–78 (Butler papers); FBI document on Carol Ellsberg interview, June 25, 1971 (WSPF, Fielding, box 18).
23. FBI document on Carol Ellsberg interview, June 25, 1971 (WSPF, Fielding, box 18).
24. Cummings interviews; Robert Ellsberg account of October 4, 1969, April 1970 (CP); Robert Ellsberg interview; FBI document on Carol Ellsberg interview, June 25, 1971 (WSPF, Fielding, box 18).
25. Robert Ellsberg interview; Ellsberg interview with Peter Davis, 1972 (SP, box 64); Schrag, 46–47.

26. Robert Ellsberg interview; Robert Ellsberg essay in 1976 War Resisters League calendar.

27. Robert Ellsberg interview.

28. FBI document on Carol Ellsberg interview, June 25, 1971 (WSPF, Fielding, box 18); Robert Ellsberg interview; Cummings interview.

29. FBI document on Carol Ellsberg interview, June 25, 1971 (WSPF, Fielding, box 18); Cummings interview.

30. FBI document on Carol Ellsberg interview, June 25, 1971 (WSPF, Fielding, box 18).

31. Cummings interview; FBI document on Carol Ellsberg interview, June 25, 1971 (WSPF, Fielding, box 18).

32. FBI document on Carol Ellsberg phone conversation, June 24, 1971 (WSPF, Fielding, box 18); Robert Ellsberg interview; Mary Ellsberg interview; Ellsberg interview with Peter Davis, 1972 (SP, box 64); Ellsberg's trial testimony, vol. 113, 19,923 (Butler papers); Cummings interview.

33. Robert Ellsberg interview; Russo interview.

34. Mary Ellsberg interview; Robert Ellsberg interview.

35. Schelling interview; anonymous source; Ellsberg interview with Peter Davis, 1972 (SP, box 64).

36. Carol Ellsberg chronology of October 1969-June 1971, undated, probably 1971 (CP); Cummings interview; Mary Ellsberg interview.

37. Cummings interview.

38. Cummings interviews.

39. LA FBI, "Daniel Ellsberg," February 18, 1970 (WSPF, Fielding, box 18); Cummings interviews; Best interview.

40. Cummings interviews.

41. Cummings interview.

42. Marshall interview; Cummings interview.

43. Marshall interviews.

44. Russo interviews; *WP,* June 25, 1971.

45. Ellsberg interview; Russo interview; Garbus interview; Garbus, "Recalling," A15.

46. Hall interview; Schelling interview; Goodman interview; Thomson interview; Kellen interview; *LAT,* June 18, 1971; Race, 167; Race interview; Sack interview; Mary Jane Vann interview; Jesse Vann interview; John Allen Vann interview; Sheehan notes on Ellsberg interview, November 20, 1976 (SP, box 64); Falk interview.

47. Shubert interview.

48. Ellsberg interviews; Garbus interview; Garbus, "Recalling," A15; anonymous source; Halperin interview.

49. Ellsberg "corrections" to Salisbury; Ellsberg interviews; Ellsberg, "Revolutionary Judo," July 24, 1970.

50. Kehler interview; Russo interview; *Minneapolis Tribune,* August 5, 1973; *National Catholic Reporter,* June 6, 1997; letter to author from Nancy Weber.

51. Patricia Ellsberg interview.

52. Nesson interview; anonymous source; Popkin interview; Butler interview.

53. Anonymous source; Peter Young interview.

54. Ellsberg interviews.

55. Schelling interview; Sheehan notes on Halberstam lunch, May 23, 1975 (SP, box 67); Nesson interview.

56. Popkin interview.
57. Ellsberg interview.
58. *LAT,* June 18, 1971; Oliphant interview; Zinn interview.
59. *BG,* June 29, 1971; McGinniss, 198; Ellsberg, *Papers,* 275–309; anonymous source.
60. Schelling interview; Cleveland interview.
61. Dowd interview.
62. Mary Ellsberg interview.
63. FBI document on Carol Ellsberg interview, June 25, 1971 (WSPF, Fielding, box 18); Ellsberg interviews; Lukas, "Month," 105.
64. Digby interview; Pauker interview.
65. Ellsberg interviews.
66. Garbus interview; anonymous source; Stanley Sheinbaum interview; Sheehan, "Vann Book Outline" (SP, box 65); Dowd interview.
67. Ellsberg's 1973 *RS* interview (reprint), 5; Sheehan, "Vann Book Outline" (SP, box 65).
68. LA FBI to FBI Director, July 12, 1971 (WSPF, Fielding, box 18); anonymous source; Kellen interview.
69. Bagdikian interview.
70. *NYT,* October 9, 1969; *WP,* October 12, 1969.
71. Anonymous source; Ellsberg interview with Peter Davis, 1972 (SP, box 64); Langer interview.
72. *NYT,* October 9, 1969; Williams interview; *WP,* October 14, 1969; Langer interview; Ellsberg interview.
73. Digby interview; Ellsberg interview.
74. Heymann interview and phone conversation.
75. Heymann interview.
76. Kwake interview.
77. Ellsberg interviews.
78. James Lowenstein interview; Lowenstein to Norvill Jones, March 23, 1973 (Jones papers); Sheehan, "Vann Book Outline" (SP, box 65); Noam Chomsky interview; Ellsberg interviews.
79. J. William Fulbright to Ellsberg, October 13, 1969 (copy in my possession); Ellsberg interview; Lowenstein press release, October 21, 1969 (copy in my possession).
80. Ellsberg interview with Peter Davis, 1972 (SP, box 64); Patricia Ellsberg interview.
81. Ellsberg interview; Sheehan notes on Ellsberg interview, November 19, 1976 (SP, box 64); Patricia Ellsberg interview.
82. Ellsberg, "Notes on the President's Speech of November 3, 1969," November 4, 1969 (copy in my possession); *Congressional Record,* November 13, 1969, E9601; Ungar, 71; Robert Sachs interview.
83. Jones, "Ellsberg matter"; KJ to Jones, March 22, 1973; Jones, "Background of Contacts with Daniel Ellsberg" and "Why the Committee Did Not Act," March 1973 (prior four items in Jones papers); Jones interview.
84. Jones interview.
85. Grant, 225; Jones interview; Lowenstein interview.
86. Jones interview.
87. Jones, "Background of Contacts with Daniel Ellsberg," March 1973; Fulbright to Melvin Laird, April 30, 1971 (prior two items in Jones papers); Lowenstein interview; Jones interview.

88. Jones, "Ellsberg matter" (Jones papers); Jones interview; McGovern interview.

89. Fulbright to Laird, November 11, 1969; other letters between Fulbright and Laird (prior two items in Jones papers).

90. Jones to Fulbright, November 7, 1969; Jones, "Background of Contacts with Daniel Ellsberg," March 1973; Richard Moose to Jones, no date; Jones, "Ellsberg matter" (prior four items in Jones papers).

91. Jones interview.

92. Kehler interview.

93. Kehler interview; Ellsberg interview.

94. Patricia Ellsberg interview; *WIN*, November 1, 1972, 12.

95. Patricia Ellsberg interview.

96. Garbus interview.

97. Garbus interview; Garbus, "Recalling," A15.

98. Ellsberg interview; Garbus interview; Russo interview.

99. Donna Wilson interview and notes (relayed over the phone).

100. Joan Libby interview.

101. Knoll and McFadden (eds.), 82–85, 127–32, 157–59; Rich, 297.

102. Grant, 324–30; Chau interview; Ellsberg to Vann, March 16, 1970 (SP, box 27); *WP*, March 4, 1970; Moose to Jones, no date (Jones papers).

103. Sheehan, "Vann Book Outline" (SP, box 65); Ellsberg to Vann, March 16, 1970 (SP, box 27); Lukas, "Month," 99.

104. Moose to Jones, no date; Jones, "Background of Contacts with Daniel Ellsberg," March 1973; Jones to Fulbright, June 21, 1971 (prior three items in Jones papers).

105. Jones interview; Grant, 219; Jones to Fulbright, April 20, 1970, June 29, 1971 (Jones papers).

106. Jones, "Background of Contacts with Daniel Ellsberg," March 1973; Jones to Fulbright, June 29, 1971 (prior two items in Jones papers); Jones interview.

107. KJ to Jones, March 22, 1973; Jones, "Background of Contacts with Daniel Ellsberg," March 1973; Jones to Fulbright, June 21, 1971 (prior three items in Jones papers).

108. FBI Director to Archibald Cox, September 26, 1973; LA FBI, "Daniel Ellsberg," February 18, 1970 (prior two items in WSPF, Fielding, box 18); Cummings interviews; Arnold Stone to William McDermott, February 23, 1970; Carol Ellsberg to "Daddy and Camille," June 19, 1971 (prior two items in CP).

109. FBI document on Carol Ellsberg interview, June 25, 1971 (WSPF, Fielding, box 18).

110. Robert Ellsberg interview; Cummings interview.

111. FBI document on Carol Ellsberg interview, June 25, 1971 (WSPF, Fielding, box 18); Cummings interviews; Carol Ellsberg chronology of October 1969-June 1971, and notes on April 4, 1970 (CP).

112. Best interview; Ellsberg interview.

113. Cott, 743; Best interview; James McGrath to Robert Mardian, July 21, 1971 (WHSF, Young, box 2); Schrag, 102; Ellsberg interview.

114. Sheehan notes on Ellsberg interview, November 19, 1976 (SP, box 64); Salisbury, 76–77.

115. FBI Director to Cox, September 10, 1973 (WSPF, Fielding, box 18); Colson to Ehrlichman, July 16, 1971 (WHSF, Colson, box 129); Ellsberg interview; Ellsberg's 1973 *RS* interview (reprint), 18; Schrag, 103.

116. Ellsberg's RAND Employee History Report (Meiklejohn); Ellsberg's 1973 *RS* interview (reprint), 18; Ellsberg interview; LA FBI to FBI Director, July 12, 1971 (WSPF, Fielding, box 18).

117. LA FBI to FBI Director, July 12, 1971 (WSPF, Fielding, box 18); *Harper's*, February 1972, 56.

118. Ungar, 61; Shubert interview; Wolf interview; Williams interview.

119. Kellen interview.

120. Ellsberg interview.

121. Kellen interview.

122. LA FBI to FBI Director, July 12, 1971 (WSPF, Fielding, box 18); Ellsberg interview with Peter Davis, 1972 (SP, box 64); Ungar, 62; *DFP*, June 20, 1971; Bundy interview; Ellsberg interview.

123. RAND form, "Approval for Access to Classified Storage," May 13, 1970 (Meiklejohn); Best trial testimony, vol. 119, 21,085–101, 21,180–200; Butler notes in Best trial testimony (prior two items in Butler papers); Best interview; LA FBI to FBI Director, July 26, 1971 (WSPF, Fielding, box 18).

124. Best trial testimony, vol. 119, 21,090–92, 21,200 (Butler papers); Best to Butler, May 20, 1970; notice of removal of top-secret material from Ellsberg's safe, May 20, 1970 (prior two items in Meiklejohn).

125. Ellsberg, *Papers*, 192; Kwake interview.

126. Ellsberg, *Papers*, 193, 197–231; Moose to Jones, no date (Jones papers); Jones interview.

127. Jones, "Background of Contacts with Daniel Ellsberg," March 1973; Moose to Jones, no date (prior two items in Jones papers); Jones interview.

128. Ellsberg's RAND "Personnel Security Clearance Change Notification," October 27, 1970; Best to Ellsberg, November 20, 1970; John Matthews to Ellsberg, February 2, March 30, 1971 (prior four items in Meiklejohn).

CHAPTER 11

1. Rodberg interview; Raskin interview.

2. Rodberg interview; Falk interview; Russo interview.

3. Rodberg interview; Barnet interview; Sheehan, "Vann Book Outline" (SP, box 21).

4. Rodberg interview; Raskin interview.

5. Rodberg interview; anonymous source.

6. Barnet interview; anonymous source.

7. Russo interview; Pentagon Papers twentieth anniversary program, June 13, 1991 (videotape).

8. Russo interview; *NYT*, August 1, 1970; Sheehan notes on Talese conversation, October 30, 1978 (SP, box 63).

9. Richard Dudman interview.

10. Ellsberg interview with Peter Davis, 1972 (SP, box 64); Russo interview.

11. Ellsberg interview with Peter Davis, 1972 (SP, box 64); Resnick interview.

12. Patricia Ellsberg interview.

13. *NYT*, August 9, 1970; Patricia Ellsberg interview.

14. Twaddell interview; Shanks, 121; Patricia Ellsberg interview.

15. Davis to Vann, August 11, 1970 (Davis papers).

16. Patricia Ellsberg interview; *Time*, July 5, 1971; Sheehan notes on Halberstam lunch, May 23, 1975 (SP, box 67).

17. Ellsberg interview with Peter Davis, 1972 (SP, box 64); Ellsberg's 1973 *RS* interview (reprint), 5; Patricia Ellsberg interview.
18. Ellsberg, "The Quagmire Myth and the Stalemate Machine" (reprint), *passim;* Ellsberg, "Escalating in a Quagmire," September 1970 (LP, box 22).
19. Schlesinger, *passim;* Herbert Kelman interview; Yarmolinsky to Ellsberg, November 18, 1970 (Yarmolinsky, box 60, JFK); Ellsberg interview.
20. John Coldwell interview.
21. Ellsberg, *Papers*, 42; Len Ackland interview; Gelb, *passim.* Ellsberg did misspell Theodore Sorensen's name—spelling it Sorenson—throughout his paper, but many people have misspelled it.
22. Ackland interview; Sheehan notes on Anthony Lake dinner, May 26, 1975 (SP, box 63); Ellsberg, *Papers*, 42.
23. Ellsberg, "Escalating in a Quagmire" (LP, box 22); Ellsberg, "The Quagmire Myth and the Stalemate Machine" (reprint), 217n, 235n; FBI, "Daniel Ellsberg: Espionage—X," August 3, 1971 (WHSF, Young, box 13).
24. Sheehan notes on Halberstam lunch, May 23, 1975 (SP, box 67); Sheehan, "Vann Book Outline" (SP, box 65); Sheehan notes on Lake dinner, May 26, 1975 (SP, box 63); Arnold interview.
25. Ackland interview; Sheehan notes on Ellsberg interview, November 19, 1976 (SP, box 64); Salisbury, 76.
26. Ackland interview and phone conversation.
27. Hersh, 328; Ellsberg's 1973 *RS* interview (reprint), 5–6.
28. Ellsberg's 1973 *RS* interview (reprint), 6–7.
29. Nesson interview; Hind Sadek Kooros interview; Larner interview; Salisbury, 22; anonymous source; Schrag, 108; Sheehan notes on Fred Graham conversation, September 16, 1973 (SP, box 65); Don Hall interview. When I visited the Ellsbergs' former flat in 1995, the tenant showed me a 2" mirror she had attached to one corner of the bedroom ceiling to commemorate the Ellsbergs' stay.
30. Priscilla McMillan interview; Helen and Stewart Perry interview.
31. Stewart Perry interview; McMillan interview.
32. Helen and Stewart Perry interview; Salisbury, 22; Ellsberg interview.
33. Helen and Stewart Perry interview.
34. Bundy interview; Edwin Diamond interview.
35. Diamond interview.
36. Bundy interview; Halberstam interview.
37. Schelling interview; Zinn interview.
38. Popkin interview; Ellsberg, *Papers*, 137, 171–73.
39. Ellsberg interview; Rich interview.
40. Anonymous source; Scott Jacobs interview.
41. Rich interview; anonymous sources; Jacobs interview.
42. Anonymous source.
43. Rich, 284; Ellsberg interview; Ellsberg's 1973 *RS* interview (reprint), 7; *WP*, November 29, 1970, hand-dated and sourced (SP, box 27); Hoffmann interview; Thomson interview; Larner interview.
44. Patricia Ellsberg interview; *WIN*, November 1, 1972, 12.
45. Rich, 284; Rich interview.
46. Popkin interview; Dowd interview.
47. Popkin interview.
48. Popkin interview; anonymous source; Dowd interview.

49. Chomsky interview.

50. Zinn interview; Ellsberg interview.

51. Zinn interview; anonymous source. Once when I was at his house, Ellsberg was checking off movies he wanted to see in the newspaper listings; they included films starring action heroes like Arnold Schwarzenneger and Bruce Willis, right-wingers in real life. Another time, when Ellsberg and I ran into his friend Seymour Hersh on the street in Washington, Ellsberg told Hersh he'd gone to three movies the night before. One of them, Ellsberg said, had been bad. "Coming from you, it must be bad," Hersh replied.

52. Zinn, 156; Zinn interview.

53. Salisbury, 612; Sheehan, "Vann Book Outline" (SP, box 21); John Kenneth Galbraith interview; Ellsberg interview with Peter Davis, 1972 (SP, box 64); Ellsberg interview.

54. Sheehan, "Vann Book Outline" (SP, box 21); Stewart Perry interview; Marva Shearer interview; Cummings interview; Salisbury, 36, 601; Breyer to Files, October 10, 1973 (WSPF, Fielding, box 20).

55. Race interview.

56. Race interview; dinner conversation with Race and his mother.

57. Document on contents of Hunt's safe, May 2, 1973 (WSPF, Fielding, box 18); Hecht to Merrill, October 10, 1973 (WSPF, Fielding, box 20).

58. Shearer, 296–99; Ellsberg's 1973 *RS* interview (reprint), 7–8; HJC, Appendix III, 92.

59. Thomson interview.

60. Jacobs interview; Oliphant interview.

61. Kelman interview.

62. Chomsky interview.

63. Zinn interview; Rich, 300.

64. Ackland interview.

65. Ellsberg interview.

66. Zinn interview.

67. Oliphant interview; Hilde Hein interview.

68. Ellsberg interview.

69. *WP,* June 24, 1971; *BG,* June 18, 1971.

70. Wierzynski interview.

71. Ellsberg, "Laos: What Nixon is Up To," *passim; NYT,* February 21, 1971.

72. Rich, 294; Ackland interview.

73. Sheehan, "Vann Book Outline" (SP, box 65); Sheehan notes, undated (SP, box 64); John Allen Vann interview.

74. Sheehan, *Bright,* 26; Sheehan, "Vann Book Outline" (SP, box 21); John Allen Vann interview.

75. Ellsberg's 1973 *RS* interview (reprint), 34; *Newsweek,* June 28, 1971, 16; Taylor Branch article in *Washington Monthly,* undated (Yarmolinsky, box 265, JFK); *BG,* March 7, 1971; *Look,* October 5, 1971, 41.

76. Oliphant interview.

77. Oliphant interview.

78. Oliphant interview; *BG,* March 7, 1971; Salisbury, 88; *Parade,* October 25, 1970.

79. Oliphant interview.

80. Oliphant interview.

81. Oliphant interview.

82. Oliphant interview; Hersh, 331.

83. Ellsberg's 1973 *RS* interview (reprint), 7; Nesson interview.

84. Jones interview; Jones, "Background of Contacts with Daniel Ellsberg," March 1973; Jones to Fulbright, June 21, 1971; Moose to Jones, no date (prior three items in Jones papers).

85. Sheehan notes on Ellsberg interview, November 19, 1976; Ellsberg interview with Peter Davis, 1972 (prior two items in SP, box 64); McGovern interview.

86. Ellsberg interview; McGovern interview.

87. McGovern interview; Nicholas von Hoffman article, undated (SP, box 65); Ungar, 82.

88. McGovern interview.

89. Ellsberg interview with Peter Davis, 1972 (SP, box 64); Ellsberg interview.

90. FBI, "Daniel Ellsberg: Espionage—X," July 20, 1971 (WHSF, Young, box 13).

91. Sheehan notes on Ellsberg interview, November 19, 1976, two sets (SP, box 64); Tschannerl interview.

92. Wierzynski interview; *BG*, July 4, 1971.

93. Wierzynski interview.

94. *BG*, July 4, 1971; David Greenway interview; Wierzynski interview; Murray Gart interview; *Time*, June 28, 1971, 18.

95. Wierzynski interview.

96. Wierzynski interview; Gart interview; Greenway interview.

97. *BG*, July 4, 1971; Gart interview; Wierzynski interview.

98. Rodberg interview; Sheehan, "Vann Book Outline" (SP, boxes 21, 65).

99. Salisbury, 88n; Rodberg interview; Sheehan, "Vann Book Outline" (SP, boxes 21, 65); Raskin interview; Ellsberg "corrections" to Salisbury; Russo interview; Barnet interview; Sheehan notes on Halberstam lunch, May 23, 1975 (SP, box 67).

100. Raskin interview; Barnet interview.

101. Rodberg interview; Sheehan, "Vann Book Outline" (SP, box 21).

102. Max Frankel note to author; Wicker interview; Salisbury, 83–84; Prochnau, 90–92, 99–100, 281–83; Sheehan to Arthur Krock, April 27, 1972; Sheehan note, May 5, 1972 (prior two items in SP, box 161); Ungar, 86; Sheehan to Jim Greenfield, October 1971 (SP, box 187).

103. Raskin interview; Sheehan note, undated (SP, box 65); Barnet interview; A. M. Rosenthal interview.

104. Sheehan, "Vann Book Outline" (SP, box 21).

105. Raskin interview; Barnet interview.

106. Barnet interview; Raskin interview; Rodberg interview.

107. Salisbury, 85–86, 87.

108. Sheehan, "Vann Book Outline" (SP, box 21); Rudenstine, 47; Ellsberg "corrections" to Salisbury.

109. Salisbury, 8, 80–81; Wicker interview.

110. Salisbury, 82–83; Sheehan, "Vann Book Outline" (SP, box 21).

111. Sheehan, "Vann Book Outline" (SP, boxes 21, 65); Sheehan, "Ellsberg-Boudin," and other Sheehan note (SP, box 65); Sheehan notes on Ellsberg interview, November 19, 1976 (SP, box 64); Salisbury, 97.

112. Frankel, 325, 326–27; Sheehan notes on Ellsberg interviews, undated (SP, box 121); Ellsberg "corrections" to Salisbury; Salisbury, 97, 99; Pentagon Papers twentieth anniversary program, June 13, 1991 (videotape).

113. Sheehan, "Vann Book Outline" (SP, box 21); Salisbury, 97; Russo interview; Sheehan notes on Ellsberg interviews, undated (SP, box 121).

114. Sheehan, "Vann Book Outline" (SP, box 21); Salisbury, 35; FBI, "Daniel Ellsberg: Espionage—X," July 20, 1971 (WHSF, Young, box 13).

115. Bill Kovach interview; Salisbury, 36; FBI, "Daniel Ellsberg: Espionage—X," July 13, 1971 (WHSF, Young, box 13).

116. Kovach interview; Salisbury, 36; FBI, "Daniel Ellsberg: Espionage—X," July 20, 1971 (WHSF, Young, box 13).

117. FBI, "Daniel Ellsberg: Espionage—X," August 3, 1971 (WHSF, Young, box 13); Kovach interview; Sheehan, "Vann Book Outline" (SP, box 21).

118. K. Dun Gifford interview.

119. Sheehan notes on Salisbury conversation, October 11, 1976 (SP, box 107); Salisbury, 167–68; Halberstam interview.

120. Sheehan to Frankel, March 26, 27, 1971 (SP, box 161); Frankel, 325.

121. Moose to Jones, no date; Jones to Fulbright, June 21, 1971; Jones, "Summary of Contacts with Daniel Ellsberg," "Background of Contacts with Daniel Ellsberg," March 1973; Jones to Fulbright, April 1, 1971 (prior five items in Jones papers).

122. Gifford interview; Sheehan notes on Gifford conversation, December 2, 1978 (SP, box 107).

123. Jones to Fulbright, June 21, 1971 (Jones papers); Jones interview; Woods, 605.

124. Falk interview; Paul McCloskey interview.

125. *Newsweek*, June 28, 1971; Falk interview; McCloskey interview; *BG*, June 23, 1971.

126. McCloskey interview; Ungar, 92.

127. McCloskey interview.

128. Charles Mathias interview; Ellsberg interview with Peter Davis, 1972 (SP, box 64).

129. Garbus interview; Zinn interview; Rich, 300; Garbus, *Tough Talk*, 72–73.

130. Anthony Austin interview and letter to author.

131. Rich, 300; Goodman interview.

132. Ellsberg "corrections" to Salisbury; Salisbury, 168; Garbus interview.

133. Russo interview.

134. Rodberg interview; Raskin interview.

135. Kehler interview.

136. Rudenstine, 67–68; anonymous source; Ungar, 16; Warnke interview.

137. Halperin interview.

138. Warnke interview; Kaysen interview; Ellsberg interview.

139. Bagdikian interview; Ungar, 15.

140. Salisbury, 207, 210; Haldeman, *Diaries*, 311; Rostow interview.

141. Salisbury, 214–215n; Sheehan notes on Halberstam lunch, May 23, 1975 (SP, box 67); Ellsberg interview with Travis-Cline, 1993; Halberstam interview; Ellsberg interview.

142. Austin interview.

143. Austin interview.

144. Ellsberg "corrections" to Salisbury; FBI, "Daniel Ellsberg: Espionage—X," July 20, 1971 (WHSF, Young, box 13); Sheehan, "Vann Book Outline" (SP, box 21).

145. Sheehan, "Vann Book Outline" (SP, box 21); Salisbury, 23–24, 214; Ellsberg "corrections" to Salisbury.

146. Gifford interview.

147. Rosenthal interview; Strober and Strober, 205; Ellsberg "corrections" to Salisbury.

148. Zinn interview.

149. Zinn interviews; Ellsberg interview.

150. Zinn interview; Ellsberg interview.

151. Zinn interview.
152. Helen and Stewart Perry interview.

CHAPTER 12

1. *NYT*, June 13, 1971.
2. Jacobs interview; Ungar, 12; Rich interview.
3. Schelling interview; Bundy interview.
4. Kolkowicz interview.
5. Oliphant interview; Ellsberg "corrections" to Salisbury.
6. Tschannerl interview.
7. Philip and Ann Heymann interview; Edelman interview.
8. Russo interview.
9. Robert Ellsberg interview; Carol Ellsberg notes on Charles Nesson conversation, summer 1971 (CP); *LAT*, June 14, 1971.
10. Cummings interview; Robert Ellsberg interview.
11. Marshall interview.
12. Resnick interview.
13. Larner interview.
14. Carol Ellsberg chronology, October 1969 to June 1971 (CP); FBI document on Carol Ellsberg interview, June 25, 1971 (WSPF, Fielding, box 18).
15. Shubert interviews; Best interview.
16. Tanham interview.
17. Shubert interviews; Best interview; Sullivan interview; anonymous source.
18. Kaufmann interview; Digby interview; Rowen conversation.
19. Shubert interview; Digby interview; Lipset interview; Langer interview; Schelling interview.
20. Shubert interview.
21. Best interview.
22. Best interview.
23. Raskin interview; Oberdorfer interview; Ungar, 131; Bradlee, 312.
24. Wierzynski interview; anonymous source.
25. *Newsweek*, June 28, 1971.
26. Rudenstine, 2, 105; Ungar, 127–28, 135.
27. Rich, 302; *WP*, June 18, 1971; *BG*, July 4, 1971; Zion interview; Garbus interview.
28. Resnick interview; *LAT*, June 18, 1971.
29. FBI Director to Archibald Cox, August 14, 1973 (WSPF, Fielding, box 18); *WP* and *BG*, June 18, 1971.
30. Bagdikian, 1.
31. Bagdikian, 3–4; Bagdikian interview; Oberdorfer interview; Ungar, 133.
32. Bagdikian, 5–7; Bagdikian interview.
33. Bagdikian interview; Bagdikian, 7.
34. Bagdikian, 7, 9; Bagdikian interview.
35. Bagdikian interview; Bagdikian, 9.
36. Bagdikian, 10; Bagdikian interview.
37. Bagdikian, 11–12; Ungar, 134; Oberdorfer interview.
38. FBI document on Carol Ellsberg interview, June 25, 1971 (WSPF, Fielding, box 18); *WP*, October 21, 1971; Ungar, 129.
39. *WP* and *DFP*, June 18, 1971; *BG* and *NYT*, June 19, 1971; Simon interview.
40. Garbus interview.

41. Nesson interview; *Meet the Press*, May 20, 1973 (transcript).

42. Nesson interview; Garbus interview.

43. Oliphant interview; *BG*, June 18, 1971; Tom Winship interview.

44. Oliphant interview.

45. Oliphant interview.

46. Oliphant interview; *BG*, June 22, 1971; Thomson interview; Robert Ellsberg interview.

47. Oliphant interview.

48. Ungar, 177–78; Oliphant interview; Winship interview.

49. Zinn interview; Hein interview; Winship interview.

50. Winship interview; Ungar, 180.

51. James Hoge interview.

52. Dudman interview.

53. *BG*, July 4, 1971; Patricia Ellsberg interview; Daniel Ellsberg interview.

54. Obst, 182; Chomsky interview; Rodberg interview; Russo interview; Pentagon Papers twentieth anniversary program, June 13, 1991 (videotape).

55. Ungar, 255–56; Bagdikian, 30–31.

56. Ungar, 259, 263; *BG*, July 1, 1971; Rodberg interview.

57. Zinn interview.

58. Lukas, "Month," 99; Ellsberg interview on "Democracy Now" radio program, Pacifica, June 13, 1996; Patricia Ellsberg interview; John Sack interview; *BG*, June 29, 1971; Pentagon Papers twentieth anniversary program, June 13, 1991 (videotape); Zinn interview; Tschannerl interview; McMillan interview; Brenman-Gibson interview.

59. Nesson interview.

60. Nesson interview.

61. Race interview.

62. Race interview.

63. Greenway interview.

64. Stewart Perry interview; Kooros interview.

65. Stewart Perry interview; Kelman interview.

66. Helen Perry interview.

67. Helen and Stewart Perry interview; Kooros interview. A journalist who went through Ellsberg's garbage found a note that referred to "the material being kept at Spencer's place," Spencer being Spencer Marx. Ellsberg later said the "material" was drapery material (Rich, 302).

68. Helen and Stewart Perry interview; Kelman interview.

69. Walter Cronkite interview.

70. Gordon Manning interview; Cronkite interview.

71. Manning interview.

72. Manning interview.

73. Manning interview; Cronkite interview; *BG*, June 24, 1971.

74. Manning interview.

75. Manning interview.

76. Manning interview.

77. Manning interview; Cronkite interview; Cronkite, 335.

78. Manning interview; Cronkite interview; Ellsberg interview with Terkel, 1980; Tschannerl interview.

79. Videotape of Ellsberg's interview with Cronkite (CBS News Archive); *NYT*, June 24, 1971.

80. Ellsberg interview; videotape of Ellsberg's interview with Cronkite (CBS News Archive); Ellsberg interview with Terkel, 1980.

81. Manning interview; Cronkite, 336.

82. Wierzynski interview.

83. Ellsberg interview.

84. *Time*, July 5, 1971; Rich, 304; Ellsberg interview; Shearer interview.

85. Cummings interviews; Marshall interview; Sheehan memo to self, December 3, 1971 (SP, box 161); Carol Ellsberg notes on Nesson conversation, July 10, 1972 (CP).

86. Carol Ellsberg to "Daddy and Camille," June 19, 1971 (CP); Robert Ellsberg interview; Cummings interview; *DFP*, June 20, 1971.

87. Cummings interview; Carol Ellsberg notes on Nesson conversation, July 10, 1972 (CP).

88. Carol Ellsberg to "Daddy and Camille," June 19, 1971 (CP); FBI document on Carol Ellsberg interview, June 17, 1971 (WSPF, Fielding, box 18); Cummings interview; Robert Ellsberg interview.

89. Carol Ellsberg chronology, October 1969 to June 1971 (CP); Cummings interviews.

90. Cummings interviews.

91. Cummings interview; Carol Ellsberg notes on Nesson conversation, July 10, 1972 (CP).

92. FBI document on Carol Ellsberg interview, June 22, 1971; FBI document on contents of Howard Hunt's safe, May 2, 1973 (prior two items in WSPF, Fielding, box 18).

93. FBI documents on Carol Ellsberg interviews, June 24 (two), June 25, 1971 (WSPF, Fielding, box 18). Dates of documents on FBI interviews do not necessarily correspond to the date of the interview itself.

94. FBI document on Carol Ellsberg interview, June 25, 1971 (WSPF, Fielding, box 18).

95. Carol Ellsberg notes on Nesson conversation, September 14, 1971 (CP); Cummings interview; Marshall interview.

96. Carol Ellsberg chronology, October 1969 to June 1971 (CP); Cummings interviews; *Look*, October 5, 1971, 40.

97. *WP*, June 26, 1971; Cummings interviews; FBI document on Carol Ellsberg interview, June 30, 1971 (WSPF, Fielding, box 18); Marshall interview.

98. Cummings interview; FBI document on Carol Ellsberg interview, June 30, 1971 (WSPF, Fielding, box 18); Shearer interview.

99. Cummings interview; Mary Ellsberg interview.

100. Marshall interviews; FBI documents on Carol Ellsberg interviews, June 30, July 9, 1971 (WSPF, Fielding, box 18); Cummings interview.

101. FBI document on Carol Ellsberg interview, June 30, 1971 (WSPF, Fielding, box 18).

102. Cummings interview; unpublished Mary Ellsberg memoir excerpt (in my possession).

103. Cummings interview.

104. Robert Ellsberg interview.

105. Cummings interview; Hall interview.

106. Robert Ellsberg interview; Cummings interviews.

107. Robert Ellsberg interview.

108. Cummings interviews; Carol Ellsberg notes on Nesson conversation, February 26, 1973 (CP); Sheehan note to self, December 3, 1971 (SP, box 161); McGinniss, 98; Carol Ellsberg, "Circumstances of my testimony and Robert's," undated (CP).

109. McGinniss, 98; Carol Ellsberg, "Circumstances of my testimony and Robert's," undated (CP); Cummings interviews.

110. Carol Ellsberg, "Circumstances of my testimony and Robert's," undated (CP); Cummings interview; Robert Ellsberg interview.

111. Carol Ellsberg, "Circumstances of my testimony and Robert's," undated (CP).

112. Resnick interview.

113. *LAT* and *WP,* June 25, 1971; Resnick interview.

114. Resnick interview.

115. Resnick interview.

116. Resnick interview. There is a pathological condition in which people lose their voice: hysterical aphonia.

117. Russo interview.

118. Russo interview.

119. Russo interview.

120. Russo interview.

121. Russo interview; Young interview.

122. *Harper's,* February 1972, 57.

123. Patricia Ellsberg interview.

124. Twaddell interview.

125. Patricia Ellsberg interview.

126. Patricia Ellsberg interview; Sheinbaum interview.

127. Patricia Ellsberg interview; Brenman-Gibson interview.

128. Patricia Ellsberg interview; Twaddell interview.

129. Shubert interview; Sullivan interview; McGarvey interview; Butler interview; Kellen interview.

130. Best interview; McGarvey interview; Komer interview; *DFP,* July 3, 1971; Sullivan interview; Ellsberg interviews.

131. *LAT,* July 3, 1971; *WP,* July 26, 1971; McGarvey interview; Heymann interview.

132. Best interview; Butler interview; Digby interview; *WP,* July 26, 1971.

133. Best interview.

134. Butler interview.

135. Sullivan interview; Best interview.

136. Sullivan interview; Butler interview; Colson affidavit, April 29, 1974 (WSPF, Fielding, box 2).

137. Sullivan interview; Butler interview; Best interview.

138. *WP,* November 16, 1971; Komer interview; Ellsberg interview.

139. Shubert interviews; Tanham interview; Rowen conversation; *NYT,* November 16, 1971; Best interview.

140. Anonymous source; Ellsberg interview.

141. Sheehan, *Bright,* 753; John Allen Vann interview; Jess Vann interview; Sheehan notes on Joe Raby interview, undated (SP, box 57); Vann to Ellsberg, September 30, 1971 (SP, box 27).

142. Lansdale to "Uncle Peter," July 23, 1971; Lansdale to "Old Team," July 1, 1971 (prior two items in Currey papers); Redick interview.

143.   Conein interview.
144.   *BG* and *DFP*, June 21, 1971; *WP*, November 30, 1971.

CHAPTER 13

1.   Haldeman, *Ends*, 110; Haldeman, *Diaries*, 300–301; Ehrlichman notes, undated (WHSF, Ehrlichman, box 22).
2.   Colson to Haldeman, June 25, 1971; Colson to Larry Higby, June 21, 1971 (prior two items in WHSF, Colson, box 129); poll data on Pentagon Papers publication; Tom Benham, "Some Comments on the June 21, 1971, Telephone Study" (prior two items in WHSF, Ehrlichman, box 22); Farrell, 80.
3.   Colson affidavit, April 29, 1974 (WSPF, Fielding, box 2); *SFC*, October 6, 1999; conversation between Nixon, Haldeman, Mitchell, Ehrlichman and Colson, September 18, 1971 (APT, NA); HJC, Appendix III, 92; Strober and Strober, 224; *NYT*, December 9, 1973; Hersh, 385; Haldeman, *Ends*, 111; Sheehan notes of Nick Thimmesch conversation, November 18, 1976 (SP, box 65); Bakes to Files, August 15, 1973 (WSPF, Fielding, box 15).
4.   Martin to Files, August 16, 1973 (WSPF, Fielding, box 15); *NYT*, December 9, 1973.
5.   Colson affidavit, April 29, 1974 (WSPF, Fielding, box 2); Martin to Files, August 16, 1973 (WSPF, Fielding, box 15); Nixon, 509; Oudes, 270.
6.   Haldeman, *Diaries*, 300, 311; Kutler, *Abuse*, 15–18.
7.   Nixon and Ehrlichman conversation, September 10, 1971 (APT, NA); Colson to Krogh, July 28, 1971 (WHSF, Colson, box 129); HJC, Appendix III, 127, 128; Liddy for the File, August 4, 1971 (WHSF, Young, box 13); Nixon, Haldeman, and Kissinger conversation, July 1, 1971 (APT, NA).
8.   Colson to Van Shumway, July 1, 1971 (WHSF, Colson, box 129); Young, Memorandum for the Record, July 20, 1971 (WHSF, Young, box 15).
9.   Liddy interview; notation on *NYT* article, November 4, 1971 (WHSF, Young, box 7); Nixon, Haldeman, Mitchell, Ehrlichman and Colson conversation, September 18, 1971 (APT, NA); Liddy to Krogh and Young, September 23, October 7, 1971 (WHSF, Young, box 13).
10.   Liddy to Krogh and Young, November 4, 1971 (WHSF, Young, box 15); Liddy to Krogh and Young, October 7, 1971 (WHSF, Young, box 13); Bakes to Files, October 16, 1973 (WSPF, Fielding, box 20).
11.   Nixon, Haldeman and Ziegler conversation, July 5, 1971 (APT, NA); Kutler, *Abuse*, 17; Krogh and Young to Ehrlichman, August 20, 1971 (WSPF, Fielding, box 2).
12.   HJC, Appendix III, 128; Liddy interview; Wise, 149–50; Krogh radio interview, October 28, 1973; Krogh, "Statement of Defendant," January 3, 1974 (prior two items in WSPF, Fielding, box 20); *NYT*, December 9, 1973.
13.   *NYT*, December 9, 1973; Akerman to Files, August 7, 1973 (WSPF, Fielding, box 20); FBI Director to Cox, September 17, 1973 (WSPF, Fielding, box 18); Cummings interviews.
14.   *NYT*, December 9, 1973; Wise, 152–53; Akerman to Files, August 1, 1973 (WSPF, Fielding, box 19); Hecht to Merrill and Bakes, August 22, 1973 (WSPF, Fielding, box 20); Bakes to Merrill and Breyer, September 25, 1973 (WSPF, Fielding, accordion file after box 3).
15.   *WP*, June 3, 1973; UPI articles, June 6, July 26, 1973 (prior two items in SP, boxes 107, 188); *BG*, July 27, 1973; notes on David Nissen interview, August 2, 1973 (WSPF, Fielding, box 21); HJC, Book VII, Part 3, 1476.

16. Colson affidavit, April 29, 1974 (WSPF, Fielding, box 2); Strober and Strober, 234; document on interview of Ellsberg and Boudin, May 1, 1974 (WSPF, Fielding, box 18).

17. "Haldeman," no date (WSPF, Fielding, box 19); Colson to John Scali, July 27, 1971 (WHSF, Colson, box 129); Merrill to Files, September 21, 1973 (WSPF, Fielding, box 22–23); Colson to Ziegler, July 7, 1971 (WHSF, Haldeman, box 81); "241-Colson," no date (WSPF, Fielding, box 22–23).

18. FBI document on Robert Beauchamp interview, October 30, 1972 (WSPF, Fielding, box 18).

19. FBI document on Robert Beauchamp interview, October 30, 1972 (WSPF, Fielding, box 18).

20. FBI document on Robert Beauchamp interview, October 30, 1972 (WSPF, Fielding, box 18).

21. FBI Director to Cox, August 31, 1973 (WSPF, Fielding, box 18); Nesson to Heymann, July 18, 1973 (WSPF, Fielding, box 21); FBI document on Beauchamp interview, October 30, 1972 (WSPF, Fielding, box 18); Strober and Strober, 234–35.

22. Colson affidavit, April 29, 1974 (WSPF, Fielding, box 2); Krogh affidavit, May 4, 1973 (Sachs); affidavit for Bekins search warrant, September 1971 (WSPF, Fielding, box 20); Krogh for Files, August 2, 1971 (WHSF, Young, box 12); Breyer to Files, October 10, 1973 (WSPF, Fielding, box 20); Liddy interview.

23. Liddy to Krogh and Young, August 18, 1971 (WSPF, Fielding, box 2); Liddy to Krogh and Young, October 7, 1971 (WHSF, Young, box 13); Liddy to Krogh, November 19, 1971 (WHSF, Young, box 12); Young, Memorandum for the Record, July 20, 1971 (WHSF, Young, box 15); Liddy, Memorandum for the File, August 11, 1971 (WHSF, Young, box 8); Kutler, *Abuse*, 24.

24. Nixon, 512; Nixon, Ehrlichman, Haldeman, and Kissinger conversation, June 17, 1971; Nixon and Haldeman conversation, June 30, 1971; Nixon, Haldeman, Laird, Mitchell, and Kissinger conversation, June 30, 1971; Nixon, Haldeman, and Kissinger conversation, July 1, 1971 (prior four items in APT, NA); Kutler, *Abuse*, 6, 17; Akerman to Files, January 24, 1975 (WSPF, Fielding, box 15).

25. Colson to Ehrlichman, July 6, 1971 (WHSF, Colson, box 129); Hersh, 390.

26. Bakes to Files, August 15, 1973 (WSPF, Fielding, box 15); Dean, 36; Bakes and Merrill to Vorenberg, August 13, 1973 (WSPF, Fielding, box 21); Bakes to Files, September 4, 1973 (WSPF, Fielding, box 15).

27. Liddy interview.

28. Nixon and Ehrlichman conversation, September 10, 1971 (APT, NA); *San Francisco Examiner*, December 8, 1996; Liddy to Krogh and Young, November 4, 1971 (WHSF, Young, box 15).

29. *BG* and *WP*, June 29, 1971; Nesson interview.

30. Best interview.

31. Ellsberg's fingerprint record, June 28, 1971 (Meiklejohn).

32. *BG*, June 29, 1971; Russo interview.

33. *WP*, June 29, 1971; Perry interview.

34. *BG*, June 29, 1971; Breyer to Files, October 10, 1973 (WSPF, Fielding, box 20); Dean to Ehrlichman, June 28, 1971 (WHSF, Ehrlichman, box 22).

35. FBI document on Carol Ellsberg interview, July 1, 1971 (WSPF, Fielding, box 18).

36. *BG*, July 1, 1971; McMillan interview.

37. Nixon, Haldeman, and Kissinger conversation, July 1, 1971; Nixon, Kissinger, and Mitchell conversation, June 30, 1971; Nixon and William Timmons conversation,

July 2, 1971; Nixon, Haldeman, Ehrlichman, and Colson conversation, July 1, 1971 (prior four items in APT, NA).

38. Nixon, Haldeman, and Kissinger conversation, July 1, 1971; Nixon, Haldeman, Ehrlichman, and Colson conversation, July 1, 1971; Nixon, Haldeman, and Ziegler conversation, June 24, 1971 (prior three items in APT, NA); Kutler, *Abuse*, 16, 19.

39. Nixon, Haldeman, Ehrlichman and Colson conversation, July 1, 1971 (APT, NA).

40. Colson to Ehrlichman, July 6, 1971 (WSPF, Fielding, accordion file after box 3); Bakes to Files, September 20, 1973 (WSPF, Fielding, box 15); Nixon, Haldeman, and Ziegler conversation, July 2, 1971 (APT, NA).

41. Nixon, Haldeman and Ziegler conversation, June 24, 1971 (APT, NA).

42. Nixon, Haldeman, Ehrlichman, and Colson conversation, July 1, 1971 (APT, NA); Colson and Hunt conversation, July 1, 1971 (WSPF, Fielding, accordion file after box 3); Nixon and Haldeman conversation, July 1, 1971 (APT, NA).

43. Colson to Ehrlichman, July 6, 1971 (WSPF, Fielding, accordion file after box 3); Ehrlichman and Robert Cushman conversation, July 7, 1971 (WSPF, Fielding, box 3).

44. "Summary of Interview with Egil Krogh," April 3, 1974; Krogh, "Statement of Defendant," January 3, 1974 (prior two items in WSPF, Fielding, box 20).

45. FBI Director to Cox, September 21, 1973; FBI document on Vernon Hebel interview, August 2, 1973; Hebel to Sam Irving [sic], July 27, 1973; San Bernardino County sheriff's report on Terry's murder (prior four items in WSPF, Fielding, box 18).

46. Kutler, *Abuse*, 15, 423; FBI Director to Cox, September 17, 1973 (WSPF, Fielding, box 18); Nixon and Richard Moore conversation, April 19, 1973 (WSPF, Fielding, box 21).

47. Patricia Ellsberg interview; Nesson to Heymann, July 18, 1973 (WSPF, Fielding, box 21); Gentry, 685; Martin to Bakes, July 26, 1973 (WSPF, Fielding, boxes 22–23); HJC, Appendix III, 112; Hoover to Brennan, September 8, 1971 (WHSF, Ehrlichman, box 21).

48. FBI Director to Cox, August 14, 1973 (WSPF, Fielding, box 18); Patricia Ellsberg interview.

49. *WP*, July 28, 1973.

50. Colson affidavit, April 29, 1974 (WSPF, Fielding, box 2); Krogh, "Statement of Defendant," January 3, 1974 (WSPF, Fielding, box 20); Liddy, 147, 158; Bakes to File, July 9, 1973 (WSPF, Fielding, box 15).

51. Krogh, "Statement of Defendant," January 3, 1974 (WSPF, Fielding, box 20); *NYT*, July 19, 1974; Haldeman, *Diaries*, 329; Krogh affidavit, May 4, 1973 (Sachs).

52. Young, "Points to be Covered in Initial Report Under Objective #1," no date (WSPF, Fielding, box 2); Liddy interview; Liddy to Krogh and Young, August 18, 1971 (WSPF, Fielding, box 2); "What Ellsberg Knows" folder (WHSF, Young, box 12); Liddy to Krogh and Young, August 3, 1971 (WHSF, Young, box 13); SSC, Book IX, 3666–67; videotape report on Ellsberg, July 30, 1971 (WHSF, Young, box 13).

53. Liddy interview; Bakes to File, July 9, 1973 (WSPF, Fielding, box 15); Bakes to Files, July 11, 1973 (WSPF, Fielding, box 20); FBI Director to Cox, September 17, 1973 (WSPF, Fielding, box 18); Liddy to Krogh and Young, August 18, 1971

(WSPF, Fielding, box 2); Bakes to Merrill and Breyer, September 25, 1973 (WSPF, Fielding, accordion file after box 3).

54. *WP,* July 25, 1971; Popkin interview.
55. Butler interview; LA FBI to FBI Director, July 20, 1971 (WSPF, Fielding, box 18); Mary Marshall interview; Strober and Strober, 235.
56. FBI documents on interviews of Carol Ellsberg, June 29, July 1, 9, 13, 1971; LA FBI to FBI Director, July 12, 20, 27, 1971; FBI document on contents of Hunt's safe, May 2, 1973; FBI Director to Cox, July 10, 1973 (prior nine items in WSPF, Fielding, box 18).
57. Document on Ellsberg and Boudin interview, May 1, 1974 (WSPF, Fielding, box 18).
58. LA FBI to FBI Director, July 20, 27, 1971 (WSPF, Fielding, box 18); Russo interview; Tschannerl interview.
59. Rich interview.
60. Robert Akeret interview; withdrawal card on FBI interview of Akeret (WSPF, Fielding, box 18).
61. Akeret interview; document on Nissen interview, August 2, 1973 (WSPF, Fielding, box 21).
62. Akeret interview.
63. Akeret interview; Patricia Ellsberg interview; *Time,* May 7, 1973; Petersen to Acting FBI Director, April 1973 (WSPF, Fielding, box 18); Ruth to Kelley, July 16, 1973 (WSPF, May 3, box 1); Akerman and Horowitz to Merrill and Ruth, March 4, 1974 (WSPF, Fielding, box 2); Hunt grand jury testimony, May 2, 1973 (Sachs); Liddy interview.
64. Patricia Ellsberg affidavit, December 29, 1972 (Meiklejohn); *NYT,* August 20, 1972.
65. LA FBI to FBI Director, July 20, 26, 1971; document on contents of Hunt's safe, May 2, 1973 (prior three items in WSPF, Fielding, box 18); Krogh and Young to Ehrlichman, August 11, 1971 (WHSF, Ehrlichman, box 21); Hecht to Merrill, August 29, 1973 (WSPF, Fielding, box 20); "Memorandum for the Record," no author listed, September 11, 1972 (WHSF, Young, box 12).
66. Polly Cronin interview.
67. FBI Director to Special Prosecution Force, June 13, 1974 (WSPF, Fielding, box 18); Liddy interview; Bakes to File, July 9, 1973 (WSPF, Fielding, box 15); document on contents of Mardian's files; Bakes to Files, July 11, 1973 (prior two items in WSPF, Fielding, box 20); Sheehan notes on Ellsberg conversation, February 9, 1974 (SP, box 64).
68. Bakes to File, July 9, 1973 (WSPF, Fielding, box 15); Hersh, 325, 392; Akerman to Files, January 15, 1975 (WSPF, Fielding, box 15).
69. FBI Director to Special Prosecution Force, June 13, 1974 (WSPF, Fielding, box 18); Strober and Strober, 227, 238; HJC, Book IV (SISBPN), 101.
70. Krogh affidavit, May 4, 1973 (Sachs); Nixon and Ehrlichman conversation, May 2, 1973 (APT, NA); Nixon and Richard Moore conversation, April 19, 1973 (WSPF, Fielding, box 21).
71. FBI document on Carol Ellsberg interview, July 9, 1971 (WSPF, Fielding, box 18); Cummings interview; Carol Ellsberg notes on Nesson conversation, summer 1971 (CP); *NYT,* August 20, 1972; document on Ellsberg and Boudin interview, May 1, 1974 (WSPF, Fielding, box 18); Larner interview.
72. Ellsberg affidavit, December 29, 1972 (Meiklejohn).

73. *LAT*, September 15, 21, 1971; affidavit for Bekins search warrant, September 1971 (WSPF, Fielding, box 20); Nixon, Haldeman, Mitchell, Ehrlichman and Colson conversation, September 18, 1971 (APT, NA).

74. FBI Director to Cox, August 14, September 17, 1973; LA FBI to FBI Director, July 27, 1971; document on contents of Hunt's safe, May 2, 1973 (prior four items in WSPF, Fielding, box 18); Hunt grand jury testimony, May 2, 1973 (Sachs); Hecht to Merrill, October 10, 1973 (WSPF, Fielding, box 20).

75. Liddy to Malloy, November 3, 1971 (WSPF, Fielding, box 3).

76. Notes on interview of Todd Hullin, "J-30–74" (WSPF, Fielding, box 19).

77. Kutler, *Abuse*, 10; Colson and Hunt conversation, July 1, 1971 (WSPF, Fielding, accordion file after box 3); Colson to Haldeman, June 25, 1971 (WHSF, Colson, box 129); HJC, Appendix III, 95; SSC, Book IX, 3781.

78. Bakes to Files, October 16, 1973 (WSPF, Fielding, box 20); SSC, Book IX, 3782; Krogh and Young to Ehrlichman, November 1, 1971 (WHSF, Young, box 15); Young to Ehrlichman, June 9, 1972 (WHSF, Young, box 2).

79. Young to Ehrlichman, June 9, 1972 (WHSF, Young, box 2).

80. Haig to Ehrlichman, December 27, 1971 (WSPF, Fielding, box 2); Sheehan, *Bright*, 754; Vann to Ellsberg, September 30, 1971 (SP, box 27); Sheehan notes on interviews with Peter and Tommy Vann (SP, box 57); Sheehan notes on Halberstam conversation, December 11, 1972 (SP, box 67); Sheehan notes on Ellsberg conversation, December 29, 1972 (SP, box 57); Sheehan notes on Ellsberg interview, November 20, 1976 (SP, box 64).

81. Mary Jane Vann interview.

82. Krogh and Young to Ehrlichman, August 20, 1971; Haig to Ehrlichman, December 27, 1971 (prior two items in WSPF, Fielding, box 2); J. T. Smith meeting notes, May 1, 1973 (WSPF, Fielding, box 21).

83. Hunt, 150–52, 255; document on contents of Hunt's safe, May 2, 1973 (WSPF, Fielding, box 18); Liddy interview; SSC, Book IX, 3886; Hunt and Conein conversation, no date (WSPF, Fielding, accordion file after box 3).

84. Nixon and Ehrlichman conversation, September 8, 1971 (APT, NA); Ehrlichman grand jury testimony, 1973 (WSPF, Fielding, box 24); "Summary of Interview with Egil Krogh," April 3, 1974 (WSPF, Fielding, box 20); Colson and Hunt conversation, July 1, 1971 (WSPF, Fielding, accordion file after box 3).

85. Jaworski to Soden, June 12, 1974 (WSPF, Fielding, box 2); "Outline of Closing Argument," no date (WSPF, Fielding, box 1); Hunt, "Devil's Advocate," no date (WSPF, Fielding, boxes 22–23).

86. Jaworski to Soden, June 12, 1974 (WSPF, Fielding, box 2); Ehrlichman to Colson, August 24, 1971 (WHSF, Young, box 12); Nixon and Ehrlichman conversation, September 8, 1971 (APT, NA); Breyer to Files, September 18, 1973 (WSPF, Fielding, boxes 22–23); Martin to Files, August 16, 1973 (WSPF, Fielding, box 15); SSC, Book IX, 3673, 3759; *Detroit News*, January 30, 1972.

87. Document on Ellsberg and Boudin interview, May 1, 1974 (WSPF, Fielding, box 18); Ellsberg's 1973 *RS* interview (reprint), 16.

88. Young to Ehrlichman, August 26, 1971 (WSPF, Fielding, box 2); HJC, Book VII, Part 3, 1215; Colson to Ehrlichman, July 14, 1971 (WHSF, Haldeman, box 81); document on Hallett interview, no date (WSPF, Fielding, box 19); Colson to Ehrlichman, September 15, 1971 (WHSF, Colson, box 130); Hullin to Krogh and Young, September 16, 1971 (WHSF, Young, box 12).

89. Nixon, Haldeman, Mitchell, Ehrlichman and Colson conversation, September 18, 1971 (APT, NA).

90. Colson to Timmons, September 22, 1971 (WHSF, Colson, box 130); Colson to Ehrlichman, July 22, 1971 (WHSF, Haldeman, box 81); "The Counter-Government and the Pentagon Papers," *National Review*, July 13, 1971; Colson to Haldeman, July 13, 1971 (prior two items in WHSF, Colson, box 3).

91. Colson to Ehrlichman, July 22, 1971 (WHSF, Haldeman, box 81); Colson to Ehrlichman, September 24, 1971 (WHSF, Haldeman, box 84); Colson to Haldeman, July 13, June 25, 1971 (WHSF, Colson, box 129); Nixon, Haldeman, Mitchell, Ehrlichman and Colson conversation, September 18, 1971 (APT, NA).

92. Colson to Haldeman, June 25, 1971, two (WHSF, Colson, box 129); Haldeman, *Diaries*, 302; Nixon, 510.

93. "EB" affidavit, May 9, 1973; Malloy affidavit, May 9, 1973; Malloy, Memorandum for the Record, August 13, 1971 (prior three items in WSPF, Fielding, box 3); Bakes to Files, July 20, 1973 (WSPF, Fielding, box 20).

94. "MB" affidavit, May 9, 1973; Malloy, Memorandum for the Record, August 20, 1971 (prior two items in WSPF, Fielding, box 3); Liddy interview.

95. Malloy affidavit, May 9, 1973 (WSPF, Fielding, box 3).

96. Malloy affidavit, May 9, 1973; Malloy, Memorandum for the Record, August 20, 1971; "MB" affidavit, May 9, 1973; "MB" to "AF," November 8, 1971 (prior four items in WSPF, Fielding, box 3); Bakes to Files, July 20, 1973 (WSPF, Fielding, box 20).

97. Bakes to Files, July 20, 1973 (WSPF, Fielding, box 20); "AF" to Helms, November 9, 1971; Hunt to Malloy, October 8, 1971 (prior two items in WSPF, Fielding, box 3).

98. Malloy, Memorandum for the Record, November 15, 1971; "AF" affidavit, May 25, 1973 (prior two items in WSPF, Fielding, box 3); Bakes to Files, July 20, 1973 (WSPF, Fielding, box 20).

99. Helms to Young, November 9, 1971; second CIA psychological profile of Ellsberg, November 1971 (prior two items in WSPF, Fielding, box 3).

100. Malloy affidavit, May 9, 1973; "MB" affidavit, May 9, 1973 (prior two items in WSPF, Fielding, box 3); Liddy interview.

101. Richard Hobson to Breyer, May 1, 1974 (WSPF, Fielding, box 20).

102. Colson to Magruder, May 1, 1972 (WSPF, May 3, box 1).

103. Akerman to Files, June 5, 1975 (WSPF, May 3, box 4); Akerman to Files, February 1, 1974 (WSPF, May 3, box 3); Akerman and Horowitz to Files, no date (WSPF, May 3, box 4); Liddy interview; Akerman and Horowitz to Files, no date (WSPF, May 3, box 4); Akerman to Files, January 24, 1975 (WSPF, Fielding, box 15); *NYT*, July 9, 1973; Horowitz to Files, November 26, 1973; Akerman to Files, July 25, 1973 (prior two items in WSPF, May 3, box 3).

104. Notes on interviews of William Rhatican, Ken Rietz, and Roger Showley, no date (WSPF, May 3, box 3); Akerman to Files, January 2, 1974 (WSPF, May 3, box 4); notes on Rhatican interview, January 25, 1974 (WSPF, May 3, box 3); Akerman and Horowitz to Ruth, September 17, 1974 (WSPF, May 3, box 4); Horowitz to Files, January 3, 1974; Horowitz to Files, October 10, 1973 (prior two items in WSPF, May 3, box 3); *New York Post*, April 24, 1972; *NYT*, April 26, 1972; *WP*, April 25, 26, 1972; *Newsweek*, May 1, 1972.

105. Akerman to File, September 10, 1973 (WSPF, May 3, box 4); Akerman to Files, July 26, 1973 (WSPF, May 3, box 20); *NYT,* July 9, 1973; Magruder, 206; notes on Rhatican interview, January 25, 1974; Horowitz to Files, January 3, 1974; Akerman to Files, February 1, 1974 (prior three items in WSPF, May 3, box 3); "Colson," no date (WSPF, May 3, box 4); notes on Rhatican, Rietz and Showley interviews, no date (WSPF, May 3, box 3).

106. Akerman to File, September 10, 1973 (WSPF, May 3, box 4); Liddy, 212; Magruder, 206; Akerman to Files, February 19, 1974 (WSPF, May 3, box 3); Liddy interview.

107. Akerman to Files, November 20, 1973 (WSPF, May 3, box 3); Akerman to Files, December 3, 1973 (WSPF, May 3, box 1); Akerman and Horowitz to Files, no date (WSPF, May 3, box 4); FBI document on interview of Humberto Lopez, August 17, 1973 (WSPF, May 3, box 3).

108. FBI document on Lopez interview, August 17, 1973; FBI document on interview of Felipe DeDiego, July 3, 1972 (prior two items in WSPF, May 3, box 3); unsourced newspaper article, May 26, 1973 (WSPF, May 3, box 1); NBC News Report, April 3, 1974 (WSPF, Fielding, box 2); FBI documents on interviews of Pablo Fernandez, September 20, 1973, July 5, 1972; FBI document on interview of John Kelly, August 22, 1973; FBI document on interview of Angel Ferrer, August 15, 1973; Akerman to Files, August 29, 1973 (prior five items in WSPF, May 3, box 3); FBI document on interview of Michael Brennan, June 24, 1972 (WSPF, May 3, box 1); FBI document on interview of Hiram Gonzalez, August 16, 1973 (WSPF, May 3, box 3); Akerman to Files, no date (WSPF, May 3, box 1).

109. FBI documents on Fernandez interviews, September 20, June 25, 1973; Akerman to Files, January 30, 1974; FBI document on Gonzalez interview, August 16, 1973; FBI document on Ferrer interview, August 15, 1973 (prior five items in WSPF, May 3, box 3).

110. Akerman and Horowitz to Files, no date (WSPF, May 3, box 4); FBI document on Gonzalez interview, August 16, 1973; FBI document on Ferrer interview, August 15, 1973; FBI documents on Fernandez interviews, July 5, 1972, September 20, 1973 (prior four items in WSPF, May 3, box 3).

111. Akerman and Horowitz to Files, no date (WSPF, May 3, box 4); Akerman and Horowitz to Merrill and Ruth, March 4, 1974 (WSPF, May 3, box 2).

112. Akerman and Horowitz to Files, no date (WSPF, May 3, box 4); Liddy interview.

113. FBI document on Ferrer interview, August 15, 1973; Akerman to Files, August 29, 1973; FBI documents on Fernandez interviews, September 20, June 25, 1973; Akerman to Files, no date (prior five items in WSPF, May 3, box 3); *Time,* October 23, 1972; Akerman and Horowitz to Merrill and Ruth, March 4, 1974 (WSPF, May 3, box 2); Horowitz to Files, December 7, 1973; Akerman to Files, June 5, 1975 (prior two items in WSPF, May 3, box 4).

114. Akerman to Files, January 30, 1974, August 29, 1973 (WSPF, May 3, box 3); Akerman to File, September 10, 1973 (WSPF, May 3, box 4); FBI document on Ferrer interview, August 15, 1973; FBI document on Fernandez interview, September 20, 1973; Akerman to Files, no date (prior three items in WSPF, May 3, box 3).

115. Akerman to Files, November 13, 1973 (WSPF, May 3, box 3).

116. FBI document on Ferrer interview, August 15, 1973; Akerman to Files, October 18, two, August 14, 1973; FBI document on Fernandez interview, June 25, 1973 (prior five items in WSPF, May 3, box 3).

117. FBI documents on Ferrer interviews, August 15, 1973, June 30, 1972 (WSPF, May 3, box 3); unsourced newspaper article, May 26, 1973 (WSPF, May 3, box 1); Barker interview.

118. Horowitz to Files, November 5, 1973; Akerman to Files, October 1, 1973; FBI document on interview of William Schaefer, December 10, 1973 (prior three items in WSPF, May 3, box 3).

119. FBI documents on Ferrer interviews, August 15, June 23, 1973; Akerman to Files, August 29, November 19, August 17, 1973; FBI documents on Fernandez interviews, September 20, June 25, 1973; Akerman to Files, no date (prior eight items in WSPF, May 3, box 3); FBI documents on interviews of two unnamed FBI agents, August 20, 1973 (WSPF, May 3, box 1)

120. Barker interview; Liddy interview; Michael Krinsky to Akerman, February 14, 1974 (WSPF, May 3, box 1); Ellsberg interview.

121. Akerman to Files, November 13, August 14, August 20, 1973 (WSPF, May 3, box 3).

122. Akerman to Files, August 17, September 6, November 13, 1973 (WSPF, May 3, box 3); FBI document on interview of unnamed FBI agent, August 20, 1973; unsourced newspaper article, May 26, 1973 (prior two items in WSPF, May 3, box 1); *Miami Herald*, April 22, 1973; Ruth to Kelley, July 16, 1973 (WSPF, May 3, box 1); FBI document on DeDiego interview, July 3, 1972; FBI document on Gonzalez interview, August 16, 1973 (prior two items in WSPF, May 3, box 3); *NYT*, March 19, 1973.

123. Akerman and Horowitz to Files, no date (WSPF, May 3, box 4); FBI document on DeDiego interview, July 3, 1972 (WSPF, May 3, box 3); Barker interview.

124. FBI document on DeDiego interview, July 3, 1972 (WSPF, May 3, box 3); Jacquelyn Barish to Akerman, August 18, 1973 (WSPF, May 3, box 1); Barker interview; Liddy, 221; unsourced newspaper article, May 26, 1973; FBI documents on Fernandez interviews, July 5, 1972, September 20, June 25, 1973; Akerman to Files, no date (prior five items in WSPF, May 3, box 3); Akerman to Files, no date (WSPF, May 3, box 1).

125. Akerman to Files, August 17, 1973; FBI document on Ferrer interview, August 15, 1973; FBI document on Gonzalez interview, August 16, 1973 (prior three items in WSPF, May 3, box 3); Barish to Akerman, August 18, 1973 (WSPF, May 3, box 1); Akerman to Files, no date (WSPF, May 3, box 3).

126. Akerman to Files, October 19, 1973 (WSPF, May 3, box 3); notes on interview of H.E. Andrews, no date; unsourced newspaper article, May 26, 1973 (prior two items in WSPF, May 3, box 1); Akerman to File, September 10, 1973 (WSPF, May 3, box 4); unsourced Sturgis statement, no date (WSPF, May 3, box 3); U.S. Capitol Police "Incident Report" (WSPF, May 3, box 1).

127. Akerman and Horowitz to Files, no date (WSPF, May 3, box 4); Akerman and Horowitz to Merrill and Ruth, March 4, 1974 (WSPF, May 3, box 1); Liddy interview; Magruder, 207; Akerman to Files, October 26, 1973 (WSPF, May 3, box 3).

128. Akerman to Files, November 20, 1973, January 30, 1974; FBI document on Fernandez interview, September 20, 1973; FBI document on Ferrer interview, June 23, 1973 (prior four items in WSPF, May 3, box 3).

129. FBI documents on Fernandez interviews, September 20, June 25, 1973; FBI documents on Ferrer interviews, June 23, August 15, 1973; Akerman to Files, August 29, 1973; FBI document on Gonzalez interview, August 16, 1973 (prior six

items in WSPF, May 3, box 3); unsourced newspaper articles, May 26, April 22, 1973 (WSPF, May 3, box 1).

130. Akerman to Files, February 19, February, 1, 1974 (WSPF, May 3, box 3); "Colson," no date (WSPF, May 3, box 4); Horowitz to Frampton, February 21, 1974 (WSPF, Fielding, box 2); Akerman and Horowitz to Files, no date (WSPF, May 3, box 4).

131. Akerman and Horowitz to Files, no date (WSPF, May 3, box 4); Magruder, 207.

132. Heymann to Cox, Ruth, and Merrill, July 17, 1973 (WSPF, May 3, box 1); Akerman to Files, June 5, 1975 (WSPF, May 3, box 4).

133. Pentagon Papers twentieth anniversary program, June 13, 1991 (videotape); Ellsberg interview.

134. Barker interview; Liddy interview.

135. Kutler, *Wars*, 115; Ehrlichman, 399.

136. Poll data on Pentagon Papers publication (WHSF, Ehrlichman, box 22); Colson to Haldeman, June 1971 (WHSF, Colson, box 3); *Time*, December 18, 1978; Rodberg interview. About six months after, to Henry Kissinger's ire, the Defense Department issued its larger, censored edition of the Papers—in part to try to "pre-empt the Beacon Press [i.e., Gravel] publication," David Young would note—Noam Chomsky went to the MIT library to see who had looked at it. "I was the only person," he recalls. "Not one faculty member, not one student, was even interested enough in the facts of the matter to bother looking at the Pentagon Papers. Now, these guys"—professors in MIT's political science department—"were all involved in Vietnam. And they were running secret seminars, and they had a villa in Saigon where students were going to work on pacification. But what the facts were was of no interest to them" (Young for the Record, September 24, 1971 [WHSF, Young, box 2]; Chomsky interview).

137. Ellsberg interview.

CHAPTER 14

1. Russo, "My Role in the Pentagon Papers Action" (copy in my possession); Weinglass interview; Libby interview; Ellsberg interview; Larner interview.

2. Libby interview; Russo interview; Lukas interview.

3. Winship interview; Schrag interview; Nesson interview; Popkin interview; *WP*, February 20, 1972.

4. Langer interview; Sheehan notes on Halberstam lunch, May 23, 1975 (SP, box 67).

5. Falk interview.

6. Ackland interview; Donovan interview; Sachs interview; Russo interview.

7. Ellsberg's 1973 *RS* interview (reprint), 39; Ellsberg interview.

8. *Newsweek*, July 26, 1971; Popkin interview.

9. *WP*, July 10, 1971; *Washington Star*, July 29, 1971; Nesson interview.

10. *NYT*, September 4, 1971; Thomson interview.

11. Thomson interview; affidavit for Bekins search warrant, September 1971 (WSPF, Fielding, box 20); *Look*, October 5, 1971, 32.

12. Linda Deutsch interview; *NYT*, August 17, 1971.

13. Lukas, "Month," 29, 95, 98; *WP*, September 24, 1971.

14. Liddy, 170–71; Liddy interview; Pentagon Papers twentieth anniversary program, June 13, 1991 (videotape).

15. Lukas, "Month," 98–99.
16. Weinglass interview; *LAT,* October 2, 1971; Russo interview; Lukas, "Month," 100.
17. Lukas, "Month," 100–101; Al Booth interview; Russo interview; Schrag, 24; Lukas interview.
18. Russo interview; Lukas, "Month," 101; Booth interview; McCloskey interview.
19. Lukas, "Month," 101.
20. Gisela and Al Booth interview.
21. UCLA *Daily Bruin,* November 15, 1971; Russo interview; McGinniss, 192; Ellsberg interview; Bella Abzug interview.
22. McGinniss, 192; Falk interview.
23. Libby interview; Donovan interview; Deutsch interview; Nesson interview; Ellsberg interview; Cummings interview; Sheinbaum interview; Schrag interview; Ungar interview.
24. FBI document on Carol Ellsberg interview, July 9, 1971 (WSPF, Fielding, box 18); Carol Ellsberg notes on Nesson conversation, summer 1971 (CP); Cummings interviews.
25. Carol Ellsberg notes on Nesson conversation, summer 1971 (CP); Cummings interview.
26. *WP,* August 6, 1971; Mark Rosenbaum interview; *NYT,* January 4, 1973; Weinglass interview.
27. *Newsweek,* February 28, 1972; Lukas interview; Ungar interviews; Sachs interview.
28. Ellsberg interviews.
29. Rich interview; Falk interview.
30. Rich, *passim;* Rich interview; Ellsberg interview.
31. Lukas, "Month," *passim;* Rich interview; Lukas interview; Ellsberg interviews; Sheinbaum interview.
32. Zion interview; Rosenthal interview.
33. Ungar interviews; Sachs interview; Arnold, 74; Sheinbaum interview.
34. Arnold interview; Theo Wilson interview.
35. Schrag interview.
36. Farrell, 79, 80, 86; videotape of Ellsberg's press conferences, 1971, 1973 (UCLA TV and Film Archive); Deutsch interview; Ungar interview; Arnold interview; Wilson interview; Sachs interview; Young interview.
37. Videotape of Ellsberg's press conferences, 1971, 1973 (UCLA TV and Film Archive); Pentagon Papers twentieth anniversary program, June 13, 1991 (videotape); Wilson interview; Sheehan notes on Halberstam conversation, January 6, 1976 (SP, box 64); Ungar interview.
38. Anonymous source; Schrag interview; Deutsch interview; Ungar interview; Donovan interview; Zinn interview.
39. Videotape of Ellsberg's press conferences, 1971, 1973 (UCLA TV and Film Archive); Russo interview.
40. Ellsberg interviews.
41. Kehler interview.
42. Harris interview; Andrew Schelling interview.
43. Pentagon Papers twentieth anniversary program, June 13, 1991 (videotape).
44. Ellsberg interview; Kellen interview; Best interview.
45. Kolkowicz interview; Ellsberg interviews; Sonnenfeldt interview; Yarmolinsky interview.

46. Ellsberg interviews; Marshall interview.
47. Ellsberg radio interview on "Democracy Now," KPFA, June 13, 1996; Libby interview; Chomsky interview.
48. Phillips interview; Conein interview.
49. Zinn interviews.
50. Goodman interview; Lukas, "Month," 105; Carol Ellsberg notes on Nesson phone conversation, January 16, 1972 (CP); Libby interview.
51. Gitlin, 448; Zinn interview.
52. Garbus interview; Rodberg interview.
53. Sachs interview.
54. *Reason,* June 1973, 10, 11, 12–13; Libby interview.
55. Lukas, "Month," 104.
56. *NYT,* July 27, August 25, 1971.
57. *NYT,* August 25, 1971; Solotaroff interview.
58. Solotaroff interview.
59. Solotaroff interview.
60. Solotaroff interview.
61. Libby interview; Sheinbaum interview.
62. Butler interview; Libby interview.
63. Solotaroff interview; Ellsberg, *Papers,* 13; *Washington Post Book World,* July 30, 1972; *New York Times Book Review,* July 23, 1972; *Time,* August 14, 1972; *Newsweek,* July 24, 1972; Brenman-Gibson interview; Lansdale to Ellsberg, September 15, 1972 (LP, box 3); Sheehan notes on Ellsberg interviews, no date (SP, box 121); Sheehan notes on Ellsberg phone conversation, August 24, 1979 (SP, box 64).
64. Solotaroff interview.
65. Russo interview.
66. Russo interview.
67. Russo interview.
68. Zinn interview.
69. Russo interview; Sheinbaum interview.
70. Libby interview; Sachs interview; Schrag interview; Sheehan notes on Fred Graham conversation, September 16, 1973 (SP, box 65).
71. Ungar interview; Nesson interview; McGinniss, 199; Russo interview; Arnold interview.
72. *NYT, WP,* December 31, 1971; Carol Ellsberg notes on Nesson phone conversation, January 16, 1972 (CP).
73. Nesson interview; Young interview.
74. Ungar interviews; Russo interview.
75. Arnold, 74; Nesson interview; Best interview; Cummings interview; Weinglass interview.
76. *New York Post,* January 8, 1972; Russo interview; Ackland interview; Sheinbaum interview.
77. Russo interview; Ungar interview; Patricia Ellsberg interview; Sachs interview.
78. Weinglass interview; Russo interview; anonymous source.
79. Russo interviews.
80. Young interview; Russo interview; Sachs interview.
81. Falk interview; Ungar interviews; Russo interview; Sheinbaum interview; Rosenbaum interview; Donovan interview; Pentagon Papers twentieth anniversary program, June 13, 1991 (videotape).

82. Russo interview.
83. Russo interview; Weinglass interview; Halperin interview.
84. Russo interview; Sachs interview; Young interview.
85. Weinglass interview; Zinn interview.
86. Donovan interview; Arnold interview; Farrell, 93.
87. Russo interview.
88. Russo interview; Falk interview.
89. Young interview; Farrell, 92.
90. Weinglass interview; anonymous source.
91. Russo interview; Farrell, 93.
92. Sheehan, *Bright*, 7, 786–89; John Allen Vann interview.
93. Sheehan notes on Ellsberg interview, November 29, 1976 (SP, box 64); Jesse Vann interview; Oliphant interview; Sheehan notes on Gene Vann interview, no date (SP, box 57).
94. Sheehan, *Bright*, 12, 14; Mary Jane Vann interview; John Allen Vann interview.
95. Jesse Vann interview.
96. Mary Jane Vann interview; Sheehan, *Bright*, 27–33; Jesse Vann interview.
97. AP article, August 25, 1972 (Indochina Archive); *Chicago Sun-Times*, hand-dated August 27, 1972 (WHSF, Young, box 7); *Newsweek*, September 4, 1972; Sheehan notes on Lake dinner, May 26, 1975 (SP, box 63). McCloskey remembers returning to his room in Miami's Doral Hotel in a depressed state late one night of the convention after having some drinks with Walter Cronkite: "I open the door at about one o'clock in the morning—I'm kind of smashed and tired and frustrated—the door goes about eight inches and it runs into a guy in a sleeping bag sleeping on the floor. I had about six people in my staff [there]. . . . And this kid looks up at me. Out of his sleep the guy says, 'Pete, you can't sleep in your room tonight.' I said, 'Why can't I?' And he says, 'Well, Dan Ellsberg and his wife are in your bed.' . . . And I said, 'Well, okay, I'll sleep in the other room.' We had a two-bedroom suite. . . . 'No,' he says, 'you can't sleep there either.' He says, 'Tom Hayden and Jane Fonda are in there.' So I said, 'To hell with it,'" and slept elsewhere. It was one hell of a way for a presidential candidate to have to act, McCloskey thought (McCloskey interview).
98. Ellsberg affidavit, November 14, 1972 (Meiklejohn); Sachs interview; Dowd interview.
99. Nissen subpoenas and letters to Carol Ellsberg, 1972 (CP); Carol Ellsberg notes on Nesson conversations, March 6, July 10, 1972 (CP); Cummings interview.
100. Carol Ellsberg notes on Nesson conversation, summer 1971 (CP); Cummings interview.
101. Cummings interviews; Robert Ellsberg interview; Carol Ellsberg notes on Nesson conversation, February 26, 1973 (CP).
102. Robert Ellsberg interview; Cummings interview; Mary Ellsberg interview.
103. Robert Ellsberg interview; Mary Ellsberg interview.
104. Cummings interview; Robert Ellsberg interview.
105. Schrag, 161; Arnold, 75, 76; Wilson interview; Arnold interview; *Time*, February 12, 1973; Sachs interview; Deutsch interview.
106. Arnold interview; Shubert interview.
107. Ellsberg interview; Schrag, 14–15, 165–66; Ungar interview; Schrag interview; jury discussion, May 20, 1973 (transcript); notes on Nissen interview, August 2, 1973 (WSPF, Fielding, box 21).

108. Garbus interview; Weinglass interview; Jamie Kalvin phone conversation; Shein-baum interview; Donovan interview; Sachs interview.

109. Liddy to Krogh and Young, September 23, 1971 (WHSF, Young, box 13); *Time*, August 14, 1972; Nesson interview; Zinn interview; Renee Vollen interview.

110. Patricia Ellsberg interview.

111. Sachs interview; Arnold, 76; Garbus interview; Donovan interview; Rosenbaum interview; Weinglass interview; Nesson interview; Young interview.

112. Sheinbaum interview.

113. Sheinbaum interview.

114. Garbus interview; Halperin interview; Sheehan notes on Rogovin conversation, December 28, 1972 (SP, box 65).

115. Arnold, 75; Rosenbaum interview.

116. Donovan interview; Halperin interview; Schrag interview; anonymous source; Deutsch interview; Nesson interview.

117. Schrag, 67; Sheinbaum interview; Sheehan notes on Krementz conversation, January 24, 1976 (SP, box 65); Deutsch interview; Wilson interview.

118. Sheinbaum interview; Carol Sobel phone conversations; Deutsch interview; anonymous source; Young interview; Farrell, 92.

119. Sachs interview; Libby interview; Weinglass interview; Sheinbaum interview; Nesson interview; Rosenbaum interview; Deutsch interview; Farrell, 86; Cummings interview.

120. Schrag interview; Sachs interview; Patricia Ellsberg interview; discussion with Patricia and Dan Ellsberg.

121. Ungar interview; Ackland interview; Sheehan notes on Fred Graham conversation, September 29, 1975 (SP, box 64); Brenman-Gibson interview.

122. Patricia Ellsberg interview; Libby interview; *New York Post*, November 24, 1971.

123. Butler interview.

124. Butler interview; Tanham interview; Heymann interview; Moorsteen and Rowen trial testimony, vols. 73, 124–25, *passim* (Butler papers); Ellsberg interviews.

125. Butler interview.

126. Donovan interview; Rosenbaum interview; Russo interview; Weinglass interview.

127. Weinglass interview; Ellsberg trial testimony, vol. 109, 19,651 (Butler papers).

128. *LAT*, April 11, 1973; Schrag, 320–21, 323; Donovan interview; Rosenbaum interview; Nesson interview.

129. Ellsberg trial testimony, vol. 109, 19,542 (Butler papers); *Washington Star*, April 12, 1973; Donovan interview; jury discussion, May 20, 1973 (transcript); Schrag, 323; Arnold interview.

130. Sachs interview; Rosenbaum interview.

131. HJC, Book VII, Part 4, 1995, 1999–2008; Russo interview; Wilson interview.

132. Best interview.

133. *Los Angeles Herald-Examiner*, April 27, 1973; Weinglass interview; Donovan interview; Schrag, 331; Young interview; Sachs interview; anonymous source; Nesson interview; *George*, June 1997, 96; Russo interview.

134. *Los Angeles Herald-Examiner*, April 27, 1973; *LAT*, April 28, 1973; video of Ellsberg press conference outside courthouse, April or May 1973 (UCLA TV and Film Archive); Fielding affidavit, April 29, 1973 (WSPF, Fielding, box 18); Goldberg interview; Rosenbaum interview.

135. HJC, Book III, Part 2, 923, 1168–69; Heymann notes on Krogh interview, June 20, 1974 (WSPF, Fielding, box 3); "Summary of Interview with Egil Krogh,"

April 3, 1974 (WSPF, Fielding, box 20); Young memo on March 27, 1973, conversation with Ehrlichman; "Closing Argument," no date; Heymann to Merrill, May 28, 1974 (prior three items in WSPF, Fielding, box 1); Ehrlichman grand jury testimony, May 14, 1973 (WSPF, Fielding, box 3).

136. HJC, Book III, Part 2, 942; Merrill and Bakes to Vorenberg, August 13, 1973 (WSPF, Fielding, box 21); Nixon and Haldeman conversation, May 20, 1973; Nixon and Ehrlichman conversation, May 2, 1973 (prior two items in APT, NA); J. T. Smith meeting notes, May 1 (two sets), 2, 4, 1973 (WSPF, Fielding, box 21); Martin to Files, August 16, 1973 (WSPF, Fielding, box 15); Merrill to Files, August 13, 1973 (WSPF, Fielding, box 21); Ehrlichman, 401–3; Ehrlichman interview; Haldeman, *Ends*, 113–15; Strober and Strober, 223, 226; Colson affidavit, April 29, 1974 (WSPF, Fielding, box 2); *WP*, October 2, 1973.

137. Nixon and Ziegler conversation, May 20, 1973; Nixon and Haldeman conversation, May 20, 1973; Nixon and Ehrlichman conversation, May 2, 1973; Nixon and Rogers conversation, May 3, 1973; Nixon and Haig conversation, May 18, 1973 (prior five items in APT, NA); Kutler, *Abuse*, 331–33, 335, 423–24, 492.

138. Notes on Kleindienst interview, July 31, 1973 (WSPF, Fielding, box 19); *LAT*, July 25, 26, 1973; Merrill to Files, August 13, 1973 (WSPF, Fielding, box 21); Breyer and Bakes to Vorenberg, October 30, 1974 (WSPF, Fielding, accordion file after box 3).

139. Ehrlichman "60 Minutes" interview, June 29, 1973, partial transcript (WSPF, Fielding, box 16); *LAT*, July 26, 1973.

140. Goulden, 230.

141. Nesson interview; Weinglass interview; Russo interview; Young interview.

142. Nesson interview; Donovan interview; anonymous source; *LAT*, May 1, 1973.

143. Deutsch interview.

144. Defense Motion to Dismiss the Indictment, May 1, 1973 (Sachs).

145. Nesson interview; Arnold interview; Schrag, 162.

146. Donovan interview; Young interview; Russo interview; Sachs interview.

147. *NYT*, May 12, 1973; *LAT*, May 11, 1973; Schrag, 347–48; Henry Petersen to Byrne, May 10, 1973 (Sachs).

148. Deutsch interview; Wilson interview; Arnold interview; Arnold, 77.

149. Kutler, *Abuse*, 462–63, 473.

150. Arnold, 152; *NYT*, May 12, 1973; Schrag, 352–56.

151. *LAT*, May 12, 1973; Arnold interview.

152. *LAT, NYT, Los Angeles Herald-Examiner*, May 12, 1973.

153. Nixon and Haig conversation, May 12, 1973 (APT, NA).

154. Nesson interview; Young interview.

155. McMillan interview.

156. Schrag, 356; Arnold interview; Young interview.

CHAPTER 15

1. *LAT*, May 17, 1973; Oliphant interview; Fain, 501–14.

2. Fain, 511.

3. Arnold, 77.

4. *People*, October 26, 1976; Arnold, 77; *WP*, May 18, 1973; Ellsberg's 1973 *RS* interview (reprint), 15–16; *NYT*, November 1, 1973.

5. *Meet the Press*, May 20, 1973 (transcript).

6. *LAT,* May 23, 1973.

7. *LAT,* June 6, 1973.

8. Sheehan notes on February 9, 1974, Ellsberg conversation (SP, box 64); Cummings interview.

9. Salisbury piece in *Esquire,* February, undated otherwise (SP, box 66); Sheehan notes on Ellsberg interviews, no date (SP, box 121); *People,* October 26, 1976.

10. Mill Valley Police Department report on burglary, October 3, 1974; San Francisco FBI, "Daniel Ellsberg," November 8, 1974; FBI Director to Special Prosecution Force, December 6, 1974 (prior three items in WSPF, DE, MV); *SFC,* December 7, 1974; *NYT,* December 8, 1974; Sheehan notes on Ellsberg interviews, no date (SP, box 121).

11. Copy of burglar's note (WSPF, DE, MV).

12. San Francisco FBI, "Daniel Ellsberg," November 8, 1974; Horowitz to Ruth, October 8, 1974; FBI document on Boudin interview, November 25, 1974 (prior three items in WSPF, DE, MV).

13. *SFC,* December 6, 7, 1974; *NYT,* December 8, 1974; FBI, Director's Office, "Alleged Burglary," December 17, 1974 (WSPF, DE, MV); *San Francisco Examiner,* December 6, 1974.

14. *People,* October 26, 1976.

15. Sheehan notes on Ellsberg interviews, no date (SP, box 121); "DE Tape Summaries" (SP, box 64); Fain, 283.

16. Sheehan notes on Ellsberg interviews, no date (SP, box 121); "DE Interview Notebooks" (SP, box 64); Sheehan notes on Raskin's comments on Ellsberg's talk (SP, box 65); *NYT,* September 14, 1974.

17. Sheehan notes on Ellsberg interviews, no date (SP, box 121); "DE Interview Notebooks" (SP, box 64).

18. Sheehan notes on Ellsberg conversation, May 14, 1976 (SP, box 63); "DE Interview Notebooks" (SP, box 64); FBI, Director's Office, "Alleged Burglary," December 17, 1974 (WSPF, DE, MV); Chomsky interview.

19. Arnold, 150, 152; Ellsberg interview; Abzug interview; Hukill interview.

20. Bethel, "Gentleman-in-Waiting" (SP, box 63); Arnold, 152.

21. Wilson interview.

22. Discussion with Dan and Patricia Ellsberg; Gitlin interview; Beneke interview.

23. Sheehan notes on Ellsberg talk, no date, mid-1970s (SP, box 64); *DFP,* October 13, 1974; Brenman-Gibson interview; *People,* October 26, 1976; Shanks, 122.

24. Sheehan notes on Tom Generous conversation, April 2, 1974 (SP, box 65); Ungar interview.

25. Ellsberg interview; Sheehan notes on Ellsberg lecture, November 17, 1976 (SP, box 64); Billy Nesson conversation; Gitlin interview; Ellsberg speech at Cranbrook, October 1975 (tape); K. Don Jacobusse to Ellsberg, November 14, 1975 (CA, Records of Headmaster's Office, series 1, box 3).

26. Anonymous source.

27. Beneke interview.

28. Ellsberg interviews.

29. Ellsberg interview; Brenman-Gibson interview.

30. Sheehan notes on Salisbury conversation, October 11, 1976 (SP, box 107); Russo interview.

31. *NYT,* May 13, 1973; Ellsberg's 1973 *RS* interview (reprint), 38–39.

32. Gitlin interview; Sheehan, "Ellsberg, Nuclear War Plans," no date; Sheehan to Ellsberg, August 10, 1979 (prior two items in SP, box 64); Sheehan notes on Ellsberg conversation, May 14, 1976 (SP, box 63).

33. Henriques interview.

34. Sterling Lord interview.

35. Ellsberg interviews; Lord interview.

36. Ellsberg interview; Pentagon Papers twentieth anniversary program, June 1991 (videotape); anonymous source; Zeckhauser interview; Falk interview; Dowd interview; Brenman-Gibson interview; Sheinbaum phone conversation; Zinn interview.

37. Brenman-Gibson interviews; Ellsberg interview; Hall interview and note to author.

38. Brenman-Gibson interview; Hall note to author; Ellsberg interviews.

39. Gitlin interview; Ellsberg interviews.

40. Brenman-Gibson interview; Ellsberg interview; Wheelis, *Quest*, 50–51, 103–25.

41. Ellsberg interview.

42. Ellsberg interview.

43. Ellsberg interview.

44. Hall interview; Brenman-Gibson interview; Ellsberg interviews.

45. Kernberg, 218–19, 243–60, 267–69, 273–76; Ellsberg interview.

46. Gitlin interview; Kolkowicz interview.

47. *People*, October 26, 1976; Brenman-Gibson interview; Zeckhauser interview; Isaacson interview.

48. *Pacific Sun*, April 27-May 3, 1979; George interview.

49. Gitlin interview.

50. Brenman-Gibson interviews.

51. Zeckhauser interview; Schelling interview; Popkin interview.

52. Brenman-Gibson interview; Gitlin interview; Kaysen interview.

53. *DFP*, October 13, 1974; Kehler interview; Sheehan, "DE Interview Notebooks" (SP, box 64).

54. Dowd interview.

55. Anonymous source; Dowd interview.

56. Dowd interview.

57. Dowd interview; Ellsberg interviews; Kehler interview; Peter Laitin interview; Joseph Laitin letter to author.

58. Ellsberg interviews.

59. Ellsberg interview.

60. Dowd interview.

61. Gitlin interview.

62. Daniel Ellsberg interview; Patricia Ellsberg interview; anonymous source.

63. Zinn interview; Chomsky interview; Ellsberg interviews; anonymous source; Beneke interview; Larner interview.

64. *People*, October 26, 1976; Popkin interview.

65. Butler interview; *People*, October 26, 1976.

66. Ellsberg radio interview on KQED, San Francisco, August 25, 1995; Dowd interview; David Cortright interview.

67. Ellsberg interview; Daniel and Pope, 10–12; *Not Man Apart*, February 1980, 23; *Nation*, May 27, 1978, 632–33.

68. Ellsberg interview.

69. Judy Danielson interview; Daniel and Pope, 14.

70. Cate Woods note to author; Daniel and Pope, 14, 23; Danielson interview; anonymous source.
71. Sachs interview.
72. Danielson interview.
73. Danielson interview.
74. Daniel and Pope, 14.
75. Danielson interview; Daniel and Pope, 9; Anne Waldman interview.
76. Daniel and Pope, 14; Kaufmann interview.
77. Ellsberg interview.
78. Daniel and Pope, 18–19; Ellsberg interview with Terkel, 1980.
79. Waldman interview.
80. David Hartsough interview; Kehler interview.
81. *NYT*, February 2, 1982; Hartsough interview; Kehler interview; Ken Butigan interview.
82. Hartsough interview; Sheehan notes on Ellsberg's *Nightline* appearance, June 27, 1983 (SP, box 63).
83. Ellsberg interview; Cortright, 209.
84. Cortright, 179; Ellsberg interview.
85. *Progressive*, July 1985, September 1989; Larner interview. Other Ellsberg interviews appear in: *Not Man Apart*, February 1980; *WIN*, November 1, 1980; *Current*, June 1981; *California*, November 1985; *RS*, November 5-December 10, 1987. Ellsberg has frequently enumerated some two dozen instances when, he says, the United States threatened use of nuclear weapons and thereby *used* those weapons in the same way that a person who points a gun at another person uses the gun. After someone else expressed the same idea without crediting him, Ellsberg complained to Margaret Brenman-Gibson that many people don't want to cite him in their writings. He feels others don't give him sufficient credit for his ideas (Brenman-Gibson interview).
86. Hartsough interview; *Oakland Tribune*, July 1985, undated otherwise (Indochina Archive); Shanks, 95.
87. Hartsough interview.
88. Butigan interview.
89. Anonymous source.
90. Ellsberg, "Manhattan Project II," 42–43; Brenman-Gibson interviews; Cortright interview; Butigan interview.
91. Warnke interview; Colby interview; Ellsberg interview with Bird, 1993; anonymous source; Ellsberg interview; Hoopes interview.
92. Garbus interview; anonymous source.
93. Call for fast, April 2, 1995 (copy in my possession); Ellsberg interviews; Cortright interview.
94. Brenman-Gibson interviews; Ellsberg interview; Cortright interview.
95. Garbus interview; Zeckhauser interview.
96. *People*, October 26, 1976; Digby interview; Shubert interview.
97. Ellsberg interviews.
98. Anonymous source; Cummings interview.
99. Anonymous source.
100. Ellsberg interviews; Sonnenfeldt interview.
101. Dowd interview; anonymous source; Don Hall interview; Ellsberg interviews.
102. Cummings interview; Brenman-Gibson interviews.

103. Zinn interview; Hartsough interview; Brenman-Gibson interview.

104. Ellsberg interviews; Patricia Ellsberg interview; anonymous source.

105. Anonymous sources; Brenman-Gibson interview; Henriques interview.

106. Anonymous source.

107. Sheinbaum interview; anonymous sources.

108. Sheinbaum interview.

109. Dowd interview; Schelling interview.

110. Dowd interview; Brenman-Gibson interview; anonymous source.

111. Anonymous sources; Henriques interview.

112. Dowd interview.

113. Dowd interview; Brenman-Gibson interview; Henriques interview.

114. Henriques interview; Brenman-Gibson interview; *Pacific Sun*, April 27-May 3, 1979; discussion with Dan and Patricia Ellsberg.

115. Dowd interview; anonymous source.

116. Henriques interview; Brenman-Gibson interview.

117. Brenman-Gibson interview; anonymous source.

118. Henriques interview and phone conversation.

119. Mary Ellsberg interview; Twaddell interview; discussion with Dan and Patricia Ellsberg.

120. Robert Ellsberg interview.

121. Robert Ellsberg interview; Ellsberg interview with Terkel, 1980.

122. Robert Ellsberg interview; Chuck Stephen conversation.

123. Robert Ellsberg interview.

124. Robert Ellsberg interview; Daniel Ellsberg interview.

125. Cummings interview; Mary Ellsberg interview; Marshall interview; excerpt of unpublished Mary Ellsberg memoir (in my possession); Hall interview.

126. Mary Ellsberg interview; Henriques interview; anonymous source.

127. Brenman-Gibson interview; Cummings interview.

128. Mary Ellsberg interview.

129. Bagdikian interview; Hall interview; Schelling interview.

130. Zinn interviews.

131. Anonymous source; Zinn interview; Dowd interview.

132. Gitlin interview; anonymous source.

133. Schrag interview; Popkin interview; Jock McDonald phone conversation; Baker interview.

134. Ellsberg interview.

135. Ellsberg interviews.

136. Anonymous source; Cummings interview.

137. Ellsberg interview; Hall interview. Ellsberg has not always wanted to be recognized in public, however. Douglas Pike remembers being on a flight from London to Hamburg in the early 1980s and noticing Ellsberg sitting in the first-class section, way at one end. You're Daniel Ellsberg, Pike said to him. No, no, Ellsberg replied. When they were deplaning later, Pike was behind Ellsberg. To hell it wasn't him, Pike thought to himself. Later, Pike heard that Ellsberg had gone somewhere on this trip and then denied to others that he'd been there (Pike interview).

138. Anonymous source.

139. Zeckhauser interview.

SELECT BIBLIOGRAPHY

Arnold, Martin. "Daniel Ellsberg at the Trial of Anthony J. Russo." *Esquire*, January 1974.

Bagdikian, Ben H. *Double Vision: Reflections on My Heritage, Life, and Profession.* Boston: Beacon Press, 1995.

Ball, Desmond. *Politics and Force Levels: The Strategic Missile Program of the Kennedy Administration.* Berkeley: University of California Press, 1980.

Beschloss, Michael R. *The Crisis Years: Kennedy and Khrushchev 1960–1963.* New York: Harper Collins, 1991.

Blauner, Bob, ed. *Our Mothers' Spirits: On the Death of Mothers and the Grief of Men.* New York: Regan Books, 1997.

Bradlee, Ben. *A Good Life: Newspapering and Other Adventures.* New York: Simon & Schuster, 1995.

Cortright, David. *Peace Works: The Citizen's Role in Ending the Cold War.* Boulder: Westview Press, 1993.

Cott, Lawrence V. "Pentagon Papers and Ellsberg: Deed and the Trial." *Human Events*, August 17, 1974.

Cronkite, Walter. *A Reporter's Life.* New York: Knopf, 1996.

Currey, Cecil B. *Edward Lansdale: The Unquiet American.* Boston: Houghton Mifflin, 1988.

Daniel, Joseph, and Keith Pope. *A Year of Disobedience.* Boulder: Daniel Productions, 1979.

Day, Gardiner M. *The Biography of a Church: A Brief History of Christ Church, Cambridge, Massachusetts.* Cambridge: The Riverside Press, 1951.

Dean, John. *Blind Ambition: The White House Years.* New York: Pocket Books, 1977.

Detroit Institute of Arts. *The Legacy of Albert Kahn.* Detroit: Detroit Institute of Arts, 1970.

Eddy, Mary Baker G. *Science and Health: With a Key to the Scriptures.* Boston: Mary Baker G. Eddy, 1889.

Ehrlichman, John. *Witness to Power: The Nixon Years.* New York: Simon & Schuster, 1982.

Ellsberg, Daniel. "Classic and Current Notions of 'Measurable Utility.'" *Economic Journal* (September 1954).

———. "Theory of the Reluctant Duelist." *American Economic Review* (December 1956).

———. "The Crude Analysis of Strategic Choices." RAND P-2183, December 1960.

———. "Risk, Ambiguity, and the Savage Axioms." *Quarterly Journal of Economics* (November 1961).

———. "Vagueness and Decision: A Rejoinder." RAND P-2705, February 1963.

———. "Vietnam Diary: Notes from the Journal of a Young American in Saigon." *The Reporter,* January 13, 1966 (published anonymously).

———. "The Day Loc Tien was Pacified." RAND P-3793, February 1968.

———. "The Theory and Practice of Blackmail." RAND P-3883, July 1968 (delivered as a lecture in March 1959).

———. "Kahn on Winning in Vietnam: A Review." RAND P-3965, November 1968.

————. "Public Goods and Public Bads: Comments on Mancur Olson's 'The Optimal Institutional Mix.'" RAND P-4029, February 1969.

————. "Some Lessons from Failure in Vietnam." RAND P-4036, July 1969.

————. "Laos: What Nixon is Up To." *New York Review of Books*, March 11, 1971.

————. "The Quagmire Myth and the Stalemate Machine." *Public Policy* (Spring 1971). Reprint.

————. *Papers on the War.* New York: Simon & Schuster, 1972.

————. "The First Two Times We Met." In *Gary Snyder: Dimensions of a Life.* Ed. Jon Halper. San Francisco: Sierra Club Books, 1991.

————. "Manhattan Project II." *Bulletin of the Atomic Scientists,* May 1992.

Emery, Fred. *Watergate: The Corruption of American Politics and the Fall of Richard Nixon.* New York: Times Books, 1994.

Fain, Tyrus G., ed., with Katherine C. Plant and Ross Milloy. *The Intelligence Community: History, Organization, and Issues.* New York: R. R. Bowker, 1977.

Farrell, Barry. "The Ellsberg Mask: Whatever It Conceals, It Always Faces the Camera." *Harper's,* October 1973.

Fine, Reuben. *Narcissism, the Self, and Society.* New York: Columbia University Press, 1986.

FitzGerald, Frances. "The Tragedy of Saigon." *Atlantic,* December 1966.

Frankel, Max. *The Times of My Life: And My Life with The Times.* New York: Random House, 1999.

Freeman, Joan, ed. *The Psychology of Gifted Children: Perspectives on Development and Education.* New York: Wiley, 1985.

Frommer, Myrna Katz, and Harvey Frommer. *Growing Up Jewish in America: An Oral History.* New York: Harcourt Brace, 1995.

Garbus, Martin. "Recalling The Papers and the Papers." *National Law Journal,* July 15, 1996.

Garbus, Martin, with Stanley Cohen. *Tough Talk: How I Fought for Writers, Comics, Bigots and the American Way.* New York: Times Books, 1998.

Gelb, Leslie H. "Vietnam: The System Worked." *Foreign Policy* (Summer 1971).

Gentry, Curt. *J. Edgar Hoover: The Man and the Secrets.* New York: Norton, 1991.

Gitlin, Todd. "Ellsberg and the New Heroism." *Commonweal,* September 3, 1971.

Gooch, Brad. *City Poet: The Life and Times of Frank O'Hara.* New York: Knopf, 1993.

Goulden, Joseph C. *The Benchwarmers: The Private World of the Powerful Federal Judges.* New York: Ballantine Books, 1974.

Grant, Zalin. *Facing the Phoenix.* New York: Norton, 1991.

Halberstam, David. *The Best and the Brightest.* Greenwich, Connecticut: Fawcett Crest, 1973.

————. *The Fifties.* New York: Villard Books, 1993.

Haldeman, H. R. *The Haldeman Diaries: Inside the Nixon White House.* New York: G. P. Putnam's Sons, 1994.

Haldeman, H. R., with Joseph DiMona. *The Ends of Power.* New York: Times Books, 1978.

Harris, Warren G. *Cary Grant: A Touch of Elegance.* New York: Doubleday, 1987.

Haushalter, Walter M. *Mrs. Eddy Purloins From Hegel: Newly Discovered Source Reveals Amazing Plagiarisms in* Science and Health. Boston: A. A. Beauchamp, 1936.

Herken, Gregg. *Counsels of War.* New York: Knopf, 1985.

Hersh, Seymour M. *The Price of Power: Kissinger in the Nixon White House.* New York: Summit Books, 1983.

Hunt, E. Howard. *Undercover: Memoirs of an American Secret Agent.* New York: Berkley, 1974.

Ise, John. *Economics.* New York: Harper and Brothers, 1946.

Jardini, David R. "Out of the Blue Yonder: The RAND Corporation's Diversification into Social Welfare Research, 1946–1968." Ph.D. dissertation, May 1996.

Kahn, Herman. *On Thermonuclear War.* Princeton: Princeton University Press, 1961.

Kantor, Martin. *Understanding Writer's Block: A Therapist's Guide to Diagnosis and Treatment.* Westport, Connecticut: Praeger, 1995.

Kaplan, Fred. *The Wizards of Armageddon.* New York: Simon & Schuster, 1983.

Kaufmann, William W. *The McNamara Strategy.* New York: Harper & Row, 1964.

Kernberg, Otto F. *Borderline Conditions and Pathological Narcissism.* New York: Jason Aronson, 1979.

Kincaid, John. "Secrecy and Democracy: The Unresolved Legacy of the Pentagon Papers." In *Watergate and Afterward: The Legacy of Richard M. Nixon.* Eds. Leon Friedman and William F. Levantrosser. Westport, Connecticut: Greenwood Press, 1992.

Klein, Pnina S., and Abraham J. Tannenbaum, eds. *To Be Young and Gifted.* Norwood, New Jersey: Ablex, 1992.

Knoll, Erwin, and Judith Nies McFadden, eds. *War Crimes and the American Conscience.* New York: Holt, Rinehart and Winston, 1970.

Kohut, Heinz. *The Analysis of the Self.* New York: International Universities Press, 1971.

Kutler, Stanley I. *The Wars of Watergate: The Last Crisis of Richard Nixon.* New York: Knopf, 1990.

―――, ed. *Abuse of Power: The New Nixon Tapes.* New York: Free Press, 1997.

Leepson, Marc. "The Cult of the Quiet American." *Regardie's,* November 1988.

Liddy, G. Gordon. *Will: The Autobiography of G. Gordon Liddy.* New York: St. Martin's Press, 1980.

Lifton, Robert Jay. *Death in Life: Survivors of Hiroshima.* New York: Random House, 1967.

Lowen, Alexander. *Narcissism: Denial of the True Self.* New York: Collier Books/Macmillan, 1985.

Lukas, J. Anthony. "A Month in the New Life of Daniel Ellsberg." *New York Times Magazine,* December 12, 1971.

―――. *Nightmare: The Underside of the Nixon Years.* New York: Penguin Books, 1988.

Magruder, Jeb Stuart. *An American Life: One Man's Road to Watergate.* New York: Atheneum, 1974.

Marshall, Andrew W., J. J. Martin, and Henry S. Rowen, eds. *On Not Confusing Ourselves: Essays on National Security Strategy in Honor of Albert and Roberta Wohlstetter.* Boulder: Westview Press, 1991.

McGinniss, Joe. "The Ordeal of Daniel Ellsberg." *Playboy,* October 1972.

McGlothlin, William H. "Long-lasting Effects of LSD on Certain Attitudes in Normals: An Experimental Proposal." RAND P-2575, May 1962.

McGlothlin, William H., Sidney Cohen, and Marcella S. McGlothlin. "Short-term Effects of LSD on Anxiety, Attitudes, and Performance." RAND P-2757, June 1963.

―――. "Long-lasting Effects of LSD on Normals." Institute of Government and Public Affairs, UCLA, MR-75, July 1967.

McNamara, Robert S., with Brian VanDeMark. *In Retrospect: The Tragedy and Lessons of Vietnam.* New York: Times Books, 1995.

Mollon, Phil. *The Fragile Self: The Structure of Narcissistic Disturbance and Its Therapy.* Northvale, New Jersey: Jason Aronson, 1993.

Newland, Constance A. [Thelma Moss]. *My Self and I*. New York: Coward-McCann, 1962.

Nixon, Richard M. *RN: The Memoirs of Richard Nixon*. New York: Grosset & Dunlap, 1978.

Obst, David. *Too Good to be Forgotten: Changing America in the '60s and '70s*. New York: Wiley, 1998.

Ogden, C. K., and I. A. Richards. *The Meaning of Meaning: A Study of the Influence of Language Upon Thought and of the Science of Symbolism*. New York: Harcourt Brace, 1936.

Oudes, Bruce, ed. *From: The President; Richard Nixon's Secret Files*. New York: Harper & Row, 1989.

Pentagon Papers, The. Senator Gravel Edition. Vols. 1–4. Boston: Beacon Press, 1971.

Pincus, Lily. *Death and the Family: The Importance of Mourning*. New York: Pantheon, 1974.

Pound, Arthur. *The Only Thing Worth Finding: The Life and Legacies of George Gough Booth*. Detroit: Wayne State University Press, 1964.

Pratt, John Clark, ed. *Vietnam Voices*. New York: Viking, 1984.

Prochnau, William. *Once Upon a Distant War*. New York: Times Books, 1995.

Race, Jeffrey. "The Unlearned Lessons of Vietnam." *Yale Review* (December 1976).

Rhodes, Richard. *The Making of the Atomic Bomb*. New York: Simon & Schuster, 1986.

Rich, Frank. "Q: Do the Claims of Conscience Outweigh the Duties of Citizenship? Testimony of the Witness, Daniel Ellsberg." *Esquire*, December 1971.

The Rolling Stone Interview: Dan Ellsberg. San Francisco: Straight Arrow Publishers, 1973. Reprint.

Rosenberg, David Alan. "The Origins of Overkill: Nuclear Weapons and American Strategy, 1945–1960." *International Security* (Spring 1983).

———. "Reality and Responsibility: Power and Process in the Making of United States Nuclear Strategy, 1945–68." *Journal of Strategic Studies* (March 1986).

Rothstein, Arnold. *The Narcissistic Pursuit of Perfectionism*. New York: International Universities Press, 1984.

Rowen, Henry S. "Formulating Strategic Doctrine." In *Commission on the Organization of the Government for the Conduct of Foreign Policy*, vol. 4. Washington: Government Printing Office, June 1975.

Rudenstine, David. *The Day the Presses Stopped: A History of the Pentagon Papers Case*. Berkeley: University of California Press, 1996.

Russo, Anthony. "Inside the RAND Corporation and Out: My Story." *Ramparts*, April 1972.

Sagan, Scott D. "SIOP-62: The Nuclear War Plan Briefing to President Kennedy." *International Security* (Summer 1987).

———. "Change and Continuity in U.S. Nuclear Strategy." In *America's Defense*. Ed. Michael Mandelbaum. New York: Holmes and Meier, 1989.

Salisbury, Harrison E. *Without Fear or Favor: The* New York Times *and Its Times*. New York: Times Books, 1980.

Savage, Leonard J. *The Foundations of Statistics*. New York: Wiley, 1954.

Schlesinger, Arthur, Jr. "Eyeless in Indochina." *New York Review of Books*, October 21, 1971.

Schrag, Peter. *Test of Loyalty: Daniel Ellsberg and the Rituals of Secret Government*. New York: Simon & Schuster, 1974.

Schwartz-Salant, Nathan. *Narcissism and Character Transformation: The Psychology of Narcissistic Character Disorders*. Toronto: Inner City Books, 1982.

Shanks, Bob. "The Middle Age of Daniel Ellsberg." *California*, November 1985.

Shapley, Deborah. *Promise and Power: The Life and Times of Robert McNamara*. Boston: Little, Brown, 1993.

Shearer, Derek. "An Evening with Henry." *Nation*, March 8, 1971.

Sheehan, Neil. *A Bright Shining Lie: John Paul Vann and America in Vietnam*. New York: Random House, 1988.

Sternberg, Robert J., and Janet E. Davidson, eds. *Conceptions of Giftedness*. Cambridge: Cambridge University Press, 1986.

Strober, Gerald S., and Deborah H. Strober. *Nixon: An Oral History of His Presidency*. New York: Harper Collins, 1994.

Talese, Gay. *Thy Neighbor's Wife*. Garden City, New York: Doubleday, 1980.

Thayer, Harry. *Management of the Hanford Engineer Works in World War II: How the Corps, DuPont and the Metallurgical Laboratory Fast Tracked the Original Plutonium Works*. New York: American Society of Civil Engineers, 1996.

Ungar, Sanford J. *The Papers* & The Papers: *An Account of the Legal and Political Battle over the Pentagon Papers*. New York: Columbia University Press, 1989.

U.S. House Judiciary Committee. *Impeachment of Richard M. Nixon, President of the United States: Report of the Committee on the Judiciary*. Washington: U.S. Government Printing Office, 1974.

U.S. Senate Select Committee on Presidential Campaign Activities. *Hearings, Final Report*. Washington: U.S. Government Printing Office, 1973–74.

Van de Velde, Th. H. *Ideal Marriage: Its Physiology and Technique*. New York: Random House, 1941.

Von Franz, Marie-Louise. *Puer Aeternus*. Santa Monica: Sigo Press, 1970.

Wells, Tom. *The War Within: America's Battle Over Vietnam*. Berkeley: University of California Press, 1994.

Wheelis, Allen. *The Quest for Identity*. New York: Norton, 1958.

———. *The Life and Death of My Mother*. New York: Norton, 1992.

Wicker, Tom. *On Press*. New York: Viking, 1978.

Wise, David. *Molehunt: The Secret Search for Traitors that Shattered the CIA*. New York: Random House, 1992.

Wohlstetter, Albert. "The Delicate Balance of Terror." *Foreign Affairs* (January 1959).

Wolfelt, Alan. *Helping Children Cope with Grief*. Muncie: Accelerated Development Inc. Publishers, 1983.

Woods, Randall Bennett. *Fulbright: A Biography*. Cambridge: Cambridge University Press, 1995.

Young, Oran R., ed. *Bargaining: Formal Theories of Negotiation*. Urbana, Illinois: University of Illinois Press, 1975.

Zinn, Howard. *You Can't Be Neutral on a Moving Train: A Personal History of Our Times*. Boston: Beacon Press, 1994.

INDEX